Mariticide Club
Wives Who Kill

William A. Stricklin

Olympus Story House

Mariticide Club
Wives Who Kill
Nonfiction Tales

Mariticide (from Latin maritus "husband" + -cide, caedere "to cut, to kill") means the killing of one's husband. Mariticide is a relevant part of homicides in general, with the killing of one's husband being far less frequent than uxoricide (a man killing his wife). This nonfiction anthology relates the sagas of over 200 wives who murdered husbands.

Nonfiction
by William A. Stricklin

Mariticide Club
Wives Who Kill

Disconcerting Stories for Grownups - Not To Tell to Children in Darkness at Bedtime

2023 1st Edition Notice and Legal Notice:
Mariticide Club – Wives Who Kill Husbands –

Wives Who Kill

nothing original. Images are presented for the purpose of research and study. Every effort has been made to credit sources and to obtain permission when appropriate. If inadvertently I have credited images or text incorrectly or without appropriate consent, or posted images or text that are neither in the public domain, nor qualify for fair use under USA copyright law, I will gladly withdraw such images or reword credits upon request. All rights reserved. No part of this publication may be reproduced, distributed, or transmitted in any form or by any means, including photocopying, recording, or other electronic or mechanical methods, without the prior written permission of the publisher, except in the case of brief quotations embodied in critical reviews and non-commercial uses permitted by the copyright laws of the United States of America. For written permission, which will be granted generously, write the request to the writer of this anthology at the address below.

William A. Stricklin

2029 Alameda Avenue

Alameda CA 94501

Writer: Stricklin, William Albert

Title: Mariticide Club – Wives Who Kill Husbands

Mariticide Club

Writer's Note: The Nonfiction Contract:

*"Part of writing non-fiction means making a commitment to telling the truth." Professor Tilar J. Mazzeo of Colby College. Part of the challenge for writers is the distinction between writing fictional and factual works. Fiction is written using imagined situations, but fictional stories may also spring from real events and involve real people. When writers present factual stories, told as non-fiction they must stay, wholly, in the realm of reality. There is a fine line between the two *****

/s/ William A. Stricklin
San Francisco, October 2023

Writer's Role: Please note that the writer of this anthology Mariticide Club – Wives Who Kill Husbands, is called "writer" never "author." Some use the words interchangeably. The words are quite different: A **writer** writes a book. This writer writes exactly as he thinks and thinks just as he writes. This writer is thankful for his fourth-grade English teacher Mrs. Conrad at Emerson School, Berkeley, California. Mrs. Conrad kept a jigger on the right side of the lavatory by her desk. From time to time, frequently Mrs. Conrad filled her one-and-a-half-ounce jigger with the amber fluid inside her soap dispenser and gulped it down. Mrs. Conrad taught us that it is pretentious for a writer to purport to be "an author". An **author** is one who professes to be the creator or originator of a written work. More broadly she taught us "an author is the person who originates or gives existence to anything" whose authorship determines what is created. An **author** originates the idea, plot, or content of what is written. In writing history, such as Mariticide Club – Wives Who Kill Husbands, with nearly everyone dead, nobody to interview, history usually is found in the writings of the longdead men and women who lived at the time the events occurred. Readers know that a writer borrows from sources. Mrs. Conrad taught us not to plagiarize and to attribute those sources and the differences between primary, secondary and tertiary sources: A secondary source relates to information originally presented elsewhere. A secondary source contrasts

Wives Who Kill

with a primary source, which is an original source of the information being discussed; a primary source can be a person with direct knowledge of a situation, or a document created by such a person. How to classify a source is not always an obvious decision. A secondary source is one that gives information about a primary source. These sources contain second- hand information that has already appeared in primary documents. In a secondary source the original information is selected, modified and arranged in a suitable format for the purpose of easy location by the users. *Primary* and *secondary* are relative terms, and some sources may be classified as primary or secondary, depending on how they are used. A third level, the tertiary source, such as an encyclopedia or dictionary, often Wikipedia, resembles a secondary source in that it contains analysis, but attempts to provide a broad introductory overview of a topic. Mrs. Conrad unshackled her students: She taught us to be comfortable that when borrowing from a writer whom we have identified and whose copyright we are not violating, whose permission has been granted, we are not limited to borrowing just a single sentence or paragraph. Why send readers to Smithsonian Archives in order to read all the anonymous Meskquwaki Fox woman's 1895 diary? Nor, to avoid plagiarism, need we substitute synonyms for another writer's words in an effort to transmogrify language, hoping to hide our source. To do so is duplicitous. To do research, then write history, inevitably a writer must use libraries and, in an earlier era, Encyclopedia Britannica. Fortunately, in the current electronic age, Wikipedia is broadly authorizing people to use their content: All their textbased content is permissible to copy/paste under a "Creative Commons" license. Cite Wikipedia as your source, then use information on Wikipedia for whatever you want, as much as you want. The bibliography evidences that I am borrowing heavily from Wikipedia in order to cobble together many stories of people and events that occurred in the past. Mrs. Conrad taught us that great literature may be the creation of order out of chaos, meaning out of meaninglessness. Writing two dozen books of my Family Secrets was not on the horizon in July 1948. I do not profess to be the originator of any of the ideas that are incorporated into Mariticide Club –

Mariticide Club

Wives Who Kill Husbands. My role in In Mariticide Club – Wives Who Kill - has been to order law and facts so as to emphasize some events, to ignore, or just to minimize, other events, ultimately to unravel secrets in order to bring characters and events of Mariticide Club – Wives Who Kill Husbands – 200 sagas in all these pages to a realistic, truthful conclusion and resolution. Please enjoy. /s/ William A. Stricklin, San Francisco, October 2023

Foreword by John Stricklin:

My father's half century of law practice in California, Washington and Hawaii has burdened him with client confidential communications that ethically he must never divulge. Percipient readers of Mariticide Club – Wives Who Kill Husbands, understandably may develop conjectures that my father is writing about clients in a manner which cannot possibly divulge or lead to their identities, as well as sharing nonfiction which perhaps may involve my father's own family or his own personal escape from deadly peril. Readers may find that my father's stories are much like being on board transcontinental airline flights from New York City to San Francisco but boarding in Chicago and debarking in Denver. My childhood memories are of my father's bedtime stories, each night lasting just long enough for fanciful dreams to start dancing in my head, his fully developed themes at bedtimes, far shorter and less elaborate than for a novel. My father's concentrated form of historical narrative pee fiction, often truncates traditional classical elements of dramatic structure: My father's short stories only rarely have an exposition; more often they start in what he calls in media res in the middle of the action Readers discover that almost every one of his manuscripts focuses on a self-contained incident or series of linked incidents, involving only a few characters, focusing more on mood than development of plot. He does his best to resist categorizations by genre and fixed formation. Plots of his short stories often have a climax, crisis, or turning point. Both his nonfiction stories and his fictionalnovels often end abruptly and are left open; some may or may not have moral or practical lessons. Few stories have the power to captivate us more than

Wives Who Kill

those that remain unresolved. Thanks to my father's Harvard Law School education and his counterintelligence training and experience, he has been successful in reconstructing from the public domain what he presents in this book. Respectful of terms of the "nonfiction contract" if facts are forever lost to history, my father tells you so and uses words "perhaps" or "it is possible that" and then labels portions of his writing as "a historical novel." Codes, puzzles and cryptic public art tease us with their intrigue: Why is their message coded? What great secrets do they hide? Despite the efforts of historians, cryptographers and determined treasure hunters, history is filled with riddles that continue to confound us; many are left unanswered in his books. British short story writer William Boyd has said in better words than I:

"[poems and short stories] seem to answer something very deep in our nature as if, for the duration of its telling, something special has been created, some essence of our experience extrapolated, some temporary sense has been made of our common turbulent journey towards the grave and oblivion."

From my own close observation for years, I know that Mariticide Club – Wives Who Kill Husbands, shares my father's personal encounters and close calls with danger as well as what he's learned from some of his law clients in California, Hawaii, and Washington about "wives who killed and got away with murder." He manages to do this without violating any client confidences. With his magnificent training at Harvard Law School, these stories of wives who kill are presented with accurate information pertaining to the legal issues and facts claimed by the prosecution and the defense in legal processes that really occurred. You will enjoy the pages that follow.

/s/ John Stricklin, San Francisco, October 2023

Mariticide Club

Dedication:

Mariticide Club – Wives Who Kill Husbands is dedicated to my father's starter wife Helen Grace Byrd who shot my father. When I met Helen in Dallas in 1948 I took the opportunity to thank her for making my life possible. If she had not shot my father in the chest with her .25 caliber Beretta pistol and then burned down his residence, never would he have escaped her, then met, romanced and married my mother who then brought me into the world I enjoy so much. My father's starter wife Helen Grace Byrd bedding with Hymie in pari delicto in 1930 shot my father when he returned home early unexpectedly from a business trip using a .25 caliber Beretta 418 Pocket Pistol that became her engagement gift to her daughter my older half-sister Dorothy calling herself "Carole" in A Perfect Crime my historical novel you may enjoy next © 2020 – Copyright Office Case No. 1-8476606391 ISBN 978-1-09830-140-8. William A. Stricklin

Beretta .25 caliber Pistol

Wives Who Kill

Table of Contents
Roster of the 200 Members of the Mariticide Club

Mariticide Club

100. Charlotte Kauffmann
101. Jean Kincaid (née Jean Livingston)
102. Gladys Kelly
103. Lizzie Lloyd King aka Elizabeth Lloyd King, Betsy King, Kate Stoddard, Kate Stoddart, Alice Howard, Minnie Waltham, Amy Snow, Amy Stone, Amy Gilmore, Amy G.
104. Sharon Kinne (née Sharon Elizabeth Hall)
105. Nancy Ann Kissel (née Keeshin)
106. Tillie Klimek (née Otylia Gburek)
107. Theresa Knorr (née Theresa Jimmie Francine Cross)
108. Kau Kobayashi
109. Koodathayi cyanide murders
110. Grace Kotani
111. Dame Alice Kyteler
112. Piroska Jancsó-Ladányi (née Piroska Mária Ladányi)
113. Bridget Larkin
114. Marie-Fortunée Lafarge (née Capelle)
115. Charity Lamb
116. Deidra Lane
117. Jane Laut
118. Raynella Dossett Leath (née Raynella Bernardene Large)
119. Marguerite Leféron (née Galart)
120. Christa Lehmann (née Ambros)
121. Janice Leidholm
122. Teresa Wilson Bean Lewis
123. Tran Thi Thuy Lieu
124. Yvonne de Ligne
125. Anjette Lyles (née Donovan)
126. Nellie May Madison (née Mooney)
127. Rhonda Belle Martin (*née* Rhonda Belle Thomley)
128. Kia Yvette Jeffries
129. Florence Elizabeth Chandler Maybrick
130. Mary Ann Young (née McCarthy)
131. Melanie Lyn McGuire (*née* Slate)
132. Elisa McNabney (*née* Laren Renee Sims)
133. Sally McNeil (née Sally Dempsey
134. Agnus McVee
135. Daisy Louisa C. de Melker (*née* Hancorn-Smith)
136. Lucille Marie Miller (née Maxwell)
137. Sharee Paulette Kitley Miller
138. Marie-Louise Victorine Bessarabo (*née* Marie-Louise Victorine Grouès pen names Héra Mirtel, Juliette de Boulogne, Juliette de Lotus)
139. Euphemia Mondich
140. Clara Moore
141. Angelina Napolitano
142. Martha Needle (*née* Martha Charles)
143. Omaima Aree Nelson
144. Hester Rebecca Nepping
145. Catherine Nevin (*née* Scully)
146. Stella Maudine Nickell(*née* Stephenson)
147. Charlotte Nixon-Nirdlinger
148. Narcy Novack (*née* Narcisa Véliz Pacheco)
149. Venera Obolashvili (*née* Lela Javakhishvili)
150. Marjorie Ann Orbin

151. Erzsébet Papp - Mrs. János Holhos - The Nicotine Killer
152. Gail Collins Pappalardi
153. Milka Pavlović
154. Najwa Petersen
155. Pamela Phillips
156. Ethel Pitts - Estranged Wife of Ernie Pitts
157. Noh - The Pocheon Poisoner
158. Susan Polk (*née* Susan Mae Bolling)
159. Milena Quaglini
160. Bessie Reece
161. Vera Renczi- The Black Widow
162. Heloísa Gonçalves Duque Soares Ribeiro (*née* Heloísa Borba Gonçalves)
163. Elizabeth Ridgeway *née* Elizabeth Husbands
164. Donna Marie Roberts
165. Sarah Jane Robinson (*née* Tennant)
166. Angelina Rodriguez
167. Mary Mabel Bennett Rogers
168. Maria Romberg
169. Kristin Margrethe Rossum
170. Margaret Rudin (*née* Margaret Lee Frost)
171. Esneda Ruiz Cataño
172. Jacqueline Sauvage
173. Nancy Ann Seaman (née D'Onofrio)
174. Alice Bradley Sheldon (née Alice Hastings Bradley) (pen name Raccoona Sheldon)
175. Melissa Ann Shepard (née Russell)
176. Frankie Stewart Silver
177. Pamela Ann Smart (née Wojas)
178. Catherine Mandeville Snow
179. May Ruth Snyder (née Brown)
180. Lyda Southard (née Keller)aka aka Lyda Trueblood Aka Flypaper Lyda Aka The Black Widow
181. Anna-Maria Farina Spaak
182. Bathsheba Ruggles Spooner
183. Barbara Stager (née Barbara Terry) aka Barbara Ford
184. Della Faye "Dante" Sutorius (née Della Faye Hall)
185. Epifania Sulu'ape
186. Edith Jessie Thompson née Edith Jesse Graydon
187. Sara Thornton
188. Julia Lynn Turner (née Julia Lynn Womack)
189. Sophie Charlotte Elisabeth Ursinus (née Weingarte)
190. Elizabeth Van Valkenburgh (née Woodley)
191. Maria Velten aka "Bilberry Mariechen""The Poison Witch from Lower Rhine"
192. Louise Vermilya (née Woolf)
193. Hattie Livermore Whitten
194. Dorothea Widmer
195. Denise Williams
196. Mary Elizabeth Wilson (née Cassidy) The Merry Widow of Windy Nook
197. Mary Winkler
198. Elizabeth Lillian Woolcock (née Oliver)
199. Elizabeth Wright
200. Susan Lucille Wright née Susan Lucille Wyche

Wives Who Kill

Nicole "Nikki"Addimando (born November 19, 1988)
Shot and killed her husband Christopher Grover in New York in September 2017. She said she tried to run away from Grover, but he threatened to kill her. There had been a fight, and Addimando shot and killed Grover while he was asleep. Sentenced to "19 years to life", her term of imprisonment was reduced on appeal to 7.5 years when she will be available to date again. If you are interested, you can write to Nikki where she is incarcerated at Bedford Hills Correctional Facility for Women.

Kiranjit Ahluwalia (born 1955)

Kiranjit Ahluwalia (born 1955) is an Indian woman who fatally burned her husband in 1989 in the UK. She claimed it was in response to ten yearsof physical, psychological, and sexual abuse. After initially being convicted of murder and sentenced to life in prison, Ahluwalia's conviction was lateroverturned on grounds of inadequate counsel and replaced with voluntarymanslaughter. Although her submission of provocation failed (under *R v Duffy* the loss of control needed to be sudden, which this was not), she successfully pleaded the partial defense of diminished responsibility under s.2 Homicide Act 1957 on the grounds that fresh medical evidence (not available at her original trial) may indicate her diminished mental responsibility. One evening in the spring of 1989, while her husband lay sleeping, Kiranjit fetched some petrol and caustic soda mixture from the

Mariticide Club

garage and mixed it to create napalm she poured over the bed and set alight. She wrote an autobiography with coauthor Rahila Gupta, Circle of Light. On September 25, 1992 Kiranjit was found guilty of manslaughter due to diminished responsibility and sentenced to three years and four months (the time she had already served). Kiranjit was released immediately. Hence, she became available for It's *Just Lunch* if you are interested in dating her.

Marguerite Alibert
aka Marguerite Laurent
aka Maggie Meller
aka Princess Fahmy

Wives Who Kill

Marguerite Marie Alibert was born on December 9, 1890, in Paris to Firmin Alibert, a coachman, and Marie Aurand, a housekeeper. At sixteen, she gave birth to a daughter, Raymonde. In the following eight to ten years, Alibert led a nomadic life until she met Mme Denant, who ran a Maison de Rendezvous, a brothel catering to a high society clientele. Under the tutelage of Denant, Alibert became a high-class prostitute. Subsequently, Alibert had a number of notable relationships. Alibert met Edward, Prince of Wales, in April 1917 at the Hôtel de Crillon in Paris. At the time, Edward was in France as an officer of the Grenadier Guards in the Western Front during World War I. Edward became infatuated with her and during their relationship he wrote many candid letters to her. Although the affair was intense while it lasted, by the end of the war, Edward had broken off the relationship. Ali Fahmy Bey became infatuated with Alibert when he first encountered her in Egypt while she was escorting a businessman. He saw her again several times in Paris, and they were eventually formally introduced in July 1922. Following that meeting, they embarked on a tour of gambling and entertainment establishments in Deauville, Biarritz, and Paris. Fahmy returned to Egypt, but soon after, he invited her to the country, feigning illness and telling her that he could not live without her. They were married in December 1922 and had a formal Islamic wedding in January 1923. On July 1, 1923, the couple arrived in London for the holidays. They stayed at the Savoy Hotel with their entourage consisting of a secretary, a valet, and a maid. On July 9, the couple and the secretary went to see the operetta The Merry Widow. Upon returning to the hotel, they had a late supper where they started one of their frequent arguments. At 2:30 a.m. on July 10, 1923, Alibert shot her husband repeatedly from behind, striking him in the neck, back, and head. She used a .32 caliber semi-automatic Browning pistol. The victim was transported to Charing Cross Hospital but died of his wounds in about an hour. The trial opened on Monday, September 10, 1923, with many queuing to enter, including some who had waited since before daybreak. The trial lasted until Saturday, September 15. During the trial, Alibert presented herself as the victim of the "brutality and beastliness" of her "oriental husband". Alibert was

Mariticide Club

defended by Edward Marshall Hall, one of the most famous British lawyers of that era. The trial judge disallowed any mention of Alibert's past as a courtesan, ensuring that the name of the Prince of Wales was never mentioned as part of the evidence during the trial. At the same time, Fahmy was described as "a monster of Eastern depravity and decadence, whose sexual tastes were indicative of an amoral sadism towards his helpless European wife". Alibert was acquitted of all charges. After the trial, Alibert sued her late husband's family aiming to lay claim to his property. A court in Egypt rejected the verdict at the Old Bailey and dismissed her claim. She lived in an apartment facing the Ritz in Paris until the end of her life. After her death, the few remaining letters from Edward (if these existed), which she had kept as insurance, were found and destroyed. In the 2013 book The Prince, the Princess and the Perfect Murder, it is speculated that the acquittal of Alibert of the charges of murdering her husband was part of a deal for returning the love letters of the Prince of Wales to him and a further guarantee by Alibert that Edward's name would not be mentioned in court. The killing of her husband was also the focus of the 1991 book Scandal at the Savoy: The Infamous 1920s Murder Case.

Wendi Elizabeth Andriano (née Ochoa); born August 6, 1970)
Wendi is an American female prisoner on death row in Arizona. She was convicted of the 2000 murder of her husband, Joe. She is incarcerated at theLumley Unit in the Arizona State Prison Complex - Perryville. If you wantto write to Wendi, her inmate number is #191593. Wendi had given birth to two children and worked as an apartment manager. She began to resent her increased responsibilities. She began to frequent bars and have affairs. She solicited a friend to pose as her husband for a life insurance pre-screening. No insurance was ever purchased. During early morning hours of October 8, 2000, Wendi Andriano bludgeoned her 33-year-old husband Joe to death with a bar stool and stabbed him in the neck with a 13-inch knife in their apartment in Ahwatukee, Arizona. Joe's autopsy revealed he had sustained 23 blows to the skull, and traces of sodium azide were found in his system.

Wives Who Kill

Approximately one hour before Joe's murder, Wendi had called 911 at the behest of a co-worker, claiming that her terminally ill husband was dying. When paramedics arrived, Wendi turned them away, stating that Joe had a do-not-resuscitate order, and that his wish was to die. Paramedics left the scene. One hour later, Wendi called 911 again, reporting she had stabbed and beaten her husband to death in self-defense. She also made claims that her husband was physically and psychologically abusive toward her. Since Joe was weak from chemotherapy and the sodium azide poisoning, he was unable to defend himself. Wendi was charged with murder. Four years after the crime, on August 23, 2004, Wendi Andriano's murder trial began. Even though she had no prior criminal record, she faced the death penalty for her crime. Prosecutors stated that Wendi's motive for murdering her husband was money. Evidence was brought up about how Wendi had tried to instate a life insurance policy on her terminally ill husband. Prosecutors alleged she was tempted by a potentially large-yield medical malpractice lawsuit filed against Joe's doctors. They attempted to prove Wendi used a pesticide, sodium azide, to poison her husband to appear as if Joe's death were the result of a heart attack. At the trial, Wendi testified in her own defense. For nine days on the stand, she testified she had been battered by her husband. She said her husband Joe flew into a rage after she told him about her affair. She said there was a struggle with a knife. Despite her dramatic testimony, November 18, 2004, Wendi's jury found her guilty of first-degree murder. A month later was the sentencing. Due to the heinousness, the cruelty, and depravity of the crime, and because the crime was financially motivated, she was sentenced to death by lethal injection on December 22, 2004. Wendi filed a post-conviction appeal in 2007, claiming that evidence of her affairs and efforts to buy life insurance on her ailing husband had unfairly prejudiced her in front of the jury. She also claimed that jurors were not allowed to consider lesser charges, such as second-degree murder or manslaughter. Her conviction was affirmed by the Arizona Supreme Court in July 2007, her case then entered post-conviction relief. For this, her appeals attorneys claimed prosecutor Juan Martinez's emphasis on her affairs ignited female stereotypes and was "prosecutorial misconduct." The

Mariticide Club

appeal, filed in 2012, has yet to receive an opinion from the Arizona Supreme Court or Maricopa County, as it is not uncommon for the highest state court and the trial county to oversee proceedings in this stage. After this level of appeal is over, Andriano could file a habeas corpus appeal. Then if this is denied at federal district court, the appeal will immediately be sent to the 9th Circuit Court of Appeals, the court that handles appeals for this federal district that includes Arizona. After this, the US Supreme Court could hear the case, although this is extremely unlikely. After this, Wendi Andriano will be executed, as by then, her appeals will be over.

As of January 2018, Wendi Andriano is one of three women on Arizona's death row; the other two women are Shawna Forde and Sammantha Allen.

Angel Makers of Nagyrév

The Angel Makers of Nagyrév (Hungarian: *Tiszazugi méregkeverők*, "Tiszazug poison-mixers") were a group of women living in the village of Nagyrév, Hungary, who, between 1914 and 1929, poisoned to death an estimated forty people. They were supplied arsenic and encouraged to use it for the purpose by a midwife, or "wise woman", named Zsuzsanna Fazekas, wife of Gyula Fazekas, née Zsuzsanna Oláh (Fazekas Gyuláné Oláh Zsuzsanna). Twenty-six of the Angel Makers were tried for killing forty to 300 husbands from 1914-1929. Eight were sentenced to death, but only two were executed. Another twelve received prison sentences. Fazekas was a middle-aged midwife who arrived in Nagyrév in 1911, with her husband already missing without explanation. Between 1911 and 1921, she was imprisoned ten times for performing illegal abortions but was consistently acquitted by judges supporting abortion. In Hungarian society at that time, the future husband of a teenage bride was selected by her family, and she was forced to accept her parents' choice. Divorce was not allowed, even if the husband was an alcoholic or abusive. During World War I, when able-bodied men were sent to fight for Austria-Hungary, rural Nagyrév was an ideal location for holding Allied prisoners of war. With POWs having limited freedom within the village, the women living there often had one or more foreign lovers while their husbands were away.

Wives Who Kill

When the men returned, many of them rejected their wives' affairs and wished to return to their previous way of life, creating a volatile situation. At this time, Fazekas began secretly persuading women who wished to escape this situation to poison their husbands using arsenic made by boiling flypaper and skimming off the lethal residue. After the initial killing of their husbands, some of the women went on to poison parents who had become a burden to them, or to get hold of their inheritance. Others poisoned their lovers, some even their sons. The midwife allegedly asked the poisoners, "Why put up with them?" The first poisoning in Nagyrév took place in 1911; it was not the work of Fazekas. The deaths of other husbands, children, and family members soon followed. Poisoning became a fad, and by the mid-1920s, Nagyrév earned the nickname "the murder district". There were an estimated 45–50 murders over the 18 years that Fazekas lived in the district. She was the closest thing to a doctor the village had, and her cousin was the clerk who filed all the death certificates, allowing the murders to go undetected.

Defendants in the arsenic poisoning case of the
Tiszazug area walking in the Szolnok prison yard

Three conflicting accounts have been cited to explain how the Angel Makers were eventually detected. In one, Szabó, one of the Angel Makers, was caught in the act by two visitors who survived her poisoning attempts. She pointed a finger at a woman with the surname Bukenoveski, who in turn named Fazekas. In another account, a medical student in a neighboring

Mariticide Club

town found high arsenic levels in a body that washed up on the riverbank, leading to an investigation. A Hungarian-American historian who is the author of a scholarly book on the subject contends the murders first were made public in 1929 when an anonymous letter to the editor of a local newspaper accused women from the Tiszazug region of the country of poisoning family members. Dozens of corpses from the local cemetery were exhumed. 34 women and one man were indicted. 26 of the Angel Makers were tried, among them Susi Oláh. Eight were sentenced to death, but only two were executed. Another twelve received prison sentences.

Áurea Vázquez-Rijos

Adam Joel Anhang Uster (March 8, 1973 – September 23, 2005) was an entrepreneur and real estate developer; he was murdered at the intersection of Calle San Justo and Calle Luna in Old San Juan, Puerto Rico in September 2005. He was leaving the Pink Skirt Nightclub/Dragonfly Club with his estranged wife, Áurea Vázquez-Rijos, from whom he was finalizing a divorce, and was knifed and beaten to death on the street. Vázquez-Rijos, known in the media as the "Black Widow", fled jurisdiction to Italy in 2006 but was discovered and extradited to Puerto Rico in 2015, and was convicted of being a co-conspirator in her husband's murder in October 2018. Vázquez-Rijos was a former Miss Puerto Rico Petite winner. Anhang and Vázquez-Rijos signed a prenuptial agreement one day before they were married, as Anhang's net worth was estimated at more than $24 million while Vazquez's was only $62,300. Anhang's father Abraham said "The motive was greed. The whole [Vázquez] family had moved into their house and basically he had to move out. There was no doubt that they looked upon him as a meal ticket and he was dispensable. In fact, they convinced themselves that he was worth to them more dead than alive." While in exile in Florence, Vazquez-Rijos gave birth to twin girls with an Italian citizen. This might have helped her avoid trial, since Italy bars the extradition of the mothers of Italian children, but the couple quickly separated after the father's family realized that she was a fugitive,

Wives Who Kill

and the father ultimately gained custody of the twins. In addition, according to US prosecutors, in June 2012, Ms Vázquez approached the Firenzebraica Jewish organization in Florence with false paperwork to attempt to certify that she and her daughters were of Jewish descent, hoping to emigrate to Israel. The trial of Vázquez-Rijos remained stalled because of the reluctance of Italy to extradite individuals facing murder charges to countries who adjudicate the death penalty. This rationale has been applied to Ms. Vázquez-Rijos, despite the fact she is not indicted in a capital case. Capital punishment in Puerto Rico is forbidden by law.

While incarcerated in Spain, Ms. Vázquez became pregnant and had a baby. Allowed to marry the father in jail, and as the mother of a Spanish citizen, she attempted to have the Spanish court prevent her extradition. She was extradited to Puerto Rico in 2015, along with her month-old baby, who was placed in local non-parental custody. As part of the extradition procedure, federal prosecutors signed a sworn affidavit to Spanish authorities that they would not ask for the death penalty in the case.

Vázquez-Rijos' extradition was completed on September 24, 2015, when she was returned to San Juan, Puerto Rico under FBI custody. Vázquez-Rijos was brought before United States Magistrate Bruce McGiverin of the United States District Court for the District of Puerto Rico, who informed her of the details of the indictment against her. McGiverin stressed to the defendant that she faces life in prison if found guilty. The Magistrate told her she would be assigned a public defender. Vázquez-Rijos was sent to the federal Metropolitan Detention Center in Guaynabo, Puerto Rico until her bail hearing on October 8, 2015. The trial was originally set to begin on August 28, 2017. After multiple delays, it began on August 21, 2018.

At trial, witnesses testified that Vázquez-Rijos watched as her husband was murdered, and then reminded Pabón-Colón that he needed to inflict an injury on her, in order to create the impression that both of them were victims of robbery. Evidence showed Pabón-Colón wrote letters attempting to collect the fee for being a hitman, but Vázquez-Rijos' sister Marcia responded to Pabón-Colón saying that they did not have the money.

Mariticide Club

On October 3, 2018, Vazquez-Rijos and two co-conspirators, her sister Marcia and ex-boyfriend José Ferrer Sosa, were all found guilty. All three face life imprisonment, with a sentencing hearing initially scheduled for January 29, 2019, and then delayed three times.

On March 15, 2019, Aurea Vazquez Rijos and her sister, Marcia Vazquez Rijos and an ex-boyfriend of hers, José Ferrer Sosa, were all sentenced to life in prison. Áurea was assigned BOP#46255-069 and Marcia was given BOP#42102-069 and are now at FMC Carswell. Jose's status is unknown.

Queen Anula of Anuradhapura

Anula was the first queen regnant in Sri Lankan history, as well as the first documented female head of state in Asia. Anula initially rose to power as consort of King Chore Naga(also known as Coranaga and Mahanaga), son of King Valagambahu of Anuradhapura. However, in her five-year reign, she poisoned her way through at least four other husbands and consorts, and she eventually governed Rajarata on her own. She should be distinguished from the other famous Anula in Sri Lankan history, king Devanampiyatissa's sister-in-law, the first woman in Sri Lanka to be ordained as a bikkhuni. The situation in Sri Lanka just before the reign of Anula was extremely unstable. King Khallata Naga was deposed in a palace coup that occurred in 104 BC; his younger brother, Vatta Gamani Abhaya (Valagambahu), overthrew the usurpers and took his dead brother's wife, also called Anula, as his own. He also adopted his nephew, Mahakuli, as his own son. Valagambahu was on the throne little more than a year when the Damilas made war upon him in a battle near Kolambalaka; and the king was vanquished. It was 16 years before Valagambahu regained the throne, and by then Mahaculika superseded Coranaga as Valagambahu's preferred heir. Mahakuli (who reigned as Mahakuli Mahatissa) inherited Valagambahu's throne in 76 BC. Coranaga on the other hand lived as a rebel; whether this constituted a struggle for the throne is unknown. If it were, then Coranaga's succession to the throne in 62 BC may well have represented an overthrow of Mahakuli Mahatissa. The Mahavamsa does

Wives Who Kill

mention that one of Coranaga's first acts was to destroy 18 temples that had refused him shelter during his time as an outlaw. Coranaga is recorded as having reigned for 12 years, before being poisoned by his consort, the infamous Anula. Anula's motives for killing her husband are not known. Coranaga's successor, King Kuda Tissa, is the son of Mahakuli Mahatissa. Kuda means little and, thus, it is possible that the new king was only a child and, effectively, under Anula's control. Kuda Tissa did not live long, because Anula was enamored of one of the palace-guards who killed Tissa also by poison and gave the government to the hands of Anula. From this point onward, the queen eclipsed her titular consorts and became the real power in Anuradhapura. The validity of these claims is debated as the main source for them is the Mahavamsa, and it has been proposed that Queen Anula was simply a victim of the misogyny of the time, and nowhere near as vicious, cunning, or licentious as she was said to be in the chronicle. After four months reigning on her own, Anula was deposed by Mahakuli Mahatissa's second son, Kutakanna Tissa. The Mahavamsa states that Kutakanna Tissa had Anula burned on a funeral pyre. Other sources indicate that Anula was burned alive in the palace where she had committed her murders.

Amy Archer-Gilligan (née Amy E. Duggan) aka Sister Theresa
Amy Archer-Gilligan was a nursing home proprietor and a serial killer from Windsor, Connecticut. She murdered at least five people by poisoning them. One of her victims was her second husband, Michael Gilligan; the others were residents of her nursing home. The authorities counted 48 deaths in her nursing home, the "Archer Home for the Elderly and Infirm". Amy Duggan married James Archer in 1897. A daughter, Mary J. Archer, was born in December 1897. The Archers first became caretakers in 1901, hired to care for John Seymour, an elderly widower. They moved into his home in Newington, Connecticut. Seymour died in 1904. His heirs converted the residence into a boarding house for the elderly, and the Archers remained to provide care for the elderly for a fee.

Mariticide Club

They paid rent to Seymour's family. They ran the boarding house as Sister Amy's Nursing Home for the Elderly. In 1907, Seymour's heirs decided to sell the house. The Archers moved to Windsor, Connecticut, and used their savings to purchase their own residence on Prospect Street in Windsor Center. They soon converted it into a business, Archer Home for the Elderly and Infirm.

James Archer died in 1910, apparently of natural causes. The official cause of his death was Bright's disease, a generic term for kidney diseases. Amy Archer had taken out an insurance policy on him a few weeks before his death. The policy benefit enabled her to continue operating Archer Home. In 1913, Amy married Michael W. Gilligan, a widower with four adult sons. He was wealthy and interested in both Amy and in investing in the Archer Home. February 20, 1914, after only three months married to Amy, Michael died. The official cause of death was "acute bilious attack" (in other words, severe indigestion). Amy was again financially secure because during their short marriage her new husband had drawn up a will which left his entire estate to her. The will would later be determined a forgery as it was written in handwriting matching Amy Archer-Gilligan's own.

Between 1907 and 1917, there were sixty deaths in the Archer Home. Relatives of her clients grew suspicious as they tallied the large number of

Wives Who Kill

deaths. Only 12 residents died between 1907 and 1910, but 48 residents died between 1911 and 1916. Among them was Franklin R. Andrews, an apparently healthy man. On the morning of May 29, 1914, Andrews was doing some gardening in the Archer house. His robust physical condition deteriorated in a single day and he was dead by evening. The official cause of death was gastric ulcer.

After Andrews' siblings (including Nellie Pierce) came into possession of some of his letters, they noted occasions where Amy Archer-Gilligan was pressing their brother for money. Amy's clients showed a pattern of dying not long after giving her a large sum of money. As the deaths continued, Nellie Pierce reported her suspicions to the local district attorney, but he ignored her. So, she took her story to the Hartford Courant. On May 9, 1916, the first of several articles on the "Murder Factory" was published. A few months later, the police started to seriously investigate the case. The investigation took almost a year to complete. The bodies of Gilligan, Andrews, and three other boarders were exhumed. All five had died of poisoning, either arsenic or strychnine. Local merchants were able to testify that Amy had been purchasing large quantities of arsenic, supposedly to "kill rats". A look into Gilligan's will established that it was a forgery written by Amy. According to M. William Phelps, author of The Devil's Rooming House, investigation appeared to show that Amy was buying the arsenic to kill large numbers of rats. However, it appears that she did not buy all of the arsenic which killed her patients. The doctor and some of the patients had signed off to purchase it. The investigation pursued Dr. King because more evidence was piling up against him, but suspicions were focused back on Amy when someone suggested to clearly check all records of arsenic purchases. When evidence was found of Amy sending her patients to the drugstore to buy quantities of arsenic, the police were able to arrest and convict her. Archer-Gilligan was arrested and tried for murder, originally on five counts. Ultimately her lawyer managed to have the charges reduced to a single count, the murder of Franklin R. Andrews. On June 18, 1917, a jury found her guilty, and she was sentenced to death. Archer-Gilligan appealed and was granted a new trial in 1919. At this trial,

Mariticide Club

she pled insanity. Mary Archer testified that her mother was addicted to morphine. Archer-Gilligan was again found guilty of murder, but this time she was sentenced only to life imprisonment. In 1924, Archer-Gilligan was declared temporarily insane and was transferred to the Connecticut Hospital for the Insane in Middletown, where she remained until her death on April 23, 1962.

Alice Brigantine Arden (1516–1551) was an English murderess. She was the daughter of John Brigantine and Alice Squire, who conspired to have her husband, Thomas Arden of Faversham, murdered so she could carry on with a long-term romantic affair with a tailor, Richard Mosbye. (or "Mosbie") The murder took place on Valentine's Day February 14, 1551. She was charged with "petty treason" viz. a wife murdering her husband, tried, convicted, and burnt at the stake for her part in the murder. The murder was described by Raphael Holinshed in his Chronicles and later had entries in both The Newgate Calendar and the Chambers Book of Days. Alice Brigantine married Thomas Arden on an unknown date. They made their home at Faversham Abbey, which had been dissolved in 1536. They had at least one daughter, Margaret, who was born in 1538. According to these accounts, Alice was "young, tall, and well-favored of shape and countenance". She began an affair with a tailor, Richard Mosbye, and then she plotted to kill her husband, Thomas Arden who was a "private gentleman". His rival Mosbye was in the service of Edward North, 1st Baron North, before setting up shop in London. Mosbye frequented the house of the Ardens and the affair was carried on rather openly. Thomas had to turn a blind eye, unwilling to sever relations with Alice's family. In time Alice came to loathe her husband and considered disposing of him. She made an early attempt on his life by poisoning him. She mixed milk and poison within a porringer, serving it to Thomas for breakfast. She had failed to account for the taste of the poison used. Thomas only took "a spoonful or two" before quitting his breakfast and complaining of its quality.

Alice decided to find an accomplice for her further efforts. Holinshed simply mentions: "They employed as their confederates one John Green, a

Wives Who Kill

Faversham tailor; George Bradshaw, a goldsmith of the same town; and one Black Will, of Calyce (Calais), a murderer, which murderer was privily sent for to Calyce by the earnest sute, appoyntment, and confederate of Alice Arden and Thomas Mosbye." The Newgate Calendar gives a more extensive account. Alice found her accomplice in the person of Mr. Green, a local man who had personal grievances with Thomas Arden. Green had claimed a piece of land on the back side of Faversham Abbey. Arden claimed the vicinity of his residence as part of his own property, successfully wresting control of Green's land. The two men had exchanged blows and threats before. Green still hated his enemy and was willing to work for his murder. Since both were inexperienced in the art of murder, they decided to hire someone else to do the deed, resolving to pay the mercenary ten pounds for the completed murder.

Green was employed by Sir Anthony Agers. Agers had business in London. He was already there for a while before asking Green to join him there. Green was reluctant to travel alone and hired Mr. Bradshaw to accompany him. Bradshaw was a local goldsmith and veteran soldier, having served under Sir Richard Cavendish during the Sieges of Boulogne. In their travel they chanced on an old acquaintance of Bradshaw, known as "Black Will". Will was also a veteran soldier who had committed "several robberies and horrid murders" in France. Armed "with a sword and buckler", Will was making his living as a highwayman since leaving military service. Green decided he had found his mercenary, hiring Will for the murder. Holinshed mentions a number of failed attempts on Thomas's life. "The conspirators watched Master Arden walking in Poule's (St. Paul's Cathedral, the nave of which was a public promenade in those days), but could not find an opportunity to murder him; they then lay in wait for him on Rainham Down, and a second time in the Broomy Close (two places near Faversham), but on all these occasions failed in obtaining an opportunity." Rainham Down probably being Rainham on the North Downs.

The Newgate Calendar again expands on the basic narrative: Black Will followed Green to London. The duo soon met Thomas Arden who had traveled there for his own purposes. Green used a walk to Old St Paul's

Mariticide Club

Cathedral to have Will take a close look at his intended victim. Arden was accompanied by a servant called Michael or Marry who was loyal to Alice. Green wanted to use the servant to gain access to Arden's lodgings in London. Black Will offered to kill both master and servant. Green informed the servant of this threat to his own life. This backfired. The servant was terrified of Black Will, making sure to bolt the doors of their lodgings at night, preventing Will or anyone else from entering.

An attempt to ambush Arden on his return journey also failed. The servant pretended that his horse went lame, having Arden travel alone. Instead, Arden convinced various acquaintances to travel with him, never actually being isolated enough for Will to ambush him. Arden returned home safely. Arden had business with Thomas Cheney, Lord Warden of the Cinque Ports in South-East England. He had his servant travel to the Isle of Sheppey and meet Cheney. The servant returned with a letter from Cheney. Alice concealed the letter and had the servant claim to have lost it. This had the intended effect. Thomas decided to travel to the Isle of Sheppey and meet Cheney in person. Black Will and George Shakebag, a fellow highwayman, were instructed by Alice to ambush him on his way there "in a broom-close between Feversham and the Ferry". Unfamiliar with the area, the highwaymen set their ambush at the wrong location, failing to meet Arden either at his journey to the Isle or on his return.

Another idea to accomplish the deed was stillborn. Valentine's Day was approaching and there would be a fair. Mosbye would have to pick a fight with Thomas in public and then end the life of his rival in a duel. With Thomas's known reluctance to fight, the idea of his accepting a challenge was deemed absurd. Holinshed continues: "The wicked wife then laid a plot for murdering her husband in his own house. She procured the services of Mosbye's sister, Cicely Pounder, and of two of Arden's domestic servants, Michael Saunderson and Elizabeth Stafford. On a particular day selected Sunday, Black Will was hidden in a closet at the end of Arden's parlor. After supper, Arden sat down to play some kind of game with Mosbye; Green stood at Arden's back, holding a candle in his hand, to shadow Black Will when he should come out; and the other conspirators

Wives Who Kill

had their cue. At a given signal in the game, Black Will came with a napkin in his hand, and suddenly came behind Arden's back, threw the napkin over his head and face, and strangled him; and forthwith Mosbye stepped to him, and struck him with a tailor's great pressing iron upon the skull to the brain, and immediately drew out his dagger, which was great and broad, and therewith cut Arden's throat." Alice herself stabbed her husband's body seven or eight times. Will helped drag the body into the closet. He then received eight pounds for his services. Cicely Pounder later helped transferring the body to the Almery Croft, a meadow behind the house. Finishing the task, "the doubly wicked Alice and her companions danced, and played on the virginals, and were merry." All this noise had a purpose. They wanted to have the neighbors think that Thomas Arden was still alive and entertaining friends. The corpse dressed in nightclothes would convince them of the hour of its death.

From here, the Newgate Calendar account diverges considerably. At last, Alice and her fellow conspirators decided to kill Thomas within the walls of their house. She arranged for most of their servants to be sent on various tasks outside the residence, "except those who were privy and consenting to the villainous design". She had Black Will hide in a closet located at the parlor of the residence, waiting for a pre-arranged signal to come out. At about 7 p.m., Thomas returned home to find Mosbye already there. He was told their supper was not ready yet. The two men agreed to a game of backgammon while waiting for Alice to call them.

The two men were in the parlor, with Arden having his back turned to the closet. Mosbye kept him distracted until voicing the signal "Now I may take you, Sir!". Will rushed from the closet and started strangling their victim with a towel. Mosbye struck Arden with a fourteen-pound pressing iron. He was knocked out. The two men then transferred their victim to his counting house. There, Will finished him. Will stole the money from the corpse's pockets and stripped it of its rings. Alice paid him his ten pounds and Green provided him with a horse to make his escape. Alice, to make certain that her husband was indeed dead, stabbed him seven or eight times. Then she had the parlor cleaned and the blood wiped

Mariticide Club

away with a cloth. The bloody knife and cloth were then discarded. When everything was prepared, guests started arriving for a delayed supper. They included Mosbye's sister, Cicely. Alice feigned ignorance at the reasons her husband was taking so long to return home. "When supper was over, Mrs. Arden made her daughter play on the virginals, and they danced, and she amongst them." Alice made sure to keep her guests around as long as possible while constantly reminding them of the suspicious absence of her husband. Then she sent most of the servants out to look for their master. Meanwhile, Alice, her daughter Margaret Arden, Cicely Pounder and the maid Elizabeth Stafford would transport the corpse outside the house. They "carried it out into a field adjoining to the churchyard, and to his own garden wall, through which he went to church." They laid it down "about ten paces from the door of that garden", making it seem that Thomas was murdered outside.

According to Holinshed, Alice waited until the following morning to alert the town that her husband had gone missing. The townspeople conducted a search and the corpse was discovered. "Some of the people saw a 'long rush or two from the parlor floor there were no carpets in those days, stuck between one of his slippers and his foot. Suspicion being aroused, the house was searched, and it was soon found that Arden had been murdered in his own parlor.' Very likely Alice's conduct as a wife had already attracted public attention; for she was at once accused of the murder."

The Newgate Calendar gives a rather different account. That night, Alice made a show of her supposed worry for her husband's disappearance. She had her servants search for him late into the night, wept and lamented, alerted the neighbors. At last, the local mayor was informed and a townwide search was contacted. When the corpse was discovered, the people involved with the search started doubting the innocence of Alice. It was a cold winter night and there was fresh snow on the ground, but the body was dressed only in "its nightgown and slippers", making it seem unlikely that he was going about his business in town when killed. The fresh snow had preserved footprints of several people in the distance between the location

Wives Who Kill

of the body and the residence of the Ardens, making it plain the body had been transported from the house to its current position.

Suspicions immediately fell on Alice. She was confronted by the mayor and "very strictly examined" on the murder of her husband. She initially denied any knowledge of the deed. But the people of the town conducted further searches near the house, discovering hair and blood of the victim, the bloody knife and the cloth, which was discarded but poorly hidden. Alice was at length forced to confess to her guilt, while also naming her associates. The two Arden ladies (mother and daughter), the servant and the maid were arrested and sent to prison. Mosbye was not present. He was found sleeping at "Fleur-de-Luce" (fleur-de-lis), the house of Adam Fowle, which he frequented. With blood found on his stockings and coin purse, this conspirator is also arrested.

A bit more controversial was the arrest of Bradshaw. He was mentioned in the correspondence between Alice and Green as the man who introduced them to Black Will. The goldsmith was then accused of being a "procurer of Black Will". He was otherwise unconnected to the case. The rest of the accused claimed to have never even met the man, much less conversed or conspired with him, but his protests of innocence failed to convince the court.

To be hanged, drawn and quartered became a statutory penalty for men convicted of high treason in the Kingdom of England from 1352 under King Edward III (1327–1377), although similar rituals are recorded during the reign of King Henry III (1216–1272). The convict was fastened to a hurdle or wooden panel, drawn by horse to the place of execution, then hanged, emasculated, disemboweled, beheaded, and quartered (chopped into four pieces). His remains would often be displayed in prominent places across the country, such as London Bridge, to serve as a warning of the fate of traitors. For reasons of public decency, women convicted of high treason were instead burned at the stake. The same punishment applied to traitors against the king in Ireland from the 15th century onward; William Overy was hanged, drawn and quartered by Lord Lieutenant Richard Plantagenet, 3rd Duke of York in 1459, and from the reign of King Henry

Mariticide Club

VII it was made part of statute law. Matthew Lambert was among the most notable Irishmen to suffer this punishment in 1581 in Wexford. Severity of the sentence was measured against the seriousness of the crime. As an attack on the monarch's authority, high treason was considered a deplorable act demanding the most extreme form of punishment. Although some convicts had their sentences modified and suffered a less ignominious end, over a period of several hundred years many men found guilty of high treason were subjected to the law's ultimate sanction. They included many Catholic priests executed during the Elizabethan era, and several of the regicides involved in the 1649 execution of Charles I. Although the Act of Parliament defining high treason still is on the United Kingdom's statute books, during a long period of 19th-century legal reform the sentence of hanging, drawing, and quartering was changed to drawing, hanging until dead, and posthumous beheading and quartering, before being abolished in England in 1870. The death penalty for treason was abolished in 1998.

Alice Arden was found guilty of the crime of murder of her husband (Petty treason) and burnt at the stake in Canterbury. Her co-conspirators were all rounded up and executed by various means at different locations. Michael Saunderson was drawn and hanged or hanged in chains at Feversham. Elizabeth Stafford, the maid, was burned at the stake in Faversham. Richard Mosbye and Cicely Pounder, brother and sister, were hanged at Smithfield; Bradshaw was hanged in chains at Canterbury.

There are two accounts given on the fate of John Green. Holinshed simply mentions that Green was hanged at Faversham. The Newgate Calendar has him evading arrest for some years. He was eventually caught and "hanged in chains in the highway between Ospringe and Boughton". Before he died, Green attempted to clear the name of Bradshaw, proclaiming the innocence of the long-dead goldsmith. Black Will ended his life on a scaffold. Holinshed mentions that Will "escaped for many years, but was at length taken, and 'brent on a scaffold at Flushing'". This could be Flushing, Cornwall. The Newgate Calendar agrees on the manner of death but places the execution at Flushing, Zeeland. Adam Fowle was also implicated and

Wives Who Kill

incarcerated for some time in the Marshalsea prison. He alone was found innocent and discharged. Chambers Book of Days mentions the event entering local legend. "It was long said that no grass would grow on the spot where Arden's dead body was found; some, in accordance with the superstitions of the times, attributed this to the murder; while others declared that 'the field he had cruelly taken from a widow woman, who had curst him most bitterly, even to his face, wishing that all the world might wonder on him.' " In 1592, the events were dramatized in the play Arden of Faversham. The paternity of the play has been long disputed, with William Shakespeare being most prominent of the candidates and, in 2020, Thomas Watson purported to be the main author. The play was adapted by George Lillo into a domestic tragedy. Alice Arden's story was also adapted into a broadside ballad, "The complaint and lamentation of Mistresse Arden of Feversham in Kent".

Shirley Jane Turner Bagby

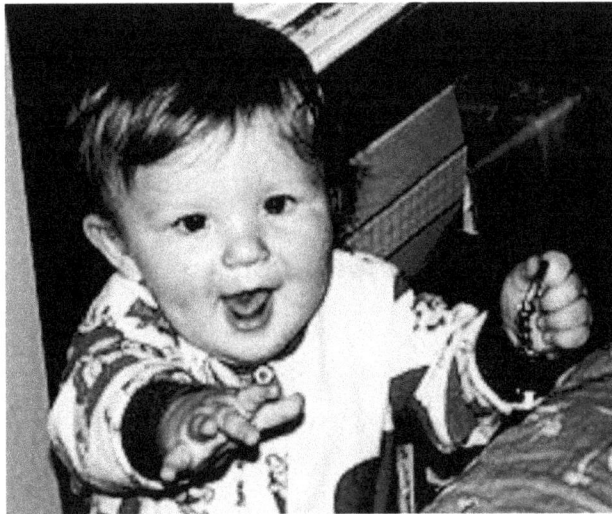

Murderer of Zachary Andrew Turner (age 1)
and Andrew David Bagby (age 28)

The deaths of Andrew Bagby and Zachary Turner became the basis for the 2008 documentary film Dear Zachary: A Letter to a Son About His Father, directed by Kurt Kuenne. Shirley Jane Turner (January 28, 1961 – August

Mariticide Club

18, 2003) was brought up with three siblings in Wichita, Kansas, but moved to Newfoundland with her mother after her parents separated; the parents later divorced. In 1980, Shirley Jane Turner enrolled at Memorial University of Newfoundland in St. John's, seeking to embark on a medical career. Beginning in early 1999, Shirley Jane Turner began dating Andrew David Bagby (September 25, 1973 – November 5, 2001), an American medical student studying at Memorial University for his third year. Bagby came from Sunnyvale, California, and was the son of Kathleen Daphne Bagby (née Barnard), a registered nurse and midwife from Chatham, England, United Kingdom; and David Franklin Bagby, an American former United States Navy serviceman and computer engineer. August 2000, Shirley Jane Turner moved to Sac City, Iowa, to begin work for Trimark Physicians Corporation. Meanwhile, after graduating from Memorial University in May 2000, Bagby landed a surgical residency at the State University of New York Upstate Medical University at Syracuse, New York. Despite the distance between states, Turner and Bagby tried to maintain a long-distance relationship. By Shirley Jane Turner's account, she visited David Bagby's residence in Syracuse seven times while he visited her once in Sac City. During one of these visits, Shirley Jane Turner burglarized David Bagby's apartment. In the fall of 2001, Bagby moved to Latrobe, Pennsylvania, and began his residency at a family practice under the supervision of T. Clark Simpson. On July 10, 2001, less than a year into her ten-year contract with Trimark, Shirley Jane Turner left their Sac City clinic and moved to Council Bluffs, Iowa, where she was hired by Alegent Health System of Omaha, Nebraska. In October 2001, Shirley Jane Turner obtained a permit to buy a firearm and purchased a Phoenix Arms HP22 handgun and .22 ammunition, which she used during firearms lessons. Meanwhile, Turner exhibited possessive behavior towards Bagby and harassed him over the phone. On October 13th, Turner told Bagby that she was three months pregnant. Bagby agreed to talk with her about the pregnancy during a wedding that Bagby was scheduled to attend. When Turner visited him in Latrobe in late October 2001—immediately after the last of her firearms lessons in Omaha—the two frequently argued over his

Wives Who Kill

relationship with a new girlfriend. On November 3, 2001, Turner confessed that she had been lying about her pregnancy in an effort to remain with Bagby permanently. Furious about this, Bagby drove Turner to the Arnold Palmer Regional Airport and broke up with her over lunch, sending her on a plane back to Iowa. Zachary Andrew Turner (July 18, 2002 – August 18, 2003) was Shirley Jane Turner's child whom she killed in a murder–suicide. Zachay's father was Shirley Jane's husband, who had been her long-time boyfriend. At the time, Shirley Jane had been released on bail and awarded custody of the infant, while in the process of being extradited to the United States to stand trial for the murder of Andrew David Bagby. The case led to a critical overview of Newfoundland's legal and child welfare systems as well as Canada's bail laws. A 2006 inquiry found serious shortcomings in how the province's social services system handled the case, suggesting that the judges, prosecutors, and child welfare agencies involved were more concerned with presuming Shirley's innocence than with protecting Zachary. The inquiry concluded that Zachary's death had been preventable. The case led to passage of Bill C-464, or Zachary's Bill, strengthening the conditions for bail in Canadian courts in cases involving the well-being of children. Upon becoming pregnant, Turner married her long-time boyfriend during Memorial University's 1981 winter recess. The child, a boy, was born on July 9, 1982. Turner's husband raised the child as a stay-at-home dad while Turner continued her studies. In 1983, Turner moved to Labrador City and worked as a science teacher. Two years later, she gave birth to a daughter. During this period, she resumed a previous relationship with a fisherman from Corner Brook. Following the end of her first marriage on January 29, 1988, Turner married her boyfriend from Corner Brook the following July. She also had an abortion that July, but the father was not known. Turner gave birth to her second daughter on March 8, 1990, one year before she and her second husband separated. Turner completed her undergraduate education while raising her children with help from her second husband. In October 1993, a man boarding with Turner confided to his therapist he had seen Shirley Jane Turner physically and emotionally

Mariticide Club

abusing two of her children. Newfoundland social service workers interviewed the children, who stated that their "disciplinarian" mother punished them with spankings and beatings by belt. Turner's second husband claimed that she used the belt only as a threat in his interview. The case was closed on January 11, 1994 without an interview with Turner. Three years later, Turner and her second husband divorced, and she was granted custody of their daughter. Within days of the ruling, Turner sent her daughter back to live with her father in Portland Creek; her other two children were sent to Parson's Pond to live with their paternal grandmother. Since 1982, Turner had taken out baby bonuses for her children from a scholarship fund, expecting to send them to college. In the summer of 2000, Turner confessed to a relative that she had spent the baby bonuses on her own living expenses and doctoral education. Turner insisted that she would earn "big money" after completing her post-residency training and would repay the savings for her children's post-secondary education. Turner received her undergraduate degree from Memorial University in May 1994; four years later, she earned her medical degree. Between 1998 and 2000, she was a resident physician at teaching hospitals across Newfoundland. During a 1999 residency at a family practice in St. John's, Turner's professionalism drew harsh criticism by her supervising physician, who stated she would become "quite hostile, yelling, crying, and accusing me of treating her unfairly." During her remedial second residency period in early 2000, Turner missed nine days of her three-month rotation and falsified clinical reports. A patient of the clinic refused to return after an encounter with Turner. The staff became "so concerned about Shirley Turner's approach to confrontation and the truth that we would never give her feedback or hold any major discussion [with her] alone." These incidents left the supervising physician with the impression that: I felt I was being manipulated whenever I spoke with Shirley Turner. When negative items would come up, she would change the topic to one of my failings. She could be charming[,] friendly and lively, but when caught in an untruth, she would become angry, accusatory, and loud. I always felt Shirley Turner was putting on a show as if she were playing the role but had no feeling for

Wives Who Kill

her work. I cannot recall a trainee like Shirley Turner in that her approach lacked personal commitment, and her relationships with people seemed, at least to me, to be superficial when compared to the over 400 residents I have supervised during the past 21 years. In a later interview with an assessment officer at the Office of the Child and Youth Advocate, the supervising physician, in hindsight, described Turner as "a manipulative, guiltless psychopath." The experience with Turner led that St. John's practice to make "constructive changes" in its residency evaluation process. By the summer of 2000, Turner had completed the requirements of her residency training and was qualified to practice medicine.

In March 1996, Turner began a relationship with a St. John's resident, Miles Doucet, who was thirteen years her junior. After Doucet broke up with Turner and moved elsewhere in Newfoundland, she began inundating him with phone calls. In November 1997, Turner confronted him in Halifax, Nova Scotia, and struck him in the jaw with her high-heeled shoe. After consulting with his parents, Doucet moved to Westtown Township, Pennsylvania, United States in 1998. Turner followed the man to Pennsylvania, leaving threatening voicemails over the following year and making unannounced visits to his apartment. On several occasions, he had summoned state troopers to order her to leave. He expressed fear to police of "what Dr. Turner would do next."

On 7 April 1999, Doucet found Turner lying semi-conscious outside of his apartment, having ingested a combined 65 milligrams of over-the-counter drugsin a suicide attempt. Turner was wearing a black dress, carried a bouquet of red roses and had two suicide notes on her. One note had been addressed to Doucet and the other to her psychiatrist; the latter read, "I am not evil, just sick." Turner was rushed to a hospital, where she received a gastric lavage. The following day Doucet received a voicemail from a female caller who stated, "Dr. Turner died last night." On November 4, 2001, Turner made a total of three phone calls to Bagby's residence in Latrobe. At approximately 1:00 p.m. local time, Turner embarked on a 16-hour, 1,523-kilometre (946 mi) drive to Latrobe with her gun and ammunition inside a gun box in her Toyota RAV4. In the early morning of

Mariticide Club

November 5, 2001, she confronted Bagby at his residence, located across the street from his practice. Bagby arrived at work in an "agitated" state and told Simpson about her appearance but dismissed Simpson's advice to not meet with her in private; Bagby subsequently promised to visit Simpson's house after talking to Turner that evening, but he never showed up. Turner later drove home and left a message on Bagby's answering machine.

The following morning, Bagby's body was found in a day-use parking lot at Keystone State Park in Derry Township, Pennsylvania. He had been shot five times in the face, the chest, the buttocks, and the back of the head with CCI .22 bullets. Acting on statements by Simpson and others, the Pennsylvania State Police contacted Turner. Despite her claim to havebeen in bed sick on 5 November, cell phone and Internet records showed that she had made cross-country calls both to and from Latrobe, accessed eBay and Hotmail from Bagby's home computer, and used his home phone to call in sick. When confronted with this evidence, Turner claimed that she met with Bagby at Keystone State Park but that he put the gun in his trunk. Turner alternately told her shooting instructor that her gun had been stolen.

Investigators interviewed Turner's shooting instructor, who explained that her handgun ejected live rounds during lessons; this was consistent with an unspent round recovered near Bagby's body. Later, a Derry resident reported having seen Bagby's Toyota Corolla parked next to Turner's RAV4 ten minutes after Bagby made his last phone call to Simpson and the Corolla parked alone the following morning. The lot number on a box of condoms found in Turner's Council Bluffs apartment matched a box purchased by Bagby in Latrobe on the night of the break-up. Also, in Turner's apartment were MapQuest printouts for road directions to Latrobe. Despite the evidence gathered, Turner had fled the country by the time authorities obtained a warrant for her arrest.

Wives Who Kill

The Supreme Court of Newfoundland and Labrador; Shirley Turner's extradition proceedings were conducted here.

On November 12, 2001, Turner abandoned her residence in Council Bluffs and flew to Toronto, eventually resettling in St. John's with her oldest son. Acting in collaboration with the Pennsylvania State Police, the Royal Newfoundland Constabulary's (RNC) Intelligence Unit conducted surveillance on her movements. On December 2, the Unit seized her trash and discovered printouts for an ultrasound taken on 29 November, showing a fetus that was conceived with Bagby the previous month. The RNC arrested Turner on December 12, the same day extradition proceedings commenced against her. However, Newfoundland Justice Gale Welsh believed Turner, then 40, wasn't a threat to society, despite the murder charges awaiting her in Pennsylvania. Turner was released from Her Majesty's Penitentiary's Clarenville Correctional Center for Women, and was required to post CAD$75,000 bail, turn in her passports, pay weekly visits to the RNC, promise not to leave the area, and make no attempt to contact Bagby's family. Turner posted bail with help from her psychiatrist, John Doucet, a former co-worker from Memorial University. The news that Turner was pregnant with Bagby's child turned the extradition case into one involving child custody, and subsequently led to a complicated legal saga. David and Kathleen Bagby moved to St. John's, Newfoundland, in order to fight for custody of their son's child, while Turner eventually moved into her own apartment on Pleasant Street in St. John's.

Mariticide Club

After Zachary's birth on July 18, 2002, Turner refused to allow David and Kathleen Bagby to see their grandson, fearing they would kidnap him. She went so far as to discharge her family law lawyer because of his positive attitude towards the Bagbys. On several occasions, it was noted that Zachary had poor attachment to his mother and preferred the company of other adults, particularly his grandparents. This preference was made especially clear during Zachary's first birthday party at a St. John's McDonald's, after which Turner said to Kathleen, "He obviously loves you more than me, so why don't you take him?" Turner was returned to jail in November 2002 pending a decision by the federal justice minister whether she should be extradited to the United States. However, in January 2003 Justice Welsh again released her, arguing that the murder "was not directed at the public at large" and that Turner was presumed to be innocent.

Conception Bay South, where Shirley Turner drowned
herself and her son Zachary

On 4 July 2003, Turner met a young man at a bar in St. John's. The pair dated and were sexually intimate on two occasions afterward. The man then broke off the relationship after learning from a friend about Turner's connection to Bagby's murder. Turner subsequently made a total of 200 threatening phone calls to the man over the following month. Turner claimed that she was pregnant by the man, but no evidence was found showing this to be the case. The man contacted the RNC on three occasions to complain about Turner's harassment, which both violated the terms of

Wives Who Kill

her bail and was considered grounds to lose custody of Zachary. However, because the man did not identify himself and declined to file any criminal complaint against Turner, no investigation was launched by the RNC. When a constable contacted Turner's lawyer about the harassment, she denied the allegations.

On 18 August 2003, Zachary was scheduled to be in his mother's custody. Turner first purchased her prescription of lorazepam from a St. John's pharmacy. She then drove with Zachary to nearby Conception Bay South, where the man she had met at the bar lived. Turner left her car parked near his home in the Kelligrews area of the town, with photographs of herself and Zachary, as well as a used tampon, on the front seat. Police concluded that she was attempting to frame the boyfriend for the planned murder–suicide. After mixing her lorazepam into Zachary's baby formula and ingesting a toxic dosage herself, Turner strapped the infant to her chest with her sweater and jumped off a fishing wharf at Foxtrap Marina into the Atlantic Ocean.0 Turner drowned. It was determined that Zachary Turner was rendered unconscious by the lorazepam and did not suffer. Turner's body was found on a beach by a vacationing couple, with Zachary's body discovered nearby. May 3, 2006, a disciplinary board convened by the College of Physicians and Surgeons of Newfoundland and Labrador found Doucet guilty of professional misconduct for his involvement in helping to post Turner's $75,000 bail. He was ordered to pay a fine of $10,000—covering one-third of the $30,000 incurred by the college for the inquiry—and was ordered to undergo psychiatric counseling. Doucet said he was "disappointed" by the verdict, while David Bagby stated that he was happy with the precedent his case would be setting. According to filmmaker Kurt Kuenne, Doucet later left Newfoundland and relocated elsewhere in Canada.

In October 2006, Winnipeg-based coroner Peter Markesteyn released the Turner Review and Investigation, which concluded that Zachary's death was preventable and criticized Newfoundland and Labrador's social services system for failing to protect the child from his mother, stating, "Nowhere did I find any ongoing assessment of the safety needs of the children." Markesteyn specifically cited poor communication between social services officials, who worked on the presumption of Turner's innocence throughout the case and became more concerned for her welfare than for Zachary's. Markesteyn ultimately concluded that internal disagreements between caseworkers and managers weren't openly discussed and that an intervention by an outside office should have been made. The provincial Government of Newfoundland and Labrador accepted the report's conclusions and its 29 recommendations. On October **23**, 2009, Scott Andrews, then a Liberal MP from Newfoundland and Labrador, introduced Bill C-464, or "Zachary's Bill", which would change the Criminal Code of Canada to allow the courts to justify refusing bail to those accused of serious crimes in the name of protecting their children. The bill received unanimous support in the Canadian House of Commons, and received support from Liberal Senator Tommy Banks. It was finally law by Governor-General David Johnston on 16 December 2010. Andrews later said that the law "gives [the Bagbys] some sense that someone has heard their cries so this will not happen again, to change the law to make sure something this tragic will never happen again." David Bagby penned a book about the case, *Dance with the Devil: A Memoir of Murder and Loss*, which was published in 2007.

Main article: Dear Zachary: A Letter to a Son About His Father

Written and directed by Kurt Kuenne, MSNBC Films and Oscilloscope Laboratories released Dear Zachary: A Letter to a Son About His Father on 31 October 2008. The film is partly composed of home movies Kuenne and Bagby shot together as teenagers in California, and features interviews with Bagby's parents, extended family, friends, classmates, and colleagues, both before and after Zachary's murder. A portion of the film also shows Kuenne meeting Zachary in Newfoundland in July 2003 to celebrate his first birthday, one month before his death; Shirley Turner is present during the visit, but Kuenne avoids her. The film premiered at the Slamdance Film Festival, and was broadcast by MSNBC on 7 December 2008.

The National Board of Review of Motion Pictures named the film one of the five top documentaries of 2008. The organizations that named it one of

Wives Who Kill

the best films of 2008 included: Time Out Chicago, The Oregonian, the Times Herald-Record, Slant Magazine, and WGN Radio Chicago. The website Film School Rejects placed the film third in their "30 Best Films of the Decade" list. The Film Vault included the film on their list of the "Top 5 Good Movies You Never Want to See Again".

The Chicago Film Critics Association nominated Dear Zachary for its Best Documentary award, and the Society of Professional Journalists presented the film with its Sigma Delta Chi Award for Best Documentary. The film also received the Special Jury and Audience Awards at the Cinequest Film Festival, was named an Audience Favorite at Hot Docs, received the Audience Awards at the St. Louis International Film Festival and the Sidewalk Moving Picture Festival, and was named Best Documentary at the Orlando Film Festival. Two scholarships have been established in tribute to Andrew David Bagby and his son. The Dr. Andrew David Bagby Family Medicine Scholarship is for medical students at Excela Health Latrobe Hospital, and almost four dozen students pursuing Bagby's specialty of family practice have benefited from the award. The Dr. Andrew Bagby and son Zachary Bursary Fund supports students at the Memorial University of Newfoundland.

Francisca Ballesteros
aka The Melilla Poisoner
The Poisoner of Melilla
Paqui Ballesteros
Francisca Ballesteros (born 1969) is a Spanish woman who poisoned to death her first baby, a five-month-old daughter, in 1990. Fourteen years later, in 2004, she killed her husband and second daughter because she had met a man on the Internet and wanted to run away from her parenting and marriage to be with her new found lover. Ballesteros then tried to poison her twelve-year-old son, although he survived after eight months of recovery. After her son's poisoning, Spanish authorities arrested her. She was convicted on three counts of murder and one count of attempted

Mariticide Club

murder and sentenced to eighty-four years in prison in 2005. Francisca Ballesteros was born in 1969 in Valencia. A few years later, she moved to Melilla. After marrying Antonio González Barribino, Ballesteros gave birth to a daughter, whom she named Florinda. In 1990, Ballesteros suffered from postpartum depression and wanted to end her marriage, but decided against it. She instead decided to kill her family and flee to Valencia. Ballesteros poisoned Florinda, then five-months old, with Colme, a drug used to treat alcoholism. After the death of her baby, Ballesteros decided to wait to kill the rest of her family. In 2004, 14 years after murdering her daughter, Ballesteros, who had met many men through the Internet, decided to kill the rest of her family, flee to the city where one of the men that she had met online was living, and marry him. On January 12, 2004 Ballesteros killed her husband Antonio González Barribino with Colme and with the sedatives Zolpidem and Bromazepam. On June 4, 2004, Ballesteros killed her daughter Sandra with the same medications and attempted to kill her 12-year-old son Antonio, who was admitted to the hospital with poisoning on June 4, 2004. The autopsy of her daughter Sandra revealed that she had been poisoned. On June 7, 2004 Ballesteros was arrested and confessed to the murders. On September 26, 2005 Francisca Ballesteros was sentenced to a term of 84 years in prison.

Maggie Velma Barfield (née Margie Velma Bullard)
Margie Velma Barfield (née **Bullard**; October 29, 1932 – November 2, 1984) was an American serial killer who was convicted of one murder, and eventually confessed to six murders. She was the first woman in the United States executed after the 1976 resumption of capital punishment and the first since 1962, and the first woman to be executed by lethal injection. Margie Velma was born in Eastover North Carolina and was brought up near Fayetteville, North Carolina. Her father was physically abusive and her mother, Lillian Bullard, did not intervene. Margie Velma escaped by marrying Thomas Burke in 1949. The couple had two children and were reportedly happy until Margie Velma had a hysterectomy and developed

Wives Who Kill

back pain. These events led to a behavioral change in Margie Velma and eventual drug addiction. Burke began to drink and Margie Velma Barfield's complaints turned into bitter arguments. On April 4, 1969, after Burke had passed out, Margie Velma and the children left the house, and when they returned they found the structure burned and Burke dead. In 1970, Margie Velma married a widower, Jennings Barfield. Less than a year after their marriage, Jennings died on March 22, 1971, from heart complications.

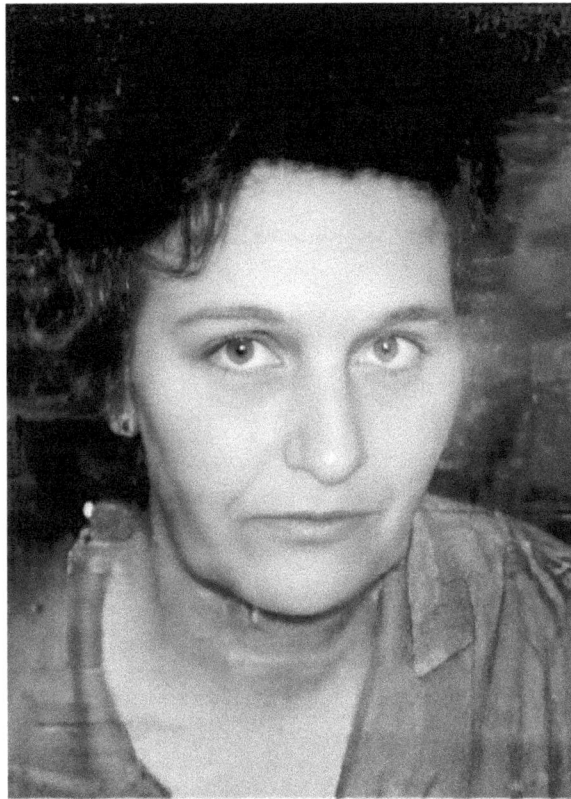

In 1974, Lillian Bullard, Barfield's mother, showed symptoms of intense diarrhea, vomiting and nausea, only to fully recover a few days later. Later that year during the Christmas season, Bullard fell ill again with the same symptoms, but died in the hospital a few hours after being admitted on December 30, 1974. In 1975, Margie Velma Barfield was convicted of seven counts of writing bad checks and sentenced to six months in prison. She was released after serving three months. In 1976, Margie Velma Barfield began caring for the elderly, working for

Mariticide Club

Montgomery and Dollie Edwards in Lumberton, North Carolina. Montgomery fell ill and died on January 29, 1977. Just over a month after the death of her husband, Dollie experienced symptoms identical to those of Bullard and died on March 1. Margie Velma Barfield later confessed to the murder of Dollie Edwards. The following year, Margie Velma Barfield took another caretaker job, this time for 76-year-old Record Lee, who had broken her leg. On June 4, 1977, Lee's husband, John Henry, began experiencing wracking pains in his stomach and chest along with vomiting and diarrhea. He died soon afterward and Margie Velma Barfield later confessed to his murder. Another victim was Rowland Stuart Taylor, Margie Velma Barfield's boyfriend and a relative of Dollie Edwards. Fearing he had discovered that she had been forging checks on his account, Margie Velma Barfield mixed an arsenic-based rat poison into his beer and tea. Edwards died on February 3, 1978, while Margie Velma was "trying to nurse him back to health"; an autopsy found arsenic in Taylor's system. After the arrest of Margie Velma, the body of Jennings Barfield was exhumed and found to have traces of arsenic, a murder that Margie Velma Barfield denied having committed. Subsequently Margie Velma confessed to the murders of Lillian Bullard, Dollie Edwards, and John Henry Lee; she was tried and convicted only for the murder of Taylor. Singer-songwriter Jonathan Byrd is the grandson of Jennings Barfield and his first wife. His song "Velma" from his Wildflowers album gives a personal account of the murders and investigation.

Margie Velma Barfield was imprisoned at Central Prison in Raleigh, North Carolina, in an area for escape-prone prisoners and mentally ill prisoners. There was no designated area for women under death sentences at the time and she was the state's only female death row inmate. A death row unit for female inmates in North Carolina was subsequently established at the North Carolina Correctional Institution for Women. During her stay on death row, Margie Velma Barfield became a devout Christian. Her last few years were spent ministering to prisoners, for which she received praise from Billy Graham. Margie Velma Barfield's involvement in Christian ministry was extensive enough that an effort was made to obtain

Wives Who Kill

a commutation to life imprisonment. A second basis for the appeal was the testimony of Dorothy Otnow Lewis, Professor of Psychiatry at New York University School of Medicine and an authority on violent behavior, who claimed that Margie Velma Barfield suffered from dissociative identity disorder. Lewis testified that she had spoken to Barfield's other personality, "Billy", who told her that Velma had been a victim of sexual abuse, and that he, Billy, had killed her abusers. The judge was unconvinced. "*One of them did it,*" Lewis quoted him as saying "*I don't care which one.*" After Margie Velma Barfield's appeal was denied in federal court, she instructed her attorneys to abandon a further appeal to the U.S. Supreme Court. Margie Velma Barfield was executed on November 2, 1984, at Central Prison. She released a statement before the execution: "*I know that everybody has gone through a lot of pain, all the families connected, and I am sorry, and I want to thank everybody who have been supporting me all these six years.*" Margie Velma Barfield chose as her last meal Cheez Doodles and Coca-Cola. Margie Velma Barfield was buried in a small, rural North Carolina cemetery near her first husband, Thomas Burke. Margie Velma Barfield's execution raised some political controversies when Governor Jim Hunt, who was challenging incumbent Jesse Helms for his U.S. Senate seat, rejected Margie Velma Barfield's request.

Albertine Barrett

Carlton "Carly" Barrett (December 17, 1950 – April 17, 1987) was a Jamaican musician best known for being the long-time drummer for Bob Marley & The Wailers. Recognized for his innovative style, which featured a highly syncopated, broken triplet pattern on the high-hat cymbals, and for his dazzling drum introductions, Barrett's prolific recordings with Marley have been internationally celebrated. He is credited with popularizing the One Drop rhythm. Carlton Barrett was born in Kingston, Jamaica in 1950, the son of Wilfred and Violet Barrett. As a teenager, he built his first set of drums out of empty paint cans he found on the street. Along with his contemporaries, drummers Sly Dunbar, Leroy "Horsemouth" Wallace, Style Scott and Carlton "Santa" Davis, Barrett was heavily

Mariticide Club

influenced by Lloyd Knibb of The Skatalites. In the 1960s, Barrett began performing with his brother Aston "Family Man" Barrett, under the names The Soul Mates, The Rhythm Force and eventually The Hippy Boys, a line-up that featured Max Romeo on vocals, Leroy Brown, Delano Stewart, Glen Adams and Alva Lewis. In 1969, the brothers joined The Wailers (later Known as Bob Marley and The Wailers). During his years with Marley, Barrett continued to record for many of Jamaica's most wellknown artists and is featured on solo albums by Bunny Wailer(Blackheart Man) and Peter Tosh (Legalize It and Equal Rights) as well as many others. On April 17, 1987, a gunman shot and killed Barrett outside his home at 12 Bridgemount Park Avenue in Kingston, Jamaica. He was 36. Carlton Barrett's widow, Albertine Barrett, was subsequently jailed on 18 October 1991, after being convicted of conspiracy to commit murder. Sentenced with her were taxi driver Glenroy Carter, 39, her lover, and Junior "Bang" Neil, 39, a mason, whom the prosecution alleged was responsible for the actual shooting.

Celeste Beard (née Celeste Johnson)

Celeste Beard Johnson (born February 13, 1963), more commonly known as Celeste Beard, is an American convicted murderer who is serving a life sentence at the Lane Murray (SHU) in Gatesville, Texas, for the 1999 murder of her millionaire husband, Steven Beard. Celeste Johnson's biological parents are unknown. She met her birth mother only one time and was told, "*I am not your mother, I was just your incubator.*" She claimed that her adoptive parent, Edwin Johnson, physically abused her as a child and that she attempted suicide during puberty. At age 17, Johnson became pregnant and gave birth to twins, Jennifer and Kristina, with her abusive first husband, Craig Bratcher. Bratcher committed suicide in 1996.

Johnson married twice more before meeting Steven Beard while she was a waitress at a country club in Austin, Texas. Beard, a retired Fox Broadcasting executive and self-made multi-millionaire more than twice her age, was a widower whose wife had died of cancer. Johnson moved in

Wives Who Kill

with Beard after he convinced her that he would legally adopt her daughters. They were married on February 18, 1995, with Beard's family and friends suspicious that Johnson had married him for his money. On October 3, 1999, Beard was shot in the stomach while he was asleep at their home in Westlake Hills, Texas. Beard was later released from the hospital, but succumbed to a blood clot on January 22, 2000. Local police tied the shooting to Tracey Tarlton, whom Johnson had met at Saint David's Pavilion, a mental health facility, after Johnson was admitted for depression. Tarlton confessed to the shooting and was arrested at home six days after the shooting, was charged with assault. The police began to hear that Johnson had spoken negatively about Beard. Their attorney, David Kuperman, refused to allow police to interview Beard while he was hospitalized, due to his grave condition. Tarlton remained silent until July 2000, when she read in a local newspaper that Johnson had remarried six months after Beard's death and realized that their relationship was a sham. Shortly before her murder trial began in March 2002, Tarlton told police that Johnson had persuaded her to shoot Beard, claiming that he had emotionally abused Johnson to the point of suicide. Tarlton was determined that getting rid of him was the only way the women could be together. Johnson has vehemently denied this persuasion. Based on Tarlton's statement, Johnson was arrested on March 28, 2002. At Johnson's trial, prosecutors charged that she had married Beard for his money and wanted him dead because he was tired of her extravagant spending and was considering divorce. The Beard attorney, David Kuperman, testified that Steven did not want a divorce and the underlying issues of the spending were addressed during joint therapy (both Beards in attendance) sessions treating Johnson's depression. According to Beard's accountant, Johnson spent $321,000 in October and November 1999, an additional $249,000 by December 10 and another $100,000 in six weeks ending March 31, 2000. Johnson's attorney, Dick DeGuerin, alleged that she had nothing to do with the shooting and that Tarlton, whom he dismissed as an unreliable witness due to documented mental instability, acted alone; Tarlton was obsessed with Johnson, who denied making sexual advances toward her. According

Mariticide Club

to Johnson and several witnesses, Tarlton tried to kiss her after she had passed out during her daughters' 1999 high school graduation. When Tarlton was arrested for drunk driving and Johnson bailed her out, Beard, angered by the relentless phone calls, demanded Tarlton stop contacting the couple. Several witnesses saw no unusual problems in Johnson and Beard's marriage, and DeGuerin alleged that Johnson's daughters lied on the witness stand because they would inherit no money if their mother were acquitted. Kristina was adverse during her testimony, answering to the defense, "*I do not remember*," 298 times.

In 2003, Johnson was convicted of capital murder, under The Texas Law of Parties, receiving a mandatory life sentence. She will be eligible for parole on April 1, 2042. Johnson continues to maintain her innocence for 19+ years and as of 2019 is imprisoned at the Texas Department of Criminal Justice Lane Murray Unit in Gatesville. Tarlton received a 10-year reduced sentence in exchange for testifying against Johnson, and was released on parole in August 2011 and lives in San Antonio. Celeste Beard's case was covered by American Justice, Snapped, Deadly Women, Vengeance: Previously unrevealed information about the lives, the crime, and the trial in the exclusive biography, The Celeste Beard Johnson Story, was released in 2019. Johnson and five other inmates published *From the Big House to Your House*, a cookbook that lists recipes that can be made in prison cells with ingredients from the prison commissary. In 2017, Celeste's daughter, Jennifer, was wounded after a shooting while attending a Halloween party. She had to undergo more than ten surgeries but survived. On June 13, 2021, Lifetime aired Secrets of a Gold Digger Killer, a TV film that featured Julie Benz as Celeste. In 2022, ABC aired two episodes titled "What the Sisters Saw - Part 1 & 2" on the show Who Do You Believe?. The show featured interviews with Celeste, her two daughters, and other people in the case.

Margery Beddingfield (née Rowe) (aka Margaret Beddingfield)
Margery Beddingfield (also known as Margaret Beddingfield) (1742–1763) was a British woman convicted and burnt for murder in 1763. Daughter to

Wives Who Kill

farmer John Rowe and his wife, Margery was named after her mother and baptized on June 29, 1742 in the Blaxhall church. She was married to John Beddingfield, a farmer, on July 3. 1759. They had one daughter Pleasance and one son John; the latter died when he was four months old. Four years into their marriage, Margery developed an illicit relationship with Richard Ringe, one of the house servants whom she promised to marry as soon as he "destroyed her husband". He at first persuaded a housemaid, Elizabeth Riches, to poison Beddingfield. After her refusal, he bought white arsenic from Aldeburgh and mixed it in John's water, who, fully unaware of their intentions, refused the cup after noticing the sediments. On the night of July 27, 1762, Margery shared the bed in the nearby kitchen chamber with Elizabeth Cleobald, another maidservant, and Ringe strangled Beddingfield while he was sleeping. To silence the maid, Margery gave her a gown. The coroner's inquest of Beddingfield's body showed signs of willful murder. He was buried on July 30, 1762. Both Ringe and Margery were tried at Lent Assizes before Baron of the Court of Exchequer Richard Adams. Ringe confessed to his crime and added that Margery's previous affection for him had turned to hatred. She eventually gave her confession. Since Beddingfield was Ringe's master and Margery's husband, both were convicted of petty treason. Margery was strangled and burnt Ringe was hanged at Ipswich on April 8, 1763 before a huge gathering of onlookers.

Betty Lou Beets (née Betty Lou Dunevant)

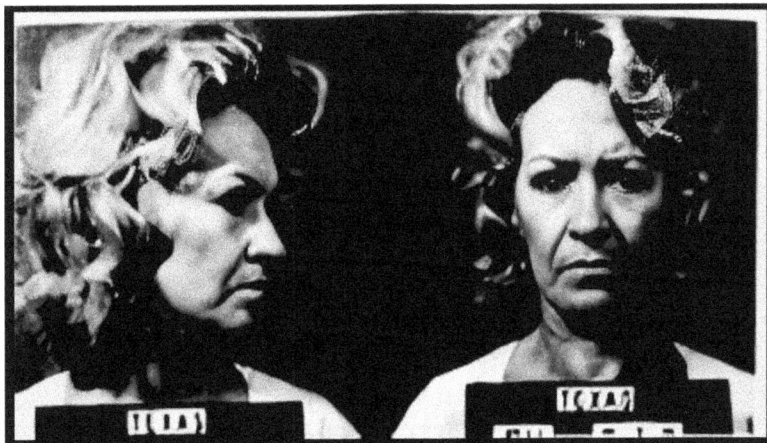

Mugshot of Betty Lou Beets

Mariticide Club

Husbands:

Robert Franklin Branson (m. 1952 – d. 1969)

Billy York Lane (m. 1970 – d. 1970)

Billy York Lane (remarried 1972 – d. 1972)

Ronnie C. Threlkold (m. 1978 – d. 1979)

Doyle Wayne Barker (m. 1979 – d. 1980)

Jimmy Don Beets (m. 1982 – murdered 1983)

Betty Lou Beets (March 12, 1937 – February 24, 2000) was a murderer executed in the U.S. state of Texas. She was convicted of shooting her fifth husband, Jimmy Don Beets, on August 6, 1983. Born Betty Lou Dunevant to Margaret Louise Smithwick (April 20, 1917 – June 16, 1993) and James Garland Dunevant (September 15, 1912 – February 14, 2003), she was born in Roxboro, North Carolina, on March 12, 1937. Beets was deaf due to a childhood bout with measles, and claimed she was sexually abused by her father. When Beets was a child, the family moved from North Carolina to Hampton, Virginia, where her father was employed as a machinist at the Langley Research Center. Her mother was institutionalized when she was 12 years old, leaving her to take care of her younger sister and brother. Beets married her first husband, Robert Franklin Branson, at age 15. All of her marriages were plagued with sexual abuse and domestic violence, Beets cited after her conviction and sentence of death. Beets had a criminal history prior to her arrest for murder, including public lewdness, and shooting former husband Bill Lane in the side of the abdomen. Married six times, twice to the same man (Bill York Lane), Beets shot Lane twice in the back in 1970; she was acquitted after Lane admitted he had threatened her life first and the two remarried, divorcing again a month later. She later tried to run over her third husband, Ronnie C. Threlkold, with her car in 1978. Both men survived and testified at her murder trial. On August 6, 1983, Beets reported her fifth husband, Jimmy Don Beets, missing from their home near Cedar Creek Lake in Henderson County, Texas. Her son, Robert Branson, later testified that Betty Lou Beets had said that she intended to kill her husband, and told

Wives Who Kill

her son to leave the house. On returning to the house two hours later, he found Jimmy Don Beets dead with two gunshot wounds. He helped his mother conceal the body below ground in the front yard of the house, after which Betty Lou Beets telephoned the police. According to her son, Beets put some of Jimmy Don's heart medication in his fishing boat the next day. Branson and Beets then abandoned the boat in the lake. It was found on August 12, 1983, washed ashore near the Redwood Beach Marina. Believing that he had fallen overboard and drowned, the police spent three weeks dragging the lake looking for Jimmy Don's body. In 1985, information was received by the Henderson County Sheriff that led to enough evidence to arrest Beets for the August 6, 1983, murder. After a search warrant was issued, a search of Beets' home found the remains of Jimmy Don in a filled-in wishing well. Also found buried in a garage were the remains of Doyle Wayne Barker, her fourth husband. Both had been shot with a .38 caliber pistol. She was never tried for Barker's murder. She was sentenced to death by lethal injection.

Mountain View Unit, where Beets was held on death row

Her trial for the murder for remuneration and the promise of remuneration of Jimmy Don Beets began on July 11, 1985, in the 173rd district court of Henderson County. She pleaded not guilty, claiming that two of her children had committed the murders. She was found guilty on October 11, 1985. The evidence of abuse was never presented to the court. During the separate penalty phase three days later, she was sentenced to death. Beets was Texas Department of Criminal Justice Death Row # 810. She

Mariticide Club

was received by Texas Department of Corrections October 14, 1985. She was incarcerated in the Mountain View Unit. An automatic appeal to the Texas Court of Criminal Appeals first overturned the conviction, saying that insurance and pension benefits were not the same as remuneration. The state requested a rehearing on September 21, 1988; this time, the Court ruled the conviction and sentence should stand. Ten years of appeals followed. The Supreme Court of the United States denied a writ of certiorari on June 26, 1989, and an execution date was set for November 8, 1989. On November 1, 1989, she received a stay from the trial court after she filed a state habeas petition. The Court of Criminal Appeals denied this request on June 27, 1990, leading to a second execution date of December 6, 1990. A federal petition for a writ of habeas corpus was filed three days before her scheduled execution, and the federal district court granted a stay of execution on December 4, 1990. Throughout the first half of 1991, evidentiary hearings were held, and on May 9, 1991, the court granted relief on one of Beets' claims, but denied all others. The United States Court of Appeals upheld the decision on March 18, 1993, and also overturned the one claim that had been granted relief. The case was sent to a federal district court, and on September 2, 1998, it denied her habeas corpus relief. After her appeals were denied throughout 1999, an execution date was set for February 24, 2000.

Huntsville Unit, where Beets died

Beets was executed by lethal injection at 6:18 pm CST on February 24, 2000, in the Huntsville Unit. She did not request a final meal, nor did she

Wives Who Kill

make a final statement. Beets was the second woman executed in the state after the reintroduction of the death penalty. At the time of the execution, she was 62 years old, and had five children, nine grandchildren, and six great-grandchildren. Like most executed criminals, Beets was cremated after her death. Her ashes were scattered over her mother's grave.

Ann Bilansky (née Mary Ann Evards Wright)

Ann Bilansky (born Mary Ann Evards Wright) (c. 1820 – March 23, 1860) was an American housewife convicted in 1859 of poisoning her husband with arsenic. She is the only woman in Minnesota to receive the death penalty and the first white person in the state to be executed by hanging. Mary Ann Evards Wright (known by her middle name, Ann) was born in Fayetteville, North Carolina, where she resided for several years with her first husband who later died in a railroad incident. She then moved to Pleasant Hill, Illinois, and then finally to St. Paul, Minnesota in April 1858 at the request of her nephew, John Walker, who was ill with typhoid fever. Shortly after, Ann married Stanislaus Bilansky, one of the first Polish immigrants to settle in St. Paul. He had moved to St. Paul from Wisconsin in 1848. Stanislaus was a poor man who drank heavily, but he owned a small cabin that doubled as a bar and grocery store. He had custody of his three young children left in his care after his second wife divorced him, and Ann frequently took care of the children when Stanislaus was ill or working. In 1859, Stanislaus was sick between March 6 and March 11, 1859, with what was thought to be indigestion, but his condition worsened rapidly as he consumed both alcohol and Graffenburg pills. Ann was seen crying at his bedside asking what she should do with the kids in case anything happened. Stanislaus died on March 11, 1859. As the funeral procession was leaving the Bilansky residence to bury Stanislaus at the cemetery, officials from the Ramsey County coroner's office arrived to conduct an inquest. A doctor examined the body and a coroner's jury was assembled to hear testimony from John Walker, a visiting neighbor named Lucinda Kilpatrick, and a housekeeper hired during Stanislaus' illness

Mariticide Club

named Roasa Scharf. The coroner's jury found that Stanislaus died of natural causes, but questioned why Ann had not called a doctor toward the end of his illness. Stanislaus was then buried on March 12, 1859, but that evening Kilpatrick changed her testimony to claim she saw Ann buying arsenic from a drugstore on February 28, 1859. Ann claimed the purchase was at Stanislaus' urging, so they might kill rats in the cellar. After taking Kilpatrick's new testimony, Stanislaus' body was exhumed for an examination and on March 13, 1859, Ann was arrested for the murder of her husband. A second coroner's jury convened to hear testimonies from Scharf and Kilpatrick, as well as from druggist W.H. Wolff and Dr. J.D. Goodrich. Wolff testified that a single crystal was found under a microscope that "resembled arsenic," but Goodrich was skeptical that Stanislaus was poisoned. The jury concluded that Stanislaus died of arsenic poisoning, a grand jury indicted Ann for the murder of her husband and a trial date was set for May 23, 1859.

The trial was conducted at the Ramsey County courthouse, and the prosecution, led by Isaac Heard, included three main arguments in their case against Ann: she had purchased arsenic and had the means to kill, she had inappropriate relations with Walker and therefore an affair gave her the motive for murder, and she had made comments that suggested she was contemplating murder. Kilpatrick was the state's principal witness, and Heard also relied heavily on Scharf's testimony, which stated that Ann made all of Stanislaus' meals separately and washed his dishes and utensils separately. Scharf also testified that Bilansky did not treat Stanislaus as a husband ought to be treated. Both Kilpatrick and Scharf testified Ann was having an affair with Walker, which County Attorney Heard argued was the murder motive. After all of the witnesses had spoken, an all-male jury began deliberations on June 3, 1859; and they took less than six hours to return with a "guilty" verdict. Upon hearing the verdict, Ann reportedly showed no visible signs of emotion or distress. Ann's defense asked for a new trial, but did not receive one as the judge considered her already found guilty in the court. Bilansky's attorney went before the Minnesota Supreme Court to try to prevent judge from imposing the death penalty, but Justices

Wives Who Kill

declined to intervene. Ann briefly escaped from the County Jail on July 25, 1859. She hid near Lake Como and eventually made contact with Walker, but was recaptured in his company on August 1, 1859. On December 2, 1859, Ann appeared in court for her sentencing where she proclaimed herself an innocent woman: *"If I die in this case, I die an innocent woman. I don't think I have had a fair and just trial."* She was sentenced to one month in solitary confinement followed by death by hanging. Governor Henry Sibley had the legal responsibility of setting the execution date, but he refused to set a date or commute the sentence, and he let his term expire at the end of 1859. The Minnesota House of Representatives made efforts to end capital punishment, but it was rejected shortly after. On January 18, 1860 another bill was introduced to prohibit the execution of women but was tabled. On January 25, 1860, newly elected Governor Alexander Ramsey set Ann's execution date as March 23, 1860. Another bill was passed by the state legislature on March 5, 1860, to try to help Ann, which stated that the first execution by Minnesota should not be that of a woman and that Ann had an unfair trial, but this was vetoed by Governor Ramsey on March 8, 1860. Ann requested a private execution, but at this point in the 19th century public executions were typical as they served civil and religious purposes to deter crime and demonstrate the danger of sin. On March 23, 1860, gallows were set up in an enclosure in Court House Square at the corner of Fifth and Cedar streets, and just before her execution Ann spoke her last words: *"I die without having had any mercy shown me, or justice. I die for the good of my soul, and not for murder. . . . Your courts of justice are not courts of justice—but I will yet get justice in Heaven."* Around 100 onlookers watched from inside the enclosure, while thousands more watched from outside the enclosure. Ann's body was left hanging for twenty minutes before she was buried in an unmarked grave in Calvary Cemetery. Throughout Ann's entire trial and execution, the St. Paul Pioneer and Democrat focused heavily on her gender. She was heavily criticized for her "lack of marital virtue," and at times the press was more focused on Bilansky's adultery than on her decision commit murder. The Democrat also criticized other women for

Mariticide Club

their eagerness to watch the execution. The day after the execution, the Democrat grew tired of the story, stating that it hoped to never have to report about Bilansky or the execution ever again. Ann Bilansky's trial and execution was the basis for Jeffrey Hatcher's stage play, A Piece of Rope, which premiered in St. Paul in March 2000.

Black Widow Gang
- **Sandra Giraldo**
- **Emilsen Yulima**
- **Nataly Rojas**

The Black Widow Gang, also known as The Black Widows of Colombia, is the nickname of a group of Colombian serial killers active during the late 2000s and early 2010s. They were charged with the murders of three men in Antioquia; and it is believed they are responsible for more crimes. The criminal network, composed mainly of women, was led by Sandra Giraldo Emilsen Yulima and Nataly Rojas. Each member had a different role within the gang, some focused on maintaining relationships with men, others on murdering them, and yet more were in charge of finding lawyers and managing life insurance collections. The total amount from insurance payments ranged from one hundred to eight hundred million pesos. One of the victims was Diego Hernández Beltrán, a 60-year-old master builder. According to the investigators, Hernández Beltrán was persuaded by an acquaintance of his to buy life insurance. When they learned of this, the gang decided to take advantage of it and invited Diego to camp at night near a reservoir called El Peñol-Guatapé on September 27, 2008. There, his hands and feet were tied and he was thrown into the reservoir, where he subsequently drowned. Hernández Beltrán's lifeless body was found the next day and claimed by Emilsen, who claimed to be his wife, with the couple having been married for two years. At the time, she claimed that she was the sole beneficiary for the life insurance, worth $150,000,000 pesos. Despite this, the family of the deceased disputed her claims, stating that Diego had never had any romantic bond with the woman.

Wives Who Kill

Black Widows of Liverpool
- **Catherine Flannagan**
- **Margaret Higgins**

Catherine Flannagan

Margaret Higgins

Mariticide Club

Catherine Flannagan (1829 – 3 March 1884) and Margaret Higgins (1843 – 3 March 1884) were Irish sisters who were convicted of poisoning and murdering one person in Liverpool, England, and suspected of four more deaths. The women collected a burial society payout (a type of life insurance) on each death, and were found to have been committing murders using arsenic to obtain the insurance money. Although Flannagan evaded police for a time, both sisters were caught and convicted of one of the murders; they were both hanged on the same day at Kirkdale Prison. Modern investigation of the crime has raised the possibility that the sisters were part of a larger conspiracy of murder-for-profit—a network of "black widows"—but no convictions were ever obtained for any of the alleged conspiracy members other than the two sisters. In 1880, unmarried sisters Catherine and Margaret Flannagan ran a rooming house at 5 Skirving Street in Liverpool. The household consisted of the two sisters, Catherine's son John Flannagan, and two lodger families—hod carrier Thomas Higgins, Higgins' daughter Mary, Patrick Jennings, and Jennings' daughter Margaret. John Flannagan, aged 22 and previously healthy, died suddenly in December 1880. His death did not raise any particular comment; Catherine collected £71 (£7120 in 2019 pounds) from the burial society with which he was registered and he was interred shortly thereafter. A brick hod is a three-sided box for carrying bricks or other building materials, often mortar. It bears a long handle and is carried over the shoulder. A hod is usually long enough to accept 4 bricks on their side. However, by arranging the bricks in a chevron fashion, the number of bricks that may be carried is only limited to the weight the laborer can bear and the unwieldiness of that load. Typically, ten to twelve bricks might be carried. Hod carrying is a labor occupation in the building industry. A hod carrier or 'hoddie' will be employed by a bricklaying team in a supporting role to the bricklayers. Two bricklayers for each hod carrier is typical. A hoddie's duties might include wetting the mortar boards on the scaffolding, prior to fetching bricks from the delivery pallet using his hod and bringing them to 2x2 wide 'stacks' upon the scaffold that may then be easily laid by the bricklayers. The carrier should plan the deliveries of bricks with

Wives Who Kill

deliveries of mortar—also carried in the hod—to ensure the bricklayers can maintain a constant work rate. At sites without premixed mortar, the mortar will also be mixed by the hod carrier. Bricks may be cut and assistance given to 'rake out' the mortar joints, if that coursing joint form is required, or in re-pointing work. The baseline rate for a bricklayer is to lay 1,000 bricks a day; if the hod carrier is serving a team of two then he must move 2,000 bricks although it is not uncommon for experienced hod carriers to serve three bricklayers. The World Record for moving 500 bricks by hod is 12 minutes set by Daren Whitmore on February 12, 2011. Song references:

- In the song Never Any Good, Martin Simpson describes his father as "not steady   enough for the office, not hard enough for the hod."
- In the Irish folk song "Finnegan's Wake", the line "...to rise in the world he carried a hod", suggests that Tim Finnegan worked as a hod carrier; hod is also a slang term for a drinking vessel.
- In the song "The Sick Note" by Pat Cooksey (performed by many), the narrator of the song is told to cart a load of bricks down fourteen floors "in me hod".
- The song "Seven Days of the Week" by Ewan MacColl and Peggy Seeger mentions "the poor old sod who'd built the world and carried the hod".
- In the song "McAlpine's Fusiliers" it says of Sir Robert McAlpine, "...McAlpine's God is a well-filled hod".
- In the song "Missing You" by Jimmy MacCarthy has the line "Your best mate's a spade and he carries a hod".
- The song "Hansel and Gretel" by Jerry Jeff Walker with Circus Maximus mentions "the stone walking away from the hod".

By 1882, a romance started between Margaret Flannagan and hod carrier Thomas Higgins; the pair married in October of that year. Thomas's daughter Mary, aged 8, died within months of the wedding after a short illness. Once again, the burial society payout was collected upon death, this

Mariticide Club

time by Margaret Higgins. In January 1883, Margaret Jennings, aged 19, also died. Her burial payout was collected by Catherine. In the face of neighborhood gossip about the death rate in the house, Catherine, Margaret, and Thomas Higgins moved their household to 105 Latimer Street and then again to 27 Ascot Street. In September 1883, Higgins, then 45, became yet another member of the household to fall mysteriously ill. His stomach pains were severe enough that a Doctor Whitford was called; he attributed Higgins' illness to dysentery related to drinking cheap whiskey and prescribed opium and castor oil. Higgins died after two days of illness. Days later, the doctor was contacted and asked to provide a death certificate. He did so, attributing the death to dysentery. Although Higgins's death by apparent dysentery raised no questions for Doctor Whitford, Higgins's brother Patrick was surprised to hear that Thomas, who had been strong and in good health, could have succumbed so easily to illness. When Patrick discovered that his brother had been insured with five different burial societies, which left his widow with a profit of around £100, he pursued the matter with the authorities. A postmortem examination was ordered on Higgins's body. To the surprise of mourners, the coroner arrived at the home to perform the examination inthe middle of Higgins's wake. Catherine, upon hearing that a full autopsy was to be performed, fled the home. When a full autopsy of Higgins's body was completed, evidence of arsenic poisoning was found: His organs showed traces of arsenic, in quantities indicating the poisoning had taken place over several days. Evidence from the home, including "a bottle containing a mystery white substance and a market pocket worn by Margaret" was examined by poison expert Dr Campbell Brown, who verified the presence of arsenic – dust in Margaret's pocket, and an arsenic solution (containing unusual adulterants) in the bottle. Margaret was arrested immediately; Catherine, after moving from one boarding house to another to avoid police for nearly a week, was taken into custody in Wavertree. On October 16, 1883, the sisters were formally charged with the murder of Thomas Higgins. Orders for the exhumation of the previously deceased members of the household were issued when it

Wives Who Kill

became clear that arsenic was the mechanism of Higgins' death. The bodies of John Flannagan, Mary Higgins, and Margaret Jennings all showed evidence of minimal deterioration, a quality associated with arsenic poisoning, and traces of arsenic were found in the remains of all three. Investigators initially assumed that the arsenic used to poison the victims had come from rat poison, but when common adulterants used in rat poison failed to show up in autopsies, they were forced to come up with a new theory. It was unlikely that the illiterate sisters would have been able to acquire arsenic through the usual method of visiting a chemist, a route open to doctors rather than spinsters. Eventually it was discovered that common flypaper at the time contained arsenic, and that by soaking the flypaper in water, a solution substantially identical – including the same adulterants – to that found in a bottle at the Higgins residence could be obtained. At the time of her arrest, Catherine claimed to her solicitor that the murders were not isolated, and provided a list of six or seven other deaths that she claimed to be killings related to burial society fraud as well as a list of five other women who perpetrated those murders or provided insurance to those who did. Catherine's list of conspirators contained three poisoners other than herself, one accomplice, and three agents of the insuring groups who had provided payouts upon the deaths. Margaret Evans, Bridget Begley, and Margaret Higgins were named as the poisoners; Margaret Potter, a Mrs. Fallon, and a Bridget Stanton were the insurers; and Catherine Ryan was alleged to have obtained the arsenic needed by one of the poisoners. According to Flannagan, Evans had been the instigator of the crime ring, beginning with the murder of a mentally handicapped teenager in which Ryan obtained the poison and Evans administered it. Although Evans did not personally receive an insurance payout from this death, there were implications that she had dealings with the boy's father and may have profited from those. The women Catherine alleged to have been involved in the conspiracy all appear often in accounts of suspicious deaths in this period; Mrs. Stanton, for example, was linked to the insurance policies of three of the deaths, and groups of two or more of the involved women were seen visiting those who died shortly before their deaths. In one case, when an insurance company supervisor requested to meet Thomas Higgins in the course of issuing the insurance on him, he was greeted at his home by a woman who was neither Flannagan nor Higgins, who presented to him a "Thomas" who he later realized, upon seeing the deceased Thomas Higgins, was an impostor. Catherine's testimony was sometimes contradictory to both herself and to what seemed to be obvious facts of the conspiracy; in one case, despite Mrs. Stanton's close links to the insurance payouts of murder victims and Catherine's identification of her as part of the conspiracy, she "exonerated" Stanton after police arrested the woman. Ultimately it was decided by the prosecuting solicitor for Liverpool that while the additional deaths were likely to be murder, it would be difficult to prove that anyone other than Catherine or Margaret had committed them, especially considering that the primary evidence against the other women was being provided by Flannagan, who had every reason to attempt to minimize her own responsibility in such crimes. As a result, only the sisters were tried for the crime of murdering Thomas Higgins, despite continuing suspicion by all investigating parties that there had been more deaths than just the four household ones, and more murderers than just the two women.

At the trial in 1884, prosecutors implicated Catherine and Margaret in the three other deaths in their household as well as that of Higgins, with which they were officially were charged. Catherine's offer to provide evidence against other conspirators for the prosecution in exchange for leniency was refused. The sisters were found guilty and sentenced to be hanged. The sentence was completed on March 3, 1884, at Kirkdale Prison, with the sisters attended to by a Roman Catholic priest. The deaths were witnessed by a reported 1,000 people. Contemporary accounts of the Flannagan sisters referred to them as "disciple[s] of Lucrezia Borgia", or as "the Borgias of the Slums", in reference to their use of poison and the tales of how Borgia had been known to do the same. Modern accounts of the sisters, such as those by Angela Brabin and television series Deadly Women, have focused more on the cooperative aspect of the crimes rather than the poison aspect, and tend to refer to them as "black widows" or "The Black Widows

Wives Who Kill

of Liverpool", particularly in reference to the allegation that the Flannagan sisters were part of a larger murder ring. Wax effigies of Flannagan and Higgins were placed in Madame Tussaud's Chamber of Horrors after their executions. A radio dramatization of the murders and following events titled Life Assurance, written by Chrissie Gittens based on the book The Black Widows of Liverpool by Angela Brabin (Palatine Books, 2003 ISBN 978-1-874181-21-7/2nd Rev Ed 2009 ISBN 978-1874181606) and directed by Claire Grove, was broadcast on BBC Radio 4 in 2005, with Sorcha Cusack as Catherine Flanagan, Gillian Kearney as Ellen Flanagan, Anny Tobin as Margaret Higgins, Robert Hastie as Inspector Keighley, Stephen Hogan as Thomas Higgins, Hugh Dickson as Dr. Whitford and Nicholas Boulton as Patrick Jennings.

The Black Widow Murders of California

The Black Widow Murders of California was a colloquial name for a pair of murders by two pensioners in California: On April 18, 2008, Helen Golay, 78, formerly of Santa Monica, California, and Olga Rutterschmidt, 75, formerly of Hollywood, California, were convicted of the murders of two vagrants—Paul Vados in 1999 and Kenneth McDavid in 2005. Golay and Rutterschmidt staged Vados and McDavid's deaths to appear as hit and run incidents in order to collect the proceeds from multimillion-dollar life insurance policies they had taken out on the men. Seventy-three-year-old homeless man Paul Vados was found lying dead in an alley in Hollywood, California, near 307 North La Brea Avenue on November 8, 1999. Vados, who had emigrated from Hungary in 1956, appeared to be the victim of a hit-and-run. Two years previously, in 1997, Golay and Rutterschmidt began applying for life insurance policies on Vados, listing themselves as the beneficiaries. After Vados's death, Golay and Rutterschmidt received benefits from eight different life insurance policies that had been taken out on him. According to a surveillance video, fifty-year-old homeless man Kenneth McDavid was hit by a silver 1999 Mercury Sable station wagon

Mariticide Club

on June 21, 2005. McDavid was originally from northern California and had attended Sacramento State University.

From November 2002 to March 2003, Golay and Rutterschmidt took out a total of thirteen policies on McDavid that totaled $3,700,000.00. On the various insurance applications, Golay and Rutterschmidt were listed as McDavid's business partner, cousin or fiancée. Before their arrest, Golay had received a total of $1,540,767.05 in insurance proceeds from McDavid's death, and Rutterschmidt a total of $674,571.89. Olga Rutterschmidt was born in Hungary in 1933. She emigrated to the United States in 1957 and owned a coffee shop in Los Angeles with her husband. Having divorced, she moved to Hollywood in the 1970s. Helen Golay was born in Texas in 1931. She lived in a $1.5 million home and also was a landlord, owning three more properties. As of November 2022, Rutterschmidt is serving her sentence at Central California Women's Facility, and Golay is at California Institution for Women. The women pleaded not guilty to the murders and nine counts of fraud. A third homeless man, Jimmy Covington, 48, testified at trial that he had been approached by Rutterschmidt. Covington asserted she took him to a Burger King restaurant for a meal, where she promised him shelter and assistance with obtaining welfare and other services for the destitute. He testified that he had moved out after a few days, due to growing suspicious when Golay and Rutterschmidt asked him to sign documents and demanded his date of birth, Social Security Number and other identifying information. By then, Golay and Rutterschmidt had already filled out one life insurance policy application for Covington. The case was described, by Deputy District Attorney Shellie Samuels, who prosecuted it, as "like Arsenic and Old Lace, but it doesn't have Cary Grant." The prosecution's case included secretly recorded conversations between Golay and Rutterschmidt when they were in jail. Rutterschmidt told Golay in one conversation "You did all these insurances extra. That's what raised the suspicion. You can't do that. Stupidity. You're going to go to jail, honey. They going to lock you up." Suspicion had in fact been raised when a detective overheard a colleague discussing a case whose features closely resembled that of another one.

Wives Who Kill

Both Golay and Rutterschmidt were convicted in Los Angeles, California, in April 2008, of conspiracy to murder Vados and McDavid, and of the first-degree murder of Vados. Golay was convicted of the first-degree murder of McDavid. Convictions on the several counts spanned a week, because one juror had to go on a trip and be replaced by an alternate. The original jury reached a deadlock over the final two counts against Rutterschmidt, but after the alternate juror was introduced the trial judge ordered the jury to re-commence deliberations. Both women were sentenced to consecutive life terms in California state prison, without possibility of parole. Appeals to the convictions and sentences were denied and judgments upheld, at first on August 18, 2009 by the Court of Appeal, Second District, Division 5, State of California, and ultimately by the California Supreme Court on October 28, 2012.

On February 10, 2010, "The Black Widow Murders" were featured on an episode of American Greed on CNBC. On September 10, 2009, the case was profiled on an episode of Deadly Women entitled "Behind the Mask". Also in 2009, the series Wicked Attraction featured an episode named "Golden Years" in its second season detailing the history and criminal acts of the two. On November 13, 2013, Elder Skelter featured a story about Ken McDavid's death. The episode was called "Death, Lies and Security Tape". On July 21, 2008, The Closer aired the episode "Speed Bump" loosely based on the Black Widow Murders, with a few changed details, such as paroled felons as victims instead of homeless men. Jenny O'Hara and Wendy Phillips guest-starred as the greedy villains. December 16, 2009, CSI: NY aired the episode "Second Chances" which mirrors a lot of Black Widow Murders, with younger cast, Kim Kardashian and Vanessa Minnillo as the money-hungry black widows. November 17, 2021, Dateline NBC released a 6 part Podcast titled "The Thing about Helen and Olga" presented and narrated by Keith Morrison.

Tommy Blake (musician)

At the age of 54, Tommy Blake was murdered by his third wife over marital disputes on Christmas Eve in 1985. Tommy Blake (born Thomas

Mariticide Club

LeVan Givens, September 14, 1931 – December 24, 1985) was an American rockabilly singer and songwriter active in the 1950s to the 1970s. Regarded as a skilled writer, Blake penned several songs that were later recorded by rock and country music artists, Johnny Horton, George Jones, and Johnny Cash among others. He also achieved modest success as a recording artist for Sun Records, but failed to record a national hit himself, a fact that frustrated Blake later in his life. Retrospectively, he has received praise for his contributions to rockabilly and was inducted in the Rockabilly Hall of Fame. Blake was born Thomas LeVan Givens in Dallas, Texas in 1931. He never knew his father nor did he develop a healthy relationship with his mother. His troubles continued into his teen years when Blake was imprisoned on statutory rape charges. In 1951, he joined the United States Marine Corps. During his service, he lost an eye, either, as Blake claimed, while on tour in Korea or more likely during boot camp. While in the Marine Corps, Blake nurtured his ambitions of being a professional musician by frequently singing and playing on the guitar for enlisted men before his discharge. He pursued his music career further when he settled in Shreveport, Louisiana to work as a deejay for the radio station KTBS and later for KRUS. In 1954, Blake persuaded the Rhythm Rebels, a duo featuring Carl Adams (lead guitar) and Eddie Hall (bass guitar), to operate as his backing group as he began touring on the live circuit and appearing on Southern television programs to gain exposure. On one such program, Louisiana Hayride, Blake closely observed the approach of Elvis Presley whose momentous performance on the show convinced Blake to adopt characteristics of rock and roll. To capitalize on the craze for rockabilly that began to dominate the American charts, Blake recorded his debut single, "Koolit", in 1956. "Koolit" was issued by Young Records in April but it failed to chart. In 1957, Blake arranged a one-off single deal with RCA Records record producer Chet Atkins in Nashville. Atkins hired a collection of session musicians, including Buddy Killen, Farris Coursey and Floyd Cramer to record the rhythm sections. The single, which included the band originals "Honky Tonk Mind" and "All Night Long", was given the full rockabilly treatment. According to music historian Shane

Wives Who Kill

Hughes, the session displayed Blake and the Rhythm Rebels' potential as songwriters; however, Blake attempted to cash-in on "Honkey Tonk Mind" offering it to Johnny Horton. RCA's competitor Columbia Records quickly released Horton's version in April 1957 under the title "The Woman I Need". Horton enjoyed a Top 10 hit on Billboard's country charts while Blake's rendition was shelved. Under advisement from RCA executives, Atkins released two songs recorded from Blake's session, "Freedom" and "Mister Hoody", then nullified his recording contract. Undeterred, Blake accepted a deal with Sun Records after Sam Philips met him at a disc jockey convention in Memphis. Blake worked at the label's famous RCA Studio B; he is the first recording artist to do so. Sun Records released Blake's single "Flat Foot Sam" on September 14, 1957: it sold well in regional markets and earned Blake his first brush with success. Furthermore, it instilled confidence in Sun Records to bring Blake back for a follow-up recording session that resulted in nine songs. Among the sides was "Ballad of a Broken Heart", his own self-penned composition that was later recorded by Johnny Cash as "Story of a Broken Heart". "Sweetie Pie" and "I Dig You Baby" were paired together for a single in 1958 but it sold poorly. Sensing he had little hope with writing pop songs, Blake struck a songwriting partnership with Jerry Ross to work for country artists. In 1959, Blake began collaborating with Carl Belew, an already established songwriter who had his first major success with Johnnie and Jack. Together, they achieved their biggest success with "Tender Years". However, they sold the rights to Darrell Edwards who pitched it to George Jones in 1961, taking the song to number one on the country charts. The Blake-Belew partnership is credited with a number of charting hits recorded by Charlie Walker, Stonewall Jackson, Jim Reeves, Del Reeves, and Mel Tillis, among others. Nonetheless, Blake was disenchanted with the music industry, embittered by his inability to record a successful tune himself. He worked for minor labels in the late 1960s before retiring the following decade. Blake suffered from alcoholism for most of his life. At the age of 54, Blake was murdered by his third wife over marital disputes

Mariticide Club

on Christmas Eve in 1985. He was posthumously inducted into the Rockabilly Hall of Fame.

Elfriede Blauensteiner

Elfriede Blauensteiner

Elfriede Martha Blauensteiner (22 January 1931 – 18 November 2003), dubbed **The Black Widow** was an Austrian serial killer who murdered at least three victims by poison. In each case, she inherited the victim's possessions. On March 7, 1997, Blauensteiner was found guilty of murdering 77-year-old Alois Pichler and sentenced to life imprisonment. Her former lawyer Harald Schmidt was jailed for seven years for being an accomplice to grievous bodily harm and for forging the will of Alois Pichler. Blauensteiner was a gambling addict and it is believed that she would deliberately date rich elderly men and poison them before gambling away the money which had been left to her in their fabricated wills. Four years later, Blauensteiner was found guilty of murdering her 64-year-old husband Friedrick Doecker and 84-year-old female neighbor Franziska Koeberl. Although Blauensteiner was convicted of a total of just three murders, Austrian police believe that Blauensteiner murdered at least ten people. Keoberl is believed to have been her only female victim.

Wives Who Kill

After serving less than seven years of her life sentence, Blauensteiner died from a brain tumor on November 18, 2003 in a Vienna hospital. She was cremated at Feuerhalle Simmering, where also her ashes were buried.

Bodenfelde Black Widows

- **Lydia L.**
- **Siegmund S.**

The Bodenfelde Black Widows were two German serial killers, who committed four murders from 1994 to 2000 in the Bodenfelde municipality. Bodenfelde is in the state of Lower Saxony, Germany. The couple were Lydia L., a former prostitute born in 1939, and her assistant, Siegmund S. Lydia invited older men to live with her in a relationship or as care for the elderly. She later murdered the men with Siegmund S.'s help. A turnaround occurred when her aide reported the crimes to the police, confessing participation. The following relationships were assigned to Lydia L.:

- Ludwig G. from Biebertal. In 1983, he met the woman at the age of 82. In September 1985, he appointed Lydia his sole heir. He died in a hospital on January 5, 1986.
- Wilhelm S., a master mason from the Sauerland.
- Paul P., who died at the age of 83 in February 1991.
- Alois M.
- Günter S., 74, strangled in June 1994.
- Adolf B. from Melsungen, was suffocated with a pillow in September 1994.
- Paul G., first stunned by Lydia L. and then strangled by Siegmund S., in April 1995.
- Gerhard G., smothered with a plastic bag by the two offenders in his house in Völksen, near Hanover, on July 13, 2000.

The court recognized the last four cases as murders. Lydia L. was sentenced to life imprisonment in 2009 by the District Court of Göttingen, and she is now serving in Vechta Prison. A revision submitted by her was unsuccessful. Siegmund S. was sentenced to 12 years imprisonment, served

Mariticide Club

in Rosdorf correctional facility. Siegmund S. was afraid of being poisoned. In 2014, Lydia L. sued the new owner of her house, for disposal of personal belongings without her permission. The claim was dismissed by the court.

Diane Borchardt

Seduced by Madness: The Diane Borchardt Story is a 1996 American television film directed by John Patterson and starring Ann-Margret, Peter Coyote, Leslie Hope, Christian Campbell, Hedy Burress, Tobey Maguire, and Freddy Rodríguez. Based roughly on real-life events, the film recounts the story of Wisconsin teacher Diane Borchardt, who hired teen students first to spy on her cheating husband and later to kill him. The film begins with the murder then traces in flashback the events leading up to it, followed by the subsequent police investigation leading to arrests and eventual murder convictions of Borchardt and the teens. This is the plot: Three teenage boys pull up to the house of Ruben Borchardt (Peter Coyote) early on Easter Sunday in 1994. They break in armed with a shotgun, intending to kill Ruben on the promise of payment. Gathering at the top of the basement steps where Ruben sleeps, the boys draw their shotgun and shoot him as he makes his way up the stairs. Having carried out their deed, the three boys flee the scene. The film cuts to seven months before the shooting, during the Fall of 1993. Diane Kay Borchardt (Ann-Margret) is a seemingly ordinary schoolteacher with a normal life. She has a loving husband, three children, and a lovely house. However, she harbors deep mental instability and possible psychosis. While she dotes on and spoils her daughter Regan, she is emotionally and physically abusive towards Ruben and his two children, Brook (Hedy Burress) and Chuck (Tobey Maguire). Ruben married Diane fourteen years prior after his wife Susan (Cynthia Lynch) died in a car crash when Brook and Chuck were young. Realizing his children needed a mother in their lives, Ruben married Diane, only to find himself in a loveless marriage in which Diane constantly abuses him. One day, Ruben goes to a neighbor's house to help him remodel his kitchen, as he is a work-at-home carpenter. There, he gets reacquainted with Claire Brown (Leslie Hope), with whom he works together to remodel the kitchen. During the remodeling, Ruben and Claire share their personal stories with

Wives Who Kill

each other, becoming increasingly close friends as the project goes on. Later that day, Ruben drops by Diane's clothes shop on account of the fact that Diane failed to pay for Chuck's new glasses, as she had spent it on new shoes for Regan despite previously agreeing to buy the glasses. Diane then accuses Ruben of spoiling his own children and neglecting Regan, and says that he ought to be making more money. Ruben tries to reason with Diane, when suddenly, without provocation, Diane hits him in the head with a label gun. Ruben later admits to Claire that his marriage was a mistake. Claire also reveals that she and her husband have also grown apart in recent years. When the project is finished, Ruben admits his true feelings for Claire, and kisses her on impulse. He then leaves her confused, only to return, and this time, the two proceed to kiss each other passionately. Upon realizing their feelings for each other, Claire and Ruben start meeting each other secretly, and contemplate leaving their spouses in order to marry. Ruben is a devout Christian who opposes divorce, yet his feelings for Claire remain strong and Ruben says he believes they can make it work. Claire agrees to make a decision when she is ready. Later, Ruben and the family go to the annual Christmas party at the Church. While Diane is away, Ruben runs into Claire at the dance and the two steal the dance floor, and Claire accepts Ruben's proposal. Diane witnesses this and confronts her husband at home, where he admits he no longer wishes to be married to Diane. Diane makes excuses for her lack of empathy toward Ruben, but Ruben is convinced that their marriage is irreconcilable. Diane drives him away and vows to get even with him. Ruben tells Chuck and Brook about his decision, and the kids admit to their father that Diane has treated them as badly as she treated him, much to Ruben's distress. Ruben goes forth with the divorce proceedings against Diane's wishes. Meanwhile at school, Diane feigns sadness in front of her students to gain sympathy from them. It becomes apparent that she maintains a close relationship with her students in order to get them to do her bidding when she feels fit. One of her closest students, Doug Vest (Christian Campbell), comforts her and Diane lies that her husband physically abuses her in front of their children, and is turning them against her. Diane hugs Doug in her drive for sympathy,

Mariticide Club

saying that Ruben would not do this to her if he knew she had him. After school, Doug meets with his friends Josh Yanke (Jonah Blechman), Cory (Michael Scott Campbell), and Elgin (Aeryk Egan) to discuss "messing up" Mr. Borchardt. Doug, whose estranged father was physically abusive towards his own mother, says that Ruben's behavior is inexcusable. One day, Ruben invites Claire to his house while Diane is away, and presents her with a necklace as a token of his affections. Unbeknownst to the couple, Cory and Elgin photograph them in the house, and when Diane shows the pictures to Shannon Johnson (Alanna Ubach), another one of her students who assists her in the shop, she declares that she wants Ruben dead. During Christmas break, Diane coaxes Doug into her car, and lets him take it for a spin. She shows him the house and says she'd be willing to let him have the car. She goes on to explain her situation with Ruben, lying to Doug about the true nature of their divorce. She then says that if she were to have Ruben killed, it would have to be someone she trusted, and to his distress, she refers to him. Later, Diane's lawyer informs her that Ruben is seeking sole custody of the house, much to her outrage, even though he is the original proprietor. In retaliation, Diane informs the pastor of their church that Ruben has strayed from the church and violated the sacredness of their marriage. Ruben is informed by the pastor that he is not to take communion at the church for committing adultery. After New Year's Day, Ruben learns that Diane is seeking custody of Chuck as part of her ploy to secure the house, prompting Ruben to confront her. Diane reacts violently and proceeds to physically beat Ruben while Chuck and Brook struggle to stop her. At the divorce proceedings, Ruben gains custody of Chuck; and Diane gains sole custody of her shop and Regan. However, to her outrage, Ruben gains custody of the house. Diane is to vacate the property within one month, and silently promises to enact revenge on Ruben. Later in March, Diane commissions another student, Tim (Johnny Strong), to do away with her husband, telling him that the one person she still trusted let her down. Tim tells this to Doug, who immediately feels guilty for turning his back on Diane. Tim also admits that Diane may be contemplating the murder of her husband. Diane later accuses Ruben of stealing her jewelry, when in reality,

Wives Who Kill

she plans on giving it to Doug to kill her husband. She also tries to secure title to Ruben's life insurance policy. Later that night, Diane approaches Doug and tells him she wants him to kill Ruben, much to Doug's horror. Once again, she makes out Ruben to be the guilty party, claiming that he is taking everything from her. She bribes Doug with her jewelry and cash to carry out the murder, and he gives in to her demands despite his reservations. Doug later commissions Josh and his cousin Michael Maldonado (Freddy Rodriguez) to help him carry out the murder. Michael rejects the proposal, insisting that he receive higher pay to carry out the deed. Diane begins to harass Claire for stealing Ruben away, going so far as to threaten her with death. Claire becomes uneasy as the harassment persists, and insists Diane is dangerous, but Ruben insists he can handle her. At school, Diane again insists that Doug carry out the murder, and lays out her plan to kill Ruben. Doug refuses to do so, until Diane bribes him with $20,000 from Ruben's life insurance policy. Doug gives in to her demands and agrees to pay Josh and Mike part of the $20,000 and they agree to help him. While Diane is packing, Ruben confides to Brook that he has a stash of emergency cash for her and Chuck should anything happen to him, and Diane listens in. She also picks a fight with Ruben when she intends to sell Susan's sewing machine, to which Ruben objects. Diane then punches Ruben and beats him when he refuses to fight back. After grabbing her arm in an attempt to disarm her, Diane uses the marks on her arm to claim to the police that Ruben hit her. Ruben denies this; and the police tell the couple to separate temporarily. Having planned on this, Diane agrees to leave the house for Easter, and has made plans to stay at Susan's parents' house with Regan. She also takes the family dog away by force. Before leaving, Diane forces Ruben to kiss her in front of the cops, and whispers to him "You're dead". On the eve of Easter morning, Ruben is wary of Diane's death threat. He tells Claire that should anything happen to him, she is to find another man to make her happy, while insisting that all will be well. Throughout the night, Shannon contemplates warning Ruben of the impending danger, but fails to make the call. In the early morning hours of Easter Sunday, Doug and his two friends break into the house while Ruben prepares for

Mariticide Club

Easter service. They gather at the top of the stairs, where they face Ruben as he goes to wake his son. Mike pulls out a shotgun and fires two rounds into Ruben, fatally wounding him. The boys then flee the scene and dump the shotgun into a vacant lot. Chuck soon wakes up to find his father bleeding to death on the stairs, and calls 911 while Ruben calls Claire. As Ruben fights for his life, he proclaims his love for her and leaves his children in her care. Ruben is rushed to the hospital where the family gathers to learn of his condition. Claire soon shows up to see Ruben, only to discover that he has died. As the family mourns their loss, Diane also learns of the murder, and feigns shock and sadness in front of Sue's parents. They become suspicious of her when she fails to ask any questions about the murder. Meanwhile, Detectives Burstyn (Cliff De Young) and Pike (Dean Norris) are assigned to track down Ruben's killer. When Diane refuses to talk to the police after the murder, she becomes the primary suspect. In the days that follow, Diane deals further insult to her grieving family by threatening to sue the funeral home for proceeding with Ruben's service without her consent, as she had not been present to arrange it. Brook accuses her of killing her father, a charge Diane immediately denies. The funeral soon takes place and the family pays their final respects to Ruben as he is laid to rest. Once again, Diane feigns sorrow in front of the open casket to preserve her innocence. Claire watches the burial from nearby, and collapses from shock.

The police soon discover that the murder weapon was a shotgun, and deduce that the shooter was an amateur, as the gun was of a cheap design. They are later tipped off about the photographs taken by Cory and Elgin, and question the boys about their activities. They learn Diane shares her personal problems with her class, thus able to manipulate them to do as she pleases. Meanwhile, Doug struggles to acquire the money promised to him by Diane. Due to her increasingly suspicious behavior in the case, Diane is denied access to Ruben's life insurance policy proceeds. Having grown impatient with Doug, Mike threatens Diane at knife-point and demands that she pay up. Frantic, Diane searches her husband's bedroom for the money he had hidden away, and soon finds a package containing $6,000. She gives

Wives Who Kill

$1,500 to the boys, who are still not satisfied with their payment. Brook meets Claire in the hospital and pleads that she come back to them, as she was more of a mother to them than Diane ever was. Claire blames herself for Ruben's death, but Brook tells her that he was more alive with Claire than he had ever been before. Upon hearing this, Claire is soon able to overcome her personal guilt and becomes an adoptive mother to Chuck and Brook. Meanwhile, Brook has moved to Madison, Wisconsin, where she starts over without Diane in her life. Brook meets a boy named Nick at her new job. The two soon fall in love. After a night in bed, Brook discovers she is pregnant with Nick's son, and the two agree to marry. Doug soon realizes that Diane will never be able to pay up, and informs his friends that he cannot obtain any more money. Mike admits to his best friend Jeb (Andrew Kavovit) that he had a hand in Ruben's death, albeit without any noteworthy remorse. Jeb is unable to bring himself to confess to the police. Five months after the murder, it becomes apparent to Diane that the cops are on to her; she tries to conceal her guilt. Shannon meets with Doug, and forces him to confess his role in the murder so that she can turn in all evidence to the cops before she commits suicide, making herself out to be the killer in an effort to protect Diane. Diane dissuades her from doing this as it will only lead the police back to her regardless. By the time school restarts, the boys are frustrated by their lack of payment, and struggle to conceal the truth about Ruben's murder. Six months into the case, Jeb breaks down and admits to his friend Jay that Mike and Doug were responsible for Ruben's murder. Rather than force Jeb to turn in his best friend, Jay goes to the cops himself and implicates Doug as an accomplice. Doug is brought in for questioning, where he accidentally let slip that he was in fact involved in Ruben's murder. When Burstyn confronts him on this, Doug makes a full confession, and provides him with the names of his accomplices. Mike and Shannon are arrested, and the two detectives rush to the high school. There, amidst the air of shock and outrage among the students, the police arrest Josh and Diane, Diane desperately protesting her innocence as she is dragged away in handcuffs. Six months later, Diane has been set free on bail as the court proceeds with the trials. Doug and Mike

Mariticide Club

are charged with first-degree murder as adults, and face life imprisonment. Josh pleads guilty to his crime in exchange for his testimony, and Shannon is charged with perjury. Josh admits his role in the conspiracy, as well as Doug's role in organizing the attack. Doug reveals the full details of the murder, and after his testimony, he is sentenced to life imprisonment. Diane is soon rearrested and brought forth to face a series of witnesses, who implicate her as the mastermind of the plot against Ruben. Among these witnesses is Shannon, who feels betrayed by Diane's reluctance to come forth to her defense. Doug also testifies against Diane, admitting that she commissioned him to carry out the murder. After the conclusion of the testimonies, the jury makes its final verdict. To Diane's horror, she is found guilty of first-degree intentional homicide, and breaks down in front of the courtroom as her daughter Regan looks on in despair. Having received justice, the Borchardt family with Brook's husband and newborn son Ruben, visit Ruben's grave along with Claire. The family reflects on the better days of Ruben's life and welcome Brook's son, named in honor of his grandfather, into their family. In the final scene, Diane is interviewed for a True Crime Documentary, from jail. Having completely lost her mind, she admits not to know what she's supposed to have learnt 'from this' her main concern is "whether Ruben had time to repent or is he lost forever?" The end of the film is followed by an epilogue outlining the sentences faced by the conspirators:

- **SHANNON JOHNSON** is found guilty of perjury, and receives an 80-day jail sentence along with two years' probation.
- **JOSHUA YANKE** pleaded no contest to second-degree intentional homicide and is sentenced to 18 years in prison.
- **MICHAEL MALDONADO** is found guilty of first-degree murder and sentenced to life in prison. He will not be eligible for parole until he has served 50 years of his sentence.
- **DOUGLAS VEST JR.** is found guilty of first-degree murder and sentenced to life in prison. He will not be eligible for parole until he has served 25 years of his sentence.

Wives Who Kill

• **DIANE BORCHARDT** is found guilty of first-degree murder and sentenced to life in prison and will not be eligible for parole until she has served 40 years of her sentence, by that time being no less than 86 years of age.

Myrtle Adkins Bennett

Bridge Murder case

The **Bridge Murder case**, also known as the **Bridge Table Murder case**, was the trial of Myrtle Adkins Bennett (born March 20, 1895, in Tillar, Arkansas), a Kansas City housewife, for the murder of her husband John G. Bennett over a game of contract bridge in September 1929. Myrtle and John spent much of Sunday, September 29, 1929, with their upstairs neighbors, Charles and Myrna Hofman. The husbands played a round of golf at the Indian Hills Country Club that morning, and then went back to the links that afternoon with their wives joining them. At dusk, they returned to the Bennett apartment at 902 Ward Parkway in the Country Club District of Kansas City. After sharing dinner, they sat down to a game of bridge in the Bennett living room, the couples playing as partners, the Hofmans versus the Bennetts. After midnight, as the Hofmans began to pull ahead, the Bennetts began to bicker. In the ultimate hand, John failed to make his four spades contract and Myrtle, frustrated by the failure, called him "a bum bridge player". He stood and slapped her in the face several times, and announced he was leaving. He said he would spend the night in a motel in Saint Joseph, Missouri. As he packed his bag, and moved from room to room, he mocked his wife. Myrtle told the Hofmans, "Only a cur would strike a woman in front of guests." After an ongoing argument, John Bennett went to pack a suitcase as he told Myrtle to retrieve the handgun he typically carried on the road for protection. Myrtle walked down the hall to the bedroom of her mother, Alice Adkins. Still sobbing, Myrtle reached into a drawer with linens and pulled out the .32 Colt semi-automatic, and walked into the den. There, she brushed past Charles Hofman, and shot at John's back twice in the bathroom of the apartment. John escaped into the

Mariticide Club

hallway, but fell to the floor in their living room. Myrtle Bennett was tried by Judge Ralph S. Latshaw. The trial began on February 23, 1931, and lasted eleven days. Her defense was James A. Reed, former three-term U.S. Senator and onetime Democratic presidential candidate. Reed showed jurors that John Bennett had been previously violent and abusive, and attempted to explain that Mrs Bennett was either insane or acted in self defense. The judge disallowed the prosecution, James R. Page, to submit John Bennett's nephew Byrd Rice, as he was not on the original list of witnesses. After an eight-hour deliberation, the jury returned a not guilty verdict. The prosecution's assistant, John Hill, said, "It looks like an open season on husbands." The case caught the public imagination, and was subject to press attention by the New York *Journal*, not for the trial itself, but for the bridge game. The case was a media sensation and a flashpoint in the bridge craze sweeping the nation. The *Journal* invited speculation from bridge experts, including Sidney Lenz, on the game, what hands had been played, and whether different play, or alternative hands, would have prevented the murder. None of the people present in the apartment at the time later recalled exactly what the hands were. When the case came to trial, Myrtle Bennett was defended by former U.S. Senator James A. Reed. Ely Culbertson, the Barnum of the bridge movement, watched the trial closely from New York. Elie Almon Culbertson (July 22, 1891 – December 27, 1955), known as Ely Culbertson, was an American contract bridge entrepreneur and personality dominant during the 1930s. He played a major role in the popularization of the new game and was widely regarded as "the man who made contract bridge". He was a great showman who became rich, was highly extravagant, and lost and gained fortunes several times over. Culbertson was born in Poiana Vărbilău in Romania to an American mining engineer, Almon Culbertson, and his Russian wife, Xenya Rogoznaya. He attended the École des sciences économiques et politiques at the Sorbonne in Paris, and the University of Geneva. His facility for languages was extraordinary: he spoke Russian, English, French, German, Czech and Spanish fluently, with a reading knowledge of five

Wives Who Kill

others, and a knowledge of Latin and classical Greek. In spite of his education, his erudition was largely self-acquired: he was a born autodidact. After the Russian Revolution (1917), Culbertson lived for four years in Paris and other European cities by exploiting his skill as a card player. In 1921 he moved to the United States, earning his living from winnings at auction bridge and poker. In 1923 he married Mrs. Josephine Murphy Dillon, a successful teacher of auction bridge and a leading woman player, in Manhattan. They were successful as both players and teachers, and later as publishers. Josephine Culbertson retained the surname after their divorce in 1938; indeed, a revised edition of *Culbertson's Contract Bridge in Ten Minutes* was published under her name in 1951. Gradually the new game of contract bridge began to replace auction bridge, and Culbertson saw his opportunity to overtake the leaders of auction bridge. Culbertson planned a far-reaching and successful campaign to promote himself as the leader of the new game. As player, organizer, bidding theorist, magazine editor, and team leader, he was a key figure in the growth of contract bridge in its great boom years of the 1930s. Culbertson was a brilliant publicist; he played several famous challenge matches and won them all. Two were played in the United States against pairs led by Sidney Lenz in 1931–32 (so-called "Bridge Battle of the Century") and by P. Hal Sims in 1935, the latter between married couples Culbertson and Sims. Four teams-of-four matches were played in England, against Walter Buller's team in 1930, against "Pops" Beasley's team in 1930 and 1933, and against Col. George Walshe's team in 1934. These matches were typically accompanied by noteworthy publicity in newspapers, on radio and on cinema newsreels, and the hands became the subject of intense discussion on bidding methods. A match did not materialize against the leading American team of the mid-1930s, the "Four Aces". Culbertson was beaten in Budapest, June 1937, in the final match of the first world championship teams tournament, by the 6-man Austria team led by Dr. Paul Stern. It was his last appearance in a tournament or match. Culbertson founded and edited *The Bridge World* magazine, which is still published today, and wrote many newspaper articles and books on bridge. He owned the first firm of playing card

Mariticide Club

manufacturers to develop plastic cards, Kem Cards, and developed and owned a chain of bridge schools with teachers qualified in the Culbertson bidding system. He continued to play high-stakes rubber bridge for many years, but gave up tournament and match competition in 1938 to write and to work for world peace. Culbertson used the Bennett tragedy to his advantage. He sold bridge and himself, telling housewives that the game was a great way to defuse the marital tensions pent-up in daily life. He told housewives that, at the bridge table, they could be their husbands' equal, and more. Culbertson wrote about the killing and trial in his new magazine, *The Bridge World*. In packed halls on the lecture circuit, he analyzed the so-called "Fatal Hand" – even as he knew the details were fabricated. In lectures, Culbertson suggested that if only the Bennetts had been playing the Culbertson System of bidding, then 36-year-old John Bennett might still have been alive. Only 35 years old at the time of her acquittal, Myrtle Bennett lived for another 61 years, dying at the age of 96 in Miami, Florida, in January 1992. She had moved into obscurity soon after the trial, her name fading from headlines. She never remarried, nor did she have children. After World War II and throughout the 1950s, she worked as executive head of housekeeping at the elegant Hotel Carlyle in New York City, living alone there in an apartment. At the Carlyle, she developed friendships with the rich and famous, including the actors Mary Pickford and her husband Buddy Rogers, and also Henry Ford II.

The widow Bennett later traveled the world, working for a hotel chain, and played bridge until nearly the end of her life. In an interview with the author Gary Pomerantz, Myrtle Bennett's cousin, Carolyn Scruggs of Arkansas, said that Mrs. Bennett never spoke with her about the shooting. Once, though, Ms. Scruggs told Mrs. Bennett, "I sometimes think of your life –" But Myrtle Bennett interrupted, and said, "Well, my dear, it was a great tragedy and a great mistake." Scruggs stammered to say, "I guess I want you to know that I understand it." But Myrtle Bennett said, "No, my dear, you don't understand it." At the time of her 1992 death, Myrtle Bennett's estate was valued at more than $1 million. With no direct

Wives Who Kill

descendants, she left most of the money to family members of John Bennett, the husband she had killed more than six decades before.

Mary Ann Britland (née Mary Ann Hague)

Mary Ann Britland (née **Hague**) (1847-August 9, 1886) was an English serial killer. She was the first woman to be executed by hanging at Strangeways Prison in Manchester by James Berry. Mary Ann Britland was born in 1847 in Bolton, Lancashire, the second eldest daughter of Joseph and Hannah (née Lees) Hague. She married Thomas Britland at St Michael's Church, Ashton-under-Lyne in 1866. They lived in a rented house at 133 Turner Lane, Ashton-under-Lyne with their two daughters Elizabeth Hannah and Susannah. Britland held two jobs; she was a factory worker by day and barmaid by night. In February 1886, Britland went to a nearby chemist's and, claiming to have had some mice infest her home, bought some packets of "Harrison's Vermin Killer". As this contained both strychnine and arsenic, she was required to sign the poison register. Britland's first victim was her eldest daughter, 19-year-old Elizabeth Hannah, in March 1886. Elizabeth's death was attributed to natural causes by the doctor who was called to attend the teenager. Mary Ann Britland then claimed £10 on Elizabeth's life insurance policy. Her next victim was her husband, Thomas, aged 44. His death on May 3, 1886, was diagnosed as epilepsy, and once again Mary Ann claimed on the insurance. Mary Ann had been having an affair with her neighbor, Thomas Dixon, and after her own husband's death was invited to stay at the Dixons' house just across the street at number 128 by Thomas's 29-year-old wife, Mary. On May 14, 1886, Mary Dixon was to become Britland's third and final victim. The three deaths, all with their near identical and somewhat unusual symptoms, raised suspicion; Mary Ann Britland was interviewed by the police in connection with Mary Dixon's death and her body was examined by a pathologist. It was found to contain a lethal quantity of the two poisons and Britland was immediately arrested along with Thomas Dixon. She confessed to Ashton Police that she had wanted to marry Dixon and that she had first poisoned her daughter, Elizabeth, because she believed that she suspected her intentions. She then killed her husband, and finally Mary

Mariticide Club

Dixon. Britland was charged with the murder of the three victims, but Thomas Dixon was found to have played no part in the murder of his wife. Britland came to trial on July 22, 1886, before Mr. Justice Cave at Manchester Assizes. Since there was an absence of motive, in her defense she argued that the small sum of money from the insurance payouts were in no way compensation for the loss of her husband and daughter. According to an eyewitness at the trial:

The case lasted two days...The evidence was overwhelming. The three deceased persons had been poisoned by strychnine. Mrs. Britland had purchased 'mouse powder' in sufficient quantities to kill them all, and there was no evidence of any mice on whom it could have been legitimately used. The case of the poisoning of Mrs. Dixon was the one actually tried, but the deaths of the others were proved to show 'system' and rebut the defense of accident. Even if there had not been sufficient evidence to secure a conviction, Mrs. Britland had many indiscreet conversations about 'mouse powder' and poisoning, and had been anxious to discover whether such poisoning could be traced after death...

It took the jury some time to convict her, although eventually they found her guilty. After she was sentenced, she declared to the court: *"I am quite innocent, I am not guilty at all."*

Strangeways Prison

On the morning of August 9, 1886, Britland was in a state of collapse and had to be heavily assisted to the gallows by two female wardens. Britland

Wives Who Kill

was screaming and asking for mercy. The women held her on the trapdoors while James Berry prepared her for execution. Two male wardens then took the place of the female wardens. On a signal from the executioner, they quickly stepped back, the trap door was released and Britland dropped. She was the first woman to be executed at Strangeways Prison

Elizabeth Broadingham

She died at York's Tyburn at Knavesmire

Elizabeth Broadingham (died March 20, 1776) was a British murderer. She was executed in 1776 with her lover for the murder of her husband in York. Her husband was considered to be her social superior so she was one of the last women to be burned at the stake (after being killed). Broadingham's early life is unrecorded. She was living with her husband, John Broadingham, in Flamborough when he was convicted for smuggling. While he was serving his sentence she started an adulterous relationship

Mariticide Club

with a man called Thomas Aikney. John Broadingham completed his sentence, but by this time his wife was living with Thomas Aikney in Lincolnshire. According to later accounts it was Elizabeth who initially proposed that her husband should be murdered. She was said to have repeated this proposal to her lover, particularly when he was inebriated. Thomas eventually agreed. Elizabeth was said to have pretended that she was reconciled with her husband and she moved back into their home. A week or so later on February 13, 1776, Thomas was said to have knocked at the door. Elizabeth woke her husband to tell him and he went to the door to investigate. John was attacked and died with a wound on his leg and a wound so deep in his abdomen that the knife was left in the wound. John made it away but with his bowels visible, he died on the following day.

Elizabeth and Thomas were arrested and tried and both were sentenced to death even though Elizabeth was just an accomplice. The key evidence was the knife which was identified as belonging to Thomas. Elizabeth was convicted of killing her social superior making the crime not murder but petty treason. For this reason she was not only strangled on 20 March but her body was burned at the stake at a place called Tyburn in York. Thomas died too and his body was sent to Leeds for dissection. She was executed in 1776 with her lover for the murder of her husband in York. She was one of the last women to be burned at the stake (after being killed). She is regarded as infamous. The place where she and several other notable people died is Tyburn in York.

Betty Broderick (née Elisabeth Anne Bisceglia)
Elisabeth Anne Broderick (née **Bisceglia**; born November 7, 1947) is an American woman who murdered her ex-husband, Daniel T. Broderick III, and his second wife, Linda (née Kolkena) Broderick, on November 5, 1989. At a second trial that began on December 11, 1991, she was convicted of two counts of second-degree murder and later sentenced to 32-years-to-life in prison. The case received extensive media attention. Several books were written on the Broderick case, and a TV movie was televised in two parts. In 2020, an 8-episode miniseries was produced and aired about

Wives Who Kill

Broderick. Betty Broderick was born Elisabeth Anne Bisceglia on November 7, 1947, and grew up in Bronxville, New York. She was the third of six children born to Marita (née Curtin; 1919–2007) and Frank Bisceglia (1915–1998), who owned a successful plastering business with relatives. Her mother was Irish American and her father was Italian American. The Bisceglias were strict parents, and much was expected of all the Bisceglia children. As Broderick later recalled, she was being trained to be a housewife since the day she was born, or as she recalled: "Go to Catholic schools, be careful with dating until you find a Catholic man, support him while he works, be blessed in your later years with beautiful grandchildren". Broderick graduated from Maria Regina High School, in Hartsdale, New York, in 1965. She graduated from the College of Mount Saint Vincent in the Bronx, where she earned a degree in early childhood education through an accelerated program. Her credits also earned her a minor in English. In 1965, Elisabeth (Betty) met her future husband, Dan Broderick (1944–1989), at the University of Notre Dame, Indiana. Dan was born in Pittsburgh, Pennsylvania, the eldest son of a very large Irish Catholic family. The couple married on April 12, 1969, at the Immaculate Conception Church in Tuckahoe, New York. Betty returned from the honeymoon pregnant with their first child, daughter Kim (b. 1970). She gave birth to four more children: daughter Lee (b. 1971), sons named Daniel (b. 1976) and Rhett (b. 1979), and an unnamed boy, who died four days after birth. After Kim's birth, Dan completed his M.D. degree. He then announced his intention to combine his medical expertise with a J.D. degree and enrolled at Harvard Law School. Betty was the main provider for the family while Dan attended law school with the help of a student loan. Dan was quickly hired by a law firm in San Diego, California, and moved his family to the San Diego community of La Jolla. Betty continued working part-time, often selling Tupperware or Avon products while raising the children. In the fall of 1982, Dan hired 21-year-old Dutch American Linda Kolkena (1961–1989), a former Delta Air Lines flight attendant, to be his legal assistant. As early as October 1983, Betty suspected that Dan was having an affair with Kolkena, but Dan denied it.

Mariticide Club

Against Betty's wishes, Dan moved out in February 1985. He eventually took custody of their children after Betty left the children on his doorstep one by one. Betty claimed that Dan confessed he had in fact been having an affair with Kolkena, and a long, drawn-out, and hostile divorce ensued. By this time, Dan Broderick had become a prominent local lawyer, serving as the president of the San Diego Bar Association. Betty claimed that Dan made it extremely difficult for her to find a lawyer willing to represent her in the divorce, which put her at a distinct disadvantage. Betty also believed that Dan used his legal influence to win sole custody of their children, sell their house against her wishes and cheat her out of her rightful share of his income. The divorce was finalized in 1989, four years after Dan filed the petition. Betty Broderick's behavior became increasingly erratic. She left hundreds of profane messages on Dan's answering machine, and ignored numerous restraining orders that forbade her from setting foot on Dan's property. She vandalized his new home, and even drove her car into his front door despite the fact that their children were inside the house at the time. On April 22, 1989, Dan and Kolkena were married. Kolkena had been concerned about Betty's behavior and even urged Dan to wear a bulletproof vest to their wedding. However, Betty did not arrive and the wedding proceeded without incident. After the wedding, Betty Broderick claimed that Linda Broderick taunted her by mailing her facial cream and slimming treatment advertisements. Eight months after buying a Smith & Wesson revolver and seven months after Dan and Linda were married, Betty Broderick drove to Dan's house at 1041 Cypress Avenue in the Marston Hills neighborhood near Balboa Park in San Diego. Betty used a key she had taken from her daughter Lee to enter the house while the couple slept, whereupon she shot and killed them. The murders occurred at 5:30 a.m. on November 5, 1989—two days before Betty's 42nd birthday. Two bullets hit Linda in the head and chest, killing her instantly; one bullet hit Dan in the chest as he apparently was reaching for the phone; one bullet hit the wall, and one bullet hit a nightstand. Dan was 17 days shy of his 45th birthday; Linda was 28. Evidence was presented at her trial that Betty had removed a phone/answering machine from Dan Broderick's bedroom

Wives Who Kill

so that he could not call for help. Medical evidence indicated that Dan had not died right away, and Betty claimed that she had spoken to him after she had shot him. After contacting her daughter, Lee, and Lee's boyfriend, Betty turned herself in to police, never denying that she had pulled the trigger. Betty's explanation at both trials was that she never planned to kill Dan and Linda and that her crime was not premeditated. Her account of the murders at her second trial was that she was startled by Kolkena screaming "Call the police!" and immediately fired the gun. Linda and Dan Broderick are listed as having been buried together, at Greenwood Memorial Park in San Diego. Criminal Defense Attorney Jack Early represented Broderick at trial. Kerry Wells prosecuted for the State of California. Broderick's defense was that she had been a battered wife, claiming that she was driven over the edge by years of psychological, physical, and mental abuse at the hands of her ex-husband. Wells portrayed Broderick as a murderer who planned and schemed to kill her ex-husband and argued to the jury that Broderick was not a battered woman. Forensic psychiatry is a subspeciality of psychiatry related to criminology, interface between law and psychiatry. According to the American Academy of Psychiatry and the Law, it is defined as "a subspecialty of psychiatry in which scientific and clinical expertise is applied in legal contexts involving civil, criminal, correctional, regulatory, or legislative matters, and in specialized clinical consultations in areas such as risk assessment or employment. " A forensic psychiatrist provides services – such as determination of competency to stand trial – to a court of law to facilitate the adjudicative process and provide treatment, such as medications and psychotherapy, to criminals. Forensic psychiatrists work with courts in evaluating competency to stand trial, defenses based on mental disorders (insanity defense), and sentencing recommendations. The two major areas of criminal evaluations in forensic psychiatry are competency to stand trial (CST) and mental state at the time of the offense (MSO). Competency to stand trial (CST) is the competency evaluation to determine that defendants have the mental capacity to understand the charges and assist their attorneys. In the United States, this is seated in the Fifth Amendment to the United States Constitution, which ensures the

Mariticide Club

right to be present at one's trial, to face one's accusers, and to have help from an attorney. CST, sometimes referred to as adjudicative competency, serves three purposes: "preserving the dignity of the criminal process, reducing the risk of erroneous convictions, and protecting defendants' decision-making autonomy". In 1960, the Supreme Court of the United States in Dusky v. United States established the standard for federal courts, ruling that "the test must be whether the defendant has sufficient present ability to consult with his attorney with a reasonable degree of rational understanding and a rational as well as factual understanding of proceedings against him." The evaluations must assess a defendant's ability to assist their legal counsel, meaning that they understand the legal charges against them, the implications of being a defendant, and the adversarial nature of the proceedings, including the roles played by defense counsel, prosecutors, judges, and the jury. They must be able to communicate relevant information to their attorney, and understand information provided by their attorney. Finally, they must be competent to make important decisions, such as whether or not to accept a plea agreement. In England, Wales, Scotland, and Ireland, a similar legal concept is that of "plead". Forensic psychiatrists are often called to be expert witnesses in both criminal and civil proceedings. Expert witnesses give their opinions about a specific issue. Often, the psychiatrist will have prepared a detailed report before testifying. The primary duty of the expert witness is to provide an independent opinion to the court. An expert is allowed to testify in court with respect to matters of opinion only when the matters in question are not ordinarily understandable to the finders of fact, be they judge or jury. As such, prominent leaders in the field of forensic psychiatry, from Thomas Gutheil to Robert Simon and Liza Gold and others have identified teaching as a critical dimension in the role of expert witness. The expert will be asked to form an opinion and to testify about that opinion, but in so doing will explain the basis for that opinion, which will include important concepts, approaches, and methods used in psychiatry. Mental state opinion (MSO) gives the court an opinion, and only an opinion, as to whether a defendant was able to understand what he/she was doing at the

Wives Who Kill

time of the crime. This is worded differently in many states, and has been rejected altogether in some, but in every setting, the intent to do a criminal act and the understanding of the criminal nature of the act bear on the final disposition of the case. Much of forensic psychiatry is guided by significant court rulings or laws that bear on this area including these three standards:

- M'Naghten rules: Excuses a defendant who, by virtue of a defect of reason or disease of the mind, does not know the nature and quality of the act, or, if he or she does, does not know that the act is indeed wrong.
- Durham rule: Excuses a defendant whose conduct is the product of mental disorder.
- ALI test: Excuses a defendant who, because of a mental disease or defect, lacks substantial capacity to appreciate the criminality (wrongfulness) of his or her conduct or to conform his conduct to the requirements of law.

"Not guilty by reason of insanity" (NGRI) is one potential outcome in this type of trial. Importantly, insanity is a legal and not a medical term. Often, psychiatrists may be testifying for both the defense and the prosecution.

Forensic psychiatrists are also involved in the care of prisoners, both in jails and prisons, and in the care of the mentally ill who have committed criminal acts (such as those who have been found not guilty by reason of insanity). Many past offenders against other people, and suspected or potential future offenders with mental health problems or an intellectual or developmental disability, are supervised in the community by forensic psychiatric teams made up of a variety of professionals, including psychiatrists, psychologists, nurses, and care workers. These teams have dual responsibilities: to promote both the welfare of their clients and the safety of the public. The aim is not so much to predict as to prevent violence, by means of risk management. Risk assessment and management is a growth area in the forensic field, with much Canadian academic work being done in Ontario and British Columbia. This began with the attempt to predict the likelihood of a particular kind of offense being repeated, by

Mariticide Club

combining "static" indicators from personal history and offense details in actuarial instruments such as the RRASOR and Static-99, which were shown to be more accurate than unaided professional judgment. More recently, use is being made also of "dynamic" risk factors, such as attitudes, impulsivity, mental state, family and social circumstances, substance use, and the availability and acceptance of support, to make a "structured professional judgment." The aim of this is to move away from prediction to prevention, by identifying and then managing risk factors. This may entail monitoring, treatment, rehabilitation, supervision, and victim safety planning and depends on the availability of funding and legal powers. These schemes may be based on published assessments such as HCR-20 (with 10 Historical, 5 Clinical and 5 Risk Management factors) and the risk of sexual violence protocol from Simon Fraser University, BC. Forensic psychiatrist and criminologist Dr. Park Dietz, for the prosecution, used the analysis of Dr. Melvin Goldzband, who previously worked on the case for the prosecution. Dietz said Broderick has histrionic and narcissistic personality disorders. Goldzband had likewise diagnosed Broderick as "severely narcissistic" and "histrionic," and clinical psychologist Katherine DiFrancesca, testifying for the defense, concluded Broderick was "histrionic" with "narcissistic features". The lead detective in the case was Terry DeGelder of San Diego Homicide, who provided testimony for the prosecution. Broderick's first trial ended with a hung jury when two of the jurors held out for manslaughter, citing lack of intent. A mistrial was declared by Judge Thomas J. Whelan. Betty Broderick was retried a year later with the same defense attorney and prosecutor. The second trial was essentially a replay of the first trial. Prosecutor Wells was successful the second time around; the jury returned a verdict of two counts of seconddegree murder. Broderick was sentenced to two consecutive terms of 15 years to life plus two years for illegal use of a firearm, the maximum under the law. She has been incarcerated since the day she committed the murders. Broderick is serving her sentence at the California Institution for Women (CIW), in Chino, California. In January 2010, her first request for parole was denied by the Board of Parole Hearings because she did not

Page 90 of 615 Mariticide Club – Wives Who Kill © 2023 TXu 2-378-397 All Rights Reserved by William A. Stricklin

Wives Who Kill

show remorse and did not acknowledge wrongdoing. She was denied parole in November 2011 and again in January 2017. She will not be eligible again until January 2032, at which date she will be 84 years old. An article about Broderick's case in the *Los Angeles Times Magazine* led to the production of a television film called (Part 1) *A Woman Scorned: The Betty Broderick Story*, and (Part 2) Her Final Fury: Betty Broderick, The Last Chapter (1992), Meredith Baxter portrayed Betty, Stephen Collins portrayed Dan, and Michelle Johnson portrayed Linda Kolkena. Baxter received an Emmy Award nomination for her portrayal of Broderick. The murder was dramatized in the season 4 episode of *Deadly Women*, titled "Till Death Do Us Part." Both before and after Broderick's trials, her story was dramatized across the United States. Broderick granted numerous television and magazine interviews. She appeared on *The Oprah Winfrey Show twice, Hard Copy, 20/20*, and *Headliners and Legends*. At least four books were written about her story (Until the Twelfth of Never: The Deadly Divorce of Dan and Betty Broderick, 1993, by Bella Stumbo; *Until the Twelfth of Never - Should Betty Broderick ever be free?*, 2013, by Bella Stumbo; *Forsaking All Others: The Real Betty Broderick Story*, 1993, by Loretta Schwartz-Nobel; and *Hell Hath, No Fury,* 1992 by Bryna Taubman). Broderick was interviewed by *Ladies Home Journal* magazine and others. The 1991 *Law & Order* episode "The Wages of Love" partially was inspired by this murder and the trial that followed. Guest star Shirley Knight was nominated for a Primetime Emmy Award for Outstanding Lead Actress in a Drama Series. Karen Kilgariff covered the case in episode 103 of *My Favorite Murder*, recorded live in San Diego. The second season of the TV series *Dirty John* features the story of Betty and Dan Broderick from the early years through the homicides. Amanda Peet played Betty and Christian Slater played Dan. In spring 2020, a true crime podcast about the Betty Broderick case was produced by the *Los Angeles Times* titled *It Was Simple: The Betty Broderick Murders*. On July 15, 2020, Oxygen aired a special episode of *Snapped* devoted to the Betty Broderick case. Betty Broderick was involved in several civil and criminal court cases, including wrongful death for murders of Dan Broderick and his wife Linda:

Mariticide Club

- Property damage case filed by Dan and Betty Broderick October 1, 1975
- Personal injury (auto) case filed against Betty Broderick April 20, 1989
- Double homicide case filed March 23, 1990
- Civil complaint filed by Betty Broderick June 28, 1990
- Wrongful death suit against Betty Broderick filed November 2, 1990
- Second wrongful death suit against Betty Broderick filed November 2, 1990
- Personal injury case against Betty Broderick filed September 18, 1991
- Betty Broderick sues County of San Diego on September 21, 1992

Elizabeth Martha Brown (née Clark)

Elizabeth Martha Brown (c. 1811 – 9 August 1856), née **Clark**, was the last woman to be publicly hanged in Dorset, England. She was executed outside Dorchester Prison after being convicted of the murder of her second husband, John Brown, July 5, 35 days earlier. The prosecution said she had attacked him with an axe after he had taken a whip to her. Among the crowd of 3,000–4,000 watching the execution was English novelist Thomas Hardy, aged 16 at the time, standing close to the gallows. He wrote seventy years later that he was ashamed to have been there. Brown was dressed in a long black silk dress. A cloth was placed over her head, but as it began to rain, her face became visible again. Hardy wrote, "I saw—they had put a cloth over the face—how, as the cloth got wet, *her features came through it*. That was extraordinary." "I remember what a fine figure she showed against the sky as she hung in the misty rain," he wrote elsewhere, "and how the tight black silk gown set off her shape as she wheeled half-round and back." Blake Morrison writes that the hanging of Tess in Hardy's *Tess of the d'Urbervilles* (1891) reflected his experience of watching Brown's

Wives Who Kill

death. A local newspaper recorded she was counseled just before her death by Rev. D Clementson, prison chaplain, and that she remained composed: *This morning (Saturday) a few minutes after 8 o'clock, Elizabeth Martha BROWN, convicted of the willful murder of her husband was executed on a scaffold erected over the gateway of the new entrance leading to Dorset County Goal from North Square. The culprit did not up to the last moment, appear to shed a tear. She on leaving her cell, shook hands with the chief warder and other officers. On her way to the scaffold her demeanor was extraordinary. The attendants on either side were entirely overcome, whilst she bore her awful position with the greatest resignation and composure. The Chaplain the Rev. D Clementson, conversed with her on spiritual subjects, and she appeared to engage in fervent [sic] devotion and prayer, with her hands clasped firmly together and upturned eyes. On arriving at the place of execution she walked with firmness up the first flight of eleven steps. On this spot the ceremony of pinioning was proceeded with. Her female attendants here left her in the care of the executioner.*

In 2016, it was reported that remains unearthed at the site of Dorchester prison in Dorset may belong to Brown. In 2018 it was reported that Martha may be re-buried with others in the Poundbury Cemetery, should she not be buried in the churchyard at Blackdown, where her husband's remains lie. A Dorset-based company, Angel Exit Theatre, produced a play *The Ballad of Martha Brown* based on the life and times of Martha Brown. The play premiered at Deverills Festival in Wiltshire on May 3, 2014 and continued on a tour of the South West and South East. In September - October 2015 it again toured the UK. In 1995, Australian band The Lucksmiths released "Thomas & Martha" based on Thomas Hardy's recollections of the event. The case was re-examined in the BBC program *Murder, Mystery and My Family* (series 4, episode 9).

Judy Buenoano (née Judias V. Welty)

Mariticide Club

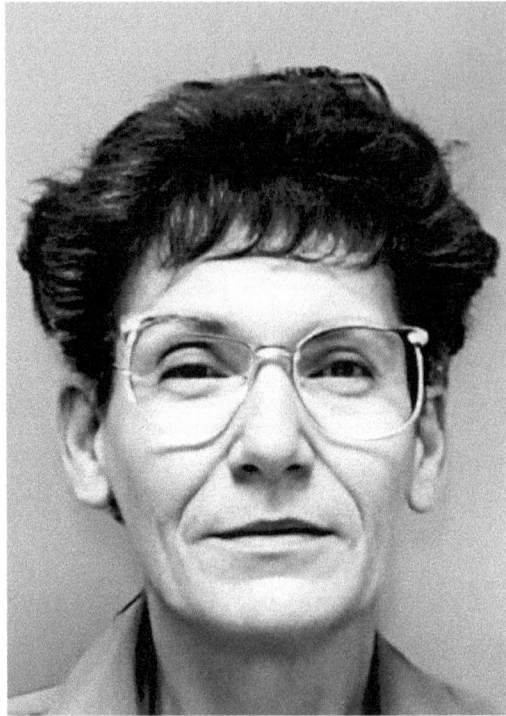

Buenoano shortly before her execution

Judias V. "Judy" Buenoano (born **Judias Welty**, also known as **Judias** Goodyear and Judias Morris; April 4, 1943 – March 30, 1998) was an American serial killer who was executed for the 1971 murder of her husband James Goodyear. She was also convicted for the 1980 murder of her son Michael Buenoano and of the 1983 attempted murder of her boyfriend John Gentry. Buenoano is also acknowledged to have been responsible for the 1978 death of her boyfriend Bobby Joe Morris in Colorado; however, by the time authorities made the connection between Buenoano and Morris, she had already been sentenced to death in the state of Florida. Buenoano is also believed to have been involved in a 1974 murder in Alabama, and in the 1980 death of her boyfriend Gerald Dossett. After her arrest, Dossett's body was exhumed and analyzed for signs of arsenic poisoning. No charges were laid in that case. Buenoano was the first woman to be executed in Florida since 1848 or electrocuted in USA since 1976. Judias Welty was born and raised in Texas, the third of four

Wives Who Kill

siblings. Her mother died when she was four, and she was sent along with her baby brother Robert, to live with her grandparents. After her father remarried, they moved to live with him in Roswell, New Mexico. She was reportedly abused by her father and stepmother, who starved her and forced her to work as a slave. When she was fourteen, she spent two months in prison for attacking her father, stepmother and two stepbrothers. Upon being released, she chose to attend reform school in where she graduated in 1960 becoming a nursing assistant. She gave birth to Michael, an illegitimate son the following year. Judy Welty was married to James Goodyear (born December 7, 1933), a sergeant in the U.S. Air Force. He died on September 16, 1971 in Orlando, Florida. His death was initially believed to be due to natural causes. In 1973, she moved in with Bobby Joe Morris (born 1939). In January 1978, he died by poison in Trinidad, Colorado. Later that year, she legally changed her name to "Buenoano" (corrupted Spanish for "good year"). In 1979, Buenoano's son Michael (March 30, 1961 – May 13, 1980) became severely ill, with symptoms including paraplegia. On May 13, 1980, Buenoano took Michael out in a canoe; the canoe rolled, and Michael, weighed down by his arm and leg braces, drowned. Following Michael's death, Buenoano opened a beauty salon. In 1983, Buenoano was in a relationship with John Gentry. Gentry was severely injured when his car exploded after a friend gathering in Pensacola, Florida. While he was recovering from his injuries, police began to find several discrepancies in Buenoano's background. Further investigation revealed that, in November 1982, she had begun telling her friends that Gentry was suffering from a terminal illness. "Vitamin pills" which Buenoano had been giving Gentry contained arsenic and paraformaldehyde. Exhumations of Michael Goodyear, James Goodyear, and Bobby Joe Morris showed that all had died of arsenic poisoning. Buenoano received substantial life insurance payouts after each death. In 1984, Buenoano was convicted for the murder of Michael and the attempted murder of Gentry. In 1985 she was convicted of the murder of James Goodyear. She received a twelve-year sentence for the Gentry case, a life sentence for the Michael Buenoano case, and a death sentence for the

Mariticide Club

James Goodyear case. She was convicted of multiple counts of grand theft (for insurance fraud), and is thought to have committed multiple acts of arson (again, for purposes of insurance fraud). She was incarcerated in Florida Department of Corrections Broward Correctional Institution death row for women. On March 30, 1998, Buenoano was executed in the electric chair at the Florida State Prison. Her last meal consisted of broccoli, asparagus, strawberries and hot tea. When asked if she had any last words, Buenoano said "No, sir." Buenoano's body was cremated after execution.

Phoebe Campbell
Murder of George Campbell

George (left) and Phoebe Campbell (right)

Phoebe Campbell (c. 1847 – 20 June 1872) was a Canadian woman who was hanged for the murder of her husband. Campbell had alleged that on the morning of July 15, 1871, in Thorndale, Middlesex County, Ontario, two black-faced men broke into George and Phoebe's log cabin home and brutally hacked George to death with an axe because he refused to hand over some money. They had attempted to use a gun which misfired.

During the investigation, six local men were arrested, including Thomas Coyle, who was George's farmhand. Doubt about Phoebe's innocence arose rapidly as she was seen talking with Coyle; she also seemed to have done nothing to help save her husband as he was being murdered and seemed very unemotional following George's funeral. A coroner's autopsy showed

Wives Who Kill

that George was murdered by Phoebe and Coyle. "I don't care. I'm innocent and I don't care", Phoebe stated. She then accused Coyle of the murder, then quickly changed her mind and accused her cousin. Phoebe's murder trial began on 1 April 1872, with much public interest. Phoebe accused George of having an affair with her cousin's wife. During the trial, the crown prosecutor produced a letter which stated, "I never shall say you done any such thing again—if I have to die for it." When asked why she changed her testimony, she claimed the ghost of her late husband visited her and declared her and Coyle innocent. The crown prosecutor responded, "You can hardly expect anyone to believe such nonsense! "After the trial, the jury took just one hour to reach a guilty verdict. Phoebe then sobbed as the judge sentenced her to hanging. She later confessed that she and Coyle murdered George so they could marry. Coyle went to trial for his crime but was acquitted. He later moved to England. She was hanged on 20 June at the age of 25 and was again said to be emotionless as she was about to be hanged, holding a lace handkerchief in her hand until after she died. The story received so much public attention that postcards depicting the crime were made, which were bought by many.

Clara Green Carl
aka Clara Gibson, "feminine Bluebeard"

Clara Green Carl (born May 1877) was an American writer and murderer from Ohio. In 1922, she was convicted of having poisoned her second husband, Frank Carl, and his father, Alonzo Carl. She was sentenced to life imprisonment but paroled after 15 years. During her time in prison, she escaped once and evaded recapture for a week. It is suspected that she killed her first husband, Robert Gibson, as well. She was "considered one of the most daring woman criminals in the country," earning the nickname "feminine Bluebeard." Green and her childhood sweetheart, Gibson, eloped on March 14, 1908, at Covington, Kentucky, moved to Cleveland where he worked as a teacher while she became a writer for a newspaper. The couple came up with a get-rich-quick scheme where they travelled from town to

Mariticide Club

town, writing and selling books of local historic areas. Their plan failed. While in Huntsville, Missouri, Gibson became ill with an unusual illness. He died March 18, 1920, leaving Clara a widow and the sole beneficiary of a $3,000 life insurance policy. A few months after her first husband's death, Green met and married Frank Carl on September 14, 1920, with the impression that he was wealthy. This was a tumultuous relationship, and at one point Mrs. Carl filed a complaint for divorce against her husband in the Hancock Circuit Court. When asked by Mrs. Lizzie Maynard what her grounds for divorce were, Clara replied that "if the law did not provide a way there was always some way. "In order to get her to drop the divorce lawsuit, Frank made her the sole beneficiary of his life insurance policy, worth $2,000.In 1921, Clara and Frank invited Frank's elderly father, Alonzo Carl, 85, to come live with them in Indiana. According to Frank's brother, Herman Carl, his father was in good health when he went to live with the couple. Like Clara's first husband, Alonzo became gravely ill by an unknown illness and died in August 1921.Expecting property from her father-in-law, Clara was furious to find that it had been given to her husband's brother-in-law Dr. Iles. Two months later, Frank was dead, suffering the same illness. The day after her husband's funeral, Clara asked Herman to meet with her to discuss obtaining Alonzo's property from Dr. Iles. Her suspicious actions aroused skepticism among her neighbors who demanded an investigation. Frank and Alonzo's bodies were exhumed, revealing that each man had enough arsenic in his system "to kill a dozen men", according to the prosecutor. "Clara was arrested and charged in January 1922. During her trial, Miss Rhoda Loehr testified that in July 1921, Clara bought arsenic citing that "neighborhood cats had been stealing her chickens [and] she said she wanted to kill the cats. "Evidence of arsenic in her second husband and father-in-law revealed this to be true. An investigation into her first husband's death revealed the same results. Clara was found guilty of second-degree murder and sentenced to life in prison at the Indiana Women's Prison at Indianapolis. She was "considered one of the most daring woman criminals in the country" earning the nickname "feminine Bluebeard." While in prison, Clara made a daring and cunning

Wives Who Kill

escape in early October 1925. She was assigned outdoor work due to ill health and became a trusty, earning the trust of prison guards after three years of good behavior. Clara was assigned to feeding the prison-yard chickens. One evening, she climbed up one of the chicken coops, hopped the prison wall and escaped. She evaded police for about a week before her re-capture. At aged 54, Clara was paroled on May 26, 1937, 15 years after she was convicted of murder.

Martha Curnutt Casto

Martha Curnutt Casto (1812 - 1887) was sentenced to five years in Missouri State Penitentiary, an all-male prison, in 1843 after murdering her brutally abusive husband, Noah Casto, with an ax while he slept in Barry County, Missouri. Her experience in the Penitentiary roused enough support from political figures in the state to petition for her pardon, which was granted in 1844. The incident drew attention to the fact that an all-female prison was necessary. Martha was born about 1812 in Tennessee, the daughter of John Curnutt. On July 6, 1839, she married Noah Casto in Missouri. Noah was from Pennsylvania and had been married at least twice before. Martha and Noah had two children together, a daughter named Mary and a son Noah, born about 1840 and 1842 respectively. On the morning of July 10, 1843, Martha's husband Noah announced that she had better make breakfast and then say her prayers because he was going to kill her afterward, then went back to sleep. In fear for her life and believing it was "his life or hers", Martha picked up the fire wood ax and brought it down on Noah's head as he slept, right through his eyes. She killed him with one blow. She then went to her neighbor and explained what had happened. She was convicted of first-degree manslaughter and sentenced to five years in Missouri State Penitentiary, where she was the only female prisoner out of about 800. Since she was not able to mix with the male prisoners, her food was brought to her cell and she was put to work outside the prison walls, in the homes of prison lessees, Captain Ezra Richmond and Judge James Brown. There, she was regularly abused by Brown's wife, to the extent than she attempted to run away but was recaptured and

Mariticide Club

temporarily placed in solitary confinement. Martha became pregnant while in the Penitentiary. Though the father remains unknown, the list of suspects is limited to those who had access to her while in prison, such as the prison guards and lessees. She gave birth in the fall of 1844 and the child, a daughter named Sarah, remained in her cell with her. With the knowledge that the baby may not survive the winter in a cold cell, 55 people, among them some prominent local figures, signed a petition for Martha's pardon which was granted in December 1844 by Governor John C. Edwards. After her release, Martha and her children assumed the use of her maiden name and lived with her father, John Curnutt, for some time. Martha's daughter Mary was married to Samuel Nixon, while her son Noah enlisted in the Union Army and died during his service in the Civil War. In her later years, Martha lived with her daughter Mary until her death on April 4, 1887, around the age of 75. Actress Cynthia Nixon is a descendant of Martha Curnutt, via her daughter Mary Nixon who was Cynthia's great-great grand-mother. Cynthia was featured on the celebrity genealogy TVshow, Who Do You Think You Are?

Stacey Castor
(née Stacey Ruth Daniels)

Wives Who Kill

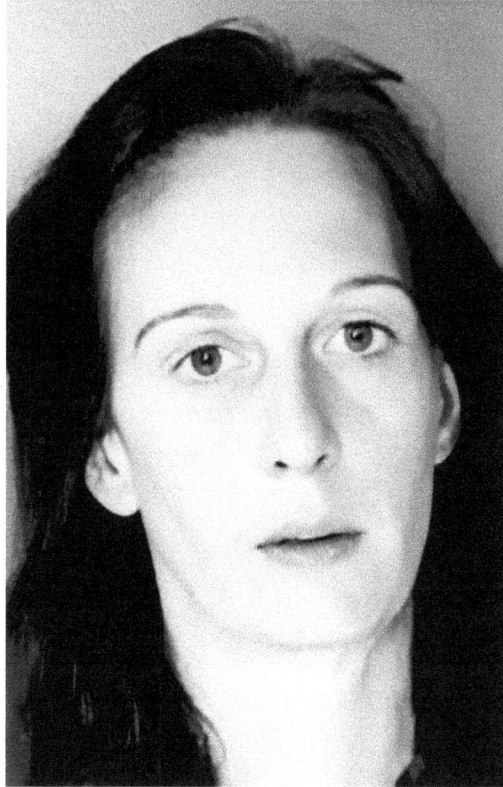

2007 mugshot, Onondaga County Sheriff's Dept

Stacey Ruth Castor (née Daniels, formerly Wallace; July 24, 1967 – June 11, 2016)was an American convicted murderer from Weedsport, New York. In 2009, she was found guilty of intentionally poisoning her then-husband David C ith crushed pills mixed in with vodka, orange juice, and Sprite in 2007. In addition, she is suspected of having murdered her first husband, Michael Wallace, in 2000; his grave lay next to David Castor's until David's remains were disinterred in 2016 and buried elsewhere by his son. The story made national news, and Castor was subsequently named "The Black Widow" by media outlets. A special twohour edition of ABC's 20/20 aired on April 24, 2009, and again on February 8, 2019, to provide the full story of the Castor case.

Mariticide Club

Stacey, the daughter of Jerry Daniels and Judie Eaton, met Michael Wallace when she was 17, in 1985, and they bonded immediately. The couple married and had their first daughter, Ashley, in 1988. In 1991, they had a second daughter, Bree. Castor was employed by an ambulance dispatch company, while Wallace worked nights as a mechanic, but the family had little money. According to Castor, Wallace was very close to Bree, showing a favoritism that Castor made up for by becoming "best friends" with elder daughter Ashley. Despite their closeness with their children, the couple grew apart; it was rumored that each was having affairs. In late 1999, Wallace began feeling intermittently ill. Family members variously remember him as acting unsteady, coughing and seeming swollen. As his inexplicable sickness persisted over the holiday season, his family encouraged him to seek medical care, but he died in early 2000 before he could do so. Their daughter Ashley was 12 at the time and had been alone with him. She had noticed his ill appearance that day, but thought nothing of it. Physicians told Castor that her husband had died of a heart attack. Although Wallace's sister was skeptical and requested an autopsy for Wallace, Castor refused, saying she believed the doctors were correct. In 2003, Stacey married David Castor, whose surname she used from that point forward. Castor was the owner of an air conditioning installation and repair company, and Stacey served as his office manager. In August 2005, at 2:00 one afternoon, Castor called her local sheriff's office to tell them that her husband had locked himself in their bedroom for a day following an argument and was not responding to his cell phone. When he did not appear at their shared workplace, she had become worried. She claimed he was depressed. Unable to get a response, Sergeant Robert Willoughby of the Onondaga County Sheriff's Department kicked in the door of the bedroom and found David Castor lying dead. Among the items near his body were a container of antifreeze and a half-full glass of bright green liquid. Willoughby says he remembers that Castor screamed, "He's not dead, he's not dead." The coroner reported that David Castor had committed suicide through a self-administered lethal dose of antifreeze, but when police found Stacey Castor's fingerprints on the antifreeze glass and

Wives Who Kill

located a turkey baster that had David Castor's DNA on the tip, they began to suspect Stacey Castor had engineered her husband's death. They believed Castor had used the turkey baster to force-feed him once he became too physically weak. The detectives on the case ordered wiretappings on Castor's house. They listened in on phone calls for any unusual conversations. In addition, they set up cameras overlooking Castor's house and the gravesites of her husbands, who had been buried side by side at Castor's request. Detectives reasoned that if Castor were truly genuine about her love for her late husbands, then she would eventually visit their graves. They wanted to observe her behavior while there. Castor, however, never visited. The investigators soon felt the only way to prove Castor responsible for both homicides was to have Wallace's body exhumed. A toxicology screening ruled that Wallace had also been killed through antifreeze poisoning. In September 2007, amid mounting evidence that Castor had murdered both of her husbands, she began to panic. After she learned police had exhumed Wallace's body and found traces of antifreeze in his system, she was believed to have devised a plan to set up her daughter Ashley for the murders. On Ashley's first day of college, investigators came to her school to question her about her father's death and to inform her that he had been poisoned instead of having died of a heart attack. An upset Ashley called Castor. Soon after, Ashley said, Castor invited her to come to the family home in Liverpool and drink together. Castor said that they had been through enough emotional stress and needed to relax. Ashley agreed because Castor was not only her mother but her "best friend". The following day, Castor invited Ashley to drink together at home again. She says that her mother offered her a "nasty-tasting" drink that she at first refused but eventually drank because she trusted Castor. Seventeen hours later, Ashley was found comatose on her bed by her younger sister Bree Wallace. Bree demanded that help be sought, and Castor made the 911 call. Ashley's sister left her side for a moment and when she returned, she found a suicide note beside Ashley. The note appeared to be Ashley's "murder confession", in which she "admits" to having killed her father and stepfather. Castor quickly took the note from the sister and later gave it to

Mariticide Club

the paramedics. Tests revealed that potentially fatal painkillers had been found in Ashley's system, and that she most likely would have died if taking her to the hospital had been just a few minutes later. When Ashley woke up, with police questioning her about the murders and the suicide note found beside her, she said that the last thing she remembered was her mother making her an alcoholic drink, something she had never done before. She told the officers that she did not write the note and was confused about their questions and accusations. For two years, investigators had collected evidence against Castor for the deaths of her husbands. In 2007, she was arrested for second degree murder in David's death and for attempting to murder Ashley and frame her for the murders of David and Wallace. Prosecutors argued that the computer-generated note where Ashley "confesses" to killing Wallace and David had actually been written by Castor. Ashley was 12 at the time of her father Wallace's death. When brought on the stand, she testified that she did not murder either her father or her stepfather nor did she write the suicide note. Onondaga County District Attorney William Fitzpatrick and Chief Assistant District Attorney Christine Garvey argued that David Castor's "suicide" had never made sense given the lack of his fingerprints on the glass or container tainted with ethylene glycol, a toxic substance found in antifreeze, and the turkey baster found in the kitchen garbage bearing both ethylene glycol and his DNA. They felt that this suggested he was force-fed antifreeze. Given evidence of the evolution of David Castor's illness, they concluded that Castor had for four days fed her husband antifreeze through the baster before trying to make it look like a suicide. She had said that her husband got the idea to kill himself with antifreeze while both were watching a news report about Lynn Turner, who murdered two past lovers by using the poison. The prosecutors presented evidence showing how antifreeze poisoning can be identified from the growth of calcium oxalate crystals in the kidneys, and that this was seen with examination of Wallace and David's bodies as well. In addition, they noted money as one of the main reasons Castor murdered her husbands. She had murdered her husbands partly to collect on their life insurance and estates, and had changed

Wives Who Kill

David's will to exclude his son by a previous marriage from the money left to him by David. "In 2005, people started to put it together," Cayuga County Sheriff Dave Gould said.

"If Mr. Wallace had been cremated, or if Mr. Castor had not died, we would never have known we had a homicide."

If there is a ceiling in terms of evil, she (Castor) is at the ceiling. — District Attorney William Fitzpatrick

Having searched Castor's computer, prosecutors had found several drafts of the suicide note Ashley was accused of writing. Forensic investigators found that based on the timestamps, it had been written while Ashley was in school, proving she couldn't have been its author. They argued that the "suicide attempt" had actually been a planned-out murder attempt by Castor against Ashley. On the stand, Ashley retold how her mother had convinced her to drink the two nights before she almost died. She repeated that she only drank the "nasty-tasting" beverage because she trusted Castor. She maintained her innocence of the two murders and the writing of the note. Castor's defense team—attorneys Charles Keller and Todd Smith—was set on creating reasonable doubt in the jury's minds about Castor having committed the murders. They wanted to "poke holes" in Ashley's version of what happened and prove that she could have been capable of murder at age 11.They noted Ashley's father, Wallace, showing favoritism toward his younger daughter rather than Ashley and cited jealousy as a possible motive for Ashley having murdered at such a young age. For her stepfather, they noted his and Ashley's tumultuous relationship and how they did not get along with each other. Castor's mother believed her granddaughter Ashley to be guilty. In a final attempt to convince the jury that she was not guilty, Castor took the stand. On cross examination, Fitzpatrick pointed out what he felt were flaws in Castor's version of that night. She maintained that it was Ashley who murdered Wallace and David, though she would not speculate about motives beyond implying that her daughter might be mentally ill. Fitzpatrick pointed out that Ashley's mother had never sought therapy for her and that at 21 Ashley exhibited no sign of mental illness.

Mariticide Club

Fitzpatrick asserted that Castor's behavior during David Castor's and Ashley's illnesses made no sense, given the years she had worked for a paramedics company. She did not seek care for Ashley for 17 hours and indicated that David Castor, who was staggering and vomiting and unable to stand, "looked OK". Likewise, he questioned how a woman who had lost two husbands to poisoning would not seek help for a daughter in Ashley's state. Fitzpatrick frequently shouted at Castor, inspiring Castor's defense attorney Charles Keller to frequently object and even to request a mistrial. Prosecutors brought up another piece of "damaging evidence" against Castor when they cited having heard "typing sounds" while Castor was on the phone. During one of the wiretapped recordings presented, "typing sounds" can be heard while Castor talks to a friend, though Castor denied memory of using the computer that day. Prosecutors argued the "typing sounds" were those of one of the several drafts Castor had written of the suicide note. Ashley had already testified to having witnessed her mother working on the computer on something she had hidden to prevent Ashley's seeing it. Fitzpatrick claimed this was the day Castor wrote the note, which had Castor's fingerprints but not Ashley's, to frame her daughter. He told the jury about the word antifreeze being written as "anti-free" in four places within the note and noted that Castor had also said "anti-free" during an interview. Castor said she had cut herself off while saying "antifreeze" because she had intended to say something else. Castor's defense team presented a pharmaceutical expert in an attempt to cast doubt on the prosecution's claim that Castor had drugged Ashley 17 hours prior to being taken to the hospital. "Professor Francis Gengo testified that after analyzing the traces of drugs and alcohol found in blood drawn from Ashley at the hospital, Ashley would have had to ingest the alcohol, Ritalin, and several other drugs just several hours before she was hospitalized." On February 5, 2009, Castor was found guilty of second-degree murder in the poisoning death of David and of attempted second degree murder for overdosing her daughter Ashley with drugs and vodka. With a "jam-packed" courtroom, most were focused on Castor. She, however, had her eyes closed as the verdicts were read. Her lead defense counsel, Keller, announced that Castor

Wives Who Kill

would appeal the verdict, including challenging the inclusion of evidence regarding the death of her first husband, for which Castor had not been charged. On March 5, 2009, at Castor's sentencing, Chief Assistant District Attorney Christine Garvey asked Fahey to impose the maximum consecutive sentences because of the brutality of David's death. Further, she criticized how Castor had "partied in her backyard with friends like nothing was happening" as Ashley was comatose in her room. "She is cold, calculating and without any emotion for what she has done," she stated. "Human life is sacred. Stacey Castor places no value on human life, not even her own flesh and blood. To Stacey Castor, human beings are disposable." David's son, whom Castor had cheated out of his inheritance, pleaded with Judge Fahey for Castor to be severely punished. "Your honor, [Castor] is a monster and a threat to society," he said. "She has created so much pain and death with this, creating multiples of pain and death, in the families of those she has hurt." Judge Fahey told Castor that he had never seen a parent attempt to murder their child in order to set their child up for a crime they themselves committed and declared Castor "in a class all by [her]self". He sentenced her to the maximum of 25 years to life for the murder of David Castor, and to another 25 years for the attempt to kill Ashley. For forging David's will, he ordered Castor to serve an additional 1⅓ to four years in prison. The trial had lasted for four weeks. An emotional Ashley told the judge she hated her mother "for ruining so many people's lives" but still loved her for the bond she originally had with her. I never knew what hate was until now. Even though I do hate her, I still love her at the same time. That bothers me, it is so confusing. How can you hate someone and love them at the same time? I just wish that she would say sorry for everything she did, including all the lies. As horrible as it makes me feel, this is goodbye mom. As hard as you tried, I survived and I will survive because now I'm surrounded by people that love me. I'm going to do good things in this world despite making me in every sense of the word an orphan.

— Ashley Wallace

Mariticide Club

Fitzpatrick said that under New York sentencing guidelines, Castor would have to serve just over 51 years before she became eligible for parole—at her age, effectively a life sentence. Castor, New York Department of Corrections inmate number 09G0209, was placed in Bedford Hills Correctional Facility for Women in Bedford Hills, New York. Even with credit for time served, her earliest possible release date was June 15, 2055—slightly over a month shy of her 88th birthday. On April 24, 2009, ABC aired a two-hour 20/20 special about Castor and the trial, which included interviews. During the trial, Castor had been dubbed "The Black Widow" by media outlets, a title previously given to Lynn Turner. Ashley said that she does not know how her mother, any mother, could try to kill her own child, a question that the public has also pondered. Castor, who professed to being shocked at the guilty verdict, maintained her innocence during the on-air 20/20 special, as well as in unaired parts of the program. She said that "Ashley brought this on" and insists that she and Ashley know what really happened. She did express sympathy for her daughter Bree. She called Bree an innocent victim, whom she lost along with her freedom and her husbands. She indicated that her mother, stepfather and some other relatives still support her. Bree, like Ashley, never spoke to Castor after the trial. Bree said that though losing her mother was hard, "I was happy that they said she was guilty, because we all know that she's guilty." Ashley said, "I would have done anything for her. But she tried to kill me instead." Both of Castor's daughters expressed concern that their mother had not yet apologized to them. Castor maintained that she was innocent of the deaths of her husbands and the attempted murder of Ashley. ABC interviewed forensic psychiatrist Dr. James Knoll for psychological perspective on the case and he answered viewers' questions via video on April 23, 2009, and via site comments on April 27, 2009. He stated that while most suicide notes focus on themes of remorse and the person not being able to go on with life, the note supposedly written by Ashley was focused on taking the blame off of Castor. He said that this theme was repeated fourteen times within the note and that he believes Castor will never admit to guilt of the murders. The code of murderers such as these,

Wives Who Kill

he said, is "deny, deny, deny" until the bitter end. When asked if Castor's behavior and body language on the stand shows any sort of clue about her mental state and guilt, Knoll reminded that body language and behavior can be affected by events during a trial (such as "side effects of medications, anxiety, fatigue and attorney instructions to the defendant on how to behave") and that their interpretation is not always reliable. Though Castor was not officially defined as a serial killer, it is likely that she would have killed again. Knoll said that killers may have many different motivations. He described Castor as a "black widow" type rather than a typical serial killer. He described a "black widow" type as a woman who kills husbands or lovers for material gain, as opposed to the typical serial killer (men who kill consecutively for sexual or sadistic motives). He relayed that "psychopathic traits and histories of childhood abuse have been consistently reported in these women" and suggested that if Castor were guilty of the crimes of which she had been convicted and accused, then she would be demonstrating psychopathic traits, including regarding even her own child as an object to be used for her convenience. Forensic Files had an episode titled "Freeze Framed" regarding Castor. In addition to the Turner and Castor antifreeze murder cases, similar cases were reported in 2008. In 2002, a man had been convicted of murdering his wife by antifreeze in 1998. A letter she had written before her death incriminated him as the murderer if she were to die eventually; the letter led to his prosecution.[28] Series Sex Lies and Murder, series 2 episode 3 as well as describing the events leading to the trial included an interview with the district attorney in the case. The DA pointed out Castor may have murdered her own father, Jerry Daniels, who died February 22, 2002, shortly after his daughter visited him in the hospital where he had a minor lung complaint. Castor's first husband's family believes Castor may have killed her father having brought an open can of soda in for her father to drink in the hospital. She was the executor of his estate. Castor was found dead in her cell on the morning of June 11, 2016. It was not immediately apparent how she died and the manner of her death was listed as undetermined. It was later determined by the D.A.'s office that Castor died of a heart attack, with no

Mariticide Club

evidence of suicide or foul play. Stacey Castor's story was adapted into the Lifetime film, Poisoned Love: The Stacey Castor Story, as part of its "Ripped from the Headlines" feature-film series; this made-for-television film was first transmitted on February 1, 2020. The film starred Nia Vardalos as Castor.

Mary Channing (née Brooks)

Mary Channing (née Brooks; May 1687 – 21 March 1706) was an English woman from the county of Dorset. Channing is known for being convicted of poisoning her husband and being burnt at the stake. Mary Brooks was born in early May 1687 to Richard and Elizabeth Brooks of Dorchester. The lack of proper parental control is said to have lowered her character. She soon established a friendship with a young neighbor to whom she often presented lavish gifts and together they spent their evenings outside. After receiving frequent complaints from neighbors, Brook's parents decided that she should be married; they thought a husband would have more control over her than they commanded. So, she married, albeit reluctantly, a grocer named Thomas Channing on 15 January 1704. Even after being married, she continued meeting her lover. Channing is said to have poisoned her husband's milk. Before dying on 21 April, Thomas Channing wrote his will, leaving everything to his father except a shilling for Mary. Her father-inlaw grew suspicious and upon post-mortem of Channing's body, he was found to have been poisoned. Mary fled Dorchester and was on the run until she found a distant relative she could stay with. When apprehended, Channing denied having killed her husband and asked the examining committee headed by Dorchester mayor to let her touch her deceased husband's body. If it did not bleed, she should be deemed innocent. Her trial began on 28 July 1705 at Dorchester Assizes and she conducted her own defense. Channing was declared guilty but the sentence was suspended when she was found to be pregnant. In prison she gave birth to a son on 19 December. Channing was burnt at Maumbury Rings on 21 March 1706. Her execution was witnessed by about 10,000 people. Thomas Hardy was somewhat "fascinated" by and "obsessed" of Channing's execution.

Wives Who Kill

David Musselwhite points out that Nance Mockridge, Mother Cuxsom and Mrs. Goodenogh, three characters in Hardy's The Mayor of Casterbridge, were an "avatar or surrogate of Channing. The Ring at Casterbridge mentioned in the novel was actually in Maumbury. In his article published in The Times (1908), Hardy noted the lack of evidences in proving that Channing poisoned her husband. Two of Hardy's poems The Mock Wife and The Bridge-Night Fire make references to her. David James' play White Mercury, Brown Rice (1995) enacted the trial of Channing. The main character in John Cowper Powys' novel Maiden Castle (1937) writes a book about Mary Channing.

Ivy Patterson Charles

Winston Holt "Win" Charles (September 26, 1903 – January 29, 1949) was a professional American football player for the American Professional Football Association's Dayton Triangles. He played in five games in the 1928 season. Charles played college football at Mary. He was shot to death on January 29, 1949.His wife, Ivy Patterson Charles, was convicted of his murder on May 11, 1949and sentenced to serve six years. She was denied a pardon by Governor Tuck on October 14, 1949.

Gama Kshatriyi

Chey Chettha III (Khmer: ជ័យជេដ្ឋាទី៣; 1639–1673) or Batom Reachea II was a Cambodian king from 1672 to 1673. Chey Chettha III was the only son of Batom Reachea. In 1671, he became the son-in-law of his uncle, King Barom Reachea V, by marrying his eldest daughter, Princess Sri Thida Kshatriyi. In December 1672, he murdered his father-in-law and seized the throne, and forced his cousin Bhagavatti Dav Kshatriyi (also the wife of his uncle Prince Ang Tan) to be his wife. Chey Chettha III was assassinated by the Chams and Malays in the employ of his wife, Gama Kshatriyi, just five months after his coronation, in April (or May) 1673.

Mariticide Club

Joyce Elaine Clarke
The Short Life and Career of Tony Clarke

Tony Clarke (April 13, 1940 – August 28, 1971) was an American soul singer and songwriter. Clarke, thought to have been born Ralph Thomas Williams in New York City, was raised in Detroit. He performed as a singer and made his first recordings for the small Stepp label in the late 1950s. He wrote the songs "Pushover" and "Two Sides to Every Story", hits for Etta James, with Billy Davis. Clarke had his first chart entry in 1964 with "(The Story of) Woman, Love and a Man", which reached No. 88 on the R&B chart. He had more success with his own song, "The Entertainer", which hit No. 10 R&B and No. 31 Pop in the U.S. in 1965. In 1966, he moved from Detroit to Hollywood for a small part in the film They Call Me Mister Tibbs!. He was fatally shot by his estranged wife when he broke into her house in Detroit. After his death, his popularity saw a resurgence in the 1970s on the United Kingdom's Northern soul scene with his recordings of "The Entertainer" and "Landslide". Tony Clarke (1940-1971) was an American soul singer-songwriter whose claim to fame during his short lifetime was his Top 40 pop/Top 10 R&B single "The Entertainer" in 1964. He was also credited as one of the writers behind Etta James' Top 40 pop hit "Pushover" and her #63 pop single "Two Sides (To Every Story)" the year before. The cause of his early death in 1971 was homicide, when he was shot and killed by his estranged wife as an act of self-defense. Clarke was only 31 years old.

Wives Who Kill

Tony Clarke's early life and struggles in his career: Soul singer-songwriter Tony Clarke was born on April 13, 1940 in New York City, New York. However, he grew up and was raised in Detroit, Michigan. Although some sources say that his real name was Ralph Thomas Williams, it seems to have never been verified. Other sources cite other possible birth names were Ralph Ferguson and Ralph Clarke. Either way, Tony Clarke inched his way to become an accomplished singer as well as songwriter. By the late 1950s he had been performing as an amateur vocalist before he secured his first recording contract with Stepp label. It was through the help of his mail man Fred Brown, who heard Clarke in one of his performances and was impressed by his singing. Clarke's first single on Stepp label was entitled "Hot Rod Car" which failed miserably. Nevertheless, Clarke was convinced and determined that singing and songwriting would be his future. He moved to another label called Fascination in 1962, and recorded another single "Cry" which again bombed. Clarke was still undaunted, though, and went on his way trying to make a name for himself.

Tony Clarke's career as a songwriter: The moment came for Clarke came when he and Billy Davis (aka Roquel Davis) teamed up to write a song for Etta James. The song turned out to be a Top 10 R&B hit for James, titled "Pushover" in 1963. It also paced the Top 40 pop charts at #25. Clarked and Davis also wrote another single for James, "Two Sides (to Every Story)" which only became a minor hit on the Hot 100. In being a songwriter, Clarke sometimes used pseudonyms such as Tony Lois and even the effeminate-sounding Thelma Williams.

Tony Clarke's hit with "The Entertainer": His link with Davis greatly helped Clarke to snag another recording deal, this time with Chicago-based Chess Records. He waxed several records for Chess, including his first charting single "Woman, Love and a Man" which peaked at #88 on the Billboard Hot 100 in 1964. "Woman, Love and a Man" was co-written by Clarke and Wlifred McKinley. However, it was his another single "The Entertainer" that raised his name into the consciousness of the recordbuying public. His self-penned hit peaked at #31 on the Billboard Hot 100,

Mariticide Club

and #10 on the Billboard R&B singles chart. The success of "The Entertainer" brought Clarke some financial cushion; it's even said that he used the money to purchase Detroit's Brute label from LeBaron Taylor. Later career after "The Entertainer": After the success of "The Entertainer," Clarke was occupied in several engagements. He starred the top bill on many big venues in Detroit. In 1966 he relocated to Hollywood and cofounded Earthquake Productions. He even dabbled in films, with his most notable appearance being a small part in the Sidney Poitier-starred They Call Me Mr. Tibbs. His own subsequent singles failed to chart again, but he wrote one hit for the Spanish beat group Los Lobos, "I Don't Care." It became Los Lobos' hit single in the UK at #16. Homesickness and missing his children (with estranged wife Joyce Elaine) prodded Clarke to return to Detroit, where he permanently settled. He was signed to M S Records where he released "(They Call Me) A Wrong Man."

Tragic end: In the wee hours of August 28, 1971, Clarke is alleged to have broken into the house of his estranged wife, with a tire jack in hand. However, his wife had a gun and, in an act of self-defense, shot him. Clarke was only 31 years old when he was killed.

Jill Coit (née Jill Lonita Billiot)

Jill Lonita Coit (née Billiot; born June 11, 1943 or 1944) is an American convicted murderer. An artist and serial bigamist who has been married 11 times to nine different men since 1961, Coit was convicted of killing her eighth husband in 1993 and is also suspected of killing her third husband in 1972. Coit is serving a life sentence with no possibility of parole at the Denver Women's Correctional Facility. Coit was born Jill Lonita Billiot in Lafitte, Louisiana; she grew up in Orleans. She is of Native American descent. Her upbringing was apparently normal and without any major trauma or unusual features, and she was described as popular at her school. However, Coit did not fare well academically and dropped out of high school in 1961 to marry her first husband. Less than a year later she filed for divorce and liquidated their shared bank accounts.

Wives Who Kill

She married for a second time, to Steven Moore, and gave birth to a son in 1964, filing for divorce soon afterwards. Coit married engineer William Clark Coit, Jr. in January 1966 in Louisiana, while still legally married to Moore. The couple had two children, William Andrew Coit (called Andrew) and William Coit III. William Coit, Jr. adopted Jill's son from her previous marriage. William Coit, Jr. was killed on March 29, 1972, shot twice in the back by an apparent intruder shortly after he filed for divorce from Jill. She was suspected of the murder, but the police could never find sufficient evidence to charge her. Additionally, she checked herself into a mental hospital to avoid further questioning. Shortly after Coit's death, Jill Coit moved to California, where she also persuaded an elderly gentleman to informally adopt her, and subsequently inherited "a large portion of his estate" after his death.

Additional marriages

Coit's fourth marriage was to Donald Charles Brodie, an officer in the U.S. Marine Corps. The couple divorced in 1975 after two years of marriage. Coit later twice married and twice divorced one of the lawyers who represented her during the investigation into William Coit's murder.

While separated from her fifth husband, Coit married Eldon Duane Metzger in Ohio. In 1983, she married husband number seven, a schoolteacher in Indiana. While renovating a bed and breakfast with her sons, Coit regularly visited Gerald Boggs' hardware store in Steamboat Springs, Colorado. They struck up a relationship and in 1991 Boggs, a 52-year-old bachelor, married her, becoming (unbeknown to him) her eighth husband. Boggs' brother Doug was concerned by Coit's excessive interest in her husband's finances. He hired a private investigator who exposed Coit as a complete fraud. She had been married nine times, had several aliases, had been involved in various financial and insurance scams, and was still legally married to her seventh husband. She had also faked a pregnancy, having had a hysterectomy. On the basis of this information, Boggs annulled the marriage after seven months. After the annulment, Coit and Boggs were involved in an acrimonious lawsuit over the bed and breakfast business. Boggs had a substantial financial interest in the

Mariticide Club

establishment that was complicated by her use of mortgage fraud, apparently to conceal her assets due to a financial judgment against her by yet another previous husband. The murder of Boggs happened shortly before the trial was scheduled to begin. Coit briefly married for a ninth time before entering into a relationship with Michael Backus and convinced him to help her murder Boggs. In October 1993, they acted on their plot. Wearing a disguise which included a false mustache, Coit and Backus broke into Boggs's home. They shocked him with a stun gun, and ultimately murdered him using a .25 caliber pistol, later fleeing to Mexico. Police quickly centered on Coit as a suspect. After she confided to her younger son about the murder and asked for his help in covering it up, he instead went to the police. She was arrested in December 1993, during a visit from Mexico. Subsequent investigation, as well as testimony at her 1995 trial, revealed that she began making plans to murder Boggs as early as the summer of 1993, going as far as to solicit several people to come to Colorado and kill him. She was convicted of first-degree murder and conspiracy to commit first-degree murder and sentenced to life without possibility of parole plus an additional 47 years on the conspiracy charge. Michael Backus was convicted and sentenced to life. Coit, Colorado Department of Corrections #86530, is serving her sentence at Denver Women's Correctional Facility. All of her appeals have been exhausted. She has repeatedly attempted to find a new husband via the internet.

In media
_____

Books

- The 1995 book Charmed to Death, by author Stephen Singular tells the story of Jill Coit's conviction for killing her husband, Gerry Boggs, and depicts her long history of bigamy and embezzlement.
- The 1995 book Poisoned Vows, by investigative journalist and true crime author Clifford L. Linedecker, is a biography of Coit and her criminal activities.

Wives Who Kill

Television

Coit was portrayed by Bonnie Bedelia in the Fox made-for-television film Legacy of Sin: The William Coit Story (1995). Coit's story is told from the point of view of her son William Coit III (played by Neil Patrick Harris). The movie is based on Stephen Singular book Charmed to Death.

Coit's exploits have been recounted by several true-crime documentary television series:

- Forensic Files, episode "Order Up" (season 8, episode 12), first aired in 2004.
- American Justice episode "Serial Wife" (season 13, episode 28), first aired in 2004 on the A&E Television Network. Host Bill Kurtis interviews prosecution and defense attorneys as well as reporters.
- The New Detectives episode "True Crime" (season 4, episode 14), aired in 1999.
- Deadly Women, episode "Fortune Hunters" (season 4, episode 3), first aired in 2010 on Investigation Discovery.
- Facing Evil with Candice DeLong, episode "The Black Widow Bride" (season 2, episode 5), first aired in 2011 on Investigation Discovery. Host Candice DeLong interviews Jill Coit in prison.

Gail Collins Pappalardi

Gail Collins (Feb 2, 1941 – Dec 6, 2013) American songwriter, record producer and visual artist. She came to prominence (as 'Miss Gail Collins') co-producing, with Pappalardi, the self-titled debut album by Energy, a group featuring Laing. She also co-produced, with Felix Pappalardi, the Felix Pappalardi and Creation album in 1976. Collins Pappalardi cowrote Cream's "World of Pain" with her husband Felix Pappalardi and "Strange Brew" with Pappalardi and Eric Clapton. Both songs are on the album Disraeli Gears. She contributed lyrics to many Mountain songs. Her artwork is on album covers by Mountain, including Climbing!, Nantucket Sleighride, Flowers of Evil, Mountain Live: The Road Goes Ever On, Twin

Mariticide Club

Peaks and Avalanche. She was associate producer on the 1978 album by Hot Tuna, Double Dose. On April 17, 1983, Felix Pappalardi was shot once in the neck in the fifth-floor New York City apartment he shared with Collins Pappalardi. He was pronounced dead at the scene and Collins Pappalardi was charged with murder. Collins Pappalardi claimed that the killing was an accident. During the trial it was revealed that the couple had an open marriage and that Collins Pappalardi had shot her husband after he had returned in the early morning from seeing his girlfriend. She was acquitted of second-degree murder and manslaughter, but found guilty of homicide and sentenced to 16 months to 4 years in prison. On April 30, 1985, she was released on parole. On December 6, 2013, Collins was found dead by her landlord in the Mexican village of Ajijic, Jalisco, a resort town with many American expatriate residents. She had been undergoing cancer treatments there. She was cremated.

Louisa Collins (née Louisa Hall)

Louisa Hall Collins

Wives Who Kill

Louisa Collins (formerly Andrews née Hall;) 11 August 1847 – 8 January 1889) was an Australian poisoner and convicted murderer. Collins, who was dubbed the "Borgia of Botany" by the press of the day, endured four trials in front of 48 men, after the first three juries failed to convict. Collins was hanged at Darlinghurst Gaol on the morning of 8 January 1889. Born Louisa Hall at Belltrees near Scone, New South Wales on 11 August 1847, one of at least seven children of Henry Hall and his wife Catherine (née Ring).Henry Hall was a native of Birmingham, England, who had been sent to Australia as a convict in 1831 on board the ship Asia; Catherine was a migrant from Ireland. At a young age, Louisa married Charles Andrews, a butcher. Louisa and Andrews had nine children, only seven of whom survived infancy. By December 1886, Andrews had moved his family to the inner-city suburb of Botany. Andrews had work as a wool washer that used chemicals, including arsenic, to wash the wool before export. To make ends meet, the family took in lodgers. One of Andrew's co-workers was Michael Collins, who took up residence in the Andrews' family home. Charles Andrews discovered the liaison between his wife and Michael Collins in December 1886. Charles Andrews confronted Michael Collins and threw him out of the boarding house. On 31 January 1887 Charles Andrews signed a will that was drawn up by a clerk at the insurance office. Soon after, he started to feel violently ill, suffering from stomach cramps, vomiting and diarrhea. Andrews died on 2 February 1887. The now-widowed Mrs. Louisa Andrews quickly applied for the life insurance of her dead husband. Acquaintances were not surprised that she took up with Michael Collins soon after the death of her first husband. Louisa Collins stated they were married on 9 April 1887, within two months of Charles Andrews' funeral. She was four months pregnant on her wedding day. Her child, John Collins, born in 1887, died and was buried in a pauper's grave. Michael Collins fell ill after he and Louisa had been married for one year. Immediately before his death on 8 July 1888, he displayed the same symptoms as Charles Andrews in 1887.
A coroner's inquest was held at the South Sydney Morgue by Mr. H. Shiell, J.P (the City Coroner)Michael Collins' life was not insured.

Mariticide Club

Neighbors were suspicious that both husbands of Louisa Collins had died with the same symptoms. Andrews' body was exhumed and a chemical analysis found the presence of arsenic. The autopsy of Michael Collins declared the cause of death to be arsenical poisoning. Louisa Collins was arrested for the murder of both men on the recommendation of the coroner, as she was the only person who nursed the men during their illnesses. One of Louisa Collins' sons from her first marriage, Arthur Andrews, gave evidence that his father was a healthy man who could work a 15-hour day if necessary. Some of the most important testimony was given by Collins' only daughter, May Andrews; just 10 years old at the time of the first trial, she gave evidence that the family kept Rough on Rats – a deadly arsenicbased poison. Sydney was suffering a rat plague in the 1880s, which led to boom sales for the product, which was the basis of the case against Collins. Collins endured four trials, the first three failed to find a verdict. She did not call any witnesses to her defense. On 8 January 1889, Louisa Collins was hanged at Darlinghurst gaol. She was the first woman to be executed in Darlinghurst Gaol. She was the last woman to hang in the state of New South Wales. The first full-length examination of the case, Last Woman Hanged: the Terrible True Story of Louisa Collins, by Australian author and journalist Caroline Overington, was published in 2014. A novel, The Killing of Louisa by Janet Lee, was published by UQP in 2018.
Victims

- Charles Andrews 52
- Michael Peter Collins 26

Marie-Josephte Corriveau (aka La Corriveau)

Marie-Josephte Corriveau (1733 at Saint-Vallier, Quebec – April 18, 1763 at Quebec City), better known as "la Corriveau", is a well-known figure in Québécois folklore. She lived in New France, and was sentenced to death by a British court martial for the murder of her second husband, was hanged for it and her body hanged in chains. Her story has become a legend in Quebec, and she is the subject of many books and plays.

Wives Who Kill

Early life

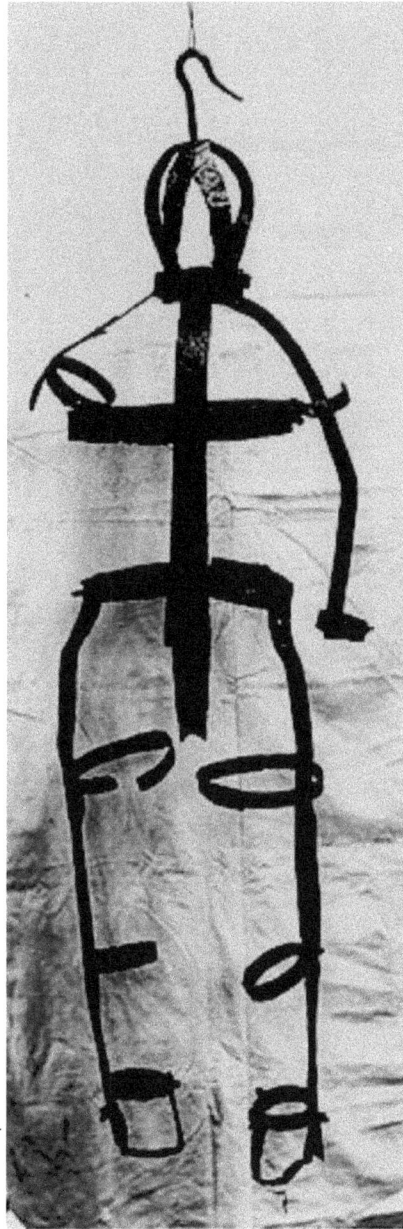

The gibbet in which Corriveau was exhibited after her execution, the "cage" of Corriveau

Marie-Josephte Corriveau was born in 1733, most probably in January or February, and baptized on May 14, 1733, in the rural parish of Saint-Vallier in New France. She was the only surviving offspring of Joseph

Mariticide Club

Corriveau, a farmer, and Marie-Françoise Bolduc. Her ten brothers and sisters all died in childhood.

Marriages and deaths of spouses

Corriveau married at the age of 16, on November 17, 1749, to Charles Bouchard, aged 23, also a farmer. Three children were born in this marriage: two daughters, Marie-Françoise (1752) and Marie-Angélique (1754), followed by a son, Charles (1757). Rumors (that only started after the death of her second husband) say that she murdered him, as there is no concrete record of his death. Charles Bouchard was buried on April 27, 1760, and she remarried fifteen months later, on July 20, 1761, to another farmer from Saint-Vallier, Louis Étienne Dodier. On the morning of January 27, 1763, he was found dead in his barn, with multiple head wounds. Despite an official recording of the cause of death being from kicks of horses' hooves, and a speedy burial, rumors and gossip of murder spread rapidly through the neighborhood. Dodier was on bad terms with his father-in-law and with his wife.

Arrest and trial

At the time, New France had been conquered by the British in 1760 as part of the Seven Years' War and was under the administration of the British Army. On hearing the rumors, the local British military authorities (charged with keeping order) set up an inquiry into Dodier's death. The inquiry opened in Quebec City on March 29, 1763, at the Ursulines of Quebec, charging Joseph Corriveau and his daughter Marie-Josephte, before a military tribunal made up of 12 English officers and presided over by Lieutenant Colonel Roger Morris. Many persons in the community had testified, including Joseph's niece and Marie-Josephte's cousin, a young woman approximately the same age as Marie-Josephte named Isabelle Sylvain. The case ended, on 9 April, with Joseph Corriveau being sentenced to death, for culpable homicide of his son-in-law. Marie-Josephte was found to be an accomplice to murder, and sentenced to 60 lashes and branded with the letter M on her hand. One of Joseph Corriveau's nieces, Isabelle Sylvain (who he employed as a servant), had

Wives Who Kill

testified but changed her story several times during the hearing; she was found guilty of perjury and given 30 lashes and branded with the letter P. Condemned to hang, Joseph Corriveau then told his confessor, that he was no more than an accomplice to his daughter, after she had killed Dodier. At a second trial, on 15 April, Marie-Josephte testified to having killed her husband with two blows of a hatchet during his sleep, because of his ill treatment of her. The tribunal found her guilty and sentenced her to hang, her body after to be "hanged in chains" (that is, put up for public display on a gibbet).

Execution

The place of execution was Quebec, on the Buttes-à-Nepveu, near the Plains of Abraham, probably on 18 April. Her body was then taken, as directed by the sentence, to be put in chains at Pointe-Lévy, at the crossroads of Lauzon and Bienville (Rue Saint-Joseph and Rue de l'Entente). The body, in its iron gibbet, was exposed to the public view until May 25 at the earliest. Following the requests of those living nearby, an order from the military commander of the district of Quebec, James Murray, addressed to the captain of the militia of Pointe-Lévy, permitted its being taken down and buried.

In 1851, the "cage" was dug up from the cemetery of the church of Saint-Joseph-de-la-Pointe-Lévy when a pit was dug.[Note 3] Soon after, the cage was stolen from the church cellar, and acquired by the American impresario P. T. Barnumand put on display as a "macabre object". After that, it was put on display at The Boston Museum. The museum slip indicated its provenance with two words: "From Quebec". Through the efforts of the Société d'histoire de Lévis, the cage was acquired from the Boston Museum and is now part of a permanent display at Musée de la civilisation in Quebec City.

In legend

Mariticide Club

La Corriveau, in her cage, attacking Father José (José's Nightmare), illustration by Henri Julien for an edition of Anciens Canadiens by Philippe Aubert de Gaspé)

The post-mortem exhibition of Corriveau's remains at a busy crossroads (a practice also in use under the French regime, and reserved in England for those found guilty of the most serious crimes);[better source needed][Note 4] the repercussions in the trial; the rumor that her father would be convicted of murdering Dodier at his daughter's instigation; and the gossip which grew up around the circumstances of the death of her first husband all stirred up the popular imagination and became legends still told today in the oral tradition — increasing the number of murdered husbands to as many as seven and likening la Corriveau to a witch.

The 1851 discovery of the iron cage buried in the cemetery of Saint-Joseph Parish (now the Lauzon district) served to reawaken the legends and the fantastic stories, which were amplified and used by 19th-century writers. The first, in 1863, Philippe Aubert de Gaspé in Les Anciens Canadiens, has a supernatural Corriveau hanging in the Pointe-Levy cage, terrorizing one night a passer-by conducting a witches' Sabbath and Will-o'-the-wisp at

Wives Who Kill

the Île d'Orléans. James MacPherson Le Moine (Maple Leaves, 1863)and William Kirby, following in his footsteps (The Golden Dog, 1877), made her a professional poisoner, a direct descendant of La Voisin, famous for her purported role in the Affair of the Poisons. Writers and historians such as Louis Fréchette and Pierre-Georges Roy have tried to give Corriveau's history, but without completely separating the facts from the anachronistic fantasies added in legend and novels.

The figure of Corriveau still inspires novels, songs and plays and is the subject of arguments concerning guilt. Oral tradition also perpetuated and has not stopped, and remains alive, as is evidenced by the numerous stories collected in the lands of many regions of Quebec.[Note 5]

In popular culture

Mariticide Club

Caroline de Saint-Castin (right) pressing to her lips the poisoned bouquet offered by la Corriveau (left). Late 19th-century illustration by J. W. Kennedy for an American edition of The Golden Dog by William Kirby.

- 1863: Les Anciens Canadiens (The Canadians of Old), novel by Philippe Aubert de Gaspé
- 1863: Marie-Josephte Corriveau, A Canadian Lafarge, in Maple Leaves by James MacPherson Le Moine
- 1877: The Golden Dog, A Legend of Québec, novel by William Kirby, translated into French by Léon-Pamphile Le May , Le Chien d'Or, légende canadienne (1884)
- 1885: La Cage de la Corriveau, novel by Louis Fréchette, first published in a special edition of the newspaper La Patrie, 24 February 1885; reprinted and rewritten many times, notably under the title Une Relique in the Almanach du peuple de la librairie Beauchemin, Montreal, 1913.
- 1966: La Corriveau, dramatic ballet choreographed by Brydon Paige, with original theme and songs by Gilles Vigneault and music by Alexander Brott. Commissioned by the Commission du Centenaire de la Confédération, the ballet was premièred by Les Grands Ballets Canadiens, with the collaboration of the Montreal Symphony Orchestra at the Salle Wilfrid-Pelletier of the Place des Arts at Montréal, 21 and 22 December 1966.
- 1972: La Corriveau, song written by Gilles Vigneault in 1966 for the ballet of the same name, is recorded by Pauline Julien on her album Au milieu de ma vie, peut-être la veille de...
- 1973: Ma Corriveau, play by Victor-Lévy Beaulieu written for the public examinations of the students of the National Theatre School of Canada, premièred at the Monument-National, its Montreal base, from 3 to 6 October 1973 with a production by Michelle Rossignol, first premièred professionally at the Théâtre d'Aujourd'hui in Montreal from 19 September to 30 October 1976 in a production by André Pagé.

Wives Who Kill

- 1978: Le Coffret de la Corriveau, fantasy story by André Carpentier , translated into English in 1982.
- 1981: La Corriveau, historical novel by Andrée LeBel
- 1990: La Cage, play by Anne Hébert, translated into English in 2009.
- 1993: La Corriveau, short story by the English Canadian Douglas Glover, translated into French the same year, and into Serbian in 1995.
- 1993: La Corriveau, play by Guy Cloutier, produced by Denise Verville and staged at the Théâtre Périscope , Quebec, from 12 to 30 January 1993. It was reprised, adapted for television with the title La Corrivaux by the director Jean Salvy, with Anne Dorval in the title role, and broadcast on the Télévision Radio-Canada network in 1995.
- 1999: La Maudite, teen novel by Daniel Mativat
- 2001: La Corrida de la Corriveau, song by Mes Aïeux (on the album Entre les branches)
- 2003: La Fiancée du vent: l'histoire de la Corriveau, née en Nouvelle-France et pendue sous le Régime anglais, novel by Monique Pariseau
- 2003: Julie et le serment de la Corriveau, teen novel by Martine Latulippe
- 2003: Her story and the alleged paranormal aspects of it were featured in Episode 1 of Season 2 of the Canadian paranormal documentary series Creepy Canada, which carried out and showed a reenactment of her story and its allegedly paranormal aspects.
- 2004: Battle of the Brave (Nouvelle-France), film produced by Jean Beaudin (loose adaptation on the theme of la Corriveau)[28]
- 2006: La Corriveau, animated film by Kyle Craig
- 2015: Corriveau is featured on a postage stamp from Canada Post
- 2022: Les Filles du QUOI?, play by Abby Paige

Mariticide Club

Mary Ann Cotton (née Mary Ann Robson)

Cotton, c. 1870

Mary Ann Cotton (née Robson; 31 October 1832 – 24 March 1873) was an English convicted murderer who was executed for poisoning her stepson. Despite her sole conviction for murder, she is believed to have been a serial killer who killed many others including 11 of her 13 children and three of her four husbands for their insurance policies. Her preferred method of killing was poisoning with arsenic. Cotton's undoing came after she tried to have the son of her deceased husband sent to a workhouse. When that failed, within days she told parish officials that Charles Edward Cotton had died. Investigations into her behavior soon showed a pattern of deaths. The body of the stepson was examined and found to contain arsenic. Cotton was convicted of his murder and sentenced to death. She was hanged at Durham Gaol. She did not die on the gallows from breaking of her neck but died by strangulation because the rope was set too short, possibly deliberately. Mary Ann Robson was born on 31 October 1832 at Low Moorsley, County Durham to Margaret, née Londsdale and Michael Robson, a colliery sinker; and baptized at St Mary's, West Rainton on 11 November. Her sister

Wives Who Kill

Margaret was born in 1834 but lived only a few months. Her brother Robert was born in 1835. When Mary Ann was eight, her parents moved the family to the County Durham village of Murton. At the time of her trial, The Northern Echo published an article containing a description of Mary Ann as given by her childhood Wesleyan Sunday school superintendent at Murton, describing her as "a most exemplary and regular attender", "a girl of innocent disposition and average intelligence", and "distinguished for her particularly clean and tidy appearance." Soon after the move, Mary Ann's father fell 150 feet (46 m) to his death down a mine shaft at Murton colliery in February 1842. Her father's body was delivered to her mother in a sack bearing the stamp 'Property of the South Hetton Coal Company'. As the miner's cottage they inhabited was tied to Michael's job, the widow and children would have been evicted. In 1843, her mother married George Stott (1816–1895), also a miner. At 16, Mary Ann left home to become a nurse at the nearby village of South Hetton, in the home of Edward Potter, a manager at Murton colliery. After all of the children had been sent to boarding school in Darlington over the next three years, she returned to her stepfather's home and trained as a dressmaker.

Husband 1: William Mowbray

In 1852, 20-year-old Mary Ann married colliery laborer William Mowbray at Newcastle Upon Tyne register office; they soon moved to South West England. At the time of her trial, there were reports of four or five of their children dying young while they were living away from County Durham. None of these deaths are registered, as although registration was compulsory at the time, the law was not enforced until 1874. The only birth recorded was that of their daughter Margaret Jane, born at St Germans in 1856. William and Mary Ann moved back to North East England, where William worked as a fireman aboard a steam vessel sailing out of Sunderland, then as a colliery foreman. Another daughter, Isabella, was born in 1858, and Margaret Jane died in 1860. Another daughter, also named Margaret Jane, was born in 1861, and a son, John Robert William, was born in 1863, but died the next year from gastric fever.

Mariticide Club

William died of an intestinal disorder in January 1865. The lives of William and of their children were insured by the British and Prudential Insurance office and Mary Ann collected a payout of £35 on William's death (equivalent to £3,560 in 2021, about half a year's wages for a manual laborer at the time) and £2 5s for John Robert William.

Husband 2: George Ward

Soon after Mowbray's death, Mary Ann moved to Seaham Harbor, County Durham, where she struck up a relationship with Joseph Nattrass. During this time, her 3½-year-old daughter, the second Margaret Jane, died of typhus fever, leaving her with one child of up to nine she had borne. She returned to Sunderland and took up employment at the Sunderland Infirmary, House of Recovery for the Cure of Contagious Fever, Dispensary and Humane Society. She sent her surviving child, Isabella, to live with her mother.

One of her patients at the infirmary was engineer George Ward. They married at St Peter's Church, Monkwearmouth, on 28 August 1865. Ward continued to suffer ill health and died on 20 October 1866 after a long illness characterized by paralysis and intestinal problems. The cause of death recorded on his death certificate is that of English cholera and typhoid. The attending doctor later gave evidence that Ward had been very ill, yet he had been surprised that his death was so sudden. Once again, Mary Ann collected insurance money in respect of her husband's death.

Husband 3: James Robinson

James Robinson was a shipwright at Pallion in Sunderland, whose wife Hannah had recently died. He hired Mary Ann as a housekeeper in November 1866. A month later, when James' baby John died of gastric fever, he turned to his housekeeper for comfort and she became pregnant. Then Mary Ann's mother, living in Seaham Harbor, County Durham, became ill with hepatitis, so she immediately went to her. Although her mother began to recover, she also began to complain of stomach pains. She died at age 54 in the spring of 1867, nine days after Mary Ann's arrival. In 1867, Mary Ann's stepfather George Stott married his widowed neighbor,

Wives Who Kill

Hannah Paley. Mary Ann's daughter Isabella Mowbray was brought back to the Robinson household and soon developed severe stomach pains and died, as did two of Robinson's children, Elizabeth and James. All three children were buried in the last week of April and first week of May 1867. Mary Ann received a life-insurance payment of £5 10s 6d for Isabella. Robinson married Mary Ann at St Michael's, Bishopwearmouth on 11 August 1867. Their first child Margaret Isabella (Mary Isabella on her baptismal record) was born that November, but she became ill and died in February 1868. Their second child George was born on 18 June 1869. Robinson, meanwhile, had become suspicious of his wife's insistence that he insure his life; he discovered that she had run up debts of £60 behind his back and had stolen more than £50 that she had been expected to bank. Then he found that Mary Ann had been forcing his older children to pawn household valuables. He threw her out, retaining custody of their son George.

Husband 4: Frederick Cotton

Mary Ann was desperate and living on the streets until her friend Margaret Cotton introduced her to her brother Frederick, a pitman and recent widower living in Walbottle, Northumberland, who had lost two of his four children. Margaret had acted as substitute mother for the remaining children, Frederick Jr. and Charles, but in late March 1870 she died from an undetermined stomach ailment, leaving Mary Ann to console the grieving Frederick Sr. Soon her twelfth pregnancy was underway. Cotton and Mary Ann were bigamously married on 17 September 1870 at St Andrew's, Newcastle-Upon-Tyne and their son Robert was born early in 1871. Soon after, Mary Ann learnt that her former lover, Joseph Nattrass, was living 48 kilometers (30 mi) away in the County Durham village of West Auckland, and was no longer married. She rekindled the romance and persuaded her new family to move near him. Cotton died in December of that year, from "gastric fever." Insurance had been effected on his life and those of his sons.

Two lovers

Mariticide Club

After Frederick's death, Nattrass soon became Mary Ann's lodger. She gained employment as nurse to an excise officer recovering from smallpox. Popular cultural sources have called him John Quick-Manning, though there appears to be no trace of a John Quick-Manning in the records of the West Auckland Brewery or the National Archives. The census records, birth, death and marriage records also show no trace of him. Richard Quick Mann was a custom and excise man specializing in breweries and has been found in the records and this may be the real name of Mary Ann Cotton's lover. Soon, Mary became pregnant by him with her thirteenth child. Frederick Jr. died in March 1872 and the infant Robert soon after. Then Nattrass became ill with gastric fever and died just after revising his will in Mary Ann's favor. The insurance policy Mary Ann had taken out on (the still living) Charles' life still awaited collection.

Death of Charles Edward Cotton and inquest

Mary Ann's downfall came when a parish official, Thomas Riley, asked her to help nurse a woman who was ill with smallpox. She complained that the last surviving Cotton boy, Charles Edward, was in the way and asked Riley if he could be committed to the workhouse. Riley, who also served as West Auckland's assistant coroner, said she needed to accompany him. She told Riley that the boy was sickly and added: "I won't be troubled long. He'll go like all the rest of the Cottons." Five days later, Mary Ann told Riley that the boy had died. Riley went to the village police and convinced the doctor to delay writing a death certificate until the circumstances could be investigated. Mary Ann's first visit after Charles' death was not to the doctor but the insurance office. There, she discovered that no money would be paid out until a death certificate was issued. An inquest was held and the jury returned a verdict of natural causes. Mary Ann claimed to have used arrowroot to relieve his illness and said Riley had made accusations against her because she had rejected his advances. Then the local newspapers latched on to the story and discovered Mary Ann had moved around northern England and lost three husbands, a lover, a friend, her mother, and 11 children, all of whom had died of stomach fevers.

Arrest

Wives Who Kill

Rumour gave rise to suspicion and scientific investigation. Doctor William Byers Kilburn, who had attended Charles, had kept samples, and tests showed they contained arsenic. He told the police, who arrested Mary Ann and procured exhumation of Charles' body. She was charged with his murder, although the trial was delayed until after the delivery in Durham Gaol on 7 January 1873 of her thirteenth and final child, whom she named Margaret Edith Quick-Manning Cotton.

Trial and execution

Cotton's trial began at Durham Assizes on 5 March 1873. The delay was caused by a problem in the selection of prosecution counsel. A Mr. Aspinwall was first considered but the Attorney General, Sir John Duke Coleridge, whose decision it was, chose his friend and protégé Charles Russell. Russell's appointment over Aspinwall led to a question in the House of Commons. However, it was accepted, and Russell conducted the prosecution. The Cotton case was the first of several famous poisoning cases he would be involved in during his career, including those of Adelaide Bartlett and Florence Maybrick.

The defense in the case was handled by Thomas Campbell Foster, who argued during the trial that Charles had died from inhaling arsenic used as a dye in the green wallpaper of the Cotton home. The doctor testified that there was no other powder on the same shelf in the chemist's shop as the arsenic, only liquid; the chemist himself claimed that there were other powders. Campbell Foster argued that it was possible that the chemist had mistakenly used arsenic powder instead of bismuth powder (used to treat diarrhea), when preparing a bottle for Cotton, because he had been distracted by talking to other people. The jury retired for 90 minutes before returning a guilty verdict.

The Times correspondent reported on 20 March: "After conviction the wretched woman exhibited strong emotion but this gave place in a few hours to her habitual cold, reserved demeanor and while she harbors a strong conviction that the royal clemency will be extended towards her, she staunchly asserts her innocence of the crime that she has been convicted of." Several petitions were presented to the Home Secretary, but to no avail.

Mariticide Club

Mary Ann Cotton was hanged at Durham County Gaol on 24 March 1873 by William Calcraft; she died, not from her neck breaking, but by strangulation caused by the rope rigged too short, possibly deliberately. Of Mary Ann's 13 children, only two survived her: Margaret Edith (1873–1954) and her son George from her marriage to James Robinson.

Television and radio drama

In 2015 ITV filmed a two-part television drama, Angel, starring Joanne Froggatt as Cotton. The series also featured Alun Armstrong, Jonas Armstrong and Fielding. The first part of the dramatization was broadcast on 31 October 2016, the second part was broadcast on 7 November. The drama was inspired by the book Mary Ann Cotton: Britain's First Female Serial Killer by David Wilson, a criminologist.

The Mary Ann Cotton case was partly dramatized on an episode of the 2022 BBC Radio podcast series Lucy Worsley's Lady Killers.

Cultural references

- A nursery rhyme concerning Cotton was composed after her hanging on 24 March 1873.

Mary Ann Cotton, she's dead and she's rotten
Lying in bed with her eyes wide open.
Sing, sing, oh what should I sing?
Mary Ann Cotton, she's tied up with string.
Where, where? Up in the air.
Selling black puddings, a penny a pair.

Mary Ann Cotton, she's dead and forgotten,
Lying in bed with her bones all rotten.
Sing, sing, what can I sing?
Mary Ann Cotton, tied up with string.

- Hardnoise recorded "Serve Tea, then Murder" (1991) as a reference to Cotton, as DJ AJ described in a 2014 interview

Wives Who Kill

- The Raveness, an English performance poet from Warwickshire, composed a spoken word piece entitled "Of Rope and Arsenic" about Cotton and featured the nursery rhyme on her album The Raveness (2003). The piece was also published in her poetry anthology, Lavinia: Volume One (2006) – ISBN 9781502313966
- The band Attrition's 2008 album was entitled All Mine Enemys Whispers – The Story of Mary Ann Cotton.
- Macabre released a song about Cotton called "Mary Ann" on their Grim Scary Tales (2011) album.

The Dead Milkmen released a song about Cotton called "Mary Ann Cotton (The Poisoner's Song)" on their 2014 album Pretty Music for Pretty People

Mary Cowan (née Mary A. Knight)

MRS. MARY COWAN.

Mary Cowan (née Mary A. Knight)

Mariticide Club

Mary A. Cowan (née Knight; March 8, 1863 – September 17, 1898), known as The Borgia of Maine, was an American serial killer who poisoned two husbands and four children between 1884 and 1894, and attempted to murder a third husband. Convicted of killing her step-son Willis Cowan in September 1894, Cowan was sentenced to life imprisonment and sent off to the Maine State Prison, where she died a few years later from an unspecified illness. Mary A. Knight was born as one of several children to Jonathan F. Knights, a veteran of the Civil War, and Apphia B. Knights (née Sidelinger). She lived on rural family home in Plymouth until the age of 20, when she married the young farmer Willis W. Bean of nearby Dixmont. The couple had three children: Gracie, Alice and Mabel. At some point during their marriage, Willis expressed a desire to become a physician, a decision encouraged by Mary, who wanted to dabble in it as well. However, the family was poor, and they also had to take care of their infants. In 1884, Gracie was found smothered to death by a neighbor at the family home. When he informed Mary of the matter, she carelessly replied that she was aware of the fact, and that the child had died about half an hour ago. No official investigation was made, but residents of Dixmont suspected that she had killed little Gracie to get rid of her. In the following two years, Alice and Mabel died from peculiar stomach aches, but yet again, no investigation was conducted, and the deaths soon forgotten after the burials at the Plymouth cemetery.

THE MODERN BORGIA AT WORK.

Illustration of Cowan's victims

Wives Who Kill

Despite these tragedies, Willis still decided to pursue his medical career, enrolling into a dubious institute that sold diplomas for $25. However, this was considered fraudulent, and soon, a state law was passed which prohibited the selling of fake diplomas, right before Bean could acquire it. Unperturbed by this setback, both husband and wife were dead-set on getting diplomas, choosing to travel to an out-of-state institution in Ohio to get them. Before their trip, Willis confided to his parents that he would invest money in a farm, in which he would live after returning to Maine. Said farm was purchased and the mortgage given to the elder Bean, but it was never recorded. After borrowing some $200, the couple traveled to Ohio to enroll into an institution. On January 6, 1888, Willis' parents received a letter claiming that their son had died mysteriously, with the cause of death later determined to be stomach pain, similar to the children who died in the previous years. Mary soon returned to stay with her late husband's parents, and soon after, the unrecorded mortgage went missing. Since she had the deed for the farm, and thus owned the land, Mary sold the farm for $2,000. Sometime later, Mary married George H. Taylor, a Dixmont laborer who worked at the Lewiston mills, where the newlyweds moved to live. Taylor, who belonged to the Independent Order of Odd Fellows, died after four days of acute stomach pain in 1891, in similar circumstances to Mary's former family. Since he was an Odd Fellow, it was supposed that he had a life insurance policy, but since George hadn't paid his dues, it was void. Nevertheless, well-meaning members contributed to a fund amounting several hundreds of dollars as a donation to the supposedly-grieving widow.

Murder of Willis Cowan and arrest

A few months after Taylor's death, Mary married Elias Cowan, a widowed farmer with an 8-year-old son, Willis. Not long after their marriage, a full set of farm buildings belonging to Elias mysteriously burned to the ground. According to neighbors who arrived to provide assistance with putting out the fires, they found the family's clothing, dishes and other items tied up in bundles and ready to be carried out. It was also rumored that young Willis was abused by his stepmother, who often beat him for the pettiest of things.

Mariticide Club

On September 14, 1894, Willis was brought down with heavy stomach pains after eating some green apples. A physician was called to the family home, who prescribed some medicine and assured that the young boy would be fine in a few hours. Two days later, the young Cowan died in agonizing pain. Due to Mary's dubious history of similar deaths, and the fact that her husband had also been taken with a similar illness but survived, Willis' body was exhumed and his organs sent for analysis at the Bowdoin College in Brunswick. The autopsy results showed that the body contained heavy amounts of arsenic, enough to kill a full-grown ox. Without wasting their time, policemen quickly arrested Mary Cowan for the murder of her stepson. Until then, she had threatened to pursue legal action if anybody accused her of poisoning, but when lodged in the prison, she started crying.

Trial and imprisonment

During her 1895 trial, an ample amount of evidence was presented, pinning Mary as the one who poisoned young Willis. One witness was a little neighborhood girl who had seen Mrs. Cowan putting white powder into the boy's medicine, which had been left by the doctor, but she did not testify per request of her father, who feared for her safety. Despite this, the prosecutor proved that the dose of arsenic present in the body could've only been put deliberately, and after a few days of deliberation, the jury returned with a guilty verdict. Cowan stood expressionless while listening to the verdict, with her counsel, J.F. Robinson, announcing that he would file a motion for a retrial. In June, however, it was announced that the proceedings for the retrial had been withdrawn.

While in prison, Mary Cowan conducted interviews with reporters and often responded to callers interested in her case. On one occasion, she confided to a reporter that she had hired a private detective who supposedly unearthed evidence in favor or her innocence, and expressed belief that she would be a free woman again one day. Her hopes were dashed on February 19, 1896, when she was officially sentenced to life imprisonment for killing Willis Cowan.

Cowan was imprisoned at the Maine State Prison, then in Thomaston, for the following two years. In 1898, her examining physician turned to then-

Wives Who Kill

governor Llewellyn Powers with the request of pardoning Mary, as she was in failing health and wished to die peacefully in her Dixmont home. Despite her ailment, Mary gave birth to a child while in prison, but it, along with herself, died soon after. Cowan, by then dubbed 'The Borgia of Maine' by the press, was first interned at Etna, where her parents lived, but her body was then moved to the Sawyer Cemetery in her birthplace of Plymouth, where she was buried on the family plot with her murder victims.

Thofania d'Adamo

Thofania d'Adamo or Teofania di Adamo, Epifania d'Adamo or La Tofania (died 12 July 1633, Palermo) was an Italian poisoner. She was executed for having poisoned her late spouse Francesco d'Adamo and for having trafficked in illegal lethal poison. She was preceded by Francesca La Sarda, who was executed for having trafficked in illegal lethal poison the year prior. The two women were accused to have sold poison together in Palermo. The case attracted a lot of attention and the investigation was conducted on the orders of Fernando Afán de Ribera. The case is first mentioned in the Compendio di diversi successi in Palermo dall'anno 1632 by Baldassare Zamparrone (1581-1648). The contemporary diarist Gaetano Alessis described in Notizie piacevoli e curiose ossia aneddoti…, in which he claimed that the poison Aqua Tofana was invented by her and named after her. Thofania d'Adamo are known in history as the alleged mother of the famous poisoner Giulia Tofana, who is claimed to be her daughter, who named the poison Aqua Tofana after her mother, and who fled to Rome after the execution of her mother, where she founded a new business selling poison. In reality, this appear to have been a myth, originated in a hypothesis from the 19th-century. Giulia Tofana, whose actual name was Giulia Mangiardi, left Palermo for Rome in 1624, not 1633, and while she do appear to have founded a business selling poison there, which she eventually left to her stepdaughter Gironima Spana, there is nothing to indicate that Thofania d'Adamo was the mother of Giulia Mangiardi, although she may have been her disciple.

Mariticide Club

Hallie D'Amore

Hallie D'Amore (August 13, 1942 – December 14, 2006) was an American make-up artist who was nominated for Forrest Gump at the 1994 Academy Awards for Best Makeup. She shared her nomination with Judith A. Cory and Daniel C. Striepeke. Hallie D'Amore killed her husband and herself on December 14, 2006.

Selected filmography

- Captivity (2007-released posthumously
- Wild Hogs (2007-released posthumously)
- The Santa Clause 3: The Escape Clause (2006)
- The Shaggy Dog (2006)
- Christmas with the Kranks (2004)
- The Princess Diaries 2: Royal Engagement (2004)
- 2 Fast 2 Furious (2003)
- We Were Soldiers (2002)
- The Princess Diaries (2001)
- Galaxy Quest (1999)
- Apollo 13 (1995)
- Forrest Gump (1994)
- Bugsy (1991)
- Steel Magnolias (1989)

Sarah Reynolds Dazley (aka The Potton Poisoner)

Sarah Dazley (1819 – 5 August 1843), The Potton Poisoner,
English murderer convicted of the poisoning of her husband William Dazley. She was suspected of, but not tried for, the poisoning of her first husband Simeon Mead and their son Jonah Mead in 1840. The murder of William Dazley took place in Wrestlingworth, England. Born in 1819 in Potton, Bedfordshire, Sarah Reynolds was the daughter of the town barber Philip Reynolds and his wife Ann Reynolds. When she was 7, her father died and her mother went on to court a series of men. She grew up to

Wives Who Kill

be tall with big brown eyes and long auburn hair, and when she was 19 she married Simon Mead. They lived in Potton for two years before moving to Tadlow in 1840. Shortly after the move, she gave birth to their son Jonah, but he became ill and died at only seven months old. In October 1840, Simon Mead died unexpectedly as well. Soon after the death of her first husband, Sarah married her second husband, William Dazley, in 1841, and they moved to the village of Wrestlingworth. She invited teenage Ann Mead, Simon Mead's daughter, to live with her and her new husband, but he was opposed to the idea. In retaliation, he became an avid drinker and beat his wife. She went on to tell a friend, William Waldock, that she would kill any man who ever hit her. William Dazley grew quite ill and his wife and her stepdaughter began to take care of him. The local doctor, Dr. Sandell, gave William prescriptions that brought on signs of recovery while under the care of Ann Mead. After seeing this, Dazley began making pills of her own for her husband. Mead didn't notice this as a problem at first. When William refused to take the new pills, Ann took one herself to show him there was nothing wrong. She was not aware that these pills contained arsenic trioxide that Sarah had intentionally added. Once Sarah saw Mead take the pill she scolded her for it. After taking it, Mead became ill and shared similar symptoms with William: vomiting and stomach pains. William eventually decided to take his wife's lethal drugs and died on 30 October 1842. After his death, suspicion rose against Dazley over the deaths of her two husbands and son. William Dazley's body was examined and found to contain traces of arsenic. An arrest warrant was issued for Dazley, who fled to London. After being discovered in London by Superintendent Blunden of Biggleswade Police, Dazley insisted she was innocent of any crimes. She claimed she had no idea about any poisonings and never got hold of poisons or anything of that nature. She was arrested and returned to Bedford. Since the news of William Dazley's death had caused suspicion about the deaths of Jonah and Simeon Mead, their bodies were also exhumed. Traces of arsenic were found in Jonah, but Simeon's body was too decomposed to test. Sarah Dazley was committed to Bedford Gaol on 24 March 1843 and awaited her trial. She used this time to concoct

Mariticide Club

defenses such as William poisoned himself, or he poisoned Jonah and Simeon, so she poisoned William as revenge for murdering her family. On 22 July 1843 Sarah Dazley was tried for the murder of William Dazley at Bedfordshire Summer Assizes. She was not tried for the murder of her son Jonah, but the case was kept if the first case against her were to fail. The chemists she bought arsenic from were able to testify against her, as well as Ann Mead and neighbor Mrs. Carver. They told the court what they had seen, including the pill making. William Waldock testified against Dazley about her statement that she would kill any man that hit her, after making claims that William Dazley had hit her. The Marsh test was used to detect the arsenic in William Dazley's body and the result was used as forensic evidence against Dazley. It only took 30 minutes for the jury to convict Dazley for the murder of her second husband. Judge Baron Alderson sentenced Sarah Dazley to death by hanging. She was executed on Saturday, 5 August 1843, at Bedford Gaol. She was the only woman to be publicly hanged at Bedford Gaol. Thousands of people came to watch the execution, and she became known as the Potton Poisoner.

Daniela Maria Delis, alcoholic wife

Wives Who Kill

Harald Reinl in 1985

Harald Reinl (8 July 1908 in Bad Ischl, Austria – 9 October 1986 in Santa Cruz de Tenerife, Spain) was an Austrian film director. He is known for the films he made based on Edgar Wallace and Karl May books and he made mountain films, Heimatfilms, German war films and entries in such popular German film series as *Dr. Mabuse, Jerry Cotton and Kommissar X.* Reinl began his career as an extra in the mountain films of Arnold Fanck. He was a screenwriter on the films*sssss*directed by and starring Leni Riefenstahl. Reinl's first movie as director was the mountain film *Mountain Crystal* (1949). He was Oscar nominated for his documentary feature *Chariots of the Gods* (1970). By the 1970s, he had semi-retired to the Canary Islands. In 1986, in his Tenerife retirement home, he was stabbed to death by Daniela Maria Delis, his alcoholic wife and a former actress from Czechoslovakia.

Marissa-Suzanne "Reese" DeVault

The murder of Dale Harrell (December 18, 1974 – February 9, 2009) occurred after he was fatally attacked on January 14, 2009, by his

Mariticide Club

wife Marissa-Suzanne "Reese" DeVault (born November 6, 1977) in Maricopa County, Arizona. Her trial made national and global headlines. The case was noted as being very similar to that of the murder of Travis Alexander by Jodi Arias, with whom DeVault was in contact and whose murder trial occurred in the same courthouse one year earlier. Though she faced the possibility of a death penalty for her crime, DeVault was sentenced to life in prison. She is imprisoned at Perryville within the Arizona Department of Corrections. On January 14, 2009, DeVault entered the master bedroom that she and Harrell shared at their home in Gilbert, Arizona. She then struck Harrell several times in the head while he was sleeping. Harrell received multiple skull fractures and was taken to the hospital. DeVault initially claimed that Harrell was beaten by an unknown assailant who had broken into the home. She later confessed that she had beaten Harrell as an act of self-defense, and alleged that Harrell was physically and sexually abusive. DeVault was arrested the same night on charges of aggravated assault and was held at a local jail, but was later released on bail. Officers noted that DeVault had reddened marks upon her neck, and that they had found a hammer covered with blood at the crime scene. In early February 2009, DeVault was indicted for attempted murder and released on bond. On February 9, 2009, Harrell died of his wounds and a grand jury indicted DeVault for first-degree murder. At 3:00 a.m. the next morning, DeVault was assaulted by an unknown assailant as she was jogging, suffering a broken jaw and ankle. Following the beating, police investigated a man who lived with DeVault, Stanley Cook, Jr., and found dirty, bloody clothing. Both DeVault and Cook initially told police that Cook had killed Harrell. Cook had a brain injury that caused him to suffer from short-term memory loss— neither he nor DeVault could provide details concerning his involvement. Police found no evidence linking Cook to the crime; indeed, forensic evidence ruled out Cook having been the assailant. When confronted with this fact, DeVault confessed that she had bludgeoned her husband with the hammer. After Harrell was cremated at a Mesa mortuary, DeVault refused to give the remains to his parents, who then filed a civil suit against her for Harrell's remains and punitive

Wives Who Kill

damages. DeVault filed a 300-page confession with the Gilbert police where she detailed the years of alleged abuse, stating that Harrell had beaten and raped her on January 14, prompting her to assault him with the hammer. She also reported that Harrell had frequently sent her to the hospital, and that he had once, in front of several witnesses, shoved her and dislocated her shoulder, which one of the witnesses helped pop back into place. During this time, police interviewed friends of DeVault and Harrell. The police found that they had no evidence to corroborate claims that Harrell had been abusive toward DeVault. They also mentioned that DeVault had lied to them in the past about receiving a large inheritance from the death of her stepfather, who was in fact not deceased. DeVault was also discovered to have lied about an older lover she was seeing, Allen Flores. She borrowed over $300,000 from Flores, who had been introduced to police as an ex-lover of her stepfather. Flores' house was searched twice, and the police located a computer with child pornography on it. Flores later agreed to testify on the Harrell murder in exchange for full immunity over the pornography charges. DeVault was initially set to go to trial in 2011, but the trial was postponed. The prosecutors in the case sought the death penalty. Defense attorneys stated that DeVault had battered woman syndrome and post-traumatic stress disorder, which they used to argue against the death penalty. Jury selection for the new trial began in January 2014, where Judge Roland Steinle commented that he did not want anyone on the jury that had been overly focused on the Jodi Arias trial. The trial for DeVault officially began on January 22, 2014, and was expected to run until April. In their opening statements, the defense and prosecutors posed different reasons for DeVault's motivations for beating Harrell with a hammer. Prosecutors alleged that DeVault killed Harrell with the intention of collecting on a total of $1,250,000 from two life insurance policies, so she could repay Allen Flores the $300,000 she had borrowed from him, while DeVault's defense attorneys claimed that DeVault acted in selfdefense. The defense also stated that DeVault had experienced abuse as a child, and that her mother had physically abused her, while her stepfather had sexually abused her. Dr. Jon Conte, a clinical psychologist that was also knowledgeable about the effects of child abuse, testified on behalf of the defense, stating that he believed that DeVault's actions were consistent with a long history of childhood abuse. One of DeVault's children also testified that she had witnessed Harrell abuse her mother.[3] The prosecution countered this with testimony from clinical psychologist Dr. Janeen DeMarte, who diagnosed DeVault as having antisocial personality disorder. She also questioned why DeVault would give custody of her children to her mother and stepfather after DeVault had earlier claimed that they had abused her. The prosecution also pointed out that DeVault had initially claimed that an unknown assailant had broken into the home and assaulted Harrell, before confessing that she was the perpetrator. On April 8, 2014, DeVault was found guilty of first-degree premeditated murder for the death of Harrell, and the jury found that excessive cruelty had been used which made DeVault eligible for the death penalty.[19] In a statement to the court, DeVault apologized for the murder, saying that she was "sorry, not only for my actions, but for everyone I hurt". She also addressed Harrell's parents, stating that, "My heart goes out to them...his mother and father have had to experience the worst loss in the world – the loss of a child. I know there is nothing I can say that will ever ease their pain." The penalty phase of the trial commenced on April 15, and deliberations began on April 22. The jury sentenced DeVault to life in prison instead of the death penalty, and Maricopa County Attorney Bill Montgomery stated that, "imposing the death penalty in any circumstance is difficult, and in this one, the jurors apparently felt that a life sentence was appropriate". On June 6, 2014, the judge sentenced DeVault to life in prison without the possibility of parole.

Hendrikje Doelen (née Hendrikje Geerts Meilofs Doelen)
Hendrikje Geerts Meilofs Doelen (June 1, 1784–December 10, 1847)
On May 7, 1819, the farmwife Hendrikje Doelen married the almost six years older Aaldert Mulder in the Drenthe town of De Wijk. Both were poor day laborers. In 1827, both were admitted to the district's poorhouse. Suddenly, in 1845 several people mysteriously died. First of all, on April 7,

Wives Who Kill

her husband Aaldert and an old woman named Jantje Wichers, who was living with the couple, died. A few days later, the three children of Arend Hut, who also lived in the poorhouse, became ill after eating oatmeal pulp that they had received from Hendrikje Doelen. Half a year later, on October 14, her neighbor Grietje van Buren died after eating pancakes made by Doelen. Her daughter, Evertje, also became seriously ill after eating those same pancakes and died ten months later on August 9, 1846. Doelen was suspected of murdering the persons mentioned. After an investigation it was established that Wichers probably died from a natural death, but both the husband and Grietje van Buren were diagnosed with the presence of arsenic. Because no legal proof could be provided for her husband's murder, she was finally sentenced to death on January 15, 1847 for the murder of Van Buren by the provincial court of Assen. Doelen denied her guilt at the hearing. But the Supreme Court rejected her cassation request, she acknowledged her guilt in her pardon request. She killed her husband because of the marital quarreling and her neighbor and daughter because of spite. The Supreme Court advised negatively about the petition, but the then minister of justice Marinus Willem de Jonge of Campensnieuwland gave a positive advice, also in view of her age. King William II granted clemency by royal order on November 14, 1847. On December 2, 1847, she was displayed for half an hour with the noose on the scaffold in Assen. The death penalty was changed to a prison sentence of 20 years. She died, however, after eight days, on December 10, 1847 in the women's prison of Gouda.

Kathleen Dorsett

Kathleen Dorsett (born July 2, 1974) is a former Neptune, New Jersey schoolteacher who was convicted of the August 2010 murder of her ex-husband, Stephen Moore, in May 2013. Her father, Thomas Dorsett, also pled guilty to the murder, and Dorsett's mother, Lesley Dorsett, a former member of the Township Board, pleaded guilty to conspiracy to commit murder in 2013. The case made headlines across New Jersey and throughout the United States. Kathleen Dorsett, was a kindergarten and third grade teacher at the Gables School in Neptune

Mariticide Club

Township, New Jersey, and Stephen Moore, a salesman at a local Honda dealership, and former speed skater, married in June 2007. The following year, Kathleen gave birth to the couple's only daughter. Shortly after though, the couple began disagreeing about how to best care for their daughter. Eventually the couple began divorce proceedings and a custody battle ensued. The divorce was later finalized in June 2010, with Kathleen receiving primary physical custody. After the divorce, Kathleen's parents, Thomas and Lesley Dorsett, planned to move to Florida with their daughter Kathleen and her daughter. However, the couple would have had to help Stephen Moore move there too, so he could have access to their daughter. This would require Thomas Dorsett providing financial assistance to Moore for the first six months following the move. On August 16, 2010, Stephen Moore was dropping off his daughter at Kathleen's parent's home in Oakhurst, New Jersey. Following the exchange, Stephen was beaten to death by Kathleen's father, Thomas Dorsett, in the driveway of their home, while Kathleen was allegedly changing the child's diaper. Later that day, when he failed to show up to work at the Honda dealership, Stephen was reported as a missing person by his employer. Two days later, on August 18, 2010, Stephen's body was found in the back of his mother's burning 2001 Nissan Altima in Long Branch, New Jersey. Shortly after the murder on August 23, Kathleen Dorsett was arrested and charged with one count of first-degree murder and one count of fourth-degree tampering with evidence. After his daughter's arrest, Thomas Dorsett attempted suicide by ingesting refrigerant outside his attorney's office. He survived and was charged with one count of first-degree murder, two counts of fourth-degree tampering with evidence, and third-degree witness tampering. Anthony Morris, was charged with arson and desecration of human remains; he had allegedly been paid $3,000 by Thomas Dorsett to burn Stephen Moore's mother's car with his body in the trunk. Kathleen and Thomas Dorsett were held at the Monmouth County jail on $1.5 million and $2.5 million cash bail. While in jail awaiting trial, Kathleen Dorsett and her mother Lesley were charged with conspiracy to commit murder and attempted murder for attempting to arrange and solicit a hit man to kill Stephen

Wives Who Kill

Moore's mother, Evlyn, who received custody of his daughter after Kathleen's arrest. During this investigation, it was also discovered that the Dorsett family was involved in money laundering, as they had attempted to conceal $96,000 worth of assets. In November 2010, all three Dorsetts were charged with money laundering. In April 2011, Anthony Morris pled guilty to conspiracy to disturb or desecrate human remains. Under his plea agreement, he was sentenced to less than seven years in prison. In May 2013, Kathleen, Thomas, and Lesley Dorsett pled guilty to all charges against them. Kathleen Dorsett was sentenced to 30 years in prison for murder, 20 years for attempted murder, and 8 years for conspiracy. She is serving her sentences, running consecutively, at the Edna Mahan Correctional Facility for Women in Union Township, New Jersey. She is eligible for parole in August 2057, when she will be 83 years old. Since her incarceration, the New Jersey Department of Education has stripped Kathleen of her teaching certificates. Thomas Dorsett was sentenced to 30 years for murder and 15 years for conspiracy to commit arson. He is serving his sentences at the New Jersey State Prison in Trenton, New Jersey. He will be eligible for parole in August 2040, he will be 93 years old. Lesley Dorsett was sentenced to 7 years for conspiracy to commit murder. She was incarcerated at the Edna Mahan Correctional Facility for Women. She became eligible for parole in December 2016 and has been released. Evlyn Moore, Stephen Moore's mother, has custody of Stephen and Kathleen's daughter. Stephen Moore's murder on Dateline NBC in April 2015 and the Oxygen channel's series Snapped in August 2015.

Nannie Doss (née Nancy Hazel)

Mariticide Club

Mugshot, October 1954

Nannie Doss (born Nancy Hazel; November 4, 1905 – June 2, 1965) was an American killer responsible for the deaths of 11 people between sometime in the 1920s and 1954. Doss was also referred to as the Giggling Granny, the Lonely Hearts Killer, the Black Widow, and Lady Blue Beard. Doss finally confessed to the murders in October 1954, after her fifth husband had died in a small hospital in Tulsa, Oklahoma. In all, it was revealed that she had killed four husbands, two children, two of her sisters, her mother, two grandsons, and a mother-in-law. Nannie was born on November 4, 1905 in Blue Mountain, Alabama, now part of Anniston. She was born to Louisa "Lou" (née Holder) and James F. Hazel. Nannie was one of five children; she had one brother and three sisters. Both Nannie and her mother hated James, who was a controlling and abusive father and husband. James would force his children to work on the family farm, refusing to let the children go to school, resulting in Nannie's poor

Wives Who Kill

academic performance. At age 9, while the family was taking a train to visit relatives in southern Alabama, Nannie hit her head on a metal bar on the seat in front of her when the train suddenly stopped. For years after, she suffered severe headaches, blackouts and depression. Doss blamed these and her mental instability on that accident. During childhood, her favorite hobby was reading her mother's romance magazines and dreaming of her own romantic future. Furthermore, her favorite part was the lonely hearts column. Nannie's father forbade the Hazel sisters from wearing makeup and attractive clothing as he believed it would prevent them from being molested by men. He forbade them to go to dances and social events.

First marriage

Nannie was first married at age 16 to Charley Braggs, her co-worker at a linen factory. With her father's approval they married after four months of dating. Braggs was the only son of a single mother who insisted on continuing to live with him after he married. Nannie later wrote:

I married, as my father wished, in 1921 to a boy I only knowed about four or five months who had no family, only a mother who was unwed and who had taken over my life completely when we were married. She never seen anything wrong with what she done, but she would take spells. She would not let my own mother stay all night...

Braggs' mother took up a lot of his attention and limited Nannie's activities. The marriage produced four daughters from 1923 to 1927. The stressed-out Nannie started drinking, and her casual smoking habit became a heavy addiction. Both unhappy partners correctly suspected each other of infidelity, and Braggs often disappeared for days on end. In 1927, the couple lost their two middle girls to suspected food poisoning. Soon after, Braggs took firstborn daughter Melvina and fled, leaving newborn Florine behind. Braggs' mother died not much later and Nannie took a job in a cotton mill to support Florine and herself. Braggs brought Melvina back in the summer of 1928, accompanied by a divorcée with her own child. Braggs and Nannie soon divorced, with Nannie taking her two girls back to her mother's home. Braggs always maintained he left her because he was frightened of her.

Mariticide Club

Her second husband was Robert Franklin Harrelson. They met and married in 1929. They lived in Jacksonville with Melvina and Florine. After a few months, she discovered that he was an alcoholic and had a criminal record for assault. Despite this, the marriage lasted 16 years.

Grandchildren

Melvina gave birth to Robert Lee Haynes in 1943. Another baby followed two years later but died soon afterward. Exhausted from labor and groggy from ether, Melvina thought she saw her visiting mother stick a hatpin into the baby's head. When she asked her husband and sister for clarification, they said Nannie had told them the baby was dead—and they noticed that she was holding a pin. The doctors, however, could not give a positive explanation. The grieving parents drifted apart and Melvina started dating a soldier. Nannie disapproved of him, and while Melvina was visiting her father after a particularly nasty fight with her mother, her son Robert died mysteriously under Nannie's care on July 7, 1945. The death was diagnosed as asphyxia from unknown causes, and two months later Nannie collected the $500 life insurance she had taken out on Robert.

Death of Harrelson

In 1945, Harrelson raped Nannie. The next day, she put rat poison in Harrelson's corn whiskey jar, and he died that evening.

Later marriages

Nannie met her third husband, Arlie Lanning, through another lonely-hearts column while travelling in Lexington, North Carolina, and married him three days later. Like Harrelson, Lanning was an alcoholic womanizer. However, in this marriage it was Nannie who often disappeared—and for months on end. But when she was home, she played the doting housewife, and when he died of what was said to be heart failure, the townspeople supported her at his funeral. Soon after, the couple's house, which had been left to Lanning's sister, burned down. The insurance money went to Nannie, who quickly banked it, and after Lanning's mother died in her sleep,

Wives Who Kill

Nannie left North Carolina and ended up at her sister Dovie's home. Dovie was bedridden and soon after Nannie's arrival she died.

Looking for yet another husband, Nannie joined a dating service called the Diamond Circle Club and soon met Richard L. Morton of Jamestown, North Carolina. They married in 1952 in Emporia, Kansas. He did not have a drinking problem, but he was adulterous. Before she poisoned him, she poisoned her mother, Louisa, in January 1953 when she came to live with them. Morton died three months later on May 19, 1953.

Nannie married Samuel Doss of Tulsa, Oklahoma, in June 1953. Doss was a Nazarene minister who had lost his family to a tornado in Carroll County, Arkansas. Samuel disapproved of the romance novels and stories that his wife adored. In September, Samuel was admitted to the hospital with flulike symptoms. The hospital diagnosed a severe digestive tract infection. He was treated and released on October 5. Samuel died on October 12, 1954. Nannie killed him that evening in her rush to collect the two life insurance policies she had taken out on him. This sudden death alerted his doctor, who ordered an autopsy. The autopsy revealed a huge amount of arsenic in his system. Nannie was promptly arrested.

Confession and conviction

Doss confessed to killing four of her husbands, her mother, her sister, her grandson, and her mother-in-law. The state of Oklahoma centered its case only on Samuel Doss. Nannie Doss was prosecuted by J. Howard Edmondson, who later became governor of Oklahoma. She pleaded guilty on May 17, 1955, and was sentenced to life imprisonment; the state did not pursue the death penalty due to her sex. Doss was never charged with the other deaths. She died from leukemia in the hospital ward of the Oklahoma State Penitentiary in 1965. She is buried at Oak Hill Memorial Park.

Roxana Druse (née Roxalana Teftt)

Mariticide Club

Roxana Druse

Roxalana "Roxana" Druse (née Teftt; born c. 1847 – hanged February 28, 1887), was the last woman hanged in the state of New York. The first woman to be hanged in four decades in Central New York, her botched execution resulted in the decision to replace the gallows with the electric chair in 1890. Mrs. Druse murdered her husband, William Druse, in their home in Warren, New York. The murder unfolded with the help of her son and daughter, George and Mary Druse, and nephew Frank Gates. The family members were threatened with death if they refused and all had an involvement with the murder case. Druse claimed that her motive was that her husband was abusive to her and was not supporting the family because he had left for a number of days after an argument. Frank Gates and George Druse were later released due to their lack of involvement in the murder. During the trial, Mary Druse admitted to assisting in the murder, and was sentenced to life at the Onondaga Country penitentiary. On October 6, 1885 Roxalana was sentenced to be hanged. On December 18, 1884, on the morning before the murder, the Druses had a fight. Fights were common

Wives Who Kill

between them, and many residents reported signs of foul play. The couple were known in the community for their arguments and disagreements (which the defense later presented to the jury to convince them that Mr. Druse was in fact abusive to his wife). During this dispute, Roxalana concealed a revolver under her apron, which she placed in another room. Upon instruction from his mother, 10-year-old George Druse left the house while his 19-year-old sister Mary remained in the house. Mary then tied a rope around her father's neck while Mrs. Druse fired the revolver, wounding Mr. Druse. She then forced her 14-year-old nephew Frank Gates to further fire at her husband. Pleading for help and unable to move, Mr. Druse was decapitated by his wife with an axe. The body parts were taken into the parlor, where they remained all day until Mrs. Druse cut up the body and burnt it to ash on the stove. She also burned William's clothes to further destroy evidence and erase evidence of his presence from the house. The conspirators produced false documents which read that Mr. Druse had left the house after an argument and his whereabouts were unknown. In order to further the idea that William disappeared, Roxalana threatened that she would kill her daughter and the boys (who were playing checkers) if they admitted to the crime. The ashes were dumped in a nearby swamp, while the axe and the revolver were wrapped up and dumped in a pond.

William Druse was later reported missing by the police on the same day. Investigation led to the murder weapon, an axe sold previously to William Druse, wrapped in paper in a pond, along with the revolver. Multiple allegations were reported against wife Roxalana, yet due to lack of evidence, nothing was officially reported. On January 16, 1885, Frank Gates admitted to the crime after consistent harassment by neighbors. Gates and Mrs. Druse were arrested and brought to trial on September 21, 1885; the trial lasted nearly two weeks. When Druse was sentenced to death in Herkimer County, New York, suspension hanging was the method of execution. The process jerked the prisoner upwards by a weighted rope instead of the dropping the body through a trap door. But Druse was a small woman, and the suspension force failed to break her neck, leaving her to die agonizingly by strangulation. The scene was so upsetting,

Mariticide Club

officials decided to switch the primary method of execution in New York to the electric chair.

Lydia Echevarría

Lydia Echevarría (born October 14, 1931) is a Puerto Rican actress who was convicted of plotting the murder of her husband, Puerto Rican television show producer, Luis Vigoreaux. Echevarría met producer Luis Vigoreaux in 1960 during the presentation of a show called "La Hora Cero" (Zero Hour), which Vigoreaux produced with actor Mario Pabón. On February 10, 1960, after they were married, Echevarría joined her husband as co-host in the 1960s and 70s in the television shows In 1982, Luis Vigoreaux began an affair with model Nydia Castillo, and in 1983, he was found burnt to death inside his car. Almost immediately, a large part of the public started pointing fingers at different people, and in 1984, Echevarría was formally accused of her husband's death. Her trial was one of the most sensational in Puerto Rican history, with a media circus atmosphere because of the celebrity status of the couple. In 1986, she was found guilty and sentenced to 208 years in a women's prison in Vega Alta, Puerto Rico. However, her health deteriorated and in 1999, Governor Pedro Rosselló allowed her to leave jail to live at home under a curfew. In 2001, she resumed her acting career with the presentation of a play titled Confinadas (meaning, women prisoners) in the same prison where she served her time. Since then she has appeared in plays and some TV shows, on the condition that she be home by 8 p.m. every night. Glendaly Vigoreaux, the couple's eldest daughter, died by suicide in her Arizona residence on July 15, 2008, however, her lawyer, Fátima Seda Barletta, stated she may have been murdered and the investigation was incomplete. Luis Vigoreaux Rivera (April 12, 1928 – January 17, 1983) was a Puerto Rican radio and television show host, announcer, comedian and producer. Vigoreaux was considered a pioneer in the television business in Puerto Rico, and enjoyed success with several radio and television shows throughout his career. Vigoreaux was brutally murdered on January 17,

Wives Who Kill

1983. His wife, Lydia Echevarría, was convicted in 1986 of planning the murder, along with hitmen Papo Newman and David López-Watts. Vigoreaux was born on April 12, 1928, in the Chupacallos ward of Ceiba, Puerto Rico. He was one of the eight children of Eulalia and Enrique Vigoreaux, a sugarcane worker at Fajardo Sugar Company. His father died when he was young, forcing Eulalia to take charge of the family. When Vigoreaux was 14 years old, they moved to San Juan, specifically Río Piedras. Vigoreaux studied at the Vila Mayo High School. As a teenager, Vigoreaux found work in a radio station named WIAC (AM), which was managed by Tomás Muñiz (father of Tommy Muñiz). There, Vigoreaux worked on a show called Alma Estudiantil. With the beginning of World War II, most of the professional hosts were enlisted for war, which led to Vigoreaux having the opportunity to work at the station. During that period, Vigoreaux worked in various areas of entertainment and show business. He served as host, presenter, commentator, among other jobs. He also became the spokesperson for Sello Rojo rice in Puerto Rico, which he did for 30 years. Vigoreaux joined Ramón Rivero "Diplo" and José Luis Torregrosa for the radio comedy El Tremendo Hotel. This radio slot enjoyed a large audience for years, and Vigoreaux continued to work as a comedian. Between 1954 and 1955, he joined fellow comedian José Miguel Agrelot in a theater show that took them to many Latin American communities in the United States. The theater show eventually led to a radio program named Torito and Company, after Torito, the character that Agrelot played. Vigoreaux himself played the character of Don Toribio. With the arrival of television to Puerto Rico in 1954, Vigoreaux began his transition hosting a show called El Show Libby's, sponsored by the company of its namesake. He then hosted the show El tren de la alegría. Vigoreaux later moved to WAPA-TV, motivated by the possibility of working with actor Mario Pabón. They wrote the story for a soap opera, but the project fell through. However, Vigoreaux moved on when he and his second wife, Lydia Echevarria, began hosting the show named La Hora Cero. The show presented many local and international singers, including Celia Cruz, José Feliciano and Marco Antonio Muñiz. The Vigoreaux family became one of

Mariticide Club

the most famous families in Puerto Rico. Some even referred to the Vigoreaux-Echevarria couple as the Lucy and Desi of Puerto Rico, in reference to the marriage of American comedians Lucille Ball and Desi Arnaz. In 1970, Vigoreaux developed a game show named Sube Nene, Sube. Hosted by Vigoreaux it became one of the most seen shows in Puerto Rican television history. Due to this success, WAPA-TV asked Vigoreaux to produce and host a few more game shows. Vigoreaux responded by creating Pa'rriba, Papi, Pa'rriba, which was a variation of Sube Nene, Sube, and Dale que Dale en Domingo. With the production and hosting of all those shows at the same time, the Vigoreaux family opened a studio, which they named Estudio CVC. They were also responsible for the transmission of the MDA television marathon in Puerto Rico. Vigoreaux later jumped to Channel 11, then named the Perez-Perry Network. He bought the Teatro Nuevo San Juan, from where he started transmitting his new show. But this show was not as successful, and soon Vigoreaux found himself off the air. In 1980, Vigoreaux went back to WAPA-TV and all his shows were rescheduled. He also became the show host of that station's lunch hour variety show, El Show Del Mediodia, and began playing the role of Pedro Navaja in a play La Verdadera Historia de Pedro Navaja. He would act in that play many times, as well as in a play named Angeles Caidos. In addition, he returned to the radio with a program named Buenos Dias, Puerto Rico, on radio station WBMJ-AM, Radio Rock, and worked, for a short period of time, as a television reporter for Noticentro 4. On the morning of January 18, 1983, Vigoreaux didn't show up to work at the radio station or at WAPA-TV, causing his co-workers to worry. When his Mercedes-Benz was found with a burned body inside, it was taken to the medical examiner's office, where it was confirmed it was Vigoreaux. His death launched a wave of rumors and speculations, and led to one of the biggest trials in Puerto Rico's history. His wife, Lydia Echevarría, was accused formally of his murder, along with Papo Newman and David López-Watts. Allegedly, Echevarría had become jealous of a relationship Vigoreaux had started with actress Nydia Castillo, and had paid Newman and López-Watts to either beat him or murder him. Vigoreaux's body was

Wives Who Kill

found gagged, stabbed, and burned inside the car's trunk. Echevarría maintained her innocence, but she was convicted to a life sentence in Vega Alta, Puerto Rico. Newman and López-Watts received similar sentences. However, Echevarría and López-Watts only served roughly 12 years in jail. Papo Newman received immunity from the Department of Justice of Puerto Rico to testify in court what happened the night of the murder. Newman did not serve time in prison as an agreement. In January 2000, Governor Pedro Rosselló granted Echevarría a pardon, which was criticized by the people. At the time of his death, Vigoreaux was about to begin another game show, A Millon, which became one of the most popular shows in Puerto Rican television history, under the hosting of Hector Marcano and produced by Vigoreaux's son, Luisito Vigoreaux. Vigoreaux was married twice. He married Rosaura Lorenzana, with whom he had three sons, Luisito, Jorge Enrique and Roberto Vigoreaux. Jorge died in 1962 of leukemia. Luisito followed his father's footsteps as an actor, comedian, producer and host. Roberto also worked as an actor, host, producer and singer. He served as a member of both the House and the Senate of Puerto Rico. In 1958, Vigoreaux met actress Lydia Echevarría, while still married to his first wife. After divorcing, they married on February 10, 1960. He and Echevarria had two daughters, Vanessa and Glendalys Vigoreaux. Glendalys committed suicide on July 15, 2008.

Julaikah Noor Aini Ellis

Robert Kevin Ellis was a British-Australian millionaire businessman who was murdered in Bali in 2014. His wife later confessed to having organized his murder. Ellis spent his early life in Otara, New Zealand. He was raised there alongside his three siblings. He later moved to Australia. He met Julaikah Noor Aini in 1986 and they were married in 1989. They had two children, in addition to the two children from Ellis' former marriage. The couple owned several businesses in Jakarta and Balo, including the telecommunications company PT Masindo Utama Nusantara and a diving company called Blue Fin. On 21 October 2014, Ellis' body was found wrapped in plastic and dumped in a ditch alongside a rice field. His throat had been slashed. Forensics searched the couple's villa and car, finding a small amount of blood. Police found Aini watching television, and she did not seem shocked when police notified her that her husband's body had been found. Aini confessed to organizing the murder and hiring her maid's boyfriend Adrianus Ngongo to murder Ellis. She claimed that he was killed because he kept her in a state of poverty and refused to give her more than a $19 per month allowance. She also claimed that he had cheated on her and withheld sex. Police arrested Adrianus Ngongo, who was carrying his share of the $A14,000 Aini had paid him and four accomplices for the murder. Police also arrested two maids who had kept the family's pet dogs quiet during the murder, before helping to clean up and move the body. Aini was sentenced to death, which was commuted to 12 years in prison. Of the five men hired to commit the murder, three received 12-year prison sentences, and two received 15-year prison sentences.

Eva Kary Faschaunerin

Eva Kary, née Faschauner (c. 1735 – 9 November 1773) was a convicted Austrian murderer. She was the last victim of judicial torture in the Austrian Hereditary Lands of the Habsburg monarchy. She was the daughter of the Faschauner family of Alpine farmers from Maltaberg in the Duchy of Carinthia. A few weeks after her marriage with Jakob Kary in February 1770, her husband died after experiencing acute pain to his upper body. An autopsy revealed that his death was caused by arsenic poisoning. Tried for murder before the Gmünd county court, Eva pleaded guilty after about three years in prison during torture. Condemned as a murderer and sentenced to death by decapitation on 20 March 1773, her clemency petition was denied by the superior court in Vienna and she was beheaded. As torture was abolished by a 1776 decree of Empress Maria Theresa and her son Joseph II, Eva Faschaunerin was the last to be a victim of judicial torture in Austria and the last person to be sent to the gallows from Gmünd.

Margaret Fernseed

Wives Who Kill

Margaret Fernseed (c. 1560 – 28 February 1608) English prostitute, brothelkeeper, and murderer. According to a pamphlet of 1608, Fernseed confessed to having run a brothel. The pamphlet details the methods by which she recruited prostitutes. Fernseed would "make spoile of young maidens who were sent out of the countrie by their friends with hope to advance themselves". Those girls were then put on the streets and compelled to hand over to Fernseed ten shillings from what they earned. Women who were discontented with their marriages were also targeted by Fernseed: once recruited, they were blackmailed if they refused to sleep with customers. Fernseed's husband, Anthony, a tailor, was found dead in Peckham Fields near Lambeth, with his throat cut; Fernseed was arrested. She had allegedly previously attempted to murder him with a poisoned broth. No motive is recorded, and Fernseed is documented as having declared her innocence of the murder. Fernseed was convicted of his murder on circumstantial evidence, in no small part due to her poor reputation. Fernseed was executed at St. George's Fields for the murder of her husband on 28 February 1608.

Margit Filó (née Margit Julianna Elek)

aka Rókus Black Widow" aka Mrs. Mihály Barna aka Mrs. Sándor Varga Margit Julianna Elek (June 10, 1914 – year of death unknown), known as The Rókus Black Widow, was a Hungarian serial killer who poisoned at least four people between 1958 and 1968. Ruled incompetent to stand trial, she was transferred to a mental hospital in Budapest, where she died. Margit Filó was born on June 10, 1914 on Attila Street in Makó. Her family was poor, and Margit was forced to work from childhood. In 1938, she was interred at a closed psychiatric hospital due to schizophrenia, and after her release, she was contracted to work at Ferenc Nagy's poultry farm in Makó. In 1949, she began quarreling with her employer over the work conditions at the farm, successfully suing him for 14,000 forints. Using this money, she bought a housing complex on 38 Hétvezér Street in Szeged's Rókus District, and allowed tenants to use the upper floor apartments. Filó

Mariticide Club

was disappointed that she had to occupy a ground floor apartment, unlike the poorer residents of the building, who were allocated flats on the upper floors by the city council. At a young age, Filó maintained relationships primarily with women, but in 1950, she met and married chimney sweeper and former veteran Mihály Barna. In 1952, she was interned at a mental hospital for a short time; when discharged, she and her husband bought a house in Debrecen. Despite being relatively well off, Filó continued to perform duties in dirty clothes. For the next eight years, the couple lived together, without issues, but over time, Barna's health deteriorated to the point that he needed constant care. As a result, his mother moved in with the couple; Margit hired 73-year-old Lajosné Biczó as a domestic aide to nurse her husband. In the late 1950s, Barna and his mother died in quick succession; it could not be proved they were murdered. In the year after her husband's death, Filó began a relationship with the 62-year-old wealthy farmer Sándor Varga, whom she had met in the market. Varga owned a good quality house and his own estate in Kiszombor, where the couple would soon settle in, bringing Biczó along with them. In October 1958, Filó incapacitated Biczó with medicine dissolved in a glass of water and then suffocated the woman while she was unconscious by pressing her hands against her mouth and nose until she couldn't breathe. The autopsy concluded Biczó was killed in a homicidal manner, and Filó was arrested. Authorities were unable to conclusively prove she was the killer; they released her. By her will, Biczó's movable property was transferred to Filó. In the autumn of 1959, Varga and Filó officially married, with Sándor naming his newlywed wife as his sole heir. Barely two months after the wedding, Christmas 1959, Filó extracted poison from thorn apple leaves collected at the edge of town, which she put into some cabbage prepared for her husband. Varga and two other family members became violently ill from the poison, but did not die, so his wife repeated the act two days later, this time poisoning a soup, from whose effects Sándor succumbed. After Varga's property was transferred to her, Filó sold it all and moved back to Rókus. The next murder occurred in 1963, when Filó came across 75-year-old Iloná Siegel, a neighbor who was very sickly. She offered to make a

Wives Who Kill

monetary contract with Siegel, who agreed, and just after the pair departed, Filó visited a tombstone manufacturer and placed an order for Siegel. Two weeks later, she poisoned Siegel with the previous medicinal extract, and while her victim was unconscious, she strangled her with a pillow or a quilt. The coroner detected nothing suspicious about the death, and thusly Siegel's properties, worth 20,000 forints, were given to Filó. Over the next few years, Filó began to grow tired of her poor tenants, wishing to kick them out and replace with some of the industrial workers who were moving to Szeged. By 1968, she managed to convince several residents to leave, but one of them, a 77-year-old widow Mrs. Mihály Tóthpál, refused. Deciding that she wanted to get rid of her, Filó signed a business deal with Tóthpál, and on July 9, 1968, she poisoned, beat and strangled her. However, while abusing her elderly victim, she unwittingly broke several of her ribs, which was noticed by the coroners. This finding was reported to the police, who immediately arrested Margit Filó as a suspect in the murder. While searching her house, authorities stumbled upon several human skulls and several kilograms of toxic substances. When questioned about these items, Filó claimed that she had stolen the skulls from the local cemetery, and that the poisons were for spells and potions which she supposedly used on acquaintances to fall in love with her. Sensing that she might've had previous experiences in killings, police exhumed the bodies of Siegel, Varga and Barna, managing to prove that, with the exception of Barna, the victims had been poisoned. Investigators also learned that the will of Lajosné Biczó from 1958 was a forgery, and that Filó's then-fiancée, Sándor Varga, had actually signed it. When brought to court, Filó tried to explain that she had killed her victims for humanitarian purposes, as, according to her, they were visibly suffering. She also claimed that their deaths benefitted the Hungarian People's Republic, as the state would no longer be required to pay pensions to them. The court, taking into account that Filó had been interred at mental institutions on two previous occasions, ordered her to undergo a psychiatric reevaluation. During the tests, Filó initially denied responsibility, but then started claiming that she had had nine husbands in total, and she would confess if the doctors gave her bread

Mariticide Club

and tomatoes. She was diagnosed with schizophrenia and dissociative identity disorder, rendering her incapable of standing trial. Because of this, Filó was transferred to the Lipótmező Mental Asylum, where she remained until her death. The building on 38 Hétvezér Street was later demolished, and later replaced by a modern residential building.

Flordelis dos Santos de Souza

Flordelis in 2019

Flordelis dos Santos de Souza (born 5 February 1961), known as Flordelis, is a Brazilian Contemporary Christian singer, Pentecostal pastor, former member of the Chamber of Deputies (representing Rio de Janeiro), and criminal convicted of the murder of her husband, pastor Anderson do Carmo. She belonged to the party Brazilian Democratic Movement (MDB) between 2004 and 2018, and was a member of Social Democratic Party (PSD) between 2018 and 2021. She has 3 biological and 51 "adopted" children, though it is unclear how many of these were legally adopted. She adopted Anderson do Carmo at the age of 14 in 1991, and married him in 1998. In 1999, they co-founded the church Comunidade

Wives Who Kill

Evangélica Ministério Flordelis. In November 2022, she was convicted of murder of Anderson and sentenced to 50 years in prison. Flordelis was born in Jacarezinho, Rio de Janeiro in 1961 to Francisco dos Santos and Carmozina Motta dos Santos. At the age of 14, she lost her father and brother in a car accident. She became a teacher and pastor, and in 1994, she adopted 37 children at once. Her charity work and adoptions attracted the attention of the media, and a film based on her life, Flordelis: Basta uma Palavra para Mudar, was released in 2009. After the release of the film, Flordelis approached the Rio de Janeiro label MK Music. Until then, she had released independent records and one distributed by Apascentar Music, a label of the then-band Toque no Altar. In 2010 she signed with MK Music and released her first album, Fogo e Unção. In 2004, Flordelis ran unsuccessfully for the São Gonçalo City Council. In 2016, she ran for mayor of São Gonçalo for the MDB. From 2019 until 2021, Flordelis was a member of the Deputies representing Rio de Janeiro after winning the 2018 elections, after having received support from Arolde de Oliveira. Early in the morning of 16 June 2019, her husband, Anderson do Carmo de Souza, was shot dead outside his home. One of the adopted children, 18-year-old Lucas dos Santos do Carmo, pleaded guilty to the murder, and also accused one of his adoptive brothers, the 38-year-old Flávio dos Santos, of complicity. In August 2020, prosecutors announced charges against Flordelis and several of her children, alleging that they had orchestrated Anderson's murder. Police could not arrest Flordelis because she held parliamentary immunity, but detectives pushed for her status as a member of Congress to be stripped. In June 2021, the Ethics Council of Brazil approved the loss of the mandate of Representative Flordelis, by 16 votes to 1. The Chamber floor approved the resolution with 437 votes for the removal, 7 against and 12 abstentions. On August 11, 2021, Flordelis had her mandate as a Congresswoman revoked by the Chamber, in a lawsuit filed by Representative Alexandre Leite. She lost her term of office for breach of parliamentary decorum and, as a result, could be tried and imprisoned for her husband's death. In addition to losing office, a Representative will be ineligible as determined by the Law of Ficha Limpa.

Mariticide Club

Flordelis had her preventive detention decreed by the 3rd Criminal Court of Niterói after being arrested on August 13, 2021 by Rio de Janeiro Civil Police. She lost parliamentary immunity when her term was revoked, thus became subject to the same treatment as an ordinary citizen. In November 2022, she was convicted of murder and sentenced to 50 years in prison.

Susana Freydoz

Carlos Ernesto Soria (March 1, 1949 – January 1, 2012) was an Argentine lawyer and Party politician. He died in the early hours of January 1, 2012, from a gunshot wound, at his farm, after the New Year celebrations. Soria was the governor of Rio Negro Province at the time. His widow was charged with first-degree murder on January 19, 2012. Soria was born in Bahía Blanca in 1949, and was raised in a nearby rural town, General Daniel Cerri. His father, Ernesto Soria, was an outspoken Peronist, and was arrested shortly after the 1955 coup against President Juan Perón. Following his release several months later, the Sorias relocated to Bariloche. The elder Soria was again arrested amid a crackdown on Peronist protests during a state visit to Bariloche by U.S. President Dwight Eisenhower in March 1959, and was imprisoned in Bahía Blanca. He was

Wives Who Kill

released in April 1962 and the family settled in General Roca, Río Negro, where they opened a neighborhood store. Carlos Soria enrolled at the University of Buenos Aires, earning a law degree in 1973. March returned Peronists to power, and Soria was elected to the local Justicialist Party (JP) chapter. He was later elected to the Provincial Council of the JP, and upon the return of democracy in 1983, won a seat in the Argentine Chamber of Deputies. Soria was elected to Congress for four consecutive terms, becoming Chairman of the Constitutional Affairs Committee. He served in the Justice, Impeachments, and Money Laundering committees; chaired the joint committee investigating the 1992 Israeli Embassy attack in Buenos Aires and the 1994 AMIA bombing (the two most significant acts of Islamic terrorism in Argentine history); and served in the Council of Magistracy of the Nation. Soria shared President Carlos Menem's opposition to trials opened in 1996 in Spanish courts against Dirty War perpetrators by Judge Baltasar Garzón, and personally led a delegation to protest these trials; when Judge Garzón turned the tables on the delegation by calling them to testify, they returned, however, creating an embarrassing diplomatic incident. He later presented a bill to restrict rights and toughen sentences for those accused of violent crime, as well as another which would have granted congressional immunity to all members in perpetuity; both bills were defeated. Soria would later be indicted for obstruction of justice in his capacity as Chair of the Joint Committee on the AMIA bombing, and though he was cleared of all charges, the Río Negro PJ dropped him from their list ahead of the 1999 elections. Soria was then offered a place in the Buenos Aires Province PJ list for Congress by Governor Eduardo Duhalde. Shortly before the October 1999 elections, moreover, Duhalde appointed Soria as Provincial Minister of Justice. His appointment took place on the heels of the September 16 Ramallo massacre, a botched Provincial Police intervention during an armed bank robbery that resulted in the deaths of two hostages. Soria promptly released hitherto sequestered police files relating to the case which confirmed that the robbery, as well as the deaths of all robbers and hostages alike, had been orchestrated by Provincial Police officers. Remaining on the electoral list

Mariticide Club

for National Deputies, Soria took his seat in Congress in December representing the Province of Buenos Aires, among leading congressional opponents of President Fernando de la Rúa's austerity package, scuttling a 2000 decree which would have cut public sector salaries (this ultimately took place the following year). President de la Rúa's resignation in December 2001, and the subsequent Congressional designation of Duhalde as provisional president resulted in Soria's appointment as Secretary of State Intelligence (SIDE) in January 2002. Taking office, as President Duhalde did, amid widespread protest, Soria's tenure at SIDE would eventually be marred by a June 26 incident in which two piqueteros, Maximiliano Kosteki and Darío Santillán, were shot in the back in Avellaneda by Provincial Police officers. SIDE had produced intelligence reports stating that the overthrow of the national government had been openly advocated in piqueteros' assemblies, and that these were attended by the extremist group Revolutionary Armed Forces of Colombia (FARC). Phone conversations between minutes before the assassinations between a policeman implicated in the incident and the Undersecretary of Intelligence at the time, Oscar Rodríguez, proved SIDE involvement in the tragedy in subsequent trials. Fallout from this incident was compounded by allegations made by Senator Cristina Fernández de Kirchner that SIDE personnel were spying on her husband, Santa Cruz Governor Néstor Kirchner, who had recently declared his intention to run for President the following year. These controversies, and Soria's own plans to run for Governor of the Province of Río Negro, prompted his resignation from SIDE in July. He was narrowly defeated in provincial elections in August 2003 by UCR candidate Miguel Saiz, though in elections held later in 2003, Soria narrowly won election for mayor of the city of General Roca (largest in the province). Duhalde and Soria continued to face charges in court related to the 2002 deaths. Soria declared at trial in 2005 that "democracy works with order, and we needed to establish order"; both were cleared of all charges. Soria was overwhelmingly reelected as mayor of General Roca in 2007, garnering 73% of the vote. He clinched the Justicialist Party nomination for Governor of Río Negro in

Wives Who Kill

2011, and ran with the support of the Front for Victory (FpV) faction of the party despite his long-standing alliance with the FpV's main rival, Duhalde. Soria's principal opponent in the race, UCR nominee César Barbeito, also professed his support of the FpV's standard-bearer, President Cristina Kirchner. The president formally endorsed Soria despite their past differences, however, while maintaining her distance from both candidates. Soria was elected governor in September with 51% of the vote, besting Barbeito by nearly 14%. Soria died on January 1, 2012, during the new year celebrations with his family at his farm near General Roca. He was shot in the face with a caliber weapon at around 5 am, and was moved immediately to a nearby hospital, where he died minutes later. The police didn't determine initially whether the death was caused by an accident or foul play; his wife was held for questioning. He had a private funeral. His widow was charged with first-degree murder on January 19, 2012. Vicegovernor Alberto Weretilneck succeeded Soria as governor. Weretilneck considered calling new elections, despite provisions in the Constitution of Río Negro Province that would allow him to complete the remainder.

Sarah Ann French - Onion Pie Murderer

The Onion Pie Murder occurred on 7 January 1852 in Chiddingly, East Sussex, England. The crime was committed by Sarah Ann French who murdered her husband William French by administering a deadly dose of arsenic to his meal, an onion pie. Sarah Ann French was found guilty of wilfully murdering her husband, William French, on 19 March 1852. French was hanged for her crime in Lewes at the HM Prison Lewes in front of approximately 4,000 people, on 10 April 1852. Her execution became a huge event with some spectators even traveling by train to see it. French was the only woman to be publicly hanged in Lewes. Lewes decided to end public hangings because they were led to believe that French had been motivated to murder her husband with poison, as three years previously she had been a spectator at the hanging of Mary Ann Gearing, who murdered her husband with the use of poison. They

Mariticide Club

came to question that public sentences had no beneficial impact on society and that they should be carried out only in front of customary officers privately inside the prison, so as not to risk influencing others to commit the same crimes and ultimately meet the same end. French murdered her husband by lacing his meal with 3d worth of arsenic in Horsebridge. The arsenic had been bought by her husband in order to kill mice in their house, and he gave it to Sarah to put away in a safe place where their child or anyone else could not find it. The meal in question, an onion pie, was served to William French on Christmas Eve in 1851. That morning, Sarah French told his co-worker William Funnell that this was a rarity in his household and in fact his favorite meal, and not even days later William French started to show symptoms of illness and rupture. Sarah's motive for murdering her husband was so that she could marry a man named James Hickman, as she on many occasions (even before her husband died) said that she had strong feelings for him. It was originally believed that Hickman had poisoned William French, however it became apparent after he testified against her that her feelings toward him were not reciprocated. On first inspection of William French's body and after an inquest held at the Gun Inn, the finding was that French had died from natural causes rather than from arsenic poisoning. However, further facts and evidence that came to light against Sarah French and her suspected involvement in her husband's death led to an inquest and then inevitably a trial so as to further investigate. William French's body was transferred to another coroner named Alfrid Swayn Taylor to see if he could find any sign of foul play. He found a number of small patches of yellow color which were then found to be that of orpiment. From these findings and the testimonies from the witnesses, Sarah French was found guilty for the willful murder of her husband William French on 2 February 1852.

Augusta Fullam (née Augusta Fairfield Goodwyn)

Augusta Fairfield Fullam (1875 – 1914) was a British Raj woman implicated in a double murder in Agra in India. Fullam was born in Calcutta in 1875 and died in Allahabad in 1914. She was the wife of

Wives Who Kill

Lieutenant Edward McKeon Fullam and lived in Calcutta, Barrackpore, Meerut and finally Agra (India). She came to notice when she was interviewed in connection with Dr Henry Clark whose wife had been hacked to death on 17 November 1912. She and Clark had been lovers since 1909, and some 400 letters Augusta had written, swiftly discovered by the police, provided unarguable evidence of conspiracy to murder their respective spouses. On 11 October 1912, days after the Fullams moved to Agra, Edward Fullam had died, supposedly of heatstroke and "general paralysis of insanity" (tertiary syphilis), but as later post mortem revealed, of arsenic poisoning., The definitive account of Augusta Fullam's life and the double murder of which she and her lover were convicted is Molly Whittington-Egan's Khaki Mischief (1990) She was born Augusta Fairfield Goodwyn in Calcutta on 23 June 1875, baptized 12 August 1875 at the Methodist Episcopal Church Calcutta, and educated in a convent, possibly Loreto House, but no school records with her name have been found. The daughter of English-born Leonard Goodwyn, a Bengal River Pilot, Augusta had a sister, Dora, and a half-sister Catherine Burridge by her mother's previous marriage to a musical instrument dealer. There is no evidence that Augusta ever left India or was in England, a confusion possibly arising from the sensitive term 'Anglo-Indian', used variously in the British Raj to define Europeans born in India and as a politer alternative to 'Eurasian' for those of mixed race. Whittington-Egan describes Augusta as "short and dumpy... vivacious and quite attractive... small, sociable, mischievous" with a "china-doll complexion" and "springy brown tresses", definitely not "a sultry siren or slinky femme fatale". On 17 June 1896 at Barrackpore, 15 miles from Calcutta, Augusta married Edward McKeon Fullam (born 1867), a rising clerk in the Indian Civil Service, whose career peaked as Deputy Examiner in the Military Accounts Department at Meerut. He was eight years older than Augusta, with a withered arm and health susceptible to the fierce climate and temperature. A Freemason, Sunday School teacher and 2nd Lieutenant in the local volunteers, "Eddie" or "hubby" (as "Gussie" called him) was perhaps a bit of a dull stick for a flirtatious, party-loving woman who enjoyed cheap romantic novels, male attention, gossip, parties

Mariticide Club

and fun. Gussie and Eddie settled into a comfortable life on cantonments, first at Barrackpore, then from 1908 at Meerut (North of Delhi). The Fullams only moved to Agra in 1911 when Eddie's health was succumbing to the poisoning campaign that killed him soon after their arrival. Meanwhile, they had three children: Leonard (born 1899), Kathleen (born 1902) and Frank (born 1906).

Affair with Henry Clark and murder of Edward Fullam

Augusta had met Henry Lovell Clark at a dance sometime in 1908, and it was at her urging that Edward Fullam invited his fellow-Mason Clark to their home in Meerut, where Clark and Augusta soon began a fully-blown affair. Clark was a raffish figure with a definite reputation. Born at Calcutta in 1868, the son of an indigo-planter, Henry was Eurasian and therefore a definite social cut below the Fullams, in the rigid hierarchy of British Raj India and the Indian caste system). He was handsome, muscular and a dedicated womaniser, despite his 1889 marriage to a former nurse, Louisa Guest, ten years older than himself, by whom he had three children: Maud, Henry and Walter. The sons were grown up when their father met Augusta, and working in the Military Accounts Department at Meerut, where Edward Fullam was deputy head. Maud was a teenager, living at home with her mother, while Clark, who regularly beat and abused his wife and children, "played the field". Clark was a medical officer in the Indian Sobordinate Medical Department: a vague status somewhere short of a fully-qualified General Practitioner. Clark had struggled to pass the examinations, but was said to have achieved his army lieutenancy serving as an assistant surgeon in the British Indian Army during the 1900 Boxer Uprising in China. Whittington-Egan describes Henry Clark as "active, restless... raffish... Versatile and bazaar-wise, he would slide off from a polite game of tennis to frequent risky native prostitutes in their questionable hovels... A bad lot... [a] brutish creature caged inside a front of gallantry...Basically he was a loser. It is surprising that a man of such known bad character ever obtained preferment at all. His undoubted success with women fueled a self-esteem that would otherwise have faltered." Augusta couldn't get enough of him. Their affair became

Wives Who Kill

increasingly indiscreet, and while Edward Fullam seems not to have cottoned on - he and Augusta had a fourth child, Myrtle, in January 1910 - Meerut was rife with gossip and in November 1910, Clark was transferred to Delhi, 45 miles from Meerut, after which, Augusta started writing him increasingly indiscreet letters, most of which he unwisely kept: 400 or so of these letters would play a crucial part in securing convictions against the couple for the murder of their respective spouses. Clark was later transferred again to Agra, 180 miles from Meerut, and there was some idea of his seniors' posting him to Aden, out of India altogether. In Spring 1911, Augusta was pregnant by Clark, who gave her abortifacient drugs to procure a miscarriage, and on a visit to Meerut, the lovers' indiscreet behavior finally alerted Edward Fullam to suspicion and jealousy. From now on the lovers' conspired to poison their respective partners, passing off the deaths as heatstroke or other common illnesses. Augusta started lacing Edward's food and drink with arsenic and other poisons posted to her by Clark, while he in turn tried to bribe the family cook Bibu to poison Louisa's food. The horrified cook went straight to Louisa, who enlisted her children's support and had the powders analyzed (by a subordinate of her husband's at the hospital): arsenic. The cook fled back home, and Clark hired a new cook Budhu, whom he suborned to help him dispose of Louisa, who was now on the alert, fully aware of his intentions. Poisoning was beginning to look problematic as a means of killing Louisa. Meanwhile, in Meerut, although the steady campaign of poisoning Edward Fullam was ruining his health, it was not finishing him off, as planned, and he was ruled unfit for work, to be pensioned off and possibly sent to a more salubrious part of India ('The Hills' or Bangalore), or even to England, where neither he nor Augusta had any real roots or connections. In October 1911, Edward was discharged from hospital and moved with his wife and family to a new home in, of all places, Agra, a short distance from Clark's bungalow. Three days later, he was dead, finished off by three injections given by Clark and witnessed by young Kathleen Fullam. He was buried in haste, and Clark soon became the Fullams' man of the house, eating most of his meals and sleeping there... beating Fullam children, as he had his own.

Mariticide Club

Murder of Louisa Clark, trial and conviction

The lovers now turned their attention to removing Henry Clark's unwanted wife Louisa, for which Clark engaged the family cook Budhu to recruit 'badmashes' (amateur criminals with daytime jobs in the local bazaars) to attack and murder Louisa as she slept in the Clark's bungalow, in what was to look like a disturbed robbery. On 17 November 1912, while Clark was cycling around Agra, establishing an alibi that would swiftly unravel on police inspection, the four hired badmashes, Sukkha, Buddha, Ram Lal and Mohan (all in their early twenties), joined by a hesitantly supervising Budhu, stole into the Clark bungalow as the ladies slept, and hacked Louisa to death in front of her daughter Maud. Clark had ruined his flimsy alibi by cycling home to lock up the dog, which was barking and preventing the assassins from entering the house, and to stop by at Augusta's. The lovers compromised themselves further by paying the killers with rupees from a cheque of Augusta's which Clark countersigned at the bank... and when police found Augusta's letters in a locked tin chest under her bed, left there "for safety" by Clark, the game was up. Edward Fullam's body was exhumed and arsenic found in the remains. Henry Clark and Augusta Fullam were arrested, and after December 1912 - January 1913 committal proceedings in the Agra Magistrates' Court, charged and sent for trial on both murders, along with the five co-conspirators, at the High Court of Justice in Allahabad (then state capital of the United Provinces of Agra & Oudh, now Uttar Pradesh). Augusta submitted a December 1912 statement, seeking to exonerate herself and attribute her letters and actions to hypnosis by Clark, but this cut little ice, and came close to a confession of her role in both murders. She later applied to the High Court to be accepted as "approver" (the equivalent of English Law's "turning King's Evidence") in the case, but this was rejected, as the canny cook Budhu had already been accepted "approver", and earned indemnity from charge or penalty by giving evidence against the others. The authorities could feel comfortable convicting Augusta, safe in the knowledge that, being pregnant with Clark's child, she would be reprieved the mandatory death sentence. The High Court trial opened on 26 February 1913 gathering international attention.

Wives Who Kill

Fullam had applied to give King's Evidence but her application was rejected. Both Maud Clark and Kathleen Fullam were key prosecution witnesses, having witnessed their respective parents' murders. It took the jury only 10 minutes to return with guilty verdicts on all those charged (except Ram Lal, who was found not guilty and discharged). Henry Clark and the other three badmashes were hanged on 26 March 1913. Augusta's sentence was indeed commuted to life imprisonment. She gave birth to Henry Clark's son on 28 July 1913, and died of heatstroke at the age of 38 in Naini Prison, Allahabad, on 28 May 1914. Her son, christened Lovell Henry William Goodwyn, was rejected by both families, brought up in a Bengal orphanage, renamed William Hope and served with distinction in the Merchant Navy, before settling in Australia and raising a family. He died in 1975 without ever knowing who his natural parents were.

Sheila Garvie

Maxwell Garvie was a Scottish farmer and businessman who was murdered in 1968, in "one of the most infamous murders in Scottish criminal history". The following year his wife, Sheila Garvie, and her lover, Brian Tevendale, were convicted of his murder after a sensational trial at the Aberdeen High Court, which included revelations about group sex and drugs. Tevendale shot Maxwell with a rifle while he was asleep. Later Tevendale disposed of the body in a tunnel at Lauriston Castle, near St Cyrus. The case against a third accused, Alan Peters, was found not proven. While alive, Maxwell enjoyed a lascivious life. He was fond of female company and maintained physical relations with many. Tevendale's sister Trudy Birse was just one of them. Maxwell frequently arranged wild parties in his house which involved orgies. At first Sheila was not eager to take part, but her husband insisted and the latter won. Sheila Garvie and Tevendale broke off contact shortly after the trial, they were both released in 1978. Tevendale died in December 2003. Garvie died from Alzheimer's disease in 2014, aged 80.

Roxanne Gay

Blenda Glen Gay (November 22, 1950 – December 20, 1976) was a defensive end in the National Football League (NFL). He played three

Mariticide Club

seasons in the NFL for the San Diego Chargers and Philadelphia Eagles and is notable for his 1976 murder by his wife Roxanne. Blenda Gay attended H. B. Sugg High School in Farmville, North Carolina. After high school, he attended Fayetteville State University in Fayetteville, North Carolina. There he started on the football team winning all-CIAA and Division II All-American. Gay was drafted in the 1973 NFL supplemental draft by the Oakland Raiders but was cut in training camp. He was picked up in 1974 by the San Diego Chargers and saw action in two games. He had also played for a semi-pro football team called the Model City Diplomats for $75 per game. In 1975, Gay was signed by the Philadelphia Eagles where he became a regular fixture on the defensive line for two seasons. Gay played in every regular season game for the Eagles in both 1975 and 1976. In December, 1976, Roxanne Gay cut her husband's throat as he slept, killing him. She was charged with the murder by the Jersey district. Roxanne claimed that the attack on her husband was purely self-defense and alleged that her husband was extremely violent and abusive. Camden police indicated that she had made over 20 calls to the police in three and a half years. Neighbors claimed that after an Eagles' loss, Gay "bounced his wife off the walls". His wife had signed a complaint against Gay after one hospital stay, but later dropped the complaint. The case became a cause célèbre for the feminist movement due to the allegations of long-term domestic violence. Gloria Steinem and Ms. magazine helped raise money for her defense. Ms. magazine alleged that when Roxanne called the police, officers would often discuss football with Blenda. A panel of psychiatrists in a sanity hearing found that Blenda Gay had not abused his wife, and Roxanne Gay's attorney admitted there was no evidence that the beatings had occurred. Roxanne Gay was determined to have schizophrenia and confined to the Trenton Psychiatric Hospital. All charges were dropped. She was released in 1980. Beginning in 1977, there was an annual "Gay Game" held each December. This ceased after the game in 1979.

Mária Gerzsány

Wives Who Kill

Mária Gerzsány (March 25, 1851 – death date unknown) a Hungarian serial killer who poisoned at least three people with arsenic in Kistelek between 1905 and 1911. She was sentenced to life imprisonment for these murders, but it's presumed that she might've been responsible for more, selling her poisons to people who wished to get rid of unwanted relatives. Mária Gerzsány was born to a Catholic peasant family in Kiskunmajsa in 1851. In an era without social security, she worked as a midwife, helping local women give birth. A later investigation by the gendarmes in Kistelek revealed that she had aided with 95 births, of which a reported 78 were reported deceased, but it was unclear whether they'd been murdered. Aside from performing abortions, Gerzsány was also suspected of prostituting trafficking girls, but despite being prosecuted in over a dozen cases, she was never convicted. At the time of the murders, she lived with shoemaker Antal Török on Szegedi Street in Kistelek, where she advertised herself as a midwife. Gerzsány had five recorded marriages, all described as "wild". Her ex-husbands (only two survived) all died in similar circumstances, issued life insurance policies by Gerzsány, as the sole beneficiary. In 1905, Gerzsány lived with a common-law husband, the farmer Ferenc Laczkó, for whom she took a life insurance policy worth 340 korona. Shortly after, the healthy peasant fell ill in December, dying on the 11th. After an autopsy was performed, the cause of death was determined to be arsenic poisoning. Following a testimony in a later trial, Gerzsány admitted to producing, selling and administering arsenic concoctions to whoever wanted to buy it, in order to get rid of relatives. Proving any such cases proved to be a difficult task, as neither the surviving victims or their family members wished to cooperate about the suspicious deaths, and their testimonies often proved inaccurate or contradictory. In an effort to prevent her activities, gendarmes imposed higher fines on Gerzsány between 1909 and 1910. In June 1911, Mária Gerzsány offered her services to a Mrs. Palinkás, who complained a lot about her husband, offering to provide arsenic in exchange for 60 korona. Palinkás refused, and instead informed the gendarmes in Kistelek, who were already keeping tabs on the suspicious old woman. They asked Palinkás to help them, providing her with marked

Mariticide Club

money, which she gave to Gerzsány in exchange for the promised arsenic. A few days later, Gerzsány came across Palinkás again, offering to give her a stronger poison for an additional six korona, to which the latter agreed. This information was relayed to the gendarmes, and on July 24, 1911, Mária Gerzsány was arrested. While examining her home, the gendarmes found the marked korona paid for the poison provided by Palinkás. Upon further searching, they uncovered numerous ointments, powders, poisons, tweezers, pliers and all kinds of instruments. Following Gerzsány's arrest, the gendarmes started exhuming bodies from the Kistelek cemetery. Despite claims from outraged villagers of death toll exceeding 50, authorities were unable to investigate all of them. Instead, they examined the bodies of six potential victims: two of Gerzsány's husbands, Mátyas Fülöp and Ferenc Laczkó, who died in 1898 and 1905, respectively; landscaper József Lévai, who died on September 13, 1908; farmer György Sisák, who died in January 1909; and widow Károly Farkas, who died in March 1910, all of whom had traces of arsenic in them.Several witnesses were summoned to the trial, claiming that they had been offered arsenic by Gerzsány, who rejected all the accusations, saying that she had feuded with the witnesses and they were taking it out on her. The evidence against her overwhelmed her claims, however, and in turn, Mária Gerzsány was sentenced to life imprisonment for murder and complicity in murder, and sent to serve her sentence at the Márianosztra prison in 1912. Mrs. Sisák was convicted as an accomplice in her husband's murder and sentenced to 15 years imprisonment. Two years later, it was revealed that she had benefitted with a 4,600 korona life insurance policy after the death of her brother Imre, who had been poisoned by his wife, but wasn't prosecuted for that case. Gerzsány spent the next seven years in prison in a cell with another infamous contemporary criminal, Verona Fekete, and was released following Hungary's defeat at the hands of the Soviet Union in World War I. She returned home to Kistelek, where she renewed her business of selling arsenic, and commissioned by a woman who wanted to poison her husband. These allegations eventually reached the police, who were afraid of letting such a dangerous criminal run loose, and March

Wives Who Kill

19, 1920, Gerzsány was rearrested and transported to prison in Szeged to finish her life sentence, where she died from an undisclosed illness.

Wife of Fawzi al-Ghazzi

Fawzi al-Ghazzi (1891–1929) (Arabic: فوزي الغزي), was a Syrian politician who wrote the first Syrian Constitution. Born in Damascus. He studied in Damascus and Istanbul, and served in the Turkish army during World War I. He was appointed secretary of the Interior Ministry of the Arab Government in 1920. He opposed the French mandate, and was imprisoned several times and exiled to Arwad. He was elected to the Syrian Parliament in the 1928 election, and became the chairman of the Constituent Assembly, that wrote the first Syrian Constitution which was approved by the Syrian Parliament July 4, 1928. He was poisoned by his wife for unknown reasons.

Janie Lou Hickox Gibbs

Mariticide Club

Mugshot Janie Lou Gibbs

Janie Lou Gibbs (née Hickox; December 25, 1932 – February 7, 2010) was an American serial killer from Cordele, Georgia, who killed her three sons, a grandson, and her husband, by poisoning them with arsenic in 1966 and 1967. Gibbs was born in Georgia on Christmas Day, 1932. She operated a daycare from her home and was a dedicated member of the local church community. She had been married to her husband Marvin for 18 years before she began killing. In 1965, Gibbs committed her first murder, poisoning her husband Marvin by putting arsenic into his dinner. While he was in hospital, she brought him homemade soup containing more poison. After Marvin's death on January 21, 1966, doctors decided the cause of death had been a liver disease. After her husband's death, Gibbs was supported by the local church community. She later donated some of her husband's life insurance money to the church. Eight months after the death of Gibbs's husband, she poisoned her youngest son, 13-year-old Marvin. He died on August 29, 1966. He was assumed to have inherited a liver disease from his father, but his death certificate listed hepatitis. Gibbs was not suspected of any wrongdoing, and she again donated a large portion of her life insurance payout to the local church. On January 23, 1967, another one of Gibbs's sons, 16-year-old Melvin, died suddenly. Doctors listed his

Wives Who Kill

cause of death as a rare muscular disorder, and for a third time, Gibbs donated life insurance money to the church. Gibbs now had only one son left, 19-year-old Robert. Robert had fathered a child named Raymond with his wife, and Gibbs was seen to be delighted that she had become a grandmother. Soon, Raymond became sick and died suddenly, followed only a month later by his father. Following the sudden deaths of a previously healthy young man and his infant son, the family physician became suspicious and referred the case to the state crime lab. An autopsy on Robert found that he had ingested a fatal amount of arsenic. Gibbs was arrested for murder on Christmas Day, and the bodies of her husband and three sons were exhumed. Autopsies conducted in the cemetery revealed each of the five murdered members of the Gibbs household had arsenic present in their bodies. Gibbs initially was found mentally unfit to stand trial and was confined to a mental institution where she worked as a cook. Later, she stood trial and was sentenced to five life sentences. She remained imprisoned until 1999 when she was diagnosed with Parkinson's disease and was released into the custody of her sister. She died in 2010 in a nursing home in Douglasville, Georgia.

Kelly Gissendaner (née Kelly Renée Brookshire)

Mariticide Club

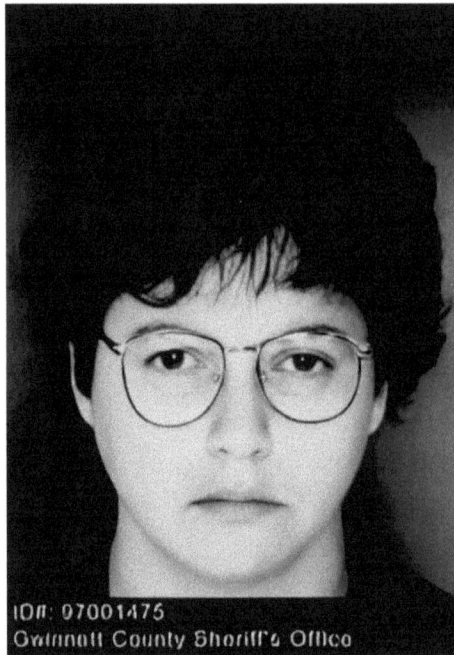
ID#: 97001475
Gwinnett County Sheriff's Office

Kelly Gissendaner

Kelly Renée Gissendaner (née Brookshire; March 8, 1968 – September 30, 2015) was an American woman who was executed by the U.S. state of Georgia. Gissendaner had been convicted of orchestrating the murder of her husband, Douglas Gissendaner (December 14, 1966 – February 7, 1997). At the time of the murder, Gissendaner was 28, and her husband was 30. After her conviction, and until her execution, Gissendaner was the only woman on death row in Georgia. Gissendaner was born into a poor cotton-farming family. She was molested by her stepfather and other men during her childhood and adolescence. During her senior year of high school, she claimed to have been date raped. Nine months later, her first son was born. In 1987, at the age of 19, Kelly Gissendaner married her first husband Jeff Banks. They stayed together for six months. Kelly married Douglas Gissendaner for the first time on September 2, 1989. They had a baby together, lost their jobs, and moved in with Kelly's mother. Douglas joined the Army and they were sent to Germany. Kelly became pregnant by another man who later died of cancer. She and Douglas were divorced in 1993.In May 1995, she remarried Douglas. In December 1996, the couple bought a house together in Auburn, Georgia. In addition to her daughter

Wives Who Kill

with Douglas, Kelly had two sons. Douglas was the stepfather to her sons. On February 7, 1997, Gregory Bruce Owen (born March 17, 1971) hid near the couple's home in Auburn. When Douglas arrived, Owen forced Douglas into his car at knifepoint and drove him to a wooded area in Gwinnett County near Harbins Park. After striking Douglas in the head with a nightstick, Owen stabbed Douglas in the neck and back multiple times. When Kelly arrived at the scene moments later, they both fire to her husband's car and hid the body in the woods. Before trial, prosecutors offered both Owen and Gissendaner a plea deal of life in prison and no chance of parole for twenty-five years. Gissendaner, however, rejected the plea deal. Gissendaner was convicted of orchestrating her husband's murder and sentenced to death in 1998, after Owen testified against her in a plea agreement in which he was sentenced to life imprisonment. Owen told a jury that Gissendaner had first approached him about "a way to get rid of" her husband three months before the murder. He further testified that Gissendaner thought murder was the only way to get Douglas out of her life and still get the house and a payoff from his life insurance policy. During the trial, Gissendaner was discovered to have threatened witnesses and also plotted to pay a witness to commit perjury.

Arrendale State Prison, where she was held

After being sentenced to death, Gissendaner was in Metro State Prison until it was closed in 2011. She was then transferred to Arrendale State Prison. While in prison, Gissendaner had a conversion to Christianity. During her time in prison, Gissendaner ministered to women living in prison with her. A group of women who were incarcerated with Gissendaner formed a

Mariticide Club

group called the "Struggle Sisters" after they were released from prison. Gissendaner had spoken to the women through an air vent and prevented some from committing suicide; other women tell how Gissendaner's words encouraged them to turn their lives around. The women released a video detailing the impact Gissendaner had on their lives. In 2010, Gissendaner enrolled in a theology studies program for prisoners, run by a consortium of Atlanta divinity schools, including the divinity school at Emory University. During theology studies, she became a student of Christian thinkers like Dietrich Bonhoeffer and Rowan Williams. Gissendaner developed a friendship with Jürgen Moltmann while she was in prison. Gissendaner sent Moltmann a paper which she had written on Bonhoeffer. He was impressed with her paper, and he responded and the two became pen-pals exchanging letters about theology and faith. Gissendaner completed a theological degree program through Emory University.

Georgia Diagnostic and Classification State Prison, the execution site Gissendaner's execution was scheduled for February 25, 2015, when a winter storm delayed it until March 2, 2015. Her execution was further delayed when one of the execution drugs (pentobarbital) was thought to have been spoiled through improper storage, though it was later determined that the drug had merely precipitated out of solution due to colder than recommended storage conditions. Archbishop Carlo Maria Viganò, on behalf of Pope Francis, urged the Georgia State Board of Pardons and Parolesto spare Gissendaner's life. Gissendaner's clemency application to

Wives Who Kill

the Board of Pardons included support from a number of correctional officers whom she had met while in prison. Norman S. Fletcher, the former Chief Justice of the Supreme Court of Georgia, urged clemency because capital punishment was not proportional to her crime. Georgia Republican Party's general counsel and Republican Bob Barr also supported clemency. The board again declined to commute her sentence on September 29, 2015. (Georgia is one of three US states in which the governor is not empowered to grant clemency to the condemned.) Gissendaner was scheduled to be executed on September 29, 2015, but was again delayed by appeals. She was executed by lethal injection at the Georgia Diagnostic and Classification Prison in Jackson, Georgia, on September 30 at 12:21 a.m. Gissendaner cried, prayed, sang "Amazing Grace", and said, *"...and I love you Sally. And I love you Susan. You let my kids know I went out singing Amazing Grace. And tell the Gissendaner family I am so sorry. That amazing man lost his life because of me and if I could take it back, if this would change it, I would have done it a long time ago. But it's not. And I just hope they can find peace. And I hope they find some happiness.* God bless you." She was the first woman executed in Georgia since Lena Baker in 1945, and the only woman executed in the United States in 2015.

Rita Gluzman

Rita Gluzman is a Ukrainian-born activist and convicted murderer who first came to prominence in the 1970s when she successfully pressured the Soviet Union to allow her husband, scientist Yakov Gluzman, to emigrate to the West with the rest of their family. In 1996, she conspired with her cousin, Vladimir Zelinin, to murder Yakov after he filed for divorce. Gluzman became the first woman to be convicted under the United States Violence Against Women Act, and was sentenced to life imprisonment. She was granted a compassionate release in 2020. Gluzman was born and raised in Soviet Ukraine. Her parents were survivors of the Holocaust. Gluzman was raped by a police officer when she was 10 years old. Her mother told her not to discuss the rape with anyone. Afterwards, Gluzman's father was sent to an internment camp. When Gluzman was 11

Mariticide Club

years old, her mother abandoned her for two years, and she had to take care of her younger sister on her own. During this time, the two survived by picking through garbage and eating handouts by neighbors. She married Yakov Gluzman in 1969. The Gluzmans had a son, Ilan Gluzman. In 1971, Gluzman launched a public campaign to pressure the Soviet government to allow her husband to emigrate with her to Israel. Gluzman's father waited fifteen years for a permit from the government to allow his family to leave, but the permit did not include Gluzman's husband. After five more years, Soviet authorities refused to grant Yakov a permit and told his family that they would leave the Soviet Union without him if they wished to leave at all. Gluzman was pregnant, and thus decided to leave for Israel with hopes that her husband could follow eventually. Yakov's appeals were continually struck down, Rita temporarily relocated to the United States. Her visa was sponsored by Congressman Jack Kemp. She spoke across the U.S. and reportedly went on an 18-day hunger strike to generate interest in her case. She also met with multiple UN officials, including then-UN Ambassador Rita Hauser. Gluzman spurred interest in her case by providing numerous interviews, and advocated for individuals to petition then-Russian ambassador Anatoly Dobrynin for her husband's release. She was able to persuade George H. W. Bush, Secretary-General U Thant, and Canadian Prime Minister Pierre Trudeau to petition for her cause. In October 1971, Gluzman spoke before the American Jewish Welfare Federation Leadership Forum in Atlanta, Georgia, and her story appeared on the front page of the Atlanta Constitution. Atlanta Alderman Wyche Fowler mistakenly thought that she was an Atlanta constituent, and took a clipping of the newspaper story with him to Kyiv. A high-ranking official learned about Gluzman's story from Fowler, and brought it to other Communist Party officials. That night, Fowler was told that Yakov would be granted leave to emigrate. On November 25, Gluzman reunited with Yakov in Vienna, Austria. Two days later, the couple reached Israel, where they settled with Rita's parents. The couple planned to study at Tel Aviv University. Yakov continued his study of biology and Rita her study of chemistry. By 1996, Yakov was an accomplished cancer researcher and

Wives Who Kill

co-owned a computer company, ECI Technologies, with Rita. However, that year, Yakov filed for divorce; he claimed that Rita was abusive and spent too much money, while Rita asserted that Yakov was having an extramarital affair with a woman in Israel. Federal agents later asserted that Rita went to Israel to collect photos of Yakov with another woman, then used the photos and illegal phone taps to blackmail him. Police asserted Rita feared a costly divorce and giving up control of ECI. Yakov was murdered on April 6, 1996 in his home in Rockland County, New York. He was stabbed and struck with an axe, and his body was chopped into pieces with a hacksaw. Rita's cousin, Vladimir Zelenin, was charged with conspiracy to commit murder after police found him preparing to throw ten garbage bags containing Yakov's body parts into the Passaic River. Zelenin was covered in Yakov's blood. Gluzman went missing for six days after her husband's death, until found by police on Long Island and arrested April 12. She was found breaking into a guest cabin owned by Yakov's former employer. Gluzman's car had a stolen license plate; a passport and travel books for Switzerland and Australia were found inside. Gluzman, who had been living away from her husband in Upper Saddle River, New Jersey, was charged with violating the Violence Against Women Act, which criminalizes crossing state lines while intending to injure or intimidate a spouse or partner. She was the first woman to be charged under this law, and the first individual to be charged for murder under the law. Federal charges were brought because there was a lack of physical evidence to corroborate the witness account of Zelenin, who turned against Gluzman. During the trial, Zelenin testified that Gluzman helped him immigrate to the U.S. and find a job at her company. Gluzman also told Zelenin that if Yakov were allowed to get a divorce, Zelenin would be out of work because ECI would go out of business. Zelenin alleged Gluzman plotted her husband's murder, and took Zelenin to Home Depot and Grand Union for an axe and garbage bags, for the murder. The two of them attacked Yakov in his apartment and killed him with two axes. Gluzman cleaned while Zelenin dismembered. Gluzman's defense claimed that Zelenin acted alone. April 30, 1997, Gluzman was sentenced to life in

Mariticide Club

prison after conviction on a federal charge of interstate domestic violence resulting in death. After sentencing, Gluzman appealed her sentence, claiming her conviction was unconstitutional. Her appeal was denied. July 28, 2020, Gluzman was granted a compassionate release after she several medical issues multiple strokes and a diagnosis of early Parkinson's disease. She was released from the Federal Medical Center, Carswell in Fort Worth, Texas and headed to Hackensack, New Jersey, where she planned to reside with her sister. She began her five year court-ordered supervised release immediately after. According to the conditions for her supervised release, Gluzman will be confined to her home with few exceptions, including doctor appointments, court appearances, religious services, employment, education, or other court-approved activities such as repairing her car that is infested with rats. Gluzman also will have to wear a GPS monitoring device. While out on probation, she will be cared for by her sister.

Gesina ("Gesche") Margarethe Gottfried (née Timm)

Gesche Gottfried (1785–1831)

Wives Who Kill

Gesina ("Gesche") Margarethe Gottfried (née Timm; 6 March 1785 – 21 April 1831), was a German killer who murdered 15 people by arsenic poisoning in Bremen and Hanover, Germany, between 1813 and 1827. She was the last person to be publicly executed in the city of Bremen. Gesina Gottfried was born into a poor family in Bremen; she had a twin brother, Johann Timm, Jr. She was affectionately known as Gesche, the low-German form of Gesina. Her parents, seamstress Gesche Margarethe Timm and tailor Johann Timm, always had a preference for her brother. Her father encouraged her to marry at the first opportunity, and at age 21 she married Johan Mittenberg who made a living as a saddler in Bremen. They had three children together. Things changed when Johan's father died and they inherited some money. Johan's behavior changed and he began drinking and gambling. In 1813 he told Gesche that they were destitute and all the money was spent. A couple of months later, after a short period of stomach pain, he died. A few months later she met Michael Kristof Gottfried, a relatively-rich wine merchant. Gesche's mother, Gesche Timm, died following stomach pain, in May 1815. Her own daughters then died, and the scope of victims widened. Coincidentally a cholera epidemic hit Germany around 1815 and helped to obscure her crimes. Moreover, Gesche helped greatly in the town during the epidemic, gaining the nickname the "Angel of Bremen". In 1826 she sold her house to Johan and Wilhelmina Rumpff and they asked her to stay on as a housekeeper. This led to Wilhemina's death. A maid left saying that illness and death followed Gesche. Johan Rumpff became ill but was now suspicious. He analyzed his food and found specks of white powder, which he took to local chemist Dr. Luce. He decided it was arsenic and notified authorities. Gesche found out and fled to Hanover, where she started killing again, starting with a Mrs. Schmidt and her daughter, who died in May 1827. In July Frederick Klein was killed. She was captured by authorities on March 6, 1828, her 43rd birthday. News of her arrest quickly spread. She confessed to killing 15 people and to trying to kill many more. The reasons behind Gottfried's crimes remain unclear and widely debated, but the emotional deprivation she suffered during her childhood and her modus operandi lead to the

Mariticide Club

assumption that she suffered from Munchausen syndrome by proxy, a very common disorder among female serial killers. Gottfried's victims included her parents, her two husbands, her fiancé, and her children. Before being suspected and convicted of the murders, she garnered widespread sympathy among the inhabitants of Bremen because so many of her family and friends fell ill and died. Because of her devoted nursing of the victims during their time of suffering, she was known as the "Angel of Bremen" until her murders were discovered. She used a rat poison called "mouse butter" (in German "Mäusebutter"), common at the time, which consisted of small flakes of arsenic mixed in animal fat. She mixed small doses into her victims' food, and when they started to get sick, she "friendly, selfless and resignedly" offered to take care of them during their convalescence, while continuing to poison them. During the period of her criminal activity, Gesche Gottfried was considered a model citizen and was well-liked in the community. Even after the constant loss of relatives who suffered, it seemed that the friendly, candid and kind Gesche chased a "cloud of misfortune". Her neighbors, moved by her zeal and resignation with caring not only for her family. Her sick friends, called her "the angel of Bremen". Gesche Gottfried's victims

---

- 1 October 1813: Johann Miltenberg (first husband)
- 2 May 1815: Gesche Margarethe Timm (mother)
- 10 May 1815: Johanna Gottfried (daughter)
- 18 May 1815: Adelheid Gottfried (daughter)
- 28 June 1815: Johann Timm (father)
- 22 September 1815: Heinrich Gottfried (son)
- 1 June 1816: Johann Timm (brother)
- 5 July 1817: Michael Christoph Gottfried (second husband)
- 1 June 1823: Paul Thomas Zimmermann (fiancé)
- 21 March 1825: Anna Lucia Meyerholz (music teacher and friend)
- 5 December 1825: Johann Mosees (neighbor, friend and advisor)
- 22 December 1826: Wilhelmine Rumpff (landlady)

Wives Who Kill

- 13 May 1827: Elise Schmidt (daughter of Beta Schmidt)
- 15 May 1827: Beta Schmidt (friend, maid)
- 24 July 1827: Friedrich Kleine (friend, creditor; murdered in Hanover)

Johann Christoph Rumpff would have been Gesche's twelfth victim if he hadn't become suspicious after finding small white granules on food she had prepared for him. He confided to his physician, Dr. Luce, who had already attended several of the earlier victims, and handed over the substance he had found. Luce determined that it was arsenic and alerted authorities, but by then Gottfried had already claimed two more victims and had moved to Hannover, where she was withering the life of her latest victim, Friedrich Kleine. On the night of March 6, 1828, her 43rd birthday, she was arrested. Sentenced to death by decapitation, she was publicly executed on 21 April 1831. It was the last public execution in the history of Bremen. Gottfried's death mask was made to study the facial patterns of criminal women, within the now-obsolete field of study of phrenology. Gottfried's crimes were the inspiration for several works of art and literature. One such work, a 2016 art book by Sarah Bodeman called GIFT: I Made This For You, ("Gift" is German for "poison") is set up like a pamphlet with fourteen recipes for each of Gottfried's victims. All of the food was cooked and photographed with the same ingredients and the same sequence of the original food that was made for Gottfried's victims. Another work titled "Gift" is a 2013 graphic novel by Peer Meter, with drawings by Barbara Yelin. It depicts Gottfried's story and her manner of poisoning her victims. Murderesses in German Writing, 1720-1860: Heroines of Horror (2009), Susanne Kord discusses Gottfried and other woman murders, and how literature has portrayed these women. Bremer Freiheit (1971) was a play by Rainer Werner Fassbinder, based on Geesche Gottfried's crimes. In 1972 Fassbinder shot a television version. In the Bremen district of Gröpelingen, a street was name Gesche-Gottfried-Weg.

Mariticide Club

Gesche-Gottfried-Weg in Bremen

Patricia Grimaldo de la Cruz

Jaime Serrano Cedillo (1967 – 16 Sept 2012) deputy of Nezahualcóyotl, State of Mexico and a member of Institutional Revolutionary Party (PRI) was assassinated on the afternoon of 16 September 2012, reportedly by his wife, inside his home in Nezahualcóyotl. Serrano Cedillo's assassination came just two days after the slaying of Eduardo Castro Luque, a deputy in the state of Sonora and a member of the PRI. Unlike other political assassinations in Mexico, Serrano Cedillo's death did not bore the signs of organized crime, and was a result of "a series of deep" marital problems.

Jaime Serrano Cedillo

Born in 1967, Serrano Cedillo was a close collaborator of the State of Mexico's current governor, Eruviel Ávila Villegas. Prior to his deputy nomination, Serrano Cedillo was the president of the Institutional Revolutionary Party(PRI) in the municipality of Nezahualcóyotl and a

Wives Who Kill

former mayoral candidate for the same locality. He had also served as the Sub-secretary of the Interior in Greater Mexico City until May 2011. On 5 September 2012, Serrano Cedillo was sworn in as deputy for the XXV District of Nezahualcóyotl. Initial reports indicate that Serrano Cedillo left his house to buy a newspaper at a nearby booth and was stabbed in the chest by someone with a sharp weapon. Serrano Cedillo was reportedly coming out of a public restroom when the attacker surprised him. The assailant then managed to flee the scene and no arrests have been made. Serrano Cedillo, on the other hand, made his way home and was transported to a nearby hospital by his family where he was later pronounced dead. The Mexican authorities indicated on 20 September 2012 that Serrano Cedillo's wife, Patricia Grimaldo de la Cruz, reportedly assassinated her husband after having a dispute that same morning for "profound series of conjugal differences." It was later proven that the assassination happened inside Serrano Cedillo's house and not outside his domicile, as previously stated. Unlike other political assassinations, Serrano Cedillo's death did not bore the signs of organized crime. Mexico's drug gangs typically target local leaders and police chiefs, not federal deputies. Moreover, stabbing is not typically a method Mexico's drug trafficking use to do their "dirty work," hinting the officials that the deputy's death was a personal attack. He was the second PRI politician killed in just two days; Eduardo Castro Luque, a deputy-elect of the state of Sonora, was shot dead by unknown assailants on 14 September 2012. In August 2012, Édgar Morales Pérez of the PRI was also shot and killed by gunmen. After the Municipal Committee of the PRI paid tribute to the fallen Serrano Cedillo on 17 September 2012, he was buried in Jardines de Oriente cemetery. The Mexican government deployed more than 1,000 troops to Nezahualcóyotl as a response to the assassination of Serrano Cedillo under a military-led program called Operation Neza. This was the first time since the start of Mexico's drug war in 2006 that soldiers have been deployed at this scale near the nation's capital. In Nezahualcóyotl, a city with around 1.1 million people and part of the Mexico City's metropolitan area, is home to a turf war between Los Zetas and La Familia

Mariticide Club

Michoacana, two drug trafficking organizations that fight for the growing drug market and illegal goods in the region. The troops were relocated from Nezahualcóyotl on 3 November 2012 after Operation Neza concluded.

Belle Gunness – 14 victims

Gunness, c. 1904

Belle Gunness, born Brynhild Paulsdatter Størseth (November 11, 1859 – possibly April 28, 1908), nicknamed Hell's Belle, was a Norwegian-American serial killer who was active in Illinois and Indiana between 1884 and 1908. Gunness is thought to have killed at least fourteen people, most of whom were men she enticed to visit her rural Indiana property through personal advertisements, while some sources speculate her involvement in as many as forty murders making her one of the most prolific female serial killers in history. Gunness seemingly died in a fire in 1908, but it is popularly believed that she faked her death. Her actual fate is unconfirmed. Belle Gunness was born Brynhild Paulsdatter Størseth in Selbu, Sør-Trøndelag, Norway, on November 11, 1859 to Paul and Berit Størseth; she was the youngest of eight children. She was confirmed at the Church of Norway in 1874.

Wives Who Kill

At age 14, Gunness began working for neighboring farms by milking and herding cattle to save enough money for the journey to New York City. She moved to the United States in 1881. When she was processed by immigration at Castle Garden, she changed her first name to Belle, then travelled to Chicago to join her sister, Nellie, who had immigrated several years earlier. In Chicago, living with her sister and brother-in-law, Gunness worked as a domestic servant, then got a job at a butcher's shop cutting up animal carcasses. She was 5'7" (170 cm) tall and weighed around 95 - 113 kg (210 - 250 lbs.) physically strong and masculine in appearance.

Deaths associated with Gunness

Mads Sorenson and children

Gunness married Mads Sorenson in 1884. The couple owned a candy store which later burned to the ground. Their home had also burned down, and both instances granted the couple insurance payouts. Two babies in Gunness' home died from inflammation of the large intestine, which can result from poisoning. Gunness had insured both of the children and collected a large insurance check after each death. Neighbors gossiped about the babies, since Gunness never appeared to be pregnant. Sorenson had purchased two life insurance policies. On July 30, 1900, both policies were active at the same time, as one would expire that day and the other would enter into force. Sorenson died of cerebral hemorrhage that day. Gunness explained he had come home with a headache and she provided him with quinine powder for the pain; she later checked on him and he was dead. Gunness collected money from both the expiring life insurance policy, and the one that went into effect that day, making a total of $5,000. With the insurance money, she moved to La Porte, Indiana, and bought a pig farm.

Peter Gunness

Belle married Peter Gunness on April 1, 1902. The following week, while Peter was out of the house, his infant daughter died of unknown causes in Belle's care. Peter died eight months later due to a skull injury. Belle explained that Peter reached for something on a high shelf and a meat grinder fell on him, smashing his skull. The district coroner convened a

Mariticide Club

coroner's jury, suspecting murder, but nothing came of the case. Belle collected $3,000 insurance money for Peter's death.

Disappearances

Gunness began placing marriage ads in Chicago newspapers in 1905. One of her ads was answered by a Wisconsin farmhand, Henry Gurholt. After travelling to La Porte, Gurholt wrote his family, saying that he liked the farm, was in good health, and requesting that they send him seed potatoes. When they failed to hear from him after that, the family contacted Gunness. She told them Gurholt had gone off with horse traders to Chicago. She kept his trunk and fur overcoat.

John Moe of Minnesota answered Gunness's advertisement in 1906. After they had corresponded for several months, Moe travelled to La Porte and withdrew a large amount of cash. Although no one ever saw Moe again, a carpenter who did occasional work for Gunness observed that Moe's trunk remained in her house, along with more than a dozen others.

Andrew Helgelien and discovery of multiple graves

Her criminal activities came to light in April 1908, when the Gunness farmhouse in La Porte, Indiana burned to the ground. In the ruins, authorities found the bodies of a headless adult woman, initially identified as Belle Gunness, and her three children. Further investigation unearthed the partial remains of at least 11 additional people on the Gunness property. After the fire at the Gunness homestead led to the discovery of bodies believed to be Gunness and her children, La Porte police authorities were contacted by Asle Helgelien, who had found correspondence between his brother, Andrew Helgelien, and Gunness; the letters included petitions for him to relocate to La Porte, to bring money, and to keep the move a secret. A visit by Asle Helgelien to the Gunness farm with a former hired hand led to attention being paid to "soft depressions" in what had been made into a pen for hogs; after briefly digging one of the depressions in the lot, a gunny sack was found that contained "two hands, two feet, and one head", which Helgelien recognized to be those of his brother. Immediate

Wives Who Kill

inspection of the site revealed that there were dozens of such "slumped depressions" in the Gunness yard, and further digging and investigation at the site yielded multiple burlap sacks containing "torsos and hands, arms hacked from the shoulders down, masses of human bone wrapped in loose flesh that dripped like jelly", from trash-covered depressions that proved to be graves. In each case, the body had been butchered in the same manner—the body decapitated, the arms removed at the shoulders, and the legs severed at the knees. Blunt trauma and gashes characterized the skulls that were found that had been separated from the bodies. Lucas Reilly, quoting The Chicago Inter Ocean in Mental Floss, noted that The bones had been crushed on the ends, as though they had been... struck with hammers after they were dismembered... [and that] Quicklime had been scattered over the faces and stuffed in the ears. After finding the parts of five bodies on the first day, and an additional six on the second—some in shallow graves under the original hog pen, others near an outhouse or a lake—"the police stopped counting". With these discoveries, the perceptions of Belle Gunness, as reported in newspaper descriptions of a praiseworthy woman—dying in the fire that consumed her house, "in a desperate attempt to save her children"—were reassessed. Despite the initial success with the identification of Andrew Helgelien, and despite the fact that widening news coverage of the mass murders invited inquiries from families with men that had gone missing, "[m]ost of the remains could not be identified."

Involvement of Ray Lamphere

Ray Lamphere was Gunness' hired hand and on-and-off lover. In November 1908, Lamphere was convicted of arson in connection with the fire at Gunness' house. Lamphere later confessed that Gunness had placed advertisements seeking male companionship, only to murder and rob the men who responded and subsequently visited her on the farm. Lamphere stated that Gunness asked him to burn down the farmhouse with her children inside. Lamphere also asserted that the body thought to be Gunness's was in fact a murder victim, chosen and planted to mislead investigators. The brother of one victim had warned Gunness that he might

Mariticide Club

arrive at the farm to investigate his brother's disappearance. According to Lamphere, this impending visit motivated Gunness to destroy her house, fake her own death, and flee. When Lamphere was arrested, he was wearing John Moe's overcoat and Henry Gurholt's watch.

Edward Bechly

Edward Bechly, a journalist, was given a secret assignment to acquire access to a confession and publish it, thus bringing a second, inconsistent Lamphere account to light. The second account is based on the report that Lamphere contacted a Reverend Edwin Schell and provided him with a verbal confession that Schell transcribed and had Lamphere sign, a document that Schell kept sealed in his personal safe. Bechly attempted to convince Schell to allow him to publish this later confession, but was denied by both Schell and Schell's wife. However, a separate newspaper published a story with speculation regarding the second Lamphere confession. Described as worried as to the peace of the families of the victims, Schell offered the confession to Bechly, which was later

Wives Who Kill

published. The Bechly narrative, entitled "Lanphere's Confession" [sic], contains this summary from Bechly: In the confession, Lanphere [sic] said that he had killed Mrs. Gunness and children with an ax, sprinkled the bodies with kerosene and set fire to them and the house. It gave details of the slaying, and told of his part in the former murders which occurred at the Gunness farm, his task usually being the burying of the bodies in the garden. The essential fact, however, was that the murderess was not alive as a fugitive. The publication of Lamphere's confession resulted in the subsequent arrest of his accomplice Elisabeth Smith. The inconsistencies between the two confessions, including the matter of the survival of Belle Gunness, remain historical issues that are not fully resolved. Belle Gunness was pronounced dead, even though the doctor who performed the postmortem testified that the headless body was five inches shorter and about fifty pounds lighter than Gunness. No explanation was provided for what happened to the body's head. Whether Gunness died in the fire or escaped remained uncertain, although the sheriff blamed a Chicago American reporter for inventing the "escaped" story. Reported "sightings" of Gunness in the Chicago area continued long after she was declared dead. At the time, police looked into reports of women suspected to be Belle, none of which led to her apprehension. In 2008, DNA tests were performed on the headless corpse in an attempt to compare the DNA in the corpse against a sample from a letter Gunness had sent to one of her victims, but due to its age the sample was not able to be properly tested. After Gunness' crimes came to light, the Gunness farm became a tourist attraction. Spectators came from across the country to see the mass graves, and concessions and souvenirs were sold. The crime became a part of area history: the La Porte County Historical Society Museum has a permanent "Belle Gunness" exhibit. Gunness is the subject of at least two American musical ballads. Method, a 2004 film starring Elizabeth Hurley as Rebecca who is portraying Gunness in a film within the film, being shot in Romania. In 2017, true crime podcast My Favorite Murder performed and later released a live episode detailing Gunness' crimes. The Farm, a 2021 film starring Traci Lords, is based on the Belle Gunness story. Hell's Princess:

Mariticide Club

The Mystery of Belle Gunness, Butcher of Men is a 2018 non-fiction book by Harold Schechter on the life of Belle Gunness. In the Garden of Spite: A Novel of the Black Widow of LaPorte is a US-published 2021 novel by Camilla Bruce with elements of "Norwegian noir and true crime" based on the life of Belle Gunness published in the UK with the title Triflers need not apply My Men, a 2023 Norwegian novel by Victoria Kielland, is a fictionalized version of Gunness's life.

Barbara Gusewelle

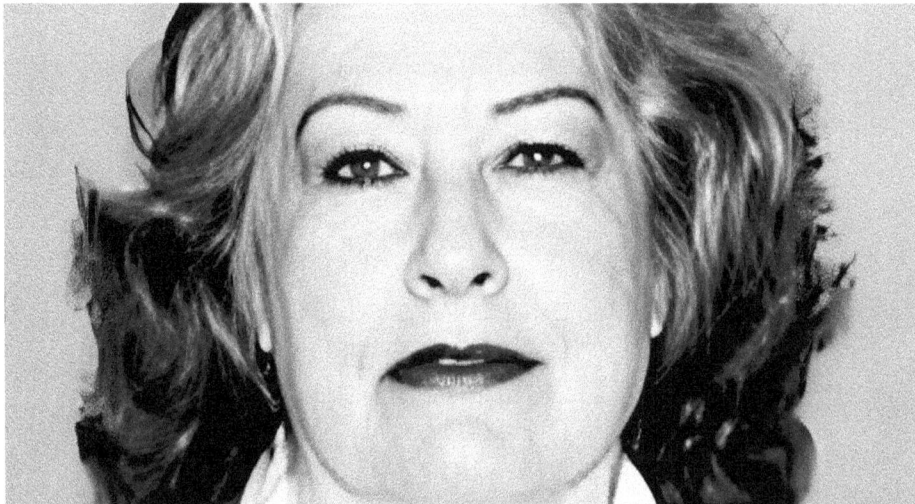

Aug 8, 2015 — Before she hooked up with Gusewelle, Barbara had a hot affair with Killer Driller St. Louis dentist who used his sexual powers to commit crime. Engleman and Barbara Gusewelle Boyle, charged with three counts of murder for the deaths of her husband and in- laws, went on trial June 20, 1985. Barbara Gusewelle Boyle, then 42, was convicted of murder in the slaying of her husband and she was sentenced Friday to 50 years in prison for "Cold-Blooded" murder of her husband in 1979. She was defended by F. Lee Bailey. When Arthur and Vernita Gusewelle were shot to death in 1976, Ron Gusewelle and Barbara Boyle had been married for about a year. Barbara Gusewelle Boyle was in on the killing of her

Wives Who Kill

husband's parents, then took part in killing him. Barbara collected $340,000 after her hubby's murder. ... in this murder," said Judge P.J. O'Neill as he sentenced Barbara Gusewelle Now, 25 years later, she is quietly paroled ...

ST. LOUIS -- Slight and balding, Dr. Glennon E. Engleman appeared to be a kindly old dentist in the quiet, south St. Louis neighborhood where he lived and practiced. But prosecutors say the mild-mannered demeanor was a facade for a madman who derived sexual pleasure from killing, and mesmerized young women into setting up their husbands as targets in murder-for-profit schemes. 'He says he does it for money, but I think that's a front,' said Gordon Ankney, the prosecutor who sent Engleman to prison. 'He never did it for enough to make it worthwhile. 'He related homicidal intimacy with sexual intimacy. There was almost a sexual excitement about killing. He's said to have quite a sexual drive. He has a very macho image of himself.' Engleman, 57, currently is serving two life terms -- with no parole for 50 years -- for two murders. But he may be forced to stand trial again in Illinois because of an indictment returned in August that names the dentist as the triggerman in the killing of an Illinois man and his parents. That pleases Ankney because a conviction could bring the death penalty. 'This guy is a dangerous man,' Ankney said. 'He's as cold-blooded a murderer as I've ever seen. 'Most believed he was a kindly old dentist in south St. Louis. But he is a Dr. Engleman and Mr. Hyde.' Ankney said Engleman had a Charles Manson-like hypnotic ability over young women. In all but one of the seven deaths in which he is implicated, Engleman worked with a woman -- sometimes hand-picking a man for her to marry. He then shared in insurance payoffs. 'I wouldn't doubt that this guy uses some hypnosis on these girls,' said Ankney. 'To get young girls to go out and get people to kill without even knowing who they were -- that's incredible.' Fred Buckles, the assistant U.S. attorney who pressed federal charges against Engleman, said he had a power over women not related to his physical looks. 'For a 50-year-old guy, he had the body of a 50-year-old guy,' Buckles said. 'Like many people his age, he has an extra pound or two.

Mariticide Club

'But he had some sort of hold on women. He's quite a talker. There's got to be so Buckles also agreed Engleman didn't kill just for money, pointing out that in one murder that took three years to pull off the dentist's share was $10,000 of a $60,000 insurance payoff. 'When I think back about it, I still think it's incredible,' Buckles said. 'I can remember the looks on the jury -- people looking at you like it was a fairy tale, like it was a TV movie.' Investigators who interviewed Engleman described him as 'super intelligent' with an IQ in the 140s. The dentist refused a UPI request for an interview in his cell in the state penitentiary at Jefferson City, but one of the last reporters to talk with him said Engleman spoke of 'parapsychology' and 'signs of the Zodiac.' 'He said he knew through the stars that he wouldn't get the death penalty,' said Bill Bryan, a veteran of 10 years as a city police reporter. 'He talks with very high self-confidence, almost cocky.' Bryan said Engleman asked him to come into his cell and help him take his coat off. The reporter said he hesitated at first. 'He's a little pipsqueak,' Bryan said. 'He's not big, maybe 5-8. If he doesn't have a gun or something, there's no reason to be afraid.' Something about his personality to convince people to do these things.' Engleman's name first made headlines in the 1958 shooting murder of James Bullock, 27 in one of the city's best-known unsolved slayings. At the time, Engleman's former wife, Edna, had been married to Bullock for six months. Mrs. Bullock got $64,500 in life-insurance benefits and later invested $15,000 in a dragstrip owned by Engleman. Engleman never was charged in the Bullock shooting, but Ankney noted the case remains open because there is no statute of limitations on murder. No charges were filed in the 1963 death of Eric Frey, an employee at the dragstrip who was killed in a dynamite explosion as he was attempting to fill an old cistern. Frey's widow received $37,000 in insurance benefits and said she later gave $16,000 of the sum to Engleman, a self-professed explosives expert. The first conviction of Engleman came in 1980 in the death of Peter J. Halm, who was shot in the back with a rifle as he stood next to his wife in a wooded area near Pacific in 1976. Halm's wife, Carmen Miranda Halm, had worked as a

Wives Who Kill

dental assistant for Engleman before she married Halm. She was granted immunity and testified Engleman 'suggested that I marry someone and that he would, uh, kill them.' Mrs. Halm said Engleman told her the plot would work because he had pulled it off before. 'He said he blew up Eric Frey,' Mrs. Halm testified, adding that she gave the dentist $10,000 of a $60,000 insurance settlement. Engleman also was convicted in the 1980 car-bombing death of Sophie Marie Barrera. Mrs. Barrera performed dental lab work for Engleman and at the time of her death was suing him for $14,500 in unpaid fees. Authorities believe Engleman constructed the bomb but a second man actually planted it. The man's identity is known, but prosecutors said they lack enough evidence to bring him to trial at this time. Police investigating the bombing were led to Engleman by his third wife, Ruth, who said she feared for her life. She agreed to tape secretly conversations with her husband. The tape was played at Engleman's trial for the Barrera killing and he was heard telling his wife he wanted to 'quietly settle down' and 'practice dentistry for a little.' 'There's no possession on my part, no driving urgency to keep getting rid of my fellow man,' Engleman said. His wife pressed him for a reason for his murderous ways and Engleman replied: 'Money, money, money, money.' He also talked of 'a nice camaraderie that you have and closeness' with the women who helped with the killings. Engleman could not be sentenced to the gas chamber for the Halm murder because Missouri did not have the death penalty when the killing occurred. He escaped death again when the Barrera jury could not agree on a sentence. But during the investigations into the two murders, police found Engleman had bragged to cohorts about 'his biggest project,' the murders of a farmer, his wife and their son in Madison County, Ill. An indictment was returned in August for the Illinois killings. Barbara Gusewelle Boyle was charged in the murder of her husband, Ronald Gusewelle, 33, in March 1979, and the deaths of his parents, Arthur, 61, and Vernita, 55, in November 1977. Mrs. Boyle was arrested in Florida where she had obtained a passport and apparently was headed to Switzerland. Ronald Gusewelle had inherited a $340,000 estate after the deaths of his parents.

Mariticide Club

In addition, Mrs. Boyle had approximately $120,000 in insurance policies on her husband. Engleman and Robert Handy, his convicted accomplice in the Halm killing, were named as unindicted coconspirators but Madison County State's Attorney Don Weber says they will be indicted on the murder charges. Weber said Mrs. Boyle planned to share the $500,000 she would make after her husband's death with Engleman. Sources said Mrs. Boyle met Engleman about 1960 when she lived in an apartment over his mother's home. Engleman and Mrs. Boyle's first husband were said to have been schoolmates. Weber has said he will seek the death penalty for Engleman because of statements by Handy that the dentist shot Ronald Gusewelle through the heart, and then beat him repeatedly on the head with a sledge hammer. Engleman, however, could escape the death chamber a third time because his health may not permit him to stand trial. His sister, Melody Gonterman, told UPI he suffers from diabetes and has lost about 75 pounds. 'He's just getting old -- old and sick,' Mrs. Gonterman said of her brother. 'He's lost a toe, lost it last year. And he has a hole in his neck. You can almost put a couple fingers in it.' Engleman once boasted to a reporter that he was a 'celebrity' in the prison and that a 'hit man' had sought out his advice on killing. Engleman advised him that a shot to the back of the head was best. 'Let's face it,' Engleman told a reporter. 'I'm a celebrity - Jesse James, the Dalton Gang and Dr. Engleman.' Mrs. Gonterman said Engleman had asked to be allowed to practice dentistry in prison but officials were afraid of lawsuits. 'It's a shame to waste all that talent,' she said. Prosecutor Ankney has a different view of Engleman's dental talents. 'There was some thinking he would practice on prisoners, but the warden stopped that talk pretty soon,' Ankney said. 'He was a lousy dentist.' Glennon Edward Engleman (February 6, 1927 – March 3, 1999) was an American dentist, contract killer, and serial killer. Engleman, a United States Army veteran and a St. Louis dentist, planned and carried out at least five murders for monetary gain over the course of 30 years. He was already serving two life sentences in a Missouri state prison when he pled guilty to the murder of a man and his wealthy parents in a

Wives Who Kill

separate contract killing that occurred in Illinois. Engleman was a sociopath, once stating that his talent was to kill without remorse, and he enjoyed planning and carrying out killings and disposing of the remains in order that it would net him financial rewards. His first known killing occurred in collaboration with his ex-wife. His ex-wife Ruth married another man, raised his life insurance and then Engleman killed him, both sharing the benefits. Later he would repeat these tactics for other murders. Engleman would use his financial worth, sex and charm to manipulate women he was close to, ex-wives, lovers and his dental assistant, in helping him formulate and execute elaborate murder schemes. This led to one of his lovers, Barbara Boyle, being convicted as an accomplice and serving just under half of a 50-year sentence. Another accomplice, Robert Handy, was also convicted and served time in prison. Methods used to kill his victims included shooting, bludgeoning with a sledgehammer and explosives. The exact number of his victims is unknown. He is the subject of Susan Crane Bakos 1988 book Appointment for Murder. The cases against him were reenacted in a rare, two-part episode of the crime documentary series "The FBI Files". Engleman was born the youngest of four children, his father was a member of the US Air Force. He was raised in the middle class and lived in a nice home his parents owned. Academically he was an above average student in school, but he didn't excel in any specific subject. He graduated in dentistry at Washington University in St. Louis, in 1954. He had been admitted under the GI Bill, having previously served in the US Army Air Corps. 1958: Engleman is suspected of the death of James Stanley Bullock, 27, a clerk for Union Electric Company of Missouri and part-time student. Shot near the St. Louis Art Museum. Edna Ruth Bullock (née Ball) and James Bullock were married on June 28, 1958, they had been married for five and half months on the date he was murdered. Edna Ruth Bullock was Engleman's ex-wife prior to her marriage with James Bullock. She collected $64,000 (equivalent to $649,000 in 2022) from James Bullock's life insurance.

Mariticide Club

1963: Engleman is suspected in the murder of Eric Frey, a business associate of Engleman at Pacific Drag Strip, in which Frey and Engleman were partners. Engleman struck him with a rock, pushed him down a well and used dynamite to blow him up afterwards. He then divided the insurance proceeds with Frey's widow.

1976: Peter J. Halm was shot in Pacific, Missouri. His wife, Carmen Miranda Halm, a former dental assistant trainee who had worked for Engleman and known him since childhood, ordered the hit to collect a $60,000 (equivalent to $309,000 in 2022) policy of life insurance on Halm. Engleman was convicted of capital murder for killing Halm and sentenced to life in prison with no possibility of parole for 50 years.

1977: Arthur and Vernita Gusewelle at their farmhouse near Edwardsville, Illinois. Arthur was shot; Vernita bashed to death. Engleman then murdered their son Ronald Gusewelle in East St. Louis, Illinois 17 months later so his widow Barbara Gusewelle Boyle could claim the millions in life insurance she had taken out on her husband, the sole heir to his parents' oil business. Boyle collected approximately $340,000 (equivalent to $1,642,000 in 2022) following her husband's murder. Boyle was convicted in her husband's murder but was acquitted of killing his parents. She was subsequently sentenced to 50 years in prison for the murder of her husband. She was released from the Dwight Correctional Center on October 10, 2009. Robert Handy, the accomplice, pled guilty to conspiring to commit the three Gusewelle killings and was sentenced to 14 years and served his time in prison. Engleman confessed to the three killings while in prison. He later pled guilty to the murders and received three life terms without parole.

1980: Sophie Marie Barrera, owner of South St Louis Dental Laboratory. Killed in car bomb explosion. Engleman owed her over $14,000 (equivalent to $50,000 in 2022). On 25 September 1980, a jury in federal court found Engleman guilty of mail fraud and conspiracy to commit mail fraud in the murder of Barrera. He was sentenced to a total of 60 years in prison for the two charges. Engleman was accused of the murder by her son, Frederick Barrera. Engleman was also convicted in state court of capital

Wives Who Kill

murder for killing Berrera, receiving a life sentence with no possibility of parole for 50 years after jurors spared him a death sentence. Engleman was married twice, first to Edna Ruth and then to Carmen Miranda Halm, with whom he had a son, David Engleman. His first marriage Edna Ruth was when they both planned and decided on their method of killing. Edna Ruth Ball married another man, raised her new husband's life insurance, Engleman killed him and they both shared the profits. Edna Ruth was never prosecuted due to lack of evidence. In March 1999, Engleman, 72, was pronounced dead in the infirmary of the Jefferson City Correctional Center, where he had a history of treatment for diabetes. A spokesman for the center said his death had been anticipated.

Lizzie Halliday (née Eliza Margaret McNally)

MRS. HALLIDAY IN HANDCUFFS.

Mariticide Club

Lizzie Halliday (c. 1859 – June 28, 1918, born Eliza Margaret McNally) was an Irish-American killer responsible for the deaths of four people in upstate New York during the 1890s. In 1894, she became the first woman to be sentenced to death by the electric chair. Halliday's sentence was commuted and she spent the rest of her life in a mental institution. She killed a nurse while institutionalized and is speculated to have killed her first two husbands. Halliday, originally Eliza Margaret McNally, was born around 1859 in County Antrim, Ireland. Her family moved to the US when she was young (given as aged three or eight). In 1879, Halliday married a Greenwich, New York, man known by the alias Charles Hopkins; his real name: Ketspool Brown. They had one son who was institutionalized. In 1881, after Hopkins' death, she married pensioner Artemus Brewer, but he also died less than a year later. Her third husband, Hiram Parkinson, left her within their first year of marriage. Halliday went on to marry George Smith, a war veteran who had served with Brewer. After a reported failed attempt to kill Smith by putting arsenic in his tea, Lizzie fled to Bellows Falls, Vermont. She married Vermont resident Charles Playstel, but she vanished two weeks later. In the winter of 1888, Halliday resurfaced in Philadelphia, at a saloon on 1218 North Front Street that was run by the McQuillans, friends she knew from Ireland. Going by the name "Maggie Hopkins", Halliday set up a shop, but was later convicted of burning it down for the insurance money. She was sentenced to two years at Philadelphia's Eastern State Penitentiary. In 1889, as "Lizzie Brown", she became the housekeeper for Paul Halliday, a twice-widowed 70-year-old farmer living in Burlingham, New York, with his sons. Their marriage was marred by what Halliday described as Lizzie's sporadic "spells of insanity". Within two years, the Halliday family's house and barn burned to the ground, and she was suspected of setting the fires. At some point, she stole a team of horses and had a neighbor help her drive them to Newburgh, New York, where she sold them. She was acquitted of the crime on the grounds of insanity (accounts vary on this happening in 1890 or 1893). In May 1891, the Halliday house was burned to the ground, killing Halliday's mentally handicapped son John. She was again suspected of setting the fire since she

Wives Who Kill

was known to have disliked John. She claimed that he died trying to save her from the flames, but his locked bedroom door was discovered in the rubble, and Halliday was in possession of the key. Soon after, she burned down the Halliday barn and mill as well. She attempted to run off with another man, but was arrested and sent to an asylum. She was transferred to another asylum, but was then declared cured and released, returning home to Halliday. Paul Halliday disappeared that August. She claimed he had gone to a nearby town to do masonry work. Following the neighbors' suspicions that something was not right about her story, a search warrant was obtained, and on September 4 the bodies of two women were found buried in hay in a barn. Both had been shot. The women were later identified as Margaret and Sarah McQuillan, New York residents who were part of the family Lizzie had stayed with in Philadelphia. Little could be ascertained from Halliday as, when questioned, she behaved in an erratic manner, tearing at her clothes and talking incoherently. She was kept in custody, and some thought she was merely faking insanity. A few days after the McQuillans were found, Paul Halliday's mutilated body was discovered under the floorboards of his house. He had also been shot. Lizzie was charged with the murders and held for trial at the Sullivan County jail in Monticello, New York. During her first few months there, she refused to eat, attacked the sheriff's wife, set fire to her own bed, tried to hang herself, and cut her own throat with broken glass, about which she said, "I thought I would cut myself to see if I would bleed." Her jailers were forced to chain her to the floor during her remaining months there. While she was in jail, Lizzie received national attention, with one sensational story after another appearing across the country in tabloid newspapers. The New York World portrayed Lizzie's case as "unprecedented and almost without parallel in the annals of crime". She was also covered by the World's Nellie, who eventually managed to get an interview with Lizzie in which she revealed her previous marriages, facts Bly was able to confirm. Another useful source for reporters was Robert Halliday, Paul Halliday's son. The Sullivan County Sheriff started a new round of speculation when he told the press that Lizzie was probably connected to the Jack the Ripper murders, although no connection was ever made. The revelation that she had been married five times before she wed Paul Halliday, that two of her husbands had died less than a year after their weddings and that Lizzie had tried to poison a third led the press to speculate that she was responsible for at least six deaths. "Whether these men died natural deaths or were murdered is not known", The New York Times noted in June 1894. Lizzie also made a claim (confided to Robert Halliday) that she had killed a husband in Belfast, but had managed to conceal the crime. On June 21, 1894, Halliday was convicted at the Sullivan County Oyer and Terminer Court for the murder of Margaret McQuillan and Sarah Jane McQuillan. She became the first woman ever to be sentenced to death by electrocution, via New York State's new electric chair. Governor Roswell P. Flower commuted her sentence to life in a mental institution after a medical commission declared her insane. Halliday was sent to the Matteawan State Hospital for the Criminally Insane, where she spent the remainder of her life. She became a model patient and was trusted with sewing privileges, giving her access to tools, including scissors. She grew close to Nellie Wicks, one of the attendants at Matteawan, but she was deeply upset by Wicks's plans to leave the institution. In 1906, she killed Wicks by stabbing her 200 times with a pair of scissors. Halliday died of Bright's disease on June 28, 1918, after spending nearly half her life in the asylum.

Bright's disease is an archaic term for what is now referred to as 'nephritis'. Nephritis is an inflammation of the kidneys, caused by toxins, infection or autoimmune conditions. It is not strictly a single disease, rather a condition with a number of types and causes.

Clara Suarez Harris

Murder of David Lynn Harris

David Lynn Harris was an American orthodontist who owned a chain of offices along with his wife, Clara Suarez Harris. The chain was particularly successful, and the couple was able to afford an upscale home and lifestyle in Friendswood, Texas. On July 24, 2002, Clara Harris confronted her

Wives Who Kill

husband in a hotel parking lot over an extramarital affair, then struck and ran over him with her Mercedes-Benz sedan, killing him in an act of mariticide. She was convicted of sudden passion and sentenced to 20 years in prison. Clara Suarez, a Colombian immigrant, was named "Mrs. Colombia Houston" and worked as a dentist. She married David Harris on February 14, 1992, at the Nassau Bay Hilton, and raised three children: twin sons Brian and Bradley, born in 1998, and David's daughter Lindsey from a previous marriage. During his marriage to Clara, David began to have an affair with his former receptionist, Gail Bridges. Suspicious, Clara hired a private detective agency to monitor David, and on July 24, 2002, the agency notified her that he was at a hotel with his mistress.

Murder and trial

That evening, Clara went to the Hilton Hotel in Nassau Bay, Texas, to confront her husband and reportedly attacked Bridges in the lobby. Hotel employees escorted Clara to her Mercedes-Benz sedan. When David and Bridges came out of the hotel, Clara struck down her husband in the parking lot as her teenaged stepdaughter Lindsey sat in the passenger seat. According to the medical examiner's office, they could only be certain there was one tire mark on the body, but Lindsey and eyewitnesses assert Clara ran over David three times. David was dead at the scene, and Clara was charged with murder. Clara's trial began the following February. Lindsey testified against her stepmother, claiming she told her to stop the vehicle. The prosecution claimed Clara's actions were more than a crime of passion, but that she "wanted to hurt" David, as she was heard saying in a police interview. Also introduced at her trial was a videotape of the crime, recorded by the detective agency Clara had hired when she suspected David of the affair. The video was especially damning, as it showed her circling her Mercedes around the parking lot three times, although David is not clearly seen in the video. Clara then parks her car next to his body. The defense's attempts to prove that Clara ran over David only once crumbled when the judge ruled their re-creation of the crime by a private consultant inadmissible in court. Her attorney explained what was in the report, using the consultant as an expert witness on the stand. They argued

Mariticide Club

that Clara could only have run over David once, and that the turning radius of her Mercedes would not have allowed for her to sharply turn and run over him a second time. The prosecution admitted that it was a good argument, but countered by bringing in a police officer who had been present at the scene who pointed out another tire track on the pavement shown in a police photograph, the angle of which went directly to where David's body had been. Clara was advised not to take the stand. However, after watching days of testimony, she decided she had to speak. Taking the stand allowed parts of Clara's original interview, which her attorneys had previously gotten ruled inadmissible, to come into question. Only part of the interview was played; the jury heard Clara state that she "wanted to hurt" her husband, but not the portion where she said later in the interview, "I didn't want to kill him." This caused her attorney to collapse from the stress, causing the court to go to recess as he was taken to the hospital and later released. Clara contends that she did not see David when she ran into him with her car. Despite the medical examiner's report, the defense was unable to prove that she did not in fact run over him multiple times. Clara was found guilty of murdering her husband. On February 14, 2003, she was sentenced to twenty years in prison – the maximum sentence allowed by the jury's "sudden passion" finding – and fined $10,000. She was incarcerated at the Mountain View Unit in Gatesville, Texas, where she converted school textbooks to Braille for blind students. Clara's sons, who are in the custody of family friends, were said to visit about once a month. She was denied parole in her first attempt on April 11, 2013, by the Texas Board of Pardons and Paroles. Her second parole request was denied in September 2016.However, she was granted parole in November 2017. Harris was released on parole on May 11, 2018, and was released from parole in February of 2023. A book titled Out of Control was written by Steven Long about the case. Published in 2004 by St. Martin's Paperbacks, the book follows the story of the murder and the reasons behind it. This was the inspiration for a chapter in Mexican series Mujeres Asesinas "Killer Women." Chapter Luz, overwhelming (Luz, arrolladora). The case was profiled on the Oxygen Network series Snapped in 2004,

Wives Who Kill

on ABC News's 20/20 in 2006, and on Investigation Discovery's Deadly Women in 2010. It was the topic of Suburban Madness, a Lifetime Original movie, starring Elizabeth Peña and Brett Cullen.

Brynn Omdahl Hartman

Hartman in character as Chick Hazard, Private Eye, c. 1978 Philip Edward Hartman (né Hartmann; September 24, 1948 – May 28, 1998) was a Canadian-American actor, comedian, screenwriter and graphic designer. Hartman was born in Brantford, Ontario, Canada, and his family moved to the United States when he was ten years old. After graduating from California State University, Northridge with a degree in graphic arts, he designed album covers for bands including Poco and America. In 1975, he joined the comedy group the Groundlings, where he helped Paul Reubens develop his character, Pee-wee Herman. Hartman co-wrote the

Mariticide Club

film Pee-wee's Big Adventure and made recurring appearances as Captain Carl on Reubens' show Pee-wee's Playhouse. In 1986, Hartman joined the NBC sketch comedy show Saturday Night Live (SNL) as a cast member, and stayed for eight seasons until 1994. Nicknamed "Glue" for his ability to hold the show together and help other cast members, he won a Primetime Emmy Award for his SNL work in 1989. He also starred as Bill McNeal in the sitcom NewsRadio, voiced Lionel Hutz and Troy McClure on The Simpsons, and appeared in supporting roles in the films Houseguest, Jingle All the Way, and Small Soldiers. After two divorces, Hartman married Brynn Omdahl in 1987, with whom he had two children. Their marriage was troubled due to Brynn's drug and alcohol abuse. In 1998, while Phil was sleeping in his bed, Brynn shot and killed him, and later committed suicide. In the weeks following his murder, Hartman was celebrated in a wave of tributes. Dan Snierson of Entertainment Weekly wrote that Hartman was "the last person you'd expect to read about in lurid headlines in your morning paper ... a decidedly regular guy, beloved by everyone he worked with". He was posthumously inducted into the Canada and Hollywood Walks of Fame in 2012 and 2014.

Hartman designed album covers for bands such as Poco.

Hartman was born Philip Edward Hartmann (later dropping one "n") on September 24, 1948, in Brantford, Ontario. He was the fourth of eight children of Doris Marguerite (née Wardell; July 17, 1919 – April 15, 2001) and Rupert Loebig Hartmann (November 8, 1914 – April 30, 1998), who sold building materials.The family was Catholic. As a child, Hartman found affection hard to earn: "I suppose I didn't get what I wanted out of

Wives Who Kill

my family life, so I started seeking love and attention elsewhere." Hartman was 10 when his family moved to the United States. They first lived in Lewiston, Maine, then Meriden, Connecticut, and then on the West Coast, where he attended Westchester High School and frequently acted as the class clown. After graduating, he studied art at Santa Monica City College, dropping out in 1969 to become a roadie with a rock band. He returned to school in 1972 to study graphic arts at California State University, Northridge. He developed and operated his own graphic art business, creating more than 40 album covers for bands including Poco and America, as well as advertising and the logo for Crosby, Stills & Nash. In the late 1970s, he made his first television appearance on an episode of The Dating Game, where he won.

Hartman's career included Groundlings and Pee-Wee Herman (1975–1985) Working alone as a graphic artist, Hartman frequently amused himself with "flights of voice fantasies". In 1975, seeking a more social outlet for his talents, he began attending evening comedy classes by the California-based improvisational comedy group The Groundlings. While watching one of their performances, he impulsively decided to climb on stage and join the cast. His first onscreen appearance was in 1978's Stunt Rock, an Australian film directed in Los Angeles by Brian Trenchard-Smith. After several years of training, paying his way by redesigning the group's logo and merchandise, Hartman formally joined The Groundlings and by 1979 was one of the show's stars. There Hartman befriended Paul Reubens, with whom he often collaborated on comedic material. Together they created the character Pee-wee Herman and developed The Pee-wee Herman Show, a live stage show that subsequently aired on HBO in 1981. Hartman played Captain Carl in the show, and reprised the role for the children's TV show Pee-wee's Playhouse. Reubens and Hartman made cameos in the 1980 film Cheech and Chong's Next Movie. Hartman co-wrote the script of the 1985 feature film Pee-wee's Big Adventure and had a cameo role as a reporter. He had considered quitting acting at the age of 36 due to the challenges of finding work; but the success of Pee-wee's Big Adventure changed his mind.After a creative disagreement with Reubens,

Mariticide Club

he left the Pee-Wee Herman project to pursue other roles. Hartman took more small roles in 1986 films such as Jumpin' Jack Flash and Three Amigos. He also worked as a voice actor in animated television programs, including The Smurfs, Challenge of the GoBots, The 13 Ghosts of Scooby-Doo, and in Dennis the Menace as characters Henry Mitchell and George Wilson. He developed a strong persona providing voice-overs for advertisements. Hartman successfully auditioned to join NBC's variety show Saturday Night Live (SNL) in its 12th season, which began on October 11, 1986. He had been recommended for the show by fellow Groundlings and SNL cast members Jon Lovitz, and Laraine Newman as well as Jumpin' Jack Flash director Penny Marshall. He told the Los Angeles Times, "I wanted to do [SNL] because I wanted to get the exposure that would give me box-office credibility so I can write movies for myself." In his eight seasons with the show Hartman became known for impressions of over seventy original characters including Eugene, Anal Retentive Chef and Unfrozen Caveman Lawyer. His impressions include Frank Sinatra, Ronald Reagan, Ed McMahon, Barbara Bush, Charlton Heston, Kelsey Grammer, Michael Caine, Oliver Stone, Phil Donahue, Telly Savalas, Barry Humphries, Kirk Douglas and Bill Clinton (considered his best impression). Hartman first performed his Clinton impression on an episode of The Tonight Show. When he met Clinton in 1993, Hartman remarked, "I guess I owe you a few apologies", adding later that he "sometimes [felt] a twinge of guilt about [his Clinton impression]". Clinton showed good humor and sent Hartman a signed photo with the text: "You're not the president, but you play one on TV. And you're OK, mostly." Hartman copied the president's "post-nasal drip" and the "slight scratchiness" in his voice, as well as his open, "less intimidating" hand gestures. Hartman opted against wearing a larger prosthetic nose when portraying Clinton, as he thought it would be distracting. He instead wore a wig, dyed his eyebrows brighter, and used makeup to highlight his nose. In one of Hartman's sketches as Clinton, the president visits a McDonald's restaurant and explains his economic policies in the metaphor of eating other customers' food. The writers told him that

Wives Who Kill

he was not eating enough during rehearsals for the sketch – by the end of the live performance, Hartman had eaten so much he could barely speak.

Hartman appears as Bill Clinton on Saturday Night Live.

At SNL, Hartman's nickname of "Glue" was coined by Adam Sandler according to Jay Mohr's book Gasping for Airtime. However, according to You Might Remember Me: The Life and Times of Phil Hartman by Mike Thomas, author and staff writer for the Chicago Sun-Times, the nickname was created by SNL cast member and Hartman's frequent on-screen collaborator Jan Hooks. Hartman was very helpful to other cast members. For example, he aided Hooks in overcoming her stage fright. SNL creator Lorne Michaels explained the name: "He kind of held the show together. He gave to everybody and demanded very little. He was very low-maintenance. "Michaels also added that Hartman was "the least appreciated" cast member by commentators outside the show, and praised his ability "to do five or six parts in a show where you're playing support or you're doing remarkable character work". Hartman won the Primetime Emmy Award for Outstanding Writing for a Variety, Music or Comedy Program for SNL in 1989, sharing the award with the show's other writers. He was nominated in the same category in 1987, and individually in 1994 for Outstanding Individual Performance in a Variety or Music Program. By 1993, almost every cast member who was there during Hartman's first year on SNL had left the show, including Jon Lovitz, Jan Hooks and Dana Carvey. Hartman said he felt "like an athlete who's watched all his World Series teammates get traded off into other directions ... It was hard to watch

Mariticide Club

them leave because I sort of felt we were all part of the team that saved the show." This cast turnover contributed to his leaving the show in 1994. Hartman said he thought it was time to leave because the show was "getting less sophisticated" and his style of humor did not fit with the less intellectual comedy of newer cast members like Adam Sandler. Hartman had originally planned to leave the show in 1991, but Michaels persuaded him to stay to raise his profile; his portrayal of Clinton contributed to this goal. Jay Leno offered him the role of his sidekick on The Tonight Show but Hartman opted to stay on SNL. NBC persuaded him to stay on SNL by promising him his own comedy–variety show The Phil Show. He planned to "reinvent the variety form" with "a hybrid, very fastpaced, high energy [show] with sketches, impersonations, pet acts, and performers showcasing their talents". Hartman was to be the show's executive producer and head writer. Before production began, however, the network decided that variety shows were too unpopular and canceled the series. In a 1996 interview, Hartman noted he was glad, as he "would've been sweatin' blood each week trying to make it work". In 1998, he admitted he missed working on SNL, but had enjoyed the move from New York City to Southern California. Hartman became one of the stars of the NBC sitcom NewsRadio in 1995, portraying radio news anchor Bill McNeal. He signed, attracted by the show's writing and use of an ensemble cast, and joked he based McNeal on himself with "any ethics and character" removed. Hartman made roughly US$50,000 (equivalent to $96,025 in 2022) per episode of NewsRadio. Although the show was critically acclaimed, it was never a ratings hit and cancellation was a regular threat. After the completion of the fourth season, Hartman commented, "We seem to have limited appeal. We're on the edge here, not sure we're going to be picked up or not", but added he was "99 percent sure" the series would be renewed for a fifth season. Hartman had publicly lambasted NBC's decision to repeatedly move NewsRadio into different timeslots, but later regretted his comments, saying, "this is a sitcom, for crying out loud, not brain surgery". He also stated that if the sitcom were cancelled "it just will open up other opportunities for me". Although the

Wives Who Kill

show was renewed for a fifth season, Hartman was killed before production began. Ken Tucker praised Hartman's performance as McNeal: "A lesser performer ... would have played him as a variation on The Mary Tyler Moore Show's Ted Baxter, because that's what Bill was, on paper. But Hartman gave infinite variety to Bill's self-centeredness, turning him devious, cowardly, squeamish, and foolishly bold from week to week." Hartman was posthumously nominated for the Primetime Emmy Award for Outstanding Supporting Actor in a Comedy Series in 1998 for his work on NewsRadio, but lost to David Hyde Pierce. Hartman provided the voices for numerous characters on the Fox animated series The Simpsons, appearing in 52 episodes. He made his first appearance in the second season episode "Bart Gets Hit by a Car". Although he was originally brought in for a one-time appearance, Hartman enjoyed working on The Simpsons and the staff wrote additional parts for him. He voiced the recurring characters Lionel Hutz and Troy McClure, as well as Duffman (on one occasion) and several background characters. His favorite part was that of McClure, and he often used this voice to entertain the audience between takes while taping episodes of NewsRadio. He remarked, "My favorite fans are Troy McClure fans." He added "It's the one thing that I do in my life that's almost an avocation. I do it for the pure love of it." Hartman was popular among the staff of The Simpsons. Showrunners Bill Oakley and Josh Weinstein said they enjoyed his work, and used him as much as possible when working on the show. To give Hartman a larger role, they developed the episode "A Fish Called Selma", which focuses on Troy McClure and expands the character's backstory. The Simpsons creator Matt Groening said that he "took [Hartman] for granted because he nailed the joke every time", and that his voice acting could produce "the maximum amount of humor" with any line he was given. Before his death, Hartman had expressed an interest in making a live action film about Troy McClure. Many of The Simpsons production staff expressed enthusiasm for the project and offered to help. Hartman said he was "looking forward to [McClure's] live-action movie, publicizing his Betty Ford appearances", and "would love nothing

Mariticide Club

more" than making a film and was prepared to buy the film rights himself to make it happen. Hartman's first film role came in 1995's Houseguest, with Sinbad. films include Greedy, Coneheads, Sgt. Bilko, So I Married an Axe Murderer, CB4, Jingle All the Way, the English Disney/GKIDS dub of Kiki's Delivery Service, and Small Soldiers, the latter of which is his final theatrically released film. At the same time, he preferred working on television. His other television roles include appearances on episodes of The John Larroquette Show, The Dana Carvey Show, 3rd Rock from the Sun, and the HBO TV film The Second Civil War as the States. He made a considerable amount of money from television advertising, earning $300,000 for a series of four commercials for the soft drink Slice. He also appeared in advertisements for McDonald's (as Hugh McAttack) and 1-800-Collect (as Max Jerome). Hartman wrote a number of screenplays that were never produced. In 1986, he began writing a screenplay for a film titled Mr. Fix-It, and completed the final draft in 1991. Robert Zemeckis was signed to produce the film, with Gil Bettman hired to direct. Hartman called it "a sort of a merger of horror and comedy, like Beetlejuice and Throw Momma From the Train", adding, "It's an American nightmare about a family torn asunder. They live next to a toxic dump site, their water supply is poisoned, the mother and son go insane and try to murder each other, the father's face is torn off in a terrible disfiguring accident in the first act. It's heavy stuff, but it's got a good message and a positive, upbeat ending." Zemeckis could not secure studio backing, however, and the project collapsed. Another film idea involving Hartman's Groundlings character Chick Hazard, Private Eye was also canceled. Hartman appeared on David Letterman's Late Night and Late Show 13 times between 1989 and 1996, where he can be seen speaking German fluently. Clean and unassuming, he had such a casual, no-nonsense way about him. It was that quality that we all find so hilarious, his delightful ability to poke fun at himself and at life with a tongue-in-cheek attitude comparable to, say, Tim Conway or Mel Brooks or Carol Burnett. — Nancy Cartwright.

Wives Who Kill

In contrast to his real-life personality, which was described as "a regular guy and, by all accounts, one of show business's most low-key, decent people", Hartman often played seedy, vain or unpleasant characters as well as comedic villains. He described his standard character repertoire as the "jerky guy" and "the weasel parade", citing Lionel Hutz, Bill McNeal, Troy McClure, and Ted Maltin from Jingle All the Way as examples. Hartman enjoyed playing such roles because he "just want[ed] to be funny, and villains tend to be funny because their foibles are all there to see". He often played supporting roles, rather than the lead part. He said: "Throughout my career, I've never been a huge star, but I've made steady progress and that's the way I like it" and "It's fun coming in as the second or third lead. If the movie or TV show bombs, you aren't to blame." Hartman was considered a "utility player" on SNL with a "kind of Everyman quality" which enabled him to appear in the majority of sketches, often in very distinct roles. Jan Hooks stated of his work on SNL: "Phil never had an ounce of competition. He was a team player. It was a privilege for him, I believe, to play support and do it very well. He was never insulted, no matter how small the role may have been." He was disciplined in his performances, studying the scripts beforehand. Hooks added: "Phil knew how to listen. And he knew how to look you in the eye, and he knew the power of being able to lay back and let somebody else be funny, and then do the reactions. I think Phil was more of an actor than a comedian." Film critic Pauline Kael declared that "Phil Hartman and Jan Hooks on Saturday Night Live are two of the best comic actors I've ever seen." Writer and acting coach Paul Ryan noted Hartman's work ethic with his impressions. He assembled a collection of video footage of the figure he was preparing to impersonate and watched this continually until he "completely embodied the person". Ryan concluded that "what made [Hartman's impressions] so funny and spot on was Phil's ability to add that perfect touch that only comes from trial and error and practicing in front of audiences and fellow actors." Hartman described this process as "technical". Journalist Lyle V. Harris said Hartman showed a "rare talent for morphing into... anybody he wanted to be". Ken Tucker summarized

Mariticide Club

Hartman's comedic style: "He could momentarily fool audiences into thinking he was the straight man, but then he'd cock an eyebrow and give his voice an ironic lilt that delivered a punchline like a fast slider—you barely saw it coming until you started laughing." Hartman claimed that he borrowed his style from actor Bill Murray: "He's been a great influence on me – when he did that smarmy thing in Ghostbusters, then the same sort of thing in Groundhog Day. I tried to imitate it. I couldn't. I wasn't good enough. But I discovered an element of something else, so in a sick kind of way I made myself a career by doing a bad imitation of another comic."

Personal life

Hartman married Gretchen Lewis in 1970 and they divorced in September 1972. He married real estate agent Lisa Strain in 1982, and their marriage lasted three years. Strain told People magazine that Hartman was reclusive off screen and "would disappear emotionally ... he'd be in his own world. That passivity made you crazy." In 1987, Hartman married former model and aspiring actress Brynn Omdahl (born Vicki Jo Omdahl, April 11, 1958 – May 28, 1998), having met her on a blind date the previous year. They had two children, Sean and Birgen Hartman. The marriage had difficulties; she was reportedly intimidated by his success and was frustrated that she could not find any on her own, although neither party wanted a divorce. She was reported to have been jealous and often verbally and/or physically abusive, even sending a letter to his ex-wife, threatening to "rip [Strain's] eyes out" if she spoke to him again. Hartman considered retiring to save the marriage. Hartman tried to get Brynn acting roles, but she became progressively reliant on alcohol and narcotics, entering rehab several times. On multiple occasions, he removed their children from the household to stay with friends or family because of her drug- and alcohol-fueled outbursts. Because of his close friendship with SNL associate Jan Hooks, Brynn "joked" on occasion Hooks and Hartman were married "on some other level". Brynn had written threatening letters addressed to Hooks, warning her to not get close to her husband, but they appeared to have never even been sent, being discovered in her belongings following her death.

Wives Who Kill

Stephen Root, Hartman's NewsRadio co-star, said few people knew "the real Phil Hartman", as he was "one of those people who never seemed to come out of character," but he nevertheless gave the impression of a family man who cared deeply for his children. Hartman befriended Joe Rogan during his time on NewsRadio and confided his marital problems to him. Rogan said that he encouraged Hartman to divorce Brynn five times, but "[Hartman] loved his kids and didn't want to leave". Hartman stated in 1997 that, though a non-practicing Catholic, he displayed a sense of religiousness. In spare time he enjoyed driving, flying, sailing, marksmanship, and playing guitar. On May 27, 1998, Hartman's wife, Brynn, visited the Italian restaurant Buca di Beppo in Encino, California, with producer and writer Christine Zander, who said she was "in a good frame of mind"; they had drinks. After returning home, Brynn and Hartman had a "heated" argument, after which he went to bed. She entered his bedroom some time before 3:00 a.m. PDT on May 28, 1998, and, as he slept, she fatally shot him once between the eyes, once in the throat, and once in the upper chest with a Charter Arms .38 caliber handgun. He was 49 years old. She was making Zoloft, had been drinking alcohol, and had recently used cocaine.

Mariticide Club

Brynn then drove to the home of her friend Ron Douglas and confessed to the killing, but he did not believe her. They drove back to the house in separate cars, and she called another friend and confessed a second time. On seeing Hartman's body, Douglas called 9-1-1 at 6:20 a.m. Police arrived and escorted Douglas and the Hartmans' two children from the premises, by which time Brynn had locked herself in the bedroom. Shortly afterward, she died from a self-inflicted gunshot. The police stated Hartman's death was caused by "domestic discord" between the couple. A friend said Brynn "had trouble controlling her anger.... She got attention by losing her temper". A neighbor of the Hartmans told a CNN reporter that the couple had marital problems. Yet actor Guttenberg said they had been "a very happy couple, and they always had the appearance of being wellbalanced". Brynn's brother, Gregory Omdahl, filed a wrongful death lawsuit in 1999 against both Pfizer, the manufacturer of Zoloft, and her child's psychiatrist, Arthur Sorosky, who had provided samples of the antidepressant to Brynn. Phil Hartman's friend and former SNL colleague Jon Lovitz has accused Hartman's then- NewsRadio co-star Andy Dick of reintroducing Brynn to cocaine, causing her to relapse and suffer a nervous breakdown. Dick claims to have known nothing of her condition. Lovitz later said he no longer blamed Dick for Hartman's murder, but in 2006, Lovitz claimed Dick approached him at a restaurant and said, "I put the Phil Hartman hex on you; you're the next one to die." Lovitz then had him ejected from the restaurant. The following year at the Laugh Factory comedy club in Los Angeles, Lovitz and Dick had another argument, with Lovitz slamming Dick's head into the bar. Dick asserted he was not at fault in relation to Hartman's death. Brynn's sister Katharine Omdahl and brother-in-law Mike Wright raised the two Hartman children. Hartman's will stipulated each child would inherit money over several years after turning 25. The total value of Hartman's estate was estimated at $1.23 million. In accordance with their wishes, both Hartman's and Brynn's body were cremated by Forest Lawn Memorial Park and Mortuary, Glendale, California, and their ashes were scattered over Santa Catalina Island's Emerald Bay. Hartman has a headstone in Thief River

Wives Who Kill

Falls, Minnesota, with wife Brynn. NBC executive Don Ohlmeyer stated that Hartman "was blessed with a tremendous gift for creating characters that made people laugh. Everyone who had the pleasure of working with Phil knows that he was a man of tremendous warmth, a true professional and a loyal friend." Guttenberg expressed shock at Hartman's death and Steve Martin said he was "a deeply funny and very happy person". Matt Groening called him "a master" and director Joe Dante said "He was one of those guys who was a dream to work with. I don't know anybody who didn't like him." Dan Snierson of Weekly concluded that Hartman was "the last person you'd expect to read about in lurid headlines in your morning paper" and "a decidedly regular guy, beloved by everyone he worked with". In 2007, Entertainment Weekly ranked Hartman the 87th greatest television icon of all time, and Maxim named him the top Saturday Night Live performer of all time. On the day of Hartman's death, rehearsals for The Simpsons and that night's performance by The Groundlings were canceled. The season five premiere episode of NewsRadio, "Bill Moves On" (aired September 23, the day before what would have been his 50th birthday) finds Hartman's character, Bill McNeal, has died of a heart attack, while the other characters reminisce about his life. Lovitz joined the show, in his place, beginning with the next episode. A special episode of Saturday Night Live commemorating Hartman's work on the show aired on June 13, 1998. Rather than substituting another voice actor, the writers of The Simpsons retired Hartman's characters. His final appearance in the tenth season episode "Bart the Mother" is dedicated to him, as is his final film Small Soldiers. Hartman was preparing to voice Zapp Brannigan, a character written specifically for him on Groening's second animated series Futurama, at the time of his death. Even though the role was specifically made for him, Hartman still insisted on auditioning and Groening said he "nailed it". After Hartman's death, Billy West took over the role. Though executive producer David X. Cohen credits West with using his own take on the character, West later said that he purposely tweaked Zapp's voice to better match Hartman's intended portrayal. Hartman was planning to appear with Lovitz in the indie

Mariticide Club

film The Day of Swine and Roses, scheduled to begin production in August 1998. In 2002, Laugh.com and Hartman's brother John published the album Flat TV, a selection of comedy sketches recorded by Hartman in the 1970s, which had been kept in storage. John Hartmann commented: "I'm putting this out there because I'm dedicating my life to fulfilling his dreams. This [album] is my brother doing what he loved." Flat TV was optioned for an animated adaptation by Michael "Ffish" Hemschoot's animation company Worker Studio in 2013. The deal came about after Michael T. Scott, a partner in the company, posted online a handwritten letter he had received from Hartman in 1997, leading to a correspondence between Scott and Paul Hartmann. A campaign was started on Facebook by Alex Stevens in 2007, and endorsed by Hartman's brother Paul, to have Phil inducted to Canada's Walk of Fame. Among the campaign's numerous publicity events, Ben Miner of the Sirius XM Radio channel Laugh Attack dedicated the month of April 2012 to Hartman. The campaign ended in success and Hartman was inducted on September 22, 2012, to the Walk of Fame, with Paul accepting the award on his late brother's behalf. Hartman was also awarded the Cineplex Legends Award. In June 2013, it was announced that Hartman would receive a star on the Hollywood Walk of Fame, which was unveiled on August 26, 2014. Additionally, a special prize at the Canadian Comedy Awards was named for Hartman. Beginning with the 13th Canadian Comedy Awards in 2012, the Phil Hartman Award was awarded to "an individual who helps to better the Canadian comedy community". In 2015, Rolling Stone magazine ranked Hartman as one of the ten greatest Saturday Night Live cast members throughout the show's fortyyear history, coming in seventh on its list of all 141 members.

Catherine Hayes

Wives Who Kill

Contemporary illustration of Catherine Hayes being burned at the stake.
Catherine Hayes (1690 – 9 May 1726), sometimes spelled Catharine Hayes, was an English woman who was burned at the stake for committing petty treason by killing her husband. Catherine Hall was born near Birmingham in 1690, the daughter of poor parents. At the age of 16, she obtained employment as a servant within the household of a Warwickshire farmer named Hayes. The son of this household was 21-year-old John Hayes, who worked as a carpenter, and who soon fell in love with her. Within a year of their acquaintance, the two were married. Several years into their marriage, the couple moved to London and set up a small shop in Oxford Road, Tyburn, while renting lodgings. Hayes also became a successful pawnbroker, and his wife would bear 12 children. Catherine would later claim that her husband was abusive, kept her isolated

Mariticide Club

from church, and murdered their newborn children. Toward the end of 1725, two men named Thomas Wood and Thomas Billings (the latter the couple's biological son, adopted out) lodged with the couple. Having been promiscuous since her mid-teens, Hayes began conducting affairs with both men, and the trio soon decided to kill John Hayes. On 1 March 1726, they persuaded him to partake in a drinking contest, then killed him once he was intoxicated. The trio then dismembered Hayes's body, subsequently discarding many of his body parts in a pond at Marylebone. The head was cast into the River Thames and was found the next day. It was displayed in the churchyard of St Margaret's, Westminster, for several days, which resulted in John Hayes being identified. On 24 March, the trunk and limbs were discovered. Catherine Hayes and Billings had meanwhile been arrested on a warrant. Wood was captured shortly afterwards, and confessed. Billings then admitted his complicity, but Hayes denied all knowledge of the murder. At the trial, Hayes pleaded 'not guilty', but was convicted of petty treason, and sentenced to be burned at the stake. Wood and Billings were sentenced to be hanged. The case excited much popular attention, and many noblemen and gentlemen attended the trial. Before 9 May, the day fixed for the execution, Wood died in Newgate Prison. Hayes unsuccessfully tried to poison herself. On 9 May, she was tied to a stake at Tyburn with a halter affixed round her neck. After 1652, it was the practice in these cases to strangle the condemned woman on a low gibbet before covering her with faggots and setting the stake alight; however, the execution of Hayes was to be botched. One early report stated that "the executioner was foiled in an endeavor to strangle her by the burning of the rope, and the woman was finally killed by a piece of wood which was thrown at her head and dashed out her brains". Later it was stated that Hayes was "the last woman in England to be burnt alive for petty treason (though the burning of women's bodies after execution continued until 1790". Billings was hanged in chains in Marylebone Fields. Ballads were written about Hayes' crime, and a correspondent of the London Journal compared the murder of John Hayes to the play Arden of Feversham. William Makepeace Thackeray based his story of Catherine,

Wives Who Kill

which first appeared in Fraser's Magazine 1839–40, on the career of Catherine Hayes. The story of John and Catherine Hayes was told in the 28 October 1953 episode of the CBS radio series Crime Classics entitled "John Hayes, His Head, and How They Were Parted." Catherine Hayes was portrayed by Betty Harford. John Hayes was played by Alistair Duncan.

Mary Hobry

Mary Hobry (sometimes spelled Mary Hobrey/Aubrey) (d. 1688) was a 17th-century midwife living in England, convicted for murdering her abusive husband and burnt at the stake. Mary Hobry was a French Catholic midwife living in London. She was married to Denis Hobry in 1684. Her husband was a drunkard, squandered the money she earned and frequently used to beat her up. She sought for his approval to their mutual separation but her husband disagreed. She reportedly considered suicide and running away from him. Fed up of the constant beatings, Hobry told her husband that if he did not change, she "would kill him". On the night of 27 January 1687, Denis returned home inebriated at five in the morning, punched Mary in her stomach, forced himself upon her and, when she resisted, beat her up violently causing her to bleed. When he was sleeping Hobry strangled him with his garter, decapitated him and chopped off his limbs. His son suggested her not to throw the body parts in river. She threw the torso on a dunghill at some distance from her house and the head and limbs in separate privies in the Savoy Palace. Mary was arrested after the identity of the deceased was discerned from the body parts and she was arraigned at the Old Bailey on 22 February. She pled guilty and the following day was sentenced to be burnt. Hobry's act caused a sensation in England and her trial and confession were reported in pamphlets and a ballad was made on her crime. She was burnt at the stake on 2 March 1688. Roger L'Estrange published A Hellish Murder based on his interrogation with her. An Epilogue to the French Midwife's Tragedy was poet Elkanah Settle's interpretation of the murder.

Mariticide Club

Lady Agnes Hungerford

Agnes, Lady Hungerford (died 20 February 1523) was a murderer and the second wife of Sir Edward Hungerford. When he died in 1522, Agnes was then charged and convicted of the murder of her first husband, John Cotell. She was hanged at Tyburn in 1523. Agnes was the widow of John Cotell, the steward of Sir Edward Hungerford. Agnes strangled her first husband at Farleigh Castle on 26 July 1518, with the aid of William Mathewe and William Inges, yeomen of Heytesbury, Wiltshire. She married Sir Edward after her first husband's body was burned in the castle kitchens. Her second husband may have been involved in the murder, or protected his wife from arrest during his lifetime. Her second husband died 24 January 1522 and Agnes was the sole executrix of his will. Around this time, proceedings were taken against Agnes and her accomplices for the murder of her first husband. She and Mathewe were convicted and hanged at Tyburn on 20 February 1523; she is likely buried in the Grey Friars' Church in London. After she died, Agnes' family left her out of documents such as genealogies due to her notoriety.

Jane Hurshman Corkum

Jane Hurshman Corkum (January 25, 1949 – February 22, 1992) was a Canadian woman best known for having killed her abusive husband Lamont William "Billy" Stafford in 1982, and for being acquitted of his murder. The Crown appealed, concerned with the legal precedent, and Corkum pleaded guilty to manslaughter, receiving a six-month sentence. She was released after two months. February 23, 1992, her body was found in a car on the Halifax waterfront, dead from a single gunshot wound.

In media

- A made-for-television film, Life with Billy was produced in 1994.
- The song Waltz For Jane by Denis Ryan's 5 Pound Spent.

Wives Who Kill

Tamara Ivanyutina (née Tamara Antonovna Maslenko)

Tamara Antonovna Maslenko Ivanyutina "The Kyiv Poisoner"

Tamara Antonovna Ivanyutina (née Maslenko, 1941–1990) was a Soviet serial killer. She was the target of a wide scale investigation in Kyiv during the 1980s. Tamara Maslenko was born in a large family as one of six children, in which her parents always told her that material security is the main thing in life. Although forensic psychiatric examination recognized Ivanyutina as sane, she was noted as self-centered, vindictive and resentful. During the investigations into the poisonings, it turned out that Ivanyutina had been convicted of speculation, and obtained employment in her school by the use of a fake employment record book, because as a former convict she wasn't allowed to work in educational institutions. Chemistry teacher Viktor Stadnik, who suffered from Ivanyutina's actions, noted such traits of her character as "perseverance and arrogance", as well as rudeness and lack of discipline. Between March 17 and 18, 1987, several pupils and employees of School #16 in the Podilskyi District in Kiev were hospitalized with signs of food poisoning. Two children - Sergei Panibrat and Andrei Kuzmenko - and two adults died almost immediately, while the remaining 9 people were in intensive care.

Mariticide Club

Doctors initially suspected influenza or an intestinal infection, but sometime later, the hair began to fall out from the victims, which is not typical for such diseases. Poisoning was suspected, and a criminal investigation and an investigative team was established. The investigators, after interviewing the survivors, found out that they all felt unwell by having lunch the day before in the school cafeteria, after eating kasha and liver. When the question arose if there was quality control in the school canteen, it was found that a dietitian named Natalia Kukharenko (according to other sources - Kukarenko) had died two weeks before the events, according to official data - from a heart disease. However, the circumstances of Kukharenko's death caused doubts in the investigators, and due to this her body was exhumed. As a result of corresponding studies, traces of thallium were found in corpse tissues. After that, searches were carried out for all persons who have access to the kitchen, including in the house Tamara Ivanyutina lived, who worked as a dishwasher in the dining room of School N#16. During the search, a "small but very heavy jar" was found in Ivanyutina's house. It interested operatives and investigators and was sent for examination afterwards. A laboratory study showed that the can contained "Clerici solution" - a highly toxic solution based on thallium used in some branches of geology. Ivanyutina was arrested and initially wrote a confession, confessing to the poisoning in the school canteen on March 16, 1987. The reason for the crime, according to Ivanyutina, was that the sixth graders who dined in the dining room refused to set up tables and chairs, and "she decided to punish them". However, she later stated that the confessions were made up from investigators who pressured her, and refused to give further testimony. Further investigation of the "Ivanyutina-Maslenko-Matzobory case" showed that Ivanyutina and her family (sister and parents) used thallium for poisoning for 11 years (since 1976); and did not poison as a mercenary goal, but simply because of personal dislikes. The family members purchased the substance from a friend who worked at the geological institute, explaining to her that the poison was for killing rats. The acquaintance admitted that for 15 years she had not less than nine times given Ivanyutina, her sister and parents a portion of the substance. At

Wives Who Kill

the beginning of her criminal activities, Ivanyutina poisoned her first husband to get his apartment. After his death, she married a second time, but then poisoned her father-in-law and mother-in-law (died at intervals of two days), later poisoning her second husband in small portions (the purpose was to take possession of her husband parents' house with a plot of land).

In September 1986, Ivanyutina got a job as a dishwasher for the school. According to investigators, she needed this work in order to gain access to food and food waste, since she kept a large farm with pigs and chickens. During her time in the dining room, Ivanyutina poisoned (in addition to the previous poisonings) the school party organizer Ekaterina Arsentyevna Scherban (died) and the chemistry teacher (survived) who prevented her from stealing food from the canteen, and two first and fifth grade students (both survived), who had asked her for the remnants of cutlets for their pets. The investigation proved that Tamara's elder sister, Nina Matzobory, using the same solution, had poisoned her husband and taken possession of their Kiev apartment. Numerous poisonings were committed by their parents as well: in particular, they killed a neighbor in a communal apartment and a cousin, who made remarks about them. While detained, Maria Maslenko explained her life position to her cellmates: "To achieve what you want, you do not need to write complaints, but to treat everybody as friends. But for especially harmful ones, just add poison to food". The geography of the criminal activities of the family was not limited to Ukraine; it was proven that some of the crimes committed by them in the RSFSR; in particular, her father Anton, while in Tula, poisoned his cousin by mixing poison in her moonshine. Also, members of the family also poisoned neighbors' pets. 45-year-old Tamara Ivanyutina, her older sister Nina Matzobory, as well as their parents - Anton Mitrofanovich and Maria Fedorovna Maslenko, appeared before the court on charges of committing numerous poisonings, including fatalities. The investigators and the court found that the family for 11 years, in selfish interests, and also personal hostility, committed numerous murders and attempted murders to kill various persons by poisoning them. According to the current deputy chairman of

Mariticide Club

the Constitutional Court of Ukraine, S.M. Vinokurov, who worked during the investigation as a senior investigator for particularly important cases in the city prosecutor's office in Kiev, proving that this was the largest case of thallium poisonings fixed in the USSR. In total, 40 cases of poisonings committed by the family were proven, 13 of which were fatal. At the same time, the largest number of poisonings (9) and assassination attempts (20) was committed personally by Tamara Ivanyutina. The trial lasted about a year, Ivanyutina did not admit her guilt and refused to apologize to the victims' families. All defendants were found guilty of murder and attempted assassination committed through poisoning. Ivanyutina was sentenced to death and executed in 1990. Her accomplices were sentenced to various terms of imprisonment: Nina was sentenced to 15 years (her further fate is unknown) and their parents to 10 and 13 years, both dying in custody. During the investigation, Ivanyutina admitted that her dream was to buy a GAZ car. She also tried to bribe an investigator, promising him "a lot of gold". Refusing to admit her guilt, she explained at her trial that she did not have "a good upbringing". This unusual case was one of only three confirmed instances of a woman executed in the post-Stalin Soviet Union – the others were the 1979 execution of Antonina Makarova for her activities on the WWII Eastern Front, and the 1983 execution of Berta Borodkina for embezzlement and bribery. Ivanyutina's case is still included in Ukraine's training materials for criminal procedures.

Katarzyna Jancarz
Murder of Edward Jancarz

Jancarz rode in the UK for the Wimbledon Dons between 1977–1982 winning the Internationale at Wimbledon in his first season, and in Poland for Stal Gorzów. He participated in ten Speedway World Championship finals, his highest placing in his first final when he finished on the rostrum in third place after run-off with Russian rider Gennady Kurilenko. He was a member of the Polish Cup winning team of 1969. He won the prestigious Embassy Internationale, at Wimbledon in 1977. After his riding career ended he was a speedway coach. He was trainer in Stal

Wives Who Kill

Gorzów, KKŻ Krosno and Polish national team. On 11 January 1992 he was fatally stabbed by his second wife, Katarzyna, during a domestic dispute caused by his alcoholism he had suffered from since the mid-1980s. Since his death the Memorial has been a semi-annual meeting at the speedway that carries his name, the Edward Jancarz Stadium in Gorzów Wielkopolski. To date, 2010 World Champion Tomasz Gollob is the only Polish rider to win the memorial, having done so in 1998 and 1999.

Edward 'Ed' Jancarz (20 August 1946 – 11 January 1992)
was a Polish international speedway rider.

Mariticide Club

Jancarz' Monument

Edward Jancarz was the first speedway rider in the World to have a monument dedicated to them. The Monument of Edward Jancarz was built in 2005 and is in the city center of Gorzów Wielkopolski.

India Juliana

Modern depiction of the India Juliana, used in the logo of a Paraguayan indigenous women's organization.

Juliana (pronounced [xu 'lja na]), better known as the India Juliana (Spanish for "Indian Juliana" or "Juliana the Indian"), is the Christian name of a Guaraní woman who lived in the newly founded Asunción, in early-colonial Paraguay, known for killing

Wives Who Kill

a Spanish colonist between 1539 and 1542. She was one of the many indigenous women who were handed over to or stolen by the Spanish, forced to work for them and bear children. Since the area was not rich in minerals as they had anticipated, colonists generated wealth through the forced labor of indigenous people—especially the sexual exploitation of women of childbearing age. The story of the India Juliana comes from the 1545 accounts of adelantado Álvar Núñez Cabeza de Vaca—who briefly ruled the territory between 1542 and 1544—as well as those of his scribe Pero Hernández. According to these sources, the India Juliana poisoned a Spanish settler named Ñuño de Cabrera—either her husband or her master—with herbs and was released despite having confessed to the crime. Upon his arrival to Asunción, Cabeza de Vaca reportedly found out about her case, and that she even boasted of her actions to her peers. In response, he ordered her execution by dismemberment, as a punishment for the crime and a warning to other indigenous women not to do the same. The India Juliana is regarded as one of the most prominent figures in the women's history of Paraguay, and her inciting other women to also kill their masters has been considered one of the earliest recorded indigenous uprisings of the era. Numerous versions of her story have emerged with various ideological connotations. Although the core of her story is usually the same, the accounts differ in details such as the date of the events, the way in which she killed Cabrera and the method with which she was executed. Although some have considered the India Juliana a collaborator of the Spanish and a builder of the Paraguayan nation, others claim her as a rebel and a symbol of indigenous resistance to colonization. Several modern interpretations describe her as an early feminist, with her figure being claimed by activists and academics. The story of the India Juliana has been the subject of numerous historical fiction works. A street in Asunción bears her name since 1992, one of the few named after an indigenous individual instead of a community as a whole.

Mariticide Club

Two engravings from 1599 illustrating explorer Ulrich Schmidl's chronicles of 1534–1554 in the Río de la Plata basin, depicting the indigenous Cario people (left) and a battle between them and Spanish colonists (right). Juliana is one of the few Cario women to be referred to in colonial sources with a (Christian) name. The first Spanish expeditions to establish settlements in Paraguay were motivated by the mistaken belief that it was a region of mineral wealth, particularly gold. In 1537, the military fort Nuestra Señora de la Asunción was founded by Juan de Salazar y Espinoza on the coast of the Paraguay River. After their encounter with the local Guaraní people, the Spanish established pacts with the caciques sealed with the delivery of women. Initially, giving women to the colonists was done under the framework of cuñadazgo, a concept through which Guaraní leaders created pacts of peace and mutual benefit, as it transformed the recipient in brother-in-law or son-in-law. Since the Spanish treatment of the Guaraní was not one of reciprocity but one of domination, these initial exchanges were soon followed by indigenous uprisings, with at least three violent situations recorded in 1538–1539, 1542–1543, and 1545–1546. The context in which the India Juliana's case took place has historically been called "Muhammad's paradise" (Spanish: "Paraíso de Mahoma"), referring to the "promiscuous" regime of sexual slavery to which indigenous women were subjected during the 1540s. In an account from 1541, colonist Domingo Martínez de Irala detailed that 300

Wives Who Kill

indigenous women lived in Asunción, who were handed over by the Cario people to serve the Spanish.

In 1541, the initial Spanish settlement of Buenos Aires—built on the coast of the Río de la Plata—was abandoned in the face of attacks from indigenous peoples, and its inhabitants moved to Asunción, which was officially founded as a city by Irala on what was once the fort. From then on, the settlement received a much larger number of Spaniards and became the center of the Spanish colonization of the southern half of South America. After discovering that the region actually lacked gold, colonists realized they could generate and accumulate wealth through the forced labor and slavery of indigenous people, especially the sexual exploitation of women of childbearing age. Mass indigenous deportations known as rancheadas took place, in which women were extracted from their communities and forced to work for the colonists. The violent rancheadas began to replace the initial period of cuñadazgo around 1543, and became generalized two years later. The native women, enslaved as servants and mothers of the mestizos, quickly became a piece of merchandise. Asunción then became a center for the deportation of indigenous slaves, supplying a human trafficking market between the city and the Portuguese port of São Vicente on the coast of Brazil.

Based in Asunción, Irala had been ruling the Governorate of New Andalusia—which was in charge of the colonization of the Río de la Plata Basin—since 1538, being elected by his peers after the appointed governor Juan de Ayolas went missing in an expedition. When the news of Ayolas' probable death reached the Spanish Court, explorer Álvar Núñez Cabeza de Vaca was named second adelantado of the Governorate, arriving to Asunción on March 11, 1542, and taking power from Irala. Upon arrival, Cabeza de Vaca "tried to establish order and discipline among the soldiers and settlers of Asunción, declaring himself protector of the [indigenous peoples]." After a failed expedition looking for a route to Peru in 1542, the discontent among the Spanish settlers led to a conspiracy led by Irala against him in 1544, re-electing the latter as governor. Cabeza de Vaca was arrested with the excuse of being too "permissive with the natives", and

Mariticide Club

sent to Spain as a prisoner. The practice of rancheadas became widespread with Irala's second government, with researcher Guillaume Candela describing them as: "without any doubt the most effective acculturation phenomenon of the conquest. Entire villages were emptied of their procreative forces, thus marking an evident trauma in the lives of the affected [indigenous people]."
Original account

Portrait of adelantado Álvar Núñez Cabeza de Vaca, who introduced the India Juliana in a 1545 account presented to the Council of the Indies. Although the historical references about the India Juliana are brief, they establish a strong counterpoint with the more usual representations of Guaraní women in the early-colonial sources of the Río de la Plata region. The main source comes from an account that Cabeza de Vaca presented to the Council of the Indies in December 1545 as judicial evidence, known as Comentarios. The text was actually written by Cabeza de Vaca's scribe Pero Hernández, at the former's request. Returning to Spain as a prisoner in 1545, Cabeza de Vaca entered into a legal dispute with the Council of the Indies that lasted

Wives Who Kill

almost eight years, in which he received a harsh sentence. In 1555, after resolving his legal problems and cleaning up his image, and upon receiving the pertinent royal authorization, Cabeza de Vaca published La relación y comentarios del gobernador Álvar Núñez cabeza de vaca de lo acaecido en las dos jornadas que hizo a las Indias, which compiled the Comentarios along with a previous account from 1542 known as Naufragios. However, he chose to omit the India Juliana passage from the book, along with other parts of the account that evidenced his use of violence, so as to "avoid any statement that allows a double reading". Section "XLII" of the original 1545 Comentarios read:

At the time I arrived in [Asunción], I was informed that an Indian named Juliana, a native of said land, had poisoned a Christian named Ñuño de Cabrera, and that Domingo de Irala had held her prisoner and had prosecuted her, and having verified the crime by confession of said Juliana, saying that out of jealousy she had of said Nuño de Cabrera, she had given him poison by which he died, and at the time [the men of Asunción] learned that I was coming they released her and said Juliana left, and to all the other Indian women who served the Christians she told that only she was the brave one who had killed her husband; which after coming to my notice I ordered to search for and arrest the said Juliana, and imprisoned, she again proceeded to confess the crime, and the said Domingo de Irala came to beg me to release her at the request of a Sancho de Salinas, his friend, first cousin of said Nuño de Cabrera, who was fond of said Juliana; I decried and reprimanded him, as well as the said Domingo de Irala as well as the said Sancho de Salinas, and by virtue of the process my mayor did justice to it, because in addition to deserving it, he agreed to remove the audacity that [other women] did not dare to such cases. An earlier reference to Juliana's case—albeit without mentioning her name—is an account authored by Hernández, dated to January 28, 1545, in which he denounced the crimes committed in the Governorate since the disappearance of governor Ayolas. In two sections of the text, Hernández referred to the India Juliana's case: ... a Christian Indian woman killed Nuño Cabrera, her

Mariticide Club

master, Cazalla's neighbor, with herbs, and Pero Díaz, her mayor, arrested her and proceeded; the Indian confessed to the crime, and at the request of Sancho de Salinas, the deceased's cousin, the Indian was released, and she left without punishment. (...)

The Governor proceeded ex officio against the Indian woman who killed her master with herbs and ordered her to be arrested and was imprisoned and by virtue of her confession of what was contained in the first process that was accumulated with the second she was sentenced to death and was quartered. Cabeza de Vaca's account of the India Juliana intended to expose the "chaos" that Irala's policies had caused in the colony, especially the promiscuity of the Spaniards with indigenous women, and to sanction these behaviors, demonstrating his "moral superiority and civilizing capacity". According to researcher Gabriela Schvartzman, the "argument of jealousy and the alleged love relationship that Juliana had with a cousin of her husband who was also close friends with Irala, are the plot that allows this interpretation." Schvartzman also noted that the story also has a "second moral" related to the disrespect of women to the sexual system imposed by the colonists. By writing that the India Juliana told the other women that she had been the only brave one to have dared to kill her master, Cabeza de Vaca implied that this made her proud and affirmed, and that she urged others to do the same. In this sense, researcher Silvia Tieffemberg felt that her revenge "crossed ethnic and gender barriers simultaneously." Based on Cabeza de Vaca's original account, several different and contradictory versions of the India Juliana's story have emerged over time, some of them through history works and others through literary works. Depending on the ideological position, some discourses portray her as a warrior and an icon of indigenous resistance, while others describe her as an enthusiastic builder of the Paraguayan nation and a facilitator of the union with the Spanish. Although versions differ in details such as the year of the events (between 1539 and 1542), how she killed Cabrera or the way in which she was executed, the core of the story is generally the same: she killed her husband and urged other women to do the same, for which she was arrested and later executed as a warning so

Wives Who Kill

that the others do not follow her example. Some nationalist discourses—both on the right and on the political left—emphasize the "bellicose character" of the India Juliana who, "in the style of the 'heroes of the homeland', wields the sword or the dagger to kill the Spanish enemy and defend the dignity of the Paraguayan nation, but not of the Guaraní people". Argentine historian Enrique de Gandía cited Cabeza de Vaca's account in his 1932 book Indios y conquistadores en el Paraguay, which in turn was cited by Paraguayan historian Carlos Pastore in La lucha por la tierra en Paraguay (1972), in which he described the "conspiracy of the India Juliana". Based on the fact that the she urged other indigenous women to also kill their masters, the India Juliana is commonly regarded as a Guaraní warrior that led an uprising of indigenous women against the Spanish rule. The rebellion of the India Juliana can thus be regarded as one of the earliest recorded indigenous uprisings against the Spanish rule. Several of these interpretations describe the India Juliana as the daughter of a cacique, as were the women who were handed over as part of the initial pacts between natives and conquerors. In his 1963 book Formación histórica de la Nación Paraguaya, Argentine professor Oscar Creydt mentions the "uprising of the female servants under the leadership of the India Juliana, who died as a heroine, executed". Paraguayan women's historian Idalia Flores de Zarza also described the uprising and execution of the India Juliana in her 1987 work La mujer paraguaya: protagonista de la historia, 1537-1870. Tomo I, although she claimed that she died by hanging. Most modern historians generally draw on these bibliographic sources, including the Argentines Felipe Pigna and Loreley El Jaber. Historian Roberto A. Romero's version—detailed in his 1995 book La revolución comunera del Paraguay—places the episode in 1542, writing: "Guaraní women were the protagonists of the great conspiracy against the Spanish colonizers, led by the India Juliana (...). She killed her Spanish husband Ñuño Cabrera and went out to walk the streets of the city, inciting the natives to do the same with their European husbands to end all the conquerors. The conspiracy was overpowered and (...) the Guaraní heroine died by hanging". Pigna

Mariticide Club

dedicated a section to the India Juliana in his 2012 women's history book Mujeres que tenían que ser, in which he claims that she cut off Cabrera's head on Maundy Thursday 1539 and her incitement caused her companions to follow her example, all of them ending up tortured and hanged. The story of the India Juliana has been the subject of historical fiction works. Uruguayan writer Eduardo Galeano mentions her case in his 1982 book Memoria del fuego. In his short story "Primeras Letras. Jueves Santo, 1539", Helio Vera portrays the India Juliana as a naive girl that falls in love with Juan de Salazar and reveals a 1539 indigenous rebellion planned for Maundy Thursday, betraying her people. This vision of the India Juliana has been described as a "Guaraní Malinche". In "¡Arde Juliana, arde!", a short story by Gloria Muñoz, Juliana's case is also set on Maundy Thursday, but in 1540; in it, she incites a rebellion of indigenous women, although the others back off and she is burned at the stake. Some versions also claim that she was beheaded. One of the facts that was made the most invisible is that the India Juliana killed Nuño de Cabrera by poisoning, with later versions indicating that it was with a sword or dagger, by beheading, or by using his own weapons. Poisoning was traditionally associated with women in the Old World and, in the Río de la Plata region, it was used effectively in the arrows of Guaraní and Timbú warriors. Schvartzman noted: "She killed him with weeds, with herbs from the mountains, those that her grandmothers used for thousands of years to heal, but which, depending on the dose, are also useful for killing. (...) She didn't kill him with force, she killed him with her knowledge, which after all is the greatest power of women in all time." Some interpretations have cast doubt on the historical existence of the India Juliana, considering her a legendary figure in the manner of Anahí, a mythical Guaraní princess. Nevertheless, these claims have been dismissed, as the contemporary writings of Cabeza de Vaca and Hernández account for her existence. Reflecting on this, Schvartzman wrote: The discourse that affirms the real non-existence of the India Juliana, or that questions this fact based on the non-existence or ignorance of reliable historical documents or records, is presented as a pretext for the invisibility of

Wives Who Kill

indigenous resistance, especially of women. It reinforces the idea that the relations between Spaniards and indigenous people, during the conquest and colonization, were relations without conflict, peaceful and even loving. (...)

Juliana's story as a traitor to her people or in love with her oppressor seems to have no support, and may be only a fiction that carries a colonialist and patriarchal discourse. Not looking for India Juliana, or not looking for her enough, are indicators that measure the interest in finding her, in making her visible, they finally constitute a political position both for those who act in the field of historical and social research, as well as for those who act from the women's movements and feminism.

Escuela India Juliana, Paraguayan indigenous women's organization named after the Guaraní rebel. Her figure is claimed by modern feminist activists and academics. Today, the figure of the India Juliana is claimed both as a historical defender of the indigenous peoples, as well as a symbol of the emancipation of women. Several contemporary authors consider the India Juliana to be an early feminist, and several feminist groups, schools, libraries and centers for the promotion of indigenous women in Paraguay are named after her. Writer Andrés Colmán Gutiérrez of Última Hora noted that the she is "carried as a banner" in the annual demonstrations of International Women's Day and the International Day for the Elimination of Violence against Women, and described her as "perhaps the first feminist indigenous Guaraní heroine, a rebel against the macho and patriarchal culture, who denies the sugarcoated official

Mariticide Club

story about the Spanish conquest in Paraguay". The figure of the India Juliana has been reclaimed as a foremother by Paraguayan academics and activists as part of a process of "recovery of feminist and women's genealogies" in South America, intended to move away from the Eurocentric vision. The same has happened in Ecuador with Dolores Cacuango and Tránsito Amaguaña; in the central Andes region with Bartolina Sisa and Micaela Bastidas; and in Argentina with María Remedios del Valle and Juana Azurduy.The government of Asunción established the India Juliana street in 1992. It is one of the few streets in the city named after an indigenous individual rather than an entire community, along with other figures such as the caciques Arecayá and Lambaré, and the servant Indio Francisco. Although the decision to name a street after an indigenous person was celebrated, the resolution has been controversial, since it credits the India Juliana with collaborating as a guide to the colonists, regarding her as a "cultural mother" in the sense of helping the union between both cultures. Considered one of the most prominent figures in the women's history of Paraguay, the image of India Juliana has been invoked in consumer products such as T-shirts or beers. In 2020, her story was adapted into a comic book released by Paraguayan publishing house Servilibro, as part of the collection "Mundo guaraní". Written by professor María Gloria Pereira and illustrated by Daniel Ayala Medina, the comic portrays her as a Guaraní heroine against Spanish domination, and uses the name Arapy as her original native name, which variously means "world", "universe", "space" or "firmament" in the Guaraní language. Paraguayan singer-songwriter Claudia Miranda included a song about the India Juliana in her 2020 debut studio album Las brujas, which was made with the support of the organization Centro de Documentación y Estudios (Spanish for "Center for Documentation and Studies" [CDE]).

Wives Who Kill

Chisako Kakehi

Chisako Kakehi (born 28 November 1946) is a Japanese serial killer who was sentenced to death for the murders of three men, including her husband, and for the attempted murder of a fourth. She is also suspected of being responsible for at least seven other deaths. Kakehi was arrested in 2014, after an autopsy on her fourth husband, Isao Kakehi, revealed traces of cyanide poisoning.

She initially pleaded not guilty, but during her 2017 trial, confessed, stating on the witness stand that she had no intention of hiding the guilt and wanted to kill her husband out of deep hatred; two days later, she retracted this confession, claiming to not remember having said it. Her lawyers subsequently argued that she suffered from dementia and could not be convicted due to diminished responsibility. In June 2021, the Supreme Court of Japan rejected her final appeal. One of the judges explained the decision based on Chisako's "ruthless crime(s) based on a planned and strong murderous intention."

Charlotte Kauffmann

San Francisco Conference from 25 April 1945 to 26 June 1945

Mariticide Club

Henrik Kauffmann in 1932

I obtained the autograph of Henrik Kauffman for my scrapbook, among others, before being summarily ushered out of the War Memorial Opera House, when I attended the United Nations Conference on International Organization (UNCIO) San Francisco Conference including delegates from 50 Allied nations that took place from 25 April 1945 to 26 June 1945 in San Francisco, California. Unfortunately, my scrapbook was tossed and lost forever during reduction of possessions by my parents wbefore moving from Berkeley to retirement in Oregon. At this convention, the delegates reviewed and rewrote the Dumbarton Oaks agreements of the previous year. The convention resulted in the creation of the United Nations Charter, which was opened for signature on 26 June, the last day of the conference. The conference was held at various locations, primarily the War Memorial Opera House, with the Charter being signed on 26 June at the Herbst Theatre in the Veterans Building, part of Civic Center. A square adjacent to Civic Center, called "UN Plaza", commemorates the conference.

Henrik Kauffmann (26 August 1888 – 5 June 1963) was the Danish ambassador to the United States during World War II, who signed over part of Greenland to the US. Kauffmann started his foreign career by serving as envoy in Rome, 1921–1923. He afterwards served in Peking in 1924–1932 when he was succeeded by Oscar O'Neill Oxholm. During this period Kauffmann became notable for three things: political reports of high quality; an ability to gain close contacts with central Chinese decision makers; and his lavish spending. After his time in Peking, Kauffmann served as envoy in Oslo 1932–1939 (when he was, again, succeeded by Oxholm), where he helped soften the Danish-Norwegian relations following the Greenland case. On 9 April 1941, the anniversary of the German occupation of Denmark, he signed on his own initiative "in the Name of the King" (Danish: I Kongens Navn) an "Agreement relating to the Defense of Greenland" authorizing the United States to defend the Danish colonies on Greenland from German aggression. The treaty was signed by the United States Secretary of State Cordell Hull and approved

Wives Who Kill

by President Franklin D. Roosevelt on 7 June 1941. Kauffmann's treaty was approved by the local officials on Greenland but declared void by the Danish government in Copenhagen. Kauffmann ignored this protest, citing the fact that Denmark was occupied by a hostile power; consequently, he considered the government incapable of protecting Danish interests. The government responded by charging Kauffmann with high treason and stripping him of his rank. Kauffmann ignored both actions. Kauffmann's line was supported by the Danish consuls general in the United States, as well as by the Danish ambassador to Iran. These diplomats were dismissed as well. Kauffmann replied by urging Danish diplomats around the world not to follow instructions from Copenhagen.

Kauffmann was nicknamed "the King of Greenland" for his independent political moves in the Greenland affair. He was married to Charlotte MacDougall, the daughter of United States Navy Rear Admiral William Dugald MacDougall. Revoking the sentence against Kauffmann was one of the first tasks done by the Danish Parliament following the Liberation of Denmark in May 1945. Kauffmann joined the Cabinet of National Unity and served as Minister without Portfolio from 12 May to 7 November 1945. While Kauffmann was unable to get Denmark to sign the Declaration by United Nations during the war, he was able as minister to join the San Francisco Conference from 25 April 1945 to 26 June 1945 and sign the Charter. Kauffmann's treaty was adapted in the early 1950s and remains the legal basis for the U.S. Thule Air Base in Greenland. In June 1963, Kauffmann, suffering from prostate cancer, was killed by his wife in a "mercy killing". His wife, Charlotte, then took her own life. The film The Good Traitor (Vores mand i Amerika) released in 2020, covers the signing of the agreement over Greenland between Henrik Kauffmann and the United States. Kauffmann is played by Ulrich Thomsen.

Jean Kincaid (née Jean Livingston)

Jean Kincaid (1579–5 July 1600) was a Scottish woman who was convicted of murdering her husband. Jean was the daughter of John Livingstoun of Dunipace, born in 1579 as Jean Livingston. She married John Kincaid of

Mariticide Club

Warriston, a man of influence in Edinburgh, related to the Kincaids of Stirlingshire, who owned huge estates in Midlothian and Linlithgowshire. In Early Modern Scotland married women did not adopt their husband's surnames. Owing to alleged maltreatment, she conceived a deadly hatred for her husband soon after being married, and a nurse who lived in her house urged her to take revenge. Robert Weir, a servant of her father, and her reputed lover, was admitted by Jean Kincaid into her husband's chamber in his house at Warriston at an early hour on the morning of 1 July 1600, and he gripped John Kincaid tightly around the throat and held him for a long time until he was dead. News of the murder quickly reached Edinburgh, and "the Lady Warristoun", "the fause nourise", and her two "hyred women", were arrested "red-handed". Weir escaped, refusing to allow Jean Kincaid to accompany him in his flight. Roger Aston, a courtier, sent news of the murder to England, mentioning that Weir was the servant who kept Dunipace's horse. Jean Kincaid and the other prisoners were immediately brought before the magistrates of Edinburgh, and a sentence of death was passed upon them. No official records of the trial are extant. Birrel wrote that: *Scho was tane to the girth-crosse, upon the 5 day of July, and her head struck from her body, at the Cannagait-fit; quha deit very patiently. Her nurische was brunt at the same tyme, at 4 houres in the morneing, the 5 of July.* According to Calderwood's History of the Kirk of Scotland, "the nurse and ane hyred woman, her complices, were burnt in the Castell Hill of Edinburgh". In the brief interval between the sentence and execution Jean Kincaid was brought, by the efforts of a clergyman, from a state of callous indifference to one of religious resignation. Weir, who was arrested three years afterwards, was broken on a cart wheel next to the Mercat Cross in Edinburgh, on 26 June 1603. The hangman used the coulter of a plough. This was a rare mode of execution in Scotland. A "memorial" of her "conversion…with an account of her carriage at her execution," by an eyewitness, was privately printed at Edinburgh in 1827, from a paper preserved among Wodrow's manuscripts. in the Advocates' Library, by Charles Kirkpatrick Sharpe. The youth and beauty of Mrs. Kincaid were dwelt upon in numerous popular ballads, which are to be

Wives Who Kill

found in Jamieson's, Kinloch's, and Buchan's collections. The songs variously ascribe blame to the husband, the wife, or the devil. "The death of Lord Warriston" is a ballad printed by Francis James Child (Child 194); Buchan's version is also in the Oxford Book of Ballads (1969).

Gladys Kelly

State v. Kelly, 97 N.J. 178; 478 A.2d 364 (1984), is a Supreme Court of New Jersey case where the defendant, Gladys Kelly, was on trial for the murder of her husband, Ernest Kelly with a pair of scissors. The Supreme Court reversed the case for further trial after finding that expert testimony regarding the defense's submission, that Kelly suffered from battered woman syndrome, was incorrectly excluded since battered woman syndrome was a proper subject for expert evidence. Kelly was represented by Charles S. Lorber who is now with Mandelbaum Salsburg of West Orange N.J. This is a notable case, both regarding the role of experts in new fields and in trials where the battered woman defense may be advanced, as is demonstrated by it being cited in other states, by universities, and by the US Government. Further, it is cited as one of the notable opinions by Chief Justice Robert Wilentz.

Lizzie Lloyd King aka Elizabeth Lloyd King, Betsy King, Kate Stoddard, Kate Stoddart, Alice Howard, Minnie Waltham, Amy Snow, Amy Stone, Amy Gilmore, Amy G.

Mariticide Club

An 1873 profile of Lizzie Lloyd King from the Canadian Illustrated News

Elizabeth Lloyd King (born 1847) was the murderer of Charles Goodrich, whom she is said to have shot three times in the head on 20 March 1873 in Brooklyn, New York, United States. The murder was headline news in the city, until her capture more than three months after the event. Her inquest drew large crowds, and prisoner church sermons drew requests for attendance from the general public, some of whom were granted entry. After a year in jail, a psychological assessment deemed that she was unfit to stand trial, and she was committed to a life sentence at the State Lunatic Hospital at Auburn. Her inquest was held on the same day and at the same court as that for Mary Ann Dwyer, who had murdered her three children, making the story even more sensational for the New York press. The Times story headline the next day was "TWO INSANE WOMEN". The chief of police who handled her case, Patrick Campbell, would recall her case

Wives Who Kill

decades later as "a great one", and one of the most memorable of his career. King was described as a "remarkable woman", who was "attractive in face, manner and figure, and was a fine musician". She was also intelligent: When she was eighteen, she commenced to go to school again; she studied very hard, graduated at the head of her class of fourteen or fifteen girls. — The New York Times

The Taunton Lunatic Asylum, now known as the
Taunton State Hospital.

King was born Elizabeth Lloyd King in Plymouth, Massachusetts to Isaac B. King and Harriet A. Hoyt, and had an older sister. She was described to have a normal childhood, for which her mother could not recall King as having "ever said an immodest word". After puberty, "she grew more and more unnatural and strange", and led a troubled youth, leaving and returning to school at her whim. When in school, she did well in her studies. She left home shortly afterward. On 25 April 1867, a probate court in Boston committed her to the Taunton Lunatic Asylum, during which time she was also known as Alice Howard. Her attending physician was Norton Folsom, who indicated the "form of her disease was mania, which was manifested by excitement, irascibility, incoherence of speech and violent conduct", and that her condition was "caused by some disease peculiar to females". He indicated that by 10 May 1867, she appeared better. She was discharged on 10 September 1867. From then until 1873, she worked as a milliner and teacher in New York City, Philadelphia, and Hartford, not returning to her hometown during this period. In New

Mariticide Club

York City, she roomed with Mary Handley at 45 Elizabeth Street from February 1872, until late June or early July of that year. Handley knew King by the name Kate Stoddard, an alias in recent use by her, and the name by which she was commonly known at the time. She was an inmate of the Working Women's Home, and worked as a milliner making straw bonnets at a warehouse on the corner of Broadway and Spring Street. King met Charles Goodrich after responding to a personal ad in a newspaper, identifying herself to him as Kate Stoddard. A relationship between King and the widower Goodrich ensued, established no later than early 1872. In a letter to Goodrich from early 1872, King refers to him as "my dear Charlie". She would write seven more letters to Goodrich between then and March 1873, and he would write to her five times. She would sign her letters to him using the alias Amy, or sometimes Kate. The letters indicate that the two had married on 20 May 1872, after which her letters to him are addressed "my dearest husband". Goodrich always addressed King as "Amy" in his letters to her. Her letters revealed that from June 1872 to February 1873, she had been living at a house on Degraw Street. His second letter to her after their marriage states that "it is better for both that we should separate". Goodrich's last letter to King states his intention of providing her with a room in New York City and to aid her financially, if she would cease to refer to herself as his wife, and not mention their relationship to his family. King refused the proposal, and on the evening of 15 February 1873 wrote a letter to his brother William W. Goodrich, sending it to his office. In that letter, King made many revelations, including that she has been living in the third Brownstone house from Fifth Avenue on Degraw Street. Seven units had been built and owned by Charles Goodrich, and were completed in the fall of 1872; he had assumed residence of the unit at 731 Degraw Street. The letter also indicated that Goodrich had married King in what she now knew was a mock marriage, since the clergyman who conducted the ceremony was Reuben Smith, a doctor by trade and a friend of Goodrich. Further, it notes that Goodrich had treated her cruelly, that they had a child in December, and that on the day she wrote her letter,

Wives Who Kill

he had evicted her, throwing her trunks and clothing into another unit. She lamented that she had neither friends nor money, and that "it seems like some dreadful nightmare". She signed the letter Amy G., intended to mean Goodrich. At the urging of his brother, Charles Goodrich temporarily separated from King for about a week, but she had returned to live with him for at least a few days before he was shot. When Goodrich attempted to finally terminate the relationship and evict her from his home, King shot him in the head three times. The murder occurred at his home. King had descended to the basement, with Goodrich following her, during an argument. He insisted that she leave his house, and reiterated that he "would do all he could afford for her". At this, she shot him in the head, dragged his body near the fireplace grate, and cleaned off the blood. A search of the house by police netted a set of letters with "only the Christian name of the writer" (that is, the given name) signed therein. During the first few days of the investigation, it was hypothesized that Goodrich had committed suicide. The post-mortem investigation revealed that he had been shot three times, the "three bullets in the brain...being as fatal to the theory of self-destruction as they were to the victim". Others persisted in the suicide conjecture; the claim was that he shot himself once, and that the person who discovered him shot him twice more to give the appearance of a murder, and then wiped away the blood. By 25 March, this conjecture was abandoned. Despite daily questioning of the neighbors up to 26 March, an accurate account of the events could not be established because they offered conflicting information. It was unanimous that a woman was either visiting or living at Goodrich's house, but little was known about her: We have very little to work on, and there is nobody to give us anything. If this woman has been visiting or stopping at the house, as is alleged, I should think it not unnatural to suppose that somebody should know her name or where she belongs, State or town. Now, I will say emphatically that there is nobody to give any information of this woman, or where she belongs, notwithstanding all that has been stated about letters, and all that. No name is known. I wish it was; the papers would have it mighty quick.
— The New York Times'

Mariticide Club

The neighbors also unanimously endorsed the hypothesis that it was murder, and that the woman was "directly concerned in the affair".

Goodrich's body was removed from his residence at 17:00 on 22 March, placed in a hearse, and transported to Cumberland Street, to the residence of his brother William Goodrich. A funeral service was conducted there on the afternoon of 23 March, and his body was then transported on that evening's train to Albany, where he was buried in a family vault the next day. Three days later, William Goodrich offered a $2,500 reward for the capture of the woman who had sent him the letter. On 2 July 1873, Brooklyn Common Council unanimously adopted the motion to offer another $1,000 in reward for the capture of King, bringing the total reward to $3,500. King had been the primary suspect from the start of the investigation, according to the New York Times:

Yesterday's developments were trivial and unimportant, going only to further establish the undeniable complicity of a woman, and her presence in the house on the night of the murder.

— The New York Times'

The name Kate Stoddard was first considered for suspicion in the murder when a book of poems was found in Goodrich's home by detectives Folk and Videtto during their search for evidence. Her name appeared on one of the pages of that book. By 1 April 1873, several suspects for the murder had been proposed: an Englishman named Barnet or Barrett; a man named James, using the alias "Pop" Tighe, and two other burglars; a Spaniard named Roscoe; and Kate Stoddard, based on several letters that were found during the initial investigation of the crime scene. The suspicion of Roscoe was based on an interview of Lucette Meyers by Chief of Police Patrick Campbell, in which she proposed that Goodrich had been "followed to his house and killed by a man—an enemy". The police efforts were by now being criticized, having failed to apprehend or even nominate a viable suspect. When a New York detective apprehended a Frenchman named Charles Dalzen, of "Hayti, West Indies" (sic),mistakenly believing him to be Roscoe, the New York Times noted:

Wives Who Kill

The clumsy and ineffectual efforts of the Brooklyn detectives were yesterday imitated by a New-York officer.

— The New York Times

Lucette Armstrong had been in jail at this time, unable to make a $1,000 bail. She had refused to divulge information she claimed to know about the murder. The police resorted to using an undercover female detective, labeled a petticoat by the press, "by whose wiles it was confidently expected Mrs. Armstrong would be induced to tell all she is supposed to know about the Goodrich murder". She was placed in the same room as Armstrong, posing as a witness named Lucy in a civil case, but failed to elicit any relevant discussion from Armstrong. Goodrich's father made a request to coroner Whitehill on 19 April 1873 to inspect the pistol used in the murder. He stated that it was not his son's pistol, which "had a white handle, ivory or pearl, while this is wood". The location of the son's pistol was unaccounted. Lucette Meyers corroborated the father's account in May. The burglar conjecture was largely ignored as implausible by this time. Various stories regarding Roscoe were known, and by July 1873, he was deemed an accomplice of King to the murder. Having failed in their search for Stoddard, increasingly the prime suspect in the case, the police hired Mary Handley, making her a detective to the chief of police, paying her a stipend of $2 per day for 40 days. Handley had revealed to the police that she was an "intimate friend" of King's, and had approached the police to assist in searching for her. At first, she dealt with a cold trail as had the other detectives on the case, but after a public tip "relating to the former haunts of Kate Stoddard" was given to the chief, Handley was "put on the track". She made trips to Glen's Falls, Gloversville and Albany, but none were productive.

Mariticide Club

PATRICK CAMPBELL
Superintendent of Police, Brooklyn

Patrick Campbell, Chief of Police of Brooklyn in 1873,
who later became Superintendent of Police for Brooklyn.

By chance, on the afternoon of 8 July 1873 Handley was returning to Brooklyn from Manhattan via the Fulton Ferry, exiting the gates at the ferry dock, when she observed King headed that way, presumably on her way to Manhattan. Handley asked officer Doherty, the on-duty ferry officer, to arrest King. He did so after some persuasion, and took both Handley and King to the Second Precinct Station of the Brooklyn police, at York Street. On the way there, King was seen to discard several letters onto the street, which were collected by the officer. Here, Handley introduced King to Chief Campbell and Captain James McConnell as the fugitive Kate Stoddard. King was interviewed, but denied the charge that she was Kate Stoddard. Campbell noticed a large gold locket pendant from a chain about her neck, and requested to see it. King denied, but Campbell took it anyway. After fumbling with it for some time, it opened, some of its

Wives Who Kill

contents falling to the floor. King picked them up and ate them. They were flakes of desiccated blood. Upon inquiry from the chief, she replied "that's blood—dried blood", then refused to answer any further questions. She was later taken to the Raymond Street Jail. Meanwhile, Campbell inspected the letters, which were addressed to individuals in Manhattan and New Jersey, and inferred that King must reside in Brooklyn. At this time, the police were reticent with the media, not yet having ascertained the identity of the woman. The police had, to their embarrassment, mistakenly arrested Lucette Meyers earlier in the investigation. ... their answers to all questions relating to it varying from weak prevarication to flat denial. Captain McConnell, of the Second Precinct, and his sergeants profess astonishment at being suspected of having charge of any prisoner connected with the Goodrich case; Chief Campbell and his detectives know, or profess to know, nothing of the arrest ...

— The New York Times

Meanwhile, detectives were continuing their search for Roscoe, who was now also considered a myth in some circles, and had summoned Dr. Reuben Smith and Charles Green to the police station. Smith and Green were friends of Charles Goodrich, and had met King during her relationship with Goodrich. This would allow the police to identify the woman in jail as Stoddard, whom they knew to be the author of the Amy G. letters. Her identity was incontrovertibly confirmed by 11 July 1873, and King confessed to being Kate Stoddard and to the murder of Goodrich. She also admitted that she had been boarding at the home of the widow Ann Taylor, at 127 High Street in Brooklyn, a three-story brick house near Jay Street. Taylor's daughter Anna Knight would later testify at the inquest, indicating that King used the alias Minnie Waltham in association with Taylor. King had been living at High Street since the third week of April, continuing to work in Manhattan. By June, however, she discontinued her work commute, instead working from her room at Taylor's house. She had friendly and frequent association with the Taylor family, who were unaware of her true identity; they became concerned about her disappearance on 8 July 1873, but King's friends suggested she had gone to

Mariticide Club

visit her parents, whom she had said lived in Trenton, New Jersey. They learned of her capture by police two days later, when as a result of the confession, an officer was dispatched to Taylor's house. Taylor was brought to the Second Precinct for questioning, where she identified King by her alias Minnie Waltham. Subsequently, a police officer and a detective executed a search of King's room at the Taylor residence, where they found two trunks, one of which contained a watch, pocket book, revolver, a ring, and two seals, all possessions of Goodrich, which were seized as evidence. If the police regarded her confession with doubt, here was corroborative and unmistakable evidence, and in a moment all mystery surrounding the affair had vanished.

— The New York Times

Handley's friends urged her to apply for the reward. By the time she was captured, King had reverted to using the name Lizzie Lloyd King, and had abandoned the Stoddard alias. She was interested in news about herself, and requested the day's papers while in jail. After tea in the prison she was provided, at her own request, with the evening papers, and seating herself under the gas-light in the corridor near the cell, she eagerly read over the reports of the earlier proceedings at the inquest, and all else pertaining to herself.

— The New York Times

An inquest was held on 12 July 1873 at the court house on Livingston Street. Stoddard arrived by carriage with Captain McConnell at 11:00 that morning, but the court room was already full by 10:00, as some had believed the inquest to start at that time. Spectators who wished to attend the inquest thus had to endure several hours of petty cases, or relinquish their seats to those waiting outside. The spectators were therefore forced either to relinquish the advantageous positions gained by early attendance or to listen patiently to the hearing of petty larceny cases for two hours.

— The New York Times

The captain escorted King to coroner Whitehill's office, where they met with the jury in consultation for about an hour. Infrequently, the coroner or a juror would enter the courtroom, causing excitement among those

Wives Who Kill

assembled of the imminent commencement of the inquest, but they returned to the coroner's office almost immediately. At 13:00, the captain entered the courtroom with Mary Handley, causing a "decided sensation, the majority of the spectators evidently mistaking Miss Handley for Kate Stoddard". By this time there was a throng of people in the hallways wishing to enter the courtroom, though "none but reporters, officials, and the influential outside few were admitted" to the already overcrowded courtroom. The jurors entered the courtroom via the clerk's office at 13:10, promptly taking their seats. King entered the courtroom shortly after via the main corridor, accompanied by Captain McConnell and her counsel William C. de Witt, to a great uproar. Nine people provided testimonials to the court. Lucette Meyers, who had been quoted in newspapers regarding the murder, identified King by several of her aliases, including Kate Stoddard, Amy Snow, Amy Stone and Amy Gilmore; "she is called by all of these names". She also identified various articles. Adeline Pabor, who had been engaged to Goodrich for months before the murder, testified that Goodrich had introduced her to King, claiming King was his sister. She also identified articles presented to her. Mary Handley testified next, and stated that she had known King when they had roomed together at an apartment at 45 Elizabeth Street, between February and June or July 1872. At the time, King was known as Kate Stoddard, and made straw bonnets. King then left for the Working-women's Home, and they did not see each other again until Handley spotted King on Fulton Street in Brooklyn, at which time she requested an officer apprehend King. Handley was employed as a detective for chief Campbell at this time. Anna Knight was the fourth person to testify. She indicated that King boarded at a home owned by Knight's mother at 127 High Street, and diligently paid her rent of $2.50 per week despite being "in rather poor circumstances". Knight indicated that King used the alias Minnie Waltham during her stay from April 1873 until her capture. She worked in New York, or sometimes brought it home with her. The father of the victim, David Goodrich, was next to take the stand. He identified various items, but noted that the wooden-handled pistols were not like that owned by his son, which was

Mariticide Club

white-handled. He also noted that in February 1872, a woman brought him a letter, signed Amy G.; he had verified some of the contents of the letter with his son, and advised him that he extricate himself from the position resultant from the association with King. Captain McConnell testified that he had seized a trunk from King's boarding room on High Street, and that it contained the items presented to the court, and two pistols, one of which was used to fire the three shots that killed the victim. He noted that King had been apprehended and brought to the Second Precinct station at noon the previous Tuesday. Charles Green noted that he had spent a night in Goodrich's house with King, during which she penned the letter signed Amy G., and identified the articles presented to the court. General Jourdan, the president of the Board of Police Commissioners, testified that the day before the trial, he had warned King "not to commit herself to the Jury without the advice of counsel". Patrick Campbell, the Chief of Police of Brooklyn, indicated that King had made statements "as to the manner in which Charles Goodrich came to his death", and that she requested that she be called Amy G. during her first interrogation at the police station. He also stated that he had hired Mary Handley as a detective "on account of her personal acquaintance with Kate Stoddard". Finally, King herself was called to the stand, and identified herself as Lizzie Lloyd King, and that she was a bonnet maker. She declined further comment regarding Goodrich, on advice from her counsel, and was dismissed. The jury retired at 16:00, and at 16:30 returned to the courtroom to announce that the testimony was sufficient to render a verdict. They received the usual instructions from the judge, then retired for final deliberations, during which time the courtroom crowd openly discussed the possible outcome.

At 18:00, the jury returned, and rendered the verdict:

We find that the said Charles Goodrich came to his death by pistol-shot wounds in the head, inflicted by Lizzie Lloyd King, alias Kate Stoddard, with intent to cause death, on the evening of the 20th or morning of the 21st of March, 1873, at his aforesaid house on Degraw-street, Brooklyn.

— The New York Times

Wives Who Kill

King was remanded into the custody of sheriff and keeper Courady of the county jail at Raymond Street, where she was assigned to a room by herself on the second floor. Three prisoners at the jail, Fanny Hyde, Mrs. Burgess, and Mrs. Simmons, were assigned to keep constant watch over her to prevent a suicide attempt. Simmons and Burgess were pardoned by the governor on 19 July 1873, and subsequently released from jail and their supervisory duties. Miss Palin, betrothed to Goodrich, visited King on 14 July 1873 and stayed until late in the evening. The police were still looking for Roscoe at this time, and sent a description of him to "the police of all the cities in the United States and Canada". On 22 July 1873, her father and brother-in-law visited her at the jail, with her counsel for the future trial, O.T. Gray of Hyde Park. During the visit, which lasted over three hours, nobody else was allowed into that part of the prison. By this time, her family resided at Walbridge, Massachusetts. Her new counsel, D.B. Thompson, made an application to the court on 2 March 1874 to release himself from "further conduct in the case", citing the actions of King to dismiss various previous counsels, and that "so many embarrassments had been put in their way". Judge Gilbert denied the request, and instructed Thompson and Lowe to act as defense counsel for King. Thompson indicated that although the defense was insanity, "the accused is not now insane, but was insane at the time of the crime, if any crime is proven, was committed". While in jail, she was deemed to be of normal disposition: Her conduct in jail continues without any marked eccentricity, although it is mysteriously whispered among the lower ranks of the police force that the prisoner is insane.

— The New York Times

She was also said to be "pretending to be very religious", reading the Bible and Episcopal prayer book. Dr. Charles Corey examined King sometime in May 1874 to evaluate her psychological condition, and on 21 July 1874 she was committed to State Lunatic Asylum in Auburn, New York. King had stated a preference for the new asylum in Poughkeepsie, and to stay at the Raymond Street Jail until that facility's completion. On 14 July 1874 the District Attorney had sent a letter

Mariticide Club

requesting information about the status of the Poughkeepsie facility, and whether it would be accepting patients. A court investigation into her state of mind concluded on 15 July 1874 that she was not fit for trial, and that an order of commitment would be issued pending a reply from the Poughkeepsie facility. Even when sent to Auburn, she inquired whether she could be transferred to the Poughkeepsie facility upon its completion: "If I go to Auburn now, I wish to know if I can be transferred to Poughkeepsie as soon as there is any room for me there". She continued to read stories about herself, even sending complaint letters to newspapers about inaccuracies in the reports she read. On 17 July 1874, she objected to the wording of the commitment announcement by Judge Moore, noting that he misrepresented the jury's indictment from the inquest: Your Honor's attention I wish to call to the wording of your commitment of me in yesterday's newspapers. It reads that I was indicted for having "feloniously, and willfully, and of her malice aforethought, killed and wounded Charles Goodrich." Please, your Honor, I was present when the indictment was read, July, 1873, and it read: "That Charles Goodrich came to his death by pistol shot wounds in the head, inflicted with intent to cause death."
— The New York Times

A syndicated report in the Oswego Daily Times of 18 May 1880 indicates that at the asylum, King had composed a curious letter: ... by cutting separate letters from a book furnished by the American Bible Society. These were arranged so as to make a readable letter, and then sowed letter by letter, word by word, sentence by sentence, until two full sheets (both sides) were covered. Even the directions on the envelope were wrought in the same way. She resorted to this method in order to carry her purpose, inasmuch as the inmates are prohibited from having either pens, ink, paper, knife or scissors.
— Oswego Daily Times

King was criticizing the New York state "lunacy law" authorizing that those indicted for a crime, but not convicted, be sent to an insane asylum. She considered this an ex post facto law. The letter was given to Alonzo B. Cornell, the Governor of New York.

Wives Who Kill

Neighborhood residents were concerned about "the unpleasant associations" of the name of their street to the murder, that within days they had petitioned to change it to "Lincoln Place", in honor of Abraham Lincoln. The name of the street, between Fifth Avenue and Sixth Avenue, was changed from Degraw Street to Lincoln Place on 15 April 1873 by the Brooklyn Common Council. Eventually, the remainder of the eastward segment, to Prospect Park, was also renamed to Lincoln Place. In May 1873, Goodrich's father filed a lawsuit against Mrs. Finlay of Staten Island. They had an apparent agreement to exchange the brownstone houses owned by Charles Goodrich for the clipper brig Hattie Haskett owned by Finlay. The suit was denied because it was signed by Finlay's husband, who "had not been shown to be an authorized agent for his wife". By 1874, Handley had made an application to claim the $1,000 reward offered by Brooklyn Common Council in June 1873. After the Law Committee of the council heard testimony on 24 November 1874 from Handley, and corroboration from Patrick Campbell and General Jourdan, it passed a resolution recommending the payment of that reward; the committee would present the resolution to council when it next convened. In a book Women Who Kill, Ann Jones argues that women like Lizzie Lloyd King, who are subjugated from childhood and then abandoned by their mates, are capable of engaging in crimes they would not otherwise commit to prevent their own destitution. Their stories are almost interchangeable. Like Amelia Norman and like the typical seduced-and-abandoned maiden sketched in the pages of the Advocate, all of these women were young, poor, friendless, and innocent. — Women Who Kill, page 153

A newspaper report in 1889 about Charles McElvaine, who murdered a grocer, recounted the Goodrich murder. It incorrectly noted that Stoddard "remained in hiding over six months" (actually three and a half months).

Those involved in the case would reminisce about it years later. In 1895, speaking to officers at police headquarters after announcing his retirement, Patrick Campbell spoke about the loyalty necessary to conduct police duties, citing the King case as an exemplary demonstration of that loyalty:

Mariticide Club

There's where the loyalty of the Captains came in. It would have been death to me to have made a failure. The community would have risen up against me for interference with personal rights. I don't think I could have lived in this city if it had been a non-success. This case is an example of your loyalty to me. I have tested your loyalty, and I say to you that I'll never forget you as long as I live.

— The New York Times

In a 1906 interview with the Brooklyn Daily Standard Union, Campbell, 80 years old at this time, recounted a few of his most memorable cases. He was chief of police for Brooklyn from 1870 until 1895, and identified the Kate Stoddard case as "a great one". Although he accurately recounted many details, he also stated that "as she made no effort to escape we got her easily enough". After she was sent to the asylum in 1874, he no longer kept track of her. "A commission adjudged her insane and she was sent to an asylum. She may be living yet, for all I know."

Sharon Kinne (née Sharon Elizabeth Hall)

Sharon Kinne

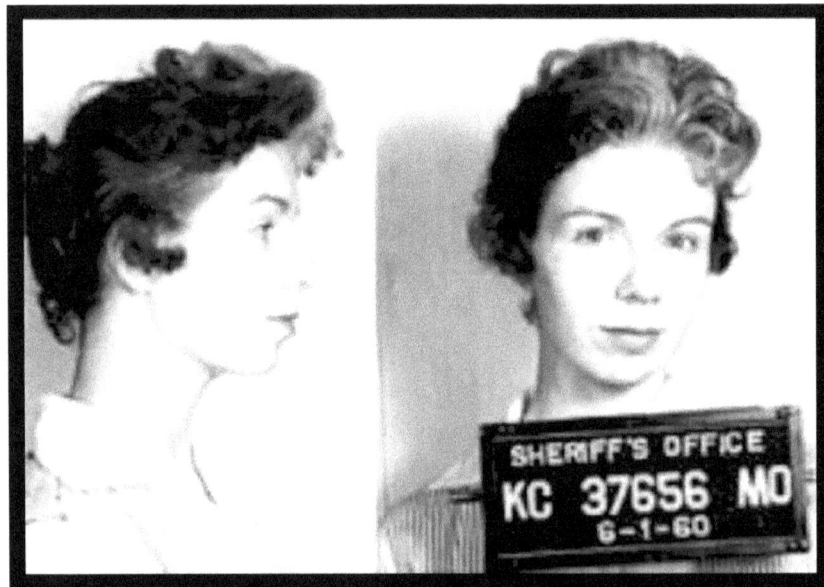

Sharon Elizabeth Hall Mugshot 1960

Sharon Kinne (born Sharon Elizabeth Hall, November 30, 1939), also known as Jeanette Pugliese and in Mexico as La Pistolera, is an

Wives Who Kill

American murderer and prison escapee who was convicted in Mexico for one murder and is suspected of two others in the United States, one for which she was acquitted at trial. As of 2022, Kinne is the subject of the longest currently outstanding arrest warrant for murder in the history of Kansas City, Missouri, one of the longest outstanding felony warrants in U.S. history. On March 19, 1960, Sharon's husband, James Kinne, was found shot in the head with the couple's two-year-old daughter playing nearby. Sharon claimed that the child, who had often been allowed to play with James's guns, had accidentally shot him, and police were initially unable to disprove her story. Then, on May 27, the body of 23-year-old Patricia Jones, a local file clerk, was found by Sharon and a boyfriend in a secluded area. Investigators found that Jones had been the wife of another of Sharon's boyfriends, and that Jones's husband had tried to break off his affair with Sharon shortly before Jones went missing. When Sharon admitted to having been the last person to speak to Jones, she was charged with her murder and, upon further investigation of his death, that of James. Sharon went to trial for Jones's murder in June 1961 and was acquitted. A January 1962 trial on charges of murdering her husband ended in conviction and a sentence of life imprisonment, but the verdict was overturned because of procedural irregularities. The case went to a second trial, which ended within days in a mistrial. A third trial ended in a hung jury in July 1964. Sharon was released on bond following the third trial and subsequently traveled to Mexico before a scheduled fourth trial could be held in October 1964. In Mexico, Sharon, claiming to have been acting in self-defense, killed a Mexican-born American citizen named Francisco Parades Ordoñez, who was shot in the back. An employee of the hotel in which the shooting occurred, responding to the sound of gunshots, was also wounded but survived. Investigation into the shootings showed that Ordoñez was shot with the same weapon that killed Jones. Sharon was convicted in October 1965 of the Ordoñez killing and sentenced to ten years in prison, later lengthened to thirteen years after judicial review. She escaped from the prison during a blackout in December 1969. Despite extensive manhunts, Sharon Kinne's whereabouts are unknown.

Mariticide Club

Sharon Kinne was born Sharon Elizabeth Hall on November 30, 1939, in Independence, Missouri, to Eugene and Doris Hall. When she was in junior high, Sharon's parents moved the family to Washington State, but by the time she was aged 15 they had returned to Missouri. In the summer of 1956, at age 16, Sharon met 22-year-old college student James Kinne at a church function, and the couple dated regularly until James returned to Brigham Young University (BYU) in the fall. Sharon, reportedly deeply interested in finding a partner with prospects who could take her away from Independence, wrote a letter to James informing him that she was pregnant by him. James took leave from BYU and returned to Independence, where he married Sharon on October 18, 1956. The couple's marriage license falsely identified Sharon as being 18 and a widow; though she later refused to address the assertion, Sharon told people at the time that she had been married when she lived in Washington, to a man who later died in a car accident. The new couple held a second, more formal wedding the following year at the Salt Lake Temple in Salt Lake City, Utah, after Sharon had completed the process of joining the Church of Jesus Christ of Latter-day Saints. After their wedding, the Kinnes returned to Provo, Utah. James resumed his studies at BYU, but put them on hold again at the end of the fall semester. The couple returned to Independence, where both took jobs—Sharon babysat and tended shops, while James worked as an electrical engineer at Bendix Aviation. Although Sharon claimed to have miscarried the child that had brought about their marriage, she soon became pregnant again. In the fall of 1957, she gave birth to a girl they named Danna. Sharon was reportedly a lavish spender who expected finer things out of life, but on James's salary they lived first in a rented home next to his parents' residence, then in a ranch-style house they had built at 17009 East 26th Terrace, Independence. James worked the night shift at Bendix, and his wife initially filled her days with shopping and, later, with other men. By the time the couple had a second child, Troy, Sharon was carrying on a regular extramarital affair with a friend from high school, John Boldizs.

Wives Who Kill

By early 1960, James was contemplating divorce, partially because of Sharon's spending habits and partially because he strongly suspected her infidelity. He spoke to his parents about the possibility of divorce on March 18, 1960, telling them that Sharon had agreed to give him one if he allowed her to keep the house, gave her custody the couple's daughter, and paid her US$1,000 in alimony. James's parents, devout Mormons, urged him to stay in the marriage. Sharon, too, was thinking about ways out of the marriage; according to Boldizs, she once offered him US$1,000 to kill her husband, or find someone who would, although he later claimed that she may have been joking.

1960 deaths

James Kinne

According to Sharon, on March 19, 1960, at around 5:30 p.m., she heard a gunshot from the direction of the bedroom in which James was sleeping. Entering the room, she found two-and-a-half-year-old Danna on the bed next to her father. Danna was holding one of James's guns, a High Standard .22target pistol, and James was bleeding from an apparent gunshot wound in the back of his head. Sharon called the police, but James was dead by the time the ambulance carrying him arrived at the hospital. Police were unable to recover any fingerprints from the well-oiled grip of the pistol, and a paraffin test for gunshot residue was not performed on either Danna or Sharon. Multiple people, including family and neighbors, told police that James had often allowed Danna to play with his guns, and in a test by investigating officers, Danna proved able to pull the trigger on a gun matching the one that had killed her father. With no evidence to the contrary, investigators ruled the case an accidental homicide. The pistol that killed James was taken into police custody and never returned to Sharon, despite her efforts to reclaim it; she later had a male friend secretly buy her a .22 caliber automatic pistol. When the friend told Sharon that he had registered the gun in her name, she requested that he re-register it under a name other than hers. With the investigation into his death closed, James was buried and Sharon collected on his life insurance policies, valued at about US$29,000 (US$230,000 today).

Mariticide Club

Patricia Jones

Patricia Jones was born Patricia Clements, one of six children born to Mr. and Mrs. Elmer Clements of St. Joseph, Missouri. After graduating from Benton High School, she married Walter T. Jones Jr., her high school sweetheart. Walter enlisted in the United States Marine Corps shortly after their marriage, and the couple relocated to the West Coast while Walter served. After his discharge from the military, they returned to Missouri and settled in Independence with their two children. By 1960, almost five years into the marriage, Jones was working as a file clerk for the Internal Revenue Service, while her husband sold cars.

Despite his marriage and children, Walter reportedly had a wandering eye. On April 18, Walter met Sharon when she bought a Ford Thunderbird from his dealership using some of the insurance payout from her husband's death. The two began an affair shortly thereafter. Sharon viewed Walter as a prospect for a second husband, but he was uninterested in leaving Patricia despite the rockiness of their relationship. When Walter declined to go on a trip to Washington with her in May, Sharon reluctantly went with her brother Eugene instead. Although the couple reunited on May 25, shortly after Sharon returned, the relationship was quickly set on the rocks when she told Walter that she was pregnant and he was the father of the baby. Walter, instead of responding with what Sharon expected to be an agreement to divorce Patricia, ended the affair. According to Sharon's later testimony, on the afternoon of May 26, she contacted Patricia at her office and told her that Walter was having an affair with Sharon's sister. Sharon then met with Patricia that evening to discuss the matter further before dropping her off near the Jones house. Patricia never made it to her house that evening, according to her husband. Walter filed a missing persons report with police the next day and began calling people he thought might have seen his wife. He got a lead when he spoke to friends of Patricia's who carpooled to work with her. They told Walter that Patricia had reported receiving a phone call that day from an unnamed woman who wanted to meet with her. She had asked the carpool driver to drop her off at a street corner in Independence, which he had done. The occupants of the

Wives Who Kill

carpool had seen a woman waiting for Patricia in another car but did not recognize her. They nevertheless provided a description of the unknown woman to Walter. Suspicious of the identity of the unknown woman based on the carpoolers' general description, Walter called Sharon and asked if she had seen or spoken to his wife. Sharon allowed that she had, indeed, seen Patricia that day; she had met her to tell her about Walter's affair. According to Sharon, she last saw Patricia where she dropped her off near the Jones house, speaking to an unknown man in a green 1957 Ford. Based on Sharon's admission over the phone, Walter met with her late Friday evening and insisted she give him more details about where his wife was; he later admitted to going so far as to hold a key to her throat threateningly. Sharon's response was, after leaving Walter, to call Boldizs and ask him to help her search for Patricia. Shortly before midnight, within hours of Sharon's conversation with Walter, she and Boldizs found the body of a woman in a secluded area approximately one mile outside of Independence. According to Boldizs, he had been the one to suggest searching the area in which they encountered the body; it was a spot to which they had often gone on dates before. The body, dressed in a black sweater and yellow skirt, was soon identified as the missing Patricia Jones. She had been shot four times by a .22 caliber pistol. Although the fatal wound was a shot to Patricia's head, entering near her mouth on an upward trajectory, she also had one through bullet wound to her abdomen and two penetrating gunshot wounds to her shoulders on a downward trajectory through her body. Powder burns on the hemline of her skirt, which had been raised to her waist, indicated that the gun had been fired from close range at least once. Initial reports and investigation placed Patricia's time of death at approximately 9 p.m. on May 27. She was buried on May 31. Investigators immediately began to question Sharon, Walter, and Boldizs. All three were questioned on May 28. Walter and Boldizs both gave written statements admitting that they had dated Sharon, and both agreed to lie detector tests; Sharon gave an oral statement to police but declined to sign a written one or take a lie detector test. She was questioned again on the morning of May 30, and Boldizs on May 31. The scheduled

Mariticide Club

polygraphs for the two men were performed on June 1, and both men were deemed to have been truthful in their statements. Sharon's brother Eugene was also questioned on May 31, but declined to answer questions.

While police questioned potential suspects and witnesses, other investigators focused on processing the crime scene. Repeated attempts were made to find the murder weapon and the bullet that had passed through Patricia's body, including the sifting of dirt at the crime scene for bullets and the deployment of a troop of Boy Scouts to search for a gun. A .22 caliber rifle slug was eventually found buried in the ground where Patricia's body had been found, providing evidence that at least some of her wounds had been sustained at the place her body was found. Although investigators went so far as to drag the bottom of nearby bodies of water, the gun that had shot Patricia—assumed to be a .22 caliber pistol—could not be found. Buildings near where the body had been located were also searched for blood and gunshot evidence, in accordance with police's theory that Patricia had been attacked elsewhere and then transported outdoors. A "white, powdery substance" found in Patricia's hair was initially believed to be trace evidence of some other crime scene area—an idea which fueled the search of nearby buildings—but was later determined to be fly eggs. Sharon was arrested at her home for Patricia Jones's murder around 11 p.m. on May 31, the same night as her funeral. The same day, the Jackson County sheriff requested that prosecutors consider a second charge of murder, this one for the death of James Kinne. Sharon's lawyers, Alex Peebles and Martha Sperry Hickman, filed a writ of habeas corpus with the court the next morning, and a hearing that afternoon resulted in her release on US$20,000 bond while she awaited a preliminary hearing originally scheduled for June 16. Police were able to rule out the .22 caliber pistol that had killed James as the murder weapon in Patricia's death; that gun was still in the possession of the sheriff's office. However, a man who worked with Sharon admitted to having secretly purchased a new .22 caliber pistol at her request in the beginning of May. Police were unable to locate the gun in question when they searched her house, though they did find an empty box that they

Wives Who Kill

believed had once held a gun. Sharon at first claimed to investigators that she had lost the gun on a trip to Washington, then stated simply that the gun had disappeared. Walter was taken into custody on June 2 as a material witness to the case and was freed the same day on US$2,000 bond. The initial autopsy performed on Patricia was criticized by police and prosecutors, who felt that the recovery of bullets and the testing of stomach contents should have been done. Dr. Hugh Owens, who had performed the autopsy, argued that he had recovered one of the presumed three bullets present in the body, and that because the body had been "prepared" by an undertaker prior to autopsy, any chemical tests on stomach contents would have been useless. Owens did add when asked that he had not seen any food apparent in the stomach at autopsy. Patricia's body was exhumed on June 17 in order to collect the bullets that had been left behind at the original autopsy, as well as to gather what samples of tissue and stomach contents were possible. Sharon's arraignment on July 11 resulted in denial of bail, but the Kansas City Court of Appeals struck down the ruling days later based on the prosecution's reliance on circumstantial evidence. She was freed on US$24,000 (worth US$188,976 in 2013 dollars) bond on July 18. After a delay in her trial date due to her advanced pregnancy, Sharon gave birth to a daughter she named Marla Christine on January 16, 1961.

Trials for 1960 murders

Trial in the death of Patricia Jones (1961)

Although charged with both murders, Sharon was tried separately for the two crimes. Her trial for the murder of Patricia Jones began in mid-June 1961, with jury selection beginning on or about June 13 and the trial commencing days later with an all-male jury. Opening arguments by both prosecution and defense set up cases based on purported times of death. Basing their assertion on pathologist-given testimony that Patricia had died about six hours after she ate lunch on May 26, the prosecution claimed that Jones had died more than 24 hours before Sharon and Boldizs found her body; defense attorneys argued that death had more likely occurred six to eight hours prior. Prosecutor J. Arnott Hill cited testimony by Walter Jones

Mariticide Club

and Chief of Detectives Lt. Harry Nesbitt as evidence of Sharon's motive for the crime: Nesbitt recalled statements by Sharon that she was afraid Walter was drifting away from her despite the financial support she offered him, and Walter testified that Sharon had told him she was pregnant by him and he had thereafter attempted to end the relationship. The prosecution was unable to firmly establish that Sharon owned or had once had the weapon that killed Patricia, though both Sharon's known pistol and the one that fired the bullets that killed Patricia were .22 caliber weapons. Roy Thrush, the man who sold the pistol to Sharon's male friend, had led police to a tree that contained what he claimed to be bullets he had fired from that pistol; however, when the bullets were extracted from the tree trunk, tests showed that the extracted bullets were not identifiable as having come from the weapon that killed Patricia. The prosecution rested its case on June 21 after calling 27 witnesses. Sharon's defense, which took less than two days and involved fourteen witnesses other than Sharon—who did not testify—focused on breaking down the State's claims of motive and means, arguing that she had no reason to kill Patricia and that the pistol she was alleged to have owned had not been proven to be the murder weapon. After slightly over one and a half hours of deliberation, the jury, citing "just too many loopholes" left in the prosecution's case, acquitted Sharon Kinne. Immediately after the delivery of the verdict, juror Ogden Stephens asked Sharon for her autograph, which she was photographed giving to him. Sharon was returned to jail the same day to await trial for the murder of her husband.

First trial in the death of James Kinne (1962)

Despite her acquittal for the murder of Patricia Jones, Sharon remained charged for the murder of her husband, James Kinne. When jury selection began on January 8, 1962, Hill noted that he did not intend to pursue the death penalty in the case. The prosecution's case rested largely on their contention that Sharon had been so interested in seeing her husband removed that she had been willing to pay for his murder, supported by the grand jury testimony of Boldizs. Boldizs, though nominally a witness for the prosecution, weakened his testimony on the stand during the trial by

Wives Who Kill

claiming that Sharon's offer to pay him US$1,000 in return for James's murder could have been a joke, and Hill was forced to attack his own witness's credibility. Further prosecution testimony alleged that the Kinnes' marriage had been on the verge of dissolution at the time of James's death, that Sharon's adultery had been a cause of this, and that Sharon had known that she would collect her husband's US$29,000 in life insurance policies only if she were still his wife. The defense, led by attorneys Hickman and James Patrick Quinn, focused on the circumstantial quality of the prosecution's evidence, noting that prior police investigation had determined James's death to be "obviously accidental" and that the jury was obligated to assume innocence on the defendant's part no matter how unpleasant they found her moral character to be. The defense, too, attacked the reliability of Boldizs' testimony, calling him a "poor, mixed-up kid" who would "sign anything". Kinne's attorneys also presented testimony from witnesses supporting the viability of the theory that Danna had shot her father, including statements that guns had been regularly left within her reach at the family home, that she was able to pull the triggers on toy guns with stiffer trigger pulls than the weapon that caused James' death, and that she had often been observed pretending to fire guns in play. The trial ended in conviction on January 11 after five and a half hours of deliberation. In April of the same year, Sharon was formally sentenced to life in prison. She began to serve her sentence in the Missouri Reformatory for Women. Later interviews with jurors from the trial revealed that "three or four ballots" had been taken before the "guilty" verdict was reached, beginning with the jury solidly divided and moving progressively toward unanimity for conviction. One juror told the Kansas City Star that Sharon's morals had not been considered at issue by the jury, and that she thought no juror had been aware of her previously being tried for the murder of Patricia Jones. Despite the verdict, James's family continued to believe the best of their daughter-in-law, telling reporters on the day of the verdict, "[W]e can't find it in our hearts to say anything bad about her" and, "We still don't feel that she committed murder." Sharon herself told reporters that she felt

Mariticide Club

the verdict was a mistake, and that she regretted her previous enthusiasm for having a woman on the jury.

The following week, Sharon's lawyers requested that she be released on bond, supported by a community petition signed by 132 supporters of her innocence. The motion was denied on the basis of first-degree murder not being a bailable offense; presiding judge Tom J. Stubbs also counseled Sharon's lawyers that he felt their involvement in such a petition at a time when a motion for bond was being considered was "highly improper". A subsequent defense motion requested that the conviction be vacated because the jury had delivered its verdict based on "surmise and speculation" rather than "substantial evidence", listing a series of procedural errors that Sharon's counsel alleged had taken place before and during the trial; these included a juror taking "incomplete" notes, disputes over Boldizs' testimony, and an incorrect number of potential jurors being provided for selection. The motion was denied by Judge Stubbs in April 1962, but appealed to the Missouri Supreme Court, which in March 1963 reversed the conviction and ordered a new trial on the basis of Sharon's defense having been denied adequate peremptory challenges during jury selection in her trial. Sharon was denied an opportunity for bail in May 1963, but that ruling was overturned in July and she was released on $25,000 bond, posted by her brother Eugene. The State's request that the Missouri Supreme Court re-consider its position on Sharon's conviction was granted, but in October 1963 that hearing resulted in further grounds being found for a new trial, this time on the basis of the prosecutor having been allowed to cross-examine a prosecution witness. A second request for a re-hearing on the validity of the conviction was denied by the Missouri Supreme Court. Sharon and her children moved in with her mother and awaited the start of her new trial.

Second trial in the death of James Kinne (1964)

Sharon's second trial for the death of James Kinne began on March 23, 1964. As jury selection got underway that day, the public was initially barred from the proceedings, but the restriction was soon loosened and journalists were allowed into the courtroom. An unusually long jury

Wives Who Kill

selection process made the first day of the trial last fourteen hours, beginning at 9 a.m. and not ending until nearly midnight; presiding judge Paul Carver noted that due to the notoriety of the case, he had been forced to choose between sequestering the entire jury pool overnight and forcing the court into a long day. The eventual jury, all men, were immediately sequestered, but days later, a mistrial was declared after it emerged that a law partner of prosecutor Lawrence Gepford had once been retained by one of the jurors.

Third trial in the death of James Kinne (1964)

Sharon's third trial, originally scheduled to begin early in June 1964, began instead on June 29. Assistant prosecutor Donald L. Mason declared at jury selection that he intended to death-qualify the jury, a process in which a prosecutor peremptorily challenges any juror who automatically opposes the death penalty, and jury selection once again took more than twelve hours in one day. Boldizs' testimony in this trial remained contradictory as to whether he believed Sharon's US$1,000 offer to have James killed had been intended seriously, but he added this time that after his death, Sharon had asked that Boldizs not tell authorities about her offer. A new witness, a female acquaintance of Sharon's, testified that she had once joked that the woman should "get rid of [the woman's] old man like [Sharon] did", but defense cross-examination highlighted inconsistencies between this testimony and a similar quote the woman had offered at a previous deposition. For the first time at any of her trials, Sharon took the stand on the last day of this trial to issue a categorical denial of all charges. The all-male jury deadlocked seven-to-five in favor of acquittal in this trial, resulting in a second mistrial.

Death of Francisco Paredes Ordoñez

A fourth trial was scheduled for October 1964; however, in September, Sharon, still free on her $25,000 bond, traveled to Mexico with an alleged lover, Francis Samuel Pugliese, leaving her children with James's father and traveling as Pugliese's wife under the name "Jeanette Pugliese". The couple later said that they had gone to Mexico to get married. Under the legal terms of her bail, Sharon was permitted to leave the country, but her

Mariticide Club

contract with the company that posted her bond prohibited her from leaving Missouri without written permission from the company's agents.

After crossing the border, Sharon and Pugliese registered at a local hotel, Hotel Gin, again as husband and wife. Sharon, saying that she felt unsafe in the foreign country, bought a pistol—which meant that the couple now possessed multiple guns, having brought one or two with them from the U.S. On the night of September 18, 1964, Sharon left the hotel without Pugliese, either to acquire money because the couple was running low or to get medicine she required. She encountered Francisco Parades Ordoñez, a Mexican-born American citizen, at a bar and accompanied him back to his room in Hotel La Vada. According to Sharon's account, she went with Ordoñez to see photographs he offered to show her, but he soon began to make sexual advances toward her and she was forced to fire her gun at him in an attempt to protect herself. Sharon maintained later that she had had no intention of harming or killing Ordoñez, and had intended only to frighten him, but her bullets struck him in the chest and killed him. Responding to the sound of gunfire, hotel employee Enrique Martinez Rueda entered the room. Sharon fired again and hit Rueda in the shoulder. Wounded, Rueda fled the room, locking Sharon inside, and called the police. Police, rejecting Sharon's story, theorized that she had gone out that evening intending robbery, and had chosen Ordoñez as her victim. When he resisted her orders to give her his money, police believed, Sharon had shot him. Police responding to Hotel La Vada arrested Sharon on charges of homicide and assault with a deadly weapon. Sharon maintained that she had not intended to harm Ordoñez, and that she had fired her weapon at Rueda because she feared that he, too, was coming to attack her. Police searched her purse, finding a gun and fifty cartridges, and then the couple's room at Hotel Gin, where they found two more guns and another supply of cartridges. Authorities took Pugliese into custody at the Hotel Gin, initially holding him without charge and later filing charges of entering the country illegally and carrying an unlicensed gun. The gun found in the couple's room that night was later proven through ballistics to be the same gun that killed Patricia Jones in 1960, but because Sharon had already been

Page 278 of 615 Mariticide Club – Wives Who Kill © 2023 TXu 2-378-397 All Rights Reserved by William A. Stricklin

Wives Who Kill

acquitted of that crime, she could not be charged again for it based on the new evidence.

Pugliese was held at the Palacio de Lecumberri in Mexico City, while Sharon was initially placed in a women's prison before being transferred to Lecumberri for her trial. The couple were arraigned on September 26 and held for trial. In October, Sharon's Mexican attorney, Higinio Lara, filed a recurso de amparo, similar to a writ of habeas corpus, asserting that the Mexican government was violating her constitutional rights by holding her for a shooting committed in self-defense. The request was denied and both Sharon and Pugliese were tried in the summer of 1965. Pugliese, cleared of the charges against him, was deported to the U.S., but Sharon was convicted on October 18 of the homicide of Ordoñez. Despite rumors that she would receive probation and be deported like Pugliese, Sharon was instead sentenced to a ten-year prison term for the murder. When she was officially notified of the sentence the next day, she asserted that she would appeal her conviction. The appeal, rather than overturning her sentence, lengthened it. The three-man superior court which heard Sharon's case overturned one aspect of her conviction—charges of attempted robbery—but upheld her murder conviction and increased her sentence from ten to thirteen years, saying that her original sentence had been too lenient. Sharon was returned to the women's prison to serve her sentence. There, she was nicknamed "La Pistolera" ("the gunfighter"), a nickname subsequently adopted by the Mexican press. On December 7, 1969, Sharon was not present for a routine 5 p.m. roll-call at the Ixtapalapan prison where she was serving her sentence. Her absence was not officially noted until she also failed to show up at a second roll-call later that evening. The news of her escape was not reported to Mexico City police until 2 o'clock the following morning. A manhunt was then arranged, initially focusing on the northern Mexican states due to authorities' belief that Sharon may have been heading for the last known whereabouts of a former inmate to whom she had grown close while they were in prison together. The search also encompassed country-wide transport hubs and eventually circled back to the Mexico City area. U.S. authorities, including

Mariticide Club

the Federal Bureau of Investigation (FBI), were also alerted of Mexican authorities' belief that Sharon may have been attempting to work her way back into her native country, but the FBI noted that it was unlikely to have jurisdiction in the case. Initial police speculation was that Sharon had bribed guards to look the other way while she escaped the prison—an unusual blackout had been reported at the prison on the evening of and at the approximate time of her escape. Investigation showed that a door that should have been locked had been left unsecured. Further questioning of prison guards and administration showed that oversight at the prison was generally lax and that it was staffed by fewer guards than it should have been. News reports of the time reported numerous theories about Sharon's escape, including that she had bribed prison guards, that she may have enlisted the help of a supposed boyfriend who was a Mexico City policeman, that her mother had been involved in the escape plan, that a former Mexican secret service agent had assisted in the escape, and that Sharon may have disguised herself as a man to effect her escape. A more modern theory speculates that Ordoñez's family had helped her escape and then killed her. The intensive manhunt for was short-lived. By December 18, the Mexican secret service and the Mexico City district attorney's office were both reporting that they were no longer involved in searching for the escaped prisoner, while the federal district attorney was reporting that responsibility for the hunt belonged to the city district attorney's office. Investigators speculated that Sharon had already crossed the border from Mexico into Guatemala, mooting the purpose of a Mexican manhunt. They noted that she was fluent in Spanish after her years in Mexican prison, and she could therefore "get along rather well" in nearly any Spanish-speaking area of the world. Despite vowing to keep the case open and their investigation running until Sharon was back in custody, authorities were forced to admit by the end of December 1969 that they had run out of investigative leads to pursue. More than fifty years after her escape, Sharon Kinne remains at large, her whereabouts and ultimate fate unknown. Sharon's arrest and conviction in Mexico had implications for the status of her Missouri legal entanglements. Because she was being held in Mexico

Wives Who Kill

on October 26, 1964—the scheduled date for her fourth trial in the murder of her husband—her US$25,000 bond was revoked on that date. Although the United Bond Insurance Company, which had posted the bond, argued that paperwork irregularities rendered the issuance of her bail illegal, the court ordered the company to forfeit the bond. Sharon was reportedly concerned about the monetary implications of this forfeiture: "I could always use the money"; the Altus, Oklahoma, Time-Democrat quoted her as saying: "I don't intend to spend all my life in jail". A US$30,000 supersedeas bond was issued in August 1965 as the United Bond Insurance Company continued to dispute the payment of Sharon's original US$25,000 bond. The supersedeas bond allowed the company to defer payment of the US$25,000 bond until a ruling on the matter was handed down by the Missouri Supreme Court, but when that court upheld the bond's forfeiture, the US$25,000 was paid to the State of Missouri in October 1965. The United Bond Insurance Company later filed suit against Sharon's family to recover the cost of the bail, lawyer's fees, and searching for Sharon after her escape. Shortly before her scheduled Missouri trial date, Sharon's Missouri counsel filed a motion to change the venue of any eventual fourth trial in the death of James Kinne, claiming that news coverage of the Kinne case had so prejudiced residents of Jackson County against Sharon that it would be impossible for her to get a fair trial there.

When Sharon failed to appear for the fourth trial, a warrant was issued for her arrest in October 1964. It is still outstanding 57 years later, making it the oldest outstanding murder warrant known to exist in the Kansas City area. Sharon's status in the Mexican system also remains outstanding, though authorities have pointed out that at the time of her escape, jailbreak was not a crime under Mexican law; if she were re-captured there, she would have only to serve out the remainder of her outstanding sentence. In a segment of Investigation Discovery (ID) series Deadly Women covering the Kinne case, author James Hays speculates that Sharon committed her first murder for monetary gain, hoping to cash in on James's life insurance policy, and that she began to derive pleasure from killing at that point. Former FBI profiler Candice DeLong supports this assertion, stating that

Mariticide Club

Sharon is a sociopath, lacking in remorse and empathy, and therefore had no compunction about killing to get what she wanted. This idea is echoed by some of those involved in prosecuting Sharon Kinne. Even those who believe in her guilt, however, note that she had a certain appeal, describing her as "rather attractive" and admitting that they grew to like her. The Mammoth Book of True Crime describes her as a relative rarity, a "pretty" criminal. In I'm Just an Ordinary Girl: The Sharon Kinne Story, Hays asserts that Sharon was inspired to kill her husband by a magazine article she read about Lillian Chastain, a Virginia woman who shot her husband during an argument and blamed the gunshot on the couple's two-year-old daughter. Charges against Chastain were filed in February 1960, weeks before James's death. Kinne's case has been featured on Unsolved Mysteries and was the subject of the ID series A Crime to Remember episode "Luck Be a Lady" (Season 4 Episode 2, 2016).

Nancy Ann Kissel (née Keeshin)
Murder of Robert Kissel

The Nancy Kissel murder case (officially called the Hong Kong Special Administrative Region v Nancy Ann Kissel) was a highly publicized criminal trial held in the High Court of Hong Kong, where American expatriate Nancy Ann Kissel (née Keeshin) was convicted of the murder of her husband, 40-year-old investment banker Robert Peter Kissel, in their apartment on 2 November 2003. It was arguably the highest profile criminal case involving an expatriate in Hong Kong's history, and was closely covered in the media. Kissel was convicted of murder in 2005 and received a mandatory life sentence. The Court of Final Appeal overturned the conviction in February 2010, citing legal errors, and ordered a retrial. At retrial 25 March 2011, Kissel was again found guilty of her husband's murder and sentenced to life in prison. She is serving her sentence at Tai Lam Centre for Women. Coincidentally Robert Kissel's brother, Andrew, a former American real estate developer, was murdered on 3 April 2006 in Greenwich, Connecticut, United States.

Wives Who Kill

Hong Kong Parkview, where the murder took place

On a return trip to the U.S. in mid-2003, Nancy Kissel met and had an affair with Michael Del Priore, a twice-married electrical repairman who had rewired the Kissel home in Vermont. Robert Kissel became suspicious of his wife's infidelity and had hired a private detective, Frank Shea, to spy on her. Robert secretly installed the spyware eBlaster on Nancy's computer. Nancy claimed that her husband had initiated proceedings for divorce and securing custody of their children. Nancy drugged Robert by having their six-year-old daughter give him a strawberry milkshake laced with a cocktail of sedatives. When the drugs had taken effect and the children were out of the apartment, Nancy bludgeoned her husband to death. She then rolled up his body in a carpet and had it placed in their storeroom in the Parkview apartment complex. After arrest, Nancy admitted to killing Robert in self-defense, claiming she was the victim of domestic violence – including repeated acts of rape and sodomy – over a five-year period. She further claimed that Robert habitually abused alcohol and cocaine. The trial began in June 2005 at the High Court, with the prosecution alleging that Nancy murdered her husband; she pleaded not guilty. Nancy admitted under cross-examination that she had bludgeoned her husband to death, but maintained that she was defending herself and further claimed memory loss, testifying she had no knowledge of how she inflicted five head wounds with a heavy metal sculpture. Nancy admitted to using Stilnox, one of the sedatives found in her husband's body, to doctor a bottle of malt whisky when they were living in Vermont in the hope that it would make

Mariticide Club

her husband less aggressive toward their children, but testified it had had no effect on him. Regardless of that, Nancy admitted to trying the same thing in Hong Kong, but testified that when she saw the sediment it left at the bottom of the bottle, she poured out the drugged liquor, bought a new bottle and used it to partially fill up the old one, and then "never thought about it again". The Kissels' neighbor, Andrew Tanzer, testified he had become drowsy and then unconscious after sampling the milkshake. Nancy admitted making it for one of her children and a visiting child, but denied drugging it, stating she would never harm her children or anyone else's. The case against Nancy Kissel was brought before Justice Michael Lunn. At the end of the trial, lasting 65 days, on 1 September 2005 the jury of five men and two women unanimously decided on her guilt after eight hours of deliberation. She was sentenced to life in prison. Kissel appealed her conviction in April 2008. That petition was rejected. She then lodged an appeal with the Court of Final Appeal on 12 January 2010. The case was heard before a five-judge panel led by then-Chief Justice Andrew Li on 21 January. The defense argued the prosecution had improperly used evidence, including hearsay, and original jury instructions were problematic. On 11 February 2010, the Court of Final Appeal quashed the conviction and ordered a retrial, citing prosecution use of inadmissible evidence. Kissel was permitted to seek bail, but ultimately chose not to apply.

Second indictment

Kissel was re-indicted on a single count of murder on 2 March 2010, with a retrial due to start on 10 January 2011.According to the defense, Robert told his wife the night of 2 November 2003, that he was filing for divorce and she was unfit to care for their children. The defense alleged she had long suffered from physical and sexual abuse. Nancy pleaded not guilty to murder, but guilty to manslaughter on the basis of diminished responsibility and provocation. She admitted to having an extramarital relationship with a TV repairman, and the prosecution alleged that she planned to run away with her lover in the U.S. after her husband's death, and that she stood to inherit her husband's estate worth US$18 million.

Wives Who Kill

On 25 March 2011, after hearing evidence from over 50 prosecution and defense witnesses over ten weeks, the jury of seven women and two men unanimously found Kissel guilty as charged. She was sentenced to life imprisonment. On 24 April 2014, the Court of Final Appeal refused to allow appeal against the verdict of her 2011 retrial, rejecting the arguments of Kissel's lawyer, Edward Fitzgerald, that the prosecution was wrong to tell the retrial's jury that his client was not suffering any psychiatric illness and the trial judge erred in directing the jury: "We are not persuaded that the two grounds submitted by the applicant are arguable," Justice Roberto Ribeiro said. Justice Ribeiro said that he and the court's two other judges, Justice Robert Tang Ching and Justice Joseph Fok, would hand down the reason for their decision later. In 2003 the murder of Kissel was the subject of a non-fiction book by Joe McGinniss, Never Enough. It was also dramatized in the 2008 Lifetime television film The Two Mr. Kissels, with Robin Tunney playing Nancy and Anson Mount playing her husband.

Tillie Klimek (née Otylia Gburek)

Mariticide Club

Klimek after her arrest in 1922

Ottilie "Tillie" Klimek (born Otylia Gburek; 1876 – November 20, 1936) was a Polish American serial killer, active in Chicago. According to accounts, she pretended to have precognitive dreams, accurately predicting the dates of death of her victims, when in reality she was merely scheduling their deaths. Klimek was born Otylia Gburek in Poland, and came to the United States as an infant with her parents. Tillie married her original husband Jozef Mitkiewicz in 1895. In 1914, he died after a short illness. The death certificate listed the cause of death as heart trouble, and she quickly remarried Joseph Ruskowski, who lived nearby. He too died in short order, as did a boyfriend who had "jilted" her. The crime for which Klimek was eventually tried was the murder of Frank Kupczyk, her third husband. He had taken ill in their apartment at 924 N. Winchester, where

Wives Who Kill

she had previously lived with a boyfriend under the name of Meyers, and she began to tell neighbors that Frank "would not live long." She mocked Frank himself, greeting him in the morning by saying "It won't be long now," and "You'll be dying soon," and joking with neighbors that he had "two inches to live." She even knitted her own mourning hat as she sat at his bedside (which she later wore to the trial), and asked for the landlady's permission to store a bargain coffin she'd found for sale in the basement. This may have been what led to the belief that she claimed to "predict" deaths. In 1921, after Frank's death, Klimek married a man named Joseph Klimek and lived with him at 1453 Tell Place (now 1453 Thomas Street). When he became ill, doctors suspected arsenic poisoning, and tests confirmed it. She was arrested. It was later said that she told the arresting officer that, "The next one I want to cook a dinner for is you." Bodies of Klimek's other husbands were soon exhumed and found to contain lethal doses of arsenic, though the soil around them was clean. Police also arrested her cousin, Nellie Koulik. Klimek told the police that she had told Nellie she was tired of her husband Frank. Nellie suggested divorce. Klimek said that, "I will get rid of him some other way," and claimed that Nellie had given her a "goodly portion" of a poison called "Rough on Rats". After Klimek's arrest, it came to light that several relatives and neighbors of the two women had died. Two neighbors Klimek had quarreled with became gravely ill after being given candy by her. A dog that annoyed Klimek in her Winchester Street house had died of arsenic poisoning. Several of Klimek and Nellie's cousins and relatives were found to have become gravely ill shortly after eating at Klimek's house. In all, the list included twenty suspected victims, fourteen of whom had died.

The papers began to speak of Klimek not as a solo murderer, but as the "high priestess" of a "Bluebeard clique" in Chicago's Little Poland neighborhood. Other wives in the neighborhood were arrested and released. Joseph Klimek would survive, though he was still in the hospital more than three months later. It was found that she had taken out life insurance policies on her husbands from which she profited greatly.

Mariticide Club

In March 1923, Klimek was found guilty of the murder of Frank Kupczyk, her third known husband. Reporters noted that unlike most of the husband killers who had been acquitted in Chicago courts, Klimek was not beautiful or charming, but a "squat" woman who spoke only broken English, despite having lived in the country since infancy. She was sentenced to life in prison, the harshest sentence that had ever been leveled against a woman in Cook County. Nellie was later acquitted after spending a year in prison during her drawn-out trial. Klimek often teased her in prison, once convincing her that she was about to be taken out and hanged. Klimek died in prison at Joliet Correctional Center on November 20, 1936 and was interred at the Bohemian National Cemetery in Chicago.

Theresa Knorr (née Theresa Jimmie Francine Cross)

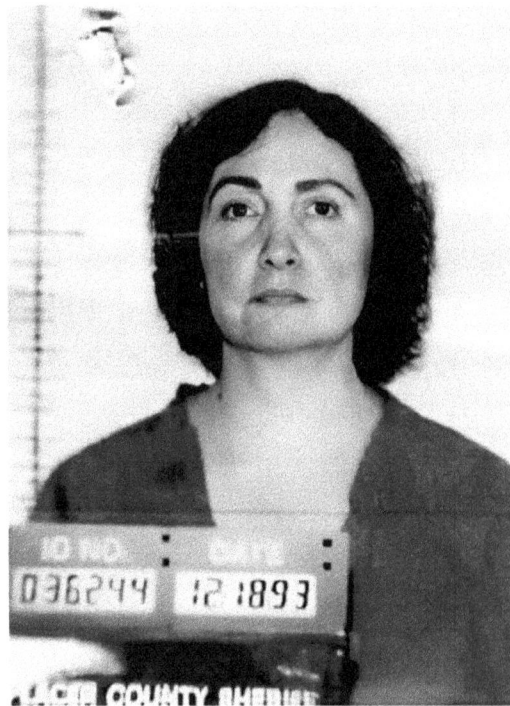

1993 mugshot of Theresa Knorr

Theresa Jimmie Francine Knorr (née Cross; born March 14, 1946) is an American woman convicted of torturing and murdering two of her six children while using the others to facilitate and cover up her crimes. She was acquitted of murdering her first husband and serving two consecutive

Wives Who Kill

life sentences at California Institution for Women in Chino, California. Theresa Knorr was born in Sacramento, California, the younger of two daughters born to Swannie Gay (née Myers) and James "Jim" Cross. Theresa's mother had a son and a daughter from a previous marriage. Her father worked as an assistant cheese maker at a local dairy, eventually saving up enough money to buy a house in Rio Linda. In the late 1950s, Jim Cross was diagnosed with Parkinson's disease, which forced him to quit his job. He developed depression and reportedly took his frustrations and anger out on his family. Swannie Cross kept the family afloat financially. Theresa was reportedly very close to her mother and was devastated when she died of congestive heart failure in March 1961. Unable to keep the family home after that, her father sold it. On September 29, 1962, 16-year-old Theresa married Clifford Clyde Sanders, a man five years her senior whom she had met a few months earlier. She immediately dropped out of high school and became pregnant, and on July 16, 1963 she gave birth to her first child, Howard Clyde Sanders. The marriage was rocky; Theresa was possessive and repeatedly accused Sanders of infidelity. The couple argued frequently and on June 22, 1964, she claimed that he had punched her in the face during one such argument. She reported the incident to police but refused to press charges against Sanders; the assault charges were subsequently dropped. On July 6, 1964, the day after Sanders' birthday, the couple were arguing because he had spent his birthday out with friends instead of at home. During the argument, Sanders informed Theresa that he was leaving her. Theresa became enraged and shot Sanders in the back with a rifle as he was walking out the door. Theresa was arrested and charged with Sanders' murder, to which she pled not guilty claiming that she was acting in self-defense. During her trial, Theresa, who was pregnant with her second child, claimed that she had shot Sanders because he was a violent alcoholic who had physically abused her. Several of Sanders' relatives testified that he was neither violent nor abusive, while the prosecution claimed that Theresa killed Sanders "maliciously" and "without provocation."

Mariticide Club

Theresa's older sister testified against her, stating that Theresa was possessive and jealous and "would kill [Sanders] before any other woman could have him." Theresa was acquitted of Sanders' murder on September 22, 1964. She gave birth to her second child, Sheila Gay Sanders, on March 16, 1965. After Sheila's birth, Theresa began drinking heavily. She regularly drank at the local American Legion hall where she met Estell L. Thornsberry, a disabled United States Army veteran. The two began a relationship and eventually moved in together. During the relationship, Theresa routinely left her children with Thornsberry while she went out drinking. Thornsberry began to question Theresa when she stayed out for days at a time and ended the relationship a few months later, after discovering that she was having an affair with his best friend. Shortly after the relationship with Thornsberry ended, she met and began a relationship with a United States Marine Corps private named Robert Knorr. She soon became pregnant and the couple married on July 9, 1966. Theresa's third child, Suesan Marline Knorr, was born on September 27, 1966. The couple had three more children: William Robert Knorr on September 15, 1967; Robert Wallace Knorr, Jr. on December 31, 1968; and Theresa "Terry" Marie Knorr on August 5, 1970. However, Theresa's marriage to Robert deteriorated after she began to accuse him of having affairs. Both spouses were known to be volatile and would constantly beat each other and the kids. Fed up with his wife's constant accusations, Robert left her in December 1970 and was granted a divorce in 1971. After the divorce, Robert attempted to see his children but Theresa prevented him from doing so. Theresa married twice more. In 1971 she wed railroad worker Ronald Pulliam, but the marriage fell apart when she began to leave her children with Pulliam while she stayed out all night drinking and partying. He divorced her in 1972 after he became convinced that she was having an affair. Her final marriage was to Sacramento Union copy editor Chester "Chet" Harris, whom she married in August 1976. Theresa's daughter Suesan grew close to Harris, which made Theresa jealous. She filed for divorce from Harris in November 1976 after she reportedly found out that Harris enjoyed taking consensual nude photographs of women.

Wives Who Kill

Theresa was physically, verbally, and psychologically abusive toward her children, behavior which escalated after her fourth divorce. She also gained a tremendous amount of weight, and became reclusive to the point of disconnecting the home phone and refusing to allow the children to have visitors. Knorr and her children lived in Orangevale, California for many years before moving into a two-bedroom apartment in Sacramento; her eldest son Howard reportedly left home before the move to Sacramento. According to neighbors, the Sacramento apartment was filthy and smelled of urine. Neighbors also noticed that the children, whom Knorr never let go outside, seemed fearful, nervous and high-strung. For years, Knorr abused and tortured her children in various ways, including beating them, force feeding them, burning them with cigarettes, and throwing knives at them. She made her children hold each other down while she assaulted them. In one instance, Knorr held a pistol to her youngest daughter Terry's head and threatened to kill her. Knorr primarily focused her anger and abuse on Terry's older sisters, Sheila and Suesan. Terry said in an interview that her mother resented that Sheila and Suesan were maturing and blossoming into attractive young women while she faced the prospect of losing her looks as she aged. Knorr also believed that her fourth husband, Chet Harris, had turned Suesan into a witch, so Suesan received the worst of Knorr's abuse. After one severe beating, Suesan ran away from home. She was picked up by police and placed in a psychiatric hospital where she told staff that her mother abused her. Knorr denied the abuse claims and told the hospital staff that Suesan had mental issues. Authorities did not investigate the matter further and released Suesan back into her mother's custody. Knorr immediately punished Suesan by beating her while wearing a pair of leather gloves, and forced Susesan's siblings to take turns in the assault. In the subsequent weeks, Knorr handcuffed Suesan to the kitchen table and ordered her other children to stand watch over her. She forced Suesan to drop out of school and forbade her to leave the house. Knorr pulled her other children out of school. They never advanced past the eighth grade. For two years, Knorr handcuffed Suesan under the dining room table making her suffer. Knorr would hand feed her from time to time, but she

Mariticide Club

had to have a mouth gag on. Suesan couldn't take the torture anymore and begged her mother to release her. The next morning, Knorr went on a psychotic rampage and started hitting all her children. She uncuffed Suesan for a minute, but handed Terry a gun to point at her to make sure she didn't move. While Knorr and the other children were in the kitchen preparing oatmeal, one of them dropped the spoon; the noise spooked Terry, and the gun went off and hit Suesan. Knorr immediately rechained her under the dining-room table; her only response to the fact that her daughter was bleeding out and begging to be taken to the hospital was to get upset that she was getting blood on the carpet. Knorr decided to nurse her back to health and made the other kids help. Suesan survived the shooting but attempts by Robert, at Knorr's request, to remove the bullet led to infection and sepsis. On July 16, 1984, Knorr packed all of Suesan's belongings in trash bags and, after binding her arms and legs and placing duct tape over her mouth, ordered her sons Robert and William to put Suesan in their car. They drove her to Squaw Valley, where Robert and William placed her on the side of the road on top of the bags containing her belongings. Knorr then doused the bags and Suesan, who was still alive, in gasoline and set fire to them. Suesan's still-smoldering body was found the following day. Due to the state of the remains, a positive identification was never made and Suesan was classified as homicide case Jane Doe #4873/84. Following Suesan's death, Knorr began directing most of her anger and abuse towards her daughter Sheila, forcing her into prostitution in May 1985 to support the family. Knorr did not work and received unemployment benefits from the State of California. Knorr was so pleased with this arrangement because of the large amounts of money Sheila was earning that she allowed Sheila to leave the house whenever she pleased. After a few weeks, Knorr became angry and accused Sheila of being pregnant and contracting a sexually transmitted disease which Knorr claimed she caught from Sheila via a toilet seat. When Sheila denied the accusations, Knorr beat her, hog tied her, and locked her in a hot closet with no ventilation. Knorr forbade her other children to give her food or water or open the closet door, but Terry disobeyed her mother and gave Sheila a beer. Terry later said, "She

Wives Who Kill

[Theresa] wanted Sheila to confess. That was Mother's way: beat them until they confess." To end the punishment, Sheila confessed to being pregnant and having an STD, but Knorr claimed that she was lying and refused to let her out of the closet. Sheila died three days later, on June 21, 1985, of dehydration and starvation. Knorr left Sheila's body in the closet for an additional three days before she discovered that she was dead. Once again she ordered her sons William and Robert to dispose of their sister's body, which had begun to decompose and fill the apartment with a foul stench. The boys placed Sheila's body in a cardboard box which they disposed of near Truckee-Tahoe Airport. Sheila's body was discovered a few hours after it had been disposed of but was never positively identified and was classified as Jane Doe #6607-85. Although Sheila's body had been removed from the closet, the smell of decomposition still lingered in the apartment, and Knorr became concerned that the smell and physical evidence in the closet could implicate her in Sheila's death. On September 29, 1986, she moved the family's belongings out of the apartment and ordered Terry to burn it down with any physical evidence. During the night, Terry dumped three containers of lighter fluid on the apartment floor and set it on fire; neighbors quickly reported it before it spread; the closet in which Sheila died was not damaged. After Knorr's arrest, investigators were able to remove the subfloor from the closet to test it for physical evidence. After leaving the Sacramento apartment, Knorr went into hiding. Her sons Howard and William, who were of legal age by then, severed all ties with her; 16-year-old Terry also escaped from her mother and used Sheila's identification card to pass herself off as a legal adult. The only child to remain with Knorr was 19-year-old Robert, Jr. Knorr and Robert, Jr. moved to Las Vegas, Nevada, and attempted to keep a low profile. In November 1991, Robert Knorr, Jr. was arrested after he fatally shot a bartender in a Las Vegas bar during an attempted robbery. He was sentenced to 16 years in prison. Shortly after Robert, Jr.'s arrest, Knorr left Las Vegas and relocated to Salt Lake City, Utah. After escaping from her mother, Terry reported her sisters' murders to the Utah police, but they dismissed her stories as fiction, as did a therapist she visited. On October

Mariticide Club

28, 1993, Terry called the hotline for Fox television program America's Most Wanted, and was told to contact detectives in Placer County, California, where Suesan's body had been found. Placer County detectives took her claims seriously and followed up with an investigation, soon linking the two Jane Does found in the area in 1984 and 1985 to Terry's detailed stories of her sisters' deaths. William Knorr was arrested on November 4, 1993, in Woodland, California, where he had been living and working. Robert Knorr, Jr. was charged with his sisters' murders while he was serving his 16-year sentence in an Ely, Nevada, prison. On November 10, 1993, Knorr herself was arrested at her home in Salt Lake City. At the time of her arrest, she was using her maiden name of "Cross" and working as a caregiver for her landlord's 86-year-old mother. On November 15, 1993, Theresa Knorr was charged with two counts of murder, two counts of conspiracy to commit murder, and two special circumstances charges: multiple murder and murder by torture. Knorr initially pleaded not guilty, but then made a deal with the prosecution after learning that her son Robert Jr. had agreed to testify against her in exchange for a reduced sentence. She pleaded guilty on the condition that she be spared the death penalty. On October 17, 1995, Knorr was sentenced to two consecutive life sentences. She is incarcerated at California Institution for Women in Chino, California. Knorr had a parole hearing in July 2019, but was denied release. Her next parole hearing will be one year from this publication in July 2024. William Knorr was sentenced to probation and ordered to undergo therapy for participating in his sister Suesan's murder. In exchange for his testimony, the prosecution dropped all charges against Robert Knorr, Jr. save for one count of being an accessory-after-the-fact in relation to Sheila's murder. Robert Jr. pleaded guilty to the charge and was sentenced to three years in prison, which was served concurrently with his 16-year sentence in Nevada. Following Knorr's arrest, police decided to reopen the murder case of Theresa's sister, Rosemary Knorr Norris. Norris was found strangled to death at the end of a dead-end road in Placer County in 1983 after she went grocery shopping in Sacramento. Police later determined that Knorr was not involved in Norris' death. After running

Wives Who Kill

away from her mother's home, Terry Knorr married twice and eventually moved to Sandy, Utah, where she lived with her second husband. She worked as a grocery store cashier in the same neighborhood where her mother lived and worked before her arrest. Theresa and Terry apparently did not know they lived in close proximity and had no contact. Terry Knorr died at 41 in 2011. The 2010 horror film The Afflicted (also titled Another American Crime) is loosely based on the Theresa Knorr case. The film follows the real-life events through a substantially-compressed timeline. Unlike the real case, the movie ends with the youngest daughter killing her mother and one of her brothers before committing suicide.

The murders were profiled on the A&E series Cold Case Files, featuring an exclusive interview with Terry Knorr Walker. The case was profiled on the series Most Evil, Wicked Attraction, Evil Lives Here, and Deadly Women.

Kau Kobayashi

Kau Kobayashi (October 20, 1908 – June 11, 1970) was a Japanese serial killer who, together with accomplice Mitsuyoshi Onuki, was responsible for murders of hotel owners Kamasuke and Ume Ikukata, called the Hotel Nihonkaku Incident. After her arrest, she confessed to fatally poisoning her husband in 1952, and was later sentenced to death and executed for her crimes. Kau Kobayashi was born on October 20, 1908 in Tamagoi, Saitama Prefecture (present-day Kumagaya), the second daughter of seven children born into an impoverished farmer couple's home. After finishing elementary school, she helped with housework until the age of 16, when she went to work as a housekeeper in Hongō, Tokyo. When she returned in 1930, she married 27-year-old Hidenosuke Hayashi, a sickly man suffering from gastroenteritis and gonorrhea who ran a store in Kumagaya. The couple would eventually have two children: a baby boy who died in infancy, and later a girl. When the Second World War broke out, Hidenosuke was called to serve, but was wounded in combat and returned to Japan. After his return, the couple built themselves a house, from where they would sell bicycle tires and contraband items such as rubber, rice and sugar. On the side, Kobayashi herself sold gokabou, which provided

Mariticide Club

additional income for the family. At one point, a 25-year-old police officer, Mataichiro Nakamura, was sent in to investigate the alleged contraband of illegal goods in the Hayashi household, but he was moved by their hospitality, and started occasionally visiting the family. Over time, Kobayashi, who was left sexually unsatisfied by her husband, began an affair with Nakamura. Despite being receptive of her advances, Nakamura told her that wanted to spend more time with her, and if that were to happen, she'd have to leave her husband. On October 2, 1952, Hayashi died from a sudden and mysterious illness, which the coroner labeled as the result of a cerebral hemorrhage. While there were suspicions that his wife was responsible for his death, the police ceased the investigation. Shortly thereafter, Nakamura moved in to live with Kobayashi, but was then fired from his job due to his behavior. Wanting to keep her new lover, Kobayashi began working even harder to run her business, eventually moving into Nakamura's house. However, this proved to be short-lived, as he eventually kicked her out and married a younger woman. A distressed Kobayashi was later observed banging at his front door and screaming for him to take her back, and even allegedly tried to poison his new wife, but still continued to provide him with money. Despite her troubled personal life, Kobayashi's business began to flourish when she began a joint venture with her sister's family, where she was hired as a saleswoman. She would travel around the various prefectures, looking for onsen-centered businesses to promote the company's services. As a result, in 1954, she found herself in Shiobara, where her most infamous crime would take place. Soon after her arrival in Shiobara, Kobayashi began familiarizing herself with the locals, and in the spring of 1956, she bought a small store in front of the Hotel Myogaya. Soon after, she began buying other stores and land in the area, eventually planning to build an onsen and work as a hostess. However, a majority of the townsfolk were unwilling to sell their properties, especially to a newcomer. In the fall of 1958, Kobayashi learned about the Hotel Nihonkaku, a small inn which was about to be closed due to poor management. The proprietor, 53-year-old Kamasuke Ikukata, desperately in need of funds to keep the inn open, he offered Kobayashi to pay a

Wives Who Kill

500,000 yen loan to his wife, Ume (49). However, when the two women met, Kau attempted to heckle the price down to 300,000 yen, which was rejected by Mrs. Ikukata. Angered by her refusal, in mid-January 1960, Kobayashi enlisted the help of 36-year-old Mitsuyoshi Onuki, offering him 20,000 yen and sexual services if she killed Ume Ikukata. Reluctantly agreeing, on the night of February 8, 1960, Onuki strangled Mrs. Ikukata with a linen string while she was sleeping. He later moved the body to the boiler room, where he dug up the floor and hid the body there, pouring concrete over it so it couldn't be located. After her disappearance, rumors starting floating around the area that she had been killed. Later in November, Kobayashi approached Onuki again, asking him to kill Kamasuke as well, but with poison this time. In mid-December, Onuki poured hydrochloric acid into Ikukata's meal and sake, but the strong taste put him off from finishing his meal. After their initial failure, on New Year's Eve, while the trio were watching TV, Kobayashi went to prepare dinner. When she was done, she snuck up behind Ikukata and started strangling him, after which Onuki joined in to help her by fatally stabbing him in the neck. The pair hid the body, and when customers came around to ask what had happened to Mr. Ikukata, they replied by saying that "he had gone to Tokyo for some money." The disappearance of the inn owners fueled the rumors of their untimely deaths even further, eventually resulting in newspapers covering the case. As a result, both Kobayashi and Onuki were arrested on February 20, 1961 on suspicion of murder. Shortly after her arrest, Kobayashi admitted her guilt in the case, additionally confessing to poisoning her husband with potassium cyanide in 1952, claiming that she had been aided by her lover Nakamura. Following these confessions, the three were put on trial, and on July 14, 1966, Kobayashi and Onuki were sentenced to death by the Supreme Court after being found guilty of the murders. Nakamura, who asserted his innocence from the beginning of the case, was acquitted due to lack of evidence. On June 11, 1970, the 61-year-old Kau Kobayashi and her accomplice were hanged at the Tokyo Detention House. She was the first woman to be executed in the country after the Second World War.

Mariticide Club

Koodathayi cyanide murders

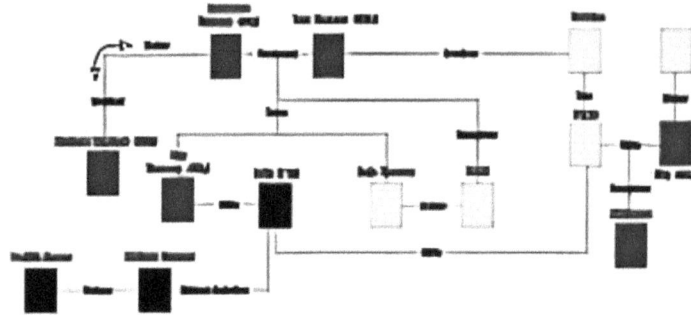

Koodathayi Cyanide Murders were a series of criminal incidents that occurred at Koodathayi in Kozhikode district, in the South Indian state of Kerala. The crimes were investigated in late 2019, involving the mystery of 6 murders over a span of 14 years. The criminal cases drew considerable media and public interest in Kerala, and eventually led to the arrest of Jolly Joseph. The case also led to a debate on the legal and moral implications. In 2002, Annamma Thomas, the mother-in-law of the accused, drank a glass of water after returning home from a walk. Immediately afterwards, she began to feel uneasy and dizzy, eventually collapsing on the floor. She was taken to the hospital where she later died, and the doctors declared that she had suffered a heart attack. In 2008, Tom Thomas, Annamma's husband passed away after swooning and collapsing. Their daughter-in-law Jolly Joseph was allegedly present on the spot on both occasions. In 2011, Roy Thomas, Jolly's then-husband, died after consuming rice and curry. He was found dead in a bathroom which was locked from the inside. The cause of death was then ruled as suicide due to financial issues as the postmortem report showed traces of poison. Roy Thomas' maternal uncle Mathew Manjayadil called for a post-mortem report and an inquiry into Roy's cause of death. In 2014, Mathew swooned and died after Jolly allegedly gave him poison-laden whisky. The deceased Roy Thomas has a cousin called Shaju Zachariah. The same year, Shaju's toddler daughter, Alphine Shaju, died after "choking on food". In 2016, Jolly allegedly gave Sily Shaju, Alphine's mother, a glass of water and the latter died on the spot with excessive frothing at the mouth. In 2018, Rojo Thomas came down to Koodathai and filed a series of RTI applications. From the government

Wives Who Kill

hospital, he received a copy of the autopsy report of his brother's body." When he read the report, he discovered what Jolly told us was wrong. Jolly told us he had food at 3.30 pm and hadn't had food after that. But it was clear in the post-mortem report that he had rice and chickpeas curry at 8.30 pm," said Bawa. "Acute cyanide poisoning can result in death in a matter of seconds. Cyanide does not accumulate in the body: it is rare to encounter it in slow death cases," explained Dr V V Pillay, head of Forensic Medicine & Toxicology, Amrita Institute of Medical Sciences in Kochi. 47-year-old Jolly Joseph is the prime suspect in the murder of six members of the family she married into. It was Rojo Thomas, Roy Thomas' brother, who complained to the police about the six unnatural deaths whose investigation led to Jolly Joseph. Following her arrest in October 2019, Jolly has confessed to using cyanide to kill the six aforementioned people. She obtained the cyanide with the help of M. S. Mathew and Praji Kumar, who also were arrested. Jolly is originally from Kattappana, Idukki district and a first-year college dropout. She married her first husband Roy Thomas in 1997. Jolly and Roy had two sons, now aged 15 and 21. According to her neighbor, Jolly lied to fellow villagers about being a M.Com. graduate and having a job at the prestigious National Institute of Technology Calicut. However, her true whereabouts during her daily outings to fake her "job" remains uncertain. In 2011, her husband Roy Thomas died under mysterious circumstances. Following the death of Shaju Zachariah's wife in 2016, Jolly married Shaju. Jolly has been described as "jovial, friendly, jolly and pious" by people who knew her. According to the police, M. S. Mathew, a jewelry shop employee who is also a relative of Jolly, provided Jolly with the cyanide. He reportedly told the police that he procured the cyanide from Prajikumar after giving him two bottles of alcohol and ₹5,000. Mathew said Jolly asked him for cyanide to kill a rat in her house. Praji Kumar is a goldsmith who gave M. S. Mathew the cyanide. He said he assumed the poison was to kill a rat.

Grace Kotani

Mariticide Club

Roland Kotani, circa 1980s.

Roland M. Kotani (June 15, 1954 – July 28, 1989) was an American politician and Democratic member of the Hawaii State House of Representatives. Kotani served as assistant majority floor leader and represented the Pearl City Pacific Palisades area. He was killed by his estranged wife Grace Kotani on July 28, 1989, at the age of 35. A Japanese American, Kotani graduated from Yale University and in 1984 he was the editor of Ka Huliau (The Turning Point), a self-described "Hawaiian Grassroots Journal." The journal was launched in early 1983 and published every six weeks, with an estimated circulation of 3,000. Kotani's particular focus was on the resurgence of the local people's movement. He worked as an editorial assistant for Herald. Kotani authored the book The Japanese in Hawaii: A Century of Struggle in 1985, writing extensively on the 100th Infantry Battalion. During this time, he worked as an assistant to the Governor of Hawaii and Lieutenant Governor of Hawaii. He was nominated to the Hawaii State House of Representatives in 1987 by the Governor John Waihee to replace representative Eloise Tungpalan who was appointed to the Hawaii State Senate. Kotani was later elected to the House unopposed in 1988. He married Grace Sadako Imura in 1979 and they had a daughter together. The couple separated in February 1989 and became estranged. On July 28, 1989, as a result of a domestic dispute, Grace attacked Kotani with a hammer and beat him to death. The killing took

Wives Who Kill

place in a rented duplex in Honolulu. The medical examination report stated Kotani sustained blunt force trauma to the head. Grace later presented herself to the Honolulu Police Department and confessed to the murder, before excusing herself to the restroom where she fatally shot herself. The University of Hawaii at Manoa launched the Roland Kotani Scholarship in his memory at the University's Department of Ethnic Studies. Kotani was also acknowledged in several state resolutions passed by the Hawaii State Legislature. Kotani's murder is studied in detail as a case study in Hawaii crime scene investigation books.

Dame Alice Kyteler

Dame Alice Kyteler (1263-1325) was the first recorded person condemned for witchcraft in Ireland. She fled the country to either England or Flanders, and there is no record of her after her escape from persecution. Her servant Petronilla de Meath (also spelt Petronella) was flogged and burned to death at the stake on 3 November 1324, after being tortured and confessing to the heretical crimes she, Kyteler, and Kyteler's followers were alleged to have committed. Kyteler was born in Kyteler's House, in County Kilkenny, Ireland. She was the only child of a Flemish family of merchants settled in Ireland in the mid- to late thirteenth century. She was married four times, to William Outlaw, Adam le Blund, Richard de Valle, and Sir John le Poer.

1. First husband c.1280–85: William Outlaw, wealthy merchant and moneylender from Kilkenny. Son: William Outlaw, was mayor of Kilkenny in 1305. Daughter: Rose?
2. Second husband (by 1302): Adam Blund of Callan, moneylender. Had children from a previous marriage
3. Third husband (by 1309): Richard de Valle, a wealthy landholder of County Tipperary. After de Valle's death c.1316, Kyteler took proceedings against one of her stepsons, Richard, for the recovery of her widow's dower. This act incited the suspicion and anger of her stepchildren,

Mariticide Club

as they would have received the money had she not intervened.

4.   Fourth husband (c.1316–24): John le Poer. He had children from a previous marriage.

In 1302, Kyteler and her second husband were briefly accused of killing her first husband. She incurred local resentment because of her vast wealth and involvement in moneylending. Her fourth husband, John le Poer, briefly defended her by imprisoning Richard de Ledrede, the Bishop of Ossory, who was attempting to arrest Kyteler. However, when le Poer fell ill in 1324, he expressed the suspicion that he was being poisoned. After his death, the children of le Poer and of her previous three husbands, her step-children, accused her of using poison and sorcery (maleficarum) against their fathers and of favoring her first-born son, William Outlaw.

Seven formal charges were brought against Kyteler. She was accused of:
1.   Denying the power of Christ and of the Church. During this period, renunciation of faith was interpreted as a shift in worship to the devil.
2.   Sacrificing animals to the demons Artis Filius and Robin Artisson.
3.   Asking demons for advice on witchcraft.
4.   Having a sexual relationship with the incubus Robin Artisson. It was alleged that Robin Artisson often took the form of animals or an Ethiopian when engaging with Kyteler.
5.   Holding coven meetings and burning candles in the church at night without permission. This group included: Robert of Bristol, Petronilla de Meath, Meath's daughter Sarah, John/Ellen'Syssok Galrussyn, Annota Lange, Eva de Brownstown, William Payn de Boly, and Alice Faver.
6.   Making dark magic-based powders and ointments or potions, from multiple alarming ingredients, including but

not limited to body parts of unbaptized children, worms, a skull, and chicken innards. It was alleged that said potions were used to corrupt her husbands.

7. Bewitching and killing her husbands to take their money for herself and her biological son, William Outlaw.

Before sentencing, Kyteler along with Petronilla de Meath's daughter, Basilia, escaped. Although at least 10 other people faced convictions in connection to Kyteler, they did not attempt to escape with their leader. There are no records of her life after her escape. Her date of death is unknown, along with the location of a burial site.

Accusers and their motives

The Husbands

Kyteler's first three husbands did not raise accusations against her regarding witchcraft or her responsibility for the deaths of her other husbands. Her last husband, John le Poer, only raised suspicions toward her once he developed the sickness that eventually led to his death. He did not mention witchcraft as a potential cause of his and his predecessors' deaths, but rather implied that poisoning was the most plausible cause of his affliction. Le Poer did not accuse her based on any perceived behaviour change from her, but rather from the physical change in his own health coupled with her previous husbands' unusual deaths.

John le Poer's children

Shortly before le Poer's death, he edited his will to financially favor Kytelerand her son. Children from his other marriage approached bishop Richard de Ledrede and claimed she had bewitched their father and was a poisoner. The phrase 'poisoner' was tied to being a witch because of the connection of herbalism and witchcraft.

Medieval Catholic Church and Richard de Ledrede

As the primary actors during the investigation of Alice Kyteler, the church had the most influence on the outcome of her and her alleged followers' trial. At the time of this trial, the church in Ireland had a secure relationship

Mariticide Club

with the judicial system. The sentence of repentance and self-betterment for Kyteler's son William Outlaw depicts this relationship as religious acts were available means of reform from convictions. Across Europe during the Middle Ages, it was common to sentence heretics to acts of religious reformation before a death sentence was brought into discussion. The belief was that heresy was comparable to an illness, which could be transferred to others as well as be cured. However, the option for reform was not offered to Kyteler or her maid after the maid confessed, which was highly unusual for the time. It is possible that the preemptive attacks against Richard de Ledrede by Kyteler and her son led to a sentence driven by resentment. The lack of confession from Kyteler herself may have implied a lack of remorse for the crimes she was accused of; however, Meath's confession did not garner her a lenient sentence either. Additionally, William Outlaw failed to produce a confession for the heretical crimes, but did apologize for his attacks against Ledrede before the trial. Outlaw received leniency in his sentence due to his apology to Ledrede, which suggests a degree of personal pride of the bishop likely was present during the sentencing of the other heretics in this case, as they did not make specific apologies to him. Additionally, although it is likely that Kyteler was responsible for at least a few of her husband's deaths, it would be difficult to persecute her to the highest extent for murder given the precedent of cross-nobility murders in the British Isles. Although murder was very uncommon amongst nobles in England, the rest of the British Isles in the 13th century had a long-lasting tradition of violent noble feuds. What made conviction even more difficult was that English jurors were unlikely to convict an accused murderer in the 13th century, as 63.5% of defendants were acquitted. It is possible that the Bishop de Ledrede and John le Poer's children accused Kyteler of witchcraft in order to secure punishment for her crimes that she would likely have been acquitted for, as witchcraft was a much more taboo topic. Additionally, heresy was considered to be the worst crime that could be committed. This would also explain why the death penalty was applied in this case compared to previous cases against heretics in Europe. What would have made this an even more appealing option for persecution was

Wives Who Kill

there was no statute for witchcraft in Ireland at this time, which meant the treatment of the case was tried with ecclesiastical law. Kyteler would be tried as a heretic not as a felon as English common law would have done. Kyteler's husbands were all notable wealthy men. When each of them died she received a large sum of their money. She may have married her husbands for love, but Kyteler's speed in remarrying and the speed of her husband's deaths after marriage suggests she was not interested in their company or personalities when she selected them. Considering their common trait was their wealth, this appears to be the most likely motive. This was also considered to be the likely motive from the perspectives of the people of Kilkenny.

Relationship values in Ireland

Another potential motive was that Kyteler's personal needs were restrained due to patriarchal values in Ireland during her time. There were two approaches to marital laws in Ireland due to discrepancies between the Anglo-Normans and the Gaelic Irish. For both groups, there were limited reasons divorce or an annulment would be approved, which included the prolonged absence of one partner, breakage of a pre-marriage agreement or contract, and impotence, among others. It is possible that Kyteler wanted to leave her husbands but did not meet any of the annulment-worthy complaints, and so resorted to murder instead. Open displays of sexuality were highly scorned in medieval Ireland. It was considered sinful to take part in or even think of committing such acts, including masturbation. During the investigation of Kyteler's room, a pipe with ointment was found in her nightstand. It has been argued that this item was a dildo. This item being in Kyteler's nightstand suggests that she was comfortable going against the sexual standards of her time. It is possible that her husbands did not satisfy her in this way or approve of her sexuality, which may have led her to try to find a husband who would. Richard de Ledrede, Bishop of Ossory, sought to uphold the laws of the church and morality. When the case was presented before him in 1324, he began his larger project of addressing witchcraft. Ledrede made initial attempts to have Kyteler arrested, and Kyteler called on the assistance of

Mariticide Club

powerful friends. The bishop wrote to the Chancellor of Ireland, Roger Utlagh (Outlaw), demanding that she be arrested. Using the decretal Ut Inquisitiones (1298), designed to protect the faith, Ledrede demanded that secular powers concede to church wishes, and this point of law became a thorny issue throughout the trial. Kyteler was related to the Chancellor (he was probably her first husband's brother) and he asked the bishop to drop the case. The chancellor demanded that Kyteler be excommunicated for at least 40 days before the trial, which caused a delay in the proceedings. This allowed Kyteler to flee to Roger Utlagh. Ledrede accused Utlagh of harboring heretics, but a commission cleared him of any wrongdoing. The bishop then charged Kyteler and her son, William Outlaw, with the crime of heresy. William was a powerful man and was related to many in the ruling classes. He called upon his friend, Sir Arnold le Poeur, a Senior Official in Dublin, who had de Ledrede thrown in prison in Kilkenny Castle. Ledrede, despite his limited political connections compared to his captors, was released from prison after he ordered the diocese be placed on an interdict. He would not allow any religious ceremonies to occur until he was released. On Ledrede's release, he renewed his efforts to have Kyteler imprisoned. Kyteler and her accomplices were accused of and investigated on the seven accounts. After some months of stalemate, one of Kyteler's servants, Petronilla de Meath, was tortured and confessed to participating in witchcraft. Her confession detailed her involvement, along with Kyteler's, in six out of seven of the above-listed crimes. One example she gave was rubbing ointment on a stick to fly. It would seem, although her testimony was likely forced and unreliable, that the accusers gained most of their information from this confession. Although the testimony did implicate Kyteler in performing heresy, questions concerning Petronella's credibility came to light, especially when examining the contents of her confession. In Ledrede's retelling of Petronilla's confession, he writes:

'On one of these occasions, by the crossroads outside the city, she had made an offering of three cocks to a certain demon whom she called Robert, son of Art (Robertum filium Artis), from the depths of the underworld. She had poured out the cocks' blood, cut the animals into pieces and mixed the

Wives Who Kill

intestines with spiders and other black worms like scorpions, with a herb called milfoil as well as with other herbs and horrible worms. She had boiled this mixture in a pot with the brains and clothes of a boy who had died without baptism and with the head of a robber who had been decapitated ... Petronilla said she had several times at Alice's instigation and once in her presence, consulted demons and received answers. She had consented to a pact whereby she would be the medium between Alice and the said Robert, her friend. In public, she said that with her own eyes she had seen the aforesaid demon as three shapes (praedictus daemon tertius), in the form of three black men (aethiopum) each carrying an iron rod in the hand. This apparition happened by daylight (de die) before the said Dame Alice, and, while Petronilla herself was watching, the apparition had intercourse with Alice. After this disgraceful act, with her own hand she (Alice?) wiped clean the disgusting place with sheets (kanevacio) from her own bed.'

Despite the clear usage of torture, Ledrede referred to the acts committed against Petronilla as floggings. His assertion that flogging occurred suggests that what she went through was an act of punishment rather than an attempt to gain a confession was potentially an attempt to give credibility to her statements. Additionally, the credibility of the physical evidence used against Kyteler was dubious. Investigators cited a 'pipe of ointment' found in Kyteler's room as evidence for the sixth charge. However, it is most likely that what they found was actually a dildo. It is said Kyteler fled to England. She appears no further in contemporary records. The Bishop continued to pursue her working-class associates, bringing charges of witchcraft against them. Petronilla de Meath was flogged and burned at the stake on 3 November 1324. Petronella's daughter, Basilia, fled with Kyteler. Kyteler's son, William Outlaw, was also accused inter alia, of heresy, usury, perjury, adultery, and clericide. Multiple courts refused to try the case, but he was eventually convicted, excommunicated, and briefly imprisoned. Outlaw was released after he begged for forgiveness from Ledrede. Additionally, he was able to reverse excommunication by visiting the Holy Land while following specific rules.

Mariticide Club

Chronology of events

- c.1280—Alice Kyteler marries her first husband William Outlaw.
- 1302—Alice and her second husband, Adam le Blund, are accused of homicide.
- c.1316—Alice's third husband, Richard de Valle, dies and she sues his heir for the widow's share.
- 1317 April—Pope John XXII appoints Richard de Ledrede as Bishop of Ossory.
- October—De Ledrede arrives in Ossory and holds a synod.
- 1320 August—John XXII sends a letter to the justiciar of Ireland regarding complaints of harassment and imprisonment made by Ledrede.
- 1324—Ledrede accuses Alice Kyteler and her associates of witchcraft and heresy.
- March/April—Arnold le Poer imprisons Ledrede for 17 days.
- Dublin parliament; the magnates, including Arnold le Poer and Maurice FitzThomas, swear to discipline their own people and followers (lineages).
- Arrest of heretics by Ledrede.
- November—Petronilla of Meath burnt for heresy and witchcraft.
- William Outlaw's penance payment is guaranteed by the magnates.
- 1325 January -- Alexander Bicknor deserts to the queen's party while on an embassy to France.
- 1326—The feud between the le Poers and Maurice FitzThomas worsens.
- Maurice FitzThomas and John le Poer, baron of Donoil, are allowed four months to discipline their followers; Arnold le Poer goes to England.
- 1327 January—Deposition of Edward II by Queen Isabella and Roger Mortimer.
- 1327/8 -- Ledrede appeals to Isabella and is given permission to come to court but fails to use it, later claiming that Bicknor and Outlaw had closed the ports against him.
- Arnold is confirmed as seneschal of Kilkenny and given custody of Kilkenny Castle.

Wives Who Kill

- The "Munster war" breaks out between the le Poers and Maurice. A jury later claims Ledrede attended a meeting to coordinate Marice's "rebellion."
- Ledrede is alleged to have instigated an attack on the le Poer castle of Moytobir.
- 1328 -- Adam Duff O'Toole burnt for heresy
- Justiciar orders the magnates to stop fighting
- Arnold returns. Ledrede charges him with heresy and has him imprisoned in Dublin Castle.
- Ledrede sends a petition to court complaining of his treatment by Arnold.
- The justiciar, Thomas FitzJohn, sends the king an indictment of Ledrede by the people of Ossory, seizes his temporalities and summons him to Dublin.
- 1329 January—Roger Outlaw purges himself at the Dublin parliament of Ledrede's heresy accusations.
- March—Arnold dies in prison.
- Archbishop Bicknor summons Ledrede to Dublin to answer charges of
  aiding and abetting heretics.
- June—Ledrede flees Ireland and England, ignoring a royal summons to appear before the king. Writs are issued for his arrest.
- Edward III warns John XXII against Ledrede. Bicknor excommunicates Ledrede.
- 1330 October—Edward III seizes control from his mother and Mortimer. He sends further letters warning the Pope against Ledrede.
- 1331 May—At the request of the papacy, Edward III restores Ledrede's temporalities.
- 1332—The cathedral roof paid for by William Outlaw collapses during a storm.
- A jury accuses Ledrede of having conspired to support Maurice in his "rebellion" of 1327.
- The dean and chapter claim Ledrede purged himself of rebellion at the Kilkenny parliament of 1328.
- 1333—Ledrede returns to England; the Pope urges Edward III to assist him and other Irish prelates against heretics.

Mariticide Club

- John XXII writes to the Archbishop of Cashel ordering him to promulgate in his province a processus pontificum against heretics.
- 1335 November—Pope Benedict XII writes to Edward III on behalf of Ledrede.
- 1339 June—Edward III orders the writs against Ledrede to be revoked.
- September—Edward III orders the escheator of Kilkenny to obey the writ issued in July restoring Ledrede's temporalities.
- Roger Outlaw dies while holding office as deputy judicier; Bicknor succeeds him.
- 1341 February—Ledrede sends a petition to the king claiming that Bicknor had planned to murder him in 1329.
- 1343—Bicknor is cited by the papacy for impeding Ledrede in his prosecution of heretics.
- Ossory is exempted from the jurisdiction of Dublin. The papacy orders an inquiry into Bicknor's protection of heretics.
- 1347 April—Ledrede receives a royal pardon and secures his temporalities back from the king; he returns to his diocese.
- 1349 July—Death of Alexander Bicknor.
- Restoration of Ossory to the jurisdiction of Dublin.
- 1351—Ledrede refuses a royal tax on the clergy, the 1347 pardon is revoked and the temporalities resumed.
- 1355—Ledrede is granted a royal pardon and his temporalities restored. He is accused of instigating a violent attack on a priory.
- 1356/7 -- The English chancellor, John Thoresby, Archbishop of York, drafts a letter to the pope asking for Ledrede's removal, accusing him of senility, madness, and persecuting his parishioners.
- 1360—Ledrede dies.

In the late thirteenth and fourteenth century, heresy was considered as evidence of the struggle with the devil, with the "dangers" of witchcraft voiced by the papacy in Avignon. Pope John XXII listed witchcraft as heresy in his bull Super illius specula. Kyteler's was one of the first European witchcraft trials and followed closely on the election of this pope (1316–1334). Kyteler's case appears to involve the first recorded claim of a witch lying with her incubus. Annales Hiberniae state that: RicardusLedered, episcopus Ossoriensis, citavit Aliciam Ketil, ut se purgaret de

Wives Who Kill

heretica pravitate; quae magiae convicta est, nam certo comprobatum est, quendam demonem incubum (nomine Robin Artisson) concubuisse cum ea viz., Kyteler had intercourse with a demon named "Robin Artisson". This case was also the first to treat the accused parties as an organized group or coven as opposed to individuals. Additionally, it was the first cased of convicted heresy resulting in the death sentence in Ireland.

Considering how Kyteler and her followers were the first people to be condemned for witchcraft in Ireland, this case set the precedent for how all following witchcraft and heresy cases would be executed. The act of burning witches in Ireland lasted until 1895. "Lady Kyteler" figures in William Butler Yeats' poem "Nineteen Hundred and Nineteen":

> But now wind drops, dust settles; thereupon
> There lurches past, his great eyes without thought
> Under the shadow of stupid straw-pale locks,
> That insolent fiend Robert Artisson
> To whom the love-lorn Lady Kyteler brought
> Bronzed peacock feathers, red combs of her cocks.
> — WB Yeats, Nineteen Hundred and Nineteen (1921)

The Stone, a novel about the times of Alice Kyteler, was published in 2008, written by a Kilkenny woman named Claire Nolan. A musical version of The Stone, based on Nolan's book, premiered in Kilkenny in 2011. Robin Morgan wrote a novel, The Burning Time, (Melville House, 2006; ISBN 978-1-933633-00-8) about Alice Kyteler. A short story by Emma Donoghue, 'Looking for Petronilla', tells the story of Alice Kyteler and her maid. The story appears in the collection The Woman Who Gave Birth to Rabbits (Virago, 2002). The Kyteler Witch is a novel that explores the relationship between Petronella de Meath and her employer Lady Alice Kyteler, written by Candace Muncy Poole, 2014. The trial is mentioned in Umberto Eco's novel The Name of the Rose in a conversation between William of Baskerville and Abo the abbot. The feminist art piece by Judy Chicago, The Dinner Party, features a place setting for Petronella de Meath. The plate features the image of a book, a candle, a bell, and a

Mariticide Club

cauldron. All of these items are encapsulated by fire. The trial is mentioned in papal chaplain Martin of Troppau's Chronicles of Popes and Emperors.

Bridget Larkin
Murder of John Hurford

The murder of John Hurford occurred on 8 April 1855 in Western Australia. His murder led to the first execution of a woman in Western Australia, for the crime of murder. Hurford arrived in the colony of Western Australia in 1830. He was granted 400 hectares of land at Augusta and purchased a further 100 hectares at Wonnerup Inlet near Busselton.: 22 By the age of 65, he had amassed a fortune of £2,000. He married Bridget Larkin in 1851. She had been widowed when her husband had drowned in Bunbury. There were six children of this earlier marriage.

The relationship was not to be a happy one. Larkin was abusive towards her new husband. Hurford alleged to a friend that Larkin had knocked out some of his teeth during an argument. By February 1855 he had had enough and left the house. He stayed with his neighbor sharing a room with a workhand, George Jones. He stayed there for six weeks refusing to return to the matrimonial home. He purchased another house with the intention of moving there and living there without his wife. Before moving to his new home, he was forced to return to his matrimonial home in late March 1855 because of the lack of space at his neighbor's premises. Jones continued to share the room with Hurford. On 8 April 1855 Hurford was not well. He had a cold and felt sore and fatigued. His wife offered him some mulled wine which he accepted. His wife also sent word to Jones that Hurford wished to sleep on his own that night because of his illness. She sent her daughter away, too. Later that night Hurford was found in bed with the sheet drawn up to his face, his eyes wide open and slightly protruding. Jones noticed a red mark on the left and right sides of Hurford's neck. An inquest was held by the Coroner. The evidence of Dr Hannibal Bryan led to a finding of natural death by the coroner. Bryan gave evidence that Hurford had died of natural causes. Later that month, Enoch Dodd confessed the murder to his friend Philip Dixon. Dixon had earlier forged Hurford's will

Wives Who Kill

in favor of Larkin. Dodd said that he had killed Hurfield at the urging of Larkin. Larkin had plied Dodd with alcohol. When Dodd had baulked at performing the murder, Larkin had stood over Dodd and made sure that Dodd had completed the deed. Larkin made noise in the kitchen to cover up the ensuing struggle. The pair were arrested and committed for trial on 28 August 1855 on murder charges. The trial was held in the Court of General Quarter Sessions on 3 October 1855 before a crowded court room. Dr Bryan was called as a defense witness and testified that he had not seen any strangulation marks on Hurfield's neck. Under cross-examination by the Crown, he admitted that he had not passed a medical examination. He was also unable to explain how to use a stethoscope. On the second day of the trial, Larkin confessed to the murder.

Both Dodd and Larkin were found guilty and sentenced to death by hanging. They were hanged on the following Monday in Perth Prison. Dixon was charged with conspiracy to forge the will. He pleaded guilty and was transported to Van Diemen's Land for the term of his natural life. Both Dodd and Larkin were the first executions in the new prison, and Larkin was the first woman to be hanged in Western Australia.

Piroska Jancsó-Ladányi (née Piroska Mária Ladányi) (15 January 1934 – 12 December 1954) was a Hungarian serial killer who killed her five female husbands, teenage girls in Törökszentmiklós between 1953 and 1954 in order to satisfy her sexual urges. Hanged in 1954, she remains one of the most infamous and insidious killers in Hungarian criminal history, with her case covered extensively in the novel Little Saints by author Szilárd Rubin. Piroska's mother, Borbála, was born on 1 May 1909, as one of 16 children of postman János and street sweeper Mária. Twelve of her siblings died in infancy, while two of her sisters would later commit suicide. Borbála lost her father at age 8, leaving the family without any income, resulting in her dropping out of school. At age 16, due to her desperate financial situation, Borbála began to offer sexual services, for which she was shunned by her peers. Officially, she worked as a maid for male farmers who paid off her living and housing expenses. As a

Mariticide Club

result of these liaisons, Borbála gave birth to five children, four of them from different men. Piroska Mária was born on 15 January 1934 in Törökszentmiklós, the offspring of Gyula Ladányi, a local farmer; her half-brother, József, was born on 5 August 1943 to Jewish merchant Lipót Weisz. Neither man recognized their paternity. Ladányi was pressured to do so in 1949, paying off an alimony of 600 forints to never deal with his daughter again. Weisz was deported to a concentration camp, and never returned. Due to change in legislation at the time, József became an heir to Weisz's fortune, with the family given a building at 171 Red Army Road (present-day Széchenyi Street). The building was regarded as a brothel by local villagers. The house was described as a *"simple farmhouse, painted in yellow, consisting of three rooms. The two windows of the room faced the street and the kitchen and the pantry looked out onto the porch. The fence was set in the winter, in the summer they just cut through their yard, trampling between meters of weeds on the path, to the kitchen door. The two street windows were covered with tar paper."* Borbála and Piroska were often visited by men to satisfy their sexual needs, for which they were paid cash, bread or tallow. Both had STDs from their partners. While Borbála often had sex with the Hungarians, 14-year-old Piroska serviced the Soviet soldiers from the local garrison at the telephone station on the Czégény farm. In her free time, she would wander around the area, stealing and getting drunk. She tried to take on several honest jobs, but often quit. Jancsó-Ladányi finished her education up to the 5th grade, but was noted for reading books and novels about human anatomy. According to one psychiatrist, she had above-average intelligence compared to her peers, wrote poems and spoke fluent Russian. By 1952, she had been prosecuted for a theft, and police had arrested her in several cities. One police officer later claimed that *"[Jancsó-Ladányi] lives an immoral lifestyle, and if she can, she would go to the Soviet soldiers, doesn't usually stay at her parents' house, goes out and lives like a tramp rather live a normal life."* She also had to undergo treatment for her STDs on three separate occasions. In the summer of 1953, Jancsó-Ladányi first met 11-year-old Marika Komáromi, who herded cows in the city's outskirts. A few months later, on 13 October,

Wives Who Kill

she met her again in front of the vegetable shop in Törökszentmiklós, standing in line for some fries. It was then that she decided to lure the little girl to her house by promising that there were more fries there. When they reached the house, Jancsó-Ladányi gave her a novel to read, and while Komáromi was reading, she was strangled from behind with an electric wire. After strangling the girl, Jancsó-Ladányi undressed the corpse and rubbed herself against it. She then covered it up with a blanket, tied a noose around the neck and dragged it out of the house, dumping it down a well. It was claimed that the little girl had disappeared near the Czégény farm populated by the Soviets, but nobody present there was questioned by local police. According to one researcher, Tibor Legát, this was a result of the fear the police department felt from the invading forces, and the contemporary belief that no violent crime occurred in socialist countries.[6] At a witness hearing in the fall of 1954, 13-year-old Mária Markoth testified that the Soviet soldiers did indeed solicit young girls for sex, which was backed up by Ilona Czene, who admitted to prostituting herself to them. However, Czene also claimed that on 27 August 1954, a drunken Jancsó-Ladányi confessed to her about killing the Komáromi girl with the help of her mother. This account was backed up by yet another witness, Rozália Lajkó, who had come across the pair near the Czégény farm. She had asked them what were they gonna do there, to which little Marika replied to "talk to the Russians", but when queried about what for, she just shrugged. Lajkó parted with them shortly after they reached the homestead, but had seen a soldier come out and greet them. When she went to the authorities, they advised her to remain quiet on the matter, and thereafter suspended the investigation out of fear for repercussions from the soldiers. Jancsó-Ladányi's presence was completely ignored, despite her known association with the troops and the fact that both of her children were born to different fathers serving in the garrison. On 9 June 1954, Jancsó-Ladányi came across 13-year-old Piroska Hóppal, who was selling chickens at the Törökszentmiklós market. Sensing an opportunity, she lured the girl to the farmhouse, ostensibly to sell her some chickens, but when they arrived, she gave her a book to distract her. While Hóppal was reading,

Mariticide Club

Jancsó-Ladányi strangled her with a wire. Then, according to her later confessions, "[she] looked at the corpse's genitalia, licked it, and then stuck a carrot in her own genitalia, causing her to ejaculate. She then inserted a long broomstick into her vagina. Later, she licked Hóppal's genitalia with her tongue while holding on to her corpse, causing her to ejaculate again". In addition, she stole 200 forints that the girl had on her. In the spring of 1954, Jancsó-Ladányi became acquaintances with 17-year-old factory worker Irén Simon, who came from Budapest. According to her, Simon was also secretly a lesbian, but rebuffed her advances, as she was afraid of somebody finding out about their intimate relationship. On 9 August 1954, Jancsó-Ladányi lured Simon to the farmhouse, where she strangled her with the electric wire. She undressed her body, but noticed that she was suffering from a venereal disease and refrained from performing any sexual acts with her corpse. She instead dragged the victim's body to the well and dumped it there, before rummaging through her clothes' pockets, stealing 30 forints and then throwing the clothes away. Two days later, she intercepted 12-year-old Marika Botos at the bus stop in front of the Törökszentmiklós council house. The girl, who came from Mezőtúr, told that she was visiting her godmother for the holidays. Jancsó-Ladányi offered to escort her there, but on the way, she asked Botos to help deliver a package to her farm. When they reached the farmhouse, Jancsó-Ladányi strangled her with a cotton cord. After satisfying her sexual urges with the little girl's naked body, she dragged it to the well and threw it in. She then hid Botos' clothes under her bed, stealing the 7 forints she found on them. On 14 August, Jancsó-Ladányi approached her fifth victim, 13-year-old Katóká Szőke, on the railway, luring her to the farmhouse under the pretext of helping to carry a package. When they entered the farmhouse, Szőke was given a book to read, while Jancsó-Ladányi snuck up behind her and strangled her with a trouser strap. She then undressed the body, mutilated it and then threw it into the well, keeping the girl's clothes. She then went to the market, selling her victims' clothes and shoes for 15-20 forints apiece. She got the most out of Hóppal's jacket, shirt and sandals, for which she was paid 45 forints. As the disappearances continued, locals

Wives Who Kill

began to panic, with parents refusing to allow their children to go out without supervision. The cases were reported to the crime department of the Szolnok Police Headquarters, with some suggesting that Soviets were responsible for the abductions. Despite this, no patrols were dispatched and authorities did not ask the parents for photographs of the children, ordering only that a car with a loudspeaker drive around the town and describe the victims. In 1954, two teenage boys disappeared: Albert Kenyeres on 2 February, and Imre Vígh on 21 June, but it later turned out that both of them had run away from home. The population became increasingly suspicious towards outsiders, especially travelling gypsies and motorists passing through the city, leading to over a thousand residents of Törökszentmiklós protesting in front of the police station, demanding that the kidnappers be apprehended. There were rumors that local Jews were kidnapping the children to "use their blood to rebuild the synagogue", and a local funeral company director was abducting them in his company car. On 2 September 1954, at 9 o'clock in the evening, Istvánné Balászi, a 21-yearold resident of Pusztakengyel, reported to the Törökszentmiklós police that Jancsó-Ladányi had attempted to rob and then strangle her with a wire. They met at the Szolnok-Alcsi railway station, where they got acquainted over their mutual search for a job. The two discussed going to the amusement park in Tiszaliget to have some fun, for which they were joined by a man who was carrying Piroska's suitcase. The next morning, Balászi realized that her new companion had stolen her package.[6] Knowing that she worked as a maid, she notified authorities, who found her on a construction site. In the end, Balászi did not make a complaint, as Piroska promised that she would return the suitcase if she accompanied her to Törökszentmiklós. When the pair arrived there, Jancsó-Ladányi gave her some brandy, causing Balászi to feel sleepy and fall asleep in the yard, since the room was dirty and the three small children were scattered around the house. In the evening, she woke up to Jancsó-Ladányi trying to strangle her with a wire, and in her fear, she wrestled off her assailant and escaped. Balászi told a friend working at the police station about the attack, who, together with two of his colleagues, brought Jancsó-Ladányi for

Mariticide Club

interrogation. Since she refused to admit whether she was guilty or not, the authorities went to the farmhouse to find the stolen clothes. While exploring the farmhouse, police found clothing belonging to the girls who had gone missing in recent months, but were unable to find Balászi's property. One of the officers reported to his superior that he had found a mineshaft with a metal cover on the porch behind the gate. When he opened it, he found a 10-12 meter deep well, built when the older house had been demolished. They lit up the mine to examine it further, only to find human remains covered in water and mud at the bottom. The first officer to go down the well reported that *"Down there, in a roughly sitting position, one could see the body of a girl. She was completely naked. Her head leaned to the side, half of her mutilated face protruding from the water. Next to her head was a sole, tossed on the corpse, and a military belt."* It took several hours to remove all the corpses, with assistance from firefighters. The discoveries shocked the nation, with even senior military and police officers, as well as ministers, arriving at the crime scene. The police believed that it was improbable that Piroska had managed to commit the murders without the knowledge of her mother, Borbála, she was detained as well. A report from the inspection described the conditions in the farmhouse: *"The building consists of two parts, a kitchen with two beds and a table. [...] There are two pillows on the bed, the color of which could not be determined due to the amount of dirt. The apartment in earthy, including the living room and kitchen. [...] In the middle of the room, there are tables, while behind the back door, there's a 5-pattern cast iron stove set on three bricks. [...] Both rooms are filthy, while the wall, which was once colored white, now cannot be distinguished due to dust and dirt. Both rooms house mice and fleas. The clothing and beddings are unwashed and dirty, as is the cutlery. [...] A side chamber is built near the building... There are two used perforated logs in the side chamber, in addition to human feces."* As the public wasn't informed on the case by officials, there were all sorts of rumors about the number of victims. Among the women gathering round the Törökszentmiklós market, there were claims that there were more girls killed elsewhere and that a boy who had been kidnapped

Wives Who Kill

from a cornfield recently was also the victim of the same killer. The investigation was marred by errors, with the authorities ignoring material signs of guilt (the rope, wire and leather strap). The corpses were placed in five cinnamon-lined wooden crates and shipped to Szolnok, but the stench from the decomposition spread over the area, which later had to be sprayed with chloride. When given to the coroners, the bodies were in very poor condition and it was hard to establish their identity, with the additional difficulty of determining whether the victims had died virgins, as it was known that Jancsó-Ladányi sodomized them with the broom post-mortem. The parents, who were either unwilling or unable to identify their own children, refused to repatriate the bodies, all of which were buried at Körösi Cemetery in Szolnok on 7 September 1954 in an ornamental tomb, with each grave marked with a wooden cross. Following the arrest of Piroska and Borbála, the remaining Jancsó children (József, Piros and Mihály) were taken to a child protection institute in Szolnok, and all were later adopted. The farmhouse was left abandoned for a few years, then bought by a new owner, who demolished it and built a new one in its place. The Sunday issue of the newspaper 'Free People', dated 3 October 1954, gave a report on the case: *"A multiple child murderer was sentenced to death. On September 29, the Szolnok County Court heard the case of Piroska Jancsó-Ladányi, a resident of Törökszentmiklós, who was accused of fivefold murder, one attempted murder, fivefold fraud and one theft. The investigation and the county court found that Piroska Jancsó-Ladányi - the daughter of kulaks who owned 40 acres - was a morally depraved woman who began her immoral life as a child. Piroska Jancsó-Ladányi committed the most serious crime: she killed children. The county court sentenced Piroska Jancsó-Ladányi to death as a final sentence. Along with her case, the court also discussed the case of her mother, Borbála Jancsó, who was accused of committing the crime of prostitution, crimes against the youth and theft of social property. She was sentenced to two years and six months in prison and banned from exercising her civil rights for another three years."* Due to the nature of her crimes, Jancsó-Ladányi's trial was held in private, attended only by the parents of the murdered girls. She was

Mariticide Club

initially brought on charges of theft, public endangerment and selling stolen property. Throughout the trial, she gave several conflicting confessions, first claiming that she had three accomplices, naming 45-year-old Józsefine Raffael, 23-year-old suitor Sándor Fekete and a Russian soldier. The former two were arrested, but later released as it was verified that neither were in Törökszentmiklós at the time of the murders (Raffael was out of town, while Fekete was serving a prison sentence). When her mother was brought in to testify, she claimed that Piroska had been a problem child who often quarreled with other children. According to her, she would attack other children, cutting them in the face and back for no apparent reason, appearing seemingly joyful when she did so. At age 10, on Christmas, she fled from home, a practice she often repeated as a teenager, and in 1951, she attempted to board a train bound for the Soviet Union from Nyíregyháza. She had been prosecuted several times for theft, and in 1953, she was convicted and sentenced to serve six months, but managed to serve only one before she was released under general amnesty. By the age of 13–14, she was already hanging around Soviet soldiers and having sex with them, something Borbála disapproved of and often quarreled with her daughter for. She also said that Piroska loved to eat raw meat, which she suspected got a taste for after killing stray dogs and cats in the neighborhood. The most harrowing revelation from Borbála's testimony was that in 1950, while she was visiting a neighbor, her sister told her that she had forgotten something and returned to the farmhouse to pick it up. When she entered, she found Piroska naked, on all fours, on the floor, forcing her then-7-year-old brother to lick her genitalia. Her sister scolded the girl, who then took a bottle of medicine and attempted to overdose on the pills. During her interrogation, Piroska herself confirmed that she "felt a pleasant feeling" while having intercourse with her half-brother. At the second interrogation, Jancsó-Ladányi gave another account, naming several Soviet soldiers as the main culprits. In particular, she blamed Nikolai Bogachov, claiming that he had taken a liking to Marika Komáromi, wanting to marry her and bring her back to the Soviet Union with him, promising Piroska that she could join them and father his second child.

Wives Who Kill

According to this claim, Bogachov raped Komáromi in the farmhouse while she had gone out for a drink, with the soldier promptly leaving after she returned. The little girl began to threaten to tell her parents, so Piroska, afraid that she would get in trouble, decided to kill Marika. She then said that she strangled the girl for about 10–15 minutes, before throwing her body down in the well. For the second murder, Jancsó-Ladányi claimed that she lured Hóppal to the farmhouse from the market, where she let her be raped by a soldier named Andrei, who subsequently strangled her and threw her body in the well. When it came to the rest of the murders, she claimed that Bogachov committed all of them using his belt, but added that at the final murder, another man, Sgt. Hammelzanov, was also present. In her defense, Jancsó-Ladányi claimed that she helped in the murders because of Bogachov's promise to take her to the Soviet Union, as she wanted to keep in contact with her child's father, fulfilling his demands for her to bring "untouched little girls" for him. On the next day, Jancsó-Ladányi changed her confession yet again. She now admitted that no Soviets were involved, and that she had committed the crimes due to her attraction towards women. In this account, she claimed to have realized this at the age of 15, when she read a book bought at the market, featuring graphic illustrations of sexual acts between women, including one in which a dog was licking a woman's genitals. Jancsó-Ladányi explained that the earlier confessions were an attempt to hide her unnatural inclinations, of which she was ashamed. Allegedly, she changed her confessions when she was informed by investigators that Bogachov had left Hungary in the summer of 1954, but it is unclear where this information originated from, and whether it was truthful. The case was forwarded to the Curia of Hungary on 14 October 1954, during which the defendants maintained their previous testimonies. The prosecutor called for a heavier sentence against Borbála Jancsó, on account of her complicity, while Piroska's attorney asked for a pardon, claiming that the girl's upbringing merited leniency. When asked to address the court for her last words, Jancsó-Ladányi said that she wished her sentence be changed, despite acknowledging the gravity of her actions, as she wanted to raise her child. Following the break

Mariticide Club

before the verdict was announced, Piroska told that she wanted to change some details of her previous testimony, confirming that her mother did indeed know about her deeds, and that for the second murder, she had asked her to "bring one from the market with good clothes and money if possible", while the others were committed due to her need for money and to satisfy her sexual needs. She claimed that she was forced into committing more murders, as her mother constantly spent the money on men, confectionaries and alcohol. As a result, the Curia reversed the initial sentence of the Szolnok County Court and sentenced both Piroska and Borbála to death, despite no evidence being uncovered in Borbala's alleged crimes. Borbála's sentence was commuted to life imprisonment, after a request for pardon was submitted to the Presidential Council of the Hungarian People's Republic. She was initially detained at a prison in Kalocsa, but due to her degrading mental and physical health, she was transferred to the prison hospital in Zalaegerszeg, where she died in the late 1960s. Several world-famous psychiatrists were recorded as attending the court hearings. Famous Hungarian actor László Mensáros was also present, as he was interested in the case. A briefing was ordered in the case, and on 12 December 1954, Piroska Jancsó-Ladányi was hanged in Szolnok Prison. Early in the evening, people gathered in front of the prison, hoping to see the execution when the gates opened. The judges, prosecutors, lawyers and doctors were seated behind a table, joined by the executioner, his assistants and the investigators in the back. Dozens of people were transported by truck from Törökszentmiklós, with the victims' family being offered a place not far from the execution site. Jancsó-Ladányi's final wish to see her son Mihály was not granted, and shortly after 10 PM, she stepped on the gallows and was summarily hanged. The only record of this event was a short notice the hanging was successful. Jancsó-Ladányi was buried in Körösi Cemetery in Szolnok, behind the old funeral home. Her grave was erected unmarked in a plot which, until the late 1950s, was reserved for people who died of suicide, a 'non-Christian' death, as well as murderers.

Marie-Fortunée Lafarge (née Capelle)

Marie Lafarge

Marie-Fortunée Lafarge (née Capelle; 15 January 1816 – 7 November 1852) was a French woman who was convicted of murdering her husband by arsenic poisoning in 1840. Her case became notable because it was one of the early trials to be followed by the public through daily newspaper reports, and because she was the first person convicted largely on direct forensic toxicological evidence. Nonetheless, questions about Lafarge's guilt divided French society to the extent that it is often compared to the better-known Dreyfus affair. Marie Lafarge was born in Paris in 1816, the daughter of an artillery officer. She is said to descend through her grandmother, Hermine, Baroness Collard, from a liaison between Stéphanie Félicité, comtesse de Genlis and Louis Philippe II, Duke of Orléans. Marie lost her father to a hunting accident when she was age 12; her mother, who remarried soon after, died seven years later. At age 18, Marie was adopted by her maternal aunt, who was married to the secretary-general of the Bank

Mariticide Club

of France. The two women did not get along. Despite that her foster parents treated her well and sent her to the best schools, Marie was kept aware of her status as a poor relative. Because she attended an elite school, Marie interacted with daughters of the moneyed aristocracy. She used every means to persuade them that she too came from a wealthy family and became envious when she saw her friends marrying rich noblemen. Marie had little say in the matter of matrimony. Her marriage dowry of 90,000 francs, while considerable, was not impressive considering her family's status, and Marie was left with feelings of inadequacy that fueled her pride and ambition. As Marie remained unmarried when she turned 23, one of her uncles took responsibility for finding her a husband. Unknown to Marie, he engaged the services of a marriage broker. This transaction produced just one candidate who fit the advice of her father that "no marriage contract should be made with a man whose only income is his salary as a subprefect."

Charles Lafarge

Charles Pouch-Lafarge was a big, coarse man, aged 28. He was the son of Jean-Baptiste Lafarge, justice of the peace in Vigeois. In 1817, Charles's father bought the former charterhouse, or Carthusian monastery, in the hamlet of Le Glandier, Corrèze, which had been run by Carthusian monks since the 13th century but fallen into disrepair after its suppression in the French Revolution. In an effort to make it profitable, Charles turned part of the estate into a foundry, a venture that plunged him into debt and bankruptcy. In 1839, Charles saw a good marriage as the only way to pay his creditors. He engaged the same marriage broker who was hired to find a husband for Marie, advertising himself as a wealthy iron master with property worth more than 200,000 francs with an annual income of 30,000 from the foundry alone. He also carried letters of recommendation from his priest and local deputy. To hide that a marriage broker was involved in facilitating their relationship, Marie's uncle passed Charles as a friend and arranged a fortuitous meeting with Marie at the opera. Marie found Charles common and repulsive, but because he advertised himself as the owner of a palatial estate she agreed to marry him. Thus, four days after the meeting,

Wives Who Kill

her aunt announced their engagement, and they were married on 10 August 1839. The couple then left Paris for Le Glandier to live at the estate.

As it could be expected, when they arrived on 13 August, Marie was disillusioned. The house, contained within the ruins of the former monastery, was damp and rat-infested. Her in-laws were peasants who disgusted her and regarded her with deep distrust. Instead of the wealth she expected, she was faced with considerable debt. In her despondency, Marie locked herself in her room the first night and wrote a letter to her husband, imploring him to release her from their marriage, while threatening to take her life with arsenic. Charles, whose affairs were desperate, agreed to make concessions except to release her from the marriage. He promised not to assert his marital privileges until he restored the estate to its original condition. She appeared to become calm, and their relationship appeared to have improved in the ensuing weeks. Despite her situation, Marie wrote letters to her school friends pretending that she was having a happy domestic life. She also tried to help her husband by writing letters of recommendation for Charles to Paris, where he hoped to raise money. In December 1839, before he left on a business trip, Marie made a will bequeathing to her husband her entire inheritance with the proviso that he would do the same for her. He did, but made another will without Marie's knowledge, leaving the Le Glandier property to his mother.

While Charles was in Paris, Marie wrote to him passionate love letters and sent him her picture, as well as a Christmas cake in the spirit of the season. He ate a piece of it and suddenly became violently ill soon after. As cholera-like symptoms were common in those days, he did not think about consulting with a physician but threw the cake away, thinking that it became spoiled in transit. When he returned to Le Glandier, having raised some money, he still felt ill. Marie put him to bed and fed him venison and truffles. Almost immediately, Charles again was afflicted with la maladie parisienne. The family physician, Dr. Bardon, agreed with its cholera-like symptoms and was not suspicious when Marie asked him for a prescription for arsenic in order to kill the rats that disturbed her husband during the evening. The next day, Charles experienced leg cramps,

Mariticide Club – Wives Who Kill © 2023 TXu 2-378-397 All Rights Reserved by William A. Stricklin Page 325 of 615

Mariticide Club

dehydration and nausea. He was so ill that his relatives kept watch on him at all times, including a young cousin named Emma Pontier and a young woman who stayed with them by the name of Anna Brun. Marie treated him with various medicaments, especially gum arabic, which, according to her, always did her good, and which she always kept a ready supply of in her small malachite box, but to no avail. Charles deteriorated so rapidly that another physician, Dr. Massénat, was called in for consultation. He also diagnosed cholera and prescribed eggnog to strengthen him. Anna noticed Marie taking white powder from her malachite box and stirring it into the eggnog. When asked, Marie said it was "orange-blossom sugar". Anna's suspicions were increased when she noticed a few white flakes floating on the surface of the eggnog after the patient took a few sips. She showed the glass to Dr. Massénat; he tasted the eggnog and experienced a burning sensation, but attributed the flakes to some ceiling plaster that may have fallen in the glass. Anna was not convinced; she put the rest of the eggnog in a cupboard and kept a close eye on Marie. She witnessed Marie stir more white powder into some soup for Charles. Again, Charles felt violently ill after a few sips. Anna took the cup of soup away and mustered courage to tell Charles's relatives of her suspicions. On 12 January 1840, while the family gathered in the sickroom fearing the worst, Emma Pontier, who had such high regard for Marie, told her of Anna's suspicions. Charles's mother implored him not to take another morsel of food from his wife. Panic ensued when it was learned that Charles's servant and gardener had bought arsenic for Marie "for the rats". Marie admitted this request, but she made the gardener confirm that she gave him the arsenic to make ratpoison paste out of it. Their fears were momentarily allayed, but the next day, white residue was found at the bottom of a glass of sugar water that Marie had administered to Charles. A third doctor, René de Lespinasse, was called on 13 January. He suspected poison, but by then it was too late: Charles died a few hours later. Already, suspicions ran high that Marie had poisoned her husband, but she seemed unfazed. While word went about regarding this suspicion, Marie went to her notary with the will, not knowing that it was invalid. Only Emma would go near her, and already

Wives Who Kill

torn by doubts, told Marie that Lafarge's brother-in-law was going to the police at Brive. Anna then took possession of Marie's malachite box. The justice of the peace from Brive, Moran, arrived at Le Glandier on 15 January. Impressed by Marie, he listened with uncertainty to the family's accusations but took possession of the soup, the sugar water and the eggnog that Anna had put aside. Then the gardener revealed that Marie had given him arsenic with which to make rat-poison paste in December as well as January. Strangely, the paste could be found all over the house, untouched by the rats. Moran had the paste collected; his suspicions aroused. He questioned the apothecary who sold the arsenic to Marie and asked Charles's doctors to perform a post-mortem examination. He also learned of a new test for the presence of arsenic that pathologists in Paris were using and asked Lafarge's doctors if they could apply the same test in this case. Dr. Lespinasse hastily replied that they could, hiding their ignorance of the test and the intricacies of its procedure.

The Marsh test

The test that Moran was referring to was actually invented in 1836 by a Scottish chemist named James Marsh, who worked at the Royal Arsenal in Woolwich. Called to help solve a murder nearby, he tried to detect arsenic using the old methods. While he was successful, the sample had decomposed and did not convince the jury of the defendant's guilt. Frustrated at this turn of events, Marsh developed a glass apparatus that detected minute traces of arsenic and measured its quantity. The sample is mixed with arsenic-free zinc and sulphuric acid, any arsenic present causing the production of arsine gas and hydrogen. The gas then is led through a tube where it is heated, decomposing into hydrogen and arsenic vapor. When the arsenic vapor impinges on a cold surface, a mirror-like deposit of arsenic forms. Despite this discovery, word on the Marsh test had not reached Brive. The doctors doing the autopsy on Lafarge only took the stomach before burial, and they subjected this body part to the old methods, which, unknown to them, proved to be unreliable; but they finally asserted that arsenic was found in quantity in the body of Charles Lafarge.

Mariticide Club

More surprising was the analysis of the rat-poison paste; it turned out to be nothing more than a mixture of flour, water and soda. This led to the possibility that Marie used the real arsenic to murder her husband. Any remaining doubts that may have lingered vanished when Emma Pontier turned over the small malachite box, and Dr. Lespinasse found that it contained arsenic. Marie was arrested and held in jail in Brive. A young French lawyer, Charles Lachaud, was appointed to her defense and was assisted by three others, Maîtres Théodore Bac (who later became mayor of Limoges during the 1848 Revolution), Paillet, and Desmont. Before they began their work, there was another surprise. The newspaper stories regarding Marie Lafarge turned up something from her past. Before she met Charles Lafarge, Marie had gone to the château one of the viscountess de Léautaud, one of her schoolmates. While there, her friend's jewels disappeared, and the sûreté was called to investigate the matter. When it was suspected that Marie was the culprit, the viscount thought that too improbable, and the matter was not pursued. In the wake of the newspaper stories regarding the murder, the viscount was reminded of the theft and demanded a search for the jewels in Marie's room in Le Glandier. When the jewels turned up during the search, some newspapers believed her and put all the blame on the viscountess. Nonetheless, when she was put on trial for theft, the court was not so persuaded. Marie was found guilty and sentenced to two years' imprisonment in the nearby town of Tulle. By this time, the Lafarge affair had generated so much interest that the curious arrived from all over Europe to watch her murder trial, elevating it to a cause célèbre. Thus, when Marie entered the assize court of Tulle for the first time on 3 September 1840, dressed in mourning and carrying a bottle of smelling salts in her hand, projecting the image of a woman unjustly accused, the spectators immediately were divided into pro- and anti-Marie factions. Coincidentally, Maître Paillet, one of Marie's defense lawyers, was also the lawyer of the renowned toxicologist Mathieu Orfila, who was the acknowledged expert on the Marsh test in France. He realized that as the case hinged largely on the tests made by the Brive doctors, Paillet wrote to Orfila and showed him the test results. Orfila then submitted an affidavit

Wives Who Kill

stating that the tests were conducted so ignorantly that they meant nothing. As soon as the Brive doctors testified that arsenic was present in Lafarge's body, Paillet read the affidavit aloud, told the court about the Marsh test, and demanded that Orfila be called. The prosecutor replied that he would consent to the test because he was confident of Marie's guilt, but he felt there was no need to call on Orfila to do it. The president of the court ruled in favor of the prosecutor's suggestion. Therefore, in lieu of Orfila, two well-known apothecaries from Tulle, M. Dubois and his son, and a chemist from Limoges named Dupuytren, were assigned to conduct the tests. While they were performed, the trial proceeded at a snail's pace. When they finally entered the courtroom, everyone waited to see what they would say. The elder Dubois testified that despite using the Marsh test carefully, they failed to find any arsenic. Almost immediately, the courtroom was in an uproar as Marie felt vindicated. By then, the prosecutor had read Orfila's book and knew that in some cases, the arsenic left the stomach but had spread to other parts of the body. He arranged for the body of Lafarge to be exhumed. Again, the three chemists performed the test on the samples taken—and again, no arsenic was found. The prosecutor had one card left to play. He had not forgotten the food items that Marie gave to Charles and were set aside. He requested that the test be performed on those as well. The defense, by then in a magnanimous mood, agreed. This time, when the chemists arrived, they declared that they tested positive for arsenic, with the eggnog containing enough "to poison ten persons". The prosecutor took this fact as a chance to recoup his earlier setbacks. He declared that in view of the contradictory results, it was apparent that the court should call upon Orfila to settle the issue once and for all. Because it was the defense who originally asked for Orfila, they could not object to this request. The defense agreed, confident of Marie's acquittal. When Orfila arrived, he insisted that the local chemists witness his experiments that night. He used the same test materials and chemical reagents that they used in the earliest tests and performed the Marsh test in an anteroom of the courthouse, behind locked and guarded doors. At last, on the afternoon of the next day, Orfila entered the courtroom, followed by the three chemists with bowed

Mariticide Club

heads. He declared that he had found arsenic on the samples taken from the body of Lafarge, excluding all other extraneous sources, such as arsenic naturally occurring in the body, from the reagents, or from arsenic from the earth surrounding the coffin. The courtroom was stunned, especially Maître Paillet, as he listened to Orfila, his client and defense witness, explain the misleading results obtained by the local experts with the Marsh test. It was not the test that gave the erroneous results, but rather, the test was performed incorrectly. Knowing that Orfila's testimony had tipped the balance against them, the defense team sought to call a known opponent of Orfila, François Vincent Raspail, to refute his testimony. While Raspail had agreed, as he had done in previous courtroom clashes with Orfila, but he arrived four hours too. In the end, despite the passionate pleadings of Charles Lachaud, Marie, no longer as composed as she was previously throughout the trial, heard herself sentenced by the president of the court to life imprisonment with hard labor on 19 September and was brought to Montpellier to serve her sentence. King Louis-Philippe, however, commuted her sentence to life without hard labor. By then, the affair had polarized French society. George Sand wrote to her friend Eugène Delacroix criticizing the perceived railroading of the case (it was worth noting that Marie, in turn, was an admirer of Sand and was said to read her works "greedily"). Raspail, as if to make up for his failure to make a difference in the trial, wrote and published incendiary leaflets against Orfila while demanding Marie's release. In effect, many have felt that Marie was a victim of injustice, convicted by scientific evidence of uncertain validity. As if to defend himself from these criticisms, in the following months after the trial, Orfila conducted well-attended public lectures, often in the presence of members of the Academy of Medicine of Paris, to explain his views on the Marsh test. Soon, public awareness of the test was such that it was duplicated in salons and even in some plays recreating the Lafarge case. At last, in June 1852, stricken with tuberculosis, she was released by Napoleon III. She settled in Ussat in Ariège and died on 7 November the same year, protesting her innocence. She was buried in the cemetery of Ornolac. For Charles Lachaud, the Lafarge case was his baptism of fire.

Wives Who Kill

He later achieved greater fame defending François Achille Bazaine against charges of treason and was able to defend successfully another woman named Marie—last name Bière—in 1880. Jeanne Brécourt, whom he defended in 1877, was found guilty. As for the monastery, it was bought again by the Carthusian monks in 1860 and flourished as before until it was sold again in 1904. It served as a shelter for children in World War I, then as a sanitarium for women and children run by the department of the Seine until 5 January 1965 when it became a shelter for semi-handicapped children. Finally, in January 2005, it was purchased by the department of Corrèze. The site of the former foundry (also that of the watermill powering it) now is privately owned. In 1937, the Lafarge case was fictionalized in the novel The Lady and the Arsenic by Joseph Shearing (a pseudonym of Marjorie Bowen). The story of Marie Lafarge got the cinematic treatment in 1938 with the release of the film L'Affaire Lafarge, directed by Pierre Chenal, with Marcelle Chantal as Marie and Pierre Renoir as Charles. The film is notable for being the first French film to use flashbacks as a narrative device. The film had controversy as the grandniece of Charles Lafarge sued the film's producers for defaming the memory of her great-uncle. The radio series Crime Classics broadcast a version of the story of Marie Lafarge in its October 14, 1953 episode, titled "The Seven Layered Arsenic Cake of Madame Lafarge". Marie Lafarge was portrayed by Eve McVeagh, and William Conrad played the part of Charles Lafarge. The broadcast claimed that Marie Lafarge committed suicide after her release from prison. Between 1989 and 1994, Czech Television produced in cooperation with some German TVs four seasons of the television series Dobrodružství kriminalistiky (Adventure of Criminalistics). The second episode of the first series, titled "Jed" ("Poison"), dealt with the case of Marie Lafarge. The whole story is narrated, including the turbulent course of the trial. Marie Lafarge was portrayed by German actress Anke Sevenich, Tomáš Töpfer played a smaller part of Charles Lafarge, while Viktor Preiss as the Lafarge's lawyer and Ladislav Frej as the prosecutor stand in the center of the story.

Mariticide Club

Charity Lamb

Charity Lamb was an American murderer who was the first woman convicted of murder in Oregon Territory. She had traveled west from North Carolina via the Oregon Trail, before settling near Oregon City with her husband and six children. On May 13, 1854, Lamb mortally wounded her husband by striking him twice in the back of the head with an axe. Rumors, and information presented by the prosecution at trial, implicated involvement with a paramour, by Charity and possibly her teenage daughter, herself acquitted of the murder two months prior. The defense argued that her husband had a long history of domestic violence, and the murder was committed in self-defense, or out of a level of fear that rose to insanity, marking her trial as an early example of the abuse defense. She was convicted of second-degree murder and sentenced to a lifetime of hard labor at the Oregon State Penitentiary. In 1862, she was transferred to Oregon Hospital for the Insane. She died there in 1879, and is likely buried on a corner of the property.

1855 survey showing the vicinity of the Lambs' cabin

Charity Lamb was born c. 1818 in North Carolina. It is not known where, but Charity had some schooling, and could read and write. She married Nathaniel Lamb, a farmer, in 1837, and their oldest child Mary Ann was born around ten months later. By 1850 they were living in White, Missouri with four children. In 1852, the family began a five-month journey on the Oregon Trail and eventually settled about 10 miles (16 km) up the Clackamas River from Oregon City, where they received a land patent to 318 acres (129 ha). By 1854, the family had six children; Mary Ann and five sons. On May 13, 1854, while the Lamb family was seated

Wives Who Kill

around the table for dinner in their cabin, Charity struck her husband Nathaniel twice with an axe to the back of his head. Nathaniel fell to the floor, and Charity ran out of the home. She later was found smoking a pipe at a neighbor's cabin around 0.5 miles (0.80 km) away. She told the constable that she "did not mean to kill the critter, … only intended to stun him." She was branded "a monster" by the local newspapers, which praised Nathaniel as "an industrious and quiet citizen, and had a good claim, which he had improved considerably with his own hands." Nathaniel would die a week later, and an autopsy was performed. Nathaniel's body was taken to the local church, which also assumed custody of the children. Rumor began to circulate that Charity and her 17-year-old daughter Mary Ann had been seduced by a drifter named Collins, with whom they were to escape to California, and that it was in pursuit of this end that the murder had been committed. Two months after Nathaniel's death on May 10, indictments were issued for both Charity and her teenage daughter. On July 13, 1854, Lamb appeared in the U.S. District Court at Oregon City. She was represented by a court-appointed attorney and the presiding judge was Cyrus Olney. Her daughter had already been acquitted days earlier in a trial that lasted less than a day, and the same attorneys who had represented Mary Ann were then appointed to represent Charity. She was charged with premeditated murder, a charge which carried the death penalty, and said nothing when asked to plead to the charges. She would then wait two additional months in the custody of the local jail, for the trial was to take place in September. When proceedings began, she arrived in court cradling her infant child in her arms. The Oregonian described her as "pale and sallow, and emaciated as a skeleton". She now pleaded not guilty. The trial would last six days. In jury selection, all but six of the all-male pool of potential jurors were eliminated, and the sheriff had to select additional candidates out of the group of spectators. The prosecution probed the candidates, asking whether they had a prejudice in favor of "the fairer sex" or whether there "needed to be more evidence to convict a woman than was needed to convict a man". At the outset of the trial, two of the requirements for a murder charge had already largely been settled:

Mariticide Club

Nathaniel had been killed, and Charity had killed him. Charity had already admitted to as much multiple times. Regarding the matter of intent, the defense turned to the matter of Collins, the traveler reported by the newspapers, supposed to have seduced either Charity or Mary Ann, or perhaps both. Around a week before the killing, Nathaniel had discovered a letter to Collins, written by one or the other, or written by Charity on her daughter's behalf. Nathaniel or Mary Ann had destroyed the letter after its discovery. The prosecution argued that the nature of the murder, attacking from behind while the victim was seated, indicated it was planned, and that Charity, disaffected and isolated on the frontier, had shown no remorse after the fact. Her defense represented one of the earliest known cases predicated on spousal abuse syndrome and the abuse defense. Two of Charity's children testified that their father often beat her, with one of the children recounting that he had assaulted her with a hammer. Lamb testified that he attempted to poison her and often threatened her with violence. The week prior to his murder, Lamb's husband claimed that he had plans to kill her, abandon the family, and head to California. It was reported during the trial, that while travelling on the Oregon Trail, Charity carried Nathaniel's gun at the head of the train, to prevent him from using it against her after he threatened to kill her. Their child Thomas testified of events that occurred on the morning of the murder: [Nathaniel] started to Mr. Cook's with the gun, and went a piece and came back to the gate, and put the gun to the paling, and pointed it at [Charity]. I was in the house and saw it. When Mary Ann rose up and saw him, he turned away the gun and shot it off at a big tree. Their child Abram testified that the week before the murder had seen renewed threats from Nathaniel over finding the letter to Collins. That she "better not run off", and that if she did "he would follow her, and settle her when she didn't know it." At the dinner table on the same day as the murder, Charity had expressed her fear that Nathaniel had made plans to take the boys and move to California, that he had sold his mare and was preparing. Thomas testified that Nathaniel had told him similarly. The defense also argued insanity, or at least that Charity was partially insane, calling her a monomaniac. Doctors who had seen her while in jail testified

Wives Who Kill

that she had seemed "excited" and "wild-like", but they thought she was faking. Others testified that she was noticeably upset the morning of the murder, but seemed rational on the same evening.

Judge Olney stressed the consideration of self-defense, instructing the jury that Charity should be found innocent if she had "acted out of a genuine belief in self-preservation". Despite this, the jury found Charity guilty of second-degree murder, as they determined that while she might have been justified in interpreting her husband's threats as inevitable, they were not imminent and her anxiety did not rise to the level of legal insanity. However, the jury sympathized with Lamb and urged leniency on the part of the judge. Standing at sentencing, Charity told the court, "I knew he was going to kill me," to which the judge replied, "The jury thinks you ought to have gone away." She responded:

Well. He told me not to go, and if I went that he would follow me, and find me somewhere; and he was a mighty good shot. He once gave me a chance to go; and I consented. I even gave up my baby and started. He told me to come back, or he would drop me in my tracks; and I had to come back.

The law mandated that she be sentenced to life in prison, the most lenient sentence the judge could impose. She spent the next two years in the local jail, before being transferred to the Oregon State Penitentiary to perform hard labor. She thus became the first woman convicted of murder in Oregon Territory, and it was only the second time an Oregon jury had decided the matter of felony charges against a woman, the first being the trial of Charity's daughter Mary Ann months earlier. She was the eighth person incarcerated in Oregon. Following the conviction, the family's belongings were auctioned and the children were raised by a number of other families. In 1862 Charity remained Oregon's only female inmate. Her duties as part of her "hard labor" included laundering the warden's clothes, and though other prisoners were said to "'elope' or escape at will from the facility", Charity did not. At some point, she received mention in the prison newspaper as a "commendation for her hardiness". More than five years after her conviction, Quaker missionaries recorded visiting the prison and talking to their lone female resident. Charity maintained that she had done

Mariticide Club

nothing wrong. There was a short-lived effort in the early 1860s to have Charity pardoned, but nothing came of it. She was transferred to Oregon Hospital for the Insane in 1862. Steve Laam, the great-great-grandson of Charity, later recounted that this was a humanitarian move, rather than being done for the reason of mental illness. By 1863 she was among 34 residents of the asylum, five of which were women. Visitation was allowed at this new facility, although no records exist to verify whether her children ever visited her.

Oregon Hospital for the Insane

The asylum, founded by James C. Hawthorne, was run so that the residents were comparatively well cared for, in a way that was "in direct opposition to earlier concepts of cruelty, punishment and imprisonment." The only surviving record of Charity's life at the asylum is the report of facility inspectors from 1865: *She sat knitting as the visiting party went through the hall, face imperturbably fixed in half smiling contentment apparently as satisfied with her lot as the happiest of sane people with theirs.*

Lamb died in 1879. The cause of death was recorded as apoplexy, likely a stroke or internal hemorrhage. She was most likely buried at the southwest corner of the Lone Fir Cemetery in Portland, just to the east of the Chinese railroad workers section, where researchers believe up to 132 patients from the mental hospital were buried. However, her name did not appear in cemetery records. Around 1930, the southwest corner was paved over to allow for Multnomah County to begin building on the property. As of 2009, the plot of landed owned by the Lambs was held as a privately

Wives Who Kill

owned parcel outside of Eagle Creek, Oregon. The remains of the family's cabin persisted on the land until at least 1969.

Deidra Lane

Fred Lane (American football)

Fred Lane running against the New Orleans Saints

Murdered by his wife July 6, 2000 (aged 24) Mecklenburg County, North Carolina, U.S. Freddie Brown Lane Jr. (September 6, 1975 – July 6, 2000) was an American football back who played professionally in the National Football League for the Carolina Panthers. Lane was born and raised in Franklin, Tennessee. His father, Fred Lane Sr., was a star at the old Natchez High School, which later desegregated with Franklin High. Attending Franklin Junior High School, it was noticed that Lane possessed uncommon speed and agility for such a young player. Lane attended Franklin High School, amassing over 1,000 yards his senior

Mariticide Club

year, while averaging 7.5 yards per carry. His number, 28, is retired by the school. He had three daughters: Régine Lane, Pilarr Lane, and Sable Lane. Lane attended Lane College in Jackson, Tennessee. He finished his career with 3,612 rushing yards, establishing himself as the school's all-time leading rusher. As of 2012, Lane still held the school records for rushing yards in a career, season (1,853 in 1995) and game (305 versus Miles College), as well as rushing attempts and per carry average. As a junior in 1995, Lane finished the season on the Harlon Hill Trophy watchlist, the NCAA Division II Player of the Year award. In the same year, Lane was named to the Heritage Radio HBCU All American team, as well as several other media services' All American teams. Lane's college number, #6, was retired by Lane College. Lane was signed as an undrafted free agent by the Panthers before the 1997 NFL season. He had a remarkable rookie season, setting several franchise records, many of which still stand (see below). Though Lane started only about half his games, he led Carolina in rushing attempts, yards, and touchdowns in 1997 and 1998, before the balance of touches tipped towards Tim Biakabutuka in 1999. During his three years with the Panthers, Lane accumulated 2,001 rushing yards (the most in franchise history at the time) and 13 touchdowns. After three years, Lane was traded to the Indianapolis Colts shortly before his death on July 6, 2000.

NFL career statistics

Year	Team	Games		Rushing					Receiving					Fumbles	
		GP	GS	Att	Yds	Avg	Lng	TD	Rec	Yds	Avg	Lng	TD	Fum	Lost
1997	CAR	13	7	182	809	4.4	50	7	8	27	3.4	7	0	4	3

Wives Who Kill

1998	CAR	14	11	205	717	3.5	31	5	12	85	7.1	16	0	4	2
1999	CAR	15	5	115	475	4.1	41	1	23	163	7.1	23	0	1	1
Carrer		42	23	502	2,001	50	4.0	13	43	275	6.4	23	0	9	6

As of 2017 off-season, Lane still held several Panthers records, including:

- Rush attempts, rookie game (34, 1997-12-08 @DAL)
- Rush yards, rookie game (147, 1997-11-02 OAK)
- Rushing touchdowns, rookie game (3, 1997-11-02 OAK; with Cam Newton)
- Total touchdowns, rookie game (3, 1997-11-02 OAK; with Cam Newton)
- Rushing yards per game, rookie season (62.2)
- 100+ yard rushing games, rookie season (4)
- Games with 3+ TDs, rookie season (1; with Cam Newton)

On July 6, 2000, Fred's wife, Deidra Lane, shot and killed him as he entered their home. His keys were still in the lock and he had been shot twice with a 12-gauge shotgun - once in the chest and a second time in the back of the head, apparently at point-blank range. Deidra Lane pleaded guilty to voluntary manslaughter in 2003. Prosecutors at her sentencing described Deidra Lane as an abusive woman who killed her husband for life insurance. Defense attorneys called her a battered wife who killed in self-defense. A judge sentenced her to seven years and 11 months, ruling her actions were premeditated and deliberate, that she acted with malice and shot him a second time after he had already been rendered helpless.

Mariticide Club

Deidra Lane received credit for jail time served waiting on a federal charge of conspiracy to commit bank larceny. She pleaded guilty and served four months for that charge. Lane was released on March 3, 2009.

Jane Laut

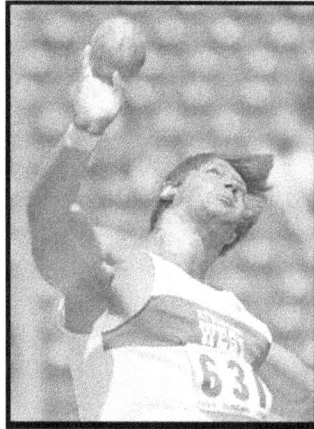

Dave Laut UCLA in 1984 Olympic Shot Put

David Lester Laut (December 21, 1956 – August 27, 2009) was an American shot putter. He was born in Findlay, Ohio, and grew up in Oxnard, California. Laut attended Art Haycox Elementary School, E. O. Green Junior High School, Santa Clara High School, Moorpark College (all in Ventura County), along with San Jose City College and UCLA, where he was a two-time NCAA champion and ranked No. 1 shot putter in the United States. Laut was shot and killed at his home, and several years later his wife was convicted for the crime. Laut won the bronze medal at the 1984 Summer Olympics in Los Angeles. He also won the gold medal at the 1979 Pan American Games and the bronze at the 1981 IAAF World Cup. He was the 1979, 1981, 1983 and 1985 United States champion in the shot put. His personal best throw was 22.02 meters, achieved in August 1982 in Koblenz. In 1985, Laut was ranked No. 7 shot putter in the world and as the No. 1 American. Laut tore tendons in both knees during an agility test to become a firefighter. He attempted to join the 1988 U.S. Olympic team, but fell short at the Olympic trials. In 1997, he was named to the Ventura County Sports Hall of Fame. After his retirement from being a professional shot putter, he became an assistant track coach at Ventura College in 1994. He served eight seasons as the track coach for Hueneme

Wives Who Kill

High School in the Oxnard Union High School District and was promoted to athletic director in 2008. Laut died at his home in Oxnard, California, on August 27, 2009, after being shot several times in the head. He was 52 years old. His wife, Jane, was arrested over five years later, and she claimed that she had shot Laut in self-defense. Clinical psychologist Katherine Emerick, who was treating Jane Laut for depression, testified that she had diagnosed Jane Laut with post traumatic stress disorder, anxiety, dependent personality disorder, and avoidant personality disorder. On March 30, 2016, she was convicted of first degree murder and sentenced to 50 years in prison. She had turned down a plea bargain for a six-year sentence.

Raynella Dossett Leath (née Raynella Bernardene Large)

Raynella Dossett Leath, from Knoxville, Tennessee, USA, is a woman who was released in 2017 from a life sentence at the Tennessee Prison for Women in Nashville for the 2003 murder of her husband David Leath. Prosecutors alleged that she shot her husband in the head, and then attempted to stage his murder as a suicide. The judge, in the third trial, directed a verdict in favor of the defendant on May 10, 2017. "The record taken as a whole does not support a finding of sufficient evidence," Judge Summers said. "The state has failed to meet its burden." Raynella Bernardene Large was born on October 25, 1948, to Annie Irene (née Owens) and Dewey Ernest Large, a nuclear scientist and raised in Oak Ridge, Tennessee. She attended Oak Ridge High School and graduated in 1966. She went on to become a registered nurse, and she married her first husband, Ed Dossett, the Knox County District Attorney, in 1970. The couple had three children, and the family lived on a farm west of Knoxville. She held a Tennessee social work license which she agreed to surrender after she was charged with murder.

Death of first husband

On July 9, 1992, Ed Dossett, who at that time was in the late stages of terminal cancer, was found dead in the couple's corral, supposedly having been trampled by cattle. Despite the medical examiner's suspicions about

Mariticide Club

a double indemnity clause in Ed's life insurance policy, his death was initially ruled to be an agricultural accident by the first medical examiner who autopsied him. Six months after his death, Raynella married her second husband, a retired barber, David Leath. Dossett's death was reinvestigated in 2006 after David Leath's death.

Death of second husband

On March 13, 2003, Raynella found the body of her second husband David Leath in their bedroom. She called 9-1-1 and reported her husband's death as a suicide. The physical evidence suggested that three shots were fired from a .38 caliber Colt revolver, but police argued that it was the second shot that killed David Leath. Following this incident, authorities reinvestigated the death of Ed Dossett. A new medical examiner revealed that the morphine levels in his system were "so extraordinarily high it is unlikely that any human could function in an ambulatory manner or continue to live". In 2006, Raynella was charged with administering an overdose of morphine. Two years later, in 2008, she was charged with the first-degree murder of David Leath.

Attempted murder charge

In 1995, after the death of her first husband, Raynella discovered that he had an affair with another woman that resulted in the birth of a child. Her late husband's mistress, Kaye Clift Walker, was in the middle of a divorce with Steve Walker; the mistress revealed to Raynella that she had an affair with Dossett and that he had fathered one of her children. Soon after, Raynella lured Walker to her farm, where she allegedly opened fire on Walker until she ran out of bullets. She was charged with attempted murder, but plea bargained to a lesser charge. She served six years on probation and her criminal record was expunged.

In May 2009, Raynella Dossett Leath went on trial for the murder of her second husband, David. She maintained that his death was a suicide. After hours of jury deliberation, there was no verdict and the judge declared a hung jury. A retrial began in January 2010. The prosecutor began his opening statement by playing Raynella's 911 call, then explaining why David's death was murder rather than suicide. The prosecutor said three

Wives Who Kill

shots were fired and the second shot killed David instantly. He also told the jury that David was also drugged with a combination similar to that used for patients undergoing surgery. In this trial, Raynella's defense argued that David's death was in fact a homicide, but Raynella had an alibi. After a day of deliberation, the jury had not reached a unanimous verdict. However, on January 25, 2010, Raynella Dossett Leath was convicted of first-degree murder and was automatically sentenced to between 51 years and life in prison. Immediately following her conviction, the charges relating to her first husband's death were dropped. Following her conviction, Raynella appealed for a new trial on the basis of Judge Richard Baumgartner's judicial misconduct relative to his drug use. She cited the murders of Channon Christian and Christopher Newsom case, which resulted in all of the defendants' convictions being overturned. She was released in May 2016 pending a retrial in January 2017. In the retrial special judge Paul Summers waited for all evidence to be presented and then declared that insufficient evidence had been presented that Raynella was the murderer and did not permit the jury to decide the case.

True crime author Diane Fanning published Her Deadly Web in 2012 about the Raynella Dossett Leath case. Her case was first profiled on Women on November 18, 2011, and subsequently on Snapped on June 17, 2012. On September 30, 2017, the TV show 48 Hours profiled her and her 2017 murder trial in the episode "The Widow on Solway Road". The title references the location of her farm, in Knoxville.

Her Case is featured on the Season 2, Episode 3, titled "High Society Sins", from the Show, Deadly Sins on January 26, 2013.

Marguerite Leféron (née Galart)

Marguerite Leferon (née Galart; d. after 1679), was an accused in the famous Affair of the Poisons. She belonged to the Parisian Bourgeoisie and was the wife of judge Leferon. In 1669, she poisoned her husband with a poison sold to her by La Voisin and married her lover, De Prade. When De Prade proved to be a fortune hunter she decided to murder him as well, which was prevented by his escape. Leferon was arrested during the Poison

Mariticide Club

Affair in 1679. La Voisin, on her way to execution, named her as her client. She was proven guilty, but was still only sentenced to exile from the capital and a fine of 1500 livres. The case against Marguerite Leferon and Françoise de Dreux, as well as that of Marguerite de Poulaillon, attracted attention as they were the first clients and the first members of the upper classes to be implicated in the affair. The light sentences imposed on them, despite their guilt, was considered damaging to the legitimacy of the court. This was obvious proof of class discrimination, as others accused for the same crime in the case, but of a different social class, were sentenced to execution. One example was Madame Philbert, who in 1673 murdered her carpenter husband Brunet by poison of Marie Bosse in order to marry her lover, Philippe Rebille Philbert: her crime was identical to that of Leferon, but she was sentenced to hang after having her right hand cut off.

Christa Lehmann (née Ambros)

Christa Lehmann (née Ambros; born 1922) is a German serial killer. Lehmann was born in Worms in 1922. She married Karl Franz Lehmann in 1944. Karl Franz died unexpectedly on 27 September 1952 within a half hour of violent convulsions. The doctor determined the cause of death as peptic ulcer disease. On 14 October 1953, her father-in-law, Valentin Lehmann, fell clinically dead from his bicycle during a trip to the city. The doctor summoned by passers-by diagnosed the death as heart failure. Christa made friends with Annie Hamann, a war widow who lived in a common household with her mother Eva Ruh, her brother Walter and her 9-year-old daughter. On Sunday 14 February 1954 Lehmann came to visit and brought five chocolate mushrooms with liquor filling. She shared four of the chocolates with Hamann, her brother, a neighbor who happened to be around, and offered the fifth one to Ruh. She politely declined and put it aside. The next day Annie came home, found the praline in the kitchen cupboard, bit into it, swallowed a part and spat the other half out disgusted on the floor. The family dog ate the rest of the praline. A short time later, Annie paled, stumbled and said she could no longer see anything. She staggered into the bedroom, accompanied by her mother, and lay plagued

Wives Who Kill

on the bed. She lost consciousness and Ruh sought help. When the doctor called by the neighbors arrived, Annie was already dead, as was the dog in the kitchen. After describing the events, the doctor informed the police. Annie's body was brought to the forensic institute in Mainz. After long investigations (inter alia on strychnine), Professor Kurt Wagner tested Annie's stomach contents on the plant protection product E 605, a poison that had been invented in Germany but at that time primarily used in the United States. The poisoning effect was very similar to that of hydrogen cyanide. By that time, however, there had been no proven case of murder or suicide using E 605. The 168 cases of poisoning documented in the United States until 1953 were due to gross negligence and were rather mild, with the exception of nine cases. Therefore, there was not method to prove E 605 forensically. Christa was arrested and interrogated. On 23 February she made a confession. It was not meant for Annie, but for her mother. On 19 March the bodies of Karl Franz and Valentin were exhumed. Both showed signs of E 605. On 20 September 1954 Christa's trial began. She was sentenced to life imprisonment. In 1971 she was transferred to the women's prison in Frankfurt. After 23 years of prison, she was released and lived freely under a new identity.

Janice Leidholm

State v. Leidholm, Supreme Court of North Dakota, 334 N.W.2d 811 (1983), is a criminal law case distinguishing the subjective and objective standard of reasonableness in a case where a woman used self-protection as a defense. Janice Leidholm had killed her husband near Washburn, North Dakota and claimed self-defense. The case clarifies between the defenses of justification and excuse.

Teresa Wilson Bean Lewis

Teresa Wilson Bean Lewis (April 26, 1969 – September 23, 2010) was the only woman on death row in Virginia prior to her execution. She was sentenced to death by lethal injection for the murders of her husband and stepson in October 2002. Lewis sought to profit from a $250,000 life

Mariticide Club

insurance policy her stepson had taken out as a U.S. Army reservist in anticipation of his deployment to Iraq. In September 2010, Lewis became the first female inmate to die by lethal injection in the state of Virginia. The state had last executed a woman in 1912. The case led to debate over capital punishment owing to Lewis's sex, as well as to questions regarding her mental capacity. Capital punishment was abolished in Virginia on March 24, 2021, making Lewis the last woman to be executed in Virginia.

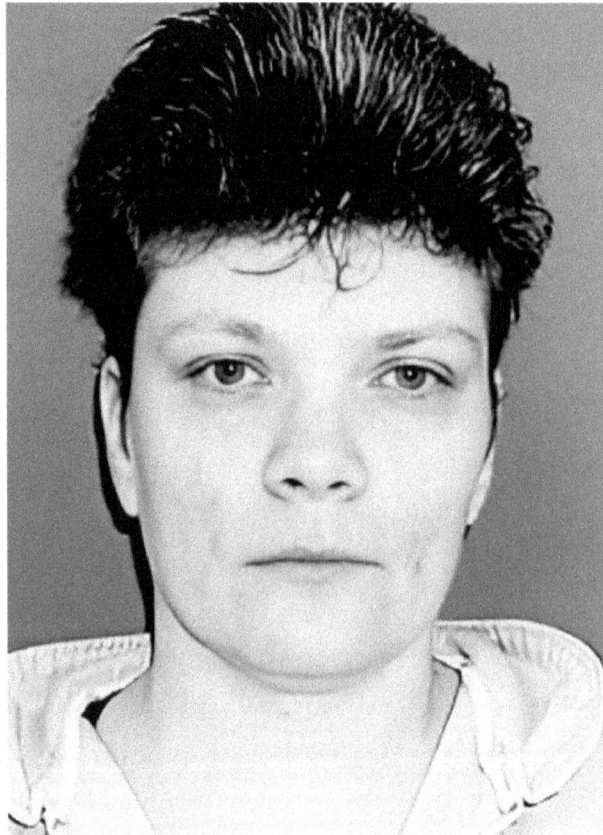

An undated photo of Lewis on death row

Teresa Wilson grew up in poverty in Danville, Virginia, where her parents both worked in a mill. Teresa sang in a church during her youth. At 16, she dropped out of school and married a man she met at that church. The couple had one daughter, Christie Lynn Bean, but the marriage soon ended in divorce, after which Teresa turned to alcohol and painkillers. Her mother-in-law, Marie Bean, described Teresa as "not right".

Wives Who Kill

Teresa Wilson Bean met future husband Julian Clifton Lewis Jr. at the now-defunct Dan River textile mill. After migrating between dozens of low-paying jobs, Teresa Wilson Bean eventually found work in the spring of 2000 at the Dan River textile mill, where her supervisor was Julian Clifton Lewis Jr. He was a recent widower with three children, Jason, Charles, and Kathy. Teresa, and her 16-year-old daughter Christie, moved into Julian's home in June 2000 and the two married soon after. In December 2001, Julian's older son, Jason Clifton Lewis, was killed in a car accident, leaving his father $200,000 from a life insurance policy. Julian used the money to buy a manufactured home on five acres of land in Pittsylvania County, Virginia. In August 2002, Julian's younger son, Charles J. Lewis, obtained a $250,000 insurance policy in preparation for his impending deployment to Iraq with United States Army Reserve. Charles designated his father as the primary and Teresa Lewis as the secondary beneficiaries.

Mariticide Club

Mug shot of Matthew Jessee Shallenberger

In the fall of 2002, Teresa Lewis met 21-year-old Matthew Jessee Shallenberger and 19-year-old Rodney Lamont Fuller at a Wal-Mart in Danville and began a sexual relationship with both of them. In October 2002, Charles came home on a visit from Army training in Maryland. On October 23, Shallenberger and Lamont were given $1,200 by Lewis to purchase firearms and ammunition to kill Julian Lewis and his son Charles for the insurance money. Their first attempt to kill Julian while on the road did not succeed. A week later, on the night of October 30, Shallenberger and Fuller entered the Lewis' trailer through a back door that Teresa had left open. While she waited in the kitchen, Shallenberger shot the sleeping Julian several times, while Fuller shot Charles in his bedroom with a shotgun. After discovering Charles was not dead, Fuller shot him twice more. Teresa waited 45 minutes before calling for help, and while waiting for the police to arrive, she removed money from her dying husband's wallet. She divided $300 with Shallenberger and Fuller before they left. However, sheriff's deputies arrived prior to Julian dying, and heard him say, "My wife knows who done this to me," while she had claimed the two had been killed by unidentified assailants in a home invasion. Shortly after, Teresa Lewis was caught attempting to withdraw $50,000 from her dead husband's account with a forged check. Within a week, she confessed to the authorities that she had offered money to have her husband killed. During the investigation, prosecutors found that Lewis had been trying to gather the assets of her late husband and stepson even before they had been buried. During the murder trial, the judge deemed Lewis the mastermind of the crime and called her "the head of this serpent." Barbara G. Haskins, a court-appointed, board-certified forensic psychiatrist, stated "Cognitive testing showed a Full Scale IQ of 72. Verbal IQ was 70, and Performance IQ was 79." Dr. Haskins also stated that Teresa Lewis was and is able to make a plea agreement and enter pleas. Lewis' lawyer stated that "She's not mentally retarded, but she is very, very close to it." In addition to a low IQ, Lewis was said by her lawyer to have an addiction to

Wives Who Kill

pain pills, and she was diagnosed with dependent personality disorder by three different forensic psychology experts.

Sentencing and appeals

Governor Bob McDonnell declined to grant clemency.

Defense attorneys thought the evidence against Lewis was overwhelming and advised her to plead guilty to the capital charges in order to avoid a jury, and hope that the judge would show some leniency since Lewis had been cooperating with investigators. Nonetheless, she was sentenced to death. The murders were capital crimes since the crimes were considered murder-for-hire. The two co-conspirators who actually did the shooting, Shallenberger and Fuller, were sentenced to life imprisonment at separate trials. Lewis was granted an automatic review by the Supreme Court of Virginia, which rejected the argument that it was unfair to execute Lewis while the co-conspirators got life sentences, as well as rejecting Lewis' challenges to the constitutionality of Virginia's death penalty law. Lewis was placed on death row at the Fluvanna Correctional Center for Women in Troy, Virginia. Lewis' daughter, Christie Lynn Bean, served five years because she knew about the plan but failed to report it.

Mariticide Club

A Supreme Court order showed that dissenting Justices Ruth Bader Ginsburg (left) and Sotomayor would have granted a stay of execution. In November 2004, a private investigator met Shallenberger at Wallens Ridge State Prison in Big Stone Gap, Virginia on behalf of Lewis. Shallenberger wrote in a partially transcribed affidavit: "Teresa was in love with me. She was very eager to please me. She was also not very smart." However, Shallenberger tore off and ate the parts of the document that he signed. Shallenberger said, "What will happen will happen." Shallenberger committed suicide at the prison in 2006. 7,300 appeals for clemency were reportedly sent to Virginia governor Bob McDonnell. Her supporters stated that "Lewis is deeply remorseful and has been a model prisoner, helping fellow female inmates cope with their circumstances." Her father, Melvin C. Wilson Sr., testified how Lewis took care of her invalid mother prior to her death. Lewis herself stated that "I just want the governor to know that I am so sorry, deeply from my heart. And if I could take it back, I would, in a minute ... I just wish I could take it back. And I'm sorry for all the people that I've hurt in the process." On September 17, 2010, McDonnell decided not to stop Lewis' upcoming execution, stating: "Having carefully reviewed the petition for clemency, the judicial opinions in this case, and other relevant materials, I find no compelling reason to set aside the sentence that was imposed by the Circuit Court and affirmed by all reviewing courts." Her attorneys moved for a writ of certiorari with the U.S. Supreme Court to stay the execution, denied September 21, 2010. Dissenting Justices Ruth Bader Ginsburg and Sonia Sotomayor said they would have granted a stay. Lewis' last meal consisted of two fried chicken breasts, sweet peas with butter, a Dr Pepper and apple pie for dessert. Lewis addressed stepdaughter Kathy Lewis Clifton, who came to witness her execution, to apologize for killing her brother and father.

I just want Kathy to know that I love you, and I'm very sorry.
— Last words of Teresa Lewis, September 23, 2010

Wives Who Kill

Lewis was executed at Greensville Correctional Center, Jarratt, Virginia. She spent her last hours praying and singing hymns. Lewis was executed on September 23, 2010, at 9 p.m. by lethal injection, at Greensville Correctional Center near Jarratt. This made her the 12th woman to be executed in the United States since the death penalty was reinstated in 1976. Lewis was the first woman to be executed in Virginia by lethal injection; it had been since 1912 that a woman has been executed in the state – Virginia Christian, who died in the electric chair. Lewis was also the first woman to be executed in the U.S. since Frances Newton in 2005 in the state of Texas, and the second woman to be executed since killer Aileen in 2002 in the state of Florida. She was cremated after her execution.

Public reaction and aftermath

Novelist Grisham publicly opposed the execution of Lewis.

Mariticide Club

Lewis' execution started a debate in the U.S. and other parts of the world concerning capital punishment, and more specifically the application of death sentences on women in murder cases. Richard Dieter, executive of the Death Penalty Information Center, argued that "so few women are involved in more heinous murders that, when they are, they cause greater offense than if they had been men. Virginia's attorney general really pushed the fact that she had committed adultery with a co-defendant and that she was somehow dishonored and should be looked down upon".

Ken Cuccinelli, Attorney General of Virginia, had stated that "the brutal nature of the crimes themselves as well as Lewis' callous, manipulating, adulterous, greedy, egregious behavior" justified the death sentence.

Thousands of supporters argued that her death sentence should have been commuted to life imprisonment. Lewis' attorney James E. Rocap III said, "A good and decent person is about to lose her life because of a system that is broken ... it is grossly unfair to impose the death sentence on her while Shallenberger and Fuller received life." Her low IQ also became a matter of discussion, with supporters citing this as a reason she should not

Wives Who Kill

have been sentenced to death. Legal novelist John Grisham echoed those sentiments and argued that evidence indicated Shallenberger, who had an IQ of 113, was the actual mastermind. Grisham quoted from an affidavit by co-conspirator Rodney Lamont Fuller: "As between Mrs. Lewis and Shallenberger, Shallenberger was definitely the one in charge of things, not Mrs. Lewis."

Iranian president Mahmoud Ahmadinejad cited the case to denounce Western media coverage of Sakineh Mohammadi Ashtiani, a woman in Iran who had been sentenced to death by stoning for adultery. He claimed the media's "heavy propaganda" campaign was perpetrating a double standard by not responding with similar outrage over Lewis' impending execution. Executive director Larry Cox of Amnesty International, which opposes the death penalty under all circumstances, stated: "Proceeding with this execution would come dangerously close to violating the U.S. Constitution, which prohibits capital punishment for those with 'mental retardation' — a precedent established thanks to Atkins v. Virginia."

Tran Thi Thuy Lieu
Murder of Lê Hoàng Hùng

BBC News reported on 23 February 2011, Tran Thi Lieu, who was 40 years old, was in police custody and authorities had discovered that she had amassed debts of "one billion dong ($47,000, £29,000)" from gambling excursions to Cambodia. Police were conducting an "expanded investigation" to check if anybody else had been involved and were holding Lieu for 4 months beginning 30 June 2011. Police discovered that Hung's wife Tran Thi Lieu had a gambling problem, Hung and his wife had argued about money and that he had an insurance policy should he be killed. Police confirmed that Lieu did owe VND1 billion (US$51,000) from gambling in Cambodia. A source told Tuoitrenews that she wanted to sell the house to settle the debt but Hung refused. An unconfirmed source told Tuổi Trẻ that the victim had bought a life insurance with a payout of VND1 billion several months before his death. Lieu, as his wife, is of course the main beneficiary. Drivers of taxis and rental cars she used to on

Mariticide Club

her gambling trips to Cambodia said that Lieu carried along VND30-100 million (US$1,500-5,100) in cash per trip. One regular driver even saved her number on his cell phone as "ZKC L.Casino". However, Lieu denied any gambling, insisting she went to casinos only to sell wet cloth tissues to gamblers there. Police found Lieu lied about the gambling. In 2010, she made 22 trips to Cambodia to visit casinos there.

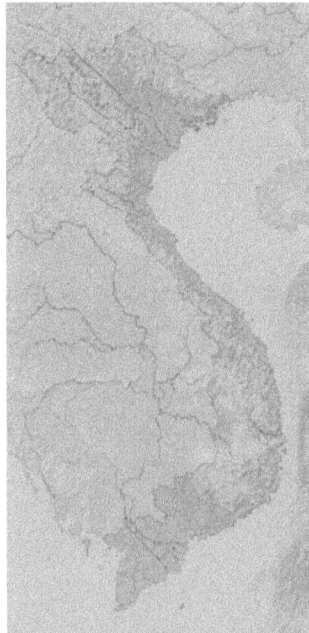

Tran Thi Lieu was convicted of murder with "vile motives" and sentenced to life in prison on 29 March 2012. Hung was a print reporter for Nguoi Lao Dong (The Worker). He covered corruption and crime stories. Hung had covered misconduct in the Mekong Delta region. He had recently covered a case about illegal appropriation of land. He reported on a wide variety of topics, including recent critical coverage of the Long An Province Market Control Department and cross-border smuggling issues. Lê Hoàng Hùng (1960 – 29 January 2011), a Vietnamese investigative journalist, worked for Người Lao Động (The Worker) in Tân An, Vietnam, where he covered corruption and crime. He was burned to death by his wife. Initially, because of his high-profile reporting and the original story told by Hung's wife about his death, police and organizations concerned with press safety believed Hung had been killed in revenge for stories he had recently published. While his wife Tran Thi Thuy Lieu originally claimed "a

Wives Who Kill

stranger broke into their house" and burned her husband, she later recanted and admitted guilt. The last journalist to have been killed in Vietnam for his journalism was Duong Hung Cuong in 1988. When the Committee to Protect Journalists listed Hung as a "motive confirmed" case after his death, this would have made Hung the first journalist who would have been killed as a result of reporting in Vietnam in 23 years, except it was learned later that he was killed by his wife for a non-reporting motive. Lê Hoàng Hung was burned in his bed and taken to the Long An General Hospital in southern Long An, Vietnam. Hung suffered from severe burns on over 20 percent of his body. Because of the severity of his burns, he was transferred to Cho Ray Hospital in Ho Chi Minh City. He died on January 29, which was ten days after the attack from his burns. Just before his death, Hung told investigators that he was sleeping when he felt someone pouring something cold on his body which immediately started to burn. Tran Thi Thuy Lieu, Hung's wife, said that an unknown assailant had broken into Hung's house in Tân An, Vietnam, in the middle of the night, doused the reporter with some sort of chemicals, and set Hung on fire. She told authorities that Hung had received several threatening text messages before the incident. Initially the Committee to Protect Journalists and Reporters Without Borders reported that Hung had been killed for his reporting of misconduct in the Mekong Delta region, and police also thought someone was getting revenge. A rope was found hanging from the second story where Hung was burnt, indicating that the culprit could have climbed up on that rope. However, police confirmed that the rope is just a ploy to distract investigators. The police said that it is very difficult to attach the rope to the second-floor balcony from the ground floor without an insider's help. Also, according to the newspaper, there was no evidence showing the rope had been climbed on. It was also regarded as suspicious that Hung went to sleep that night alone without closing the main door or the windows although the night was very cold. A photograph of Hung's torched bed was published in Vietnam shortly after his death and created public awareness about the journalist's death. Fatal attacks against journalists in Vietnam have been rare. Most journalists who had died in Vietnam had died

Mariticide Club

covering the Vietnam War, such as Larry Burrows or Dickey Chapelle. The last foreign journalist to be killed in Vietnam was in 1979 when Japanese journalist Isao Takano was shot near the Vietnam-Chinese border in Lạng Sơn. The last case of a Vietnamese journalist having been murdered on account of duties was Duong Hung Cuong in 1988 while he was being held by authorities. Investigative journalists, like Hung, have been important in changing the media culture of Vietnam, which has allowed government corruption to be exposed. Hung had to write about sensitive issues in a country where media are state owned, the media support the government in a communist press model, and journalists face restrictions. While the killing of journalists seldom happens in Vietnam, Reporters Without Borders ranked Vietnam 165 of 178 countries on press freedom in 2010. Hung's colleagues in Vietnam had called for an investigation into his death because of his reporting on sensitive issues and police were initially also focused on this motive. This brought international attention to press safety concerns in Vietnam. The Committee to Protect Journalists has been active in order to make sure that there is no impunity in cases where journalists are murdered. Shawn Crispin, CPJ's senior Southeast Asia representative, said shortly after his death, "The government signaled its commitment to protecting journalists in a media decree earlier this month and until this crime is solved that commitment will have gone unfulfilled." Irina Bokova, director-general of UNESCO, issued the following statement shortly after his death: "I condemn the brutal attack on Le Hoang Hung that caused his death. Freedom of expression is a key ingredient of democratic societies, vital to the rule of law, and it must be protected. Le Hoang Hung's death must be fully investigated and his attacker brought to justice." Police investigated the murder and even reopened the case later after the wife had already admitted to the killing after inconsistencies between the confession and the evidence were noticed. The result of the further investigation was reported in October by Tuổi Trẻ news that police believe that Lieu had acted alone.

Yvonne de Ligne

Wives Who Kill

Yvonne de Ligne (née Geurts, 18 May 1902 – 1952) was a Belgian figure skater. She competed in the ladies singles event at all major competitions from 1929 to 1936, including Winter Olympics, world and European championships. Her best achievements were sixth place at the 1929 and 1932 world championships and 1932 Olympics, and fifth place at the 1933 European Championships. She was born Yvonne Geurts, and changed her last name after marrying speed skater Charles de Ligne. During World War II she fell in love with Dutch figure skater Jacob Hartog, who then lived in Antwerp. She arranged the murder of her husband, for which she was sentenced to 15 years. She was released after 6 years as she was suffering from tuberculosis, from which she died shortly thereafter.

Mariticide Club

Yvonne de Ligne at the 1932 European Championships

Charles de Ligne (speed skater)
Charles de Ligne (12 September 1895 – 14 November 1944) was a Belgian speed skater. Aged 40, he competed in four events at the 1936 Winter Olympics with the best result of 28th place over 10,000 m.
De Ligne was a successful businessman and a decorated officer, who fought in World War I and was part of the Belgian underground movement

Wives Who Kill

during World War II, helping to rescue downed Allied pilots. He was married to figure skater Yvonne de Ligne, who fell in love with a young Dutch figure skater in 1944. She hired a man to kill de Ligne and made it look as if he was killed by the Gestapo. The murder was solved in 1945. Yvonne de Ligne was sentenced to 15 years, but was released after six years due to poor health, and died from tuberculosis shortly afterwards.

Anjette Lyles (née Donovan)

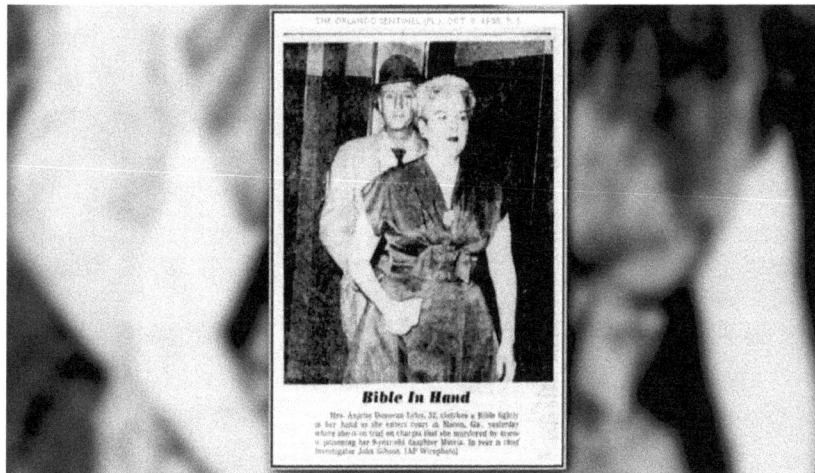

Bible In Hand

Mrs. Anjette Donovan Lyles, 32, clutches a Bible tightly in her hand as she enters court in Macon, Ga., yesterday where she is on trial on charges that she murdered by arsenic poisoning her 9-year-old daughter Marcia. In rear is chief investigator John Gibson. (AP Wirephoto)

Anjette Lyles (née Donovan; August 23, 1925 – December 4, 1977) was an American restaurateur and serial killer responsible for the poisoning deaths of four relatives in Macon, Georgia, between 1952 and 1958. Initially sentenced to death upon her conviction, Lyles was eventually diagnosed with paranoid schizophrenia and instead sent to the Central State Hospital in Milledgeville, where she spent the rest of her life. She was a small-town cook with a big-time secret. 61 years ago, a Bibb County jury convicted Anjette Lyles of poisoning her 9-year-old daughter. She was also accused of killing both of her husbands and her mother-in-law. It's a bizarre case that's become the plot of books, plays, and TV specials. Decades later, it's still something that haunts some people in Macon. "Macon, at that time, had a small-town vibe. People were very close," says longtime Macon resident, Patricia Sanderfer. And at the center

Mariticide Club

of the small southern town, there was a popular diner on Mulberry Street called Anjette's. "Lawyers, attorneys, judges -- all kinds of folks -- would come and eat dinner at the diner," says Shannon Ray with Middle Georgia Paranormal Investigations. Owned by a buxom blonde with a personality to match, almost everyone in town knew Lyles. 61 years ago, a Bibb County jury convicted Anjette Lyles of poisoning her 9-year-old daughter. She greeted customers with tight hugs and warm conversation, an added bonus to her delicious southern fare. "It was what we call 'country kitchen food' -- good, wholesome vegetables and meat -- just everyday southern food," says Sanderfer. Between the fried chicken and mashed potatoes, it was a popular joint for many years, until people discovered murder might be on the menu. Over the course of six years, four of Lyles' immediate family members had died from what appeared to be natural causes -- her first husband, Ben Lyles, her second husband, Joe Gabbert, her mother-in-law, Julia Lyles, and Anjette's oldest daughter, Marcia. In May 1958, Bibb County deputies arrested Lyles and charged her with the murders of all 4 family members, but how had she done it? "I was shocked, like everybody," says Sanderfer. "To kill a 9-year-old child takes a very sociopath mind that goes beyond any pale of the imagination and narcissistic behavior," says Macon playwright Denver Pickard. When investigators searched her home, they found voodoo paraphernalia, candles, potions, and powders, along with bottles of Terro Ant killer. The pesticide contains arsenic, the same chemical found in the body of each of Lyles' dead family members after fresh toxicology tests. "It was hard to imagine anyone killing people that they were supposed to love," says Sanderfer. A medical examiner later testified that small doses of arsenic had been administered to all four victims over time, most likely disguised in food and drink. "Well, how could she do that? Well, it was money. The root of all evil -- money," says Pickard. In October 1958, Lyles' trial began at the Bibb County Courthouse, drawing hundreds of spectators and reporters from around the world. "Well, it was on the news and in the papers. It was everywhere. Many, many people were there," says Sanderfer. Former state judge Bill Adams' father co-prosecuted the case in 1958, after the district

Wives Who Kill

attorney recused himself for being a distant relative of Lyles. "This was a sensational trial, because Anjette was charged with murdering her daughter with arsenic poisoning," says Adams. "The theory of the case was Anjette was doing this for the money, for life insurance money." During the weeklong trial, the prosecution presented the jury with evidence that Lyles had spent money like, "a drunken sailor." She reportedly bought herself a new white Cadillac with her second husband's life insurance payout. "They were able to prove she had done some "funny business," if you will, with the way some of the insurance matters had been handled," says Adams. The prosecution also brought in a handwriting expert who testified that the signature on Julia Lyles' will had been forged. "She thought she could charm the all-male jury into believing her when she said she did not do this," says Adams. But, in the end, she couldn't. Anjette Lyles clutched her small, white Bible in a Bibb County Superior Court room and listened to the guilty verdict before being sentenced to death. "She was never executed, though, because the governor, some said, did not want to sign a death warrant for a white woman," says Adams. Lyles was later deemed "insane" by a group of psychologists, and spent the rest of her days at Central State Hospital in Milledgeville where people say, ironically, she worked in the kitchen. "I feel like it's part of Macon's tarnished history that people don't like to talk about very much," says Ray. In 1977, at age 52, Lyles died of a heart attack. She and her first husband and daughter are all buried together at Coleman's Chapel Cemetery in Wadley, Georgia. It's true that Anjette Lyles' case is one that has fascinated investigators as well as writers and storytellers for many years. One such writer is Jaclyn Weldon White, author of "Whisper to the Black Candle," a book that explores the Lyles case in great detail. If you are interested in learning more about this dark moment in Macon history, visit White's website.

Nellie May Madison (née Mooney)

Mariticide Club

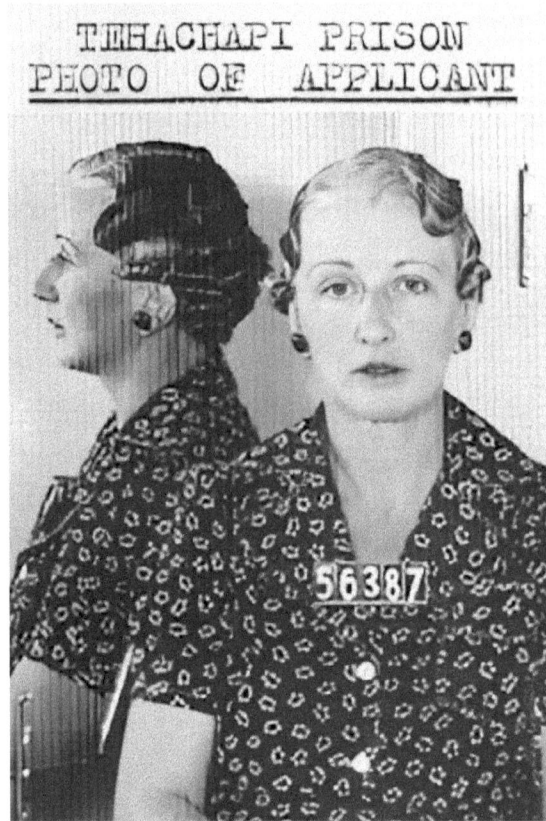

TEHACHAPI PRISON
PHOTO OF APPLICANT

56387

Parole application photo of Madison (1941)

Nellie May Madison (née Mooney) (April 5, 1895–July 8, 1953) was an American woman who was convicted of murder in 1934 for killing her husband. She was the first woman to be sentenced to death in the state of California. Due to public outcry, her sentence was later commuted to life in prison and she was eventually released. Her case helped garner legitimacy for the abuse defense, a concept virtually unknown at the time in criminal cases. The case was the subject of a 2015 episode of Investigation Discovery's series A Crime to Remember. Nellie May Mooney was born in Red Rock, Montana and brought up in the nearby community of Dillon. She was trained to be a natural survivalist of the mountains. Prior to her marriage to Eric Madison, she had an annulment from a 23-year-old ex-convict when she was 13. She later married and divorced three different men. She had no children. On March 24, 1934 at their home in Burbank, California, after alleged repeated spousal abuse episodes by her husband Eric Madison, Nellie Madison pointed a gun at Eric while he was changing

Wives Who Kill

out of his day clothes with the intent on threatening him. He quickly reached under the bed for a box of butcher knives and allegedly threatened to cut her heart out. As he was reaching for a knife, Nellie shot Eric in the back five times, killing him. Nellie Madison was later arrested and tried for the murder of her husband. Even before he knew all the facts, Los Angeles County District Attorney Buron Fitts sought the death penalty for Madison. On advice of her lawyers, Madison made no mention of the spousal abuse and claimed she was not at the scene of the murder. As her story was implausible, a jury convicted her and Judge Charles Fricke sentenced her to death. On appeal, the California Supreme Court upheld the conviction. After sentencing, Madison's ex-husband, with whom she was still friends, urged her to make the spousal abuse episodes public. When pleading her case to Fricke, he refused to reduce the sentence and dismissed the allegations of domestic violence as "ridiculous." Madison began receiving public support, including from prominent journalist "Aggie" Underwood. Underwood discovered that Eric Madison had beaten both Nellie and his ex-wife into signing a similar confession stating they were unfaithful in their marriage, when in fact, it was Eric who had been unfaithful and having affairs with teenage girls. All of the jurors who convicted Madison petitioned Governor Frank Merriam to commute the sentence. September 1935, Merriam commuted Madison's sentence to life in prison. After she waged a letter-writing campaign from prison to reduce her sentence, Governor Culbert Olson had Madison freed from prison on March 27, 1943, exactly nine years and three days after the murder. In the fall of 1943, she settled in San Bernardino, where she married her sixth husband, house painter John Wagner. It was her longest marriage. She died there on July 8, 1953 after a stroke.

Rhonda Belle Martin (née Rhonda Belle Thomley)

Rhonda Belle Martin (Rhonda Belle Thomley; c. 1907 – October 11, 1957) was an American serial killer and family annihilator who was executed by the state of Alabama for the murder of Claude Carroll Martin, her fourth husband, in 1951. Martin's method of murder was rat poison; she was also

Mariticide Club

accused of poisoning and murdering her mother, and five of her seven children, all of whom were below the age of 12 at the times of their deaths. Only one of her victims, her former son-in-law and fifth husband Ronald Martin, was known to have survived. She confessed to all the murders she was accused of committing, and later recanted her confession in the murders of two of her children. Martin's execution made her the third and final woman to be electrocuted in Alabama before the *Furman v. Georgia* ruling, and the last woman put to death in the state until 2002. Rhonda Belle Thomley was born around 1907 in Alabama, to James Robert Thomley and Mary Frances (née Grimes). Prior to her arrest, she worked as a waitress. At the time of arrest, she lived in Montgomery, Alabama. She confessed in March 1956 to poisoning her mother, two husbands, and three of her children. She denied killing two other children. According to *LIFE Magazine* in an article published at the time, she loved getting the get-well cards, and later the sympathy cards that came when the victims died, as well as taking great care to have them buried side by side in a private plot. Her fifth husband, Ronald Martin (her step-son, the son of Claude Carroll Martin), was poisoned like the others. He survived, left as a paraplegic. His illness led authorities to look into the strange deaths surrounding Martin. Prosecutors said collecting insurance proceeds prompted her killing spree, although this is unlikely, since she collected only enough to cover burial costs, and she never admitted this was the case. Martin was arrested in March 1956. Martin was convicted of murdering fifty-one-year-old Claude Carroll Martin in 1951 by surreptitiously feeding him rat poison. Although Martin was convicted of only one murder, she admitted committing every murder she was suspected of, except for two of the children. Because Martin had a heart condition, prison officials withheld information from her regarding her scheduled execution date until the date was near. The day before her execution, Martin had a clemency hearing that lasted two hours, during which her defense attorney unsuccessfully attempted to stop the execution on grounds of Martin's sanity not having been adequately tested. Martin was housed in the Jefferson County jail until late May 1957; as her execution was set for May 31, she was transferred to Kilby Prison,

Wives Who Kill

where Alabama's electric chair was located. When that execution date was postponed, she was sent to the Julia Tutwiler Prison for Women. Eight days before her execution, Martin gave an interview in which she said, "Well, you've never seen anybody who was ready to sit down in the electric chair. But if that's what it's got to be, that's what it will be." She was housed at the Julia Tutweiler Prison until four hours before her execution, when she was sent back to Kilby Prison. Seven hours before execution, Martin had a last meal consisting of a hamburger, mashed potatoes, cinnamon rolls, and coffee. October 11, 1957, Martin was led to Alabama's electric chair while she held a Bible in her hand. Martin was reportedly calm but quietly weeping at her execution as she recited the 23rd Psalm alongside the prison chaplain. She received the first shock at 12:10 am, and she was pronounced dead at 12:16 am and removed from the death chamber at 12:25 am. She declined to make a final statement. Martin's execution featured a slight mishap prior to the time she received the first shock, as her executioners threw the switch activating the electricity before the electrodes were ready for use. Martin had to wait several minutes until the electric cycle was finished before authorities could complete her execution. In 1956, Martin had expressed a desire for her body to be sent to an unspecified "scientific institution" for autopsy, so scientists could analyze her and find out why she committed her crimes. After her execution, prison officials found a note expressing a similar sentiment. Martin's note read, in part, that she wanted physicians "to find out why I committed the crimes I committed. I can't understand it, for I had no reason whatsoever. There's definitely something wrong." Instead, after her execution, some family members received her body in a funeral home in Montgomery. Martin was the last woman executed in Alabama until 2002, when Lynda Lyon Block was executed for the murder of a policeman.

Kia Yvette Jeffries Wife of Ernest Abdul Mateen

Mariticide Club

Ernest Mateen

Ernest Mateen (June 3, 1966 – November 6, 2012, in Bedford-Stuyvesant, Brooklyn, New York) nicknamed 'M-16' a USA and IBU Cruiserweight (boxing) champion, shot to death by his wife in probable self-defense. As an amateur boxer in New York City, M-16 Mateen won two New York Golden Gloves Championships. Mateen won the 1988 and 1989 178-pound Open Championships. In 1988, Mateen defeated Clinton Mitchell of the Police Athletic League in the finals to win the Championship. Mitchell then turned pro and defeated Bernard Hopkins on December 11, 1988, in their professional debuts. M-16 Mateen remained an amateur, and in 1989 repeated as 178-pound Open Champion again by defeating Jade Scott of the Police Athletic League in the New York Golden Gloves championship final. Mateen trained at the Bedford-Stuyvesant, Brooklyn BA in 1988 and at Gym in 1989. He was trained in the amateurs by his father, Ernest Mateen Sr., an auto mechanic and a father of nine, who was shot and killed in mid-afternoon in a crowded open-air vegetable market in Canarsie, Brooklyn May 1990. M-16 Mateen turned pro in Light heavyweight boxing division on January 13, 1991, and won by decision over undefeated David Telesco, who went on to become the USBA Light heavyweight champion ranked # 1 by the WBC, WBA and IBF. Mateen drew with, then later defeated Tim Wilson, and won by decision over David Telesco again. M-16 Mateen went undefeated in his first twenty professional bouts, including wins over 12-0 Steve Pannell and 20-0 Billy Lewis. M-16 Mateen also defeated Kevin Watts, Dale Jackson, and Drake Thadzi (who later defeated James Toney), fighters with a combined 65 wins, en route to

Wives Who Kill

winning the Nevada State and World Boxing Council Continental Americas Light heavyweight boxing title and rising as high as # 2 in the world ratings, before losing his title in the tenth round to Charles Williams (boxer). Williams fought in 11 consecutive IBF Light heavyweight world title fights before fighting Mateen. In a controversial ending, M-16 Mateen was later disqualified in the fifth round of a Light heavyweight world title bout against champion James Toney. M-16 Mateen went on to decision John Scully twice, later to become trainer of Chad Dawson, and drew with future Cruiserweight (boxing) champion O'Neil Bell. M-16 won the United States Boxing Organization Cruiserweight title by 12-round decision over Joey DeGrandis. M-16 Mateen went on to win the International Boxing Union version of the Cruiserweight (boxing) title, stopping Uriah Grant twice in title bouts. Grant went on to stop Thomas Hearns. M-16 Mateen finished with a professional record 30-12-3 with 10 knockouts. In his last two fights, M-16 Mateen lost to future top contender Matt Godfrey, but finished his career with a ten-round unanimous decision over veteran Terry Porter in Memphis, Tennessee, on June 10, 2006, leaving the ring a winner at age 40. Mateen worked as a licensed professional boxing trainer in New York and New Jersey, with particular attention to the career of his brother, rising light heavyweight boxer Hamid-Abdul Mateen. Police outside Atlanta say they consider the shooting death of a former professional boxer to be a case of self-defense; and no charges were filed. Gwinnett County police Cpl. Jake Smith said homicide detectives determined that Earnest Mahir Abdul-Mateen used a handgun to repeatedly hit his wife Kia Yvette Jeffries early Tuesday morning. Smith said Abdul-Mateen struck her so many times that he became exhausted, and at that point Jeffries managed to turn the gun on her husband and pull the trigger. The shooting happened at an extended say hotel near Duluth. Smith said officers found Jeffries with injuries to her head and face. Abdul-Mateen was lying in a hallway, suffering from a gunshot wound. Smith tells The Gwinnett Daily Post detectives consider the case "a self-defense shooting."

Florence Elizabeth Chandler Maybrick

Mariticide Club

Florence Elizabeth Chandler Maybrick (3 September 1862 – 23 October 1941) was an American woman convicted in the United Kingdom of murdering her husband, cotton merchant James Maybrick.

Chandler Mansion in Mobile, Alabama, birthplace of Florence Chandler. Florence Maybrick was born Florence Elizabeth Chandler in Mobile, Alabama. She was the daughter of William George Chandler, a one-time mayor of Mobile and a partner in the banking firm of St. John Powers and Company, and Caroline Chandler Du Barry, née Holbrook. Florence's

Wives Who Kill

father had died before her birth. Her mother remarried a third time in 1872 to Baron Adolph von Roques, a cavalry officer in the Eighth Cuirassier Regiment of the German Army. While travelling by ship to the United Kingdom, Florence met James Maybrick, a cotton merchant from Liverpool. Other passengers were either amused or shocked by a 19-year-old girl spending so much time alone in the company of Maybrick, who was 23 years her senior. On 27 July 1881, the couple were married at St James's Church, Piccadilly, in London. They settled in Battlecrease House, Aigburth, a suburb of Liverpool. Florence made quite an impression on the social scene in Liverpool, and the Maybricks were usually to be found at the most important balls and functions, the very picture of a happy, successful couple. But Maybrick, a hypochondriac, was a regular user of arsenic and patent medicines containing poisonous chemicals and had a number of mistresses, one of whom bore him five children. Florence meanwhile, increasingly unhappy in her marriage, entered into several liaisons of her own. One was with a local businessman, Alfred Brierley, which her husband was told about. A violent row ensued after Maybrick heard reports of Florence's relationship with Brierley, during which Maybrick assaulted her and announced his intention of seeking a divorce. The wish for divorce seemed mutual.

James Maybrick was taken ill on 27 April 1889 after self-administering a double dose of strychnine. His doctors treated him for acute dyspepsia, but his condition deteriorated. On 8 May, Florence wrote a compromising letter to Brierley, which was intercepted by Alice Yapp, a nanny who hated Florence. Yapp intercepted all letters sent by Florence and passed them on to Maybrick's brother, Edwin, who was staying at Battlecrease. Edwin, himself by many accounts one of Florence's lovers, shared the contents of the letter with his brother Michael Maybrick, who was effectively the head of the family and who also hated Florence. By Michael's orders, Florence was deposed as mistress of her house and held under house arrest. On 9 May, a nurse reported that Florence had surreptitiously tampered with a Valentine's Meat Juice bottle that was afterwards found to contain a halfgrain of arsenic. Florence later testified that her husband had begged her to

Mariticide Club

administer it as a pick-me-up. However, he never drank its contents. Maybrick died at his home in Aigburth on 11 May 1889. In her memoir, *Mrs. Maybrick's Own Story: My Fifteen Lost Years*, Florence describes the following, as she knelt down by her late husband's bedside: Death had wiped out the memory of many things. I was thankful to remember that I had stopped divorce proceedings, and that we had become reconciled for the children's sake. His brothers, suspicious as to the cause of death, had his body examined. It was found to contain slight traces of arsenic, but not enough to be considered fatal. It is uncertain whether this was taken by Maybrick himself or administered by another person. In April 1889, Florence Maybrick was accused of using flypaper containing arsenic from a local chemist's shop and later soaked in a bowl of water. After an inquest held in a nearby hotel, Florence was charged with murder and stood trial at St George's Hall, Liverpool, before Mr. Justice Stephen. She was convicted and sentenced to death. Her trial was reported in newspapers as a miscarriage of justice, as the prosecution evidence was baffling. After the verdict, crowds shouted in favor of Florence, believing she was accused of a murder she did not commit. After public outcry, Henry Matthews, Home Secretary, and Lord Chancellor Halsbury concluded 'that the evidence clearly establishes that Mrs. Maybrick administered poison to her husband with intent to murder; but that there is ground for reasonable doubt whether the arsenic so administered was in fact the cause of his death'. The death sentence was commuted to life imprisonment as punishment for a crime with which she was never charged. During the 1890s, new evidence was publicized by Florence's supporters, but there was no possibility of an appeal, and the Home Office was not inclined to release her in spite of the strenuous efforts of Lord Russell of Killowen, the Lord Chief Justice. The case became something of a *cause célèbre* and attracted considerable newspaper coverage on both sides of the Atlantic. Arsenic was then regarded by some men as an aphrodisiac and tonic, and Maybrick had certainly taken it on a regular basis. A city chemist confirmed that he had supplied Maybrick with quantities of the poison over a lengthy period and a search of Battlecrease House later turned up enough to kill at least fifty

Wives Who Kill

people. Although her marriage was clearly over in all but name, Florence had little motive to murder her husband. The financial provision Maybrick had made for her and his children in his will was paltry and she might have been far better off with him alive but legally separated from him. Many people held the view that Florence had poisoned her husband because he was about to divorce her which, in Victorian society, would see her ruined. An even more compelling motive might have been the prospect of losing the custody of her beloved children.

After fifteen years of research, writer and film director Bruce Robinson published They *All Love Jack: Busting the Ripper* (2015), a massive study of Jack the Ripper, in which he makes a case that Florence and her husband were the victims of her brother-in-law, Michael, whom Robinson claims was actually the Ripper.

HM Prison Aylesbury, shortly after construction in 1847

Following the commutation of Florence's sentence, she was transported to Woking District Female Convict Prison, where she remained until 1896 when she was moved to Aylesbury Prison. Florence spent her first nine months in solitary confinement before being moved to a different cell but remaining under the strictures of the silent system, whereby silence was enforced at all times. Her memoirs reveal the physical and mental toll that solitary confinement had on her. She dubbed the practice 'by far the most cruel feature of English penal servitude' and emphasized the 'desolation and despair' that the 'hopeless monotony' of confinement led her to feel. During

Mariticide Club

her time at Woking, Florence suffered from insomnia and frequent ill health caused, she claimed, by the frequent shrieking and destruction of the content of cells during the night by weak-minded inmates, which left her with 'quivering nerves' and unable to sleep. Having passed through the first stages of solitary confinement and a probationary period, Maybrick then entered a third stage of hard labor whereby she was permitted to leave her cell during the day to assist in carrying meals from the kitchen. Her day commenced at 6.00 a.m. and ended at 5.30 p.m., during which she had, according to her memoirs, to wash ten four-quart cans, scrub one twentyfoot table and two twelve-foot dressers, clean knives, wash a sack of potatoes, assist in serving the dinners and scrub a piece of floor twenty by ten feet. During 1896, Maybrick entered into the prison infirmary for two weeks, suffering from a 'feverish cold' caused, she claimed, by the inadequate clothing, bedding and draughty cells. At the end of her time in the infirmary on 4 November 1896 she was transferred to Aylesbury prison. Maybrick did speak well of the warders she encountered during her incarceration, describing their 'patience, civility, and self-control'. After detention in Woking and Aylesbury prisons, Florence was released in January 1904, having spent more than 14 years in custody. Although she had lost her U.S. citizenship when she married her British husband, it was restored when she returned to her home country. Initially she earned a living on the lecture circuit, speaking on prison reform and protesting her innocence. In later life, she moved to Connecticut and used her maiden name, Florence Elizabeth Chandler. After months spent unsuccessfully as a housekeeper, Florence became a recluse, living in a squalid three-room bungalow in Gaylordsville, Connecticut, a village in New Milford, Connecticut, with only her cats for company. A few sympathetic residents discovered Florence's true identity but kept her secret. Florence Maybrick died alone and penniless in her home in New Milford on 23 October 1941, and the next day her obituary was published at the top of Page One of *The New York Times*. She was buried at her request next to her dear friend, Clara Dulon, in South Kent, Connecticut on the grounds of South Kent School. Among her few possessions were a scrapbook with newspaper

Wives Who Kill

clippings of her former life and a tattered family Bible. She never saw her children again; they were brought up by the family's doctor. Her son, who became a mining engineer, died in 1911 of accidental poisoning when he mistook a cyanide solution for a glass of water. Soon after her release, Florence wrote a book about her experiences, *Mrs. Maybrick's Own Story: My Fifteen Lost Years*, which is available online. A rare copy is still held by Liverpool City Libraries.

Non-fiction books and pamphlets about the case

- Boswell, Charles, and Lewis Thompson. *The Girl with the Scarlet Brand* (1954).
- Christie, Trevor L. *Etched in Arsenic* (1968).
- Colquhoun, Kate. *Did She Kill Him?: A Victorian Tale of Deception, Adultery and Arsenic* (2014).
- Daisy Bank Print. and Pub. Co. *Full Account of the Life & Trial of Mrs. Maybrick: Interesting Details of her Earlier Life* (ca. 1901).
- Densmore, Helen. *The Maybrick Case* (1892).
- Graham, Anne E. and Carol Emmas. " The Last Victim : The extraordinary life of Florence Maybrick" (1999).
- Irving, Henry B. *Trial of Mrs. Maybrick* (Notable English Trials series, 1912).
- Irving, Henry B. "Mrs. Maybrick", in James H. Hodge (ed.), *Famous Trials III* (Penguin, 1950) pp. 97–134
- J.L.F. The Maybrick Case: *A Treatise Showing Conclusive Reasons for the Continued Public Dissent from the Verdict and "Decision."* (1891).
- L.E.X. *Is Mrs. Maybrick guilty?: A Defence Shewing that the Verdict of Guilty is not Founded on Fact, and is Inconsistent with the Presence of a Strong Element of Doubt; with Reasons for Mrs. Maybrick's Release* (1889).
- Levy, J. H. *The Necessity for Criminal Appeal: As Illustrated by the Maybrick Case and the Jurisprudence of Various Countries* (1899).
- MacDougall, Alexander. *The Maybrick Case* (1891 and 1896).
- Mason, Eleanor. *Florie Chandler: or, The Secret to the Maybrick Poisoning Case* (1890).
- Maybrick, Florence E. *Mrs. Maybrick's Own Story: My Fifteen Lost Years* (1904).
- Morland, Nigel. *This Friendless Lady* (1957).

Mariticide Club

- Robinson, Bruce *They All Love Jack: Busting the Ripper* (Fourth Estate, 2015)
- Ryan Jr., Bernard. *The Poisoned Life of Mrs. Maybrick* (1977).
- Tidy, Charles Meymott and Rawdon Macnamara. *The Maybrick Trial: A Toxicological Study* (1890).
- Hutto, Richard Jay, "A Poisoned Life: Florence Chandler Maybrick, the First American Woman Sentenced to Death in England," McFarland Publishers (2018). www.poisonedlife.com

The Maybrick case was dramatized on the radio series *The Black Museum* in 1952 under the title of "Meat Juice". The 1952 film noir, *A Blueprint for Murder*, mentions Florence Maybrick, along with other notorious poison murderesses Madeleine Smith, and Lyda Trueblood. The BBC Radio series *John Mortimer Presents Sensational British Trials* featured an episode about the Maybrick case, entitled "The Case of the Liverpool Poisoner". Maybrick is mentioned in an episode of television show *Law & Order: Criminal Intent* called "Sound Bodies" from season 3, episode 8 about an arsenic poisoning at a church. The case was reexamined in the BBC program *Murder, Mystery and My Family* (series 4, episode 2) and revisited in *Case Closed?* (Series 4, episode 1). Examined in the TV Series "In suspicious circumstances", Series 4 episode 1: 1994 "Poisoned whispers" Fiction inspired by the case:

- Ackroyd, Peter. *Dan Leno and the Limehouse Golem* (1994).
- Berkeley, Anthony. *The Wychford Poisoning Case* (1926).
- Edwards, Martin. *The Case of the Choleric Cotton Broker* (2015).
- Fessenden, Laura Dayton. *Bonnie Mackirby* (1898).
- Lowndes, Mrs. Belloc. *Letty Lynton* (1931).
- Lowndes, Mrs. Belloc. *Story of Ivy* (1928).
- Purdy, Brandy. *The Ripper's Wife* (2014).
- Sayers, Dorothy L. *Strong Poison* (1930).
- Shearing, Joseph. *Airing in a Closed Carriage* (1943).
- Goodland, David. *The Voice of Angels* (BBC Radio, 2003)

Wives Who Kill

Mary Ann Young (née McCarthy)

Mary Ann McCarthy, born County Galway, Ireland in 1834, was an Irish orphan who fatally stabbed her husband Edward Young in Gulgong, New South Wales after he beat her with a horsewhip. McCarthy was a victim of the Great Famine of Ireland which created widespread starvation. People were dying of starvation and McCarthy was forced to go to a workhouse. At 17 she was selected to take part in Earl Grey Famine Orphan Scheme.

Prison photo Mary Ann Young née McCarthy at Darlinghurst Gaol 1872 After a three months at sea on the Thomas Arbuthnot McCarthy arrived in Sydney in February 1850. Earl Grey's Famine Orphan Scheme transported 4114 Irish orphan girls to the New South Wales colony. The Irish Famine of 1848 to 1850 created widespread famine throughout the land. Thousands of orphans were sent to workhouses in all 32 counties of Ireland. At the height of the Irish Famine, the Earl Grey scheme fashioned a plan to ease overcrowding in the workhouses of Ireland, while providing serving staff and a way to help settle the new Australian colony. The arrival of the Irish

Mariticide Club

women was not universally popular. They were subject to abuse, exploitation and mistreatment by their employers. McCarthy got a job as a milliner but it was cancelled and her wages withheld because of "disobedience". The Irish Orphan young women were housed in the former convict barracks in Macquarie Street, Sydney. Glass panels of Sydney's Famine Memorial feature the names of some of the over 4,000 "Irish Brides" orphan girls and women who were resettled in the colony between 1848 and 1850 under a transportation plan during the Great Famine. Mary Ann was married twice - the first time in Bathurst to George Cooper and the second time to Edward Young in Dubbo. Mary Ann died in 1887 after taking a dose of Chlorodyne, a laudanum-based pain-relieving mixture containing cannabis and chloroform. Early on Tuesday morning of 20 February 1872 a violent argument broke out in Black Lead Lane, Gulgong between Mary Ann and her husband Edward Jacob Young. Witnesses testified that the deceased had beaten his wife with a horse whip. The pair were seen quarreling, fighting and pulling each other's hair. At one point Edward Young struck his wife so hard that she fell to the ground. She recovered and was going inside the shop when her husband made a remark which must have offended her. She seized a butchers knife and stabbed her husband in the navel, penetrating the liver. Young died instantly. When the police arrived Mary Ann confessed: "I am the person who did the deed. I don't deny it. I did not do it willfully. I did it in the heat of passion. The knife was beside me, and I took it up and stabbed him." The case was the talk of town as it was extremely rare for a woman to kill a man. Mary Ann was initially charged with murder in Gulgong police court however the prosecutor recommended that the charge be manslaughter. Witnesses testified that Edward Young had beaten her with a horse whip. Mary Ann was committed for trial in Bathurst. The fact that a wife had killed her husband attracted the attention of newspapers across the state. The jury at Parramatta Police Court found her guilty but recommended her for mercy. She was sentenced six months imprisonment for manslaughter.

Wives Who Kill

Melanie Lyn McGuire (née Slate)

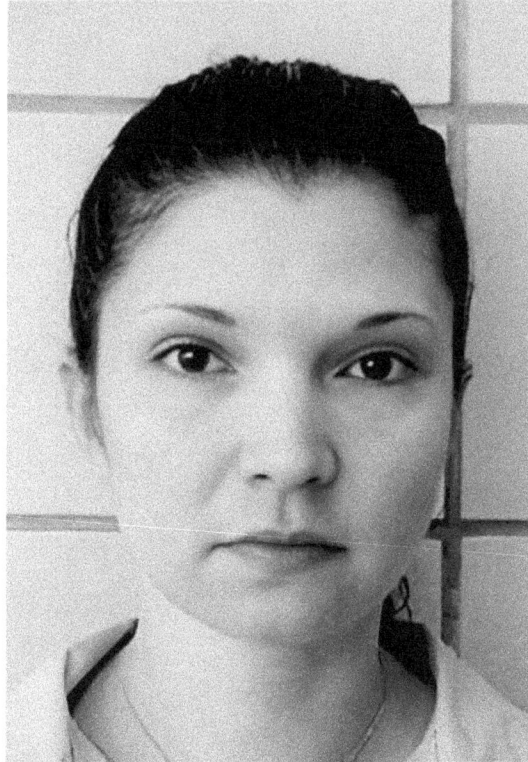

Melanie Lyn McGuire

Melanie Lyn McGuire (née Slate; born October 8, 1972) is an American former nurse who was convicted of murdering her husband on April 28, 2004, in what media dubbed the "suitcase murder". She was sentenced to life in prison on July 19, 2007, and is serving her sentence at the Edna Mahan Correctional Facility for Women in Clinton, New Jersey. She will not be eligible for parole until she is 101 years old. Melanie Lyn Slate grew up in Ridgewood and Middletown Township, New Jersey. She attended Middletown High School South. She enrolled at Rutgers University with a double major in math and psychology and graduated in 1994. She graduated, second in her class, from the Charles E. Gregory School of Nursing (now Raritan Bay Medical Center) in 1997 with a nursing diploma. She married United States Navy veteran William T. "Bill" McGuire (born September 21, 1964) in 1999. By April 2004, the McGuires had been married for five years. Melanie was a nurse at a fertility clinic and Bill was a computer programmer. The couple had two sons and lived in

Mariticide Club

a Woodbridge Township, New Jersey, apartment, but planned to move that month to a larger home in Warren County. They closed the documents on their new house on April 28, but never moved in. That night, according to the prosecution, McGuire drugged her husband, shot him dead, and subsequently dismembered his body. She put his remains into a 3-piece suitcase set, and those three pieces were later found in Chesapeake Bay. On May 5, 2004, the first suitcase, containing human legs, was found floating near the Chesapeake Bay Bridge–Tunnel's fourth artificial island, by two fishermen and two children, and a murder investigation was launched. On May 11, a second larger suitcase was found on the beach of Fisherman Island National Wildlife Refuge, by a graduate student cleaning up litter on the beach. This suitcase was found to contain the head and torso with three bullet wounds, two in the chest and one in the head. The third and smallest suitcase, containing arms, was recovered floating in the water near the Chesapeake Bay Bridge–Tunnel's second artificial island on May 16. Police released a facial reconstruction sketch of the victim, which an acquaintance of Bill McGuire's recognized. Melanie became the prime suspect in the investigation. Because the murder did not occur in Virginia, authorities turned over their investigation to the New Jersey State Police. During the investigation, incriminating evidence against Melanie was uncovered. April 26, 2004, Melanie had purchased a .38 caliber handgun from a store in Easton, Pennsylvania; Bill had been killed with a .38 caliber handgun with wadcutter bullets. Melanie's receipt for the gun also listed an unspecified purchase of $9.95; there were only two items in the store for that amount, and one of them was a box of wadcutter bullets. Police received a tip from a private towing company employee who said he towed a 2002 Nissan Maxima (Bill McGuire's car) from the Flamingo Motel in Atlantic City, on May 8, 2004. Upon further investigation, police discovered a security video of the car being moved in the early morning hours of April 30, 2004. The footage was blurry and the police weren't able to identify the person in the video. Melanie later claimed she had moved the car as a "prank", even though she had applied for a protection from abuse order days earlier after allegedly being slapped by her husband.

Wives Who Kill

Police also learned that Melanie had been having a long-term affair with a co-worker named Bradley Miller. Her E-ZPass tag was recorded at a toll booth in Delaware two days after the murder; she claimed that this was the result of her going furniture shopping in Delaware, since it has no sales tax. Before she was charged with murder, Melanie contacted E-ZPass and attempted to have the $0.90 charge removed from her account history. Days later, an unidentified man, believed by many to be her stepfather, also contacted E-ZPass and attempted to have the charge removed. The plastic bags that contained Bill's body parts and the bags that contained Bill's clothes, which Melanie had given away to a friend, were demonstrated by forensics to have been manufactured on the same assembly line within hours of one another. Melanie admitted that the couple owned the same set of luggage that the body was found in, a matching three-piece set of Kenneth Cole suitcases. Green fibers had been found on one of the bullets lodged in Bill's chest; the fibers were identified as polyester fill, a common material found in household furniture. Bill and Melanie owned a green couch, and investigators theorized that the murderer used a pillow or couch cushion as a makeshift silencer to shoot Bill. Similarly, a medical grade towel found with Bill's body matched those stocked at the clinic where Melanie worked. A witness testified that Melanie used the same towels to protect furniture when she moved house. Police believed that she used a syringe and prescription from her work to obtain the drug used as a means to incapacitate her husband. On June 2, 2005, more than a year after the murder, Melanie dropped her children off at child care and preschool. After exiting the older child's school, Melanie started walking toward her vehicle when law enforcement emerged from the bushes, taking her into custody without incident. She was immediately booked into the Middlesex County Adult Correctional Center on first-degree murder charges, but made her USD$750,000 bail (USD$1.12 million today). Through her attorneys, Joe Tacopina, Steve Turano, and Marc Ward, she pleaded not guilty to the charges. After being released on bail, Melanie faced additional charges on October 11, 2005. A four-count indictment came down from a state grand jury. Her bail was raised to USD$2.1 million (USD$3.1 million today), but

Mariticide Club

she was again released. More than a year later, on October 26, 2006, McGuire was charged with two counts of hindering apprehension for allegedly writing letters to police aimed at getting them off her trail. She again pleaded not guilty and was released after posting USD$10,000 bail. Almost three years after the crime, McGuire's murder trial commenced at the Middlesex County Courthouse in New Brunswick, New Jersey on March 5, 2007. Prosecutors contended her motive for murder was to take up a new life with her lover. McGuire persisted in claiming she was innocent, and claimed her husband had become increasingly moody and unpredictable and was a compulsive gambler. April 23, 2007, McGuire's murder trial jury found her guilty of first-degree murder, finding that the evidence established her culpability for the murder beyond a reasonable doubt. She was convicted of the lesser charges of perjury, desecration of human remains, and possession of a weapon for an unlawful purpose. McGuire was acquitted of the two counts of hindering apprehension, and tampering with evidence and possession of Xanax without prescription. Shortly after her conviction, but before sentencing, McGuire appealed for a new trial on the basis of the story of jailhouse informant Christopher Thieme that her husband was deeply in debt and may have been killed by Atlantic City mobsters. Prosecutors established that the informant was "entirely incredible and routinely and habitually fabricates stories" according to a New Jersey State Police investigation, before recanting and accusing McGuire's attorney of suborning perjury. With the story debunked, the request for a new trial was withdrawn. On July 19, 2007, at the age of 34, McGuire was sentenced to life in prison. During her arraignment on murder charges, McGuire's case was dubbed the "Suitcase Murder" by various media outlets. Author John Glatt wrote a book about the case, entitled *To Have and To Kill*. The case has been profiled on television outlets: Snapped Oxygen Network; *Dateline NBC; 48 Hours Mystery CBS; and The Investigators TruTV; Deadly Affairs* Investigation Discovery, and *Forensic Files II*, among other true crime television shows. McGuire's conviction was affirmed by an appeals court on March 16, 2011. She must serve more than 63 years before she is eligible for parole. On September 20,

Wives Who Kill

2011, the New Jersey Supreme Court declined to hear her further appeal. On April 29, 2014, McGuire filed a motion for post-conviction relief, alleging ineffective assistance of counsel and newly discovered evidence. On September 25, 2014, McGuire appeared in court with her new attorney Lois DeJulio, a public defender, to try to get a hearing that could overturn her 2007 murder conviction, on the grounds that her previous legal representation by Joe Tacopina was inadequate or ineffective. The request was subsequently denied.

Elisa McNabney (*née* Laren Renee Sims)

Larry (right) and Elisa (left)

Larry McNabney (December 19, 1948 – September 12, 2001) was a Sacramento, California attorney whose body was found buried in a vineyard on February 5, 2002. After a nationwide manhunt, his wife, Elisa McNabney, was captured in Florida and arraigned for firstdegree murder. The case made national headlines when police learned that her real name was actually Laren Sims, and that she had served time in a Florida prison for fraud and identity theft. Before Elisa could stand trial however, she hanged herself in her jail cell. Elisa's friend Sarah Dutra was later convicted of voluntary manslaughter and sentenced to 11 years in prison for murdering Larry McNabney. Elisa McNabney (January 20, 1966 – March 31, 2002) was born Laren Renee Sims to parents Jesse and Jackie Sims in Attleboro, Massachusetts, before moving to Florida. Laren was

Mariticide Club

a cheerleader and excellent student at Hernando High School; she had an IQ of 140. Despite her intelligence, she dropped out of high school, had two children with two different fathers, and started stealing. Laren was arrested for stealing a L'Oreal hair color kit from a Woolworth's in Tampa, Florida. After being released on that charge, she violated her probation by illegally using a credit card. She cut off her ankle monitor and headed to Las Vegas, Nevada with her daughter Haylei (born January 29, 1985). Over the years, Laren Sims had a total of 38 aliases, including:

- Melissa Godwin
- Tammy Keelin
- Elizabeth Barasch – a woman she met in Florida prison
- Elisa Redelsperger – the name she used when she met Larry McNabney
- Shane Ivaroni – the name she used while she was on the run

Elisa Redelsperger met Larry McNabney in 1995 when she applied for a job at his Las Vegas law office. She worked as his office manager and settled large cases. However, in late 1995, Larry's law firm was investigated by the Nevada State Bar, which determined that Elisa embezzled more than $140,000 from clients. Larry closed his offices in Reno and Las Vegas in Nevada and moved his practice to Sacramento, California. Despite this, Elisa became McNabney's fifth wife in 1996.On September 10, 2001, following a horse show, Elisa McNabney and her fellow employee and friend Sarah Dutra, with whom she worked at the law office, injected Larry with the horse tranquilizer drug xylazine at a Los Angeles hotel. McNabney, 52, was last seen alive being pushed in a wheelchair by Sims at a Los Angeles horse show September 10. A day later, authorities said, Elisa (or Sims) started clearing out his office and sold his $110,000 horse trailer and truck. According to her later confession, Elisa drove to Yosemite National Park to bury Larry, but he was still alive and she returned with the unconscious Larry McNabney in the back seat to Sacramento. After his death the next day, September 12, from receiving the initial tranquilizer injection along with numerous later doses of other

Wives Who Kill

tranquilizer injections and mouth drops, it was estimated by the forensic examiners that Elisa and Sarah presumably had kept McNabney's body in the refrigerator in the McNabney garage for months. His body was later moved to the nearby winery near where it was finally discovered by San Joaquin County Sheriff's Office detectives in a shallow ditch near Linden, California on February 5, 2002. By that time however, Elisa had liquidated the couple's assets, over USD$500,000, and disappeared. After the discovery of Larry's body, Elisa was the subject of a nationwide manhunt. She was going by the alias Shane Ivaroni and was hiding out in Destin, Florida. On March 20, 2002, Elisa was at her daughter Haylei's friend's house in Fort Walton Beach when she turned herself in. She was booked into the Hernando County Jail and was to be extradited to California. While awaiting extradition, Elisa gave a full confession to law enforcement while in custody at the Okaloosa County, Florida Sheriff's Department. One week later, on Easter Sunday 2002, Elisa hanged herself in her jail cell. Sarah Dutra went on trial for the murder of Larry McNabney in 2003. She faced life imprisonment without parole if convicted of first-degree murder, but she was instead found guilty of voluntary manslaughter and being an accessory to murder. She was sentenced to the maximum of 11 years, 8 months in prison. In Elisa McNabney's suicide note, she asked her lawyer to sue the Hernando County Jail for not preventing her suicide. She also asked that her children receive any funds raised from the lawsuit. "This is all I can give to my children... My actions now will allow them to move into the future without this heavy burden. They won't have to watch my trial on Court TV. It should all die with me," she wrote in the note. She also claims that she was not checked regularly in her cell, but an investigation has since disputed the charge. Sarah Dutra was released from the Central California Women's Facility on August 26, 2011, after serving eighty-five percent of her eleven-year sentence. This case was the basis for the made-for-TV movie *Lies My Mother Told Me* which aired on Lifetime in 2005. The film starred Joely Richardson as Elisa, Kailin See as Sarah, and Hayden Panettiere as Haylei. The case was featured on the television

Mariticide Club

programs Dateline, Evil Stepmothers, Deadly Wives, and Snapped. The case is the basis for true-crime novel, Marked for Death by Brian J. Karem.

Sally McNeil (*née* Sally Dempsey)

Sally McNeil (born September 30, 1960) is a professional bodybuilder, who was convicted for the murder of her husband Ray McNeil, a Mr. Olympia competitor. McNeil was born Sally Dempsey in Allentown, Pennsylvania and describes her upbringing as tough, including exposure to violence so frequently that she had thought it to be commonplace in every home. Sally's father, Richard Dale Dempsey, was a raging alcoholic who was frequently abusive to her mother. Her mother remarried when Sally was 3 years old, and they had two daughters, Judy and Jill, who were Sally's half-sisters, according to the *Killer Sally* documentary. McNeil attended Dieruff High School in Allentown, where she was on the school's swimming and diving and track and field teams. She enrolled at East Stroudsburg State College with aspirations of becoming a gym teacher. After three and a half years in college, however, she ran out of money to fund her education and dropped out. Like her brother and her uncle before her, McNeil served in the United States Marine Corps at Camp Pendleton. She rose to the rank of Sergeant.

First marriage to Anthony Lowden

McNeil met her first husband, Anthony Lowden, at Parris Island while in the Marines, and were married for four years and had two children together: Shantina, John, and a third child. From another man Sally described Anthony as abusive towards the end of their marriage. As she was being transferred to Camp Pendleton, McNeil filed for divorce from Anthony, winning custody of their two oldest children in the process. During their divorce, the third child was put up for adoption. She won the U.S. Armed Services Physique Championship twice in the late 1980s. In 1990, McNeil was demoted from her position as a sergeant for a continuously poor behavioral record, including anger issues, violence, and

Wives Who Kill

lashing out at others. Her behavioral record also resulted in her being discharged from the military.

Second marriage to Ray McNeil

McNeil started bodybuilding during her service at Camp Pendleton, where a friend introduced her to Ray McNeil, another competitive bodybuilder, in June 1987. They dated for about two months before getting married. Three days later, Ray began abusing both Sally and her two children. Sally was choked and punched by Ray. The family settled in Oceanside, California. When she was discharged from the military, Sally began a career wrestling men on video for $300 an hour, earning her the moniker 'Killer Sally.' She made enough money to enable Ray to leave the Marines and concentrate on his own bodybuilding career. Ray started using steroids, which Sally blamed for his violent behavior. Sally would even go to Tijuana, Mexico with her children to buy steroids for Ray. Sally would admit she was not proud of this and considered this to be 'bad parenting'. During this time, Ray won the heavyweight and overall titles in both the 1991 NPC California Championships and the 1991 IFBB North American Championships, and competed in the 1993 Mr. Olympia competition, placing 15th. He also began participating in professional wrestling and did stand-up comedy, performing his material in free shows at The Comedy Club in La Jolla, San Diego. According to his friend, Dwayne "DJ" Jeffers, Ray got into an altercation with another man one night whilst working as a bouncer at a nightclub and ended up sticking his fingers through his eyes. Shantina, Sally's daughter, spoke about the same night to verify this, as she recalled seeing Ray coming home covered in blood and how he told her he had to do what he did because the others were trying to kill him. Ray had been dating another woman at the time and had decided to leave Sally for her. According to DJ, Ray actually planned to spend Valentine's Day in 1995 with the other woman, not his wife. Ray apparently even told DJ he would tell Sally about ending their relationship. DJ warned him about the shotgun in their house, saying she might shoot him. But he said Ray only laughed it off. McNeil was arrested in 1990, for brandishing a firearm at Lowden and smashing the windows of his vehicle with a metal bar. She

Mariticide Club

had been arrested previously for assaulting a mailman who had slapped her son John after he had a fight with his son. McNeil attacked one of Ray's lovers at a bodybuilding show, pinning her to the floor and hitting her repeatedly. This resulted in the National Physique Committee suspending her for a year. It is thought she also physically took her anger out on her husband, pulling a gun on him for the first time before being peppersprayed by police officers. In 1993, Sally was confronted by a club bouncer for dancing on the tables. Drunk and not wanting to do what he told her, Sally kicked him in the face three times. When police arrived, she threatened to kill them. On February 14, 1995, Sally called 9-1-1, telling them: "I just shot my husband because he just beat me up." Earlier in the night, Ray was on a date with Marianne Myers, a fellow member of Golds Gym, instead of Sally on Valentine's Day. Sally was about to go out and find where Ray was, but he turned up after 9:15pm. Sally claimed and maintains that she shot Ray in self-defense when he, spurred by road rage, began choking her after she accused him of adultery. The police transcript reads that Ray, "slapped her, pushed her down on the floor, and started choking her. McNeil squirmed away, ran into the bedroom, and took her sawed-off shotgun out of its case in the closet." Sally then shot Ray twice: once in the abdomen and once in the jaw. Evidence arose during Sally's trial that questioned the validity of the story she had given, including her body language during the initial police interview, the trajectory of the rounds fired into Ray (one of which must have been fired while he was on the floor), and the blood splatter on their living room lamp. In addition, no DNA of Sally's was found on Ray, which eliminated any forensic evidence to back up her story. In 1996, she was convicted of second degree murder and sentenced to 19 years to life. After numerous appeals on a variety of grounds, including improper jury instructions, McNeil's conviction was initially overturned by the U.S. 9th Circuit Court of Appeals which resulted in the granting of a writ of habeas corpus. The State of California then appealed to the US Supreme Court which reversed the 9th Circuit's ruling and remanded the case back to that same venue for further action. Relying on information and instructions from the SCOTUS

Wives Who Kill

opinion, the 9th Circuit reconsidered the matter and on March 29, 2005, issued their opinion ruling in favor of the State and reinstating McNeil's original conviction. McNeil served her sentence at the Central California Women's Facility in Chowchilla, California. Her parole was granted by the California Department of Corrections and Rehabilitation on May 29, 2020. Following her release, McNeil married Norfleet Stewart, whom she met through her Veterans Transition Center support group. She currently resides in Northern California.

Bodybuilding

Year	Body	Competiton	Division	Placing
1998	NPC	US Armed Forces Championship	Middleweight	1st
1998	NPC	US Armed Forces Championship	Overall	1st
1991	NPC	Junior USA	Lightweight	5th
1991	NPC	Nationals	Middleweight	13th
1991	NPC	Palm Springs Classic	Middleweight	4th
1992	NPC	Junior USA	Middleweight	2nd
1992	NPC	Nationals	Middleweight	12th
1992	IFBB	North American Championships	Middleweight	9th

Mariticide Club

1992	NPC	USA Championship	Middleweight	5th
1994	NPC	Nationals	Heavyweight	16th
1994	IFBB	North American Championship	Heavyweight	6th
!994	NPC	National Championships	Middleweight	5th

In October 2022, Netflix released a three-part docuseries, *Killer Sally,* covering the case and its aftermath directed by Nanette Burstein, whose credits include *On the Ropes* (1999) and *Hillary* (2020).

Agnus McVee

Agnus McVee was a Canadian serial killer. McVee ran a hotel and store at 108 Mile House on the Cariboo Wagon Road from 1875 to 1885 during the Cariboo Gold Rush. Along with her husband Jim McVee and her son-in-law Al Riley, she is said to have killed many miners for their gold and kidnapped women for sale to miners as white slaves. The story has achieved local prominence, but documentary evidence is absent. Her story was the subject of the 2019 graphic novel *Agnes, Murderess* by Canadian writer Sarah Leavitt. The actions attributed to Agnus McVee and her accomplices are multiple murders, kidnappings, torture, and white slavery. The murders were of traveling gold miners (most likely killed for their gold). The kidnappings were of eight young women who were tied up in the hotel basement. The women were mistreated until they were obedient and then sold to miners. The story goes that a miner, Jim MacDonald, wished to buy a young girl from the McVees. Agnus agreed to sell MacDonald a 17-year-old girl. The next morning, Jim McVee followed MacDonald down the Cariboo Wagon Road. McVee murdered MacDonald and took all his money. The next morning, Agnus McVee poisoned her

Wives Who Kill

husband in retaliation for this murder. The girl, however, was able to escape and to identify Jim McVee to the North West Mounted Police. Upon investigation, the police found McVee, Al Riley (her brother-in-law), Jim McVee's body, and eight young girls in the basement of the McVee's hotel. The police arrested McVee and Riley and the pair were taken to Fort Kamloops. They were charged and convicted of murder and kidnapping. They were then transported to New Westminster and incarcerated in the New Westminster jail. McVee killed himself in 1885 while in the jail by swallowing poison. Riley was hanged shortly after. The Agnus McVee story seems to have originated from a single source: According to Maryanne Rutledge, president of the 100 Mile and District Historical Society, the story comes from an out-of-publication booklet titled "Lost Treasure in BC #3" by Larry Lazeo of Fort Langley. The author received the details from an old-timer. The tale has become widespread in the 100 Mile district and has expanded beyond it. In 2006, Red Barn Productions filmed the story for CTV's *Travel and Discovery* series, intended for satellite broadcast in late September or October 2006. The story is also on a BC Government web page of historical information. One form of evidence that is sometimes given is that caches of gold have been found in the area. Rutledge states "In 1929, there was a farmer who unearthed a cache of gold in bags. More recently, when a nearby airport was built, excavation dug up a sum of cash from that era." However, documentary evidence for the story is absent. An article by Greg Joyce in the *Prince George Citizen* newspaper discusses the story of the McVee murders. He states that there are no documents of ownership of the 108 Mile Hotel during the decade that McVee is supposed to have run it. Missing persons records do not list anyone who lodged at the hotel between 1875 and 1885 as reported missing. No police records of the arrest or trial have been found "despite Rutledge's extensive searches in Kamloops, New Westminster, and in the provincial archives in Victoria." Furthermore, there are no death certificates for either McVee or Riley.

Mariticide Club

Daisy Louisa C. de Melker (née Hancorn-Smith)

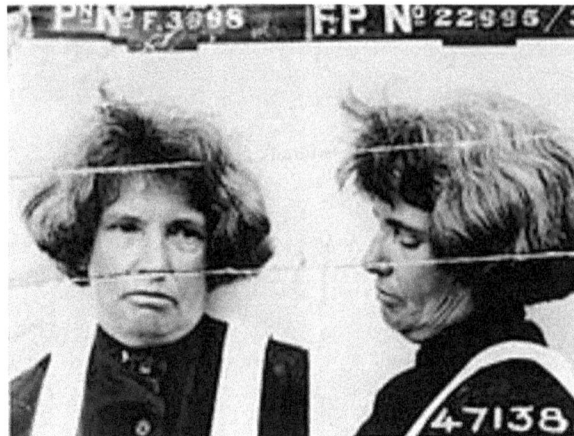

Daisy de Melker

Daisy Louisa C. de Melker (née Hancorn-Smith; 1 June 1886 – 30 December 1932) simply known as Daisy de Melker, was a South African nurse who poisoned two husbands with strychnine for their life insurance money; she also poisoned her only son with arsenic for reasons which are still unclear. De Melker is the second woman to have been hanged in South African criminal history. De Melker was accused of three murders but only convicted of one, the killing of her son. The charges of poisoning her husbands were never proven in a court of law. It was William Sproat, the younger brother of her second husband Robert, who accused De Melker because he wanted Robert's will in favor of De Melker declared invalid. De Melker refused to refund an alleged loan from her mother-in-law, Jane Sproat, to Robert; she regarded it as a gift and argued that it was not stipulated in the will as a loan. William won the civil case on the will, which ran concurrently with the murder trial, and was awarded costs. De Melker withdrew on the date Justice Greenberg sentenced her for murder. William's was a pyrrhic victory, however; to pay her exorbitant legal costs, De Melker had to sell off all her assets. She was declared insolvent and was eventually buried in a pauper's grave. Daisy de Melker was born Daisy Hancorn-Smith in Seven Fountains in what was then the Cape Colony. She was one of eleven children. When she was twelve, Daisy went to Bulawayo, Rhodesia (now Zimbabwe) to live with her father and two of her brothers. Three years later, she became a boarder

Wives Who Kill

at the Good Hope Seminary School in Cape Town. She returned to Rhodesia in 1903, but soon moved to the Colony of Nataland enrolled at the Berea Nursing Home in Durban. On one of her holidays in Rhodesia, Daisy fell in love with a young man named Bert Fuller, a civil servant in the Native Affairs Department at Broken Hill. They planned to marry in October 1907. However, Fuller contracted blackwater fever and died, with Daisy at his bedside, on the very day they had planned to marry. Fuller left a will bequeathing £100 to his fiancée. In March 1909, about eighteen months after Fuller's death, Daisy married William Alfred Cowle, a plumber in Johannesburg. She was 22 and he was 36. The couple had five children, four of whom died. The first two were twins who died in infancy; their third child died of an abscess on the liver; and the fourth suffered convulsions and bowel trouble and died at fifteen months old. Their last, and only surviving child, Rhodes Cecil, was born in June 1911.

First murder: William Cowle (first husband)

Early on the morning of 11 January 1923, William Cowle became ill soon after taking epsom salts prepared by his wife. The first doctor who attended Cowle did not consider his condition serious and prescribed a bromide mixture. But Cowle's condition deteriorated rapidly; he took a turn for the worse soon after the doctor left. Daisy summoned the neighbors to help and called for another doctor. Cowle was in excruciating pain when the second doctor arrived. He foamed at the mouth, went blue in the face, and screamed in agony if anyone touched him until he died. Faced with these symptoms, the second doctor suspected strychnine poisoning and refused to sign the death certificate. A postmortem was subsequently performed by the acting District Surgeon, Dr. Fergus. The cause of death was certified to be chronic nephritis and cerebral hemorrhage. Daisy, the sole beneficiary of her husband's will, inherited £1795.

Second murder: Robert Sproat (second husband)

On 11 January 1926, 36-year-old Daisy married another plumber, Robert Sproat, who was ten years her senior. In October 1927, Robert became violently ill, suffering excruciating pain and severe muscle spasms similar to those experienced by Cowle. Robert recovered, only to suffer a second

Mariticide Club

attack a few weeks later after drinking beer in the company of his wife and stepson Rhodes. He died on 6 November 1927. Dr. Mallinick, the attending physician, certified that the cause of death was arteriosclerosis and cerebral hemorrhage. No autopsy was performed. Following Robert's death, his widow inherited over £4000, plus a further £560 paid by his pension fund.

Third murder: Rhodes Cecil Cowle (son)

On 21 January 1931, Daisy married for the third time. Her husband was a widower, Sydney Clarence de Melker; like her two previous husbands, he was a plumber. Late in February 1932, Daisy had travelled from Germiston on the East Rand to Turffontein, to obtain arsenic from a chemist. She used her former name, Sproat, and claimed that she required the poison to destroy a sick cat. Less than a week later, on 2 March 1932, Rhodes, aged 20, fell ill at work after drinking coffee from a thermos flask his mother had prepared for him. A fellow worker, James Webster, also become violently sick. Webster, who had drunk very little of the coffee, recovered within a few days, but Rhodes died at home at midday on 5 March. A postmortem followed and the cause of death was given as cerebral malaria. Rhodes was buried at New Brixton cemetery the following day; on 1 April, de Melker received £100 from Rhodes' insurance policy. Daisy's motives for killing her son Rhodes remain unclear. In the case of her first two husbands, the motive seemed to be financial gain. Rhodes seems to have been under the impression that he would come into an inheritance at age 21. One theory is that he was demanding more than his mother could give him and was becoming a burden to her. The most obvious answer is that he had become a disappointment to Daisy; she had pampered him all his life, but he rarely showed her any consideration in return. By this time, Daisy's former brother-in-law, William Sproat, raised his suspicions concerning his brother Robert's death to the authorities. On 15 April 1932, the police obtained a court order permitting them to exhume the bodies of Robert, Cowle and Rhodes. Rhodes' remains were found to be in an unusually good state of preservation, which is characteristic of the presence of arsenic in

Wives Who Kill

large quantities. A state forensic pathologist was able to isolate traces of arsenic in the viscera, backbone and hair. Although the bodies of Cowle and Robert Sproat were largely decomposed, traces of strychnine were found in the vertebrae of each man. Their bones also had a pinkish discoloration, suggesting that the men had taken pink strychnine, which was common at the time. Traces of arsenic were also found in the hair and fingernails of James Webster, Rhodes' surviving colleague. One week later, De Melker was arrested and charged with the murders of all three men. Public interest in the case grew, and newspapers gave the story a great deal of coverage. The Turffontein chemist, Mr. Abraham Spilkin, from whom she had bought the arsenic that killed her son, contacted police after he recognized de Melker from a newspaper photograph as being "Mrs. D.L. Sproat", who had signed the poisons register. The De Melker trial lasted thirty days. Sixty witnesses were called for the Crown and less than half this number for the defense. To present the forensic evidence, the Crown employed the services of Dr. J.M. Watt, an expert toxicologist and professor of pharmacology at Witwatersrand University. In summing up, before giving his verdict, the judge pointed out that the Crown had been unable to prove conclusively that Cowle and Sproat had died of strychnine poisoning. "It does not convince me, nor does it convict the accused," he said. On the third count, however, he had come to the "inescapable conclusion" De Melker had murdered her son. This was evident because:

- Rhodes Cowle had died of arsenic poisoning
- The coffee flask held traces of arsenic
- The accused had put the arsenic into the flask
- The defense of suicide was untenable

When the judge finally turned to pass sentence on De Melker, her face went pale but she still proclaimed her innocence. De Melker was condemned to death by hanging. The sentence was carried out on the morning of 30 December 1932 at Pretoria Central Prison.

Mariticide Club

Lucille Marie Miller (née Maxwell)

Lucille Marie Miller (née Maxwell) (January 17, 1930 – November 4, 1986) was a Canadian-American housewife and mother who was convicted of first-degree murder in the death of her husband. Prosecutors alleged Miller was inspired by the eponymous plot device of the film *Double Indemnity*, a provision in which the proceeds of a life insurance policy pay double the face value for accidental deaths. Joan Didion whom I met in Ireland wrote a 1966 essay about the case, "Some Dreamers of the Golden Dream", which appeared in *The Saturday Evening Post* as "How Can I Tell Them There's Nothing Left" (a quote from Lucille Miller the morning of the fire); it was included in her 1968 book *Slouching Towards Bethlehem*. At the time of the murder, Lucille Miller was just a few months shy of 35 years old, married to dentist Dr. Gordon "Cork" Miller, a mother of three, and pregnant with their fourth child. The Millers were Seventh-day Adventists (SDA), and had met and married when they attended the SDA owned Walla Walla College. The family had recently moved from Oregon to a new house at 8488 Bella Vista Drive in the then-unincorporated Alta Loma area of San Bernardino County, California, due to Cork's stated desire to attend the medical college at the nearby SDA-owned Loma Linda University Medical Center so he could move from dentistry to general medicine. Their oldest child, Debra J. Miller, recalled that her father wanted to be an airline pilot, but had reluctantly followed her grandfather into dentistry in order not to have college funding cut off. Cork had also showed signs of depression and suicidal behavior, including one incident where Lucille hid the keys to the couple's 1964 Volkswagen Beetle with Debra, and had been taking sedatives to help him sleep at night. October 7, 1964, Lucille Miller had poured Cork a glass of milk to settle his stomach, and discovered she needed to make a late-night trip to the store to purchase milk so the children would have it for breakfast. Cork asked to come along. He was sleeping next to the passenger door, which she locked to ensure he didn't fall out. They went to an all-night Mayfair Market where she purchased the milk. At about 12:30 AM on October 8 on the way home, Lucille claimed, the Beetle had a tire blow out, causing the car to catch fire

Wives Who Kill

as she drove off Banyan Street above a lemon grove. She claimed she tried to break a window but the fire was too hot to reach in and unlock the door, and that she then used a big tree branch to try to move her husband out of the car, but he was fast asleep. She then went to get help on the deserted section of Banyan Street and finally found a house from which she called the police Initial evidence matched her story, until authorities more closely examined the skid marks, which were much shorter than they would be in a loss of control as Lucille reported. They also noticed an empty can of gasoline lying on its side on the back seat, while the charred milk cartons were still standing upright and not jostled by the sudden stop. The car was still in low gear (unusual for a 35mph crash), and was also dug in, implying that someone had tried to push it the rest of the way over the embankment. Miller was arrested later that day and held pending charges. A complaint was filed October 13; an indictment for first-degree murder was returned October 20. Further investigation led to the discovery of a $125,000 (some sources say $140,000) life insurance policy with a double indemnity clause for accidental death. The couple was also found to be roughly $64,000 in debt, including a nearly $30,000 mortgage on the Bella Vista house. Lucille was also discovered to have had an affair with lawyer Arthwell Hayton, a widower father of three, one of them a friend of Debra, who said Hayton's wife, Elaine, had died under mysterious circumstances. Both Lucille and Hayton told police that the affair had ended several months before Cork's death. Miller was convicted on March 5, 1965, and sentenced to life imprisonment. Her conviction was upheld on appeal to the California Supreme Court in 1966, and also by the U.S. Supreme Court in 1968 (with F. Lee Bailey as part of her legal team). After serving seven years of her sentence, she was paroled in 1972. Her attorneys, convinced of her absolute innocence, continued to appeal her conviction.

In addition to the trial, Didion's essay contains details of the fire, the Hayton affair, and a biographical sketch of Lucille and Cork Miller. Didion would later meet Lucille Miller's daughter Debra in 1996. Arthwell Hayton later married Wenche Berg, his children's governess. San Bernardino County authorities never further investigated the death of Elaine Hayton,

Mariticide Club

which had been ruled an accidental overdose of sedatives, despite the discovery of the affair between Hayton and Lucille Miller and the fact that both their spouses had had high levels of sedatives in their systems when they died. Debra, Guy and Ron Miller all married, but had no children. Debra and Ron both became teachers (Ron is also a writer), and Guy became a third-generation Miller dentist. Kimi Kai Miller, born in June 1965 during their mother's incarceration at California Institution for Women in Corona, CA, died at age 25 from lung cancer. Debra and Ron were two of the on-camera interviewees for "Accident on Banyan St.," an episode of A Crime to Remember that dealt with the case. It first aired on December 16, 2014, on Investigation Discovery. Little was revealed about Lucille's post-parole life, except that the prison-educated stenographer and model prisoner had three job offers in Los Angeles upon her release from prison and she planned to change her name. Lucille was also "hopelessly entangled" with her kids until her death on November 4, 1986, as Debra reported in a 2006 newspaper article she wrote about her mother's case.

Sharee Paulette Kitley Miller

Sharee Paulette Kitley Miller (born October 13, 1971) is an American woman convicted of plotting the murder of her husband, Bruce Miller, over the Internet with her online lover Jerry Cassaday, who later died by suicide. Bruce Miller was found dead at his junkyard in Mt. Morris, Michigan on November 8, 1999, killed by a 20 gauge shotgun. After Sharee was arrested in February 2000, she was held without bail until her trial. On December 12, 2000, the trial began and her case made national headlines. According to the prosecution, Sharee wanted Bruce dead for his money and that a divorce would not have given her enough. After two days of deliberation, on December 22, the jury found Sharee Miller guilty on all charges. On January 29, 2001, Genesee County Circuit Court Judge Judith Fullerton sentenced Miller to life in prison for the conspiracy to commit murder charge, and 54 to 81 years for second-degree murder. She served part of her term at the Robert Scott Correctional Facility in Plymouth, Michigan and as of 2019, was serving a life sentence at the Women's Huron Valley

Wives Who Kill

Correctional Facility in Ypsilanti, Michigan. Her mother currently has custody of one of her three children. In 2007, while in prison, Miller was diagnosed with posttraumatic stress disorder and other mental illnesses. She claimed she wanted to give back to people she had selfishly taken from. In August 2008, a federal court judge overturned her conviction and ordered that she receive a new trial. The judge found that the suicide note from Cassaday (her boyfriend and the one who committed the homicide) should never have been admitted into court and seen by the jurors because Cassaday was dead and could not be cross examined. On July 16, 2009, a federal court judge ordered Sharee Miller's immediate release from prison on bond pending the new trial which was ordered in August 2008. In response, on July 17, 2009, Genesee County Prosecutor David Leyton ordered that Miller immediately be re-arrested from prison where she was taken to the Genesee County Jail and held without bond to await new charges. Sharee Miller was arraigned on July 22, 2009, again on charges of second-degree murder and conspiracy to commit premeditated first-degree murder. The new trial was scheduled to begin on October 20, 2009. Miller's attorneys appealed this action. The retrial was put on hold pending the federal appeal. On July 29, 2009, Sharee Miller was released from the Genesee County Jail on a $100,000 recognizance bond until her trial began. In December 2009, Sharee Miller was found using the popular social networking site Facebook. Miller's lawyer David Nickola said that there was no reason for his client to be barred from using a computer, but Sharee's Facebook page was temporarily deactivated when it attracted publicity. "I don't think there's anything inappropriate about it," Nickola said. He states that Sharee used Facebook to keep in touch with her family members and her son who is overseas in the military. "She's an innocent person out in society and she's doing positive things," Nickola said. "Having a Facebook page to communicate with her son who is serving in the military overseas is nothing inappropriate whatsoever." While having a Facebook page is not a violation of Miller's bond, Genesee County Prosecutor David Leyton said this is a perfect example of why people need to be careful when they're online. "People have to be careful when they're communicating with others who they don't know on the Internet.". On June 21, 2010, a panel of the U.S. Court of Appeals upheld the August 2008 federal ruling that the Cassaday suicide note was not admissible. On November 14, 2011, the US Supreme Court vacated the Court of Appeals decision and remanded the case back to the Sixth Circuit Court of Appeals to reconsider the case based on recent U.S. Supreme Court case law. On February 16, 2012, the Sixth Circuit remanded the case to the District Court. On August 2, 2012, the District Court entered its opinion and ordered reinstatement of Miller's convictions and revoked her bond. The court held the suicide note possessed sufficient guarantees of trustworthiness to satisfy defendant's constitutional right of confrontation. It also found that the Michigan Court of Appeals' factual determination, that the statements were spontaneous, voluntary, made to Cassaday's parents, and less likely to be fabricated because he was about to kill himself, were reasonable findings. On February 11, 2014, the United States Court of Appeals for the Sixth Circuit affirmed the federal district court's reinstatement of Miller's convictions and sentences. In 2016, Sharee Miller, in a four-page typed letter sent to Judge Fullerton, admitted to her role in her husband's death. On August 28, 2017, Judge Judith A. Fullerton of the Genesee County Circuit Court, issued an opinion denying Miller's motion for relief from judgment.

Marie-Louise Victorine Bessarabo (née Marie-Louise Victorine Grouès and pen names Héra Mirtel, Juliette de Boulogne, Juliette de Lotus) Marie-Louise Victorine Bessarabo (pen names, Héra Mirtel, Juliette de Boulogne, Juliette de Lotus; 24 October 1868 - 21 March 1931) was a French writer, woman of letters, militant feminist, salonnier, lecturer, and ardent suffragist. She was also a spiritist and a believer in the Black Mass, a stock exchange gambler, a plotter for the restoration of the royalist regime in France, as well as an advisor of other women in matrimony and affairs of the heart. Mirtel was famous for the murder of her second husband, Georges Bessarabo, whose body was sent in a "bloody trunk" "from Paris to Nancy, by rail. Brilliantly defended by Vincent de Moro

Wives Who Kill

Giafferi, she was sentenced to twenty years' imprisonment. She was suspected of having murdered her first husband as well.

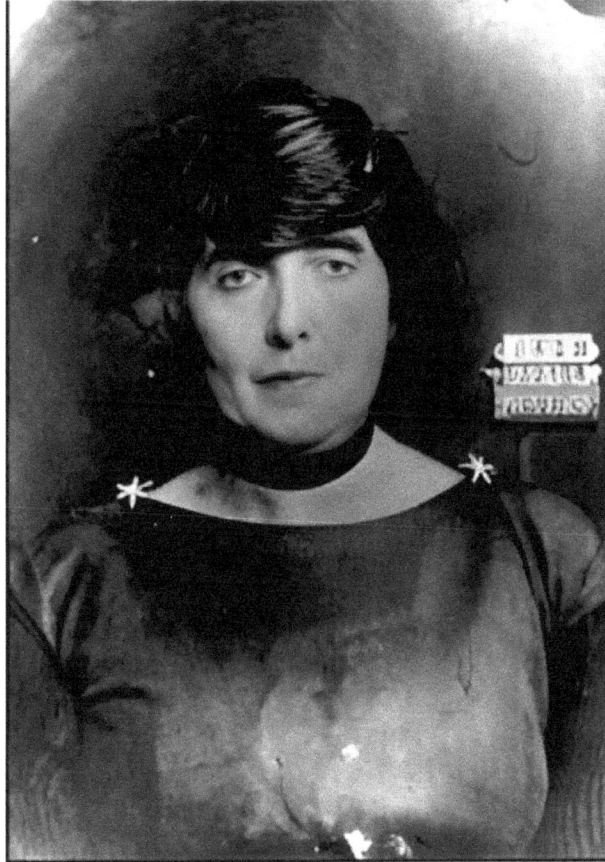

Marie-Louise Victorine Bessarabo Mugshot 1920

Marie-Louise Victorine Grouès was born in Lyon on 24 October 1868. She was the aunt of Abbé Pierre. Known by her pen name, Héra Mirtel, she wrote novels, poems, plays, and many articles, including columns for *Le Sillon de Bordeaux*, magazine exclusively written by women; *Le Soleil*, daily; *La Renaissance Contemporaine*, literary review; and *Le Divan*. She was the founder of the newspaper *L'Entente*, and secretary general of the editorial staff of *La Renaissance contemporain*. In addition, Mirtel worked in advertising, and lectured at Université Populaire de Montmartre. Mirtel advocated a matriarchal feminism inspired by the theses of Johann Jakob Bachofen. In 1897, in Saltillo, Mexico, she married Pierre Paul Antoine Jacques, a trader of the Ubaye valley. After becoming financially enriched in Mexico, she became a widow in March 1914, with two daughters, Paule

Mariticide Club

(1898) and Louise (1900). In 1915, in Mexico, she married Ishmael Jacob Providence Weissmann, a commissioner born in Romania, who called himself Georges Bessarabo. Mirtel murdered Bessarabo in Square La Bruyère, Paris, on 31 July 1920. On 4 August 1920 his corpse, shot dead by a revolver, was discovered at the bottom of a trunk in the Nancy rail station, having been sent by train from the Gare de l'Est. On 21 June 1922 Mirtel, defended by Vincent de Moro-Giafferi, was sentenced to twenty years of forced labor. During the investigation, suspicions weighed on the death of his first husband, who feared that his wife would poison him, and who committed suicide with a revolver in March 1914. But the investigation confirmed the suicide. His daughter, Paule, present at the scene of the crime and judged for complicity, was acquitted. Many dailies followed the trial, rich in theatrics: Le Petit Parisien (17 issues), Le Temps (12 January 1922), Le Matin (22 June 1922), Le Figaro (29 April 1921), Le petit journal illustré (18 June 1922), L'Ouest-Éclair (June 9, 1922) and Le Gaulois (29 April 1921). Arthur Bernède recounted the lawsuit in the Bessarabo case (Tallandier, 1931). In 1929, after recognizing that Paule had lied, there was a request for the revision of the trial. Mirtel, incarcerated in Rennes and on the verge of obtaining a conditional release, died on 21 March 1931. She was buried with her first husband, in Saint-Paul-sur-Ubaye, in the Alpes de Haute-Provence.

The trial of Mme. Bessarabo

Wives Who Kill

In *The Police Journal* (1920), L. Czapski provided a narrative of the case:—*"I am not a woman who kills. Everything in my past life protests against such an accusation. All my works radiate with proof that I am a creatress. Being that, I cannot destroy."* These were the words from Madame Bessarabo, suspected murderess of her first husband and confessed assassin of the second one. When a police investigator came upon an abandoned trunk at a railway station, as was the case with the trunk consigned by Hera Mirtel to Nancy; when, moreover, he espies blood trickling through the bottom onto the cement floor of the baggage room; and when on opening the trunk he finds therein a man's dead body folded in two, ankles strapped to neck and the whole bundle hastily wrapped up in a mackintosh—he somewhat naturally concludes that a murderer or murderess has been at work. When, in addition, after a story woven of futile lies, the dead man's wife confesses that it was she who killed him the French authorities place the woman in a cell at St. Lazaire prison, precisely as they did Hera Mirtel charged with murder. Not a single one of her attitudes since the imprisonment has indicated that Hera Mirtel as much as recognizes her guilt for the killing. One of her intimate literary friends, likewise a woman, has, indeed, publicly suggested that at the moment of the shooting Hera might have been in the grip of an occult power. Certain it is that throughout the latter part of the war Hera's quaint salon in the Place La Bruyere attracted a group of nondescript marquises and c0untesses who made the evocation of spirits a weekly practice. Hera, aided by a dilapidated Italian priest, acted as the high priestess at the seances. On one occasion it is said she called in the ghost of Madame de Pompadour, and so impressive was the confab held between the hostess medium and the Eighteenth-Century beauty that the witnesses thereafter denounced the decadence of the French Republic as hotly as they extolled the blessings of the bygone Empire. It would remain to be seen by what means Hera Mirtel managed to work herself up into a trance at that midnight hour when, lying in her bed, she reached over for the revolver, placed it to her sleeping husband's right temple and fired. If the theory advanced by Hera's literary friend he the right one, the shot that rang out in the darkened bedchamber

Mariticide Club

failed to rouse the murderess into a consciousness of the hideous reality that lay beside her there in the form of a corpse. So little so that Hera languidly put the weapon on its wonted place on the bedside chair, turned over and calmly fell asleep. Her daughter Paulette, from her chamber a few yards down the corridor, heard the sound of the shooting and rushed to her mother's bedroom door. Doubly reflected in some wall mirrors, she espied her stepfather's head reposing on a reddened pillow. When morning came Hera put on her blue silk bathrobe, ate breakfast, and then set about the packing. Georges Bessarabo's corpse was of considerable bulk. Finding it hard to handle unaided, Hera revealed the truth to the daughter, and from that moment on at least Paulette schemed with the murderess to get the inconvenient baggage out of the way. They brought one of the family trunks down from the garret on the seventh floor. As the mother held the body in position Paulette strapped the ankles to the neck whereupon the corpse was covered with a raincoat and tucked into the trunk, laid on its side for the purpose. After lunch, the two women procured some rope at a nearby market-place fastened down the lid (there was some doubt as to whether the lock would hold), hauled the trunk downstairs, had it loaded on a taxi and driven to the Gare de l'Est, addressed to an imaginary woman at Nancy. Were the whole truth of the murder confined to these limits it would be odd but still possible to accept the theory which attempts to throw the moral responsibility for the crime on some bloodthirsty sprite in possession of Hera Mirtel's soul. There might have been room for the other defense put forward by the woman's partisans—namely that the motive behind her act was her imperious desire to make reality out of some of the romance which, as a poetess, she had dreamed and written during most of her life. But the police soon learned that, a couple of days before the murder, Hera Mirtel had booked a passage to Mexico for herself and Paulette. It became known that the dead broker's pocket-book, containing what was believed to be a large sum of money, had mysteriously disappeared. Here surely it is not so much Hera Mirtel, the poetess desirous of living her romance, but Madame Bessarabo, wife of the oil promoter, that comes to the fore. It is the same woman who played on the money

Wives Who Kill

market and so frequently lost. She had a big settlement to make at the Bourse on the day following the murder. She knew that her husband had just made 'a vast deal in Mexico oil property, on which his commission was to amount to nearly a million francs. Could she have expected that he would bring the entire amount of the commission home with him, when as a matter of fact he had often told his brother that he feared as much as to go to his home himself? In the morning of the day he was destined to die at his wife's hands Georges Bessarabo deposited several hundred thousand of the newly earned francs at his bank, retaining but some odd thousands in the pocketbook. That was all the wife got out of it after all her planning of murder and the commission of the crime itself. None of the more sordid accompaniments of her act seem to have impressed Hera Mirtel's mind. In her prison cell she haughtily protested against the accusation of vulgar killing. "I am a creatress," she wrote, "and I cannot destroy. I am not a woman who kills." Back in her flat for a while, Hera Mirtel calmly reconstructed the tragic scene of the shooting and that of the packing of the corpse for its railway trip to Nancy. Police officers present noticed that on the mattress covering beneath the spot where lay. dead man's pillow the linen had been washed and carefully ironed over—so carefully that the hot iron left a trace. As for the pillow itself Madame Bessarabo took it with her to Montmorency villa the day after the murder and burned it in the kitchen stove. She flung the revolver into a little lake near the villa, rowing out in the company of Paulette. She gave the police these and other details with the nonchalance of a woman talking to her grocer. Passion? Yes there was some talk of passion in her first defense after the arrest at Montmoreucy. Her husband she said had been for long enamored of a stenographer. She reproached him for it on the night of the murder, she said, and he then grabbed her by the shoulders and shook her. She fired in self defense, she insisted, as he had threatened to kill her. In the early flutter of lying, when an examining judge confronted her with the story of the trunk found at Nancy, Madame Bessarabo blundered into a yarn to the effect that her husband had fled from Paris because of an approaching financial catastrophe. She had sent her daughter to his office the morning after the

Mariticide Club

murder with a forged letter announcing the flight. Seven years ago, when her first husband was found dead in his study, with a note in what seemed his handwriting saying he had committed suicide Hera Mirtel. then Madame Jacques, gave it out to all who would hear that he killed himself to escape the shame of bankruptcy. Some months later, however, in Mexico, where her dead husband's property was located she realized nearly a million francs from the sales of his real estate alone. Now police want M. Jaeques' body exhumed for another examination. In both cases. the fatal bullet entered at the right temple and came out at the left.

Euphemia Mondich

Euphemia Mondich Mugshot (c. 1924)

Wives Who Kill

Euphemia Mondich (1884 – August 20, 1961), known as Lady Bluebeard, was a Polish–American bigamist, murderer and suspected serial killer who killed at least one husband and a lover in Detroit, Michigan, on two separate occasions in 1921. Convicted for the final murder, she was sentenced to life imprisonment and remained imprisoned until her death in 1961. Little is known of Mondich's background. Born in 1884 in Austrian Galicia, she first married George Woodwood, who died three years later under mysterious circumstances. In 1910 she emigrated to Toronto, Canada, where she married a man named George Woropchuk. Their marriage lasted until she deserted him in 1914 and moved to United States, settling in Detroit. There, she married Joseph Sokolsky on June 14, 1921. The couple lived in a small house on Osborne Street, where a third man, a 39-year-old emigrant John Udurovich, also resided.

Shortly after becoming acquainted, Udurovich fell in love with Mondich, but they could not facilitate their relationship while Sokolsky was still around. And so, on July 7, the trio went out for a ride on a dirt road outside the town. Along the way, Udurovich stopped the car, claiming that a tire had gone flat. Sokolsky then exited the car to help him out, but Udurovich then hit him on the head with a wrench, killing him on the spot. Afterwards, both he and Mondich dragged the body to a nearby brick manufacturing company and dumped the body into a hole used for unloading building materials, covering it with rubbish. Mondich would later be questioned about her husband's disappearance on July 12, but as there was no credible evidence for an arrest, she was let go. She filed for divorce on the grounds of cruelty and desertion, which she won and was given ownership of their house on Osborne. After the murder, Udurovich proposed to Mondich, but she denied his advancements on the grounds that the neighbors would get suspicious because of her husband's recent disappearance. Mondich then moved to a house on Dwyer Street, but only three weeks later, Udurovich found her again and threatened her at gunpoint to marry him. Mondich initially pretended to accept his offer, but when he sat down to read the newspaper, she grabbed his revolver and shot him in the abdomen. Frightened, Udurovich attempted to flee through the window, but was shot

Mariticide Club

in the back and fell, whereupon Mondich got closer and shot him in the neck, killing him. On the following morning, she buried the body under the house and moved away yet again. Mondich eventually remarried, this time to a man named Steve Mondich. The couple lived together with seemingly no issues for around three years, until Euphemia suddenly deserted him in September 1924, taking $5,700 with her for a supposed move back to her native Poland. Distressed by this, Steve went to the police station and begged the officer in charge to find his wife, mentioning that she had taken some clothing and all their money. In an attempt to bring further attention to his pleas, he mentioned that she had previously been questioned in the disappearance of a previous husband. Steve was brought to the Homicide Division's room to give further details. Looking further into her case, detectives not only discovered that she had won a successful divorce lawsuit against her missing husband, but that another man who had been in her company had also gone missing. Four days later, they received an anonymous tip that Mondich was attempting to sell her property at the County Building, where she was arrested and jailed on a murder charge. After refusing to admit her guilt for more than four hours, she finally confessed to shooting a man and burying his body under the house on Dwyer Street, agreeing to show detectives exactly where she had buried him. After excavating the house and uncovering a complete human skeleton, initially believed to be Sokolsky, the investigators were shocked to learn that this was her lover, John Udurovich. Mondich was then brought back to the police station for further questioning, where they learned that she had been in a total of nine relationships across Poland, Canada and the United States, but authorities were unable to locate all of her husbands and suitors. In the end, Mondich was charged solely with the Udurovich killing, as authorities were unable to locate Sokolsky's body. While awaiting trial, she hoped that she would be acquitted of the murder charge, but this did not occur; and she was ordered to stand trial. At the trial, she entered a plea of self-defense, arguing that she was deathly afraid of Udurovich and had no choice but to kill him; to counter this, the prosecution brought parts of Udurovich's skeleton to show where he had been shot, indicating that the

Wives Who Kill

killing had been premeditated. Upon seeing them, Mondich burst into tears. Mondich was eventually found guilty of the murder charge and sentenced to life imprisonment. After her trial, her two surviving husbands met up and congratulated one another on staying alive before bidding her farewell. Mondich was then transferred to the Detroit House of Correction in Plymouth Charter Township, where she remained until her death of a heart attack on August 20, 1961, aged 77. According to Superintendent Jonathan Goldsmith, Mondich had no visitors during the last ten years of her life and spent most of her time tending to the prison flower garden and feeding stray animals. She turned religious during her imprisonment, and occasionally received letters from The Salvation Army.

Clara Moore

Murdered her husband Wilbur John Moore August 9, 1965 (aged 49) Wilbur John Moore (April 22, 1916 – August 9, 1965) was an American football running back in the National Football League (NFL) for the Washington Redskins. He played college football at the University of Minnesota and was drafted in the ninth round of the 1939 NFL Draft. On August 9, 1965, Moore was shot to death in front of his wife's home in Mitchellville, Maryland. He and Clara Moore had been separated for three months, and had been seen arguing before she killed him with a single shot from a .22 caliber revolver. Wilbur Moore, Grid Ace, Slain", Chicago Tribune, August 10, 1965, p1

Angelina Napolitano

Angelina Napolitano (1March 12, 1882 – September 4, 1932) was an immigrant to Canada who murdered her abusive husband in 1911, igniting a public debate about domestic violence and the penalty. She was the first woman in Canada to use the battered woman defense on a murder charge and brought domestic abuse to national awareness. Napolitano was found guilty. The jury recommended clemency, but she was sentenced to death, which led to a flood of petitions asking to have her life spared.

Mariticide Club

MOTHER OVER WHOSE HEAD THE CRUEL NOOSE HANGS

ANGELINA NAPOLITANO.

Murder defendant Angelina Napolitano in the press at time of her 1911 trial After an international outcry, however, the Canadian federal cabinet eventually commuted her sentence to life imprisonment. She served 11 years before being paroled. In 2005, the story of Napolitano's marriage and dramatic trial became an award-winning film, *Looking for Angelina*. Angelina was born in Italy about 1883, probably in a small town not too far from Naples. Her family name is not known. She married Pietro Napolitano about 1898 and the couple emigrated to America shortly after the turn of the century. They lived in New York City for seven years and moved to Canada in 1909—first to Thessalon, Ontario, then to Sault Ste. Marie, where there was a sizable Italian immigrant community. The couple had four children. The marriage was not good; Pietro beat and threatened his wife. In November 1910, he attacked her with a pocket knife, stabbing her nine times in the face, neck, shoulder, chest and arms and wounding her badly. He was charged with assault, but received a suspended sentence.

Wives Who Kill

After her conviction, newspapers across North America gathered petition signatures calling for Napolitano's sentence to be commuted or for her to be released. As the winter of 1910–1911 continued, Pietro, who worked on and off as a laborer, began to pressure Angelina to earn money (to build the family a house) by prostitution. On April 16, 1911, Easter Sunday, when Angelina was six months pregnant, Pietro told her to go out and make money through sex or he would beat her, kill her, or kill her unborn child. He was going to sleep and she had until he woke to get some money. That afternoon, as Pietro slept in their top-floor apartment on James Street, Angelina took an axe and hit him four times in the neck and head, killing him. She immediately sought out a neighbor and confessed, adding "I just killed a pig", then waited for police to come. They found her with her arms wrapped around her youngest child, and charged her with murder. The trial began on Monday, May 8, 1911, in Sault Ste. Marie, with Justice Britton presiding and Edmund Meredith as the crown attorney. When the court realized that Napolitano did not have a lawyer, the trial was adjourned for a day to allow the court-appointed lawyer, Uriah McFadden, to prepare a case. When the trial resumed on Tuesday, May 9, Meredith called nine witnesses to testify to Napolitano's guilt. McFadden called only Angelina herself, who did not speak English well. McFadden's case rested on what was essentially the battered woman defense; he argued that Pietro's abuse had forced a desperate Angelina to murder, and cited the November stabbing. Britton, however, ruled the incident inadmissible evidence, arguing that "if anybody injured six months ago could give that as justification or excuse for slaying a person, it would be anarchy complete". The jury returned a guilty verdict. The trial took just three hours.

Mariticide Club

Although the jury recommended clemency, Britton sentenced her to hang because murder required a mandatory death sentence. The execution was scheduled for August 9, one month after Napolitano's due date.

Napolitano's pregnancy at the time of sentencing was emphasized, helping to make her an international cause célèbre. Once the story hit the newspapers, however, a media frenzy began—not just in Sault Ste. Marie, but especially in the United States and even Europe. Though some of the coverage was negative, arguing from racist stereotypes that Napolitano, as an Italian, was a "hot-blooded foreigner" and deserved to pay the penalty for her crime, most of it revolved around those sympathetic to the abuse she had suffered, and agitating for her sentence to be commuted to jail time or even a pardon. The federal minister of justice, Sir Allen Bristol Aylesworth, received many letters from individuals (including McFadden), as well as petitions organized by groups in Sault Ste Marie, Toronto, New York City, Chicago, England, Austria, and Poland. A doctor in Ohio, Dr. Alexander Aalto, even offered to be hanged in Angelina's place, saying: "It would only be fair to Mrs. Napolitano for a man to give his life for her, inasmuch as her life is in peril on account of a

Wives Who Kill

man's persecution of her, and because men condemned her." Dr. Aalto's remarks reflect a theme among Napolitano's supporters, who included women in the fledgling feminist movement. These early feminists argued that Pietro's beatings meant the murder was in self-defense, and that Britton was being sexist when he threw out the evidence of abuse. The British suffragette journal *Common Cause* excoriated not only the law that had condemned Angelina, but also the justice system that upheld it as "both bad, for they are exclusively masculine". Other arguments presented in the letters included the idea (put forward by the area's MP, Arthur Cyril Boyce) that Angelina must be not guilty because her pregnancy made her temporarily insane, and the argument that Napolitano's fear of her impending doom would adversely affect her unborn baby, therefore she should be pardoned. This last was a common psychological view at the time. Whether any of these arguments had an impact, the federal cabinet eventually did commute Angelina's sentence to life imprisonment on July 14, 1911. Napolitano's later life is not well known. She did give birth, but the baby died within a few weeks. Her older children were placed in foster homes. She was granted parole on December 30, 1922, after serving 11 years at Kingston Penitentiary. Napolitano rdied September 4, 1932, at Hotel Dieu Hospital in Frontenac County, Ontario.

In 2003, independent film director Sergio Navarretta began researching Angelina's life for a documentary, but expanded the project into a film "once we realized how dramatic the facts were". The film, *Looking for Angelina*, was shot in two weeks in 2004 in Sault Ste. Marie, on a shoestring budget of $250,000. The writers, Alessandra Piccione and Frank Canino, took inspiration from Canino's play *The Angelina Project*. The film *Looking For Angelina* includes a domestic violence awareness campaign component. The film's producers, Platinum Image Film, screened the movie before a panel discussion of domestic violence experts, and put on screenings to raise money for organizations such as the Shelter from the Storm Campaign. As of October 2008, the film DVD sells packaged with a 114-page companion book, *Child Abuse Prevention and Intervention*.

Mariticide Club

Martha Needle (née Martha Charles)

Martha Needle

Martha Needle was an Australian serial killer known for poisoning her husband, three children, and prospective brother-in-law. She was hanged on 22 October 1894, when she was 31. She was convicted for the murder of Louis Juncken, brother of her fiancé Otto Juncken, on 15 May 1894. Although Needle collected substantial sums of insurance money, her exact motive for murdering her family has not been determined. Several times she stated her innocence, but she was eventually hanged. Needle was born Martha Charles on 9 April 1863 in Morgan, South Australia; her father died when she was quite young. In 1870, her mother, Mary Charles, married Daniel Foran and had two more children. They were poor and lived in a small two-room house in North Adelaide. Needle claimed that she was often beaten with a stick or rope by her mother and at 12 she was indecently assaulted by her stepfather.[a] She left home at 13 and started

Wives Who Kill

working as a housekeeper, [b] and married Henry Needle in 1882 when she was 18. The marriage was happy and the couple had three daughters - Mabel, Elsie, and May - before the family moved to the Melbourne suburb of Richmond in 1885. After the move the relationship between Martha and Henry Needle deteriorated; she was an attractive woman and enjoyed the company of men; he was a shy, jealous man who often beat her. On 23 February 1885, Mabel Needle died after a short illness. Needle stated that she "seemed to fade" and later collected £100 (Au$40,000 in 2010) life insurance on Mabel's death. Henry Needle, who was insured for £200, died of a mysterious illness on 4 October 1889, followed by Elsie and May in 1890. Doctors were baffled. Needle spent almost all the insurance money on an elaborate family grave which she visited regularly. Louis Juncken, a friend from Adelaide, operated a saddlery business with his brother Otto Juncken at 137 Bridge Road, Richmond and, in 1891, Needle sub-let the attached house and took in lodgers. Needle began an affair with Otto in 1893 but Louis and his other brother Herman disapproved and attempted to prevent their engagement. The following year Louis became ill and died of suspected typhoid. In June 1894, Herman travelled to Melbourne from Adelaide to handle his late brother's affairs, he ate a meal prepared by Needle and suddenly became ill. He recovered but became ill again the next day after eating breakfast. Two days later, Herman had fully recovered but while eating a lunch prepared by Needle, he was seized by painful violent cramps. Doctor Boyd treated Herman for suspected poisoning and took a sample of Herman's vomit and sent it to the government laboratory for analysis. The analyst reported that the sample contained arsenic. Boyd informed the police of his suspicions and a trap was set, the police asked Herman to ask Needle to make lunch. After being served a cup of tea, Herman literally "blew the whistle", summoning detectives who arrived as Needle was struggling with Herman to upset the teacup, which was found to contain enough arsenic to kill five people. Needle was charged with attempted murder. The body of Louis Juncken, interred in Lyndoch, South Australia was exhumed and samples sent to Melbourne. The bodies of Henry Needle and the three girls, interred in Kew, were also exhumed. All

Mariticide Club

five bodies were found to contain fatal levels of arsenic and Needle was charged with the murder of Louis Juncken. The trial lasted three days; Needle pleaded not guilty, but was found guilty and sentenced to death. During her time in gaol, Needle received continued visits from her friends. In her final letter to friend, Mrs. Owen, she writes "Try not to grieve too much for me." She was executed at 8.00am on 22 October 1894. When asked for her last words, she replied, "I have nothing to say." Needle was the third of four women hanged at the Old Melbourne Gaol, where her death mask can be seen. The others were Elizabeth Scott (1863), Frances Knorr (1894), and Emma Williams (1895). On 15 July 1920, Alexander Newland Lee, the son of Needle's older sister Ellen, was hanged at Adelaide Gaol for the 1 April murder of his wife Muriel, who had been poisoned with strychnine. During the Great Depression, the Brighton City Council built bluestone walls to protect local beaches from erosion. The stones were taken from the outer walls of the Old Melbourne Gaol and included the headstones, with initials and date of execution, of all those executed and buried on the grounds. Although most were placed with the engravings facing inwards, Needle's stone was faced outwards, and the initials MN and the date are still clearly visible in the Green Point wall. Over time, sand drifts buried her headstone until its precise location was rediscovered near Wellington Street.

Notes

---

1. Foran was charged with the offence of indecent assault on Martha Charles and the jury took 30 minutes to return a verdict of guilty. Foran was sentenced to the maximum of 2 years imprisonment on 3 April 1876 by Justice Stow.
2. Reports of Needle's age when she left home vary, however, she was indecently assaulted at age 12 by her stepfather; at that time, she was still living at home.

Omaima Aree Nelson

Omaima Aree Nelson (born c. 1968) is an Egyptian former model and nanny who was convicted of murdering her husband, Bill Nelson. She is serving a life sentence at California Institution for Women, as of 2020. Her case made international headlines due to allegations of bondage

Wives Who Kill

sex, decapitation, castration and cannibalism. Omaima Aree Nelson was born and raised in Egypt, and immigrated to the United States in 1986. She met her husband William E. "Bill" Nelson, a 56-year-old pilot, in October 1991, when she was 23. Within days of meeting, the couple married, but Omaima would later claim that during the couple's month-long union, she suffered sexual abuse by her husband. Omaima claimed that on 28 November 1991, Bill had sexually assaulted her in their Costa Mesa, California apartment. Following this, Omaima stabbed Bill with scissors, then began beating him with a clothes iron. After killing him, she began dismembering his body, and cooked his head and boiled his hands to remove his fingerprints. She then mixed up his body parts with leftover turkey and disposed of him in a garbage disposal. Neighbors claim they heard the disposal unit running for hours after the time of Bill's death. She castrated him in revenge for his sexual assaults. She told her psychiatrist that she had cooked her husband's ribs in barbeque sauce and eaten them. Omaima was arrested on a suspicion of murder charge in December 2, 1991, and her trial began almost exactly one year later on December 1, 1992. During the trial it was revealed that as a child living in Cairo, she had undergone female genital mutilation and sex was traumatic and painful for her, only increased by the assaults she allegedly sustained during her marriage. She was convicted of second-degree murder on January 12, 1993. She was sentenced to 27 years to life in prison. Omaima first became eligible for parole in 2006, but was denied when "commissioners found her unpredictable and a serious threat to public safety." She became eligible again in 2011, but was denied by the parole board again, citing that she had not taken responsibility for the murder, and would not be a productive citizen if she were freed. She will not be able to seek parole again until 2026. Omaima Nelson has been compared to fictional serial killer and cannibal Hannibal Lecter, from *The Silence of the Lambs*. Her case has been televised on the Investigation Discovery programs *Happily Never After and Women*, "*Model Killers*", as well as an episode of *Snapped* and her case was again put into limelight by a popular YouTuber Bailey Sarian on her weekly series Murder, *Mystery and Makeup Monday.*

Mariticide Club

Hester Rebecca Nepping

Hester Rebecca Nepping (baptized October 9, 1774 - June 15, 1812) was a Dutch serial killer and poisoner who was guillotined in 1812. Nepping was born in Amsterdam in 1774, the only child of master painter Johannes Nepping and Cornelia Schram. At the age of 19, she married tobacco retailer Jan Brummelkamp in Amsterdam. Due to debts, they left the capital in 1800 for Loenen (present-day Hilversum), where Brummelkamp again opened a tobacco shop. After that business also failed, they moved to the village of Hall in 1805, where they both worked at a paper mill. In 1808, Nepping acquired a considerable inheritance, including a house in Wijk bij Duurstede and five thousand guilders in cash. The couple moved there, with Jan buying a paper dyeing shop, which again, also failed. In the meantime, Hester had an extra-marital affair with the city messenger, Gerrit Verkerk. The inheritance ran out, and the couple had to take boarders: the elderly Beerenburg-Vinjole couple and their sister-in-law. The couple paid three thousand guilders for the services, with an additional amount to be paid in case they died. Mrs. Beerenburg turned out to be a woman with a nasty attitude, and so Nepping, together with her maid Adriana van Rijswijk, planned to murder the woman. Beerenburg died on August 31, 1811. On November 9, Hester's elderly father, who lived with her, died as well, followed two days later by her husband Jan. The deaths aroused suspicion, and the bodies were exhumed. The autopsy reports indicated that they had been poisoned with arsenic. Nepping and Van Rijswijk were arrested, as was Verkerk, who had provided the arsenic. In January 1812, they were detained in Amsterdam, where the trial was to take place. All three of them made partial confessions, and the Assizes considered two of the killings proven, handing down death sentences to all three of the accused. From 1810 onwards, because of the annexation of the Netherlands to the First French Empire, French criminal law was applied and an appeal had to be made to the court of cassation in Paris. The court upheld the verdict, and on June 15, 1812, all three were publicly guillotined in front of the Nieuwmarkt in Amsterdam. It was the only time that a death sentence was applied that way in the city's

Wives Who Kill

history and is often considered to be the first execution by guillotine in the Netherlands, although the guillotine was already used in Maastricht in 1798, but Maastricht was back then an integral part of France.

Execution of Nepping andaccomplices Adriana van Rijswijk and Gerrit Verkerk Nieuwmarktin Amsterdam, 1812 (print by Gerrit Hulseboom)

Catherine Nevin (*née* Scully)

•Jack White's Bar Location of the murder site in Ireland

Catherine Nevin (née Scully; 1 October 1950 – 19 February 2018) was an Irish woman who was convicted in 2000 of murdering her husband Tom Nevin at Jack White's Inn, a pub owned by the couple in County Wicklow. The jury in her trial also found her guilty on three charges of soliciting others to kill him after five days of deliberation, then the longest period of deliberation in the history of the Irish State. She was subsequently dubbed the *Black Widow* by the press. Nevin was the subject of significant

Mariticide Club

coverage by the tabloid press and Justice Mella Carroll ordered a ban on the press commenting on Nevin's appearance or demeanor during the trial. Catherine Scully met Tom Nevin in Dublin in 1970 and they were married in Rome in 1976. Within ten years, they owned two houses and managed a pub in Finglas, Dublin. In 1986, they opened Jack White's Inn. On 19 March 1996, Tom Nevin was killed with a shot from a nine pellet shotgun while counting the day's takings in Jack White's pub near Brittas Bay in County Wicklow. According to Catherine Nevin, she was woken by someone pressing her face into a pillow. She said: "It was a man shouting: 'f**king jewelry, f**king kill ya'. He had a knife in his left hand. Everything in the room was coming down around." IR£13,000 was taken from the pub, and the Nevins' car was stolen and was found abandoned in Dublin. Nevin served her sentence at the Dóchas Centre, Dublin. She lost an appeal in 2003, and in 2010 also lost an application to have her conviction declared a miscarriage of justice.

Nevin in 2016 was diagnosed with a brain tumor and given only months to live by doctors at the Mater Hospital. She received compassionate release

Stella Maudine Nickell(*née* Stephenson)

Stella Maudine Nickell (née Stephenson; born August 7, 1943) is an American woman who was sentenced to ninety years in prison for product tampering after she poisoned Excedrin capsules with lethal cyanide, resulting in the deaths of her husband Bruce Nickell and Sue Snow. Her May 1988 conviction and prison sentence were the first under federal product tampering laws instituted after the 1982 Chicago Tylenol murders. Stella Maudine Stephenson was born in Colton, Oregon, to Alva Georgia "Jo" (née Duncan; later changed her name to Cora Lee) and George Stephenson. She grew up in a poor family. At age 16, following the birth of her first daughter, Cynthia Hamilton, Stella moved to Southern California, where she married and had another daughter. Stella soon found herself in various legal issues, including a conviction for fraud in 1968, a charge of spousal abuse for beating Hamilton with a curtain rod in 1969, and a

Wives Who Kill

conviction for forgery in 1971. She served six months in jail for the fraud charge, and was ordered into counseling after the abuse charge. Stella met Bruce Nickell in 1974. Bruce was a heavy equipment operator with a drinking habit, which suited her lifestyle, and the two were married in 1976. In the course of their ten-year marriage, Bruce entered a drug rehab and gave up drinking, which Stella reportedly resented as she later felt he had "turned into a boring man". When her bar visits were curtailed by Bruce's sobriety, she began requesting evening shifts at her security screener job at Seattle–Tacoma International Airport and cultivated a home aquarium as a new hobby. On June 5, 1986, the Nickells were living in Auburn, Washington, when Bruce, 52, came home from work with a headache. Stella said he took four extra-strength Excedrin capsules from a bottle in their home for his headache and collapsed minutes later.[note 1] Bruce died shortly thereafter at Harborview Medical Center, where treatment had failed to revive him. His death initially was ruled to be by natural causes, with attending physicians citing emphysema. A second death, less than a week later, forced authorities to reconsider the cause of Bruce's death. On June 11, Sue Snow, a 40-year-old bank manager, took two Excedrin capsules for an early-morning headache. Her husband, Paul Webking, took two capsules from the same bottle for his arthritis and left the house for work. At 6:30 am, their 15-year-old daughter Hayley found Snow collapsed on the floor of her bathroom, unresponsive and with a faint pulse. Paramedics were called and transported Snow to Harborview Medical Center, but she died later that day without regaining consciousness. During an autopsy on Snow, Assistant Medical Examiner Janet Miller detected the scent of bitter almonds, an odor distinctive to cyanide. Tests verified that Snow had died of acute cyanide poisoning. Investigators examined the contents of the Snow-Webking household and discovered the source of the cyanide: the bottle of Excedrin capsules that both Snow and Webking had used the morning of Snow's death. Three capsules out of those that remained in the 60-capsule bottle were found to be laced with cyanide in toxic quantities. A murder by cyanide was sensational news in Washington State. When another tainted bottle from the same lot was

Mariticide Club

found in a grocery store in nearby Kent, Bristol-Myers, the manufacturers of Excedrin, responded to the discovery with a heavily publicized recall of all Excedrin products in the Seattle area, and a group of drug companies came together to offer a $300,000 reward for the capture of the person responsible. In response to the publicity, Stella came forward on June 19. She told police that her husband had recently died suddenly after taking pills from a 40-capsule bottle of Excedrin with the same lot number as the one that had killed Snow. Tests by the Food and Drug Administration (FDA) confirmed the presence of cyanide in her husband's remains and in two Excedrin bottles Stella had turned over to police.

Initial suspicions were directed at Bristol-Myers, with Stella and Webking filing wrongful death lawsuits against the company. The FDA inspected the Morrisville, North Carolina, plant where the tainted lot had been packaged, but found no traces of cyanide to explain its presence in the Washington bottles. On June 18, Bristol-Myers recalled all Excedrin capsules in the United States, pulling them from store shelves and warning consumers to not use any they may already have bought; two days later the company announced a recall of all of their non-prescription capsule products. On June 24, a cyanide-contaminated bottle of Anacin-3 was found at the same store where Snow had bought her contaminated Excedrin. On June 27, Washington State put into effect a 90-day ban on the sale of non-prescription medication in capsules. Examination of the contaminated bottles by the FBI Crime Lab found that, in addition to containing cyanide powder, the poisoned capsules also contained flecks of an unknown green substance. Further tests showed that the substance was an algaecide used in home aquariums sold under the name Algae Destroyer. With contamination of the Excedrin at the source having been ruled out, investigators began to focus their investigation on the end-users of the product. The FBI began an investigation into possible product tampering having been the source of the poison. At the time, Excedrin was packaged in plastic bottles with the mouth of the bottle sealed with foil and the lid secured to the bottle with plastic wrap. Both Stella and Webking were asked to take polygraph examinations. Webking did so, but Stella,

Wives Who Kill

who had started drinking heavily, declined. A lawyer representing Stella told reporters that she was too "shaken up" to be subjected to the examination. Investigators' suspicions began to turn to Stella when they discovered that she claimed that the two contaminated Excedrin bottles that she had turned over to police had been purchased at different times and different locations. A total of five bottles had been found to have been contaminated in the entire country, and it was regarded as suspicious that Stella would happen to have acquired two of them purely by chance. With investigatory focus turned to Stella, detectives uncovered more circumstantial evidence pointing to her as the culprit. She had taken out a total of about $76,000[note 2] in insurance coverage on her husband's life, with an additional payout of $100,000 if his death was accidental. She was also known to have, even before Snow's death, repeatedly disputed doctors' ruling that her husband had died of natural causes. Further FBI investigation showed that Bruce's purported signatures on at least two of the insurance policies in his name had been forged. Investigators were also able to verify that Stella had purchased Algae Destroyer from a local fish store; it was speculated that the algaecide had become mixed with the cyanide when Stella used the same container to crush both substances without washing it in between uses. Stella finally consented to a polygraph examination in November 1986. She failed and investigators narrowed their focus to her even further. Concrete evidence proving that she had ever purchased or used cyanide was lacking, and despite their relative certainty that she had orchestrated the poisonings as either an elaborate cover-up for an insurance-motivated murder of her husband or a desperate attempt to force her husband's death to be ruled an accident to increase her insurance payout, they were unable to build a strong case supporting arrest. In January 1987, Stella's now-grown daughter, Cynthia Hamilton, approached police with information: her mother had spoken to her repeatedly about wanting Bruce dead, having grown bored with him after he quit drinking. Stella, Hamilton claimed, had even told her that she had tried to poison Bruce previously with foxglove hidden in capsules. Bruce had taken them to no effect save for complaining of sudden drowsiness. Following

Mariticide Club

that failure, Stella had begun library research into other methods and hit upon cyanide. Hamilton also claimed that Stella had spoken to her about what the two of them could do with the insurance money if Bruce was dead. Records from the Auburn Public Library, when subpoenaed, showed that Stella had checked out numerous books about poisons, including *Human Poisonings from Native and Cultivated Plants and Deadly Harvest*. The former was marked as overdue in library records, indicating that she had borrowed but never returned it. The FBI identified her fingerprints on cyanide-related pages of a number of the works she had checked out during this period. By the summer of 1987, even Stella's attorneys acknowledged that she was the prime suspect in the case. On December 9, 1987, Stella was indicted by a federal grand jury on five counts of product tampering, including two which resulted in the deaths of Bruce and Snow, and arrested the same day. She went on trial in April 1988 and was found guilty of all charges on May 9, after five days of jury deliberation. Stella's legal team sought a mistrial on grounds of jury tampering and judicial misconduct. One of the jurors had been a plaintiff in a case involving a pill baked into Pepperidge Farm Goldfish crackers. While it was deemed to be a manufacturing error, the defense thought that it involved product tampering and therefore should have been disclosed during jury selection. However, the motion was denied. Stella was sentenced to two terms of ninety years in prison for the deaths of Bruce and Snow, and three ten-year terms for the other product tampering charges. All sentences were to run concurrently, and the judge ordered Stella to pay a small fine and forfeit her remaining assets to the families of her victims. She was denied parole in 2017. As of publication, Stella Nickell is housed at female-only low security/minimum security Federal Correctional Institution, Dublin in California, just east of San Francisco. She will be eligible for release in 2040, with credit given for good behavior, by which time she will be 96 years old. Nickell petitioned for compassionate early release in 2022, stating that her health is failing, and this request was denied. Stella continued to maintain her innocence after her trial. An appeal based on jury tampering and judicial misconduct issues was rejected by the United States Court of Appeals for

Wives Who Kill

the Ninth Circuit in August 1989. A second appeal, beginning in 2001, was filed by her new attorney, Carl Park Colbert, based on evidence obtained by private detectives Al Farr and Paul Ciolino, requesting a new trial on the basis of new evidence having been discovered that the FBI may have withheld documents from the defense. The appeal was denied, though Stella and her team continue to assert her innocence. Stella claimed that her daughter, Cynthia Hamilton, lied about her involvement in the case in order to reap the $300,000 of reward money being offered. Hamilton eventually collected $250,000 of that money. Stella also alleges that the evidence actually points to another person as the killer, and that the testimony about various smaller details in the case, such as the store owner who testified about her having purchased Algae Destroyer, was influenced by promises of payment. After 1982 Chicago Tylenol murders, new FDA regulations went into effect which made it a federal crime—rather than just a state or local crime—to tamper with consumer products. Local and state authorities are not, however, prevented from also filing charges in such cases. Under this law, Stella Nickell's crime was prosecutable as a federal product tampering case as well as a state murder case, and she was not convicted of murder, but of product tampering that caused death. The possibility of state charges for the actual murders of Bruce and Snow continues to exist.

Seattle author Gregg Olsen wrote about the Nickell case in his 1993 book *Bitter Almonds: The True Story of Mothers, Daughters and the Seattle Cyanide Murders*. The case was also featured in episodes of *Autopsy, Forensic Files, The New Detectives, Mysteries at the Museum*, and *Snapped*, as well as two episodes of Deadly Women. The murders are discussed in the Jodi Picoult novel *House Rules*, published in 2010. It was also featured in episode 93 of Casefile True Crime Podcast in August 2018. The case was referenced in an episode of *In Plain Sight* titled "Kill Pill", aired November 23, 2018 on the Investigation Discovery channel. The 2000 TV film *Who Killed Sue Snow?* was to be made about the Nickell case to air on USA Network, but it was cancelled shortly before production began. One factor was strong objections from advertisers, including Johnson & Johnson, owner of the Tylenol brand of painkillers

Mariticide Club

which had been affected by the 1982 Chicago case. Additionally, network executives feared the film would inspire copycat crimes. The film was to have been directed by Jeff Reinerand starring Katey Sagal as Stella Nickell.

Charlotte Nixon-Nirdlinger

Fred G. Nixon-Nirdlinger

1903 portrait (Associated Press)

Born	1877
Died	1931
Nationality	American
Occupation	Theater Operator

Wives Who Kill

Fred G. Nixon-Nirdlinger (1877–1931) was an American theater operator who obtained control of all the main theaters in Philadelphia. He was shot dead by his wife in their apartment on the Riviera. The trial caused a huge sensation. Fredrick G was the son of Samuel F. Nixon (originally Samuel Frederic Nirdlinger) and Sallie Strauss. His father and J. Fred Zimmerman Sr. were partners. By the mid-1890s Nixon and Zimmerman controlled the Broad, the Park, the Chestnut and the Chestnut Street Opera House, the four most important theaters in Philadelphia. They also owned first-class theaters in Pennsylvania, West Virginia and Ohio. Fredrick G Nixon Nirdlinger became a partner in the Nixon & Zimmerman theatrical firm. He managed Park Theatre and People's Theatre in Philadelphia. An Associated Press story distributed in December 1903 said "…Nixon Nirdlinger is the richest and most powerful theatrical manager and promoter in America…. His son, Frederick G. Nixon Nirdlinger, is an assistant to his father, and has won (his own) fame in his profession…" Marcus Loew developed a growing chain of vaudeville theaters. They competed with the agency run by Fred G. Nixon-Nirdlinger, who filed a complaint with the U.S. Department of Justice alleging that Loew and others had established a virtual monopoly of the vaudeville business. The "Philadelphia Vaudeville War" continued until an agreement was struck on 13 December 1913 by which Loew gave up his holdings in the Metropolitan Opera House and Chestnut Street Opera House, and in exchange gained a stake in a new company being formed by Benjamin Franklin Keith. Samuel F. Nixon, Fred Nixon-Nirdlinger, J. Fred Zimmerman and Edward Franklin Albee were parties to the agreement. Nirdlinger became the owner of four theaters in Philadelphia, and others in Pittsburgh, Harrisburg, Reading and smaller places. As head of the organization he operated the 1,400-seat Maryland Theater in Cumberland. In 1913 he leased the Metropolitan Opera House in Philadelphia. In 1920 the lease was transferred to the Lu Lu Temple of the Nobles of the Mystic Shrine. Fred G. Nixon-Nirdlinger was living in an apartment on the French Riviera in 1931 when he was shot

Mariticide Club

and killed by his wife, Charlotte. Their infant children were present. The sensational story of the murder and subsequent trial, in which Charlotte was acquitted on the grounds of self-defense, made headlines for months.

Narcy Novack (née Narcisa Véliz Pacheco)
Murders of Bernice and Ben Novack Jr.

Ben Novack Jr. at a desk in the lobby of the Fontainebleau in 1972

In 2009, Bernice Novack and her son, Fontainebleau Miami Beach hotel heir Ben Novack Jr., were murdered three months apart. Narcy Novack (née Narcisa Véliz Pacheco; born 1956), Ben's estranged wife, was convicted of orchestrating the murders and after a highly publicized trial, was sentenced to life in prison without the possibility of parole. April 5, 2009 Ben's 87-yr-old mother Bernice (December 2, 1921 – April 4, 2009), was found dead in her Fort Lauderdale, Florida garage. Her husband Ben Novack Sr., who built the hotel and owned it until 1977, had died in 1985. Her death was initially ruled to be the result of an accidental fall while trying to get out of her car in her garage, but after her son's murder three months later, a subsequent police investigation revealed that her death was a homicide. On the morning of July 12, 2009, her son, who was 53, was found bludgeoned and suffocated to death in the penthouse suite at the Hilton Hotel in Rye Brook, New York. He was bound with duct tape and his eyes were gouged out. At the time of his death, he was having an affair with actress Rebecca Bliss. He was also the heir to a multimilliondollar estate. Narcy Novack, from Fort Lauderdale, was arrested for the murders of her husband and mother-in-law in July 2010, three days shy of a

Wives Who Kill

year after her husband's death. Her brother, Cristóbal Véliz, was also accused of enlisting Alejandro Gutiérrez-García, Joel González, and Denis Ramírez to participate in both murders. Narcy Novack and Cristóbal Véliz were tried together in a federal courtroom in White Plains, New York in 2012. The duo's defense was to blame Narcy's only daughter from a previous marriage, May Abad, for having orchestrated the killings, stating that she was motivated to collect on Ben Novack Jr.'s estate, including a large collection of Batman memorabilia. Prosecutors alleged that Narcy was afraid that her husband would leave her for his mistress, and that a prenuptial agreement would only leave her $65,000 instead of the bulk of her late husband's estate. They claimed she was motivated by "hatred, greed, and vengeance." At the conclusion of the trial, Narcy and Veliz were each convicted of murder, conspiracy to commit murder, domestic violence, stalking, money laundering, and witness tampering. Narcy waived her right to appear in court when the guilty verdict was read. She also did not appear in court when she was sentenced to life in prison without parole. Novack is currently incarcerated at the Federal Correctional Institution Tallahassee in Florida. Eliz was also sentenced to life in prison without parole and he is currently incarcerated at the United States Penitentiary, Big Sandy in Kentucky. Gutiérrez-García, González, and Ramírez all pleaded guilty to lesser charges. In accordance with the slayer rule, Narcy Novack is ineligible to inherit her husband's estate. Ben Novack Jr.'s estate, valued at $4.2 million, is expected to go to Novack's daughter, May Abad, and Abad's two sons. The Novack murders have been televised on several programs including *Deadly Rich, My Dirty Little Secret (ID), 48 Hours, NBC, Snapped, True Crime with Aphrodite Jones and Dying to Belong*. The story was also the basis for the 2015 made-fortelevision Lifetime movie *Beautiful & Twisted*, directed by Christopher Zalla and starring Rob Lowe as Ben Novack Jr., Paz Vega as Narcy, and Candice Bergen as Bernice Novack.

Mariticide Club

Venera Obolashvili (née Lela Javakhishvili)

Venera Obolashvili (Georgian:**ვენერა ობოლაშვილი**; born 1954) is a Soviet-Georgian murderer, fraudster and self-confessed serial killer who murdered a female relative in 2009 in order to sell her apartment - she also confessed to killing one of her husbands and a boyfriend but was never charged due to a lack of evidence. Found guilty of one murder and sentenced to 23 years imprisonment, she was released on parole in 2023. Little is publicly available about Obolashvili's life. Born in 1954 in the Georgian SSR, she would go on to marry to three separate husbands and have three children, although she would also live with boyfriends on common-law grounds. Sources report that graduated university and held a license as a dentist, but is not known to have practiced professionally. Murders

---

Yuri Yurkin

The first suspicious death linked to Obolashvili dates back to 1984, with the death of her 43-year-old husband Yuri Yurkin. Officially, he was thought to have died after accidentally falling of a train near Tbilisi, but after her arrest, Obolashvili claimed that she had pushed him to his death. After this, she sold his apartment for the equivalent of $4,000.

Anatoli Kalinka

No other serious crime was allegedly committed by Obolashvili until 2008, when she started dating 52-year-old Anatoli Kalinka. According to her testimony, one day she hit him on the head and dragged the unconscious man to a bridge, where she threw him into the Kura River. Kalinka's body was found not long after, but his death was written off as an unfortunate accident. Obolashvili later sold his apartment for $50,000.

Maria Arzamaseva

By 2009, Obolashvili was living with 79-year-old Maria Arzamaseva, who had been her uncle's girlfriend for some time. In August of that year, they invited a young man over to discuss selling the apartment, but according to Obolashvili, Arzamaseva got drunk and chased him away, claiming that this was her home. Angered by this encounter, Obolashvili confronted

Wives Who Kill

Arzamaseva and the two got into an argument. During their scuffle, Obolashvili strangled Arzamaseva and then put her body on the bed, before going out to buy a large sack to stuff her body in. With the help of a cab driver - who was unaware that there was a body inside - she transported it a factory and dumped it into a sewer. The sack containing Arzamaseva's body was later washed ashore, but she was mistaken for a homeless woman and buried in a pauper's grave. Soon after her death, Obolashvili successfully sold Arzamaseva's apartment to a stranger, using the money to pay off some of her debts and buy a new Audi. Unbeknownst to her, bank employees noticed that there was something suspicious going on with her purchases, as she was using Arzamaseva's credit cards. As a result, she was arrested on December 15, 2009, and charged with forgery and fraud, but a murder charge was soon added after it was established that Arzamaseva had been killed. It was quickly established that both her husband and boyfriend had died in similarly suspicious circumstances, but as prosecutors lacked sufficient evidence to charge her in these cases, Obolashvili was charged solely with the murder of Arzamaseva and the corresponding fraud charges. During her trial, she claimed that her death was an accident, but her claims were disregarded and she was found guilty on all counts. As a result, the court sentenced Obolashvili to 23 years imprisonment. During her time in prison, Obolashvili was initially avoided by fellow inmates due her notoriety, but eventually managed to befriend some with whom she developed a strong bond. She claims that during her time in prison, she spent most of her studying and learning new skills, earning a total of 27 certificates in different fields. Obolashvili also claims that she got two master's degrees in automation and agrobiology from two separate Russian universities and to be fluent in English and German.

In late January 2023, Obolashvili was released on parole after serving less than half of her original sentence. Upon her release, she gave an exclusive interview to a local news outlet in which she told of her life in prison and apparently expressed remorse over her actions.

Mariticide Club

Marjorie Ann Orbin

Marjorie Ann Orbin (born October 29, 1961) is an American woman who murdered her husband Jay Orbin in Phoenix, Arizona, on or about September 8, 2004, which would have been his 45th birthday. Jay Orbin was a jewelry dealer. In September 2004 he returned home to Phoenix from a road trip to Florida. Police said he arrived at his home on September 8, based on cell phone and credit-card records. He was never seen alive again. Prior to her crime, Marjorie Orbin was a 43-year-old former Las Vegas showgirl. According to officials, she had been having affairs with several men. When Jay Orbin returned home from a business trip, investigators believe his wife shot and killed him, then dismembered his body with jigsaw blades in an attempt to keep the affairs a secret and inherit Jay's money. The husband's body was found several weeks later, when his torso was discovered on October 23 in a plastic container on the outskirts of Phoenix. The rest of his body was never found. Marjorie was convicted of the murder in 2009 after a trial lasting eight months. On October 1, 2009, Marjorie Orbin was sentenced to life imprisonment without the possibility of parole by an Arizona court. As of publication of this book, she is currently serving her time at the Arizona State Prison Complex - Perryville. Marjorie Orbin's case was featured in an episode of Killer in Plain Sight, an episode of *Deadly Women*, an episode of the CBS newsmagazine *Hours and* in the investigation series *Scorned: Love Kills*. A book titled *Dancing with Death* by author and journalist Shanna Hogan was released about the case in May 2011. Author Camille Kimball released a book about the case in 2010 titled *What She Always Wanted*. The case was also covered in an episode of *Snapped*. In August 2016 Reelz Channel show *Copycat Killers* covered Marjorie Orbin's case in an episode titled "Saw". The case is covered in an episode of the TV show Corrupt Crimes on the True Crime TV Network. The Investigation Discovery show, *Betrayed* highlighted Jay Orbin's disappearance and subsequent death in the episode entitled "Life and Limb" on October 19, 2016.

Wives Who Kill

Erzsébet Papp - Mrs. János Holhos - The Nicotine Killer Erzsébet Papp (January 28, 1935- January 23, 1962) The Nicotine Killer or her married name "Mrs. János Holhos", was a Hungarian serial killer who poisoned four people with nicotine between 1957 and 1958. She was sentenced to death and subsequently hanged for her crimes in 1962. Erzsébet Papp was born on January 28, 1935, in Penészlek, one of two daughters born to farmers János and Julianna Papp (née Krivacs), who also had two sons. According to contemporary accounts, Erzsébet was considered an intelligent woman in comparison with her peers, but was also considered to have a warped sense of morals. All of Papp's killings were carried out using a formula mixing nicotine in tobacco leaves provided by her unsuspecting brother, a fruit grower, and using the concoction on her unsuspecting victims, who were all killed for menial reasons. The first victim was 5-year-old Ilona Tarnóczi in Pereces, who, according to the investigators, had been a victim of opportunity - at the time, Papp was experimenting with her poison, first giving it to a dog and then mixing it in a brandy bottle, which she gave to the little girl. The high amounts of nicotine quickly made Tarnóczi dizzy and unable to walk, making Papp drag her to the road, where Ilona collapsed. When she was found, police quickly wrote off the death as drowning, and closed the case. Papp's second victim was her best friend, Mrs. József Fürtös, whom she had decided to kill after the former began spreading unsavory rumors about her. In what appeared to be an attempt at reconciliation, she brought Fürtös a bottle of pálinka, which had secretly been laced with nicotine. When Fürtös' body was found, an autopsy was conducted that revealed that she had been pregnant, and her death was written off as a botched abortion attempt. Papp was interrogated on the circumstances of her friend's death, claiming that she had gone to her after she had had a fight with her husband, pointing towards the empty nicotine bottle on the table to back up her claims. Her third murder was that of her husband István Rostár, an alcoholic who often verbally abused her when he was drunk. In August 1957, Rostár offered that they go to a restaurant in Lillafüred for dinner. When he wasn't looking, Papp poisoned his drinks with nicotine, and due to his alcoholic tendencies,

Mariticide Club

Rostár drank it without a second thought, collapsing not long after. After an autopsy was conducted on the body, the coroner erroneously concluded that the cause of death the result of alcohol poisoning due to the high levels of alcohol in his blood, the strong smell of gastric acid and the discoloration of the gastric mucosa present in alcoholics. Papp, who had gotten pregnant from István with two children, miscarried the first one, while the second child died at three months old after falling from a hay cart. In 1959, while working at a sovkhoz, Papp met János Holhos, whom she soon married. She tried to poison him as well, but failed, with the angry Holhos beating and then abandoning her, without reporting his wife's attempted murder. After that, she began living with a Romani man, but their relationship was poorly received by her family and friends, who disowned Papp and made her sister, Mrs. Ferenc Juhos, the family heir. Wanting to exact revenge on her family, she went to Nyírbátor, where her sister lived, pouring the nicotine in her glass and successfully killing her. Like the previous murders, it was considered a non-homicidal death in nature. While she wasn't a suspect in her sister's death, Papp's downfall came when she accidentally placed the brandy bottle on the liquor store shelf, with the shopkeeper selling it to a customer. As a result, two people drank from it, receiving severe poisoning, but managed to survive. Curious about what had caused it, authorities examined the bottle, discovering that it had a lethal dose of nicotine in it. Upon further investigation, it was revealed that the brandy bottle originally belonged to the later widow Erzsébet Papp, who had a suspicious history of close family and friends dying around her. An investigation was launched and the bodies of Tarnóczi, Rostár and her sister were exhumed for testing, confirming the authorities' suspicions that they had been poisoned. Erzsébet Papp was then arrested and charged with fourfold murder, but then released, as the authorities had insufficient evidence to detain her. This changed during the course of the investigation, as they gathered witness testimony that increasingly weighed in favor of her guilt. Papp was then rearrested and charged anew, and despite initially protesting her innocence, she would eventually break down and confess to all four murders. At trial, Papp was found guilty and sentenced to life imprisonment, but upon appeal to the Curia, she was resentenced to death. On January 23, 1962, she was executed in Miskolc.

Gail Collins Pappalardi

Felix Pappalardi

Felix A. Pappalardi Jr. (December 30, 1939 – April 17, 1983) was an American music producer, songwriter, vocalist, and bassist. He is best known as the bassist and co-lead vocalist of the band Mountain, whose song "Mississippi Queen" peaked at number 21 on the *Billboard* Hot 100 and has become a classic rock radio staple. Originating in the eclectic music scene in New York's Greenwich Village, he became closely attached to the British power trio Cream, writing, arranging, and producing for their second album *Disraeli Gears*. As a producer for Atlantic Records, he worked on several projects with guitarist Leslie West; in 1969 their partnership evolved into the band Mountain. The band lasted less than five years, but their work influenced the first generation of heavy metal and hard rock music. Pappalardi continued to work as a producer, session musician, and songwriter until he was shot and killed by his wife Gail Collins in 1983. Pappalardi was born in the Bronx, New York City. A classically trained musician, he graduated from New York City's The High School of Music & Art and attended the University of Michigan. In 1964, Pappalardi was a member of Max Morath's Original

Mariticide Club

Rag Quartet (ORQ) in their premier engagement at New York's Village Vanguard with several other musicians. Along with Pappalardi on guitarrón (Mexican acoustic bass) were pianist-singer Morath, who revived classic ragtime played in the Scott Joplin manner, Barry Kornfeld, a New York studio folk and jazz guitarist, and Jim Tyler, a Baroque and Renaissance lutenist, playing four string banjo and mandolin. The ORQ then toured the college and concert circuit during the following year, and opened four engagements with the Dinah Shore show in Las Vegas and elsewhere. Pappalardi studied classical music at the University of Michigan. Upon completing his studies and returning to New York, he was unable to find work and so became part of the Greenwich Village folkmusic scene where he made a name for himself as a skilled arranger; he also appeared on albums by Tom Paxton as well as Vince Martin and Fred Neil for Elektra Records. From there he moved into record production, initially concentrating on folk and folk-rock acts for artists such as The Youngbloods and Joan Baez.

As a producer, Pappalardi is perhaps best known for his work with Cream, beginning with their second album, *Disraeli Gears*. He contributed instrumentation for his studio arrangements and he and his wife, Gail Collins, wrote the Cream hit "Strange Brew" with Eric Clapton. He also produced The Youngbloods' first album. As a musician, Pappalardi is widely recognized as a bassist, vocalist, and founding member of the American hard rock band (and heavy metal forerunner) Mountain, a band born out of his working with future bandmate Leslie West's soulinspired rock and roll band The Vagrants, and producing West's 1969 *Mountain* solo album. The band's original incarnation actively recorded and toured between 1969 and 1971. Pappalardi produced the band's albums, and co-wrote and arranged a number of the band's songs with Collins and West. The band's signature song "Mississippi Queen" is still heard regularly on classic rock radio stations. They also had a hit with the song "Nantucket Sleighride" written by Pappalardi and Collins. Pappalardi generally played Gibson basses on Mountain's live and studio recordings. He was most often seen with an EB-1 violin bass but there are

Wives Who Kill

also photographs of him playing an EB-0 live (likely because they had the same pickup configuration and scale length). Pappalardi obtained his sound by playing Gibson basses with a single Humbucker in the neck through a set of Sunn amplifiers that, he claimed, once belonged to Jimi Hendrix.

The grave of Felix Pappalardi in Woodlawn Cemetery

Pappalardi was forced to retire because of partial deafness, ostensibly from his high-volume shows with Mountain. He continued producing throughout the 1970s, released a solo album (*Don't Worry, Ma*) and recorded with Kazuo Takeda's band Creation (who had opened for a reunited Mountain during their 1973 tour of Japan).

In May 1973, the British music magazine *NME* reported that Pappalardi would be producing and playing bass on *Queen of the Night*, the debut album for Maggie Bell, former singer of Stone the Crows, but this proved to be false.

He also worked on the NBC show *Hot Hero Sandwich* in 1979. Pappalardi was shot and killed by his wife, Gail Collins Pappalardi, on April 17, 1983, in their apartment on the East Side of Manhattan, with a derringer he had given her as a gift a few months previously. She was subsequently charged with second-degree murder and was found guilty of the lesser criminally negligent homicide. He is interred next to his mother at Woodlawn Cemetery in the Bronx, New York City.

Mariticide Club

Milka Pavlović

Milka Pavlović (1905 – 18 May 1935) was a Croatian serial killer. A peasant woman living in Stari Pavljani, near Bjelovar, she poisoned family members, relatives and servants with arsenic between March and July 1934, succeeding in killing six and wounding ten others so she could acquire their inheritance. After being convicted of the crimes, she was sentenced to death and subsequently executed. Little documentation of Pavlović's early life exists. She was born in 1905 in the small of village of Kokinac, and at some point, she married Rade Pavlović of nearby Stari Pavljani, moving into his home and finding work as a milkmaid. A childless, bitter woman, Milka was regarded poorly by her fellow villagers. Around March 1934, she bought arsenic from a local pharmacy under an alias, claiming that it was for killing rats. She then took the poison home and put it into the food served to her husband Rade, who soon after began vomiting violently and died. His death was not regarded as suspicious, and Milka inherited his estate, since the couple had no children. Over the next few months, dozens

Wives Who Kill

of other relatives and their servants were poisoned in the same fashion, mainly the Jagodić household. As a result, four people were admitted to a clinic in Zagreb with complaints of terrible cramps in their stomachs: the widow Slavka Jagodić, her daughter Sava, an unnamed servant and a close relative of the family. Shortly after their admission, all of the victims died. The nine other living members of the Jagodić family survived, but were left with the after effects of the poisoning. However, on 2 July that year, another strange death occurred: the family's Romani blacksmith, Miso Gjurgjević, died writhing in agony, much alike the others before him. This arose suspicions from local villagers, who were quick to point out a possible culprit: the widow Milka Pavlović, whose husband had passed in eerily similar circumstances just months before. Milka was arrested, and the prosecutor's office ordered that all of the deceased be exhumed and tested for traces of arsenic poisoning. While she protested her innocence at first, Pavlović eventually admitted that she had poisoned her victims because of her desire to acquire their wealth, a statement backed up when the autopsies concluded that Rade Pavlović, the Jagodić family members and Miso Gjurgjević had been poisoned with lethal quantities of arsenic. According to Milka, she poured the poison into biscuits, salt and any other food while she was alone cooking in the kitchen, and thereafter served it to her unaware victims. After a six-day long trial, Milka Pavlović was found guilty on all counts and sentenced to death. During her trial, it was additionally revealed that she had planned to dispose of a two-year-old child, the heir to an inheritance, with a poisoned loaf, but was stopped in the nick of time by the child's mother. For her crimes, she was brought to Bjelovar, where she was executed by hanging on May 18, 1935.

Najwa Petersen

Taliep Petersen (15 April 1950 – 16 December 2006) was a South African singer, composer and director of a number of popular musicals. He worked most notably with David Kramer, with whom he won an Olivier Award. One of "South Africa's best known theatre personalities", Petersen was born in the multi-cultural neighborhood of Cape Town, District Six. He

Mariticide Club

first sang publicly aged six, at the Coon Carnival. His first theatre performance was a part in a 1974 production of *Hair*, followed by *Godspell* and *Jesus Christ Superstar* . After a period studying classical guitar at the Fitznell School of Music in England, he wrote his first revue, called *Carnival a la District Six*, based on the New Year celebrations in Cape Town. In the 1980s, Petersen formed a band, called Sapphyre, that played interpretations of traditional Cape Malay songs. In 1986 he and David Kramer collaborated on the first of a number of musicals together, District Six: The Musical, exploring the culture and history of the Colored community in Cape Town. This was followed by Poison, Fairyland, Crooners, Kat and the Kings, Klop Klop and Spice Drum Beat: Ghoema. A number of these toured internationally; Kat and the Kings had runs in Las Vegas, New York's Broadway and in London's West End. Ghoema had opened in London's Tricycle Theatre shortly before Petersen's death. In 1999, he and Kramer won the Best New Musical Olivier Award for Kat and the Kings, with the cast sharing the Best Actor in a Musical award. In 2001, he presented a television series about District Six called O'se Distrik Ses and has featured on South Africa reality talent shows, Idols and Joltyd. in 2002, he created a sitcom called Alie Barber. In 2005, a second season of Alie Barber was shown and Petersen released songs from the series on the 2006 album Deur Dik en Dun, his first in Afrikaans. Petersen, a practicing Muslim, was twice married and fathered six children. He was shot dead at his home on 16 December 2006. In tribute Ebrahim Rasool, premier of the Western Cape, praised Petersen's ability to "capture our entire history, express our deepest pain, articulate our joy, and demonstrate our humanity through music and drama." On 18 June 2007, Najwa Petersen, the wife of Taliep Petersen, was arrested at the family home in connection with the murder. Together with three men she was charged with his "planned and/or premeditated" murder. Najwa Petersen was convicted in the Cape High Court on 2 December 2008 along with two hitmen, Abdoer Emjedi and Waheed Hassen. All three were found "guilty of murder and of robbery with aggravating circumstances". Judge Siraj Desai postponed the matter to 4

Wives Who Kill

February 2009 for sentencing procedures, at which Najwa Peterson was sentenced to 28 years in prison. The Cape *Town Taliep Pietersen Bridge* crosses over Woodstock, Nelson Mandela Boulevard.

Pamela Phillips

Murder of Gary Lee Triano

Gary Lee Triano (November 6, 1943–November 1, 1996) was a millionaire real estate developer from Tucson, Arizona who was killed in Catalina Foothills by a pipe bomb explosion in his Lincoln Town Car on November 1, 1996. His former wife, Pamela Anne Phillips, a onetime model, real estate agent and socialite, was charged with orchestrating her ex-husband's death. In a sensational trial nearly 18 years after Triano's murder, Phillips was convicted of first-degree murder and conspiracy to commit murder and was sentenced to life in prison. Phillips, who is now incarcerated at the Arizona State Prison Complex – Perryville, claims that Triano's death was a mob revenge killing. Ronald Young, who was hired by Phillips as a hit man, also was convicted and sentenced to life in prison. Gary Triano was a longtime Tucson, Arizona resident. He graduated from Rincon High School and earned a degree in accounting from the University of Arizona. He also attended the University of Arizona's law school. He married Mary Cram, and they had two children, Heather and Brian. Triano married his second wife, Pamela Phillips, on October 4, 1986 in San Diego, California. During their marriage, the couple had two children, Trevor and Lois, before their bitter divorce in 1993. At the time of the divorce, Triano filed for Chapter 11 bankruptcy, claiming $40 million in debt after several failed business dealings regarding Indian casinos. Phillips moved to Aspen, Colorado with the couple's two children, where she continued her career in commercial real estate. On November 1, 1996, Gary Triano was killed when a pipe bomb exploded in his car at the La Paloma Country Club in Arizona. Within weeks, the investigation centered around his ex-wife Pamela Phillips, who was still living in Aspen. It was discovered that she had taken out a $2 million life insurance policy on Triano shortly before his death. The couple's two children were the

Mariticide Club

beneficiaries of the policy, which was paid out to Phillips in 1997. Evidence also linked Phillips to Ronald Young, a small-time criminal with whom Phillips developed a relationship while in Aspen. Shortly before the bombing, a van rented by Young was found abandoned in Yorba Linda, California, and inside the vehicle there were documents pertaining to Phillips and Triano's divorce, a map of Tucson, Arizona, and a sawed-off shotgun. Nine years after the murder, on November 19, 2005, an episode of America's Most Wanted profiled Ronald Young, who was then wanted for forgery and embezzlement. The episode also mentioned his suspected involvement in Triano's death. Two days later, Young was apprehended in Fort Lauderdale, Florida. He served a 10-month sentence in federal prison for weapon possession before being extradited back to Aspen. Following Young's arrest, investigators found records of phone calls and email correspondence between Young and Phillips related to Triano's murder. In 2008, Ronald Young was charged with the murder of Gary Triano. On December 3, 2009, Pamela Phillips was also arrested for Triano's murder in Vienna, Austria, when she fled after her indictment in October 2008. She was later returned to the United States to stand trial. Ronald Young went to trial for Gary Triano's murder in 2010. Prosecutors showed records that Phillips agreed to give Young $400,000 to kill her exhusband. Also introduced into evidence were the tapes and recordings outlining the conspiracy. At the conclusion of his trial, Young was convicted of first-degree murder and conspiracy to commit murder. He was sentenced to two life terms. Following her extradition to Arizona to stand trial, Pamela Phillips was held on $5 million bond at the Pima County Jail. In December 2011, she was initially ruled mentally incompetent for trial. In October 2012, she was ruled competent to stand trial after undergoing treatment at the jail. Phillips' trial began in 2014 and lasted for seven weeks. Prosecutors used similar evidence in her trial that was used to convict Young. Phillips was convicted of first-degree murder and conspiracy. Like Young, she was also sentenced to life in prison; she has no possibility for parole. The murder of Gary Triano has been televised on several programs, including Dateline NBC, Dateline on ID, 48 Hours, Snapped, American

Wives Who Kill

Greed (2015 episode "A Widow's Web"), Fatal Vows and Vengeance: Killer Millionaires. In January 2012, the case was a subject of a true crime book by Kerie Droban.

Ethel Pitts - Estranged Wife of Ernie Pitts

San Francisco 49ers 1957 NFL draft selection

Ernie Pitts (March 8, 1935 – September 24, 1970) was a Canadian Football League wide receiver and defensive back for the Winnipeg Blue Bombers and the BC Lions in a 14-year career in the CFL from 1957 to 1970. He won four Grey Cups with Winnipeg. In August 2019 he was inducted into the Canadian Football League Hall of Fame. Ernie Pitts played intercollegiate baseball and football at University of Denver.

Professional career - Winnipeg Blue Bombers

Ernie Pitts was a standout wide receiver who also played defensive back for the Bombers from 1957 to 1969. For all those years except the last two, Ken Ploen was at quarterback. Together, along with Jim Van Pelt [1958-59], Pitts and Ploen were major factors in Winnipeg's six Grey Cup appearances (1957, 1958, 1959, 1961, 1962, 1965), including four victories: 1958, 1959, 1961, 1962 and two losses: 1957, 1965. His highest totals in caught passes was 68 in 1959 and 62 in 1962. In 1959, he scored 16 touchdowns. He once caught 5 touchdown passes in one game and scored on a 107-yard touchdown pass play. Evidence of his prowess on defense included 7 interceptions in 1968 and 5 more in 1969. Pitts ended his career with the BC Lions in 1970. Pitts, on September 24, 1970, was fatally shot (by a .38 caliber revolver) in the neck by his estranged wife during a domestic dispute on the porch of their home in Thornton, Colorado. They had six children. She was charged, tried for murder, and, in June 1971, acquitted, for reasons of self-defense of a forcible entry by Ernie Pitts. One of Pitts brothers, George E. Pitts (1925–1987), was an influential and longstanding newspaper entertainment columnist, notably with the *Pittsburgh Courier*. One of his nephews, George Pitts (1951–2017) was a photojournalist. The Canadian Football League Hall of Fame induction ceremony marks a time for happiness and a strong sense of pride

Mariticide Club

for all involved. One player who will be posthumously recognized on Friday is former Winnipeg Blue Bombers wide receiver and defensive back, Ernie Pitts. Over a 13-year professional career, he helped lead the team to four championships after opting for the CFL over the NFL in 1957. Then-Bombers head coach Bud Grant received a tip from a scout regarding Pitts, and Grant (later the Hall of Fame head coach for the Minnesota Vikings) moved quickly to sign the University of Denver alum. The San Francisco 49ers also selected Pitts, but he'd made up his mind While the Pitts family certainly relates to a feeling of pride for his accomplishments, the day will also be complicated by mixed emotions. Daughter Tanya and son Ernie will reflect on the lessons their father taught them and all of the feats they witnessed, but will also remember one painful time that would cause them to grow up faster than they imagined. In 1970, at his home in Brighton, Colorado, Pitts was shot by his wife, Ethel. He died in Tanya's arms. Tanya describes the night of her father's death as one that started with confusion and escalated quickly before it ended in great tragedy. "Of course, us kids, we thought he was here to celebrate my birthday and just be with us," she remembers. "We were all sitting around the dinner table. I had cooked dinner, and they got in a big argument and then they finally told us that they were separating, and we didn't know what that really meant. My dad asked where we wanted to live, because my dad was going to be moving to California to pursue a theater or Hollywood dream of being an actor with Jim Brown. Our other choice was to stay with my mom in Denver, and of course we all said 'Nope, we'll just go to California with our dad.' "That night was a very tumultuous night, and basically when my mom shot my dad, it was a turning point in my life. I went into shock, I went into immediately protecting my brother and sisters."

Wives Who Kill

(Courtesy of the Pitts Family)

The day after that fateful evening, Tanya attended a football game with her friends. While she felt a wave of negative emotions, she was also left with a very positive takeaway. "The very next day, I was in a football stadium, and I'm sitting there in the stands just watching and just thinking, 'God, that was my dad,'" Tanya said. "It was surreal, and I literally heard a voice, audibly just saying that this is going to shape my life in a way that's going to help lots of people and that's the message I heard. At that point, I became even more protective, not only of myself, but of my family." Tanya's mother was ultimately found innocent of murdering her father in one of the first United States cases of a murder acquittal due to a battered woman defense. Ethel was reunited with her children. As one can imagine, Tanya had to become an adult much earlier than most. She says she grew up in what she calls a "Leave It to Beaver" family that appeared harmonious and popular on the outside before her father's death, but had a lot of trauma, abuse and turmoil under the surface. "I grew up very early," Tanya said. "I cooked dinner, I did all the things, ordered food, went grocery shopping, all the things my mom would have done. But, I did it instead. I was trained to do it, obviously. I watched my mom and then my aunt and my uncles, so I learned at a very early age to do that." She also learned lessons of leadership and conducting herself from her father's high level of fame as a child. "My dad was very famous. We never went anywhere that my dad didn't give autographs. We grew up with lots of

Mariticide Club

people, lots of parties, a lot of entertaining. Of course, I grew up with that as well. So, I had lots of friends, was very social." After he was gone, she learned a lot of things about who she was at her core and recognized the choices in life she had to make that were fully in her control. "Never give up. Stand in truth. Be real with what is," Tanya said. "One of the lessons I've learned over the years is that I pretended a lot. I thought that was a survival technique. I pretended that things were OK when things weren't OK. That's how we were wired. We kept lots of secrets people didn't know about, and that's really not the way to live your life." She also notes her faith as something that helped her to get through such a trying time. "The lesson is to really speak truth, be your authentic self and the other piece in all this is that I have a great faith base," Tanya said. "I know that God helped me through all this in many, many ways by sending me people and resources for me to really learn from and respect and honor over the years."

Despite the complications surrounding Ernie's death, Friday's induction will provide a reason to celebrate for his family. "The entire family is elated," Tanya said of the induction. "There will be a total of 36 family members from two generations attending, including grandchildren. Ernie Sr. did set a tremendous positive example during a different time. He provided many special moments for his children off the field which has resulted in the development of our personal and professional happiness." In the past, stars such as Jets quarterback Joe Namath lived extravagant lifestyles filled with fancy cars, beautiful women and the spotlight. Pitts enjoyed a luxurious lifestyle in his own way. "Football was just coming into its own when my dad played. There was the race issue, you know, blacks and whites living together. Getting along together and becoming good friends. The football industry has shifted in recognizing that it's not just about the players," Tanya said. "It's now about a family unit, and that family equals community. In the past, I believe it was really just about the players. Protecting the players, making sure the players get all the things that they need. Putting them on a pedestal, things like that, while the families were pretty much on the sidelines. Today, it's much more inclusive. The players,

Wives Who Kill

even though they still are put on pedestals, the public is holding players accountable for their actions way more than they used to."

Her brother sees a similar trend. "In early times, I feel like players pretty much controlled what they wanted to do. They were stars. The people that others look up to. Now, people are more conscious of what the rules are and the regulations in place and can avoid some of the mistakes of the past." Today, Ernie Jr. and Tanya have built successful careers. Tanya works as a business coach, helping victims of domestic, emotional and physical abuse, while her brother is a respected restaurateur in Atlanta who serves as a mentor to the underprivileged teenagers he employs. As they move forward, though, they keep their father's undying sense of passion and what they've learned close to them. "Even in my sixties, that day and those memories will always be with me," Tanya says. "But it's also shaped me to be a much more compassionate, empathetic, loving person. Hate brings hate, and love brings love. For me, it's making that choice in helping people to really decide to stand for truth and authenticity. I think there's so much tragedy that happens to people, and I was thrust into that, My mom brought me into that situation. She had me watch it. There are many things people do that are thrust upon you. You're basically, at that point, a victim. "The lesson there is to not stay a victim and understand you are a part of the story, but that wasn't your story. You get to choose." His son believes that even after death, his father's ability to persevere lives on. "He overcame quite a few things. Even to this day, I feel like his perseverance continues even now — just because it took so long for him to get the recognition he deserves." The Canadian Football Hall of Fame ceremony will take place at Tim Hortons Field in Hamilton, Ontario, on Aug. 9. Doors are set to open at 6:30 p.m. ET, with the ceremony beginning at 7:30 p.m. ET.

Noh - The Pocheon Poisoner

The Pocheon Poisonings were a series of murders committed in Pocheon, South Korea between 2011 and 2014. An unidentified woman,

Mariticide Club

known only as Noh, killed three family members using herbicides and left one in critical condition. She was sentenced to life imprisonment for her crimes. In 2011, Noh's ex-husband was poisoned with a lethal amount of herbicide. It was initially deemed a suicide, with an eyewitness statement claiming that he killed himself after drinking a poisoned glass of water. Three years later, both the mother-in-law and husband, who suffered from lung diseases, died. Herbicides had been added to a fatigue-relieving drink for the mother-in-law, while the husband died after being slowly poisoned over a long period of time. Then, in February 2015, Noh was arrested. Even more shockingly, she tried to also poison her daughter, who suffered from lung fibrosis. Noh, who killed her relatives for money, was indicted by the court in 2015, with the prosecutors asking that she be given the maximum penalty available. At her first trial, she was sentenced to 10 years imprisonment and was required to wear an electronic bracelet. In her appeal trial, she was resentenced to life imprisonment.

Susan Polk (*née* Susan Mae Bolling)

Susan Polk (born Susan Mae Bolling in 1957) is an American woman convicted in June 2006 of second degree (unpremeditated) murder for the 2002 death of her husband, Dr. Frank "Felix" Polk. Polk's trial, described by one Associated Press correspondent as "circus-like", drew extensive media attention with its sensationalist elements. Her Case is featured on the Season 1, Episode 2, titled "Deadly Desire", from the Show, *Deadly Sins*. Susan Polk met Dr. Polk, a psychotherapist, in 1972 when administrators at her high school recommended she see him to treat her attacks. Susan Polk later made the "undisputed" claim that Dr. Polk first had sex with her when she was fourteen and still under his treatment, a taboo and a violation of professional ethics in the relationship between therapist and patient, which is now illegal in California. At the time, Dr. Polk had a wife and two children, though that couple subsequently divorced in 1982. After graduating from high school, Polk attended Mills College and San Francisco State University Graduated magna cum laude before, in 1982, marrying Dr. Polk, who was then an instructor at the California Graduate School of Family Psychology, and an occasional consultant as well as a

Wives Who Kill

private practitioner. At the time of their wedding, Polk was 24 and her husband 50. During their marriage, the couple had three sons. In 2001, Susan Polk filed for divorce, a complicated and contentious proceeding during which each contacted police with allegations of domestic violence. When asked by police whether Ms. Polk had made threats or been violent, Mr. Polk said she hadn't. In 2002, while Susan was living in Montana, Dr. Polk was able to petition the courts, ex parte, without providing Ms. Polk any form of official notice in advance. The courts then granted Dr. Polk sole custody of the couple's minor son, Gabriel Polk, and sharply reduced Susan's alimony. Dr. Polk also received sole possession of their house. On Wednesday, October 9, Polk went to the home to retrieve her belongings and complete her dental procedure by having a permanent crown put on her tooth. That Friday, October 11, the eldest son, Adam, came home from UCLA to pick up his dog. On Sunday, October 13, Dr. Polk, Adam, and the youngest son Gabriel drove Adam and the dog back to UCLA. Dr. Polk and Gabriel returned home at around 9:30 pm. Dr. Polk, then 70, was found dead the next day, Monday, October 14, 2002. At trial, prosecutors sought a conviction of murder in the first degree, contending that Susan Polk planned the murder of her multimillionaire husband for money. Susan Polk claimed self-defense, asserting that, after years of abuse, beginning with his "Therapy Sessions," in which Dr. Polk performed "guided visualizations" (i.e. hypnosis), he brandished a kitchen knife against her. She stated that she took control of the weapon and stabbed him instead. As an expert witness for the defense, forensic pathologist Dr. John Cooper testified that Felix Polk's death was caused by heart disease and that his stab wounds were not life-threatening and were evidence that Susan Polk delivered them in self-defense. Dr. Cooper failed to appear in court the following day to continue being cross-examined and to present documents he claimed to have received from Susan Polk, sending a written explanation to the judge. He returned with the letters a week later to resume testimony. Prosecuting attorneys dismissed Susan Polk's claim, arguing that she had no defensive wounds from her husband's alleged attack, which was disproved by expert testimony for the defense (Dr. John Cooper). The court

Mariticide Club

was forced to declare a mistrial when the wife of Susan Polk's thencounsel, Daniel Horowitz, was murdered in an unrelated incident. Susan fired her attorneys to represent herself. She supported her defense with allegations of a history of marital and professional misconduct, including claims that Dr. Felix Polk had drugged and raped her when she was a teenager, brainwashed the couple's children, and threatened to kill her if she tried to leave him. Susan Polk repeatedly requested a second mistrial, lodging accusations of conspiracy against the prosecutor and the judge.

Each of Susan and Felix's children testified at the trial. The youngest son, Gabriel, who had found the body, testified that his mother had speculated about means of killing her husband in the weeks before his father's death. The oldest son, Adam, also testified against his mother, receiving widespread media coverage when he referred to her on the stand as "cuckoo for Cocoa Puffs". The middle son, Eli, testified on Susan's behalf, that Felix was the aggressor, controller, manipulator and responsible overall. Jurors, obeying the judge's jury instruction order, disagreed that the crime was premeditated, finding her guilty of second-degree murder. Susan Polk was sentenced to prison for a term of 16 years to life. Her appeal was denied. Susan Polk was transferred to the California Institution for Women (CIW), a dorm-like prison, in Corona (near Chino), CA, in December 2012 and was eligible for parole in 2018. On May 29, 2019, Polk was removed from her parole hearing for being uncooperative and was subsequently denied parole. Polk will be eligible again for parole and may be available for "It's Just Lunch" in May 2029 if you are interested in romancing Susan.

Milena Quaglini

Milena Quaglini (March 25, 1957 – October 16, 2001) was an Italian woman, who in the late 1990s murdered three men who tried to rape her. Quaglini was born in 1957 in Mezzanino, near Broni in the Oltrepò Pavese. After graduating as an accountant in Pavia, at 19 she ran away from home to live between Como and Lodi, working occasionally as a cashier, caregiver and cleaning lady. She married and had a son, but her husband became seriously ill with fulminant diabetes and died, causing her to fall

Wives Who Kill

into a depression that would accompany her throughout her life, also beginning to drink. Quaglini moved to live in Travacò Siccomario, and after finding a job in San Martino Siccomario, she met Mario Fogli, who would become her second husband. He proved to be an obsessive, closed and jealous alcoholic who occasionally worked as a truck driver. Both Mario and Milena were also activists for the Lega Nord. Quaglini had two sons from him, but when the bailiffs arrived at their house for an attachment of assets because of the husband's debts, she decided to separate from him and move to Este, with her second daughter. In Veneto, she worked as a concierge for a gym. The money wasn't enough, so Quaglini found work as a caregiver for an elderly gentleman, 83-year-old Giusto Dalla Pozza, who lent her 4 million lires and then tried to blackmail her. On October 25, 1995, Dalla Pozza told Milena that she could repay him 500,000 lires for a month or pay him in another way. When she refused, he tried to rape her. A scuffle broke out, in which Quaglini struck him on the head with a lamp. She then left the house and left the agonized Dalla Pozza, who was still alive, calling an ambulance. He died ten days later. Milena was accused of this murder, and instead was filed as an accidental fall until her confession. For this reason, she was sentenced to 20 months' imprisonment due to excessive legitimate defense. Quaglini returned to Broni in attempt to reconcile with her former husband Mario Fogli; but the quarrels started again, with Milena returning to drinking and taking antidepressants. On August 2, 1998, after another quarrel, in a state of strong drunkenness, she killed her husband: she waited for him to fall asleep, put the two girls in bed, then snatched a rope from a shutter and wrapped it around Mario's neck to scare him. This resulted in a scuffle in which Fogli tried in vain to overwhelm her. Quaglini hit him with jewelry box and then strangled him with the shutter rope. She then wrapped her husband's body in the bloodstained blankets and then in a carpet, which she put on the balcony. At 4 PM, she called the Carabinieri of Stradella, saying she had killed her husband: the Carabinieri kept her on the phone while she told them the address. After she gave the phone to her daughters, they said with certainty that the carpet with the body was on the balcony. Milena was

Mariticide Club

arrested, and for this murder was sentenced to six years and eight months, also selling her house because her sentence was reduced due to her semiinsanity. Quaglini was sent to a recovery community for alcoholics, but after a few months she started drinking again. She was taken into a new community, where she met a former carabiniere named Salvatore, who offered her hospitality, but tried to rape her two days later. Quaglini met Angelo Porrello through an announcement. On October 5, 1999, she killed him in his home in Bascapè after he told her to dress provocatively, which she refused to do. He then slapped her, and proceeded to rape her three times. After the situation subsided, in the early afternoon she prepared a coffee for him, dissolving 20 tranquilizer tablets into it. Porrello fell asleep, and then Milena moved his body into the bathtub, filling it with water. She returned a few hours later to check on him, and he had drowned. In the evening, she moved the corpse to the garden. Drugs found in the home and DNA traces brought her to confess, after Quaglini was arrested in Porrello's car and returned to prison. On October 20, two weeks after the murder, the corpse was discovered in an advanced stage of decomposition. Condemned to serve her sentence in the Vigevano Prison, Quaglini tried to overcome depression by resuming her passion for painting, but she eventually hanged herself with a bed sheet on October 16, 2001. She was found still alive by a guard at 1:50 AM, but she died in the Emergency Room at 2:15 AM.

Milena Quaglini's story had a dedicated episode on *La linea d'ombra* with Massimo Picozzi Rai 2; her story was compared to that of American serial killer Aileen Wuornos, a prostitute who killed seven clients in Florida. In March 2015, Sky Crime dedicated the first episode of *Profondo Nero* with Carlo Lucarelli to the story of Milena Quaglini. April 7, 2016, Rai 3 aired the 4th episode of the 4th season of *Black Stars* conceived and conducted by Marco Marra, dedicated to Milena.

Victims

- Giusto Dalla Pozza, 83, died in Este November 4, 1995 following injuries
- Mario Fogli, 52, killed on August 2, 1998 in Broni
- Angelo Porrello, 53 years old, was killed on October 5, 1999 in Bascapè

Wives Who Kill

Bessie Reece

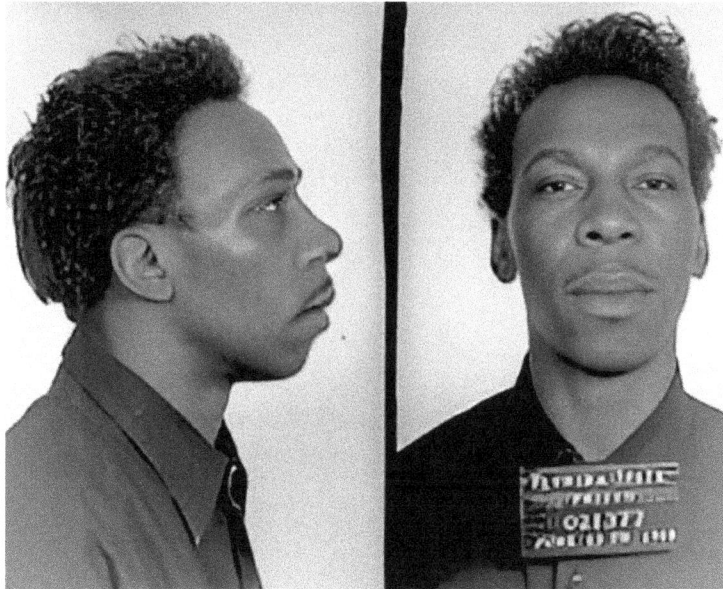

James Joseph Richardson

$2 million paid by State of Florida to James Joseph Richardson for falsely accusing him of the mass murder (2016) James Joseph Richardson (born December 26, 1935) is an African-American man who was wrongfully convicted and sentenced to death in 1968 for the October 1967 mass murder of his seven children. They died after eating a poisoned breakfast containing the organic phosphate pesticide parathion. At the time of the murders, Richardson was a migrant farm worker in Arcadia, Florida living with his wife Annie Mae Richardson and their children. At a trial in Fort Myers, Florida, the jury found him guilty of murdering the children and sentenced him to death. As a result of the United States Supreme Court's 1972 *Furman v. Georgia* decision finding the death penalty unconstitutional, his sentence was commuted to life imprisonment. He was then exonerated in 1989 after 21 years, when his case was revisited by appointed Miami-Dade County prosecutor Janet Reno. After Richardson's exoneration, the babysitter of the Richardson children, Bessie Reece, has been named as the key suspect. Reece died in 1993. In 2016 he began receiving compensation under a state law narrowly tailored to his case.

Mariticide Club

Murders of the Richardson children
7 Deaths
(Betty, aged 8
Alice, aged 7
Susie, aged 6
Dorreen, aged 5
Vanessa, aged 4
Dianne, aged 3
James Jr., aged 2

On October 25, 1967, the seven Richardson children, ranging in age from two to eight, consumed food poisoned with parathion. Six of the children died that day: Betty, age 8; Alice, age 7; Susie, age 6; Dorreen, age 5; Vanessa, age 4; and James Jr., age 2. The seventh child, Dianne, age 3, died the next day. Betty and Alice were from Annie Richardson's previous marriage while James was the father of the five youngest.

The night before, Annie Mae Richardson, James' wife, had prepared a lunch of beans, rice, and grits for the children. The meal was placed in a locked refrigerator overnight. In the morning the Richardsons left to work at the orange groves 16 miles away. A neighbor, Bessie Reece, was delegated to take care of the children while their parents were at work. The oldest four were enrolled in school; they went home to eat lunch. After they returned to school that afternoon, their teachers noticed they were showing strange symptoms, and the principal immediately took them to

Wives Who Kill

hospital. One of the teachers went to check on the three children at home, found them to be sick as well, and they were also taken to the hospital. Word was sent to the parents that just one of their children was ill and that a parent needed to come to the hospital. Both left the groves to go to the hospital, unaware that six of their children were dead by that time.

Investigation and accusation

Joseph H. Minoughan of the Arcadia Police Department was the first officer to arrive at the hospital. Determining that all of the sick children were from the same family, he promptly went to their apartment building to search for and quarantine any potential poison. He found nothing in the apartment indicative of a poison except an insect spray, and did not believe that it could have been the cause of the children's poisoning, so he rushed back to the hospital. Arcadia Police Chief Richard Barnard and County Sheriff Frank Cline were among the next law enforcement officers to examine the apartment. Minoughan came back from the hospital for a second examination of the apartment and found them there. Barnard and Cline went into the unlocked apartment and noticed a very strong smell, but no sign of any poison. Cline believed that the poison might be a pesticide and went to the shed behind the apartment building to search it; he found no poison there, either. Reporters started flocking to Arcadia to cover the breaking news. Richardson and the law enforcement officers were repeatedly questioned, but did not make any preliminary statements. Frank Shaub, a prosecuting attorney in the area, did respond to reporters and gave them accounts of his investigation of the house. The next morning, after the death of the last child, Dianne, a two-pound sack of parathion was discovered in the shed. Cline, Barnard, their staffs, and Shaub all agreed that the bag of parathion had not been there the day before, when the premises had been searched five times. They thought that whoever had placed the parathion sack was also probably the person who had poisoned the children. Conflicting reports on how the parathion sack was found were given to law enforcement officers. Minoughan was the first officer to arrive and was told by Bessie Reece, the babysitter, that Charlie Smith, a black resident of Arcadia's Quarters, had discovered the parathion. When

Mariticide Club

Minoughan asked Barnard who called in the discovery to the police station, he was informed that it was an anonymous male caller. The next day Cline and Shaub's local assistant, John Treadwell, III, told reporters that Richardson had "discussed insurance policies for the children the night before their deaths". It was determined that the insurance salesman, George Purvis, talked to Richardson just hours before the children were poisoned. According to authorities, Richardson and Purvis gave conflicting stories on the insurance policies. No additional evidence was found for two days. The children's funeral was held on Sunday. Both Richardson and his wife collapsed in sorrow at the service. National news magazines, television, and radio networks covered the funeral. This put Sheriff Cline at the center of nationwide attention. Barnard later told attorney Mark Lane: "Cline saw the chance to make a big name for himself. He needed to make an arrest real bad." Two days after the funeral Cline charged Richardson with murder in the first degree. However, Police Chief Barnard said, "There just is no case against that man." Treadwell, charged with prosecuting the case if it came to trial, agreed with Barnard. The murder warrants were dropped, but both Richardsons were formally charged with child neglect. Hayes agreed with Cline and summoned a coroner's inquest "to substantiate evidence already on hand". At the press conference the next day Cline announced that Richardson had five other children who had died under mysterious circumstances in another Florida city and that his motive for this crime was to collect the insurance money on the children, which would total almost $14,000. Judge Hayes said that both Richardson and his wife had taken lie-detector tests and that the results showed that Richardson had knowledge of the poisoning, which indicated he was guilty.

The coroner's jury held a hearing on November 2, 1967, at which Judge Hayes said: "We will meet today to instruct Frank Cline to file murder charges against Richardson." This statement carried considerable weight in Arcadia, including with the hand-picked jury, because of Hayes' prominent standing in the county and the fact he had been a judge in Arcadia for more than 31 years. John S. Robinson, a 30-year-old white lawyer, became concerned over the media coverage of the Arcadia murders. He believed

Wives Who Kill

the case was being handled unfairly as the judge constantly claimed that Richardson was guilty. He contacted people who knew Richardson and they told him he had a reputation as a family man and they could not believe he would kill his children. Robinson then called the president of the NAACP in Florida, Joel Atkins, and convinced him that the NAACP chapter in Arcadia should ask Richardson whether he wanted to be represented by them and should give him a list of potential lawyers. Richardson decided to let the NAACP represent him and chose Robinson as his attorney. Robinson went to talk to Richardson while he was being held in the county jail before the trial took place. Richardson was adamant that he had not killed his children, because he loved them very much. Richardson said Sheriff Cline was pushing him around, calling him a nigger, and questioning him "in a very mean way" every day. Cline had told Richardson that he would be let off easy if he confessed to the crime, but he denied that he had ever harmed any of his children. Through Ernell Washington, another prisoner, Robinson also discovered that Cline placed an eavesdropping device in Richardson's cell whenever Robinson was going in there to talk to Richardson. Robinson later found the microphone and removed it, letting Sheriff Cline know that he had found it. Robinson filed for a writ of Habeas Corpus after examining the available evidence and finding nothing substantial that could indicate Richardson was guilty. He then contested the high bond that had been set, which started at $100,000. After negotiations, the bail was reduced to $7,500, and Robinson was able to have Richardson released on bail. Ernell Washington, James Weaver, and James Cunningham, who had all been cellmates with Richardson in the Arcadia jail, said that Richardson had admitted to them that he had killed the children. Judge Justice revoked the bail, ordered Richardson to be jailed again, and asked for a change in venue, to Fort Myers, in the next county. Attempts by Robinson to move the trial to a potentially fairer county were denied. The trial began on Monday morning, May 27, 1968, at the Lee County Courthouse. All of the chosen jurors were white; despite numerous challenges, Robinson was unable to secure a different jury. During the trial, the most sensational development was when

Mariticide Club

Cline claimed that there was evidence that at least three of Richardson's children had been killed in another county and a further three who had become ill but had not died. Bessie Reece gave evidence that she divided up the meal into seven equal parts once the children came home from school at five minutes to twelve. Treadwell, who was conducting the examination of Reece, established that she was on parole at the time but did not ask what charge she had been convicted on; Treadwell did not want the jury to find out that she was on parole for having murdered her husband. No other questions about her involvement in the preparation of the food were asked. When asked about finding the sack of parathion, Reece became more specific, claiming that Charlie Smith wanted to look for the sack and went straight to the shed, pulling a board off the window and discovering the sack, implying that Charlie Smith had prior knowledge of the location of the parathion. Then an unknown woman saw them retrieving the sack and called authorities. Charlie Smith was in the courtroom but was not asked to testify at that time. The next witness was Gerald Purvis, the insurance salesman. He claimed that he called at the Richardson household on the 24th. It was not determined whether he was invited or was soliciting from door to door. Purvis testified that he talked about family plans with Mr. Richardson, but Richardson could not pay the necessary premiums; Purvis decided that he would come back in a week. Treadwell insisted that Purvis left with the impression that a policy was in place, but Purvis adamantly denied this. A pathologist and a chemist concluded that the children had in fact died from the organic phosphate parathion, which was found in their stomachs and on utensils in the Richardson apartment. Several law enforcement officers, including Barnard, Cline, and Minoughan, testified that they had searched the shed and had not seen the bag of parathion there on October 25. Charlie Smith testified about finding the bag of parathion in the shed. His story agreed with Reece's, and he was quickly excused. The jury then retired to consider the evidence, and a half hour later, on May 31, 1968, returned with a unanimous verdict: "Death with premeditation at the hands of James Richardson and party or parties unknown". Jurors recommended the death penalty for

Wives Who Kill

Richardson. Judge Hayes had Charlie Smith arrested as a material witness and set bond for him at $2,000; no other witness was jailed. After the hearing, Chief of Police Barnard still believed that there was no case against Richardson. Richardson was sentenced to die by the Court and was on death row for nearly five years. He was saved by the U.S. Supreme Court ruling in 1972 that the death penalties in the U.S. at the time were unconstitutional. His sentence was commuted to life in prison, with eligibility for parole in 1993. Many clues had been overlooked or hidden that would have pointed to Richardson's innocence. Mark Lane, an internationally known trial attorney and author, had visited Richardson on death row. Richardson asked Lane to represent him. Lane began an exhaustive investigation and in 1970 published his findings in the book *Arcadia*, in which he revealed that the baby sitter, Bessie Reece, was a convicted murderer, and indicated that Richardson and his wife were innocent. At the time of the children's murders, Reece was on parole for killing her ex-husband using poison. The prosecution had worked hard to keep this fact from coming up at trial. Little had been done to pursue her involvement with the children's deaths at all, including the facts that she had given them the food and that she had initially lied, saying that she had not gone into the apartment. As of 1988 Reece, suffering from Alzheimer's disease and in a nursing home in Arcadia, had reportedly confessed to the murders more than 100 times, but her confessions were not taken seriously because of her condition. She died of Alzheimer's in 1992. Also, the last surviving witness to Richardson's alleged jail-cell confession recanted his testimony to state legislators, saying that he had been offered a lighter sentence in return for the testimony. Further, the investigation into the children's deaths had been inadequate: leads were never pursued, critical questions were not answered, and inconsistencies were never resolved. Remus Griffin, a man who had been dating the secretary of one of State Attorney Frank Schaub's deputies, "Red" Treadwell, met Lane and his wife at a town meeting called "End the Silence: Free James Richardson", and then took one of the three copies of the complete original file on the case and gave it to Lane. Lane then met with the Governor's counsel and

Mariticide Club

turned the entire file over to the Governor, asking for a full investigation and a hearing on the Richardson case. The Governor, Robert Martinez, appointed the State's Attorney from Miami-Dade County, Janet Reno, to be the special prosecutor on the investigation. A number of months thereafter, on October 25, 1989, a hearing was held in Arcadia, in the same courthouse where Richardson had been convicted more than 21 years earlier. Lane appeared on behalf of Richardson and Reno appeared on behalf of the State of Florida. Lane argued and Reno agreed that a grievous injustice had been done and the wrong person had been convicted of the crimes. Reno cited the withholding of Brady material from the defense: six separate exculpatory elements of evidence. There was evidence of a cover-up by Sheriff Frank Cline, State Attorney Frank Schaub and his deputy, Treadwell, as well as the local judge. On April 25, 1989, after looking at all of the evidence presented by both sides and noting the inconsistencies and the injustice that had been done in Arcadia over two decades ago, retired Circuit Judge Clifton Kelly said that Richardson had not received a fair trial, and released him into the custody of his attorneys, Lane and the local counsel. After his release Richardson went to work for nutritionist Dick Gregory at a health resort in Fort Walton Beach; Gregory had previously spoken out for Richardson, amid a groundswell of celebrities including famed Miami attorney Ellis Rubin. He filed a lawsuit against DeSoto County for his wrongful prosecution, and settled for $150,000. On August 25, 2008, after his legal claims had been rejected based upon the precedent of "prosecutorial immunity", Richardson filed a claim under Florida's wrongful conviction compensation law, which provides compensation for wrongful imprisonment of $50,000 a year. Richardson had meanwhile suffered a series of setbacks after being released from jail. The job at the health resort ended. He suffered from severe heart problems, which he attributed to prison food, poor medical care, and constant stress; he had had open-heart surgery in prison. He and his wife, who had remained loyal to him for part of the time he was in jail, eventually divorced. The settlement by the county went to pay the costs of his local lawyers, while Richardson had been in prison so long that he became eligible for Social

Wives Who Kill

Security. In August 1995, he had a heart attack at his home in Jacksonville. He was flown with a long-time friend, media expert Steve Jaffe, to Wichita, Kansas, for emergency treatment by cardiologist Dr. Joseph Galichia, a friend of Jaffe's. Galichia performed an angioplasty and offered Richardson a job as a caretaker on his ranch. As of 2013, he was living in Wichita. In 2014, Florida Governor Rick Scott signed into law House Bill 227, which provides compensation to a wrongfully incarcerated person who was convicted and sentenced prior to December 31, 1979, and who is otherwise exempt from other state provisions for compensation because the case may have been reversed by a special prosecutor's review and *nolle prosequi* rather than being overturned by a court. The law is so narrowly circumscribed that it is likely that Richardson will be the only individual eligible for compensation under it. He was expected to be awarded $1.2 million. In 2016 he received his first check toward compensation, totaling $50,000 for each year of his wrongful imprisonment. In 2015, a documentary film about Richardson was produced called *Time Simply Passes*. It tells the story of his life until the vote to grant him compensation.

Vera Renczi- The Black Widow

Vera Renczi (dubbed the Black Widow, Mrs. Poison or Chatelaine of Berkerekul), was a Romanian serial who was charged with poisoning 35 individuals including her two husbands, multiple lovers, and her son with arsenic during the 1920s. Journalist Otto Tolischus published the earliest known article in the United States in May 1925 based on letters from the readers without naming any reference. Renczi's story has surfaced repeatedly, but without traceable details such as specific dates of her birth, marriages, arrest, conviction, incarceration or death. Most sources place the murders at Berkerekul, Yugoslavia (present-day Serbia), or Bečkerek, which changed the name to Zrenjanin in 1946; although, the spelling Berkerekul is unknown for this city. In 1972, the *Guinness Book of World Records* found no authoritative sources to support the claim that 35 people were killed by Renczi in early 20th-century Austro Hungarian Empire. Renczi was born in Bucharest in 1903, but in view of the dates of her

Mariticide Club

alleged crimes, a date in the late 19th century would be more appropriate. The accounts of her life are lacking in verifiable documentary supporting evidence. Her mother died when she was 13 and she moved with her father to Nagybecskerek (today Zrenjanin, Serbia) where she attended a boarding school. By the age of fifteen, she had become increasingly unmanageable and had frequently run away from home with numerous boyfriends, many of whom were significantly older than she was. Early childhood friends described Renczi as having an almost pathological desire for constant male companionship and possessing a highly jealous and suspicious nature. Before she was twenty, her first marriage was to a wealthy Austrian banker named Karl Schick, many years her senior. They had a son named Lorenzo. Left at home daily while her older husband worked, she began to suspect that her husband was being unfaithful. One evening, in a jealous rage, Renczi poisoned his dinner wine with arsenic and began to tell family, friends, and neighbors that he had abandoned her and their son. After approximately a year of "mourning", she then declared that she had heard word of her supposedly estranged husband's death in a car accident. Shortly after allegedly hearing the news of her first husband's "automobile accident", Renczi remarried, this time to a man nearer her own age. However, the relationship was a tumultuous one and Renczi was again plagued by the suspicion that her new husband was involved in extramarital affairs. After only months of marriage the man vanished and Renczi then told friends and family that he had abandoned her. After a year had passed, she then claimed to have received a letter from her husband proclaiming his intentions of leaving her forever. This would be her last marriage. Renczi did not remarry: she spent the next several years carrying out a number of affairs, some clandestine with married men, and others openly. The men came from an array of backgrounds and social positions. All would vanish within months, weeks, and in some cases, even days after becoming romantically involved with her. When connected to men she was openly having an affair with, she would invariably concoct stories of them being "unfaithful" and having "abandoned her". She was caught after having poisoned her last lover, a bank officer named Milorad; his wife reported his

Wives Who Kill

disappearance to the Police, who ignored her. But she pursued her own investigation and rapidly found that Vera was her husband's mistress. She went back to the Police, who send two inspectors to the chateau. She admitted to them that Milorad had been her lover, but that he had quit her. Impressed by her beauty, wealth and excellent reputation, the Police abandoned their search. The wife went back to the Police and started to ask questions which should have been asked long time ago: where was her husband Joseph? Where was their son? What happen to the numerous other men who people knew they were her lover and had also disappeared? The Police went back to see her; not only she then denied that Milorad was her lover, which she had admitted before, but the Police had a proof, a love letter sent by her to her lover. The Police got a search warrant and discovered a locked round cellar underground. In it were 35 spaces, each with a zinc-lined coffin inside. In the middle of the cellar were a red armchair, a big church candle and an empty bottle of champagne. She told them that it was all family members, but they insisted in opening one coffin, in which was the decomposed body of a man ; they then opened all the others ones, in which they found the same thing. Arrested, she confessed that she had poisoned all of them with arsenic when she suspected they had been unfaithful to her or when she believed their interest in her was waning. She also confessed to the police that, on occasion, she liked to sit in the armchair, surrounded by the coffins of all her former lovers. She was convicted of 35 murders and sentenced to death, but, at that time, Yugoslavia did not execute women. She was instead condemned to life in prison. During her trial, she had started showing signs of dementia. It became worse and worse in prison (she ended up talking to her victims and screaming obscenities). She died in 1960. Some have speculated that Renczi's story may have inspired Joseph Kesselring's play *Arsenic and Old Lace,* yet this is incorrect. It was the Amy Archer-Gilligan case which the playwright used as his model. In 2005, The Discovery Channel's three-part series *Deadly Women* recounted the history of Renczi, portrayed through reenactments and commentaries from FBI agents and criminal profiler Candice DeLong and a forensic pathologist. Renczi was featured in

Mariticide Club

the series' first episode titled "Obsession", where she is described as having killed her victims in the "1930s in Bucharest, Romania". As for her motivation, the voice-over says that "modern analysis suggest she was simply looking for love". On 17 March 2012, a depiction of Renczi appeared in the *Daily Mirror*, but it was proved to be a misidentified 2004 photograph, and an apology was printed.

Heloísa Gonçalves Duque Soares Ribeiro (*née* Heloísa Borba Gonçalves born March 13, 1950) Black Widow (Portuguese: *Viúva Negra*), is a Brazilian–American criminal, murderer and accused serial killer. Convicted for the murder of one husband and bigamy/fraud charges *in absentia*, Gonçalves has been accused in at least three other murders and multiple other violent crimes dating back to 1971, but has so far evaded capture. As of February 2023, she is one of Brazil's most wanted criminals and has a red notice issued for her arrest from Interpol. Due to her tendency to use aliases and not talk about her life, little can be verified about Gonçalves' past. She was born on March 13, 1950, in Porto Alegre, Rio Grande do Sul, as Heloísa Borba Gonçalves, and had her first child at age 19 with then-boyfriend Carlos Pinto da Silva. She then began a simultaneous relationship with a doctor named Guenther Joerg Wolff, and became pregnant with his child as well. On December 27, 1971, the 4-months-pregnant Gonçalves and Wolff decided to go on a trip from Porto Alegre to Taquara in the latter's Volkswagen Karmann Ghia. According to official records, they collided with a truck, as a result of which 38-year-old Wolff died on the spot, but Gonçalves and her unborn child managed to survive. A daughter was born soon after, with Gonçalves inheriting Wolff's house in Porto Alegre as his widow. A year after that, she became a mother for a third time, having her second child with Pinto. Criminal charges: Suspicious deaths

The first violent crime attributed to Gonçalves took place on December 20, 1977, while she, Pinto, and their children were on vacation in Salvador, Bahia. On that date Pinto was shot five times in the chest, but managed to

Wives Who Kill

survive and identified the assailant as Gonçalves. For reasons unknown, he decided to withdraw the complaint for attempted murder and the case was dropped. In 1980 Gonçalves was arrested on fraud charges for signing a document under the name "Matilde Irene Gomes da Silva". Unwilling to be imprisoned again, from then on she would legally adopt her future husbands surnames to avoid trouble. A year after this, she began a relationship with security guard Irineu Duque Soares and had a child with him that same year, but the pair did not officially marry until May 13, 1983. In October of that year, the family and their nanny were en route to Magé, Rio de Janeiro, when they suddenly got flagged down by another car – when Duque got out to see what was going on, the other driver shot him twice in the chest and then stole his money before fleeing. Officially, the case was registered as a robbery-homicide. In the late 1980s Gonçalves bigamously married two different men: military policeman Roberto de Souza Lopes and Colonel Jorge Ribeiro, having a child with the latter born in 1987. On May 8, 1990, she married yet another man, an elderly Syrian businessman named Nicolau Saad – both Saad and Ribeiro would then claim to be the fathers of a child born in that same year, but was known under two different names. On December 29, 1991, Nicolau Saad was found dead at his home – the official cause of death was attributed to his advanced cancer and a heart attack, but coroners found that he had somehow broken his arm in unexplained circumstances beforehand.

Murder of Jorge Ribeiro

By the beginning of 1992 Gonçalves and Ribeiro had already divorced, but she still wanted to acquire his personal properties and assets. To do this, she hired an unidentified individual to break into her ex-husband's office in Copacabana and kill him. When he did so, the man bound and gagged Ribeiro with a plastic bag and nylon ropes, before proceeding to hit him several times in the face and head with a sledgehammer. Ribeiro's skull was fractured, killing him almost instantly. Upon his death Gonçalves inherited his phone line service, earning her a nickname "The Queen of Telephones" (Portuguese: *Rainha dos Telefones*), taken after her late ex-husband nickname "The King of Telephones" (Portuguese: *Rei dos Telefones*).

Mariticide Club

On November 28, 1992, Gonçalves married yet again – this time to Lebanese-born merchant Wagih Elias Murad. She became a godmother to his family on his son's side, all of whom were unaware of her shady past. Five months after Murad's son Elie had married and only ten days after his grandson had been born, Wagih was hanging around with his friend Wagner Laino in Recreio dos Bandeirantes when an unidentified man approached from a taxi and shot them both to death before fleeing. Convinced this was on the behest of his godmother, Elie Murad used his position as a business administrator to hire private detectives that would look into her past. To his shock, he discovered that Gonçalves was a bigamist and fraudster whose ex-husbands and boyfriends had either been murdered, died in suspicious circumstances or were almost killed by persons unknown – allowing her to inherit their possessions and properties. On October 11, 1993 Murad and police officer Luiz Marques de Motta, who was helping him with his private investigation, were driving to a local police station in the Barra neighborhood when they were ambushed by two unidentified men driving in another car. The gunmen opened fire on both, hitting De Motta at least three times and killing him on the spot, while Murad was hit in the head, but managed to survive after spending two weeks in an intensive care unit. After spending some time to recover from the attempt on his life, Murad continued his investigation into Gonçalves, which eventually culminated into an aggravated murder charge being filed against her in August 2005 for the murder of Jorge Ribeiro. However, she appealed the decision and the trial date was postponed for several years. Sometime circa 2010 Gonçalves went into hiding and has been on the run ever since. As a result, prosecutor Patrícia Glioche issued two arrest warrants on the aggravated murder and bigamy charges, as well as announcing a R$2,000 prize for any information that could led to Gonçalves' arrest. It was eventually decided that she should be tried *in absentia*, as a result of which she was swiftly convicted and sentenced to 18 years imprisonment. As of publication 2023, Gonçalves remains one of the country's most dangerous and most wanted fugitives, ranking among drug lords and gang members. A warrant has been issued for her arrest by

Wives Who Kill

Interpol, and she is currently sought in a total of 188 countries. Prosecutors following her case have indicated that she may be hiding somewhere within Brazil, with possible locations being her home state of Rio Grande do Sul, Paraná, the Barra da Tijuca and Jardim Botânico neighborhoods of Rio de Janeiro and Niterói. Information posted from Interpol indicates that she likely fled to the United States in 1994, gaining dual citizenship and continuing to marry and divorce husbands. Her last reported sighting was in May 2010 in Boca Raton, Florida, with her then-husband, Peruvian national Vicente Lopez Huaman, and it is said that Gonçalves has family members living in the states of California, Virginia and New York. The current reward for her arrest stands at more than R$11,000.

Elizabeth Ridgeway *née* Elizabeth Husbands

Elizabeth Ridgeway (died 24 March 1684) was an English woman convicted of poisoning her husband. While awaiting execution by burning at the stake, she confessed to previously poisoning her mother, a fellow servant, and a lover. Ridgeway poisoned each of her victims by mixing white mercury or arsenic into her intended victim's food or drink. Elizabeth Ridgeway, née Husbands, was born in the mid-17th century on a farm outside Ibstock, Leicestershire, England. She lived at home until about age 29, poisoning her mother after an argument, about a year before she took a job in town as a household servant. She poisoned a male coworker in her household with arsenic, reportedly after developing a grudge against this individual. Ridgeway had many suitors during this time and poisoned John King in 1682 after she had backed herself into a corner romantically, having promised too much to King. She far preferred the wealthier Thomas Ridgeway and married him on 1 February 1683 after waiting through the winter.

Mariticide Club

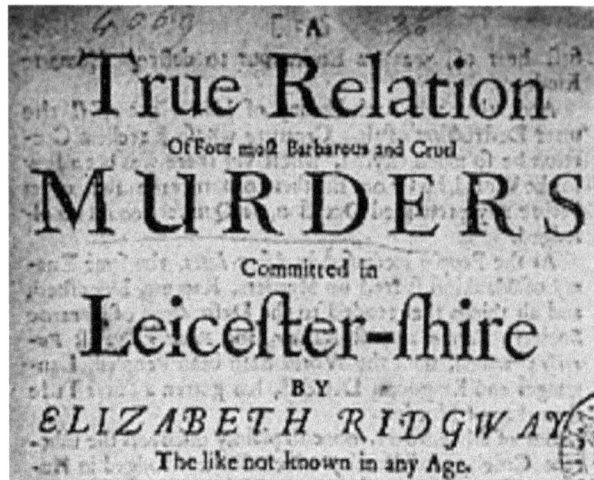

"A True relation of four most barbarous and cruel MURDERS committed in Leicester-shire by ELIZABETH RIDGWAY; The Like not Known in any Age. With the Particulars of Time, Place, (and other Circumstances)..." Printed by George Croom, 1684 All was not bliss as Ridgeway's sister called in his £20 debt to her shortly after the marriage, which nearly bankrupted the couple. She contemplated suicide for a time, but ultimately stirred some arsenic that she had purchased earlier in Ashby-de-la-Zouch into her husband's broth while he was at church. He ate most of it although he complained to his apprentices that it was gritty. Thomas Ridgeway died that evening, three weeks and three days after their wedding. The apprentices suspected poisoning and, after her attempt to feed them arsenic-laced porridge failed, she attempted to bribe them into silence. One of them reported his suspicions to Ridgeway's in-laws and the local justice of the peace ordered an inquest by the coroner. Examination of the body confirmed that he had been poisoned and Elizabeth Ridgeway was jailed in Leicester to await trial. To test her guilt, she was supposedly forced to touch her husband's body in the belief that the body of the victim would spontaneously bleed in the presence of the murderer (cruentation) and the body gushed blood at the nose and mouth. During her trial on 14 March, she pled not guilty, but was convicted and sentenced to burn.

Despite some protests over the severity of the sentence, the judge refused to relent, but did ask John Newton, a local clergyman, to counsel Ridgeway. She had no interest in making her peace with God and toyed with him by promising full confessions multiple times before changing her mind. She

Wives Who Kill

finally admitted on the morning of her execution that she had poisoned her mother, a fellow servant, John King, and her husband and confessed she thought of suicide at the time of her mother's death three years previously.

Donna Marie Roberts

Donna Marie Roberts (born May 22, 1944), an American convicted of being an accomplice to murder, is the only woman on death row in the State of Ohio. Roberts was born and raised in Youngstown, Ohio and was a student of Austintown Fitch High School. She enrolled at Youngstown State University for two years, and in 1966, she married her first husband, William Raymond, and moved to Miami, Florida. She had one child, Michael Raymond, in 1969. She and William Raymond divorced in 1971. She remarried her second husband, Burton Gelfand, in 1972 and later divorced him in 1980. Roberts converted to Judaism while living in Miami, Florida, and worked as a surgeon assistant for over 20 years in North Miami Beach. Roberts met her late husband, Robert Fingerhut, in 1980. They married and bought a home in Miami, near Miami Gardens and Ives Estates in 1983. They later sold their home and moved to Richmond, Virginia for one year, and in 1993, the couple moved back to Roberts' hometown of Youngstown, Ohio. Roberts purchased their new home in Warren in 1994 on Fonderlac Avenue. During this time, Roberts and Fingerhut managed the Avis Car Rental franchise at the Youngstown–Warren Regional Airport for several years. They later managed both the Youngstown and Warren Greyhound bus stations and turned them into successful locations. For a short period, Roberts also ran a small restaurant located within the Youngstown Bus Terminal called "Just the Ticket." Roberts was convicted in 2003 of complicity in aggravated murder and conspiracy to commit murder. Roberts was having an affair with Nathaniel E. Jackson before he was sent to prison for a separate offense. While Jackson was still in prison, he stated in letters and phone calls that he would kill her ex-husband, Robert Fingerhut, which he did on December 11, 2001, in the house Roberts and Fingerhut shared. In Roberts' appeal, it was alleged that the police performed an illegal search of her car parked inside the garage since the search warrant was only for the home. Jackson stated that Roberts had no knowledge of his planned actions, videotaped during his confession by the police; he also stated this during his trial. Jackson was sentenced to death for his role in the murder. In addition to phone calls and letters between Roberts and Jackson, investigators said Roberts bought Jackson a mask and gloves to wear while committing the crime, even allowing him into the home where the murder occurred. On June 25, 2020, the Ohio Supreme Court ruled that carrying out the execution of Roberts would be placed on hold until all state post-conviction proceedings, including any appeals are exhausted. In the years since their conviction, Roberts and Jackson's case has been featured on *Deadly Women, Snapped: Killer Couples, Calls From the Inside, Season 2, and For My Man.*

Sarah Jane Robinson (*née* Tennant)

Sarah Jane Robinson (née Tennant; May 26, 1838 – January 3, 1906), known as The Boston Borgia, was an Irish-born American serial killer who poisoned her family members and other people from 1881 to 1886,with the help of her accomplices Thomas R. Smith and Dr. Charles C. Beers. She was initially sentenced to death for the poisoning of her brother-in-law, but the verdict was later changed to life imprisonment, with Robinson dying behind bars. Sarah Jane Robinson was born in Newton Hamilton, Ireland, and immigrated to Massachusetts with her sister when she was fourteen or fifteen years old. She married Moses Robinson in July 1858. Over the course of their marriage, the couple had eight children, five of whom survived infancy. They initially settled in Sherborn, Massachusetts, moving around the Boston area throughout their marriage. Robinson became a member of the Cottage Street Methodist Church, where she later on would meet her future partner-in-crime: Thomas R. Smith, a prominent church leader and one-time superintendent of the local Sunday school in Hyde Park. Both of them were well known in the community, with Robinson standing out for her constantly changing addresses in order to avoid paying rent and other bills. From 1881 and 1886, several members of the Robinson family passed away from mysterious illnesses, all with similar symptoms

Wives Who Kill

such as excruciating stomach pain and vomiting. Each time, the sickly were attended to by Sarah Jane Robinson, who supervised the administration of all medicine. When the victims eventually needed medical attention, Robinson called a different physician each time. Curiously, all of the deceased except for Oliver Sleeper had life insurance policies through the United Order of Pilgrim Fathers. Mr. Sleeper, the Robinson's landlord, was nursed by Sarah Jane during his illness, and died of what, at the time, was deemed heart disease. She tried to bill the family $50 for nursing services. They instead gave her a break on her rent. His family discovered $3000 missing from his apartment. Though it was never proven, it was assumed that Sarah Jane stole it. Already the deaths of Robinson's eldest daughter Elizabeth (24) and her nephew Thomas Freeman (7) had caused suspicion and were under investigation, but the breaking point came when her son, William, was taken sick with the previous symptoms. Although he died shortly, he still managed to point at his mother as the one responsible for his condition. Using this knowledge, Dr. White preserved parts of William's stomach for later analysis at Harvard College, which revealed large quantities of arsenic. White then informed the authorities, who swiftly arrested Robinson and Smith, who had just arrived at the house. After a quick prayer for the mother and the son, the duo were taken to the police station for questioning. While the police were still investigating, they made one further arrest: that of Dr. Charles C. Beers, of Boston. In October 1886, the trio were indicted for William and Lizzie's murders, with all of them pleading not guilty on every charge at their arraignment on December 14, 1886. Then, surprisingly, in January 1887, the grand jury revealed four more indictments against Sarah Jane for the killings of Oliver Sleeper, Sarah's husband Moses, her brother-in-law Prince Arthur Freeman, and little Thomas Freeman. During this whole ordeal, Robinson tried to feign insanity, but this was later refuted by Dr. Kelly of the McLean Asylum.

Before the trial started, a *noelle prosequi* was entered by Attorney General A. J. Waterman, dismissing the charges against Thomas Smith and Charles Beers. On December 13, 1887, the trial against Sarah Jane for the murder of her son, William, began. The six-day long trial was followed by twenty

Mariticide Club

four hours of jury deliberation and resulted in a hung jury. On February 6, 1888, Sarah Jane was put on trial for the murder of her brother-in-law, Prince Arthur Freeman. On February 11, 1888, Sarah Jane Robinson was convicted of murdering Prince Freeman and sentenced to death by hanging. The following year, when Robinson's house had already been sold at auction and the new owner was making improvements, a box of rat poison was discovered behind the furnace, in a hole of the cellar wall, which was quickly tied back to Robinson. After her sentence was announced, and despite the fact a majority of the public disdained her, a petition was started to commute Robinson's sentence. Although the Governor's Council allegedly was against such a decision, they later decided to indeed commute the sentence to life in prison, much to the surprise of both the press and the citizens of Boston. Robinson died behind bars on January 3, 1906. All but one of Robinson's victims were poisoned with the aim of collecting insurance money. She poisoned:

- Oliver Sleeper, landlord, age 72, poisoned on August 10, 1881
- Moses Robinson, husband, age 45, poisoned on July 25, 1882. Moses, who lived in Cambridge, was alleged to have died due to drinking cold water after overheating himself. This was challenged by the insurance company, who refused to pay Robinson a cent. She then moved out of Cambridge.
- Emma M. Robinson, daughter, age 10, poisoned on September 6, 1884
- Annie Freeman, sister, age about 45, poisoned on February 28, 1885
- Prince Arthur Freeman, brother-in-law, age 33, poisoned on June 27, 1885. After his death, Robinson adopted his son and received the $2000 he had been insured for in order to care for the child.
- Elizabeth "Lizzie" A. Robinson, daughter, age 24, poisoned on February 22, 1886
- Thomas Arthur Freeman, nephew, age 7, poisoned on July 23, 1886
- William "Willie" J. Robinson, son, age 22, poisoned on August 12, 1886

Robinson could have attempted to poison upwards of a thousand people by putting arsenic into the ice cream offered at a festival at the Sunday School in June 1885. This conjecture, however, was promptly dismissed in court.

Wives Who Kill

Angelina Rodriguez

Rodriguez in 2011

Angelina Rodriguez (born May 31, 1968) is an American woman from Montebello, California who was sentenced to death for the September 2000 murder of Jose Francisco "Frank" Rodriguez, her fourth husband. She also was accused of killing her infant daughter in 1993 by suffocating her with a pacifier. Rodriguez is incarcerated at the Central California Women's Facility in Chowchilla, California, where she is on death row awaiting execution. Rodriguez met her husband Frank, a special education teacher, while they were employed at a camp in San Luis Obispo, California. The couple married in April 2000. It was her fourth marriage. Prosecutors argue that within months of the marriage, Rodriguez took out a $250,000 (2018 value of $366,000) life insurance policy on Frank and began plotting to kill him. She was suspected of poisoning Frank's tea with oleander leaves, loosening the gas cap on their clothes dryer, and finally adding antifreeze to her husband's Gatorade. Frank Rodriguez died on September 9, 2000. His death was initially ruled undetermined, but the lack of a cause of death meant that Rodriguez could not get a death certificate or Frank's life insurance. She pushed for more

Mariticide Club

testing, and these results showed that he intentionally had been poisoned. Rodriguez was arrested for murder in Paso Robles, California in February 2001. Three years after Frank's death, Rodriguez's murder trial began in the fall of 2003. During the years since her arrest, prosecutors discovered that her 13-month-old daughter Alicia died suspiciously in 1993. Rodriguez claimed that her daughter choked on a pacifier that became dislodged, but investigators believe that Rodriguez removed the pacifier's nipple and used it to suffocate Alicia. Rodriguez then sued the pacifier manufacturer and was awarded a settlement of $700,000. After Alicia's death was ruled accidental, she also received a $50,000 life insurance policy. Although she never was charged with her daughter's death, this evidence was presented at her trial to show that Rodriguez's motive for the murder was financial.

In October 2003, Rodriguez was convicted of first-degree murder with special circumstances, murder for financial gain, and attempt to dissuade a witness. She was not convicted of the charge of soliciting murder. The following month, the jury rendered a sentence of death. Rodriguez was sentenced to death by lethal injection on January 12, 2004. In her sentencing, Los Angeles County Superior Court Judge William R. Pounders stated that she killed her husband in an "exceptionally cruel and callous" way and that her guilt had been proved to be "an absolute certainty...In the past 20 years, I have never seen a colder heart." Despite her conviction and death sentence, Rodriguez argued her innocence and maintained that her husband's death was a suicide by antifreeze poisoning. Rodriguez was awarded a new sentencing hearing in 2010 but was resentenced to death in November 2010. Her most recent appeal was denied by the Supreme Court of California in February 2014.Rodriguez remains on death row at the Central California Women's Facility in Chowchilla, California. However, she is planning to appeal her case to the United States Supreme Court. The murder of Frank Rodriguez has been profiled on several television shows, including *North Mission Road* on truTV, *Deadly Women and Happily Never After* on Investigation Discovery, *Snapped* on the Oxygen Network, and *It Takes a Killer* on Escape TV. The crime was featured on an episode of NBC's Dateline, titled "The Devil in Disguise".

Wives Who Kill

Published in February 2016, the book *A Taste for Murder*, by Burl Barer and Frank C. Girardot, has details of the crimes committed by Rodriguez.

Mary Mabel Bennett Rogers

Mary Mabel Bennett Rogers (March 9, 1883 – December 8, 1905) was the last woman legally executed by Vermont. Rogers was hanged for the 1902 murder of her husband, Marcus Rogers. Mary Mabel Bennett was born to Charles and Johanna Bennett. Her father was reportedly a mentally ill alcoholic who was unable to hold down a job. As a result, he was abusive and tried to kill her a number of times. At age 15, Mary Bennett married Marcus Rogers. She was noted for being immature and restless, and often stayed away from home when she was upset with her husband. Rogers gave birth to a daughter in 1901. When the child was six months old, Rogers ran into a neighbor's home crying that she had dropped the baby, who later died of a fractured skull. Her husband's family, however, believed she had intentionally killed the child. These suspicions were heightened after Marcus Rogers became violently ill after drinking tea that his wife had prepared for him. Mary Rogers moved out of the house shortly after this incident, but her husband hoped they could reconcile. Marcus Rogers found work as a laborer in Hoosick Falls, New York, while Mary lived in Bennington, Vermont. Although Marcus pleaded with his wife to join him in Hoosick Falls, she refused. Mary Rogers struck up relationships with a laborer, Morris Knapp, and two brothers living in the same residence house as Knapp, Leon and Levi Perham. Rogers first approached Levi Perham with an offer of $500 if he would kill her husband. Levi initially agreed to help her, but he was intoxicated at the time and later backed out; he did not tell the police because he felt it was just idle talk. Rogers then proposed the idea of murdering her husband to Leon Perham while they lay in bed in early August 1902; Leon agreed to help her kill her husband, even though Rogers made it clear that her reason for disposing of her husband was to leave her free to marry Knapp. Rogers arranged to meet her husband in a Bennington picnic grove on the evening of August 12. Leon Perham was with Mary when Marcus arrived, but apparently

Mariticide Club

Marcus did not question Leon's presence. That evening, Mary pretended to be happy to have seen her husband and spoke with him of reconciliation. At some point during the picnic, Mary offered to show her husband a rope trick she had learned from a friend. Mary tied Perham's hands several times, and each time Perham easily broke free of the restraint, with Mary pretending to be disappointed when he did so. Mary then challenged her husband to try the trick. She tied his wrists a few times, and he also easily broke free. Then Mary "convinced" Perham to try the trick on her husband. When Perham bound Marcus's wrists behind his back, Rogers could not break free. Mary took a vial of chloroform from her purse and forced her husband to breathe it in for about 20 minutes, until he stopped struggling. Mary went through Marcus's pockets and removed his life insurance payment book. Mary and Perham then rolled the body into the nearby river and Marcus Rogers drowned. Mary tacked Marcus's hat to a tree with a forged suicide note. The investigation began after the body was discovered; Perham made a full confession. At Rogers's trial in 1904, Perham was the state's key witness against her. Due to his testimony and his youth, Perham avoided the death penalty and was sentenced to life imprisonment. Rogers was found guilty of first-degree murder and sentenced to death by hanging.Following Rogers's conviction, there was a concerted effort to have her death sentence commuted. State Representative Frank C. Archibald of Manchester, who was also one of Rogers' attorneys, introduced a bill in the Vermont House of Representatives that would have commuted Rogers' sentence to life imprisonment. The bill was referred to the judiciary committee on October 12, 1904. On December 6, the committee reported in favor of its passage. On December 7, a vote on the bill in the House of Representatives was defeated by a vote of 139 to 91. On December 9, Representative Archibald proposed a joint resolution of the Vermont House and Senate to investigate Rogers's physical and mental condition at the time of the commission of the crime and at the present time, and to prepare a report as to her condition for the governor. The resolution stated that if it should appear that Rogers either at the time she committed the crime or at present was mentally or physically unsound, that a reprieve

Wives Who Kill

should be requested and her execution delayed until after the 1906 Vermont Legislative Session. The House adopted this resolution but the Senate did not. On May 30, 1905, Governor Charles J. Bell granted a reprieve to Rogers after the Vermont Supreme Court denied Rogers's appeal by a 5–2 vote; the reprieve was intended to allow the appeal to be heard by the United States Supreme Court. The U.S. Supreme Court heard the case on November 6 and held on November 27 that the Court could not find that Rogers had sustained any violation of her Federal Constitutional rights by the proceedings of the executive or judicial departments of the State of Vermont. In 1904, the Vermont Commission to Investigate State Institutions began investigating charges of sexual misconduct at the Vermont State Prison, where Rogers was being held. A large portion of the commission's investigation focused on allegations of inappropriate sexual relations between Rogers and two other prisoners. Evidence of issues at the prison included the fact that a child was born to Rogers after she had been incarcerated for over a year. After the U.S. Supreme Court decision, Bell signed Rogers' execution warrant and the execution was scheduled for December 8, 1905. Rogers inquired on December 7 whether the gallows were being erected, despite efforts having been made to muffle the construction noise. During the ten days between the signing of the warrant and her execution, Rogers ate and slept well, but she declined breakfast on the morning of her execution. Governor Bell granted leave to hear an appeal from Rogers's counsel at 8 a.m. on her scheduled execution day; however, he found no reason to commute her sentence. With no new evidence, he declined to stay the execution and Rogers was hanged at the Vermont State Prison later that day. She was pronounced dead at 1:17pm. A scandal later ensued because of the circumstances of Rogers' death. The executioner reportedly used a rope that stretched when Rogers was dropped from the gallows, causing her to strangle as her feet scraped the floor. After several minutes, sheriff's deputies pulled on the end of the rope until Rogers was suspended, then held it in place until she finally died. Rogers is buried at St. Mary's Cemetery in Hoosick Falls, New York. Advocates for clemency later attempted to have a large monument to her memory placed

Mariticide Club

at the cemetery. The Augustinian fathers who managed the site refused to allow it, citing a family request that no memorial mark Rogers' grave.

Maria Romberg

Maria Romberg (1697 – 14 April 1725) was a Swedish convicted murderer, the central person in a murder story well known in her time. She was convicted along with her three accomplices, among them her lover, for the death of her husband. In 1716, at the age of 19, Maria Romberg was arranged to marry merchant Anders Broberg, 27 years her senior, in Borås, against her will. Broberg was said to abuse Maria; he was called brutal and Maria's stepfather accused him of alcoholism. In 1719, Maria started a relationship with her childhood friend, Haqvin Wijndruf, a member of one of the most wealthy and influential families in Borås. The relationship was well known in the city, and many people acted as messengers for their letters. In 1722, her husband called upon two vicars to lecture her. After this, Maria and Haqvin made two attempts to poison Broberg, but failed. Maria then hired a cunning woman called Romans Ingeborg, who was reputed to be able to perform magic, and who assured her that she had performed many murders for hire in the past. The three accomplices then made plans. On one occasion, they tried to strangle him, but failed. In 1724, they informed the maid Karin Andersdotter of their plans: Broberg had abused her, and she wanted revenge. On 28 December 1724, Maria was again lectured by the vicars, and the same night, Maria, Haqvin, Ingeborg and Karin planned the murder. The three women went to Broberg's bedroom, where he was asleep, and Ingeborg hit him in the head until he died. They then placed his body to look as if he had tripped and hit his head. When the corpse was examined, he was thought to have been murdered, and so Maria and her three accomplices were accused of murder. Karin was the first to confess. When Maria heard this, she also confessed, and told Haqvin to do the same. Haqvin denied everything, claimed that she had several lovers beside him, and tried to escape, but was arrested and forced to confess. On 23 February, Maria, Haqvin, Ingeborg, and Karin were found guilty and sentenced to death. They were all decapitated, with some

Wives Who Kill

variations. Maria was decapitated and burned, Haqvin was decapitated and had his head nailed to a pole, Ingeborg had her hand cut off, and was then decapitated and burned. Karin was simply decapitated, and buried. The sentence was carried out 14 April 1725. The affair ended influence of the Wijndruf family in the city. Haqvin's brother Andreas was ordained a priest four days later and emigrated to North America in the summer of 1725.

Kristin Margrethe Rossum

Kristin Margrethe Rossum (born October 25, 1976) is an American former toxicologist who was convicted of the murder of her husband Gregory T. de Villers, who died from a lethal dose of fentanyl on November 6, 2000. Rossum is serving a life sentence at the Central California Women's Facility in Chowchilla. Kristin Rossum was born in Memphis, Tennessee. She grew up in Claremont, California, the oldest child of Ralph and Constance Rossum. Her father is a professor and her mother worked at Azusa Pacific University. She has two brothers. In 1991, after her father accepted the position of President of Hampden–Sydney College, the family moved to Virginia and Kristin enrolled at the allgirls St. Catherine's School in Richmond. There, Rossum began drinking beer and smoking cigarettes. She also tried marijuana, but said it had little effect. Starting in 1992, she began using methamphetamine.

In 1994, Rossum moved back to California and enrolled part-time at the University of Redlands and moved into a dormitory on campus, but eventually left following a relapse. After overcoming her addiction and beginning her relationship with Greg de Villers, Rossum enrolled at San Diego State University and graduated with honors in 1998. After graduating, she worked as a toxicologist at the County medical examiner's office. Rossum and de Villers married in 1999. The following year, she began an extramarital affair with her boss, Dr. Michael Robertson. In late 2000, de Villers had learned about both the affair and her resumption of her meth habit, threatening to expose both to the medical examiner if she did not quit her job. Robertson, who also knew Rossum had relapsed, learned of this threat prior to the death of de Villers. On November 6, 2000, just

Mariticide Club

after 9:15 p.m., Rossum dialed 9-1-1 and reported that de Villers had committed suicide. Paramedics found him lying unresponsive on the couple's bed, which was sprinkled with red rose petals; he was pronounced dead on arrival at the hospital. Rossum told authorities he had committed suicide. Despite her claims, de Villers's family – particularly his brother, Jerome – were adamant that he was not suicidal. However, San Diego police were initially reluctant to open an investigation. One month after de Villers' death, Rossum and Robertson were both fired from the medical examiner's office – Rossum for hiding her meth habit, and Robertson for enabling her meth habit, as well as for fraternization with a subordinate. Due to potential conflicts of interest, the San Diego medical examiner outsourced de Villers' autopsy to an outside lab in Los Angeles. The tests showed de Villers had seven times the lethal dose of fentanyl in his system. Under questioning, Rossum told detectives that her husband had been depressed before he died, while her father stated that he seemed to be deeply distressed and that he drank heavily on the night he died. As the investigation continued, police learned about Rossum's relapse, and about a phone call she made to de Villers's employer telling them he would not be coming in to work the day of his murder. On June 25, 2001, seven months after de Villers' death, Rossum was arrested and charged with murder. On January 4, 2002, her parents posted her $1.25 million bail.

At trial, the prosecution contended that Rossum murdered her husband to keep him from telling her bosses about both her affair and her use of meth stolen from the drug lab. Defense attorneys argued that de Villers was suicidal and poisoned himself. Rossum's brother-in-law, Jerome de Villers, testified that it was difficult to believe his brother had committed suicide because he hated drugs. Rossum's account of the day of death was that she went to work in the morning, then returned in the early afternoon to check on her husband and serve him a bowl of soup. She returned to work, then came home around 7 P.M. where she said she showered and shaved her legs. Upon drying herself, she went to the bedroom where she found her husband not breathing, and called 911. The 9-1-1 tape played in court appeared to indicate Rossum was administering CPR to her husband. The

Wives Who Kill

prosecution had presented a store card receipt from Vons where it was shown she had acquired a single red rose. Crumpled rose petals were found on de Villers' corpse akin to the film American Beauty. The defense claimed de Villers' had put the petals on himself for his final action out of suicidal grief, which was refuted by the prosecution who argued that a man of de Villers build having overdosed on fentanyl would lack the energy to accomplish this. The clinching evidence was the credit card receipt, having been timestamped 12:42 P.M., the same time Rossum having claimed to be at home nursing her husband. On November 12, 2002, Rossum was found guilty of first degree murder. On December 12, she was sentenced to life in prison without the possibility for parole, and a $10,000 fine. She was transferred to the Central California Women's Facility in Chowchilla, the largest women's correctional facility in the U.S.

Recent events

In 2006, both Rossum and San Diego County were named as defendants in a wrongful death lawsuit filed by de Villers' family. A jury ordered Rossum to pay more than $100 million in punitive damages, while San Diego County was ordered to pay $1.5 million. The family had originally asked for $50 million in punitive damages, but jurors awarded double that amount after estimating Rossum could have made $60 million from selling the rights to her story. John Gomez, the lawyer for the de Villers family, acknowledged that the family may never see the money, but wanted to make sure Rossum does not profit from her crime. A judge later reduced the punitive damages award to $10 million, but allowed the $4.5 million compensatory award to stand. In September 2010, a three-judge panel of the 9th U.S. Circuit Court of Appeals ruled that Rossum's lawyers should have challenged the prosecution's assertion, by doing its own tests, that she poisoned her husband with fentanyl. The panel ordered a San Diego federal court to hold a hearing into whether the defense's error could have affected the trial's outcome. On September 13, 2011, the U.S. Court of Appeals withdrew its opinion and replaced it with a one-paragraph statement that under a new Court precedent, Rossum's petition was denied. Following his termination by the San Diego medical examiner's office, Robertson

Mariticide Club

returned to his home in Brisbane, Queensland, Australia, ostensibly to care for his ailing mother. In September 2013, the *San Diego Reader* reported that, in 2006, prosecutors secretly filed a criminal complaint charging Robertson – who was named as an unindicted co-conspirator at Rossum's trial – with one count of conspiracy to obstruct justice. If the Australian government elects to extradite Robertson or he voluntarily returns to the US, he could face up to three years in prison. As of 2014, Robertson is running a forensic consulting service in Brisbane. Rossum was featured in true crime documentary Oxygen's true crime series *Snapped*, truTV's *The Investigators*, and Investigation Discovery's *Deadly Women*. Her story was also featured on newsmagazines such as CBS's *48 Hours*.Caitlin Rother, who was interviewed for each episode, wrote *Poisoned Love*, a book about the case: ISBN 0-7860-1714-7. Another book about Rossum was *Deadly American Beauty* by John Glatt: ISBN 0-312-98419-7.

Margaret Rudin (*née* Margaret Lee Frost)

Margaret Rudin (born Margaret Lee Frost; May 31, 1943) is an American woman convicted of the December 1994 murder of her husband, Vegas real estate magnate Ronald Rudin. She was incarcerated at Florence McClure Women's Correctional Center in North Las Vegas, Nevada. In May 2022, Rudin's conviction was vacated. Rudin was born in Memphis, Tennessee, one of three daughters. The family moved frequently, and before graduating from high school, Rudin had lived in 15 states. Rudin had married four times before meeting Ronald Rudin at the First Church of Religious Science in Las Vegas. The couple wed on September 11, 1987. Ronald Rudin (born November 13, 1930, Chicago) disappeared on December 18, 1994, aged 64, after walking to Margaret's antique shop which was in the same strip mall as his real estate office. On January 21, 1995, his charred dismembered remains were discovered near Lake Mojave along with the burnt remains of an antique steamer trunk. He had been shot in the head at least four times with a .22 caliber gun. Police later searched the Rudin residence and found blood spatter in the bedroom as well as semen on the floor that had been removed from the house by

Wives Who Kill

authorities to test. On July 21, 1996, a .22 caliber Ruger handgun was found in Lake Mead and was traced back to Ron Rudin. The handgun was later confirmed to be the murder weapon. Ron Rudin had reported the gun missing in 1988, shortly after he married Margaret. On April 18, 1997, the grand jury handed down a murder indictment against Margaret Rudin, but by this time, she had left the state. She spent the next 31 months in hiding until she was arrested in Massachusetts in November 1999 and was extradited to Nevada to face murder charges in the death of her husband. Margaret Rudin went on trial on March 2, 2001. Her defense claimed that her husband was killed due to illegal activities he was involved in. The prosecutor argued she had killed her husband to prevent him from divorcing her and losing what she would inherit from his estate. She was found guilty on May 2, 2001, and on August 31 she was sentenced to life in prison with the possibility of parole after 20 years. In 2002, the Nevada Supreme Court denied Margaret Rudin's appeal, finding she was not denied effective assistance of counsel. As of 2008, no record of federal collateral review could be found. In 2008, Rudin was given a new trial. Clark County District Judge Sally Loehrer ruled that lawyers for Margaret Rudin, then 65 years old, were not prepared to defend her at her 2001 trial, according to lawyers on both sides of the case. She also ruled that Michael Amador, Rudin's lead attorney at the time, was not effective, according to Christopher Oram, Rudin's new attorney. On May 10, 2010, the Nevada Supreme Court ruled that Rudin would not get another trial, as reported by KLTV-8 News. The lower appeals court's ruling was overturned, and the original conviction stood. The *Las Vegas Sun* reported on April 26, 2011 that Margaret Rudin had filed a habeas corpus petition in federal court seeking a new trial and reversal of her conviction based on ineffective assistance of trial counsel, impermissible hearsay testimony, faulty jury instructions and other points. On January 25, 2012, U.S. District Court Judge Roger L. Hunt dismissed Margaret Rudin's federal habeas corpus case with prejudice. In a nine-page decision, Judge Hunt found that Rudin's federal petition was not filed in a timely manner. The ruling paves way for an appeal to the Ninth Circuit Court in San Francisco. On September 10,

Mariticide Club

2014, in a split decision by a three-judge panel, the United States Court of Appeals for the Ninth Circuit affirmed the district court's order dismissing Rudin's federal habeas corpus case despite what it acknowledged to be serious issues with her representation and prosecution, both pre- and post-conviction. The court deemed that it was compelled to deny her petition, and it acknowledged that it was "troubled" by the case. Excerpts from the Opinion's Conclusion: *We are troubled by the outcome of this case for many reasons. Margaret Rudin's direct appeal and collateral review proceedings have been pending in either state or federal court for a combined total of 13 years. She has potentially meritorious claims that she has suffered prejudice at the hands of her own attorneys' egregious misconduct. Yet she has never had an opportunity to present those claims in court.* Rudin's defense counsel, Amador, indisputably engaged in egregious professional misconduct during the course of her underlying criminal trial. On direct appeal of her judgment of conviction, the Nevada Supreme Court acknowledged that Rudin's trial was plagued not only with inadequacies on the part of defense counsel, but also with prosecutorial misconduct and legal error on the part of the State and the court. Although two members of the Nevada Supreme Court found the record sufficiently clear as to the *"inherent prejudice created by [trial counsel]"* to require immediate reversal of Rudin's judgment of conviction, a majority of the court declined to address the effect of those errors, finding them more appropriate for resolution on collateral review. At this point, Rudin is still in prison, having served 13 years of her life sentence for murder. We know from the state post-conviction court that the State's "proof of guilt [at that trial] was not a slam dunk by any stretch of the imagination." We also know from the post-conviction court that, had Rudin been represented by competent counsel, the jury's verdict may have been different. Thus, what we do not know is whether Rudin is lawfully imprisoned. And, regrettably, that is something we may never know. On March 10, 2015, the Ninth Circuit Court of Appeals withdrew its opinion of September 10, 2014 and issued a revised opinion affirming the trial court's decision that Rudin was

Wives Who Kill

entitled to a new trial as a direct result of the professional misconduct and prejudicial conflict of interest by Michael Amador, her original trial lawyer. On February 29, 2016, the United States Supreme Court denied a petition by the attorney general of Nevada challenging the Ninth Circuit's ruling. In May 2022, United States District Judge Richard F. Boulware vacated the murder conviction of the 78-year-old Rudin after she had spent 20 years in prison. Boulware ruled that Rudin received ineffective legal representation from her late defense attorney. Margaret Rudin was released on parole from the Florence McClure Women's Correctional Center on January 10, 2020. She told the *Las Vegas Review-Journal* that she intended to relocate to Chicago to be closer to her daughter, granddaughter and great-grandchildren, and that she was "optimistic her murder conviction will one day be tossed." She was 76 years old at release. After her conviction was vacated in 2022, the possibility was left open that she could still be re-tried for her husband's murder. She's available for It's Just Lunch.

Esneda Ruiz Cataño

Esneda Ruiz Cataño (born 1968), known as The Predator and The Black Widow, is a Colombian serial killer. She collected millions of financial proceeds through life insurances of her husbands. Cataño could have received about 150,000,000 pesos. She was arrested in the municipality of Ebéjico and is serving her sentence in a prison for women. Esneda Ruiz Cataño was born in Dabeiba, in the Antioquia Department. According to the investigating Colombian authorities, the murders occurred between 2001 and 2010, all against her husbands, with Cataño acquiring their life insurance after. The first victim was identified as Juan Pablo Aristizábal Gutiérrez, who was killed on June 16, 2001 in a village called El Tablazo, in the municipality of Rionegro, dating on Father's Day. Cataño was investigated for the murder, but was released, so she returned to Medellín to get the insurance. The second person killed was José Valencia Guzmán, which occurred in 2006 in the commune of Aranjuez, on Valentine's Day. He was killed near a pool, after Cataño stabbed him in the neck. The authorities again conducted an investigation, but nobody was

Mariticide Club

arrested. The third and last victim was Miguel Ángel Beleño Mejía, who died in 2010 of a stab in the neck, acquiring a life insurance of 80 million pesos. Cataño was issued an arrest warrant for the three murders. The police sought her for 2 years, when she was finally detained in Ebéjico, where she lived. She was tried and convicted for aggravated homicide. She is currently being held in El Pedregal Prison in Medellín.

Jacqueline Sauvage

Jacqueline Sauvage (27 December 1947 — 23 July 2020) of Montargis, France, killed her husband Norbert Marot by shooting him in the back three times with a hunting rifle on 10 September 2012. This occurred the day after Sauvage's son committed suicide. Sauvage stated that Mr. Marot had physically and sexually abused his wife, daughters and possibly his son. A criminal case was then filed against Mrs. Sauvage, that resulted in her being condemned to ten years in jail by a cour d'assises. She then filed an appeal motion, but the verdict remained unchanged, pronounced on 3 December 2015. On 31 January 2016, the French president François Hollande announced his giving a partial presidential pardon to Mrs. Sauvage. This resulted in a reduction of her jail time of two years and nine months. On 28 December 2016, M. Hollande pronounced a full pardon, announced both on his personal Twitter account and by a release made by the Elysée. This decision led to immediate release from the detention center of Réau. Jacqueline Sauvage was convicted by two different Cours d'assises, in accordance with the French judicial system. Because of this, only a motion presented to the Court of Cassation was possible. However, this court does not re-examine the facts of the case, it merely examines the application of the law within the context of the case. Therefore, the verdict itself could not be questioned, but the sentence could be altered, with a presidential pardon being the only avenue to a full verdict nullification. A demand for a presidential pardon was then filed by the daughters of Mrs. Sauvage, who publicly expressed relief at their father's death. President Hollande was known to be reluctant to use the presidential pardon, and had granted a pardon only once since his election in 2012. Nevertheless, he

Wives Who Kill

agreed to a meeting with Mrs. Sauvage's daughters and lawyers at the Élysée Palace in January 2016. This case was the main topic covered by the French media after the Sauvage sisters' demand was presented to M. Hollande. The media coverage was as diverse as it was intense. Since the end of 2015, feminist associations' websites, traditional media and public channels, and French social media coverage was entirely focused on the case. A petition launched on the website Change.org to ask the French president to grant a pardon to Mrs. Sauvage garnered 435,971 signatures. On 26 February 2017, a French TV show named "Sept à Huit" received extremely high ratings with five million viewers, due to a segment profiling Jacqueline Sauvage. The political establishment took a stand for Mrs. Sauvage to create a support committee, including Anne Hidalgo and Jean-Luc Mélenchon. After the presidential pardon was pronounced, a major debate was launched by lawyers and specialists of criminal law on whether the State of law had been respected. Their stance was that the media had overruled two successive court decisions by influencing the public, who then pushed for the presidential pardon. From the woman, guilty of murder to the wife, victim of abuses After the Cour d'assises of first instance found Jacqueline Sauvage guilty of murder, French feminist associations such as Osez le Féminisme released information on Mrs. Sauvage's past. These articles depicted a woman, trapped in an abusive relationship for 47 years, beaten, raped and whose three daughters were also raped. This information was meant to defend the thesis of Mrs. Sauvage being a victim of domestic and sexual abuse, who acted to defend herself, instead of a cold-hearted murderer. This group also called for the definition of self-defense to be modified, as to include "female victims of violence". In addition, other outlets reported failure by authorities to help the Sauvage family. When Jacqueline Sauvage tried to kill herself, the doctor did not ask why. When one of her daughters reported being raped by her father to police, the officer called the alleged perpetrator. It was also noted that an average of 223,000 women a year in France are abused by their husbands, and that 134 (on average) are killed by them. There was controversy on the royal power of the pardon: Régis de Castelnau, lawyer and author of the blog Vu du

Mariticide Club

Droit (In Terms of Law) mentioned a "cult of the innocent guilty" created by the public opinion through the media, with only partial information given about the case. For him, public opinion was mobilized based on a story radically different from the one constituted by a regular and contradictory procedure. He considered the presidential pardon granted to Mrs. Sauvage as an insult made to the independence of the judiciary, to the legal profession and to the Republic. This was backed-up by the lawyer Florence Rault, who denounced the media treatment on this case, first on her blog and later published by the Figarovox, saying there was a will to "promote a victimizing feminism and to affirm the impossibility of the existence of female violence". These opinions were a minority voice and do not incorporate the complexity of the case, as established by the judicial system itself. In an article published by Le Figaro, the philosopher Robert Redeker also contested the pardon, which he considered to be "an insult to democracy motivated by a victimizing ideology". Another philosopher, Michel Onfray, questioned the relevance of the pardon, undermining multiple court decisions and potentially opening the way to self-defense and personal vendettas. For Marie-Jane Ody, Secretary General of the Union Syndicale of Magistrates, the whole work done during the trial is being denied by the executive power which rules only according to a support committee. She asked for the removal of the presidential pardon, "survival of the royal power", considered incompatible with democracy and the idea of a fair and independent justice.

Nancy Ann Seaman (née D'Onofrio)

Nancy Ann Seaman (née D'Onofrio; born May 13, 1952) is an American woman and former teacher at Longacre Elementary School in Farmington Hills, Michigan, who was convicted of first-degree murder in 2005 for killing her husband with a hatchet. Jurors rejected her argument that she killed her husband in self-defense and decided that the murder was premeditated. She is currently serving her life sentence at the Women's Huron Valley Correctional Facility. Nancy Ann D'Onofrio was born on May 13, 1952, in Lincoln Park, Michigan, to Lenore and Eugene D'Onofrio.

Wives Who Kill

She was the valedictorian of her high school class. She met her husband Bob Seaman in 1972 and they married a year later. Bob worked at Ford Motor Company while Nancy stayed home. In 1979, Nancy and Bob welcomed their first son Jeff, followed by another son Greg in 1981. In 1995, she began working as an elementary schoolteacher. Shortly into the couple's marriage, Nancy cites her first incident of spousal abuse, where her drunken husband attempted to push her out of a moving car. She later claimed that other incidents of physical abuse occurred in her marriage sporadically, but intensified after her husband lost his job at Borg Warner Automotive. She stated that "Bob would shove. That's what he liked to do, shove and push against walls. Most of my bruisings were either that he would grab me by an article of clothing or an arm. He would squeeze my arm and push me against the wall. Sometimes I'd get knocked down." Nancy's younger son Greg stated that he saw his father both physically and mentally abuse his mother; however, her older son Jeff denies that any abuse ever occurred. By 2004, Nancy and Bob Seaman were planning to divorce. The couple were living on different floors of their home. In February, Nancy was planning to move out of the couple's home and into a condo, which she told her husband was for their younger son, Greg. Nancy claimed that on the morning of Monday, May 10, 2004, after Bob had been away for the weekend, an argument ensued over Nancy moving out. She claimed that her husband was holding a kitchen knife, became enraged, and started chasing her into their garage. According to physical evidence, Nancy grabbed a hatchet in the garage and struck her husband with it at least 20 times. Following the murder, Nancy went into school that day after she failed to find a substitute teacher. Nancy Seaman was arrested by police on the Wednesday following the murder. A relative of Bob's informed police that Bob was missing, and when police went to question Nancy, they found Bob's body wrapped in a tarp with duct tape in the back of her Ford Explorer. Police also found the knife that was used to stab Bob to death inside the tarp. Despite Nancy's claims of self-defense, police had a different version of events. Instead of Bob attacking Nancy, police alleged it was the other way around, claiming that Nancy ambushed her

Mariticide Club

husband in their kitchen with the axe, then dragged his body into the garage where she stabbed him with a knife and beat him with a sledgehammer. The police had evidence to support their claims, too. Just a day before the killing, video surveillance captured Nancy purchasing the hatchet at the Home Depot, which she said was used to cut down a stump in their front yard. The following day, Nancy returned to Home Depot, where she purchased duct tape, the tarp, bleach, and other cleaning products. A third trip to Home Depot revealed that Nancy shoplifted a hatchet, and then attempted to return it with the receipt she received after purchasing the first hatchet. On the Friday following the murder, Nancy was formally charged with first-degree murder; she pleaded not guilty to the charge. Six months after the murder on November 29, 2004, Nancy Seaman's murder trial began. She had spent the last six months in the Oakland County Jail. While Nancy claimed that she had killed her husband in selfdefense, prosecutor Lisa Ortleib-Gorcyca alleged that Nancy killed her husband out of rage, stating how Nancy was angry that although she planned to leave her husband, Bob was about to leave her first. Ortleib-Gorcyca also stated how Nancy believed that her husband was having an affair with another woman, although this wasn't the case. She alleged that after a marital fight, Nancy went straight to Home Depot where she purchased the hatchet she would use to kill her husband. Despite the prosecutor's statements, Nancy persisted in her arguments of self-defense. She testified in her own defense on December 7, 2004, saying that she and Bob got into "the grand finale of all fights" on May 10 because she planned to leave. Nancy went on to describe the violent struggle that ended in Bob's death. In the end however, Nancy was convicted of first-degree, premeditated murder, which in Michigan carries an automatic life sentence. Following this conviction, trial judge John McDonald reduced this conviction to second-degree murder, citing a lack of evidence to support a first-degree murder conviction. This decision was later overturned by the Michigan Court of Appeals back to first degree murder. She is serving her sentence in Women's Huron Valley Complex.

Wives Who Kill

After Nancy Seaman's appeals in state court were exhausted, she petitioned for a new trial in federal court. On November 4, 2010, her conviction was overturned by United States federal judge Bernard A. Friedman on the basis that her defense attorneys were not fully able to develop their theory of battered woman syndrome. A new trial was ordered, until January 19, 2011, when another federal judge ordered a stay of proceedings in her appeal. However, on November 25, 2012, it was announced that a threejudge panel for the Sixth Circuit of the United States Court of Appeals denied Nancy's motion for a new trial, citing that: "Battered spouse syndrome (Battered person syndrome) is not itself a defense under Michigan law."

Alice Bradley Sheldon
(née Alice Hastings Bradley) (pen name Raccoona Sheldon)

Mariticide Club

Alice B. Sheldon

James Tiptree Jr.

Raccoona Sheldon

Alice Bradley Sheldon (born Alice Hastings Bradley; August 24, 1915 – May 19, 1987) was an American science and fantasy author better known as James Tiptree Jr., a pen name she used from 1967 until her death. It was not publicly known until 1977 that James Tiptree Jr. was a woman. From 1974 to 1985 she also used the pen name Raccoona Sheldon. Tiptree was inducted into the Science Fiction Hall of Fame in 2012. Tiptree's debut story collection, Ten Thousand Light-Years from Home, was published in 1973 and her first novel, Up the Walls of the World, was published in 1978. Her other works include the 1973 novelette "The Women Men Don't See", the 1974 novella "The Girl Who Was Plugged In", the 1976 novella "Houston, Houston, Do You Read?", the 1985 novel Brightness Falls from the Air, and the 1990 short story "Her Smoke Rose Up Forever". Alice Hastings Bradley came from a family in the intellectual enclave of Hyde Park, a university neighborhood in Chicago. Her father was Herbert Edwin Bradley, a lawyer and naturalist, and her mother was Mary Hastings Bradley, a prolific writer of fiction and travel books. From an early age she traveled with her parents, and in 1921–22, the family made their first trip to central Africa. During these trips, she played the role of the "perfect daughter, willing to be carried across Africa like a parcel, always neatly dressed and well behaved, a credit to her mother." This later contributed to her short story, "The Women Men Don't See."

Wives Who Kill

Alice Sheldon with the Kikuyu people, 1920s

Between trips to Africa, Bradley attended school in Chicago. At the age of ten, she went to the University of Chicago Laboratory Schools, which was an experimental teaching workshop with small classes and loose structure. When fourteen, she attended finishing school in Lausanne in Switzerland, before returning to attend boarding school in Tarrytown in New York. Bradley was encouraged by her mother to seek a career, but her mother also hoped that she would get married and settle down. In 1934, at age 19, she met William (Bill) Davey and eloped to marry him. She dropped out of Sarah Lawrence College, which did not allow married students to attend. They moved to Berkeley, California, where they took classes and Davey encouraged her to pursue art. The marriage was not a success; he was an alcoholic and irresponsible with money and she disliked keeping house. The couple divorced in 1940. Later on, she became a graphic artist, a painter, and—still under the name "Alice Bradley Davey"—an art critic for the Chicago Sun between 1941 and 1942. After the divorce, Bradley joined the Women's Army Auxiliary Corps where she became a supply officer. In 1942 she joined the United States Army Air Forces and worked in the Army Air Forces photo-intelligence group. She later was promoted to major, a high rank for women at the time. In the army, she "felt she was among free women for the first time." As an intelligence officer, she became an expert in reading aerial intelligence photographs. In 1945, at the

Mariticide Club

close of the war, while she was on assignment in Paris, she married her second husband, Huntington D. Sheldon, known as "Ting." She was discharged from the military in 1946, at which time she set up a small business in partnership with her husband. The same year her first story ("The Lucky Ones") was published in the November 16, 1946 issue of The New Yorker, and credited to "Alice Bradley" in the magazine. In 1952 she and her husband were invited to join the CIA, which she accepted. At the CIA, she worked as an intelligence officer, but she did not enjoy the work. She resigned her position in 1955 and returned to college. She studied for her bachelor of arts degree at American University (1957–1959). She received a doctorate from George Washington University in Experimental Psychology in 1967. She wrote her doctoral dissertation on the responses of animals to novel stimuli in differing environments. During this time, she wrote and submitted a few science fiction stories under the name James Tiptree Jr., in order to protect her academic reputation. Bradley began illustrating when she was nine years old, contributing to her mother's book, Alice in Elephant Land, a children's book about the family's second trip to Africa, appearing in it as herself. She later had an exhibit of her drawings of Africa at the Chicago Gallery, arranged by her parents. Although she illustrated several of her mother's books, she only sold one illustration during her lifetime, in 1931, to The New Yorker, with help from Harold Ober, a New York agent who worked with her mother. The illustration, of a horse rearing and throwing off its rider, sold for ten dollars. In 1936, Bradley participated in a group show at the Art Institute of Chicago, to which she had connections through her family, featuring new American work. This was an important step forward for her painting career. During this time, she also took private art lessons from John Sloan. Sheldon disliked prudery in painting. While examining an anatomy book for an art class, she noticed that the genitals were blurred, so she restored the genitals of the figures with a pencil. In 1939, her nude self-portrait titled Portrait in the Country was accepted for the "All-American" biennial show at the Corcoran Gallery in Washington D.C., where it was displayed for six weeks. While these two shows were

Wives Who Kill

considered big breaks, she disparaged these accomplishments, saying that "only second-rate painters sold" and she preferred to keep her works at home. By 1940, Bradley felt she had mastered all the techniques she needed and was ready to choose her subject matter. However, she began to doubt whether she should paint. She kept working at her painting techniques, fascinated with the questions of form, and read books on aesthetics in order to know what scientifically made a painting "good." She stopped painting in 1941. As she was in need of a way to support herself, her parents helped her find a job as an art critic for the Chicago Sun. Bradley discovered science fiction in 1924, when she read her first issue of Weird Tales, but she wouldn't write any herself until years later. Unsure what to do with her new degrees and her new/old careers, she began to write science fiction. She adopted the pseudonym of James Tiptree Jr. in 1967. The name "Tiptree" came from a branded jar of marmalade, and the "Jr." was her husband's idea. In an interview, she said: "A male name seemed like good camouflage. I had the feeling that a man would slip by less observed. I've had too many experiences in my life of being the first woman in some damned occupation." She also made the choice to start writing science fiction she, herself, was interested in and "was surprised to find that her stories were immediately accepted for publication and quickly became popular."

Her first published short story was "Birth of a Salesman" in the March 1968 issue of Analog Science Fact & Fiction, edited by John W. Campbell. Three more followed that year in If and Fantastic. Other pen names that she used included "Alice Hastings Bradley", "Major Alice Davey", "Alli B. Sheldon", "Dr. Alice B. Sheldon", and "Raccoona Sheldon". Writing under the pseudonym Raccoona, she was not very successful getting published until her other alter ego, Tiptree, wrote to publishers to intervene. The pseudonym was successfully maintained until late 1977, partly because, although "Tiptree" was widely known to be a pseudonym, it was generally understood that its use was intended to protect the professional reputation of an intelligence community official. Readers, editors and correspondents were permitted to assume gender, and generally, but not invariably, they

Mariticide Club

assumed "male". There was speculation, based partially on the themes in her stories, that Tiptree might be female. In 1975, in the introduction to Warm Worlds and Otherwise, a collection of Tiptree's short stories, Robert Silverberg wrote: "It has been suggested that Tiptree is female, a theory that I find absurd, for there is to me something ineluctably masculine about Tiptree's writing. "Silverberg likened Tiptree's writing to Ernest Hemingway's, arguing there was a "prevailing masculinity about both of them—that preoccupation with questions of courage, with absolute values, with the mysteries and passions of life and death as revealed by extreme physical tests, by pain and suffering and loss." Tiptree's work is proof of what she said, that men and women can and do speak both to and for one another, if they have bothered to learn how. —Ursula K. Le Guin, Khatru "Tiptree" never made any public appearances, but she did correspond regularly with fans and other science fiction authors through the mail. When asked for biographical details, Tiptree/Sheldon was forthcoming in everything but her gender. According to her biographer, Julie Phillips, "No one had ever seen or spoken to the owner of this voice. He wrote letters, warm, frank, funny letters, to other writers, editors, and science fiction fans". In her letters to fellow writers such as Ursula K. Le Guin and Joanna Russ, she would present herself as a feminist man; however, Sheldon did not present herself as male in person. Writing was a way to escape a male-dominated society, themes Tiptree explored in the short stories later collected in Her Smoke Rose Up Forever. One story in particular offers an excellent illustration of these themes. "Houston, Houston, Do You Read?" follows a group of astronauts who discover a future Earth whose male population has been wiped out; the remaining females have learned to get along just fine in their absence.

In 1976, "Tiptree" mentioned in a letter that "his" mother, also a writer, had died in Chicago—details that led inquiring fans to find the obituary, with its reference to Alice Sheldon; soon all was revealed. Once the initial shock was over, Sheldon wrote to Le Guin, one of her closest friends, confessing her identity. She wrote, "I never wrote you anything but the exact truth, there was no calculation or intent to deceive, other than the signature which

Wives Who Kill

over 8 years became just another nickname; everything else is just plain me. The thing is, I am a 61-year-old woman named Alice Sheldon—nickname Alli—solitary by nature but married for 37 years to a very nice man considerably older [Huntington was 12 years her senior], who doesn't read my stuff but is glad I like writing". After Sheldon's identity was revealed, several prominent science fiction writers suffered some embarrassment. Robert Silverberg, who had argued that Tiptree could not be a woman from the evidence of her stories, added a postscript to his introduction to the second edition of Tiptree's Warm Worlds and Otherwise, published in 1979. Harlan Ellison had introduced Tiptree's story in the anthology Again, Dangerous Visions with the opinion that "[Kate] Wilhelm is the woman to beat this year, but Tiptree is the man". Only then did she complete her first full-length novel, Up the Walls of the World, a Doubleday Science Fiction Book Club selection. Before that she had worked on and built a reputation only in the field of short stories. "Tip" was a crucial part of modern SF's maturing process. "He"… wrote powerful fiction challenging readers' assumptions about everything, especially sex and gender. —Suzy McKee Charnas, The Women's Review of Books A constant theme in Sheldon's work is gender; she was influenced by the rise of Second-wave feminism. A strong example is "The Women Men Don't See" (1973), where Sheldon, as in most of her stories, devises a convincing male point of view. We see the two women in the story (Ruth Parsons and her daughter) through the eyes of Don Fenton, who assesses them critically as possible sexual partners and is also concerned to protect them. He is confused when Ruth shows courage and common sense, failing to "fulfill stereotypical female roles," according to Anne Cranny-Francis. Ruth tries to explain the alienation of women in general and herself in particular, but to Fenton it seems nonsense. The Parsons' decision to leave Earth on an alien spaceship jars him into, if not understanding, at least remembering Ruth's words. The title of the short story itself reflects the idea that women are invisible during Sheldon's time. As Cranny-Francis states, "'The Women Men Don't See' is an outstanding example … of the subversive use of genre fiction to produce an unconventional discursive

Mariticide Club

position, the feminist subject." Sheldon continued writing under the Tiptree pen name for another decade. In the last years of her life, she suffered from depression and heart trouble, while her husband began to lose his eyesight, becoming almost completely blind in 1986. In 1976, then 61-year-old Sheldon wrote Silverberg expressing her desire to end her own life while she was still able-bodied and active; she said that she was reluctant to act upon this intention, as she did not want to leave her husband behind and could not bring herself to kill him. Later, she suggested to her husband that they make a suicide pact when their health began to fail. On July 21, 1977, she wrote in her diary: "Ting agreed to consider suicide in 4–5 years." Ten years later, on May 19, 1987, Sheldon shot her husband and then herself; she telephoned her attorney after the first shooting to announce her actions. They were dead, hand-in-hand in bed, in their Virginia home. According to biographer Julie Phillips, the suicide note Sheldon left was written in September 1979 and saved until needed. Although the circumstances surrounding the Sheldons' deaths are not clear enough to rule out murder–suicide, testimony of those closest to them implies a suicide pact. In her personal life, Bradley had a complex sexual orientation, and she described her sexuality in different terms over many years. For example, she explained it at one point: "I like some men a lot, but from the start, before I knew anything, it was always girls and women who lit me up."

The James Tiptree Jr. Award, honoring works of science fiction or fantasy that expand or explore our understanding of gender, was named in her honor. The award-winning science fiction authors Karen Joy Fowler and Pat Murphy created the award in February 1991. Works of fiction such as Half Life by Shelley Jackson and Light by M. John Harrison have received the award. Due to controversy over the circumstances of her and her husband's deaths, the name of the award was changed to the Otherwise Award in 2019.

Melissa Ann Shepard (née Russell)

Wives Who Kill

Melissa Ann Shepard (née Russell; born May 16, 1935), aka Melissa Ann Weeks, Melissa Ann Friedrich, Melissa Ann Shephard and Melissa Ann Stewart, sometimes given the sobriquet of Internet Black Widow, is a Canadian murderer and habitual offender. Friedrich has been convicted of manslaughter in the death of one of her husbands, convicted of poisoning another, and convicted of numerous fraud offenses. According to The Washington Post, Shepard's first husband, Russell Shepard, was her only husband not to "become [a victim] of a methodical, practiced ruse". This marriage ended in divorce. From 1977 to 1991, she served prison sentences for more than 30 convictions of fraud. In 1992, Shepard was convicted of manslaughter of Gordon Stewart, her 44-year-old second husband, after running him over twice with a car in 1991. He had tranquilizers in his system at the time. She told police that he had raped her and that she ran him over while trying to escape. She was sentenced to six years in prison but was released early on good behavior, serving just two years. Following her release, she toured the country, giving speeches on battered woman syndrome and killing in self-defense. She received a government grant to help others. During her tenure as a speaker, she sued journalist Barb McKenna of the Canadian newspaper The Guardian for writing an article in which she doubted Shepard's claims. In 2000, Shepard married American Robert Friedrich, her third husband, shortly after meeting him online through a Christian dating site. He died 14 months later, leaving her with tens of thousands of dollars in assets. His sons made a criminal complaint against her, alleging that she caused his death by overdosing him with prescription medicine. She was never charged with a crime related to his death, but his sons later won back $15,000. In 2005, she settled with a man that she met online in Pinellas Park, Florida. The man's son alerted police after his father was hospitalized a half-dozen times and he noticed unusual activity in his bank account. Hospital tests showed the man tested positive for tranquilizers but police could not prove she

Mariticide Club

poisoned him; they instead charged her with grand theft, forgery and using a forged document, to which she pleaded guilty. She was sentenced to five years in prison. In 2012, she was charged with attempted murder of Fred Weeks, her fourth husband, and after pleading guilty to lesser charges, she was sentenced to three and a half years in prison. Police found a substantial drugs stockpile (primarily lorazepam and temazepam) together with prescriptions from five different doctors and several sets of identity documents in different names among her possessions. Chief Justice Joseph Phillip Kennedy, sentencing, said: "People who have contact with this lady should be careful." On March 18, 2016, Melissa was released in Truro, Nova Scotia on a number of strict conditions. Halifax Regional Police released that she would be residing in the Halifax area, and that she had been assessed and found to be at a high risk to reoffend. On April 11, 2016, Shepard was seen at the Halifax Central Library accessing the internet by a community response officer and was found with a device capable of accessing the internet during this incident, which were breaches of the release conditions she received a month before. She was charged with breaching the terms of her release. On August 4, her lawyer entered not guilty pleas for three counts of breaching a recognizance, including a ban on accessing the internet, on her behalf. Her trial was set to begin February 1, 2017, but the charges were dropped on December 22, 2016. After being released from prison in 1994, Friedrich appeared in the documentary When Women Kill and was interviewed by Peter Gzowski. In 2012, she was the subject of an episode of CBC's the fifth estate, titled "The Widow's Web". She was featured on the Investigation Discovery channel series Deadly Women in Season 8, Episode 11 "For the Money, Honey." In 2017, she was also the subject of an episode of the Investigation Discovery channel series Web of Lies.

Wives Who Kill

Frankie Stewart Silver

On July 12, 1833, Frankie Silver became the first woman in the state of North Carolina to be hanged for murder. Burgess Gaither, the 1832 Clerk of the Court for Burke County, narrates the story from her arrest to her execution. As he began to understand the true nature of events, he wonders if there is such a thing as equal justice under the law.

The grave of Charles Silver in Kona, North Carolina.

Frances Stewart Silver (born 1814 or 1815; died July 12, 1833) was hanged in Morganton, Burke County, North Carolina for the axe murder of her husband Charles Silver. Frankie Silver, as she was known, is believed to have been the first white woman put to death in Burke County. She was born Frances Stewart, the daughter of Isaiah and Barbara (née Howell) Stewart. The family moved to Burke County when Frankie was young, around 1820. They lived in the town of Kona near the home of Jacob Silver who had lost his wife Elizabeth in childbirth. His son Charlie Silver was a year older than Frankie. Charlie and Frankie married and initially seemed a good pair. On 3 November 1830 their first daughter, Nancy, was born. They lived in a wooden cabin on land gifted by Jacob Silver. At Christmas 1831 Charlie apparently went missing whilst out hunting. A search party could not find him. Jack Colliss decided to investigate while Frankie was in the village. He found bones in the fireplace and bloodstains on the floor. He called the sheriff. They found a head. Frankie and her mother and brother were arrested. The motive for the murder is still not clear. It was claimed during the trial that Frankie was a jealous wife seeking revenge. Later

Mariticide Club

theories asserted that she was an abused wife. There is no definitive evidence for either theory. Despite claims made by journalists at the time, Frankie never confessed, nor did she discuss her motive. There is a theory that Frankie wanted to move west with her parents to join other family members, but Charles Silver refused to do so. There was also speculation that her frustration with Charles's refusal was the motive for the murder. Although not discovered until January 1832 it was revealed that on December 22, 1831, Charles Silver (aka "Johnny Silver") was hacked to death with an axe and later dismembered in the cabin he shared with his wife, Frankie, and their 13-month-old daughter, Nancy. Shortly after the murder, suspicion fell on Charles's wife Frankie, her mother Barbara Stuart, and her brother Jackson aka; "Blackstone" Stewart. All three were arrested. Barbara and Blackstone Stewart plead not guilty before a magistrate on January 17, 1832, and were discharged. Frankie alone stood trial for the murder. The trial of Frankie began on 29 March 1832. Evidence would now be considered circumstantial. The jury were undecided but on an instruction had a further meeting and found Frankie guilty. The investigation into the whereabouts of Charles Silver found a fireplace full of oily ashes, a pool of blood that had flowed through the cabin's puncheon floor, and blood spatters on the inside walls of the cabin. Pieces of bone and flesh were discovered in ashes poured into a mortar hole near the spring, as well as a heel-iron similar to those worn by Charles on his hunting moccasins. According to Silver family lore, the evidence showed that Charles had been murdered and his body had been burned to hide the evidence. Frankie could either be interpreted as a family ties murderer for the possibility that she manipulated family members to help kill her husband, or a battered woman murderer for the possibility that she killed him in self-defense during one of the beatings he would give her. Whatever happened that night inside the family cabin remains a mystery. It is probable that she was a victim of abuse from her husband due to the fact that a petition was signed by townswomen and several members of the all male jury in Frankie's favor. However, this petition did not sway the Governor. Another reason this will always remain a mystery is because as

Wives Who Kill

Frankie was asked about her last words, legend has it her father yelled out from the crowd "Die with it in you, Frankie!". This made some believe, along with them helping her escape, that family members were involved in the killing of Charles Silver. During the time between her sentencing and hanging, Frankie was broken out of jail by someone who entered by way of one of the basement windows. With the aid of false keys, this person opened the doors leading to the prisoner's apartment. Frankie was arrested again seven days later in Henderson County walking behind her father's wagon heading for Tennessee. When taken, she was dressed in men's clothes, and her hair been cut short. Her father and uncle were committed to jail as accessories to her escape. The story goes as follows:

Her family broke her out of jail, cut her hair short, and dressed her in men's clothes. A sheriff's posse found them trying to make their get-away in a hay wagon. Frankie was in the hay until she was out of sight; she then walked beside the wagon. Someone in the posse yelled to her, "FRANKIE!" She called back to him in a deep voice, "I thank you sir, but my name is Tommy." Her uncle then added, "Yeah, HER name's Tommy!" Saying "HER" gave them away, so back to jail she went. Frankie was hanged at Morganton, North Carolina on Friday 12 July 1833. Frankie's father had intended to bring his daughter's body home and bury it in the family burial plot. However, extreme heat and humidity in North Carolina that year forced him to bury it in an unmarked grave behind the Buckhorn Tavern, a few miles west of Morganton. For many years, the exact location of the grave was unknown, but it is now believed to be in a remote corner of the present day Devault farm. In 1952, a granite stone marking the probable location of the grave was placed by Beatrice Cobb, editor of the Morganton newspaper. The marker misspells Frankie's married name as "Silvers."

Popular culture

- As a young college student in September 1963, author Perry Deane Young discovered the letters and petitions to the governor which turned upside down the traditional story of a jealous wife seeking her revenge. Thus began a lifelong crusade by Young to show through documentation that Frankie Silver was unjustly hanged. At the height of the Watergate hearings, Sen. Sam Ervin wrote to Young to concur that Frankie should never have been hanged. Young's book, The

Mariticide Club

Untold Story of Frankie Silver, reproduced all of the documents which proved Frankie's innocence. His later play, Frankie, fictitiously gave the long-dead woman a chance to tell her side of the story. These accounts are known to be controversial, especially among descendants of the Silver family, who claim that "there were no documents to ever officially exist as this author suggests."

•The case of Frankie Silver served as the basis of Sharyn McCrumb's 1999 novel, The Ballad of Frankie Silver. In it, McCrumb's series character Spencer Arrowood takes a fresh look at the Frankie Silver case and at a (fictional) modern murder with many parallels.

• The 2000 film The Ballad of Frankie Silver and its re-release in 2010 as The Ballad of Frankie Silver:(Special Edition) DVD was written, directed, and produced by Theresa E. Phillips of Legacy Films Ltd. This film has a different theory of what happened.

• In a 2013 episode of the Investigation Discovery show Deadly Women, Frankie Stewart Silver appears. The episode was titled "Brides of Blood."

•A petition to have Frankie officially pardoned for the murder was formed unsuccessfully on April 9, 2013.

• In 2016 Parkway Playhouse in Burnsville, North Carolina adapted Sharyn McCrumb's book into a stage show.

Pamela Ann Smart (née Wojas)

Pamela Ann Smart (née Wojas; born August 16, 1967) is an American woman who was convicted of being an accomplice to first-degree murder, conspiracy to commit murder, and witness tampering in the death of her husband, Greggory Smart, in 1990. Smart, then aged 22, had conspired with her underaged boyfriend, then 15-year-old William "Billy" Flynn, and three of his friends to have Greggory (24) murdered in Derry, New Hampshire. She is currently serving a life sentence at Bedford Hills Correctional Facility for Women, a maximum security prison in Westchester County, New York. Pamela Smart was born Pamela Wojas in Coral Gables, Florida, on August 16, 1967, the daughter of John and Linda Wojas. She grew up in Miami, Florida, before her family moved to Derry, New Hampshire, when she was in the eighth grade. Pamela attended secondary school at Derry's Pinkerton Academy, where she was a cheerleader, and graduated from Florida State University (FSU) with a degree in communications. At FSU, she had been the host of a college radio program. Pamela met Greggory Smart while she

Wives Who Kill

visited New Hampshire over Christmas break in 1986. They formed a relationship in February 1987 and married two years later, with Greggory moving to Florida to live with Pamela during her senior year at FSU. Seven months into their marriage, the couple began having difficulties in their relationship. Pamela took a job as a media coordinator at Winnacunnet High School in Hampton, New Hampshire, where she met sophomore student William "Billy" Flynn at Project Self-Esteem, a school drug awareness program where both were volunteers. Pamela also met another intern named Cecelia Pierce, who was friends with Flynn. On May 1, 1990, Pamela came home from a meeting to find her condominium ransacked and her husband Greggory murdered. Police officials said the crime scene looked like a disrupted burglary. Pamela was accused of seducing 15-yearold Flynn and threatening to withhold sex from him unless he killed her husband. Flynn did so with help of friends Patrick "Pete" Randall, Vance "J.R." Lattime, Jr., and Raymond Fowler. During the investigation, Lattime's father brought a .38 caliber pistol he had found in his house to the police, believing it might have been the murder weapon. On May 14, an anonymous tip also indicated that Pamela's friend Cecelia Pierce was aware of the plan. Police talked to Pierce, who agreed to wear a wire and record conversations with Pamela in hopes that she would say something incriminating, which she did. On August 1, 1990, Detective Daniel Pelletier approached Pamela in her school's parking lot. Smart recognized him, having spoken to him on at least six other occasions. Taken by surprise, she asked, "What's up?" "Well, Pam," Pelletier said in the recording, "I have some good news and I have some bad news. The good news is that we've solved the murder of your husband. The bad news is you're under arrest." "What for?" Smart asked. "First-degree murder." Smart was then handcuffed and arraigned at the Derry District Court and jailed at the New Hampshire State Prison for Women, which was in Goffstown at the time. Smart's trial was widely watched and garnered considerable media attention, partly because it was one of the first in the U.S. to allow TV cameras in the courtroom. She faced life in prison if convicted. The prosecution's case relied heavily on testimony from Smart's

Mariticide Club

teenaged co-conspirators, who had secured their own plea bargains before her trial began. When oral arguments began March 4, 1991, Assistant Attorney General Diane Nicolosi portrayed the teenagers as naïve victims of an "evil woman bent on murder." The prosecution portrayed Pamela Smart as the cold-blooded mastermind who controlled her underaged sex partner. Nicolosi claimed that Smart seduced Flynn to get him to murder her husband, so that she could avoid an expensive divorce and benefit from a $140,000 life insurance policy. In her testimony, Smart acknowledged that she had what she termed an "affair" with the underaged boy, but claimed that the murder of her husband was solely the doing of Flynn and his friends as a reaction to her telling Flynn that she wished to end their "relationship" and repair her marriage. She insisted that she neither participated in the murder plot nor had any foreknowledge of it. Though Flynn claimed he had fallen in love with Smart when he first met her, Cecelia Pierce testified at trial that Smart and Flynn were originally just friends. Pierce first noticed a change about February, when Smart confessed to her that she "loved Bill." Flynn testified at trial that he was a virgin before he had sex with Pamela Smart. After a 14-day trial that culminated on March 22, 1991, in the Rockingham County Superior Court, Smart was found guilty of being an accomplice to first-degree murder, conspiracy to commit murder, and witness tampering. The tampering stemmed from Smart's coercing Pierce not to say anything to authorities or to lie. The conviction was largely the result of the testimony of her co-conspirators and secretly taped conversations in which Smart appeared to contradict her claims of having wanted to reconcile with her husband and of having no knowledge of the boys' plot. She could have been charged with capital murder, but the prosecution decided against it. Later that day, she was given a mandatory sentence of life in prison without the possibility for parole. Smart argued that the media had influenced her trial and conviction, as she explained in the 2014 HBO documentary Captivated: The Trials of Pamela Smart. In March 2023, the New Hampshire Supreme Court dismissed Pamela Smart's chance of freedom. This came after asking the Supreme Court to reverse Gov. Chris Sununu's decision to deny her a

Wives Who Kill

commutation hearing. Smart is serving her life sentence at the maximum security Bedford Hills Correctional Facility for Women in Westchester County, New York, where she was transferred in 1993 from the New Hampshire State Prison for Women in Goffstown. At the time, New Hampshire officials said the transfer was for unspecified "security reasons." Co-defendants William Flynn and Patrick Randall were also transferred out-of-state, in both cases to the Maine State Prison in Warren, Maine. The specific reasons for Smart's transfer are unclear. In 2007, a senior assistant in the state attorney general's office told the Keene State Equinox that Smart was transferred due to discipline problems. While she had accrued 22 disciplinary reports, all but two of them were for minor offenses. Deputy Compact Administrator Denise Heath claimed that at the time, there were fears that the State Prison for Women was not suitable for a high-profile inmate like Smart, and that it would be too easy for someone to break her out. However, New Hampshire has never had a formal transfer agreement with New York; Heath believed the transfer was a "commissioner to commissioner" arrangement. Smart's family maintains they were never informed of the transfer. She maintains her innocence; Smart has conceded that her husband would still be alive if she had not had what she continues to describe as an "affair" with Flynn, a minor. While in prison, Smart has tutored other inmates and has completed two master's degrees with concentrations in literature and legal studies from Mercy College, which were paid for with private funds from Mercy College. Smart became a member of the National Organization for Women, campaigning for rights for women in prison. In October 1996, Smart was severely beaten by fellow inmates Mona Graves and Ghania Miller. She sustained a fractured nose and a broken eye socket, which resulted in the insertion of a plastic plate in the left side of her face. The two inmates beat Smart after they accused her of snitching on them about their prison relationship. Graves and Miller were convicted of second-degree assault in the attack on Smart at Bedford Hills Correctional Facility and were subsequently transferred to separate prisons. As a result of the beating, Smart takes medication for chronic pain and sometimes thinks of suicide.

Mariticide Club

Her counselor, Dr. Eleanor Pam, says that "she has many, many, many dark days." Smart says she still keeps track of Flynn because she regards him as being the key to her freedom, before the 2023 ruling. "He is one of the few people that could actually get me out of here, by coming forward and telling the truth, but he's never gonna do that," said Smart. In 2003, photos of a scantily clad Smart were published in the National Enquirer. She filed a complaint against the prison and was placed in solitary confinement for two months. Smart sued in relation to her placement in solitary, but the lawsuit was dismissed. In 2004, Smart and fellow inmate Carolyn Warmus sued officials of Bedford Hills, claiming sexual harassment, and sexual assault by a corrections officer, who they said coerced them into posing for the suggestive pictures published in 2003. On November 5, 2009, a U.S. District Court Judge approved a $23,875 judgment to Smart from the State of New York. Smart received $8,750, while her attorney received the remaining balance for attorney fees. While serving her sentence, Smart took part in a writer's workshop, which was facilitated by playwright Eve Ensler. The workshop and Smart's writing were exhibited in the 2003 PBS documentary What I Want My Words to Do to You. In April 2004, the First U.S. Court of Appeals upheld a 2002 ruling by a federal judge who rejected her federal habeas petition. Prior to her federal appeal, Smart had exhausted all judicial appeals at the state level. In July 2005, the New Hampshire Executive Council unanimously denied a pardon request for "any conditions the governor may seek to impose." In an interview with ABC News, Smart indicated she is afraid of growing old and dying in prison and would rather have been given the death penalty.

On March 29, 2023, it was reported that Smart lost her final appeal, cementing that her life sentence would now be permanent. In 1992, Bill Flynn was sentenced to life in prison for second degree murder; not eligible for parole for 40 years with 12 years of the minimum sentence deferred if he maintains good behavior. Flynn was incarcerated at the Maine State Prison in Warren, where he earned his GED, has been active in charity work and worked as an electrician at the prison. In 2007, Flynn sought a sentence reduction after serving 16 years, stating that he had vowed not to

Wives Who Kill

do so until he had spent as many years behind bars as he had spent free. He also apologized to Gregg Smart's family for murdering him. The Smart family opposed the request. On February 12, 2008, the request was denied, although Flynn's earliest parole eligibility date was reduced by three years to 25 years, making him eligible for parole in 2015. In July 2014, Flynn was moved to a minimum security facility in Warren, Maine; the transfer allowed him to participate in a work release program. Flynn was granted parole by the state parole board on March 12, 2015, and was released from prison with lifetime parole on June 4, 2015, a few days past the 25th anniversary of Gregg Smart's death. Like Flynn, Patrick Randall was also sentenced to life in prison for second degree murder, eligible for parole after 40 years with 12 years deferred, making him eligible as early as 2018. He too served his sentence at the Maine State Prison in Warren, Maine. In March 2009, a judge reduced Randall's minimum sentence by three years to 25 years, making him eligible for release as early as June 2015. Randall was granted parole by the New Hampshire Parole Board after a hearing on April 9, 2015. He was released on June 4, 2015, on lifetime parole, the same day as co-conspirator Flynn's release and a few days past the 25th anniversary of Gregg Smart's death. Co-conspirator and driver Vance Lattime was sentenced to life in prison as an accomplice to second-degree murder, eligible for parole after 30 years with 12 years suspended. In 2005, his minimum sentence was reduced by three years, and he was paroled that same year, 15 years after Gregg Smart's death. Coconspirator Raymond Fowler (who waited in the car during the killing) was sentenced to 30 years for conspiracy to murder and attempted burglary, and parole eligibility after 15 years. Fowler was paroled in 2003, 13 years after Gregg Smart's death, but was sent back to prison in 2004 for violating his parole terms. He was paroled again in June 2005.

Catherine Mandeville Snow

Catherine Mandeville Snow, (c. 1793 – July 21, 1834) was the last woman hanged in Newfoundland. Born between 1791 and 1793 in Harbor Grace, Conception Bay, Newfoundland, Snow as a young woman moved to

Mariticide Club

Salmon Cove near Port de Grave. Snow lived common law and then married an abusive planter, John William Snow, in Port de Grave. Together they had seven children, and married on October 30, 1828. Their marriage was unhappy, and there were frequent fights. According to reports, Catherine would fight back and throw things at him. On the night of August 31, 1833, John Snow disappeared, and neighbors wondered quietly and then loudly if he had been murdered. Magistrate Robert Pinsent launched an investigation, and the general suspicion was confirmed when dried blood was discovered on John Snow's fishing stage. On September 12, it was noted in the newspaper The Newfoundlander, A most atrocious and unnatural murder has lately been perpetrated at Port-de-Grave, in Conception Bay. Mr. JOHN SNOW, a respectable planter of that place, having suddenly and mysteriously disappeared enquiry was set on foot, and from certain suspicious circumstances, a servant of SNOW'S named ARTHUR SPRING, and another man of the name of MANDEVILLE, were arrested, but there not being sufficient evidence to criminate them, they were, we understand, released on bail. We learn, however that on Saturday last, SPRING made a voluntary confession, in which he stated that his master had actually been murdered, at the instigation of his own wife, that he had been shot by MANDEVILLE in his (SPRING'S) presence; and that after the deed was accomplished they had attached the body to a grapnel and thrown it into the sea. MANDEVILLE, we understand, on being arrested and examined, admitted part of SPRING'S evidence, but denied having been the actual perpetrator of the crime – alleging that SPRING was the principal. MANDEVILLE and SPRING were brought to this town, and committed to Gaol on Sunday evening. The woman had previously quitted Port-de-Grave, but although an active search has been made for her, she had not, at the time of writing this article, been discovered. SNOW and his wife were the parents of a large family, and had been married about 17 years. The two prisoners underwent a long examination yesterday – the particulars of which have not transpired; but we understand it to have been similar to the former examinations. Catherine and her first cousin Tobias Mandeville were implicated in the

Wives Who Kill

murder, along with Arthur Spring, one of Snow's indentured servants. Catherine ran away to the woods, but eventually turned herself in to the courthouse at Harbor Grace. According to the confession, John Snow was shot while going from his boat to the stage head, but his body was never found. The trial took place at St. John's on January 10, 1834, and despite their confessions, all had pleaded not guilty. Chief Justice was Judge Bolton; jury members were Thomas Buckham, John Lang, Thomas Edstrom, George Lewis, Patrick Byrne, William Buckley, James Tubrid, Patrick Maher, Richard Trelegan, Robert Radford, Valentine Merchant, and Andrew Stewart. Snow and Mandeville were represented by George Henry Emerson, while Spring's lawyer was Bryan Robinson. The attorney general told the all-male jury, "I can't prove which one fired the shot, both were present for the murder. As to Catherine Snow, there is no direct or positive evidence of her guilt. But I have a chain of circumstantial evidence to prove her guilty." On Friday the 10th, Tobias Mandeville, Arthur Spring, and Catherine Snow, were put to the Bar, on their trial for the willful murder of John Snow, a respectable planter of Port-de-Grave – the husband of the prisoner Catherine Snow, and the master of the prisoner Spring. – This trial excited the most painful interest, – and occupied the attention of the Court for upwards of twelve hours; – when the Jury brought in a verdict of "Guilty" against all the Prisoners; and after a most eloquent and affecting address from the Chief Judge, sentence of Death was passed on them by his Lordship – to be carried into effect on the following Monday (yesterday). Tobias Mandeville, being found Guilty of Murder, was sentenced to be hung by the neck until dead; and his body to be dissected and anatomized: – Arthur Spring, the servant, and Catherine Snow, the wife, of the deceased, were declared Guilty of Petit-Treason, and accordingly sentenced to be drawn to the place of execution on a hurdle, – and their bodies, after death, also to be given to the surgeons for dissection. During their trial, Snow claimed to be pregnant with her eighth child. Following this, "the Court ordered that a Jury of Twelve respectable Matrons should be Empaneled to decide on the truth or falsity of the Prisoner's allegation; a Jury of that description accordingly met on Saturday morning, and returned a verdict

Mariticide Club

(in substance) that the Prisoner was in the situation stated in her plea." On January 13, 1834, both Arthur Spring and Tobias Mandeville were hanged. Instead of being dissected, their bodies were ordered to be taken to Port de Grave, and from there to be displayed in a gibbet at Spectacle Head, near Cupids. This did not happen, in part due to the "interference" of Roman Catholic priests, and in March, a funeral for both was held in Harbor Grace, preceded by a mock execution held over the corpses.Many in Newfoundland were determined that Snow not meet the same fate. Bishop Michael Fleming made Snow a cause célèbre. The governor, Thomas John Cochrane delayed her hanging until the baby was born. She gave birth to the child, baptized Richard Snow, and nursed him for three months in her prison cell. On July 21, 1834, at 8:45 am, as crowds gathered on Duckworth Street, Snow walked out on the platform. Three priests, Fathers Troy, Ward and Waldron, attended her on the scaffold. The Public Ledger reported, "The unhappy woman, after a few brief struggles, passed into another world." Snow declared herself innocent to the end. She died declaring she was a wretched sinful woman, but as innocent of any participation in the crime for which she was about to suffer as the child unborn, and that she had not even the most distant presentiment, at any time, that her husband would have fallen under the hand of an assassin. After her death, Bishop Fleming took over guardianship of her children. The eldest three of Snow's children signed a petition calling for the dismissal of Judge Bolton for his handling of the case. The story of Catherine Snow has inspired two novels by Nellie P. Strowbridge, "Catherine Snow" and "The Hanged Woman's Daughter;" the play "What Hangs in the Balance" by Petrina Bromley; the song "The Nameless Murderess" co-written by Jody Richardson and the Newfoundland folk trio The Once, the short story "Catherine Snow" and the short two-hander play "Catherine Snow: a duologue" both by Grace Butt, the play "Offensive to Some" by Bernadine Stapleton, an episode of the TV show Lore, and an episode of the podcast Tales, Tunes, and Toutons. On April 1, 2012, a restaging of Snow's trial was held in St. John's. It was organized by the Newfoundland and Labrador Historical Society, with Supreme Court

Wives Who Kill

justices Seamus O'regan and Carl Thompson, with defense lawyer Rosellen Sullivan. Approximately 400 local residents attended. Snow's modern-day defense lawyer argued, "the evidence of the affair is so prejudicial, it's impossible to extricate it from the statements ... there's no way she could have a fair trial." After hearing the evidence, the modern jury acquitted her. Snow's great-great-granddaughter is former CNN news anchor Mary Snow.

May Ruth Snyder (née Brown)

May Ruth Brown Snyder Mugshot for transfer to Sing Sing Prison 1927 May Ruth Snyder (née Brown; March 27, 1895 – January 12, 1928) was an American murderer. Her execution in the electric chair at New York's Sing Sing Prison in 1928 for the murder of her husband, Albert Snyder, was recorded in a highly publicized photograph. May Ruth Brown met Albert Edward Snyder (né Schneider) in 1915 in New York City, when she was 20 years old and he was a 33-year-old artist. The couple had little in common; Brown, who went by her middle name Ruth to most people and was known as "Tommy" to close friends, was described as vivacious and gregarious, while Snyder was described as very reserved and a "homebody". Despite their differences in personalities and age, the couple married and settled in a modest house in Queens. In 1918, Ruth gave birth to their only child, a daughter named Lorraine. Albert Snyder worked as an art editor for Motor Boating magazine, published for most of its run by Hearst Magazines, and

Mariticide Club

made one-hundred dollars a week. In 1925, Ruth began an affair with Henry Judd Gray, a married corset salesman who lived in the New Jersey suburbs. She began to plan the murder of her husband Albert, enlisting Gray's help, but he was reluctant. Some claim that Ruth's distaste for her husband apparently began when he insisted on hanging a picture of his late fiancée, Jessie Guischard, on the wall of their first home and named his boat after her. Guischard, whom Albert described to Ruth as "the finest woman I have ever met", had been dead for 10 years. However, others have noted that Albert Snyder was emotionally and physically abusive, blaming Ruth for the birth of a daughter rather than a son, demanding a perfectly maintained home, and physically assaulting both her and their daughter Lorraine when his demands were not met. Ruth first persuaded Albert to purchase insurance, and with the assistance of an insurance agent (who was subsequently fired and sent to prison for forgery), "signed" a $48,000 life insurance policy that paid extra if an unexpected act of violence killed the victim. According to Gray, Ruth had made at least seven attempts to kill Albert, all of which he survived. On March 20, 1927, the couple garroted Albert with a picture wire, stuffed his nose full of chloroform-soaked rags, and beat him with a sash weight, then staged his death as part of a burglary. Detectives at the scene noted that the burglar left little evidence of breaking into the house. Moreover, Ruth's behavior was inconsistent with her story of a terrorized wife witnessing her husband being killed. Police discovered that the property Ruth had claimed had been stolen was still in the house, but hidden. A breakthrough came when a detective found a paper with the letters J.G. on it (it was a memento Albert had kept from former lover Guischard) and asked Ruth about it. A flustered Ruth's mind immediately turned to Gray, whose initials were also J.G., and she asked the detective what Gray had to do with the murder. It was the first time Gray had been mentioned, and the police instantly became suspicious. Gray was found in Syracuse, New York. He claimed he had been there all night, but it was found out that a friend of his had set up Gray's room at a hotel to support his alibi. Gray proved far more

Wives Who Kill

forthcoming than Ruth about his actions. He was caught, returned to Queens, and charged along with Ruth.

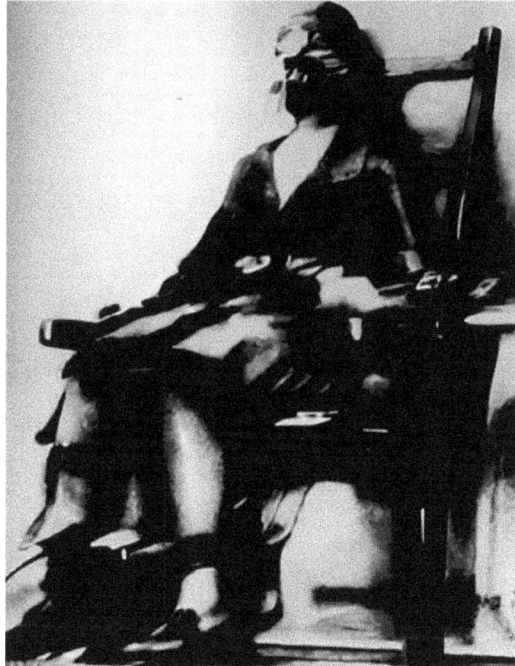

Ruth Snyder's mid-execution photo taken by Tom Howard
and published the next day in the New York Daily News

Ruth and Gray turned on each other, contending the other was responsible for killing Albert; both were convicted and sentenced to death. Ruth was imprisoned at Sing Sing in Ossining, New York. On January 12, 1928, she became the first woman to be executed at Sing Sing since Martha Place in 1899. She went to the electric chair 10 minutes before Judd Gray, her former lover. Her execution (by New York State Electrician Robert G. Elliott) was surreptitiously photographed at the moment electricity was running through her body with the aid of a miniature plate camera strapped to the ankle of Tom Howard, a Chicago Tribune photographer working in cooperation with the Tribune-owned Daily News. Howard's camera later was owned by inventor Miller Reese Hutchison and later became part of the collections of the Smithsonian Institution's National Museum of American History. Ruth was interred in the Woodlawn Cemetery in the Bronx. Her footstone reads "May R." and includes her date of death. Gray was interred in Rosedale Cemetery in Montclair, New Jersey.

Mariticide Club

Lorraine Snyder

Following the pronouncement of the death sentence on Ruth Snyder in May 1927, legal disputes arose between the relatives regarding the care of Ruth and Albert's daughter, Lorraine, who was nine years old at the time. Warren Schneider, brother of Albert, petitioned to be allowed to appoint a legal guardian who was not a member of Ruth's family. Josephine Brown, mother of Ruth, also petitioned for custody of the girl. Lorraine had been in the care of Brown since the murder. Lorraine was formally placed by her maternal grandmother in the Catholic institution where she had been residing at the time of her mother's execution. Ruth requested that her daughter not be brought to the prison for a final visit. On September 7, 1927, Josephine Brown was awarded guardianship of the girl. During this time, there were disputes with the insurance company Ruth had used to insure her husband's life. Although one policy, worth US$30,000, to Gray's daughter, was paid without contest, they filed suit to void two other policies, worth $45,000 and $5,000 (the three combined policies worth $1.35 million in 2022). By May 1928, the insurance company made available $4,000 for the maintenance of Lorraine. In November 1928 a ruling in the case was reached, with a court finding the policies could not

Wives Who Kill

be collected because they had been issued fraudulently. At the time of the judgment, the lawyer acting on behalf of Ruth's family asked the court to allow them to appeal without a printed record on the basis that the family was destitute and unable to sell the house due to the notoriety of the case. By May 1930, it was ruled on appeal that the two policies were invalid.

The grave of Ruth Brown Snyder in Woodlawn Cemetery

While incarcerated on death row, Ruth Snyder wrote a sealed letter which she requested be given to Lorraine "when she is old enough to understand". One year after her mother's execution, Lorraine was apparently aware that her parents were both dead, but not of the manner of either of their deaths.

Lyda Southard (née Keller) aka Lyda Trueblood
Aka Flypaper Lyda Aka The Black Widow

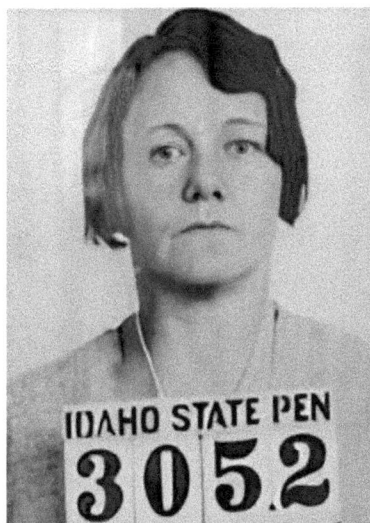

Mariticide Club

Lyda Southard (October 16, 1892 – February 5, 1958), also known as Lyda Anna Mae Trueblood, was an American female suspected serial killer. It was suspected that she had killed her four husbands, a brother-in-law, and her daughter by using arsenic poisoning derived from flypaper in order to obtain life insurance money. Lyda Keller was born on October 16, 1892, in Keytesville, Missouri, 60 miles northeast of Kansas City and in the central flatlands of Missouri. Keller married Robert Dooley on March 17, 1912. The couple settled with his brother Ed Dooley on a ranch in Twin Falls, Idaho, and had a daughter, Lorraine, in 1914. Lorraine died unexpectedly in 1915, Keller claimed, as a result of drinking water from a dirty well. Edward Dooley died soon afterward in August 1915; the cause of death was ruled ptomaine poisoning. Robert Dooley subsequently fell ill and died of typhoid fever on October 12, 1915, leaving Keller as the sole survivor in the family. Keller collected on the life insurance policies of each person shortly after their death. Two years after Robert Dooley's death, Keller married William G. McHaffle. Shortly afterward, Keller's three-year-old daughter fell ill and died, prompting the McHaffles to move to Montana. A year later, McHaffle suddenly fell ill of what was thought to be influenza and died in Montana on October 1, 1918. The death certificate stated the cause of death as influenza and diphtheria. In March 1919, she married Harlen C. Lewis, an automobile salesman from Billings, Montana. Within four months, Lewis fell ill and died from complications of gastroenteritis. Keller married a fourth time in Pocatello, Idaho, to Edward F. Meyer, a ranch foreman, in August 1920. He mysteriously fell ill of typhoid; he died September 7, 1920. List of marriages:

1. Robert Dooley (March 17, 1912 – October 12, 1915)
2. William G. McHaffle (June 1917-October 1, 1918)
3. Harlen C. Lewis (March 1919-July 1919)
4. Edward F. Meyer (August 1920-September 7, 1920)
5. Paul V. Southard (?, divorced)
6. Harry Whitlock (March 1932-?, divorced)
7. Hal Shaw (possibly divorced)

Wives Who Kill

Twin Falls chemist Earl Dooley, a relative of Keller's first husband, began to study the deaths surrounding her. Along with a physician and another chemist, he soon discovered that Ed and Bob Dooley were murdered by arsenic poisoning. Twin Falls County Prosecutor Frank Stephan began an investigation and started exhuming the bodies of three of Lyda Keller's husbands, her 4-year-old daughter, and her brother-in-law. Stephan discovered that some of the bodies contained traces of arsenic, while otherswere suspected of arsenic poisoning by how well the bodies were preserved, and found her motive in the records of the Idaho State Life Insurance company of Boise. All four of Keller's husbands had held a life insurance policy where they listed her as the beneficiary. Keller was able to collect over $7,000 over the years from the deaths of her first three husbands. She was found by law enforcement in Honolulu, married for the fifth time to Navy petty officer Paul Southard. Following extradition to Idaho, she was arraigned on June 11, 1921.

Victims

Husband	Insurance Money
Robert Dooley	$4,600
William McHaffle	$500
Harlan Lewis	$3,000
Ed Meyer	$10,000
Paul Vance Southard	$10,000

Mariticide Club

Southard was returned to Idaho to face murder charges on Meyer. She pleaded not guilty in court but ultimately was convicted of using arsenic to murder her husbands and then taking the insurance money. It was determined that her motive for murder was money, since she had taken out and collected on the life insurance policies of each of her dead husbands. Following a six-week trial, Southard was convicted of second degree murder and sentenced to ten years to life in the Old Idaho State Penitentiary. She escaped from prison on May 4, 1931 and took up residence in Denver, Colorado, as a housekeeper for Harry Whitlock, a man she married in March 1932 but who ultimately assisted in her arrest in Topeka, Kansas, on July 31, 1932. Southard returned to the penitentiary in August 1932. She was released on probation in October 1941, and received a final pardon. Lyda Southard died of a heart attack on February 5, 1958, in Salt Lake City, Utah. Her body was interred at Sunset Memorial Park in Twin Falls, Idaho.

Anna-Maria Farina Spaak

Murder of Fernand Spaak

Fernand Paul Jules Spaak (8 August 1923 – 18 July 1981) was a Belgian lawyer and diplomat. The son of Paul-Henri Spaak and Marguerite Malevez, he was born in Forest and was educated at Cambridge University and at the Université libre de Bruxelles, receiving a Doctor of Laws from the latter institution. From 1950 to 1952, he worked for the National Bank of Belgium. In 1952, he became chief of staff to Jean Monnet, president of the High Authority of the European Coal and Steel Community. Then, in 1960, he assumed the position of director general for the Agence d'approvisionnement Euratom. From 1967 to 1975, Spaak was director general for the Directorate-General for Energy (DG XII). From 1976 to 1980, he was delegate for the European Economic Community Executive Commission in the United States. In April 1981, Spaak initiated the Paul-Henri Spaak Lectures, named in honor of his father, at Harvard University. In 1953, Spaak married Anna-Maria Farina in London; the couple had three children. His daughter Isabelle became a journalist and

Wives Who Kill

author. His sister Antoinette Spaak was head of the Democratic Front of Francophones. Spaak was shot dead in his flat in Brussels in 1981 by his estranged wife with a hunting rifle; she had previously threatened to kill him on a number of occasions. She then replaced the rifle in its bag and committed suicide by electrocuting herself with an electric iron in a bath. At the time of his death, Spaak was chief of staff for Gaston Thorn, then president of the European Commission.

Bathsheba Ruggles Spooner

Bathsheba Ruggles Spooner (February 15, 1746 – July 2, 1778) was the first woman in American history to be executed following the Declaration of Independence. The daughter of prominent Loyalist brigadier general and jurist Timothy Ruggles, Bathsheba Ruggles had an arranged marriage to wealthy farmer Joshua Spooner. After becoming pregnant by her lover, Continental Army soldier Ezra Ross, she enlisted the assistance of Ross and two others to murder her husband. On the night of March 1, 1778, Spooner was beaten to death and his body deposited in a well. Bathsheba and the three conspirators were soon arrested, tried, and convicted of Spooner's murder and sentenced to death. Bathsheba petitioned to have her execution delayed because of her pregnancy, which was first denied and then supported by some members of a group charged with examining her to verify the pregnancy. After the four were executed, a postmortem examination revealed that she was five months pregnant. Historians have pointed out that the trial and execution may have been hastened by anti-Loyalist sentiment. Bathsheba Ruggles Spooner was the daughter of Brig. Gen. Timothy Ruggles, a lawyer who had served as chief justice of the Court of Common Pleas in Worcester, Massachusetts, from 1762–64. Timothy Ruggles refused to sign the Stamp Act protest when serving as Massachusetts representative to the Stamp Act Congress in 1765. An avowed Loyalist who threatened to raise an army to protect his and other Loyalist farms against attacks by Patriot forces, Ruggles joined forces with the British Army in Boston in 1775. Bathsheba Ruggles married Joshua Spooner on January 15, 1766. He was a well-to

Mariticide Club

do Brookfield farmer, the son of a wealthy Boston merchant. The Spooners lived in relative affluence in a two-story house in Brookfield, and had four children between 1767 and 1775. Spooner was later described as an abusive man for whom his wife developed "an utter aversion." In the spring of 1777, sixteen-year-old Ezra Ross, a soldier in the Continental Army, fell ill en route to his home in Linebrook, a village in Ipswich. Bathsheba nursed him back to health. On his travels to and from army service, Ross visited the Spooner home in July and December 1777.On the latter occasion he stayed into the new year, traveled with Spooner on business trips and had an affair with Bathsheba. She became pregnant mid-January and began urging Ross to kill her husband. In February 1778, Ross accompanied Spooner on an extended trip to Princeton, bringing along a bottle of nitric acid given to him by Bathsheba with the aim of poisoning Spooner. Ross backed out of the plan and returned directly to his Linebrook home. While Ross and Spooner were in Princeton, Bathsheba invited two runaway British soldiers—escaped prisoners of war Pvt. Williams Brooks and Sgt. James Buchanan—to stay at the Spooner home and discussed ideas for killing her husband with them. When Spooner returned, she recruited them to assist her. She also wrote to Ross to inform him of these developments, and he returned to Brookfield on February 28. When Spooner returned home from a local tavern the following evening, Brooks committed the murder and Buchanan and Ross helped hide the body in the Spooners' well. Bathsheba distributed paper money from her husband's lockbox and articles of his clothing to the three men, who then took one of the Spooner horses to Worcester, fourteen miles away. Brooks and Buchanan spent the remainder of the night drinking, and the next morning Brooks showed off Spooner's silver shoe buckles engraved with his initials. Once the murder was discovered, the three men were arrested in Worcester within 24 hours. When Ross was discovered hiding in the attic of a tavern, he asked for a confessor. The trio implicated Bathsheba and three of her household servants in the crime. Brooks was charged with the assault on Spooner; Buchanan and Ross with aiding and abetting in the murder; and Bathsheba with inciting, abetting and procuring the manner and form of the

Wives Who Kill

murder. All were arraigned and pleaded not guilty. The Spooner murder case was the first capital case in the U.S. history. Robert Treat Paine, later the first Attorney General of Massachusetts, prosecuted the case. At the trial on April 24, 1778, the household servants testified for the prosecution. Levi Lincoln, later U.S. Attorney General under President Thomas, defended the accused. Brooks and Buchanan had no defense to offer, having signed lengthy confessions. Though Ross had signed a similar confession, Lincoln argued that he had no intention of harming the deceased, was not aware of the plan until a few hours before the murder, had not assisted in the murder and pretended to support it to maintain his affair with Bathsheba. He argued that Bathsheba had a "disordered mind," that her actions were irrational as evidenced by the lack of a getaway plan. All four defendants were found guilty the next day and sentenced to death, with the executions set for June 4, 1778. Bathsheba petitioned for a postponement, citing her pregnancy, based on common law principle that protected the life of a fetus if it had quickened. Bathsheba was examined by a panel of twelve women and two male midwives. All swore that she was not "quick with child." When Bathsheba and her confessor, the Rev. Thaddeus Maccarty, protested the report, four of the examiners joined by another midwife and Spooner's brother-in-law, Dr. John Green, conducted a second examination and supported the claim of pregnancy. The court did not accept those findings and Bathsheba was hanged alongside Ross, Brooks and Buchanan on July 2 in Worcester's Washington Square before a crowd of 5,000 spectators. A post-mortem examination, performed at Bathsheba's request, showed that she was pregnant with "a perfect male fetus of the growth of five months." Bathsheba's body was claimed by her sister, Mary Ruggles Green, wife of Dr. John Green. She was buried in an unmarked grave on the Green Estate, which today is the site of Green Hill Park in Worcester. Shortly after the executions, on July 5, Rev. Ebenezer Parkman, minister of the nearby town of Westborough, delivered a sermon entitled The Adultress Shall Hunt for the Precious Life in which he said: So keep thee from the Evil woman, from the flattery of the tongue of a strange woman. Neither let her take thee with her eyelids. There are a *thousand dangers, that poor young wretches are in by reason of the snares & traps which are everywhere laid ... particularly the poor beardless youth not quite 18.*

One historian says the judgment of the first panel that examined Spooner– "they refused to acknowledge what must have been obvious"–and blames "vindictiveness". Others question the motivation of the Massachusetts Executive Council. Some suggest Bathsheba was executed because the community opposed her father's Loyalist stance. John Avery Jr., the deputy secretary and leader of the Massachusetts Executive Council, who signed Bathsheba's death warrant, belonged to a group of Patriots called the Loyal Nine, who formed the innermost circle of the Sons of Liberty and was a step-brother of the murder victim. CBS radio program Crime Classics dramatized the case in an episode entitled "The Crime of Bathsheba Spooner" that aired on June 15, 1953.Bathsheba Spooner's case was also featured in Season 11, Episode 10 of Deadly Women.

Barbara Stager (née Barbara Terry) aka Barbara Ford

Barbara Stager (born October 30, 1948) is an American woman who was convicted in 1989 of murdering her husband, Russell Stager, in 1988. Russell was shot while in bed; Barbara reported the shooting as accidental. Her first husband also died under similar circumstances. "Til Death Do Us Part: The Barbara Stager Story", is an episode of A&E's television series American Justice, which profiled the case. Jerry Bledsoe also wrote a book in 1994 about the case, entitled Before He Wakes: A True Story of Money, Marriage, Sex and Murder, which was later made into a TV movie in 1998 starring Jaclyn Smith. A&E's City Confidential presented its perspective on the case in the 2003 episode "Durham: Dangerous Housewife". Investigation Discovery's Deadly Women series portrayed the story in the 2010 "Fortune Hunters" episode and their Scorned: Love Kills revisited the case in its own "'Til Debt Do Us Part," in 2012. The Forensic Files series had an episode "Broken Promises" about this case; Investigation Discovery examined the case a third time in 2015, with an episode entitled "No Accident" in its Fatal Vows series. In 1999,

Wives Who Kill

the Discovery Channel's The New Detectives series, Season 4, Episode 6, "Women Who Kill" featured Barbara Stager's crime.

Della Faye "Dante" Sutorius (née Della Faye Hall)

Della Faye "Dante" Sutorius (August 8, 1950 – November 20, 2010) an American woman who was convicted of murdering her husband in 1996. Dr. Darryl Sutorius, a prominent heart surgeon in Cincinnati, married Dante Britteon in 1995. Sutorius was found dead in the basement of the house he shared with his wife in Symmes Township, Ohio on February 19, 1996. A gunshot to the head had been the cause of death; authorities were unsure whether his death was homicide or suicide. Dante Sutorius was arrested the same day when investigating police found a supply of cocaine. Though released on bail the next day, Dante Sutorius was re-arrested on February 27 when it was determined that she had purchased the weapon that had killed her husband and gunshot residue tests and autopsy results indicated that she had been the one who fired the weapon on the day of Sutorius's death. This time the charge was aggravated murder with prior calculation. Investigation into the background of Dante Sutorius revealed that her real name was Della; she had begun using the name "Dante" sometime in her 20s. It also showed it was not the first time she had been associated with violence. Her third husband alleged that she had repeatedly threatened to kill him during their marriage; after the couple divorced, she was charged with threatening another man, this time a boyfriend, with a gun. One husband had found knives hidden around the house he shared with her and had been surprised when she told him she "could kill you", while her fourth husband told investigators that she was mentally abusive and he feared her to the point of hiding the bullets to his gun to prevent her from being able to use them. Dr. Sutorius had discovered that virtually everything Della/Dante had told him about her background was false. She claimed to have graduated from UCLA, but in truth had never finished high school. She claimed to have owned a day care business, but had never held a steady job in her life. When he learned about these lies and her violent history, he cut Della out of his will and began divorce

Mariticide Club

proceedings. A week before his death, he was planning to formally serve her with papers and have her thrown out of their house. Hamilton County, Ohio prosecutor Joe Deters theorized that Della Sutorius had "a serious problem with rejection" after colleagues of her husband reported that he had been considering divorce. According to her sister Donna Hall, Sutorius's approach to men had long been colored by monetary gain: "She said you find a wealthy man and, when they die, you'd get their money". Sutorius declined to take the stand in her own defense at her trial. Though her lawyers argued that police had failed to prove that Darryl Sutorius's death was anything but suicide and their client's statements to police had not been preceded by a Miranda warning, she was convicted on June 7, 1996, with the jury deliberating for fewer than five hours before finding her guilty of aggravated murder, use of a gun in a crime of violence, and drug possession. Later the same month, she was sentenced to 23 years to life in prison, the maximum penalty allowed. Judge Richard Niehaus said that contrary to her media portrayal as a "black widow," she was more akin to a lionfish, who attracts prey with its brilliant stripes before using its poisonous spines to kill them. Della Sutorius appealed her conviction in the spring of 1997, claiming that the trial jury having been allowed to hear hearsay evidence of statements her dead husband had made and that prosecutors had made improper comments to the jury. The appeal was declined in June of the same year and Sutorius returned to serving her sentence at the Ohio Reformatory for Women. In order to defray the costs of prosecuting Sutorius, the Hamilton County Sheriff's department seized and auctioned off Sutorius's 11-piece jewelry collection. Despite the coverage the press devoted to the auction, bidders failed to meet the minimum necessary total for the pieces to sell separately and the lot was sold for a $5,100 lump sum. According to the Ohio Department of Rehabilitation and Correction, Della Sutorius died of natural causes at the Franklin Medical Center on November 20, 2010, where Sutorius had been serving her life sentence since her conviction. She was 60 years old. Sutorius would have been eligible for parole in 2014. Della Sutorius's dramatic history with her husbands and the public perception of her as

Wives Who Kill

being a "black widow" attracted high levels of coverage from the press; her lawyer, ex-husbands, and ex-boyfriends were all reportedly approached by talk show hosts and news broadcasts such as Geraldo and Hard Copy. A spokeswoman for the Sally Jessy Raphael talk show Sally, which also pursued the story, explained that the case was "highly dramatic" and would appeal to daytime television watchers. Despite jury selection being slowed down by already widespread news coverage of the case, Court TV was permitted to televise coverage of the May 1996 trial. A 2010 episode of Dateline NBC covered the case in detail, interviewing Sutorius's family and friends as well as people who had been involved in her legal cases. Crime reporter Aphrodite Jones covered Sutorius's case in her 2002 book Della's Web. Her case is one of the thirteen famous murders reported on in the book The Cincinnati Crime Book (1998), by George Stimson. The Sutorius case was featured in 2005: Oxygen Network series Snapped, and the Investigation Discovery series Deadly Women and Fatal Vows, and Forensic Files episode "Second Shot at Love".

Epifania Sulu'ape

Su'a Sulu'ape Paulo II

Mariticide Club

Su'a Sulu'ape Paulo II (1949/1950 – 25 November 1999) was a *tufuga ta tatau* (master tattooist) born in Matafa'a near Lefaga, Samoa but based in New Zealand since the 1970s. He was born into one of the leading families of tattooists *tufuga ta tatau* in Samoa. The tattooists in these families, are loosely organized in a guild like system of master and apprentices. In the late 20th and early 21st centuries *tufuga ta tatau* were known internationally for their culturally distinctive and highly skilled work. The word tattoo is believed to have originated from the word tatau. In Samoan mythology the origin of the tatau is told in a legend about two sisters, Tilafaiga and Taema who brought the tools and knowledge of tattooing to Samoa. The Samoan male tattoo (tatau) is the pe'a. The female tatau is the malu. Paulo was axed to death by his wife, Epifania Sulu'ape, after she learned that he planned to leave her for his Swedish lover, Heidi Hay. Sulu'ape Paulo's father was Sulu'ape Paulo I, who was a well-established tattooist in Samoa. Paulo's brothers Su'a Sulu'ape Petelo, Su'a Sulu'ape Alaiva'a Petelo and Su'a Sulu'ape Lafaele are respected master tattooists today. In his teenage years, Paulo was a student at Chanel College, a Catholic [boarding] school near Apia. He began tattooing in 1967, and migrated to Auckland, New Zealand in 1973. Paulo would work during the day and tattoo in the evenings and on weekends for a growing local Samoan community. He tattooed several prominent Samoans from this community including artist Fatu Feu'u and activist and lawyer Fuimaono Tuiasau. He also tattooed well known New Zealand artist Tony Fomison and developed strong connections with Maori, the indigenous people of New Zealand. In 1985, Paulo's brother Su'a Sulu'ape Alaiva'a Petelo visited a tattoo convention in Rome at the invitation of American tattooist Don Ed Hardy. Over the next decade, Sulu'ape Paulo followed in his brothers footsteps finding new opportunities to share his work and knowledge in Europe. He developed relationships with tattooists across the world and the family name became known throughout the tattooing conventions in Europe.

Wives Who Kill

He did residencies at the Tattoo Museum in Amsterdam at the invitation of tattooist Henk Schiffmacher and received international guests and customers at his home in Auckland. Sulu'ape and his brothers also served a growing Samoan diaspora in New Zealand, Australia and the United States. He was a much celebrated and at times a controversial figure amongst Samoans, mainly for his efforts to innovate in his work and share the art form beyond the Samoan community. Since Paulo's sudden death in 1999, Su'a Sulu'ape Alaiva'a Petelo has maintained and extended the influence of the Sulu'ape family in the Pacific region and internationally. He has been joined by his sons who have also picked up the tools. In 2009, Su'a Sulu'ape Paulo's life and tattoo work was documented and published in a photographic book *Tatau: Samoan Tattoo, New Zealand Art, Global Culture* published by Te Papa Press. The book features photographs by New Zealander Mark Adams a close friend of Sulu'ape and observer of his work for close to 30 years. it includes interviews and essays reflecting on his tattooing career. In November, 1999, Paulo's wife Epifania Sulu'ape clubbed him to death with the blunt edge of an axe after he told her that he planned to leave her for a Swedish lover, Heidi Hay. Sulu'ape's trial was a major media event in New Zealand. She was convicted of manslaughter and sentenced to 7.5 years in prison.

Edith Jessie Thompson née Edith Jesse Graydon
'Hanged for Adultery, the Tragic Fate of Edith Thompson'

Bywaters (27 June 1902 – 9 January 1923) were a British couple executed for the murder of Thompson's husband Percy. Their case became a cause célèbre. Edith Thompson was born Edith Jessie Graydon on 25 December 1893, at 97 Norfolk Road in Dalston, London, the first of the five children of William Eustace Graydon (1867–1941), a clerk with the Imperial Tobacco Company, and his wife Ethel Jessie Graydon (née Liles) (1872–1938), the daughter of a police constable. During her childhood, Edith was a happy, talented girl who excelled at dancing and acting, and was academically bright, with a natural ability in arithmetic. After leaving

Mariticide Club

school in 1909 she joined a firm of clothing manufacturers, Louis London, near Aldgate station in London. Then, in 1911, she was employed at Carlton & Prior, wholesale milliners, in the Barbican and later in Aldersgate. Edith quickly established a reputation as a stylish and intelligent woman and was promoted by the company several times, until she became their chief buyer and made regular trips to Paris on behalf of the company.

Edith Jessie Thompson

In 1909, at the age of 15, Edith met Percy Thompson who was three years her senior. After a six-year engagement, they were married at St Barnabas, Manor Park on 15 January 1916. At first, the couple lived in Retreat Road in Westcliff-on-Sea, before buying a house at 41 Kensington Gardens in the then-fashionable London suburb of Ilford in July 1920. With both their careers flourishing they lived a comfortable life.

Acquaintance with Bywaters

Wives Who Kill

Frederick Bywaters Edith Thompson, circa 1920

In 1920, the couple became acquainted with 18-year-old Frederick Bywaters, although Bywaters and Edith Thompson had met nine years earlier when Bywaters, then aged nine, had been a schoolfriend of Edith's younger brothers. Frederick Bywaters had enlisted in the merchant navy. The 26-year-old Edith was immediately attracted to Bywaters, who was handsome and impulsive and whose stories of his travels around the world excited Edith's love of romantic adventure. To Edith, the youthful Bywaters represented her romantic ideal; by comparison, 29-year-old Percy-seemed staid and conventional. Percy—oblivious to the emerging romantic attraction between his wife and Bywaters—welcomed the youth into their company. Shortly thereafter, the trio—joined by Edith's sister Avis—holidayed in Shanklin on the Isle of Wight. Upon their return, Percy invited Bywaters to lodge with them.

Frederick Bywaters; Edith; and Percy Thompson. 10 July 1921

Mariticide Club

While holidaying upon the Isle of Wight in June 1921, Edith and Bywaters began an affair. Initially, Percy was unaware of this, although he gradually noticed his wife was drifting away from him. Matters came to a head barely a month after the affair started. A trivial incident in the Thompsons' garden triggered a violent row during which Percy Thompson struck his wife and caused her to fall over some furniture. Bywaters intervened and Thompson ordered him out of the house. The Thompsons' sitting tenant, a Mrs. Lester, commented on Mrs. Thompson's bruises in one of her statements to police. From September 1921 until September 1922 Bywaters was at sea, and during this time Edith Thompson wrote to him frequently. After his return, they met up again. On 3 October 1922, the Thompsons attended a performance at the Criterion Theatre in Piccadilly Circus, London, together with Edith's uncle and aunt, Mr. and Mrs. J. Laxton. They left the theatre at 11 pm and all went to Piccadilly Circus tube station, where they separated. The Thompsons caught the 11:30 pm train to Ilford. As they walked along Belgrave Road, between Endsleigh and De Vere Gardens, a man jumped out from behind some bushes near their home and attacked Percy. After a violent struggle, during which Edith Thompson was knocked to the ground, Percy was stabbed. Mortally wounded, he died before Edith could summon help. The attacker fled. Neighbors later reported hearing a woman (here assumed to have been Edith) screaming hysterically and shouting "Oh don't, oh don't" several times. By the time police arrived Edith had not composed herself. At the police station the following day she was distressed. She was unaware that Bywaters was already a suspect: he was arrested that evening and taken to Ilford Police Station. The police confronted her with Bywaters. One of the inspectors, Frank Hall, untruthfully told her that Bywaters had already confessed. She then admitted to the police that she knew who the assailant was and provided the police with details of her association with Bywaters. The police investigated further and discovered a series of more than 60 love letters from Edith Thompson to Bywaters. The letters were the only tangible evidence linking Edith Thompson to the killer. In Stratford, London Magistrates Court her defense argued that the letters did not

Wives Who Kill

connect Mrs. Thompson to the place or manner of the murder. Accordingly, they did not allow for consideration of common purpose, namely that if two people agree to achieve the death of a third, and one of these people acts on the expressed intentions of both, both are equally guilty. The presiding magistrate decided that the letters should be admitted and that the court at the Old Bailey would rule on it again. Edith Thompson and Frederick Bywaters were each committed for trial, charged with murder. The trial began on 6 December 1922 at the Old Bailey, with Bywaters defended by Cecil Whiteley KC, and Thompson by Sir Henry Curtis-Bennett KC. The prosecution for the Crown was led by the Solicitor-General Sir Thomas Inskip, assisted by Travers Humphreys. Bywaters had cooperated completely. He had led police to the murder weapon he concealed after the murder, and consistently maintained that he had acted without Edith's knowledge. Edith Thompson's love letters were produced as evidence of incitement to murder. The extant letters date from November 1921 to the end of September 1922. They run to over 55,000 words and afford a dayto-day account of her life in London when her lover Bywaters was at sea. In a few passages of these letters, she writes about her longing to be free of her husband, Percy. She refers to grinding glass light bulbs to shards and feeding them to Percy mixed into mashed potato, and on another occasion feeding him poison. She wrote of a woman who had lost three husbands and remarked "I can't even lose one." Thompson described how she had carried out her own abortion after becoming pregnant by Bywaters. Edith Thompson's counsel urged her not to testify, stressing that the burden of proof lay with the prosecution and that there was nothing they could prove other than that she had been present at the murder. But she rejected his advice. She was determined to give evidence, imagining that she could save Bywaters. As Curtis-Bennett later observed, she had no conception of the danger she was in. She made a poor impression on the judge and the jury, particularly when she repeatedly contradicted herself. She had claimed that she had never attempted to poison her husband, and references in her letters to attempting to kill him were merely attempts to impress her paramour. In

Mariticide Club

answer to several questions relating to the meaning of some of the passages in her letters, she said "I have no idea."

(L to R) Frederick Bywaters, Percy Thompson, Edith Thompson July 1921

Bywaters stated that Edith Thompson had known nothing of his plans, nor could she have, as he had not intended to murder her husband. His aim had been to confront Percy, he claimed, and to force him to deal with the situation, and when Percy had threatened to shoot him and reacted in a superior manner, Bywaters had lost his temper. Edith Thompson, he repeatedly claimed, had made no suggestion to him to kill Percy, nor did she know that Bywaters intended to confront him. In discussing the letters, Bywaters stated that he had never believed Edith had attempted to harm her husband, but that he believed she had a vivid imagination, fueled by the novels she enjoyed reading, and in her letters she viewed herself in some way as one of these fictional characters. On 11 December the jury returned a verdict of guilty against both defendants. Both Thompson and Bywaters were sentenced to death by hanging. Edith Thompson became hysterical and started screaming in the court, while Bywaters loudly protested Edith Thompson's innocence, stating: "I say the verdict of the jury is wrong. Edith Thompson is not guilty." Before and during the trial, Thompson and Bywaters were the subjects of highly sensationalist and critical media

Wives Who Kill

commentary. But after they had been sentenced to death there was a dramatic shift in public attitudes and in media coverage. Nearly a million people signed a petition against the death sentences. Bywaters in particular attracted admiration for his fierce loyalty and protectiveness towards Edith Thompson but she was widely regarded as the controlling mind that had set it all up. It was generally considered abhorrent to hang a woman (no woman had been executed in Britain since the baby farmer Rhoda Willis 1907). Despite the petition and a new confession from Bywaters (in which he once again declared Thompson to be completely innocent) the Home Secretary, William Bridgeman, refused a reprieve. A few days before their executions, Edith Thompson was told that the date of execution had been fixed, at which point she lost her composure. She spent the last few days of her life in a state of near-hysteria, crying, screaming, moaning, and unable to eat. On 9 January 1923 in Holloway Prison, the 29-year-old Edith Thompson collapsed in terror at the prospect of her hanging. Heavily sedated by the prison governor, almost unconscious, she was carried to the gallows by four prison warders. In Pentonville Prison, the 20-year-old Frederick Bywaters, who had tried since his arrest to save Thompson from imprisonment and execution, was himself hanged. The ordeal of executing Edith Thompson had a profound effect on her hangman John Ellis. The two executions occurred simultaneously at 9:00 am, only about 1/2 mile (800 m) apart. Holloway and Pentonville prisons (respectively for women and men) are close together in North London. Later, as was the rule, the bodies of Edith Thompson and Frederick Bywaters were initially buried within the walls of the prisons in which they had been executed.

Mariticide Club

Edith Thompson's former grave in Brookwood Cemetery.
Her body was exhumed in 2018

Edith Thompson's new grave in the City of London Cemetery, June 2019

The body of Edith Thompson was initially buried in an unmarked grave within the walls of Holloway Prison, as was customary. In 1971 the prison underwent an extensive program of rebuilding, during which the bodies of all the executed women were exhumed for reburial outside the confines of the prison. With the exception of Ruth Ellis, the remains of the four women executed at Holloway (Edith Thompson, Styllou Christofi, Amelia Sach and Annie Walters) were reburied in a single grave at Brookwood

Wives Who Kill

Cemetery in Surrey. The new grave (in plot 117) remained unmarked for over 20 years. It was acquired in the 1980s by René Weis and Audrey Russell, who had interviewed Avis Graydon (Edith Thompson's surviving sister) at length in the 1970s. On 13 November 1993, a grey granite memorial was placed on plot 117, and dedicated to the memory of the four women buried there. The grave and plot were formally consecrated by the Reverend Barry Arscott of St. Barnabas, Manor Park, the church in which Edith Thompson was married in January 1916. Edith Thompson's details appear prominently on the face of the tombstone, together with her an epitaph: "Sleep on beloved. Her death was a legal formality". The names of the other three women are inscribed around the edges of the tombstone. The precise location of Thompson's former grave within Brookwood Cemetery is 51°18′13.67″N 0°37′33.33″W. Representatives of the Home Office did not inform Avis Graydon of the exhumation and the fact that she had the right to take control of her sister's funeral arrangements. The remains of Frederick Bywaters still lie in an unmarked grave within the walls of HMP Pentonville, where they were buried shortly after his execution in January 1923. The precise location of the cemetery within the prison is 51°32′44.05″N 0°06′54.62″W. The remains of Percy Thompson are buried at the City of London Cemetery and Crematorium. In her will, Avis Graydon expressed a wish for Mass to be said for members of the Graydon family every 9 January, the anniversary of her sister Edith's death. This annual service of remembrance was restarted after the publication of Weis's book in 1988. Since the early 1990s, an annual service of remembrance has taken place at St. Barnabas, Manor Park (East Ham) every 9 January at 8:30 am.

In July 2018 an exhumation order was granted by the Ministry of Justice to René Weis, Edith Thompson's executor and heir. On 20 November 2018 Edith Thompson's remains were exhumed from Brookwood Cemetery, and on 22 November 2018 she was formally buried alongside her parents, in accordance with her mother's wishes, in the City of London Cemetery. René Weis echoes a trend of recent and older suggestions that Edith Thompson was innocent of murder. In his letter to the Home Secretary in

Mariticide Club

1988, he notes that the Crown used a selection of her letters in Court to generate a climate of prejudice against her as an immoral adulteress who seduced a young man eight years her junior. Weis writes: 'Despite the fact that there is no evidence of any kind in the letters or otherwise that Edith Thompson knew that her husband would be assaulted that night in that particular place and in that manner, the Solicitor-General stated in his opening address to the jury that 'there is the undoubted evidence in the letters upon which you can find that there was a preconcerted meeting between Mrs. Thompson and Bywaters at the place'. As only half of Edith Thompson's correspondence was submitted in Court, the jury may well have been led to believe, by this erroneous claim, that a reference to the place, the time, and the manner occurred in one of the letters withheld from them. That the jury was furthermore influenced by the judge's openly expressed disgust concerning the sexual immorality of the correspondence is on record in a letter which a juror wrote to The Daily Telegraph thirty years later: 'It was my duty to read them [the letters] to the members of the jury ... "Nauseous" is hardly strong enough to describe their contents ... The jury performed a painful duty, but Mrs. Thompson's letters were her own condemnation'. It is true that Mr. Justice Shearman did instruct the jury to find Edith Thompson guilty only if they were convinced that she had lured her husband to the place where he was murdered. In his charge to the jury, he noted 'Now, I am going to ask you to consider only one question in your deliberations, and that is, was it an arranged thing between the woman and the man? ... if you think that when she saw him [Bywaters] there that evening he came there under her direction and information that she had given him as to where she would be about that time – if you think she knew perfectly well as soon as she set eyes on him that he was there to murder, she is guilty of murder too.' The judge then turned to Edith Thompson's letters, focusing on the ones referring to poison and ground glass, directing the jury to 'look at these words' when Edith related to Bywaters how she had pretended to Avis that Percy's state of health worried her. Avis had testified in court that this incident was a fabrication regarding a bottle of medicinal tincture of opium which she, Avis, had

Wives Who Kill

poured down the sink. The judge saw it differently and restated the prosecution's case: 'It is said that she is already preparing for witnesses in case there should be a murder case; that is what is said'. He failed to acknowledge that this point had been tackled head-on by the defense, as it was his duty to do. Again, commenting on a passage in the letters in which Edith Thompson refers to 'this thing that I am going to do for both of us, will it ever at all make any difference between us, darling, do you understand what I mean; will you ever think any the less of me?', the judge simply restates the Crown's interpretation, after pretending to the jury that he will resist interpreting the passage: 'The meaning of that is for you to judge; you will fully understand that it is not for me to tell you what the letters mean … It is said the meaning of that is 'If I poison him is it going to make any difference to you afterwards'; that is what is suggested as the plain meaning of the words.' The Court of Appeal would interpret the passage similarly as self-evident proof of intent to murder, overlooking the fact that this was not a charge that was being tried. The judge discredited Edith Thompson's account of the murder. She swooned (according to her, the judge notes) and she lied to shield the killer. Above all the witnesses who claimed to have heard her scream of 'Oh don't, oh don't!' may not be reliable. In his closing comments Mr. Justice Shearman impugned the integrity of the important witness John Webber, whose house overlooked the scene of the murder. Webber's is, according to the judge, a 'very curious piece of evidence'. If Webber can be trusted to tell the truth, then there is corroborative proof of Edith Thompson's spontaneous panic and hysteria during the fight and stabbings. The judge directs the jury: 'You know he [Webber] is some way off; I am not saying it is true; it is for you to say whether it is accurate, or whether it is imaginary, or whether he has made a mistake.' Such direct undermining of a bona fide witness chimed with the judge's evident hostility towards Edith Thompson. His wider antifeminist bias at the trial was evident and extensively commented on at the time. Thus, he consistently referred to the jury as "gentlemen" in spite of the fact that the jury included a woman juror. Shearman labelled Edith an 'adulterer' and therefore deceitful and wicked and, by implication, easily

Mariticide Club

capable of murder. Her letters were full of "insensate silly affection". He similarly repeatedly called Bywaters an 'adulterer'. However, Filson Young, in writing contemporaneously with the trial in Notable British Trials (1923), suggests that it was the young of that generation who needed to learn morality: 'Mr. Justice Shearman frequently referred to Bywaters as "the adulterer," apparently quite unconscious of the fact that, to people of Bywaters' generation, educated in the ethics of dear labor and cheap pleasure, of commercial sport and the dancing hall, adultery is merely a quaint ecclesiastical term for what seems to them the great romantic adventure of their lives. Adultery to such people may or may not be "sporting," but its wrongness is not a matter that would trouble them for a moment. Sinai, for them, is wrapped in impenetrable cloud. And if we are not prepared to adapt the laws of Sinai to the principles of the night club and thé dansant, I see no other alternative but to educate again our young in the eternal verities on which the law is based'. The Court of Appeal endorsed the Judge's description of the accused as adulterers: "Now, the learned judge, in his summing-up to the jury, spoke of the charge as a common or ordinary charge of a wife and an adulterer murdering the husband. That was a true and appropriate description." The deficit in evidence as to direct arrangement was conceded by the Court of Appeal. However, it pursued a line of reasoning to the effect that proof of instigation of murder in a community of purpose without evidence of rebuttal raises an "inference of preconcerted arrangement". The Court of Appeal held that her earlier prolonged incitement to murder revealed in her letters, combined with her lies about what happened on the night of the murder told to several witnesses, up until her second witness statement, which was open to being found untrustworthy, her meetings with Bywaters on the day of the murder, and the content of her last letter, was sufficient to convict her of arranging the murder. The Court of Appeal seemed to take a narrower approach to "principal in the second degree" than the Court, but it is unclear, because "preconcerted arrangement" admits of different shades of meaning. The Court of Appeal seemed determined to forestall any argument based on the mere method or timing of the murder being

Wives Who Kill

unagreed to, if there was other plausible evidence of a preconcerted object of murder. Its narrow judgment is unsatisfactory to those who now allege Edith played no part in the murder itself. However, its judgement is limited in extent to the point it was addressing, which was continuity of purpose up until the commission of the murder. If non-agreement as to the means and timing of the murder be conceded, there was merit to its claim that the case "exhibits from beginning to end no redeeming feature." In his address to the jury Curtis-Bennett attempted to cast her adultery as defensible in the context of the "glamorous aura" of a "great love," seeking to overlook the point continually being made by the Judge at the trial that the case concerned only an adulterer and an (adulterous) wife. In his summing-up, Curtis-Bennett said of Edith: 'This is not an ordinary charge of murder....Am I right or wrong in saying that this woman is one of the most extraordinary personalities that you or I have ever met? ...Have you ever read...more beautiful language of love? Such things have been very seldom put by pen upon paper. This is the woman you have to deal with, not some ordinary woman. She is one of those striking personalities met with from time to time who stand out for some reason or another....You are men of the world and you must know that where there is a liaison which includes someone who is married, it will be part of the desire of that person to keep secret the relations from the other partner. It is not the sort of thing that they would bring to the knowledge of their partner for life'. Sir Henry Curtis-Bennett KC later claimed that he could have saved her had she not rejected his advice not to take the witness stand. His failure to secure her acquittal had affected him deeply. He maintained her innocence of murder throughout his life, claiming that Edith "paid the extreme penalty for her immorality." In Notable British Trials, Filson Young takes a similar approach, suggesting that Curtis-Bennett should have resigned his brief at her insistence on going into the witness box, although his quest for fame and fortune could never have allowed it. The famous defender Sir Edward Marshall Hall KC similarly stated that he would have surrendered his defence brief if she had defied him the way she did Curtis-Bennett. Curtis-Bennett said to Mr. Stanley Bishop, a journalist, "She spoiled her chances

Mariticide Club

by her evidence and by her demeanor. I had a perfect answer to everything which I am sure would have won an acquittal if she had not been a witness. She was a vain woman and an obstinate one. She had an idea that she could carry the jury. Also, she realized the enormous public interest, and decided to play up to it by entering the witness-box. Her imagination was highly developed, but it failed to show her the mistake she was making." One mistake that Edith appeared to make was in testifying that Bywaters had led her into the poison plots. Delusion was no defense to murder and this could not save her. Curtis-Bennett argued a more legally secure but evidentially weak defense based on Edith acting the part of poisoner, or engaging in a fantasy. The fact that the two Home Office pathologists, Sir Bernard Spilsbury and Dr John Webster both concluded categorically in their independent post mortem reports that there were no traces of poison or glass in Percy Thompson's body should have been proof of the fantasy defense. One of her main lines of defense, that she was constantly seeking a divorce or separation from her husband, and that it rather than murder was the main object of the attested five-year compact between her and Bywaters shown in her letters, was dismissed by the Judge as a sham. "If you think these letters are genuine, they mean that she is involved in a continual practice of deceit; concealing the fact of her connection with Bywaters, and not reiterating it with requests for her husband to let her go." Filson Young argues that the Defense used the wrong tactics. He said: "If the defense had said on behalf of Mrs. Thompson, 'I did not murder Percy Thompson, I had nothing to do with it. I had no knowledge of it, and I was stunned and horrified when it took place, and I defy the prosecution to introduce any evidence with which that denial is not absolutely compatible,' and had rested on that, I do not think you could have found a British jury to convict her." There is undoubtedly an air of a presumption of guilt surrounding her trial. However, Young's point, that the burden of proof was on the Crown, to prove murder, rather than on the Defense to rebut a presumption of murder, is certainly a valid one. The Judge, Mr. Justice Shearman, placed much weight on inconsistencies in her evidence, particularly her statements to the police concerning the night of the murder that suggested she had

Wives Who Kill

intended to conceal her witness of the crime, and perhaps conversations of criminal intent with Bywaters preceding it, although she always vigorously denied foreknowledge of it. In The Innocence of Edith Thompson, Lewis Broad states that the Judge's summing up was considered to be at the time "deadly, absolutely against her" and that he 'was pressing the case much more strongly than the Solicitor-General had done.' The Defense did succeed in some points, showing that guesswork by the prosecution over ambiguous content of some of the letters was fanciful and wrong. An autopsy on Percy Thompson had failed to reveal any evidence that he had been fed ground glass or any type of detectable poison. That her letters did not necessarily reflect her deeds in respect of the so-termed poison plots was fairly clear. Even though perceived in her favor by Lewis Broad, Filson Young, Edgar Lustgarten, René Weis, Laura Thompson and others students of the case, the Court of Appeal held the poison-plots against her and against him: "if the question is, as I think it was, whether these letters were evidence of a protracted, continuous incitement to Bywaters to commit the crime which he did in the end commit, it really is of comparatively little importance whether the appellant was truly reporting something which she had done, or falsely reporting something which she merely pretended to do." Moreover, "it matters not whether those letters show or, at any rate, go to show, that there was between this appellant and Mrs. Thompson an agreement tending to the same end. Those letters were material as throwing light, not only upon the question by whom was this deed done, but what was the intent, what was the purpose with which it-was done" said the Court of Appeal to Bywaters. James Douglas, the chief reporter for the Express papers covering the trial in 1922/23, also took issue with the verdict, writing 'I think the hanging of Mrs. Thompson is a miscarriage of mercy and justice ... I believe she was an adulteress. But we do not hang a woman for adultery. The Mosaic Law stoned the adulteress to death. Our law punishes adultery by divorce, not by death. Therefore, in judging Mrs. Thompson we must not mix up the crime of murder with the sin of adultery. ... Let us condemn her as being guilty of all she charges herself with in her letters. Having done so, let us see what

Mariticide Club

she is not guilty of. 1. It was not her hand that struck down her husband. 2. Her husband did not die by poison or powdered glass administered by her hand. 3. There is no evidence that she put poison or glass in his food. 4. There is no evidence that at any time in any way she ever made any attempt on the life of her husband. 5. There is no evidence that she was guilty or premeditated connivance, collusion, or complicity in the actual crime. 6. There is no evidence that she was an accessory before the fact, apart from the incitements in her own letters. 7. There is no evidence that she actually aided and abetted the striking of the fatal blows. 8. There is no evidence of willful murder against her. Therefore, in her case murder is not murder, but merely a legal extension of the legal definition of murder. It is a moral, not a physical, crime. It is a sin of the soul, and not a consummation of sin in the act of slaying. I might amplify this catalogue of the innocence or nonguiltiness of Mrs. Thompson, but my eight points suffice to drive home my argument that her guilt stopped short of willful murder if only by a hair's breadth was a broad abyss separating the will from the deed. One last word. If Mrs. Thompson had not been walking with her husband when he was murdered, would the jury have found her guilty of willful murder? Why should she be hanged by reason of what may have been the unforeseen accident of her presence? In Verdict in Dispute (1949), Edgar Lustgarten states that "The Thompson verdict is now recognized as bad, and the trial from which it sprang stands out as an example of the evils that may flow from an attitude of mind." He continues with 'There was no failure of law; there was no failure of procedure; there was no failure to observe and abide by all the rules. It was from first to last a failure in human understanding; a failure to grasp and comprehend a personality not envisaged in the standard legal textbooks and driven by forces far more powerful and eternal than those that are studied in the Inns of Court.' From this it may be reasonably surmised that his essay is something of an apology for Edith, whose culpability he diminishes on the basis that "she was a woman of quality whose talents were frustrated." He adds "She was a remarkable and complex personality, endowed with signal attributes of body and of mind. She had intelligence, vitality, a natural grace and poise, sensitiveness,

Wives Who Kill

humor and illumining all these that quintessential femininity that fascinates the male." He writes "[In the absence of her letters] all that could be said against her was that she had lied in a futile attempt to protect and cover Bywaters. That might make her an accessory after the fact. It could not bring her into danger of the rope." Although Lustgarten does not allege any defect in legal procedure, he says that the Court was unable to understand questions of "sex and psychology" and the consequent possibility of fantasy. A critique of the conduct of her trial and the state of the law was made by Lewis Broad. He argued that it was the misfortune of Edith Thompson that she was unable to separate herself from the prejudice due to her immorality whereas, if it had been a former crime, she was entitled not to have it mentioned. He also attacked the judge for using morally prejudiced language to incite the prejudice of the jury. He concedes that it was within the rules for the jury to decide what the words in Edith's letters meant and what was intended by them. Broad went on to attack the general conduct of the trial: 1. She should have been granted a separate trial in that she was handicapped by having to appear alongside Bywaters. 2. The judge allowed the jury to be inflamed by prejudice on account of her immorality. 3. Suspicion based on prejudice was allowed to take the place of proof of meaning, motive and intention in respect of her letters. Broad also levels criticism against the prosecution for the unfair use of her letters at trial, covering such matters as: a) 1,500-word extract used at trial from 25,000 words in total, which in turn were less than half of her total of 51,000 or so words. Many of the letters were censored by the court during the trial, because they dealt with subjects such as menstruation and orgasm, subjects that were not then considered fit for public discussion. b) There was only one unambiguous reference to poison in the five months preceding the murder. c) The meaning of uncertain phrases were allowed to be suggested by the Crown and were determined to prejudice the jury. d) The context of the murder suggested no element of planning. e) Despite their meandering and casual discussion of the subject matter, Percy's murder, there is nothing in the letters that amounted to agreement or one. f) There was a break in the chain of causation after Bywaters had indicated he did not want to continue

Mariticide Club

to see Edith, evidenced from her letters 20 June - 12 September 1922. g) That the letters were part of a fantasy between the parties was not put forth to the jury. The 'broken chain' theory of the case, favored by Broad, arguing that there is no causal link between Edith's letters and the actual murder, because of the length of time separating them and the manner of the murder, is developed by the UCL professor of jurisprudence William Twining. In Rethinking Evidence: Exploratory Essays (2006), pp. 344–396, Twining argues that a Wigmorean, 'decompositional' analysis of the charges brought against Edith Thompson demonstrates how unsatisfactory the verdict against her was in law. Twining writes that 'For the prosecution to convict Edith, they had to prove that the attack was premeditated. Even if one totally discounts Freddy's evidence about the events of the evening (and his story of the period up to 11 p.m. was generally consistent and was largely corroborated by the Graydons), there is almost nothing to support the proposition that the attack was premeditated. There was no evidence to support the proposition that the knife was purchased recently in order to attack Percy; there was no evidence in support of the proposition that Bywaters put the knife in his pocket that morning because he planned to attack Percy — the best that the prosecution could do was point out that there was no corroboration for his claim that he was in the habit of carrying it.' The 'tea-room' passage (exhibit 60) - "Don't forget what we talked in the Tea Room, I'll still risk and try if you will — we only have 3 1/2 years left darlingest. Try and help." - was interpreted by the judge as referring to either poisoning Percy Thompson or to using a dagger. This was also the prosecution theory, that 'what' referred to killing Percy; the defense claimed that 'what' referred to Freddy trying to find Edith a post abroad so that they could elope. Twining argues that a close Wigmorean analysis allows for the following conclusions: 'For example, the judge's suggestion can be attacked on the following grounds: 1. it is sheer speculation, with no evidence to support it; 2. it involves a petitio principii in that it assumes what is seeks to prove; 3. it does not make sense of the passage: 'Don't forget what we talked in the Tea Room [about whether to use poison or a dagger], I'll still risk and try if you will we have only 3 1/2 years left

Wives Who Kill

darlingest.' Twining continues with 'Even if we totally discount testimony of both accused that it referred to eloping (the 'risks' being financial and/or of social stigma), the context of the letter as a whole and the words '31/2 years left' both tend to support the judgement that an innocent explanation is a good deal more likely than the prosecution's interpretation. At the, very least, such factors seem to me to cast a reasonable doubt on that interpretation, yet this passage was the main item of evidence in support of the conspiracy theory.' A feminist review of the case occurs in Laura Thompson's 2018 book, Rex V Edith Thompson: A tale of Two Murders. Thompson (not a relative) claims that Edith Thompson was the victim of a highly prejudicial 'gendered' trial, with the trial judge's and the Appeal Court judges' bias against the accused woman playing a key part in her conviction. In March 2018 the BBC presented a thoughtful evaluation in an episode of the series Murder, Mystery and My Family in which barristers Sasha Wass and Jeremy Dein reviewed the case. Although they were unable to determine any new evidence they agreed that there were serious issues to be addressed regarding the final summing up by the trial judge, Mr. Justice Shearman. Despite acting as prosecution and defense, Wass and Dein presented a joint submission to Senior Crown Court Judge David Radford for consideration, arguing that there was no case to answer by Edith Thompson with regard to the charge that was brought against her. Judge Radford gave his opinion that the summing up in the case was deficient and had failed to offer correct direction to the jury. He considered that it had been unfair and unbalanced and that there were grounds for coming to a decision that the conviction of Edith Thompson was both unsafe and unsatisfactory. This was followed by a second BBC 2 program in 2019, with the same participants, to take account of the reburial of Edith Thompson in November 2018. In January 2023 it was reported that an application for a posthumous pardon for Edith Thompson, using the royal prerogative of mercy, would be reconsidered by the Ministry of Justice; the application, made on behalf of Thompson's heir and executor, René Weis, had initially been rejected in 2022 by the then Justice Secretary Dominic Raab. On 6 March 2023 BBC News reported that the Secretary of State for

Mariticide Club

Justice, Dominic Raab, had referred René Weis' application on behalf of Edith Thompson to the Criminal Cases Review Commission (the CCRC), 'as a potential miscarriage of justice'. The BBC quotes Mr. Raab's letter to Prof Weis stating that this will 'allow a full investigation of your application to take place'. The Times of 7 March 2023 heads its piece on the CCRC referral with 'Pardon for hanged woman is step nearer after 100 years'. The Thompson and Bywaters case has provided the basis for several fictional and non-fictional works and depictions. The couple were the subject of waxworks at Madame Tussauds Chamber of Horrors. Alfred Hitchcock expressed the wish to make a documentary film on the case, several times commenting that the Thompson and Bywaters case was the one he would most like to film. At the start of the 1920s Hitchcock had been taught to dance by Edith Thompson's father at the Golden Lane Institute, at a time when he worked for the Cable Car Company. His sister and Avis Graydon became close friends later, as they served in the same Catholic church in Leytonstone. Hitchcock exchanged Christmas cards with Avis Graydon but they never discussed the case. He asked his authorized biographer, John Russell Taylor, not to mention the case of Edith Thompson in case it caused her sister distress, even after all those years. Some aspects of the case have similarities to the plot of Hitchcock's film Stage Fright (1950). According to the ODNB's entry on the novelist E. M. Delafield, her 1924 novel Messalina of the Suburbs was based on the Thompson/Bywaters trial. She ends the novel before the verdict is announced. In 1934, F. Tennyson Jesse published A Pin to See the Peepshow, "a fictional account of the Thompson-Bywaters case despite the usual disclaimer at the front that all the characters are imaginary. The title refers to the children's entertainment at which (she) first met her lover-tobe". This was dramatized on TV in 1973 with Francesca Annis, John Duttine and Bernard Hepton playing characters based on Edith Thompson, Bywaters and Percy Thompson respectively. Annis received a nomination for British Academy Television Award for Best Actress. A play based on the case was written in the 1930s by Frank Vosper, People Like Us, remained unperformed until 1948 when it premiered at the Wyndhams

Wives Who Kill

Theatre, London, in the West End. In non-fiction, Lewis Broad wrote The Innocence of Edith Thompson: A Study in Old Bailey Justice in 1952. René Weis published a biography of Thompson, entitled Criminal Justice: The True Story of Edith Thompson, in 1988. Weis's biography, with a new preface about the case and his letter of appeal to the Home Secretary, appeared in 2001. Also in 2001, the film Another Life was released, telling the story of the case, in which Natasha Little played Edith Thompson, Nick Moran played Percy Thompson and Iona Gruffudd played Frederick Bywaters. In 2014, Sarah Waters published the novel The Paying Guests, which does not directly represent the events of this case but was partly inspired by it. In 2018, Laura Thompson published Rex v Edith Thompson: A Tale of Two Murders. The case of Edith Thompson was featured in Murder, Mystery, and My Family, with barristers Jeremy Dein KC and Sasha Wass KC investigating whether Edith Thompson had suffered a miscarriage of justice. In light of their submissions in the program, Judge David Radford determined that Edith's conviction was indeed unsafe. In January 2020 the Edith Thompson website was launched, a comprehensive data archive with detailed accounts of Edith Thompson's 2018 exhumation and funeral, a complete set of her letters, a 90-minute interview with her sister in 1973, and unpublished photographs of Mrs. Thompson, her friends and family, and locations relating to the case. On 9 January 2023, the centenary of Edith Thompson's death, Chris Forse, formerly of Shakespeare Crescent, Manor Park, East Ham, published, online, 'Hanged for Adultery, the Tragic Fate of Edith Thompson', an indepth, extensively illustrated re-examination of the case. He concludes that she was the victim of a biased trial and of the moral climate of post-World War I Britain.

Sara Thornton

Sara Thornton (born 1954/1955) is a British woman who was sentenced to life imprisonment after being convicted of the 1989 murder of her violent and alcoholic husband, Malcolm Thornton. Thornton never denied the killing, but claimed it had been an accident during an argument. The

Mariticide Club

prosecution at her trial argued that she had carried out the act for financial gain, and she was found guilty of murder. The case became a cause célèbre among women's groups, and ignited a political debate on how the courts should deal with the issue of domestic violence. At a retrial in 1996 Thornton was found guilty of the lesser charge of manslaughter and freed from custody. Malcolm Thornton died in hospital after he was stabbed at the home he shared with his wife Sara on 12 June 1989 following an argument. At her trial in 1990, Sara Thornton pleaded guilty to manslaughter due to reasons of diminished responsibility, claiming that she had stabbed Malcolm accidentally following a row as he lay drunk on the sofa. The court heard that the police had been called to the house in Atherstone, Warwickshire on several occasions when she was being assaulted by her husband. A representative from Alcoholics Anonymous saw Malcolm punch his wife on one occasion, while a neighbor spoke of how Sara Thornton had been beaten "black and blue" to the point where she became unconscious and required hospital treatment. The prosecution claimed that Sara was a "pathological liar" who had carried out the killing for financial gain. A jury convicted her of murder. Sentencing her to life imprisonment, the judge told Thornton that she could have walked out of the house or gone upstairs. Thornton appealed the conviction, but it was rejected in 1991. The original trial had been largely ignored by the media. Thornton's case was taken up by Justice for Women, who were pressing for a change in the way cases of domestic violence are dealt with by the courts. The group, founded by Harriet Wistrich and Julie Bindel, began life as the "Free Sara Thornton campaign". Following the high-profile campaign, Thornton was eventually granted leave to appeal. At a hearing at the Court of Appeal in December 1995, lawyers argued she was a victim of "battered woman syndrome" as a result of her husband's repeated violence, something which had resulted in her losing control and killing him. Her murder conviction was quashed, and a retrial ordered for the following year.

Thornton faced her second trial in May 1996, and the twelve-day hearing took place at Oxford Crown Court. The prosecution presented evidence that

Wives Who Kill

Thornton had talked of killing her husband to a colleague. Psychiatrists successfully argued that Thornton suffered from dissociation—a personality disorder that causes an individual to react inappropriately to events. She was convicted of manslaughter, and sentenced to five years imprisonment. She was released from custody as a result of time already served. Speaking shortly afterwards, Thornton said that she believed her sentence was fair. "I am not saying that every woman should be sent to prison, but for me it was fair. I took a life at the end of the day." Despite the high-profile campaign, the verdict at Thornton's trial did little to resolve the issue of how the courts should deal with such cases. In 2008, the Labor Government of Gordon Brown put forward proposals to look at the issue as part of a planned reform of the laws governing murder. Jennifer Nadel's acclaimed non-fiction book about the case, Sara Thornton: The Story of a Woman Who Killed (1993), highlighted the ways in which the legal system discriminates against victims of domestic violence. Nadel's book was subsequently adapted into the film, Killing Me Softly (1996), which aired on BBC1 within six weeks of Thornton's release in July 1996.The drama, written by Rebecca Frayn and starring Maggie O'Neill and Peter Howitt, appeared under the Screen One strand. The case inspired the song "Woke Up This Morning" by the British band Alabama 3. The song was later adopted as the theme song to The Sopranos.

Julia Lynn Turner (née Julia Lynn Womack)

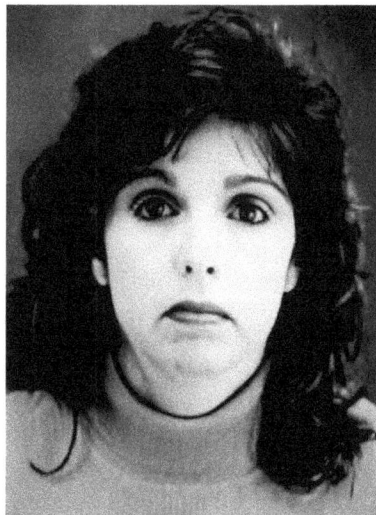

Mariticide Club

Gary Lee Triano (November 6, 1943–November 1, 1996) was a millionaire real estate developer from Tucson, Arizona who was killed in Catalina Foothills by a pipe bomb explosion in his Lincoln Town Car on November 1, 1996. His former wife, Pamela Anne Phillips, a onetime model, real estate agent and socialite, was charged with orchestrating her ex-husband's death. In a sensational trial nearly 18 years after Triano's murder, Phillips was convicted of first-degree murder and conspiracy to commit murder and was sentenced to life in prison. Phillips, who is now incarcerated at the Arizona State Prison Complex – Perryville, claims that Triano's death was a mob revenge killing. Ronald Young, who was hired by Phillips as a hit man, also was convicted and sentenced to life in prison. Gary Triano was a longtime Tucson, Arizona resident. He graduated from Rincon High School and earned a degree in accounting from the University of Arizona. He also attended the University of Arizona's law school. He married Mary Cram, and they had two children, Heather and Brian. Triano married his second wife, Pamela Phillips, on October 4, 1986 in San Diego, California. During their marriage, the couple had two children, Trevor and Lois, before their bitter divorce in 1993. At the time of the divorce, Triano filed for Chapter 11 bankruptcy, claiming $40 million in debt after several failed business dealings regarding Indian casinos. Phillips moved to Aspen, Colorado with the couple's two children, where she continued her career in commercial real estate. On November 1, 1996, Gary Triano was killed when a pipe bomb exploded in his car at the La Paloma Country Club in Arizona. Within weeks, the investigation centered around his ex-wife Pamela Phillips, who was still living in Aspen. It was discovered that she had taken out a $2 million life insurance policy on Triano shortly before his death. The couple's two children were the beneficiaries of the policy, which was paid out to Phillips in 1997. Evidence also linked Phillips to Ronald Young, a small-time criminal with whom Phillips developed a relationship while in Aspen. Shortly before the bombing, a van rented by Young was found abandoned in Yorba Linda, California, and inside the vehicle there were documents pertaining to Phillips and Triano's divorce, a map of Tucson, Arizona, and a sawed-off

Wives Who Kill

shotgun. Nine years after the murder, on November 19, 2005, an episode of America's Most Wanted profiled Ronald Young, who was then wanted for forgery and embezzlement. The episode also mentioned his suspected involvement in Triano's death. Two days later, Young was apprehended in Fort Lauderdale, Florida. He served a 10-month sentence in federal prison for weapon possession before being extradited back to Aspen. Following Young's arrest, investigators found records of phone calls and email correspondence between Young and Phillips related to Triano's murder. In 2008, Ronald Young was charged with the murder of Gary Triano. On December 3, 2009, Pamela Phillips was also arrested for Triano's murder in Vienna, Austria, when she fled after her indictment in October 2008. She was later returned to the United States to stand trial. Ronald Young went to trial for Gary Triano's murder in 2010. Prosecutors showed records that Phillips agreed to give Young $400,000 to kill her exhusband. Also introduced into evidence were the tapes and recordings outlining the conspiracy. At the conclusion of his trial, Young was convicted of first-degree murder and conspiracy to commit murder. He was sentenced to two life terms. Following her extradition to Arizona to stand trial, Pamela Phillips was held on $5 million bond at the Pima County Jail. In December 2011, she was initially ruled mentally incompetent for trial. In October 2012, she was ruled competent to stand trial after undergoing treatment at the jail. Phillips' trial began in 2014 and lasted for seven weeks. Prosecutors used similar evidence in her trial that was used to convict Young. Phillips was convicted of first-degree murder and conspiracy. Like Young, she was also sentenced to life in prison; she has no possibility for parole. The murder of Gary Triano has been televised on several programs, including Dateline NBC, Dateline on ID, 48 Hours, Snapped, American Greed (2015 episode "A Widow's Web"), Fatal Vows and Vengeance: Killer Millionaires. In January 2012, the case was a subject of a true crime book by Kerie Droban. Julia Lynn Turner (July 16, 1968 – August 30, 2010), originally Julia Lynn Womack, was an American convicted murderer. In 1995, her husband, Glenn Turner, died after allegedly being sick with the flu. In 2001, the death of what had been

Mariticide Club

described as her common-law husband, Randy Thompson, under remarkably similar circumstances, aroused the suspicion of law enforcement. After investigation, it was determined by authorities that Lynn Turner had murdered both her husbands by poisoning them with ethylene glycol–based antifreeze. She was tried for Glenn Turner's murder in 2004. She was found guilty and went to trial in 2007 for the murder of Randy Thompson, ultimately being convicted. Turner died in prison on August 30, 2010.The cause of death was an apparent suicide by toxic overdose of blood pressure medication. Julia Lynn was adopted by the Womack family shortly after her birth mother gave her up. The Womacks divorced when Lynn was five, after which Helen Womack took custody of Lynn. Shortly afterwards, Helen Womack married again, and Lynn did not get on well with her new stepfather, D.L. Gregory. As a teenager, Lynn took to substance abuse and was admitted to a clinic in Atlanta for drug problems. By the 1990s, Lynn Womack was working as a 911 dispatcher for Cobb County, Georgia. Lynn attempted to become a police officer, but she failed the psychological exam.

Marriage to Glenn Turner In 1991 she met a Cobb County police officer named Maurice Glenn Turner and began to pursue him. She married Glenn Turner in August 1992. Glenn began to work a job at a gas station to support himself and Lynn after she left her job. Shortly after they married, Glenn and Lynn began to have problems in their marriage due to Lynn spending more money than Glenn could make and soon were sleeping in different bedrooms. Around the same time Lynn began an affair with Forsyth County firefighter Randy Thompson who was from Warner Robins, Georgia. Glenn was unaware of his wife's affair and by 1995 he began plans to move out and file for divorce. However, before he could go through with it, he fell ill and went to the room on March 2, 1995, complaining of flu-like symptoms. He was treated there, and when he felt better he went home. The next day, he was found dead when Lynn came home. Glenn's cause of death was ruled natural causes due to an irregular heartbeat. After Glenn's death she moved in with Randy Thompson and collected $153,000 from her husband's death and pension. Lynn and Randy

Wives Who Kill

bought a house together and had a son and daughter. By 2000 Randy and Lynn were having problems in their relationship, causing Randy to move out. On January 22, 2001, Randy Thompson, age 32, was found dead in his apartment. Thompson had reported feeling ill with flu symptoms and had gone to the emergency room complaining of a stomach ache and constant vomiting. He was treated and released on January 21. Lynn made him some Jell-O and by the next day, he was dead. She only collected $36,000 in her boyfriend's death because his $200,000 insurance policy had lapsed. Thompson's reported cause of death was an irregular heartbeat, the same cause of death as Lynn's previous husband. Shortly after Randy Thompson's death, police reopened the case of Glenn Turner's death after finding that both men died under nearly the same circumstances. Suspecting something sinister, Glenn Turner's mother read Randy Thompson's obituary and called a named relative saying she lost her son very mysteriously as well and stated that both her son and Randy had a common connection to Lynn Turner. Blood tests later found that ethylene glycol–based antifreeze was found in Thompson's system. Police discovered that Lynn had visited an animal shelter, asking about how to put down a stray animal and what poison to use. Glenn Turner's body was exhumed and ethylene glycol was also found in his kidneys. Crime scene photos from Glenn Turner's death contained a photograph of the garage where antifreeze was visible.

Ten months after Randy Thompson's death, Lynn was arrested for Glenn's murder. She was tried for Glenn Turner's murder in 2004 and was found guilty. She went to trial in 2007 for the murder of Randy Thompson, ultimately being convicted. The state contended that she poisoned both men by placing the antifreeze in their food as it is odorless with a sweet taste. She faced execution for the murder of Randy Thompson, but was instead sentenced to life imprisonment without parole. According to the Georgia Department of Corrections website, Turner was serving her sentences at Metro State Prison. Turner was found dead in prison on August 30, 2010. Her death was ruled a suicide. An episode of Murder She Solved on the Oprah Winfrey Network claimed that she intentionally accumulated

Mariticide Club

enough prescription medication to cause an overdose. Turner's case has been profiled on many different television programs. Her case first aired on Forensic Files in 2007 in an episode entitled "Cold Hearted". Her case aired on season six of Snapped on the Oxygen Network that year, and three programs on the Investigation Discovery network: Deadly Women, Main Street Mysteries, and Motives and Murders. On July 18, 2012, the ABC show Final Witness told the story from the perspective of her first husband, in an episode entitled Vixen's Elixir. Oxygen True Crime, Charmed to Death "Dispatched" (S1 E6) aired August 22, 2021.

Sophie Charlotte Elisabeth Ursinus (née Weingarte)

Sophie Charlotte Elisabeth Ursinus (née Weingarten; 5 May 1760 – 4 April 1836) was a German serial killer believed to have been responsible for poisoning her husband, aunt, and lover, and of attempting to poison her servant. Her trial led to a method of identifying arsenic poisoning. Sophie Weingarten was born in Glatz (now Kłodzko), a city in Lower Silesia, Prussia, the daughter of the secretary of the Austrian legation. Her father having lost his position, at the age of 19 she married the much older counselor of the Supreme Court Theodor Ursinus. She lived with him in Stendal until 1792 and afterwards in Berlin. Privy Counsellor Ursinus died there, suddenly, on 11 September 1800, a day after celebrating his birthday. His wife came under suspicion for not summoning a doctor, after the medicine she administered to him made his condition worse. During her marriage Sophie had started an affair with a Dutch officer named Rogay, possibly with the consent of her elderly husband. He left Berlin for a time, but later returned and died three years before her husband. At the time his death was attributed to tuberculosis. It was later discovered that shortly before his death Sophie Ursinus had purchased a quantity of arsenic.

Wives Who Kill

Sophie Ursinus

On 24 January 1801 an aunt of Sophie Ursinus, Christiane Witte, died in Charlottenburg after a short illness, leaving her a large inheritance. It was again later discovered that Sophie Ursinus had purchased a large quantity of arsenic shortly before her aunt had died. At the end of February 1803 Sophie Ursinus's servant, Benjamin Klein, became ill, after having quarreled with her sometime earlier. She gave him an emetic, then soup, which made him worse. He became suspicious and when she gave him some plums, he secretly had them examined by a chemist, who confirmed that they contained arsenic. Sophie Ursinus was arrested and soon came under suspicion of having poisoned her husband. His body was exhumed, but at the autopsy the examiners, the chemist Martin Heinrich Klaproth and his assistant, Valentin Rose, could not confirm that he had been poisoned with arsenic. But there was a suspicion, from the general condition of the bodily organs and convulsive contraction of the limbs, that arsenic had been used to poison him. She was next charged with murdering her aunt. Again, the body was exhumed but this time the examiners, contrary to what

Mariticide Club

the doctors had said at her death, had no doubt that the aunt had died from arsenic poisoning and that Sophie Ursinus had administered the poison. The trial for murder ended on 12 September 1803. In her attempt to save her life and honor, Sophie Ursinus had disputed every point, but was found guilty of the murder of her aunt and the attempted murder of her servant, and was sentenced to life imprisonment. She was allowed a certain amount of comfort while in prison in Glatz; she was even allowed to have parties with guests and to dress in fine clothes. After 30 years, she was pardoned in 1833 and rejoined the upper-class society of Glatz until her death in 1836. The work of Valentin Rose in proving that the victims in this case were actually poisoned showed that the evidence of doctors who were present at death was not sufficient. In 1836 the Marsh test, a highly sensitive method in the detection of arsenic, was developed by the chemist James Marsh.

Elizabeth Van Valkenburgh (née Woodley)

Elizabeth Van Valkenburgh (née Woodley; July 1799 – January 24, 1846) an early American murderer who was hanged for poisoning her husband. Elizabeth Woodley was born in Bennington, Vermont. Her parents died when she was around 8 years old, and she was sent to Cambridge, New York to live; she had little education or religious upbringing. She first married at the age of 20, moving with her husband, with whom she had four children, to Pennsylvania. After living there for six years, the family moved near to Johnstown, New York, where she remained for the next 18 years. In 1833, her first husband died, which she initially stated was due to dyspepsia and exposure. Later, she admitted that she had poisoned him by adding arsenic to his rum, because she was "provoked" by his drinking in bars. In an addendum to her confession to Van Valkenburgh's murder, she noted that her first husband had been able to go to work the following day after being poisoned, although he suffered after effects until he died, and that she did not intend to kill him.

Second marriage and murder

Wives Who Kill

She married John Van Valkenburgh, with whom she had two more children, in 1834. In her confession, she stated that he was an alcoholic, that he "misused the children", and that "we frequently quarreled" when he was drunk. Her son had offered to buy "a place" for her and the other children in the west, but John Van Valkenburgh opposed this. She stated in her confession that "John was in a frolic for several weeks, during which time he never came home sober, nor provided anything for his family." She managed to purchase arsenic and poison his tea, although he recovered from the first dose of poison. Several weeks later, she mixed another dose in his brandy. So gruesome was his death, however, she said that "if the deed could have been recalled, I would have done it with all my heart."

She ran away, hid in a barn, and broke her leg in a fall from the haymow. She was captured, tried and convicted. She was sentenced to death by hanging. Many people, including ten of the jurors, petitioned Governor Silas Wright for clemency, but having studied the materials related to the crime, and despite being moved by her gender and poverty, he could find no new evidence to stop the execution. She was executed on January 24, 1846. Because of her broken leg and her obesity, Van Valkenburgh was hanged in an unusual way. She was carried to the gallows in her rocking chair and was rocking away when the trap was sprung.

Maria Velten aka "Bilberry Mariechen"
"The Poison Witch from Lower Rhine"

Maria Velten (1916 – 2008) was a German serial killer, who was sentenced to life imprisonment for three murders. Maria Velten died in 2008 in a nursing home after having been released from prison for health reasons. Velten was a war widow with six children, two of them conceived after the war. In 1983, she was arrested after one of her daughters-in-law told her lawyer that her mother-in-law had poisoned her two husbands. Following investigations by the police revealed that Velten had killed in about 20 years - from 1963 to 1982 - a total of five people: her father, an aunt, two husbands and a partner. She mixed parathion with bilberry pudding, as the color of the pudding covered the blue warning color of the poison.

Mariticide Club

Therefore, she was referred to in the tabloid press as "Bilberry Mariechen" and "The Poison Witch from Lower Rhine". Maria Velten killed mainly for financial reasons; however, most of the time she did not spend on herself, but gave it to her children and grandchildren. In 2009, a documentary about Velten was broadcast on German television (ARD). The accompanying text from the film states: "Here we have the classic case of a poison murder series committed by a woman. Women usually kill out of a situation of weakness to protect themselves or their families in a situation that is considered unbearable. If the deed succeeds because it has gone undetected, the temptation to undertake the seemingly simple way of solving conflicts again becomes great. Also witnessed in women who had always been perceived as weak and as victims, the killings give a sense of power: they will master over life and death in their environment."

The case was also featured in a RTL series Anwälte der Toten.

Louise Vermilya (née Woolf)

Louise Vermilya (née Woolf; July 1868 – December 1913)was an American "black widow" whose activities spanned the turn of the 20th century. Light was shed on her murders only after she resorted to murdering outside of her immediate family, beginning with the death of policeman Arthur Bissonette. Authorities were alerted and suspicion arose over the peculiar and similar fates experienced by her two husbands, several immediate family members and two associates known to her.

Wives Who Kill

Sketch by journalist Marguerite Martyn,
November 1911 while awaiting her trial

Louise Vermilya was born Louesa Woolf in Cook County, Illinois, to parents Wilhemina (née Munaroe) and John Woolf, Prussian immigrants. She was the oldest daughter of five girls and third oldest child out of 11 siblings. She married 24-year-old Fred Brinkamp on April 2, 1885, at the age of 16 and moved to the village of Barrington within the Cuba township of Lake County in northern Illinois. The string of homicides began in 1893, when Vermilya claimed the life of her first husband, Fred Brinkamp, while living on their farm near Barrington, Illinois. The coroner ruled Brinkamp's death to be attributed to a heart attack. Following his death, she inherited $5,000 from a life insurance policy Brinkamp had which named her as the beneficiary. Due to Brinkamp's age at death, no suspicions arose as it was thought to be due to natural causes. Brinkamp left behind six children, two of whom met similar fates to their father shortly after his death. Cora Brinkamp was the first to die at age eight, with her sister Florence following at four and a half years old. Undertaker E.N. Blocks, who owned a mortuary in Barrington, recalled that Louise enjoyed working around bodies. Despite not being a salaried employee, Vermilya seemed too eager to work in the mortuary with Blocks "while I never employed her for a couple of years I couldn't

Mariticide Club

keep her out of the office". Blocks also stated that "at every death she would seem to hear of it just as soon as I and she would reach the house only a little behind me." Vermilya moved to Chicago in 1906 with her minor charges in tow. It was while living in Chicago that Vermilya claimed the life of her stepdaughter, 26-year-old Lillian Brinkamp. The coroner, however, ruled her cause of death as "acute nephritis". Due to the unusually high number of deaths within the Brinkamp family, they were thought to be cursed. Around this time, Vermilya remarried to a man named Charles Vermilya, aged 59. Three years later, he died, apparently victim to sudden illness. He left his widow with $1,000 in cash and a home in Crystal Lake, Illinois, forty-five miles northwest of Chicago. Her stepson, Harry Vermilya, followed his father in death shortly after quarreling with Louise over the sale of the Crystal Lake estate. No suspicions arose after the deaths, and coincidence was blamed. The following year, in 1910, Vermilya inherited $1,200 after the death of her 23-year-old son from her first marriage, Frank Brinkamp. Frank had been married to a widow and divorced her, receiving $1,200 from the divorce proceedings. On his death bed, he voiced suspicion involving his stepmother to his fiancée, Elizabeth Nolan, stating he was "going the way his father did." Uncharacteristically, Vermilya began poisoning acquaintances. Jason Rupert, a railroad fireman, fell ill after dining with Vermilya on January 15, 1910. He died two days later, but was only the first in a series of deaths of boarders in Vermilya's home. In February 1910, Vermilya married Richard Smith, a train conductor and boarder at her home. On March 11, 1910, two days after eating a meal prepared by Vermilya, he met a similar fate to Vermilya's prior boarder. His death was determined to be caused by gastritis.

Smith was still married at the time of his supposed nuptials to Vermilya. His estranged wife believed that the circumstances surrounding her husband's death were suspicious. She believed that Smith was murdered for one of three reasons, "either Mrs. Vermilya loved Smith and was afraid that he would desert her, or he was murdered for his money, or C. C. Boysen, the undertaker, thought to be in love with Mrs. Vermilya, was jealous". While her motive in the earlier deaths of her family members was

Wives Who Kill

pursuit of financial gain, they became unclear after the deaths of her boarders, for whom she gained no monetary rewards. It wasn't until Arthur Bissonette came to dine with Vermilya did she experience her undoing. While dining with his father at the Vermilya home in October 1911, both of the Bissonettes started experiencing abdominal pain. Homicide detectives became suspicious after questioning Bissonette's father who states he saw Vermilya sprinkling "white pepper" over their meals prior to serving them. This led the Chicago Police Department to do an autopsy on Bissonette's body revealing arsenic poisoning. Vermilya was taken into custody soon after its discovery. There is some speculation as to whether Bissonette's death was precipitated by financial motives. With Vermilya's assistance, Bissonette was accepted into the Home Guard, a militia-like entity for those men who were unable to qualify for the military. In return, Bissonette was to make a will naming Vermilya as the sole beneficiary of the insurance policy he would carry as a result of this employment. Vermilya was to name him as her beneficiary for the life insurance that she carried after their nuptials. Bissonette authored a will shortly before his death, but named his fiancé who lived in nearby Kankakee, Lydia Rivard, as the beneficiary of his estate. Though Vermilya was listed as the witness, she claimed to have no knowledge of ever signing the document. On November 4, Vermilya was rushed to the hospital after playing victim to her own modus operandi. Authorities reported Vermilya had been ingesting the "white pepper" since her house arrest on October 28. By November 9, she was reported as being near her death with comorbidities such as valvular heart problems adding to her demise. Vermilya was discharged from the county hospital on November 24, 1911. By December 9, she was stricken with paralysis, which physicians stated was a permanent condition. Nevertheless, Vermilya was required to attend all her court proceedings, and usually did so in a wheelchair. Vermilya was arraigned before Municipal Judge Walker on 6 November 1911 for the death of Arthur Bissonette. On 7 March 1912, nolle prosequi was filed after it had been found that Bissonette had been taking medication containing arsenic. In an effort to expedite court proceedings, a conference was held between the

Mariticide Club

presiding judge, Judge Kersten, attorney Joseph R. Barres, and the prosecutor on the case. The prosecutor was reticent as to the strongest points and the motive in Smith's death stating "There are several cases as to which Mrs. Vermilya may be tried and I don't want to try her more than once...For that reason, I want to pick out the strongest one and I have concluded the Smith one is the strongest one." Vermilya was rearrested and charged for the murder of Richard Smith. Evidence of arsenic poisoning was found in Smith's liver via autopsy conducted by Prof. Walter S. Haines, the Rush Medical College expert chemist. His findings showed "arsenic in sufficient quantities in the viscera of the two men to cause death." Vermilya was taken into custody and detained in the county jail where she attempted suicide again. The trial began on 21 March 1912 and lasted 16 days. The case was resubmitted for trial ten days later, ending in another hung jury as evidence against her was deemed circumstantial. There were subsequent difficulties that further complicated the progression of the trial. Juror selection had become an arduous process as men were unsure of if they could inflict the death penalty on a woman as freely as they would on a man. Nearly every man called forward had established a bias based on current newspaper accounts of the crime. A good percentage of these were sure that because of the impression made by the newspaper stories, they could not give a fair verdict. About 50% of those who passed this barrier had a prejudice against circumstantial evidence which necessitated their being excused. Up to this point, the jury had been composed of an all-male panel, who were unable to not only impose a death sentence on a woman, but whose attitudes toward female defendants in murder cases also came into question. By 12 October 1912, Vermilya was still in custody awaiting trial along with fellow murderer Louisa Lindloff. On 28 June 1913, Vermilya was released on $5,000 bail due to concerns for her continued failing health and exposure to the summer heat in a non-airconditioned jail, pending her trial for the poisoning of Richard Smith. On 18 April 1915, a conference was held between the Assistant State's Attorney, Michael Sullivan, and the State Attorney Hoyne regarding continuation of the trial. It was decided that it would be impossible to obtain a conviction on the

Wives Who Kill

Smith indictment, with Sullivan remarking "We could only see that another trial would entail a heavy cost without any assurance of being able to show any strong evidence." Per the request of Vermilya's attorney, all charges were dropped. Vermilya led a quiet life following the dismissal of her charges as no further documentation exists of her in local papers past this point. It is estimated that Vermilya amassed a total of $15,000 from the nine deaths.

Hattie Livermore Whitten

Hattie Livermore Whitten (July 24, 1862 – November 30, 1902) was an American serial killer who poisoned her husband and two daughters in the early 20th-century. Arrested after attending her daughter's funeral, Whitten hanged herself while in prison custody, and thus was unable to be put on trial for her crimes. Little is known of Hattie's early life prior to her moving to Dexter. It was reported that she came from a respectable family in Dover, one of two daughters born to David and Esther (née Lord) Livermore. At some point in her life, she married Harry E. Whitten and gave birth to three children: Fannie, Jennie and Lewis. In 1900, Harry died suddenly under suspicious circumstances, most likely as a result of poisoning from his wife. In the following two years, friends and acquaintances noted that Mrs. Whitten's behavior became odd, evidently from a morphine addiction. Sometime in September 1902, the Whittens moved to Dexter, with Hattie running a boarding house for a short time period. On September 19, 11-year-old Fannie died suddenly, with the coroner ruling the cause of death as meningitis. This was suspicious, however, as the little girl appeared to be in good health, with no obvious signs of any ailment. Nevertheless, Hattie had insured her daughter, receiving $85 from the insurance company. About a month after Fannie's death, Jennie and Lewis began to notice that their mother's mental health rapidly deteriorating. Not long after, tragedy struck again - the 9-year-old Jennie also died suddenly on November 27, from what was supposed to be heart failure. But authorities were suspicious, as the Whitten girl was insured for $50 by her mother, and requested that coroner George M. Barrows examine the little girl's corpse. To his shock,

Mariticide Club

Barrows discovered traces of arsenic and strychnine in Jennie's body, which led him to issue an arrest warrant for murder. The day after, Hattie Whitten was arrested at her home immediately after returning from her daughter's funeral. While Hattie was held in custody, Fannie's body was exhumed and tested as well. While the autopsy results were never publicly disclosed, it is very likely that traces of poison were found in her as well. Not long after, Mrs. Whitten was arraigned before the court for Jennie's murder, pleading not guilty to the charge. She was to be held until Tuesday in the custody of Dep. Leslie Curtis, but stayed the night in the house of her son Lewis, sleeping soundly next to her elderly mother. On November 30, the deputy took the suspected poisoner into his home, where he kept her under house arrest. Around noon, Curtis briefly left the house so he could feed his horse in the barn. Seizing the opportunity, Hattie Whitten took two towels and tied them together into a noose, with which she hanged herself from the bed post. When Curtis found her lifeless body, he called in medical staff to help resuscitate her, but to no avail. Along with her daughters, Hattie was buried at the family plot in Evergreen Cemetery, in Milo. Sometime after her death, some peculiar facts were revealed to the public, including a possible motive for her filicides: ever since coming to Dexter, Hattie had been courted by a weaver named Surto, whom she planned to marry. However, Surto refused to engage with a woman who had children of her own, which likely led to Whitten's decision to end her kids' lives. Circumstantial evidence supporting her guilt was also disclosed, as a day prior to Fannie's death, she was seen buying laudanum, arsenic and castor oil; similarly, while the still-healthy Jennie was out selling wares so she could buy her mother a present for Christmas, Hattie was seen buying the arsenic and strychnine she would later kill her with. Dr. Murphy, who attended both of the children, voiced his opinion that the poisons were likely ingested in the form of oil, so they could easily pass through the stomach into the intestines. When it came to the death of Jennie, Hattie had apparently left a postal card calling for the doctor to treat her, despite him living only half a mile away from her residence, and having a telephone.

Wives Who Kill

Dorothea Widmer

A copper engraving of Widmer's head by Matthias Stumpf.

Dorothea Widmer (1758 - 1781), was a Swiss woman who was abused by her husband until she killed him. Her crime attracted tremendous public attention in Switzerland. Widmer's husband was an alcoholic who habitually abused her. With her accomplice Bartholome Gubler, Widmer murdered him. Widmer and Gubler were both convicted of murder and sentenced to execution. After a postponement until her child was born, Widmer was executed on 29 August 1781 in Zürich. Widmer attracted great public sympathy because of her youth, beauty and her longstanding abuse. She was compared with Beatrice Cenci and became the subject of poems and inscriptions.

Mariticide Club

Denise Williams

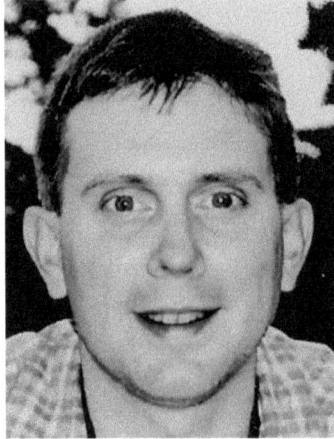

Photo of Williams circulated since his disappearance

Jerry Michael "Mike" Williams (October 16, 1969 – December 16, 2000) was an American man. Williams was initially presumed to have drowned on a 2000 hunting trip to Lake Seminole, a large reservoir straddling the Georgia-Florida state line; investigators later came to suspect he had been the victim of foul play, possibly at another location. His body was found in October 2017 near Tallahassee, and Florida Department of Law Enforcement (FDLE) officials confirmed he was a victim of homicide. After Williams' boat was found abandoned on the lake, the initial theory was that he had fallen out of it after a collision while duck hunting. However, a lengthy and exhaustive search of the lake bed in the area failed to find his body: at that time, it was the only known occasion when no remains or body had been discovered after a drowning death in the lake. It was eventually concluded that his body had been eaten by alligators. After waders and a jacket containing Williams's hunting license were found in the lake six months later, he was declared legally dead, following a court petition by his widow, Denise. She went on to marry Brian Winchester, a mutual friend who had helped her take out a large life insurance policy on Williams shortly before his disappearance. Some investigators felt aspects of the case were not consistent with the alligator theory. After years of pressure from Williams's mother, Cheryl, the case was reopened in 2004 by the FDLE. By then, officers had learned that alligators do not, in fact, eat during the winter months, as the water is too cold, and as such, it was

Wives Who Kill

suspected that foul play might have occurred. But it did not produce any new evidence, as the potential crime scene had not been secured during the search for Williams. Cheryl Williams wrote letters daily to the governor, asking him to have the state reopen the investigation even though two later investigations were likewise unable to uncover any significant new information, alienating many of the law enforcement officials she had previously persuaded to reopen it. The Investigation Discovery channel series Disappeared devoted an episode to the case in 2012. In 2016, Winchester was arrested on charges stemming from an incident where he allegedly kidnapped Denise, the missing man's widow, who was now divorcing him; he was sentenced to 20 years in prison on the day before the FDLE announced that Williams's body had been found. In May 2018, Denise Williams was arrested and charged with first-degree murder, conspiracy to commit murder, and accessory. She was found guilty that December, after Winchester testified to shooting Michael at Denise's behest when their original plan to stage a boating accident failed, and was sentenced to life in prison in January of 2019. In 2020, a Florida appellate court overturned her murder conviction but upheld her murder conspiracy conviction, for which she will serve 30 years. Jerry Michael Williams was known as Michael or Mike. He grew up in Bradfordville (north of Tallahassee), the son of a Greyhound bus driver and a day care provider who raised him and his older brother Nick in a double-wide trailer. Instead of building a house, the parents saved their money so both boys, who helped by working nights at supermarkets, could attend North Florida Christian High School. There Mike excelled, serving as student council president, playing football and being active in the Key Club. At the age of 15, he began duck hunting as a hobby, and also came to know fellow student Denise Merrell. After North Florida Christian, he attended Florida State University, where he majored in political science and urban planning. Before graduation, he was hired by Ketcham Appraisal Group as a property appraiser. He distinguished himself as "the hardest-working man I ever saw", according to the company's owner. After he married Merrell in 1994, he would often go home for dinner and return to work after she (and

Mariticide Club

later, his daughter as well) went to bed, and he sometimes went into work after going duck hunting in the morning. According to his mother, Mike was making US$200,000 annually by the time of his disappearance. He and Denise had bought a home in a small upscale subdivision on the east side of the city. In 1999, Williams's only child, a daughter, was born. His coworkers said he was as devoted to her as he was to his work. The following year his father died. Midway through the year, the couple bought a $1 million life insurance policy on him through Brian Winchester, a childhood acquaintance of Merrell who had also become best friends with her husband. Later that year, Williams told his mother, whom he had been consoling, that he would have liked to have $50,000 to take the next year off. Two days before his disappearance, Mike and Denise told his mother, as well as his brother Nick, that they were planning to have another child soon. In 2001, she said, they were planning to go on a cruise in Hawaii that spring; later in the year he expected to travel to Jamaica for work as well.

According to Denise Williams, on the morning of December 16, 2000, a Saturday, her husband awoke early, leaving the house on Centennial Oaks Circlewell before dawn, boat in tow, to go duck hunting at Lake Seminole. The lake is a large reservoir approximately 50 mi (80 km) westnorthwest of Tallahassee located in the southwest corner of Georgia along its border with Florida, where three other streams merge to form the Apalachicola River. The couple had plans to celebrate their sixth wedding anniversary that night in Apalachicola. At noon, Denise called her father to tell him that Mike had not returned; Brian Winchester's (Mike's best friend) father drove with Winchester to the areas of the lake where they knew Mike Williams frequently went duck hunting. They found his 1994 Ford Bronco near a remote boat launch in Jackson County, on the Florida side. After investigators with the Florida Fish and Wildlife Conservation Commission (FFWCC) were called, a search began, but soon had to be called off after a storm blew in.

Wives Who Kill

Shoreline on the west side of Lake Seminole

The initial search investigation was handled by the FFWCC. Since it had been reported to them as a missing hunter, the agency handled the case that way, focusing on search and rescue or recovery. "We didn't have a whole lot to go on except there was an empty boat and the guy didn't show up," one of the agency's officers recalled later, after his retirement. "There was nothing there that we had from the scene that suggested foul play at all." Deputies with the Jackson County Sheriff's Office were present but primarily worked in a support capacity. Searchers focused on the 10 acres (4.0 ha) of the lake surrounding the cove where Williams's truck was parked. His boat was soon found roughly 225 feet (69 m) from the ramp by a helicopter pilot, who initially assumed it was a boat being used in the search. After retrieving the boat, investigators found Williams's shotgun, still in its case, but no sign of Williams himself. The cove is locally believed to have been an orchard before the Chattahoochee and Flint rivers and Creek were dammed to create the lake. It took its name, Stump Field, from the many remaining stumps that protruded above and below the water level, requiring careful handling of any powerboat in the area. Searchers thus assumed that Williams had hit a stump with his boat, fallen out, sunk into waters 8–12 feet (2.4–3.7 m) deep when his waders filled, and then drowned when he was unable to extricate himself. Had Williams drowned, his body would have been expected to eventually float to the surface.

Mariticide Club

It would be easier to discover at the surface. Investigators assured the Williams family that his body would surface, like other drowning victims, within three to seven days, or perhaps slightly longer due to the cold front that had moved in after the first night's storm. No body was found, however. Ten days into the search, a camouflage-patterned hunting hat was found, but it could not be connected to Williams. Efforts continued until the search was called off in early February. It has since been suggested that the search might have been continued had Denise Williams indicated an interest in such. At that time, the case was still considered open. "Nothing in investigative or search and rescue efforts has produced any definitive evidence of a boating accident or a fatality as of this date," read the final report, issued in late February 2001.

If Williams had drowned after accidentally falling out of his boat, his body would be the only one of 80 known deaths in the lake never to have been found. The head of a private search firm that supplemented official efforts

Wives Who Kill

near the end of the search offered a possible explanation. "With the wildlife around, I would guess that the alligators have dismembered and have stored the remains in a location that we would not be able to find," he wrote in a report. Early searchers had reported seeing many of them, and some of the officials were willing to accept the possibility. "Everyone knows the lake is full of alligators," said the FFWCC's David Arnette. "You look for other answers: 'Why hasn't the body appeared?'" It was suggested that Williams's body could have been caught in the lake's dense underwater hydrilla beds. It was suggested that perhaps Williams's body had become entangled in the beds of dense hydrilla beneath the lake surface, and then found by the alligators later, with turtles and catfish finishing what they had left behind. Denise Williams, who had avoided media attention during the search for her husband, accepted that her husband had died. She arranged for a memorial service for Mike to be held the day after the search ended. In June, an angler in the Stump Field area discovered a pair of waders floating in the lake, and divers called to search the area then recovered from the lake bottom a lightweight hunting jacket and a flashlight: in one of the jacket pockets, there was a hunting license with Williams's name and signature. However, there were no teeth marks or any other damage on the waders, none of the recovered items showed signs of having been in the water for anything like the period Williams had been missing, and there was no DNA evidence found to link the clothing to him. Nevertheless, a week later, a Leon County judge granted Denise Williams's petition to have Mike declared legally dead on the basis of those recovered items and an assumption that alligators and other water life had consumed the body in its entirety. The court decision allowed Denise Williams to immediately proceed with claims on her husband's life insurance policies, from which she received $1.5 million. Five years later, she married Brian Winchester, who had sold Mike some of the policies a few months before he disappeared. The couple went on to live in the same house where Denise and Mike had lived prior. Denise and Brian have mostly declined to discuss the case publicly The private search team that surmised the alligator theory had been hired near the end of the original search by Williams's mother,

Mariticide Club

Cheryl. After it ended, and after her son was declared legally dead (proceedings she said in 2008 she would have contested had she been aware of them), she was still not convinced that he had drowned in the lake, but her attempts to bring about a further investigation were unsuccessful. She has stated that she received threats to discourage her. For the next several years, she investigated on her own when not operating a day care at her home. She ran advertisements in local newspapers, and put up billboards seeking information. All the subsequent investigations of the case have resulted from her efforts. She believed her son might still be alive. "I get criticized a lot for not admitting that Mike's dead," she told the Tallahassee Democrat in 2007. "All I know is I can't stop looking for him until I find him." Her efforts had severely strained her relationship with her former daughter-in-law. In 2004 the Florida Department of Law Enforcement (FDLE) agreed to reopen the case after lobbying by Cheryl Williams and a friend. It does not normally have jurisdiction in missing-persons cases and cannot get involved in investigations purely on the basis of a citizen's request, although it can offer assistance to local agencies, as it did in this case. In retrospect, many officers agreed with her that the circumstances surrounding Michael Williams' apparent drowning four years before were unusual, and were strongly at odds with that conclusion:

- The boat launch where his Bronco was found, which he would presumably have used to put his boat in the lake, was an undeveloped patch of mud. Yet nearby were finished concrete launches that he was known to have used in the past.
- The storm the night after he was reported missing had westerly winds that should have blown the abandoned, unmoored boat across the lake to the Georgia side.
- When the boat was recovered, its engine was off, yet the gas tank was full. According to a representative of the manufacturer, if the engine had been running when Williams allegedly fell out of the boat, as investigators had theorized, it should have stayed on, with the boat running in circles until its

Wives Who Kill

fuel was exhausted. "Something sounds fishy on that deal," the representative said when the situation was described to him. Investigators also learned that Williams didn't usually hunt alone. "Some things looked unusual right off the bat," said the FFWCC's Arnette, who had initially thought the situation was a typical case involving a missing hunter and a possible boating accident. "Then after a couple, three days and after the weeks went on, those first things looked even more out of place." Alligator theory debunked Doubts that Williams had drowned became much more serious when investigators learned that, in fact, alligators do not generally feed during the winter months due to the colder temperatures. During the search period, daytime temperatures averaged around 55 °F (13 °C), with overnight lows below freezing. Some nights got as cold as 19 °F (−7 °C); a fire was built in a 55-gallon drum on the shore for searchers to stay warm. The water, already at 58 °F (14 °C) the day of Williams's disappearance, dropped to 46 °F (8 °C), and the lake iced out to as much as 20 feet (6.1 m) from shore. In those conditions, "it [i]s highly unlikely an alligator would have been active" said Matt Aresco, a local herpetologist authorities had consulted. "All they are doing is maintaining their body temperature ... Fifty-eight degrees is too cold for an alligator to be interested in food at all." And even if an alligator had "defied all known gator behavior," and eaten Williams's body, as another investigator, Ronnie Austin, then with the state's attorney's office, put it, it would likely have left something behind. Williams was 5 feet 10 inches (1.78 m) and 170 pounds (77 kg). Aresco considers any theory that attributes the missing body to alligators and any other aquatic animals a "stretch ... It would be very, very unusual to have the complete disappearance of a full-grown man." The waders, discovered almost six months after Williams's disappearance, further undermined the alligator theory. While the diver who retrieved them reported that they were in an area of disturbed weeds with alligator excrement nearby, consistent with the original belief that Williams had drowned while wearing them, he allowed it was "anyone's guess" as to whether they had been later planted in that spot. "These waders, we don't know where they came from," Austin said. Investigators suspicions' were further raised by the waders' condition—undamaged, without any tooth marks, and lacking any of the residues that would be expected to accumulate on an object submerged in the lake for as long as the waders had supposedly been. Arnette filtered the water in them after they were recovered, and did not find any human remains. The hunting jacket and flashlight were likewise in much better condition than expected, with the latter even working when turned on. Apart from the condition of the waders was the question of why Williams would have been wearing them when he supposedly fell out of the boat. According to a friend who hunted with him frequently, including one week before his disappearance, Williams took safety very seriously, keeping his guns at work, away from his daughter, among other precautions. On the water, he never put his waders on until he had reached the point where he planned to get out and start hunting, following a common safety procedure in order to avoid the type of accident from which he was later believed to have died. "As much as he preached that to me," the friend said, "why would he be wearing his waders while driving the boat?"

Lack of evidence "My gut feeling is Mike did not die in Lake Seminole", Austin said in 2006, after leaving the state's attorney's office for the FDLE. He added that that belief was shared by all the investigators at that point. "I would say this is a suspicious missing person." However, the new investigation was made extremely difficult by the deficiencies of the original search, when criminal activity had not been considered. "They did not protect the crime scene at all," recalled a Williams family friend with law enforcement experience, who had tended the drum fire during the search. "They botched it." By the time investigators began to realize that they should have asked some more questions, the opportunity was gone. Williams's Bronco and the boat had been returned to his family and friends, the footsteps of the many volunteers and searchers all over the lakeshore had made it impossible to collect any evidence from that area, and the items later recovered from the lake had not been retained. Without any of that evidence or Williams's body, it was impossible for police to make a case. "[We're] at a brick wall ... pounding our heads against it," said Austin.

Wives Who Kill

Derrick Wester, an investigator with the Jackson County sheriff's office, agreed that they were "trying to make up for" not having considered the possibility that things might not have been what they seemed in 2000. His office kept the case open, and had some persons of interest, although he did not identify them.

2007

The FDLE closed its case, convinced that the alligator theory was wrong, but without any leads or evidence that could allow it to further investigate. By 2006, its cold case investigators were no longer returning Cheryl Williams's phone calls. She continued to do what she could to publicize the case, taking out ads in the Tallahassee Democrat.

A possible new lead emerged in October 2007, when Michael Williams's older brother found a photograph and the serial number of a .22-caliber Ruger pistol that had once belonged to their father. Michael had inherited it after his father's death, and after Michael was declared legally dead it was the only one of his firearms that Denise Williams had not returned to her former in-laws. After Jackson County sheriff's investigator, Wester, asked the federal Bureau of Alcohol, Tobacco and Firearms (ATF) to look for it, agents visited Denise and Brian Winchester, now married, in their house (the same one she had lived in with Michael), to interview them. Several days later, their attorney delivered the gun to the FDLE. It was sent to a state forensics laboratory for DNA testing: the results have not been reported. On the anniversary of Williams's disappearance that year, the Winchesters made one of their few public statements on the case: "For seven years we have prayed and hoped to find out with certainty what happened to Mike," Brian said in an email to the Democrat, and "Nobody wants Mike found more than we do." Rumors were circulating around Tallahassee that a grand jury had been hearing evidence and would soon hand down indictments.

2008

In 2008, the Services' Division of Insurance Fraud (DIF), in conjunction with FDLE, began investigating the case from that angle. Normally, under Florida law, the statute of limitations on that crime is five years,

Mariticide Club

meaning it would have expired in 2005. But it can be extended by three years under certain circumstances.

"The circumstances surrounding this case raise many serious and troubling questions," said DIF's lead attorney, Mark Schlein. Perry, the FFWCC officer who had been heavily involved in the original search, added at the time that if he or any other person investigating had known that there was a large life insurance policy on Williams, and who the beneficiary was, that search might have been handled differently. It was noted that Denise Williams's court petition to have her husband declared legally dead mentioned only the Kansas City Life Insurance Company policies Winchester had sold him, omitting policies through other companies that Michael Williams had obtained through other sources. However, Brian Jones, an expert in insurance law at Florida State University, told the Democrat that any fraud case would have to rest on more than just those facts already known to have aroused investigative interest. "The mere fact that they can't locate the body isn't necessarily something the insurance industry would care about," he said. But if Michael Williams was to be proven dead and the beneficiary were to have shown to have been involved, or if he was still alive (as his mother and many residents of Jackson County believed possible), then an insurance company would strongly consider pursuing a case. By the eighth anniversary of Williams's disappearance, however, the DIF closed the case. "Our job was difficult, and we were unable to develop enough evidence to proceed with the investigation," Schlein said. He added that if new information were received, the investigation could be reopened. "We have suspicions, but what we need is evidence." Another possible lead that year proved fruitless as well. Carrie Cox, a self-described psychic and certified forensic psychological profiler from Kentucky reviewing the case had identified a possible location of Williams's body. She gave investigators the coordinates of a location in Wakulla County near another boat launch. Cadaver dogs were brought to the area and sniffed it out, but found nothing. Cox nevertheless concluded that "we are moving in the right direction... I think something is there." FDLE officials said in 2011 that Cox had not found anything requiring further investigation.

Cheryl Williams's lobbying efforts

Despite the failure of a third investigation to discern the fate of her son, Cheryl Williams persisted. Her efforts led to the Investigation Discovery cable channel doing a segment on Michael's disappearance and the later investigations in late 2011. "We don't know what the smoking gun is, but we hope someone will find it," she said. By then, she had become disillusioned with the FDLE, believing that it was either incompetent or uninterested in resolving the case. In particular, she came to believe the investigation was hampered by the involvement of agent Mike Philips, a friend of both her son and his then-wife. Philips had told her early on in the search that Michael had probably been eaten by alligators, so she had assumed he had been involved in the investigation at that point. He said later he never was and was merely trying to comfort her; FDLE said his involvement was limited to asking his superiors if the agency could help with the search; it did not see a need to formally investigate his role.

Starting on New Year's Day in 2012, Cheryl began writing one letter a day to Governor Rick Scott, asking him to either have another agency besides FDLE investigate or appoint a special prosecutor to do so. After she had written over 200 letters without even an acknowledgment that they had been received, she began inquiring personally as to why. It turned out that the governor's office had forwarded them, unopened, to FDLE's headquarters, where they were placed in the case file. She was outraged. "They could not have hurt me more if they had punched me in the face." In 2012, Denise and Brian Winchester separated, reportedly due to his sex addiction; she filed for divorce in 2015. Brian opposed it initially and had to be ordered to comply. As part of that order, he was to provide an appraisal of the couple's house, due early in August 2016. Denise told Leon County Sheriff's Office investigators that, on August 5, the day when the appraisal had to be filed with the court, she left her home to drive to her job at Florida State University. While she was talking on her phone to her sister, she saw someone climb over the back seat of her car. It turned out to be

Mariticide Club

Brian. He took her phone away and began yelling directions at her. She did not comply until he showed her a gun. She said later that he claimed this was necessary since she was not taking his calls and was blocking his text messages. Instead of going where he wanted her to, she pulled into a CVS drugstore parking lot, close to the door. Brian told her that he was planning to kill himself with the gun. He did not want the divorce and felt he had nothing to live for if it went through. He assured her he did not want to kill her. She was able to calm him down and took him back to where he had parked his own truck at a nearby park. Before he went to it, he took a tan sheet, a different-colored plastic sheet, a spray bottle of bleach, and a tool from Denise's car. After she left, Brian pulled up to her and apologized for his actions. Despite her promise to him not to tell police about the incident, she drove straight to them afterwards. According to a friend of Winchester's later interviewed by police, he had been increasingly concerned that as a result of the divorce Denise would tell the police what she knew about "this guy who died 10 or 12 or 15 years ago". She had not answered his many phone calls, so he came up with his plan to wait in her car and hold her at gunpoint. Brian was arrested and charged with kidnapping, domestic assault, and armed burglary, with two of the charges being felonies. Denise requested protection orders, saying she feared for her life and her daughter's. After a hearing the next week at which she said she could neither eat nor sleep since the incident, the court decided to hold Brian without bond. Cheryl Williams expressed hope that this development could lead to the resolution of her son's disappearance. "[Brian]'s not going to let Denise run around alone with all that money," she told the New York Daily News. "I'm praying he doesn't commit suicide; I'm praying he'll tell us what actually happened." She added that she is alone among her family in holding out hope that her son is still alive. In December 2017, Winchester was sentenced to 20 years in prison for the kidnapping, with credit for 502 days time served, to be followed by 15 years' probation. His attorney told the court that he was suicidal that day, due to not only the divorce but also his mother's recent terminal cancer diagnosis and the decision by his teenage son from his first marriage to

Wives Who Kill

move in with his mother, and argued for the 10-year mandatory minimum. Prosecutors countered that Winchester's actions that day indicated he planned a murder-suicide that was only averted by Denise's quick thinking, and asked the court for the 45-year maximum. Winchester is now imprisoned in the Wakulla Correctional Institution. No mention was made of the Williams case at Brian Winchester's sentencing, although State Attorney Jack Campbell told the media that he hoped the case against Winchester would help authorities solve that disappearance. Later it was reported that he had reached an agreement with prosecutors before the sentencing that they would neither seek a life sentence on the kidnapping charge nor introduce certain evidence at the hearing. What that agreement required of Winchester, if anything, beyond his guilty plea has not been disclosed. The next day, at a news conference, Mark Perez, the FDLE's special agent in charge, announced to assembled reporters that Williams's body had been found and it had been determined he was the victim of a homicide. However, they declined to release any details of how he had been killed, who might be a suspect or person of interest, or where the body had been found, saying they were withholding that information since only the perpetrators would be expected to know it. Subsequently, the FDLE revealed they had found Mike Williams's remains at the end of dead-end Gardner Road in northern Leon County, five miles (8.0 km) from where he grew up; they were confirmed as his following a match to his mother's DNA. No other details were provided. After Denise Williams was arrested, the FDLE disclosed that they had received information on where the body was in early October 2017. County public works employees brought in backhoes for what they were told was a training exercise. After five 16-hour days of digging 9-foot-deep (2.7 m) holes in the mud at that corner of the lake, all the while holding back the lake waters by dams and pumps amid the constant presence of eels and water moccasins, the FDLE was ready to hire a private contractor to finish the job. On October 18, the team of search dogs and officers finally found Mike Williams's remains in the piles of dirt stacked on plywood sheets. An FDLE source told the Tallahassee Democrat that 98% of his bones were recovered, all very well preserved, as was some of the clothing he had been wearing, such as winter gloves and booties. Two DNA tests matched the remains to his mother's sample. On May 8, 2018, Denise Williams was arrested at Florida State University as she left work to celebrate her daughter's 19th birthday, minutes after a grand jury had indicted her on charges of first-degree murder, conspiracy to commit first-degree murder, and accessory after the fact. Prosecutors continued to keep details of the crime to themselves, saying they would share them in court when the time came. They did say that they would seek to have her denied bail. Denise's attorney declined to comment at that time, saying he had not had time to review the case. Denise's estranged husband, Winchester, was serving his sentence at Wakulla Correctional Institution near Tallahassee; his attorney said his client would take the stand at trial if legally compelled to do so. However, the attorney did not think Winchester would be charged in the case as well. Two FDLE officers went to Cheryl Williams's house immediately following the indictment to inform her. She did not speak to the media about how she reacted to the news. The three-page indictment was released two days later. It revealed that prosecutors believed Denise allegedly began conspiring with Winchester in March 2000, nine months before her first husband disappeared. Winchester is alleged to have killed Michael with a gun. The accessory charge suggested that sometime between August 2014 and the day Winchester was sentenced, Denise had allegedly helped Winchester avoid prosecution or arrest for the crime. Ethan Way, Denise's lawyer, said his client was innocent of all the charges. "[She] had absolutely nothing to do with Mike Williams's disappearance and had absolutely nothing to do with any of the crimes that Brian Winchester committed." He found it convenient that the indictment came after Winchester had been imprisoned for several months. On Denise's behalf, Way entered a plea of not guilty. In late June 2018, Denise Williams was ordered held without bond, with trial date set for September 24. Audio of Brian Winchester's interview with the FDLE was played in court. In it, Brian confessed to pulling the trigger but claims the killing was Denise's idea. Her defense argued that the tape should not have been admitted as

Wives Who Kill

evidence since Winchester was not charged with anything despite his admission; the prosecution said it simply asked him to tell the truth about what happened. She went on trial in December. The state's star witness was Brian Winchester, who testified at length about how he and Denise had never really ended their high school relationship, even after they both married others. Kathy Thomas, Winchester's first wife, told the jury that she had suspected the two of having an affair in the late 1990s, when they frequently double-dated with Mike and Denise. Brian said in his confession, a tape of which was played for the jury, that the affair had started in 1997 and just "snowballed". After discreetly rekindling the relationship, the two began to consider killing Mike so they could marry, as Denise's family frowned on divorce for religious reasons. Denise suggested staging a boating accident on the Gulf of Mexico where they could throw both Mike and Kathy Thomas overboard, but Winchester did not want to kill his children's mother. After rejecting plans for a murder at Mike's office meant to look like a robbery, Winchester hit on the idea of an apparent hunting accident after he saved Mike from quicksand when the two were hunting in Arkansas. On the day Mike disappeared, Winchester said, he had enticed him to Lake Seminole. Out on the water, he had gotten Mike to put the waders on, then pushed him out of the boat, thinking he would be unable to resurface and thus would drown. But instead, he managed to get to a tree stump, so Winchester fired a single shotgun blast to the face. Since Mike's death could no longer be passed off as a boating accident, Winchester buried the body where it was later found, then cleaned out his truck and went to a family Christmas party, where he learned that a search was underway. He and Denise took it slow after Mike's "accident", both to let the insurance money earn further interest and to allay any suspicion. The kidnapping that had led to his present imprisonment, he explained, was his reaction to fear that Denise would reveal the truth about what had happened to her first husband now that she and Brian were divorcing. Prosecutors also played a taped phone conversation in which Kathy Thomas, who was working with police at the time, had told Denise she knew the truth about the crime. Each time she brought it up, Denise attempted to change the

Mariticide Club

subject, but at one point asked "What do you know?" Assistant state attorney Jon Fuchs said this evasiveness, as well as Denise's dispassionate response when Winchester told her how he had killed Mike, demonstrated how cold-bloodedly she helped plan the crime that happened on her behalf. Way argued in response that there was no physical evidence linking Denise to the crime and that it had been entirely Winchester's idea; he expressed incredulity that Winchester was not on trial despite having admitted to committing the crime himself. After four days of testimony, the jury took eight hours to convict Denise of all the charges. Way said his client would appeal the conviction. In February 2019, Denise was sentenced to life in prison. She did not speak or offer any argument on her behalf. The only person to address the court besides the lawyers was Cheryl Williams, who said that justice had finally been served, and that Denise had taken not only her son but also her granddaughter from her. Five months later, Mike and Denise's daughter Anslee was awarded all assets of her late father's estate and insurance monies due to Denise, after her mother signed them over to her to avoid prosecution on three counts of insurance fraud. As part of the deal, Anslee may not use any of the money on her mother's legal fees; if she did, she would owe the state a US$150,000 penalty. Denise is now imprisoned at the Florida Women's Reception Center. In January 2020, Denise Williams appealed her conviction and life sentence. Her attorney argued before the Florida First District Court of Appeals that there was no evidence she was involved in the commission of the murder. In November 2020, the murder conviction was overturned, but the conspiracy to commit murder conviction was upheld including the 30 year sentence that accompanied it. In the early 2000s, Cheryl Williams had posted flyers, put up signs, and run newspaper ads soliciting information about the case. One of the ads drew the attention of Jennifer Portman, a reporter at the Tallahassee Democrat. In 2006, after the closure of the first FDLE investigation, she wrote a lengthy story about the case. She followed the story through Denise's conviction, making a point of keeping the poster for the case on her cubicle wall. In 2011, the case made it into two other media formats. Carrie Cox, the psychic and profiler who had identified a possible

Wives Who Kill

burial site at which no body was found, published Alligator Alibi, a lengthy book with documents from the investigation, Cheryl Williams's notes, and her own commentary. She supported it with an eponymous Facebook page, where she regularly publishes whatever updates she can and news about other, similar cases. Near the end of that year, the Investigation Discovery cable channel series Disappeared devoted an episode to the case. Cheryl Williams promoted it heavily in the days before it aired. Portman, said she could always tell when it got rerun due to the increase in email she got, many of which asked questions she herself had tried in vain to get authorities to answer. After one such re-airing in 2015, she expressed the hope that "one day ... instead of a question, there will be an answer". The Crime Junkie podcast featured the case in an episode that was released 2019. On November 13, 2020, True Crime Network featured the case in season 1, episode 11, of Meet, Marry, Murder. In August 2021, the seventh season premiere of the A&E Network series Cold Case Files featured the case.

Mary Elizabeth Wilson (née Cassidy) The Merry Widow of Windy Nook

Mary Elizabeth Wilson (née Cassidy; 1889–1962), also known as The Merry Widow of Windy Nook, was an English murderer and the last woman to be sentenced to death in Durham, in 1958. However the sentence was commuted to a prison sentence. Wilson was born Mary Elizabeth Cassidy on 11 June 1889, in Catchgate, Stanley, County Durham, and christened on 30 June 1889 at Our Blessed Lady and St. Joseph, Brooms, Co. Durham. She married her first husband John Knowles around November 1914. They settled at a house in Windy Nook, Gateshead. Her lover John Russell eventually moved in with them. In 1955, Knowles died. Five months later she married Russell. He died in 1956 (or early in 1957). The attending physician declared that both men had died of natural causes. Wilson inherited their money, £42. In June 1957, Wilson married her third husband, Oliver Leonard, a retired estate agent. He died only 12 days into their marriage, leaving her £50. She soon married a fourth husband, Ernest Wilson. His estate included up to £100, a bungalow and life insurance. He

Mariticide Club

died within the year. This time, she did not even bother to attend the funeral. By this time Wilson had become a figure of local gossip, concerning both the frequency at which her spouses died and her rather cheerful attitude towards the pattern; she had joked at her latest wedding reception that left-over sandwiches would be fresh enough to use at the next funeral. She had also asked for a trade discount from the local undertaker, for providing him with plenty of business. These instances of morbid humor brought her to the attention of the police. An exhumation of the bodies of her last two husbands revealed high levels of phosphorus. Her defense claimed the substance was contained in their medication. Wilson was convicted of murdering two of her four husbands with beetle poison in 1956 and 1957. The remains of her earlier two husbands were exhumed at a later date and pointed to the same cause of death. There was no reason, however, to have a second trial. Wilson was sentenced to death but her advanced age allowed her to get a reprieve and her sentence was commuted to life imprisonment. She died of natural causes on 5 December 1962 while incarcerated at Holloway Prison. In popular culture

- Her story was depicted in the season 11 premiere episode of Deadly Women, entitled "Mid Life Murder".

Mary Winkler
Who murdered her husband Matthew Winkler (minister)

Former Winkler residence in Selmer, Tennessee

Wives Who Kill

Mary Carol Winkler (born on December 10, 1973) is an American woman who was convicted of voluntary manslaughter in the 2006 shooting of her husband, Matthew Winkler, the pulpit minister at the Fourth Street Church of Christ in the small town of Selmer, Tennessee. Winkler gained national attention because of public speculation regarding her motives and mental health, allegations of abuse by her husband, her brief flight from the state, and again for the brief length (150 days in jail plus 60 days in a mental health facility) of her sentence. In August 2008, Winkler was granted full custody of her three daughters. According to police, Mary Winkler confessed to the March 22, 2006 fatal shooting of her husband, whose body was discovered in their home by church members after he missed that evening's service. He had been shot in the back with a 12-gauge shotgun. The couple had been married since 1996. One neighborhood family reported that Matthew Winkler had repeatedly threatened to shoot that family's dog after it strayed onto the Winklers' lawn. Also, other people as well as Mary Winkler's family alleged that Matthew Winkler had been abusive to Mary. Winkler maintained this was the reason for the shooting. After police issued an Amber Alert due to fears of kidnapping, Mary Winkler and the children (Patricia, then 8; Mary Alice, then 6; Breanna, then 1) were discovered in Orange Beach, Alabama. Winkler was placed into custody there and later extradited to Tennessee to stand trial. When asked by investigators about what had happened to her husband, Winkler stated that she and her husband had argued about money and offered "I guess that's when my ugly came out." A grand jury indicted Winkler on June 12, 2006, accusing her of first-degree murder. On June 30, 2006, Mary Winkler's bond hearing was held. A Tennessee Bureau of Investigation agent read a statement Winkler gave to authorities in Alabama, where she was arrested a day after her husband's body was found; in it, Winkler says she did not remember getting the gun but she did know her husband kept a shotgun in their home. The next thing she heard was a loud boom. Matthew Winkler was shot in the back as he lay in bed. He rolled from the bed onto the floor, and, still alive, he asked his wife, "Why?" to which she responded, "I'm sorry." When she left the home,

Mariticide Club

Matthew Winkler was still alive in the bedroom, and the phone had been disconnected from its socket. According to the statement, she and her husband had been arguing throughout the evening about many things, including family finances. She admitted some of the problems were "her fault." Mary had lost money in what her lawyer said was a scam. She had deposited checks that came from "unidentified sources" in Canada and Nigeria into bank accounts belonging to her and her husband. The checks amounted to more than $17,000. Winkler had become caught up in a swindle known as the "Nigerian scam", which promises riches to victims who send money to cover the processing expenses. She added "He had really been on me lately criticizing me for things — the way I walk, I eat, everything. It was just building up to a point. I was tired of it. I guess I got to a point and snapped." Bond was later set at $750,000, an amount that defense lawyer Steve Farese Sr. claimed was excessive and "tantamount to no bond at all". A plea for reduction of bond was filed and subsequently denied. Winkler's lawyers, Leslie Ballin and Steve Farese Sr., also filed motions to throw out her confession on a technicality, to require prosecutors to state whether or not they would seek the death penalty (they did not), to give potential jurors an extensive questionnaire, and other motions relating to voir dire. Winkler's entire defense team (her attorneys Steve Farese Sr., Leslie Ballin, Tony Farese, Steve Farese, Jr. and Investigator Terry Cox) represented her pro bono throughout the criminal case. Winkler made bond on August 12, 2006 and was set for release from jail. Initially, problems stemming from a 1999 suspension of the bail bond company kept her in jail. However, Winkler was able to post $750,000 bond and was released on August 15, on the stipulation that she live with Rudolf and Kathy Thomsen, friends in McMinnville, Tennessee. The trial commenced on April 9, 2007, with the prosecution resting on April 16. The defense rested two days later. On April 18, 2007, Mary Winkler took the stand in her own defense. She told a jury of ten women and two men that her husband often "berated" her and forced her to wear "slutty" costumes for sex. As proof she displayed a pair of high-heeled shoes and a wig at which those in attendance gasped. Winkler claimed that she only shot her

Wives Who Kill

husband accidentally. She said that she went to the bedroom closet and retrieved a shotgun because she wanted to force him to work through their problems. "I just wanted him to stop being so mean," she said through tears. Winkler denied she ever actually pulled the trigger, but told the jury "something went off". She heard a boom, then ran from the house because she thought he would be mad at her. On April 19, 2007, the jury came back with the verdict: guilty of voluntary manslaughter. Prosecutors had asked that Winkler be convicted of first-degree murder, but the jury settled on the lesser charge after deliberating for eight hours. The sentencing phase was set to begin on May 18, 2007, but was delayed due to a scheduling conflict by one of the attorneys. On June 8, 2007, a Tennessee judge sentenced Mary Winkler to 210 days in prison for the conviction of voluntary manslaughter. She had credit for already serving five months and the judge permitted her to spend up to 60 days in an undisclosed mental health facility in Tennessee. She was to be put on probation for the rest of her sentence. Some men's rights activists argue the sentence did not constitute justice for the killing of Matthew Winkler. They argued that society sees males only as victimizers[self-published source] and say that the definition of emotional abuse has been expanded to include mere criticism, thereby giving anyone who does not like being criticized justification to commit murder in order to end the criticism. Mary Winkler's family alleges that she was reacting to a combination of emotional, sexual, and physical spousal abuse. In a 2007 interview with Oprah Winfrey, Winkler stated that her jail time was too short. "There's no amount of time I think you can put on something like this. I was just ready for them to lock the door and throw away the key", she told Winfrey. The song "The Wig He Made Her Wear" from Southern alt-rock band Drive-By Truckers' 2010 album The Big To-Do describes the case and the details surrounding the actions of the Winklers, particularly that of Mary. The transcript of Mary's police interview was used by Lithuanian artist Ignas Krunglevicius in a piece called "Interrogation" in 2009, in which he changed her last name to show some respect for her privacy. Mary Winkler's murder trial was the subject of the 2011 TV film The Pastor's Wife starring Rose McGowan. In April

Mariticide Club

2020, this case was in a new episode "The Pastor's Secrets" in the Sex and Murder series on HLN cable network. Matthew Brian Winkler (November 21, 1974 – March 22, 2006) was the minister who was the victim in 2006. Winkler was raised in Woodbury, Tennessee; Huntingdon, Tennessee; and Decatur, Alabama. He attended college at Freed-Hardeman University in Henderson, Tennessee in 1990s and moved to Tennessee after he got married. He had three daughters named Patricia, then 8; Mary Alice, then 6; Brianna, then 1, whose custody was given to their mother later. Winkler was serving as the pulpit minister at the Fourth Street Church of Christ in Selmer, Tennessee, at the time of his death. Members of his congregation found him dead inside his home after he failed to appear at the church for a Wednesday-night service he was to lead on March 22, 2006. He had been shot in the back. Mary Winkler, his wife; and the couple's three small daughters were reported missing along with the family's minivan. The state of Tennessee issued an Amber Alert, and Mary and the children were located the next day in Orange Beach, Alabama. Mary would confess to killing her husband and be charged with first-degree murder after extradition to Tennessee. She was released on bond, and her trial began on April 9, 2007. At trial, Mary claimed that she had suffered extensive physical and emotional abuse at her husband's hands. She was convicted of manslaughter and sentenced to 150 days in prison plus 60 days in a mental health facility.

Elizabeth Lillian Woolcock (née Oliver)

Elizabeth Lillian Woolcock (née Oliver; 20 April 1848 – 30 December 1873) was an Australian murderess who was hanged in Adelaide Gaol for the murder of her husband Thomas Woolcock by mercury poisoning. She remains the only woman ever executed in South Australia and is buried between the outer and inner prison walls of Adelaide Gaol. It has been argued that she may have been a victim of domestic violence and suffered from battered spouse syndrome. Elizabeth was born on April 20, 1848, and lived with her family in Burra Burra in South Australia. In January 1852, Elizabeth's father joined the Victorian gold rush and the family moved

Wives Who Kill

to Ballarat, taking residence in a tent on the goldfields. When Elizabeth was four years old, her mother moved to Adelaide, leaving the girl to be raised by her father. In 1855, seven-year-old Elizabeth was raped and left for dead by an itinerant Indian. Two years later her father died of consumption.

Thomas and Elizabeth Woolcock

In 1865, after receiving news that her mother was alive and looking for her, Elizabeth travelled to Moonta, South Australia and moved in with her mother and stepfather. She taught Sunday school at the Wesleyan Church. Thomas Woolcock emigrated from Cornwall and settled in Moonta with his wife and two children in 1865; the next year, his wife and one son died of fever. A widower left with his namesake son Thomas to look after, he hired Elizabeth as a housekeeper. Elizabeth's stepfather disliked Woolcock,

Mariticide Club

and when he heard rumors of more than a work relationship going on between the man and Elizabeth, he threatened to cripple her if she kept seeing him. To stop the gossip, Woolcock married 20-year-old Elizabeth in his cottage's front parlor on October 2, 1867. Woolcock turned out to be a heavy drinker, a bully, and a wife-beater. Elizabeth attempted to leave him several times, but he continued to find her and bring her back to Moonta. Feeling depressed and alone after her mother and stepfather moved to Adelaide, Elizabeth attempted suicide. She was given Morphine to help with insomnia and melancholy. The situation improved somewhat when Woolcock took in a boarder whose presence lessened the abuse she suffered, but eventually the two men had a dispute and the boarder left. Not long afterward, the family dog died after being poisoned and Thomas suspected the boarder and reported him to the Police. Around this time Elizabeth was seeking medication, mainly morphine, for her ailments, but the chemist refused to prescribe any and she resorted to sending her stepson to pharmacies with notes. She visited a chemist, claiming she needed morphine to "get ink stains out of a skirt", then claimed it was for scurf in her hair. Her desperation to acquire drugs became common knowledge in the community. A month after the dog died, Woolcock became ill with stomach pains and nausea, Elizabeth called in three doctors over the following weeks who each diagnosed different illnesses and prescribed different medications. Dr. Bull prescribed syrup and pills laced with a third of a grain of Mercury each (21 mg) for a sore throat, but Woolcock became considerably worse and Elizabeth then called Dr. Dickie who diagnosed a gastric disorder and prescribed Rhubarb tablets and cream of tartar, which had no effect. Finally, Dr. Herbert treated him for excessive 'Salivation by Mercury'. This treatment worked and Woolcock improved, but two weeks later he could no longer afford Dr. Herbert's fees so returned to Dr. Dickie, who resumed the treatment for a gastric problem. When his condition failed to improve, Elizabeth suggested returning to Dr. Bull, but according to neighbors and friends who were present and later testified at her trial, Woolcock replied: "I certainly don't want Dr. Bull again, as it was his medicine that made me bad in the first place". At 3 am on 4 September

Wives Who Kill

1873, Thomas Woolcock died. Dr. Dickie initially stated his patient had died from "pure exhaustion from excessive and prolonged vomiting and purging". Woolcock's cousin, Elizabeth Snell, suggested to the doctor that as everyone knew Woolcock's wife had been getting "Morphia" she could have poisoned him with it, and rumors of foul play began spreading. An inquest was ordered. The inquest was opened in the front parlor of Woolcock's cottage. Dr. Dickie testified on the drugs taken by the deceased and the chemist, Mr. Opie, testified regarding Elizabeth's attempts to get morphine. Elizabeth stated she had nothing to gain from her husband's death. An autopsy was ordered and performed in the cottage that day while Elizabeth waited outside. The next day the inquest resumed at the Moonta courthouse where Dr. Dickie described the state of the body and suggested that mercury poisoning was a strong probability, Dr. Herbert concurred. Dr. Bull admitted prescribing pills with mercury but insisted Woolcock only took one. Police told the inquest that they had exhumed the Woolcock's' dead dog and found the body too contained large traces of mercury (a known treatment for Ringworm). Several jars considered 'poison' were found in the cottage and the jury decided that Woolcock was poisoned by his wife, and she was arrested. Elizabeth pleaded not guilty and the trial in Adelaide was a sensation with crowds filling Gouger Street outside the Supreme Court. Elizabeth was provided with an inexperienced lawyer who failed in court against the accomplished Crown Solicitor, Richard Bullock Andrews QC, who argued that Elizabeth had poisoned the dog as an experiment, the ringworm powder was the means and that motive was an affair with the boarder. Defendants at this time were barred from testifying on their own behalf so Elizabeth was unable to answer the accusations. Following a three-day trial, the jury, after deliberating for 20 minutes, found her guilty with a recommendation for mercy on account of her youth. The plea for mercy was declined by Governor Anthony Musgrave and she was sentenced to death. On 30 December 1873, dressed in a white frock and carrying a posy of fresh flowers, Elizabeth gave a letter to be opened after her death to her minister, the Reverend James Bickford, and then walked calmly to the gallows. The letter, describing her

Mariticide Club

life, was badly written with poor spelling and inaccuracies including even getting her own age wrong:

The last Statement and confession of Elizabeth Woolcock to Mr. Bickford. Sir I was Born in the Burra mine in Provence of South Australia in the year 1847 my parents' names were John and Elisabeth Oliver they were Cornish they came to this Couleney in 1842 but they went to Victoria in 1851. I was left without the care of a Mother at the age of 4 years and I never saw her again until I was 18 my father died when I was 9 years old and I had to get my living until I was 18 and then I heard that my Mother was alive and Residing at moonta mine she wrote me a letter asking me to come to her as she had been very unhappy about me and she was very sorry for what she had done I thought I should like to see my Mother and have a home like other young girls so I gave up my Situation and came to Adelaide my mother and my stepfather received me very kindly and I had a good home for 2 years my Mother and Stepfather were members of the Wesleyan Church and I became a Teacher in the Sunday school for 2 years at the End of that time I first saw my late husband Thomas Woolcock I believe my stepfather was a good man but he was very passionate and determined my late husband was a widower with two Children his Wife had been dead about 8 months when I went to keep house for him against stepfathers wishes I kept house for him for 6 Weeks when someone told my stepfather that I was keeping Company with Thomas Woolcock he asked me if it was true and I told him it was not but he would not believe me but called me a liar and told me he would Cripple me if I went with him any had not been with the man but I would go with him now if he asked me if the Divel said I should not this took place on the Thursday morning I saw my husband in the evening and he asked me what was the matter and I told him what had taken place the following Sunday he asked me to go with him for a walk instead of going to Chapel I went and my stepfather missed me from the Chapel and came to look for me and found us both together so I was afraid to go home for has he had said he would break both of my legs I was afraid he would keep his word ,as I never knew him to tell a willful lie so I went to a cousins of my husbands and stopped and my husband asked me if I

Wives Who Kill

would marry him and for my words sake I did. We were married the next Sunday morning by license after the acquaintance of 7 weeks I was not married long before I found out what sort of a man I had got and that my poor stepfather had advised me for my own good but it was too late then, so I had to make the best of it, I tried to do my duty to him and the children, but the more I tried the worse he was, he was fond of drink but he did not like to part with his money for anything else and god only knows how he ill-treated me I put up with it for 3 years during that time my parents went to Melbourne and then he was worse than ever I thought i would rather die than live so I tried to put an end to myself in several different ways ,but thank the Lord I did not succeed in doing so as he did not treat me any better and I could not live like that. I thought I would leave him and get my own liven so I left him but he would not leave me alone he came and fetched me home and then I stopped with him twelve months and I left him again with the intention of going to my Mother I only took 6 pounds with me I came down to Adelaide and I stopped with my sister I was here in Adelaide 6 weeks when he came and fetched me back again but he did not behave no better to me I tried my best to please him but I could not there is no foundation at all for the story about the young man called Pascoe he was nothing to me nor I did not give the poor dog any poison for I knew what power the poison had as I took it myself for some months and I was so illtreated that I was quite out of my mind and in an evil hour I yielded to the temptation he was taken ill at the mine and came home and quarreled with me and Satan tempted me and I gave him what I ought not but thought at the time that if i gave him time to prepare to meet his god I should not do any great crime to send him out of the World but I see my mistake now I thank god he had time to make his peace with his maker and I hope I shall meet him in heaven for I feel that god has pardoned all my sins he has forgiven me and washed me white in the precious blood of Jesus I feel this evening that I can rejoice in a loven Savior I feel his presence here to night he sustains me and gives me comfort under this heavy trial such as the world can never give. Dear friend if I may call you so I am much obliged to you for your kindness to a poor guilty sinner but great will be your reward

Mariticide Club

in heaven I hope I shall meet you there and I hope that god will keep me faithful to the End o may I be able to say that I live is Christ but to Die will be gain Bless the Lord he will not turn away any that come unto him for he says come unto me all ye that labor and are heavy laden and I will give you rest I feel I have that rest I hope to die singing Victory through the Blood of the lamb I remain sir Yours truly a sinner saved by grace Elizabeth Woolcock. —Adelaide Observer, 3 January 1874 Source Since her execution, flowers have been placed by her grave regularly, a tradition that has continued despite the closure of the Gaol. Experts agree that Elizabeth's "confession" was religiously inspired and prompted by a desire for salvation with an exaggeration of her sins. Police historian Allan Peters says she was "more interested in impressing the Reverend than setting the record straight". It is unlikely that Elizabeth was having an affair and she had nothing to gain from Woolcock's death. That she cared for him while he was ill was evidenced by his lack of bed sores and witnesses testified that Elizabeth showed no ill will towards her husband. The dog was treated for ringworm with mercury laced powder and could have died from mercury poisoning after licking the powder on its body. Woolcock's symptoms were consistent with tuberculosis and dysentery, both of which were found at autopsy, and typhoid, although this was not found. Woolcock's organs, removed at autopsy, had been left unattended and exposed to the air for 24 hours before they were examined which could have compromised the diagnosis. It was never proven at trial that Woolcock had died of mercury poisoning or that Elizabeth had administered it. Dr Bull prescribed mercury laced syrup and tablets which would have killed Woolcock if he had taken more than Bull testified to. Bull was a drug addict for thirty years and consumed atropine, sulphuric ether, chloroform and opium in large and frequent doses. He was reportedly in a "drug be-fuddled state" when treating Woolcock and several witnesses testified that Thomas has told them that it was Bull's medicine that had made him so sick. Dr Bull was committed to a psychiatric hospital after the trial and committed suicide several months later. Two recently discovered letters sent by Samuel Way to relatives in England shortly before he was

Wives Who Kill

appointed Chief Justice of South Australia were commentary on the now lost report into the hanging commissioned by the government of the day and headed by his brother Dr Edward Way. Edward he wrote, concurred with the analytical chemist that the evidence on administration of the poison was "unreliable" and that the "medical evidence mistaken". The implication is that she did not poison Woolcock and that even if she had been guilty she did not receive justice based on the available evidence. In January 2009, after 30 years of research, Police historian Allan Peters applied to the State Attorney General Michael Atkinson for a posthumous pardon. In 2010, Peters and his daughter Leeza distributed petitions throughout the Copper Coast and online, urging people to sign and support a posthumous pardon for Elizabeth. The signed petitions along with detailed documentation and evidence was delivered to the Governor of South Australia Rear Admiral Kevin Scarce on 28 September 2011. The request was declined. Records show that Elizabeth and Thomas had a baby named Thomas Woolcock on March 23, 1873, who died on April 9, 1873.

Elizabeth Wright

Lorenzo Christopher Wright (December 9, 1926 – March 27, 1972) was an American athlete. A Detroit native, he started at Miller High School and Wayne State University; Wright is renowned for his noteworthy accomplishments in the sport of track and field. Lorenzo C. Wright's crowning athletic achievement would come as a member of the gold medal winning 4×100 meter relay team at the 1948 Olympic Games. During those same London Games, Wright finished fourth in a fiercely contested long jump competition. Willie Steele of the U.S. won the gold medal at 25 feet 8 inches (7.825 m); Australia's Bruce came in second, taking the silver medal at 24 feet 9+1⁄2 inches (7.555 m). Herb Douglas of the United States captured the bronze medal with a jump of 24 feet 9 inches (7.545 m), and Lorenzo Wright ended up in fourth place at 24 feet 5+1⁄4 inches (7.45 m) – a hand's width from a second trip to the medals podium. At Miller High, Wright was a two-time Detroit Public Secondary Schools Athletic League champion in the long jump. Upon

Mariticide Club

graduating from high school, LC Wright served eighteen months in the U.S. Army. Then, as a student-athlete for Wayne State University, Wright was an NCAA All-American in 1947 and 1948; placing second and third respectively in the long jump. Lorenzo Wright was a Central Collegiate Conference indoor champion in the 60-yard dash; he was also the inaugural Mid-American Conference titlist in the 100 and 220-yard dash, 220-yard low hurdles, and the long jump. During his career, Wright won two individual and two relay squad titles at the prestigious Penn Relays. Wright also won the long jump event at the 1948 and 1952 National AAU Championships. Wright's indoor and outdoor long jump marks, along with his performances in the 100-meter and 220-yard dash, are still Wayne State University varsity records – having stood the test of time for nearly seventy years. After his athletic career, L.C. Wright served many seasons as the track and swimming coach at Miller, Eastern and Southwestern High School; during the 1960s, Wright's athletes were some of the best in the United States. Wright was later appointed Director of the Detroit Public Secondary Schools Athletic League (DPSSAL). Wright was honored posthumously as a 1973 inductee to the Michigan Sports Hall of Fame and -in 1976- as a charter member of the Wayne State University Athletic Hall of Fame. One of Detroit's major interscholastic athletic facilities, adjacent to Martin Luther King High School, is named Lorenzo C. Wright Field. In 1972, at age 45, Wright was stabbed to death by his wife Elizabeth during a dispute about their possible separation.

Susan Lucille Wright née Susan Lucille Wyche

Susan Lucille Wright (born April 24, 1976) is an American convicted murderer from Houston, Texas, who made headlines in 2003 for stabbing her husband, Jeff Wright, 193 times in an act of mariticide and then burying his body in their backyard. She was convicted of murder in 2004, and was given a 20-year sentence at the Crain Unit in Gatesville, Texas. She was denied parole on June 12, 2014, and July 24, 2017. She was granted parole in July 2020 and released from prison on December 30, 2020. Susan Lucille Wright was born on April 24, 1976, in Houston, Texas,

Wives Who Kill

to Sue Wella (née Tschoepe) and Jimmy Lawrence Wyche. At the age of 17, she worked as a topless dancer at Gold Cup for two months. In 1997, while working as a restaurant waitress in Galveston, Texas, she met Jeff Wright and they married in 1998 while she was eight-and-a-half months pregnant with their first child. In 2002, a daughter was born. Mrs. Wright claims her husband began to abuse her the first few years of their marriage.

Susan Wright, right, listens along with her attorney Neal Davis, left, as the jury's verdict of guilty is read in her murder trial Wednesday, March 3,

Mariticide Club

2004, in Houston. Wright, who claimed she acted in self-defense when she stabbed her husband Jeffrey Wright 193 times, was found guilty of murder. Susan Wright, a Houston mother of two who made national headlines for stabbing her husband 193 times in 2003, was released on parole Wednesday after 16 years in prison, according to the Texas Department of Criminal Justice. Wright, now 44, was originally sentenced to 25 years in prison after a jury found her guilty of killing 34-year-old Jeffrey Wright at the couple's northwest Harris County home. A second trial in 2011 shaved five years off that sentence. She was granted parole last July and ordered to complete a rehabilitation program, TDCJ records show. At the time of her release, Wright was being held at the Murray Unit in Gatesville, about 30 miles north of Killeen. Wright asked for privacy when KTRK-TV spoke with her at home Tuesday. "Please don't do this to my family. Please stop. Have a heart. Please," she told the station. According to earlier reports in the Houston Chronicle, Wright, a former topless dancer and homemaker, argued that the Jan. 13, 2003, slaying was in self-defense against a husband who abused her for years. She testified that the night of the murder, he raped and beat her after she confronted him about his cocaine problem. At the 2004 trial, Harris County prosecutors contended that the killing was a ploy to benefit from his $200,000 life insurance policy. Prosecutors said Wright, who was 26 at the time, seduced Jeffrey Wright and tied him to the bed, leaving him helpless against a barrage of jabs to his head, neck, chest and genitals. She then buried his body in the backyard and confessed to the stabbing five days later. Assistant District Attorney Kelly Siegler also grabbed headlines during the trial with her elaborate re-creation of the crime. Siegler hauled the Wrights' blood-stained bed into the courtroom, straddled another prosecutor tied to the bedposts and re-enacted the stabbing while questioning police investigators. Jurors found Wright guilty after a roughly five hours of deliberation. She served a portion of her sentence at the Crain Unit for women in Coryell County, according to earlier reports. The case was the basis for a 2012 made-for-TV movie, "The Blue-Eyed Butcher," on the Lifetime channel. It also had been featured in 2014 on a weekly TV series, "Secret Lives of Stepford Wives ." The crime

Wives Who Kill

occurred at the Wright family house in the White Oak Bend subdivision in an unincorporated area of northwest Harris County, Texas. January 13, 2003, Susan Wright, 26, tied her husband, Jeff Wright, 34, to their bed and stabbed him 193 times with two different knives. She buried his body in their Houston backyard. She attempted to cover up the crime scene by painting the bedroom. The next day, Wright filed a false domestic abuse report in order to get a restraining order against her husband. January 18, Wright asked her attorney, Neal Davis, to come to her home and admitted to stabbing her husband. Davis contacted the Harris County's district attorney's office to inform it that a body was buried under Susan Wright's house and that she had confessed to the killing. Wright turned herself in to authorities at the Harris County Courthouse on January 24 and was arraigned on murder charges the following Monday. Thirteen months after her arraignment, Wright's murder trial commenced on February 24, 2004. She had already pleaded not guilty to killing her husband by reason of self-defense. Assistant district attorney Kelly Siegler depicted Wright as a scheming wife who seduced her husband into bed, tied him up, repeatedly stabbed him, and then buried his body in their backyard in hopes of collecting a $200,000 life insurance policy. Wright's defense attorney Neal Davis claimed that his client had suffered years of physical and emotional abuse by her husband and killed him to protect herself and her two young children. At her trial, Susan Wright testified in her own defense. In her emotional testimony on the stand, Wright claimed: "I couldn't stop stabbing him; I couldn't stop. I knew as soon as I stopped, he was going to get the knife back and he was going to kill me. I didn't want to die." She testified that on the night of the murder, Jeff Wright was on a cocaine binge and was violent, having allegedly beaten her. Wright again insisted that she stabbed her husband in self-defense. Susan Wright's mother testified for the defense, claiming they witnessed Wright's bruises. Siegler said Wright's tears were faked to try and sway the jury. The prosecution presented an unusual demonstration by bringing the Wrights' actual bed into the courtroom. During closing arguments, Siegler brought up to the jury how Wright had been a topless dancer and said she believed Wright's emotions were insincere. She contended that Susan Wright was a "card-carrying, obvious, no-doubt-about-it, caught-red handed, confirmed, documented liar" whose frequent shows of emotion during the trial were deliberate efforts to influence the jury.

Verdict

On March 3, 2004, after more than five hours of deliberations, the jury convicted Wright of murder. Wright showed little reaction to the guilty verdict. Wright was sentenced on the following day. Prosecutors were hoping for at least a 55-year sentence, and Wright's attorneys argued for probation for their client. The jury sentenced Wright to 25 years in prison. She was imprisoned at the Unit, under SID Number: 04835513. In 2005, the Fourteenth Court of Appeals of Texas in Houston upheld Susan Wright's conviction. With a re-appeal in 2008, a new witness, Misty McMichael, the wife of former NFL Super Bowl champion Steve McMichael and ex-fiancée of Jeff Wright, came forward to tell her story of how she endured abuse and violence during her four-year relationship with Jeff Wright. In 2009, the Texas Court of Criminal Appeals granted Wright a new sentencing hearing, after determining that Wright's "counsel rendered ineffective assistance during the punishment phase of trial" in 2004. On November 20, 2010, Wright had her sentence reduced to 20 years in prison, five years less than her original sentence. Wright was first eligible for parole on February 28, 2014, at the age of 38. She was denied parole on June 12, 2014, and again on July 24, 2017. Wright was approved for parole on July 2, 2020. On Wednesday, December 30, 2020, Wright was released on parole at the age of 44. Wright's murder trial had been nationally televised on Court TV. Wright's case was also profiled on Snapped in 2004, 48 Hours Mystery in 2005, on an Especial entitled Women Who Kill, on the Deadly Women episode "Lethal Love" on ID in 2011, and on an episode of Secret Lives of Stepford Wives in 2014. Wright's case was also the subject of the 2012 Lifetime original movie Blue Eyed Butcher, starring Sara Paxton as Wright and Lisa Edelstein as Kelly Siegler. In 2014, Canadian director Chloe Bellande released a 17-minute short film titled Will of Fortune, which was inspired

Wives Who Kill

by the murder trials of Wright and Guy Turcotte, a man who had stabbed his two children to death in Canada. The film premiered at the Cannes Film Festival in May 2014. Susan Wright who was released on parole 16 years after conviction for killing her husband is now 46 years old and available. to share Its Just Lunch if you are interested in becoming her next husband.

About the Writer William A Stricklin:

Mariticide Club

Military Training and Service
- Life Member of "Military Order of World Wars",
- Bill received training initially at Ft. Lewis; basic infantry training, Ft. Benning, Georgia; followed by Fort Holabird, Counterintelligence Corps training for US Army service at Ft. McNair and in the Pentagon
- Honorable Discharge two years active service (wartime); and four years US Army Reserve

Professional License History
- State Bar of California 036559 Active 1964-2023
- Hawaiʻi State Bar Association JD0962 Active 1970-2023
- Washington State Bar Attorney 10456 Active 1969-2023
- State of Washington General Contractor: Type I steel/concrete 1968-1970 Denny Building
- State of Hawaiʻi "B" General Contractor CT6406: 2/16/1973-4/30/1996 Amfac Center HI
- State of Hawaiʻi Real Estate Broker 1968-2015("inactive")
- State of California Real Estate Broker: Commercial, Residential real estate sales and leasing 1958-1999
- Financial Consultant, Montecito Bank & Trust. Santa Barbara 1997-1998

Courts Admitted to Practice
- Supreme Court of the United States 1964-2023
- United States Court of Appeals for Ninth Circuit
- United States Tax Court 1964-2023
- United States District Court for the Northern District of California 1964-2023
- United States District Court, District of Hawaiʻi
- Supreme Court of State of California 1970-2023
- Supreme Court of Hawaiʻi 1970-2023
- Washington Supreme Court (Rule 18 reciprocity in 26 states) 1969-2023

Bar Affiliations, Activities and Memberships
- Hawaiʻi Bar's Model Rules Committee, rules of lawyers' conduct
- Hawaiʻi Bar's Government Lawyers Section
- Hawaiʻi Bar's Litigation Section
- Hawaiʻi Bar's Natural Resources Section
- Founding Charter Member Washington State Bar Association Civil Rights Section. Active Member of Bar Association of San Francisco (BASF) 162968
- Environmental Law Section of BASF
- Conference of Delegates Committee of the BASF
- Ethics Committee of BASF
- Member Race and Ethnicity Committee of BASF
- Member of Disability Rights Committee of BASF

Honors Philanthropic Affiliations and Awards
- Order of Golden Bear to promote statewide unity of University of California campuses
- Chair, University of California Alumni Association, Washington DC 1960-61
- Listed in National Trust for Historic Preservation Directory of Historic Preservation Lawyers
- Chair, Hawaiʻi Advisory Committee, American Arbitration Assn 1975 to 1985
- Master Mason 3° Berkeley 363 Blue Lodge 1959

Wives Who Kill

- Scottish Rite 32° Mason Oakland Temple 1959
- Hawai'i Shriners Temple 1968
- Hawai'i Shriners Hospital Clown Corps
- Hawai'i Opera Theater Board of Trustees
- Hawai'i Ballet Board of Trustees
- National Board of Trustees, American Arbitration Assn, New York, 1990-1994
- Santa Barbara Board Trustees, Planned Giving Chair, American Red Cross 1998-2000
- Member Santa Barbara Board of Trustees, Catholic Charities, 1998-2000
- Member Santa Barbara Board of Trustees, Cottage Hospitals, 1998-2000
- Elected Member Montecito Santa Barbara All Saints by the Sea Episcopal Church Board, 2000-02
- Hawai'i's "Mediator of the Year" 1989 American Arbitration Association
- Robinson Cox Visiting Fellow, Law School, University of WA (Perth) 1989 to 1990, teaching dispute resolution to the Law Society and students
- Facilitated the Australian Minister of Land's return of land the size of Rhode Island called Silver Plains Station Queensland to the traditional owners, Lama Lama Peoples
- Charter Member Founding Secretary, Hawai'i Lambda Alpha (Land Economics Honor Society)
- Confrere Order of Knights of the Hospital of St. John of Jerusalem, appointed by HerMajesty Queen Elizabeth II to help serve medical needs of children of all faiths caught up in the wars of the Middle East

Confrère of the Venerable Order of St. John

Breast star of a Knight of Grace of the Most Venerable Order of the Hospital of St John of Jerusalem. Perhaps recognition of fundraising for Friends of Covent Garden, Metropolitan Opera National Council, Hawai'i Opera Theater, Historic Hawai'i and Shriners' Children's Hospital, Queen Elizabeth II appointed me to become a confrère in the Venerable Order of St. John.

Mariticide Club

Concurrently Queen Elizabeth II appointed my son John Stricklin as a confrère. The Order of St John, formally The Most Venerable Order of the Hospital of St. John of Jerusalem (French: l'ordre très vénérable de l'Hôpital de Saint-Jean de Jérusalem) and also known as St John International, is a British royal order of chivalry first constituted in 1888 by royal charter from Queen Victoria. The Order traces its origins back to the Knights Hospitaller in the Middle Ages, which was later known as the Order of Malta. A faction of them emerged in France in the 1820s and moved to Britain in the early 1830s, where, after operating under a succession of grand priors and different names, it became associated with the founding in 1882 of the St John Ophthalmic Hospital near the old city of Jerusalem and the St John Ambulance Brigade in 1887.

The order is found throughout the Commonwealth of Nations, Hong Kong, the Republic of Ireland, and the United States of America, with the worldwide mission "to prevent and relieve sickness and injury, and to act to enhance the health and well-being of people anywhere in the world." Recommendations are made by the Grand Council and those selected have generally acted in such a manner as to strengthen the spirit of mankind—as reflected in the order's first motto, Pro Fide—and to encourage and promote humanitarian and charitable work aiding those in sickness, suffering, and/or danger—as reflected in the order's other motto, Pro Utilitate Hominum. As the Sovereign Head, Queen Elizabeth II confirms all appointments to the order as she, in her absolute discretion, shall think fit. Individuals may not petition the Grand Council or the Queen for admission. The Order of St John is perhaps best known for the health organizations it founded and continues to run, including St John Ambulance and St John Eye Hospital Group. As with the Order, the memberships and work of these organizations are not constricted by denomination or religion. The Order is a constituent member of the Alliance of the Orders of Saint John of Jerusalem. Its headquarters are in London and it is a registered charity under English law.

Wives Who Kill

Library – 6th and Final Wife of King Henry VIII married July 1543 Catherine Parr (1512-1548) Peacemaker Outlived Henry- Nonfiction - Copyright © 2017 Case 1-5607493201 – TXu 2-060-893

King Eadgar's Secret - Oblate Expectations - Nonfiction - Copyright © 2017 Case 1-5600182531

Nun of My Dreams © 2018 TXu 2-093-545 ISBN 978-1-48098-155-3

Dollie's Secret – Survivor of the DeKalb, Texas, Indian Raid - Nonfiction – © Case 1-5564559089 © 2017 TXu 2-067-664

A Pregnant Nun a historical novel - Nonfiction – Copyright © Case 1-8558966897 © 2019 Pau 3-833-744 - ISBN 978-1-09830-437-9

A Hundred Secrets Volume 1 Books 1-20 nonfiction Copyright © Case 1-7072486931 © 2018 TXu 2-105-513 - ISBN 978-1-64530- 435-7 - &

A Hundred Secrets Vol 2 Books 21-100 nonfiction 100 secrets © Case 1-6749127961 © 2018 TXu 2-105-513 - ISBN 978-1-64530-435-7

Why Weren't the Kurds at Normandy? Parody Lyrics © 2019 Pau 3-998-562

S'more Secrets - Sleepover Stories to be Told in Darkness Volume 1 Bedtime stories for kids ©2019 - TXu 2-129-150 - ISBN 978-1-64426-708-0

S'more Secrets - Sleepover Stories to be Told in Darkness Volume 2 for tweens and teens - Fiction -© 2018 Case 1-7262889391 © 2018 TXu 2-129-150 - ISBN 798-1-64530-433-3

S'more Secrets - Sleepover Stories to be Told in Darkness Volume 3 scary stories to be told in darkness to grownups – Fiction - © 2018 TXu 2-189-150 - ISBN 798-1-64530-454-0

The Nurse's Secret - Kjellfrid's Secret - Nonfiction - ©2019 Case 1-5985073311 © 2019 TXu 2-074-508 –

Emily's Secret – Emily's Cargo Cult of 40 Mates in Irian Jaya - Nonfiction - © Case 1-5985016941 © 2019 TXu 2-074-514

Katie's Secret – The Arsenic Murder Trials of Katie Browder Stricklin - Nonfiction - © 1-5714428421 © 2019 TXu 2-065-209

Bad Breakup at 430 Lafayette Street - Nonfiction - Copyright © 2017 Case 1-5592907361 - ©2017 TXu 2-060-686

Aesop Fables and The Candy Rabbit bedtime stories for kids - © 2019 - ISBN 978-1-54399-921-1

The Prince and I - Miss Olive - historic novel - Unsolved murder of my nanny's former charge © 2019

TXu 2-139-737 - ISBN 978-1-64530-432-6

One Corinthians nonfiction sermon delivered at Saint Clements' Church, Berkeley, at 11AM December 11, 1949 © 2020 - ISBN 978-1-54389-951-8

Senatorial Courtesy – nonfiction life-saving senatorial courtesy Senator John William Warner III - Nonfiction - Copyright © 2020 1-837259272592781 ©2020 - ISBN 978-1-54399-891-7

Ladies Day – nonfiction account of misogyny at Harvard Law School professors during 1960s © 2020 ISBN 978-1-5499-920-4

A Perfect Crime a historical novel © 2020 - Case No. 1-8476606391 ISBN 978-1-09830-140-8

Four Score and More – nonfiction autobiography of a long life Case © 2019 TXu 2-167-560 ISBN 978-1-54399-922-8

Easter Parade nonfiction COVID-19 © 2020 - ISBN 978-1-09830-945-9

Mariticide Club

Ambrose Bierce anthology of Ambrose Bierce's 70 best of his 249 short stories © Case 1-8725184511 Copyright © 2020 - ISBN 978-1-09831-080-6

George Sterling A Wine of Wizardry anthology of George Sterling's 20 best poems 1-8731197451 © 2020 - ISBN 978-1-09831-102-5

The Boss – nonfiction my 18-months service to Vice President Richard M. Nixon Copyright © 2020 - ISBN 978-1-09830-750-9

Epilogue – nonfiction account of crimes of President Richard M. Nixon and Presidential staff 1-8592617481 © 2020 - ISBN 978-1-54399-891-7

White Fox and White Buffalo – Comanche abduction my maternal grandmother's maternal grandmother:

White Fox – Book 1 Prequel to White Buffalo -Nonfiction Copyright © 2020 – Case 1-8842056821 and White Buffalo – Book 2 Sequel to White Fox -Nonfiction © 2020 – Case 1-8862149151 TXu2-093-545 ISBN 978-1-09831-836-9

Roses among the Thorns -The Founders of the Bohemian Club ©2020 TXu 2-195-987 ISBN 978-1-09831-738-6

© 2020 Case No. 1-8791258541

Crazy – Nonfiction plus five short stories that are fiction historical novels © 2020 Case No. 1-8946543741 – first edition ISBN 978-1-09832-149-9 and second edition ISBN 978-1-0983-2399-8

Thistlewood Non©2020 TXu 2-206-871 ISBN 978-1-09832-390-5

Twice Upon A Time – ©2020 Case 1-9245623151 ISBN 978-1-09833-861-9

Alice Blue Gown –©2020 Nonfiction Case 1-9105640341 - ISBN 978-1-09833-191-7

Day of Infamy – Pearl Harbor Day – The Ni'ihau In cident - Nonfiction - © Case No. 1-9381160911 © 2020 TXu 2-222-380 ISBN 978-1-09834-126-8

The Plumbers Introduction – © 2020 TXu 2-217-462 Case No. 1-9185174771 ISBN 978-1-09833-500-7

The Plumbers Volume 1 – United Airlines Flight No. 553 - Unsolved Mystery of Missing $2,000,000 – Watergate Burglars - Nonfiction Copyright © 2020 TXu 2-217-462 Case No. 1-9185174771 - ISBN 978-1-09833-400-0

The Plumbers Volume 2 – Nonfiction Copyright © 2020 TXu 2-217-462 Case No. 1-9185174771 - ISBN 978-1-09833-401-7

Ted historical novel ©2020 Case 1-9620202411 TXu 2-225-762 - ISBN 978-1-09834-717-8

Trump Plague – What did he know and when did he know it? Nonfiction - © 2020 TXu 2-219-947 Case No. 1-9264731081 ISBN 978-1-09833-825-1

Reverse Santa Nonfiction Case 1-9990314981 © 2020 TXu 2-234-240 ISBN 978-1-09835-902-7

Pardon Me Nonfiction Case 1-10029277321 © 2021 TXu 2-237-084 ISBN 978-1-09836-275-9

Tiny Hands Loser Non© 2021 TXu 2-237-155 Case No. 1-10029325830 ISBN 978-1-09836-204-1

Widow of Friedrich Christian Anton "Fritz" Lang Non©2021 TXu 2-251-784 Hardcover ISBN 978-1-09837-577-5 ISBN 978-1-09837-157-9

The Man in the Brown Suit by Agatha Christie - Fiction Republished 2021

Poirot Investigates by Agatha Christie - Fiction 2021

Wives Who Kill

The Mysterious Affair at Styles by Agatha Christie - Fiction Republished 2021

Ghost Stories –The Speluncean Explorers © 2022 TXu 2-295-124 Case No. 1-10977740461

125 Bedtime Stories Still Untold to My Most Beloved Daughter Sarai Stricklin (09.28.1959 – 06.19.2021) - Book 1 – Stories 1-52 - Fiction by original authors Republished 2021- © 2021 ISBN 978-1-09837-566-9

125 Bedtime Stories Still Untold to My Most Beloved Daughter Sarai Stricklin (09.28.1959-06.19.2021) Book 1 Stories 1-52 - Fiction Anthology Republished in June 2021- © 2021 ISBN 978-1-09837-566-9

Mary Eliska's Untold Stories - Bedtime Stories Still Untold to my Daughter Mary Eliska Books 1-26 © 2021-

Mary Eliska's Untold Bedtime Stories of Japan, China, India, Israel, Europe and America - © 2021 TXu 2-254-154

Mary Eliska's Untold Stories - Book 1 The Yellow Fairy Tales Book - © 2021 ISBN 978-1-09838-368-8

Mary Eliska's Untold Stories - Book 2 The Red Fairy Tales Book - Tales of India by Rudyard Kipling - © 2021 ISBN 978-1-09838-424-1

Mary Eliska's Untold Stories - Book 3 The Blue Fairy Tales Book - Jungle Books by Rudyard Kipling - © 2021 ISBN 978-1-09838-425-8

Mary Eliska's Untold Stories - Book 4 The Orange Fairy Tales Book - Kim by Rudyard Kipling © 2021 ISBN 979-1-09838-438-4

Mary Eliska's Untold Stories - Book 5 The Purple Fairy Tales Book – The Wind in the Willows by Kenneth Grahame; The Tale of Jimmy Rabbit by Albert Scott Bailey; The Velveteen Rabbit by Margery Williams; The Adventures of Danny the Meadow Mouse and The Adventures of Reddy Fox by Thornton W. Burgess; and, by Beatrix Potter: an anthology of Bedtime Stories; The Tale of Peter Rabbit; The Tale of Benjamin Bunny; The Tale of Johnny Town-Mouse; The Tale of Squirrel Nutkins; The Tale of Ginger and Pickles; and The Story of a Fierce Bad Rabbit. Mary Eliska's Untold Stories - Book 5 The Purple Fairy Tales Book – © 2021 Case 1-10518564131

Mary Eliska Girl Detective – Vol 1 Books 1-13 Mildred Augustine Wirt Benson's Penny Parker Stories -© 2021 ISBN 978-1-09837-244-6

Mary Eliska Girl Detective - Book 1 - Clue of the Silken Ladder -© 2021 – Behind the Green Door - © 2021 – and The Deserted Yacht - © 2021 Case 1-10130208421 ISBN 978-1-09837-625-3

Mary Eliska Girl Detective - Book 2 - Ghost Beyond the Gate - © 2021 – The Missing Formula – © 2021 - The Vanishing Comrade - © 2021 Case 1-10130208421 ISBN 978-1-09837-626-0

Mary Eliska Girl Detective - Book 3 - Guilt of the Brass Thieves – The Little French Girl - © 2021 Case 1-10130208421 ISBN 978-1-09837-627-7

Mary Eliska Girl Detective - Book 4 - Hoofbeats on the Turnpike - © 2021 Case 1-10130208421 ISBN 978-1-09837-249-1 ISBN 978-1-09837-628-4

Mary Eliska Girl Detective - Book 5 - Saboteurs on the River - ©2021 Case 1-10130208421 ISBN 978-1-09837-245-3 ISBN 978-1-09837-629-1

Mary Eliska Girl Detective - Book 6 - Signal in the Dark - © 2021 Case 1-10130208421 ISBN 978-1-09837-630-7 Hardcover 978-1-09837-251-4

Mariticide Club

Mary Eliska Girl Detective - Book 7 - Swamp Island © 2021 – The Clue of the Gold Coin - © 2021 TXu 2-265-659 – and The Silver Ring Mystery Book 570-© Case 1-10156100271 ©2021 TXu 2-265-652 Case 1-10574287601 and 1-10574287730 ISBN 978-1-09837-631-4

Mary Eliska Girl Detective - Book 8 - The Wishing Well – The Lorelei Rupert Mystery – The Old Maid Fiction Case 1-10130208421 Case 1-10156100271 Case 1-10582290111 ISBN 978-1-09837-632-1

Mary Eliska Girl Detective - Book 9 - The Cry at Midnight - © 2021 – The Stowmarket Mystery - © 2021 Case 1-10130208421 Case 1-10595752961 ISBN 978-1-09837-633-8

Mary Eliska Girl Detective - Book 10 - The Secret Pact – © 2021 Case 1-10130208421 The Mystery at Dark Cedars Book 572 - © 2021 Case 1-10602161171 – The Mystery of the Fires Book 573 - © 2021 Case 1-10676148519 – The Mystery of the Secret Band Book 574 - © 2021 Case 1-10676090161 ISBN 978-1-09837-634-5

Mary Eliska Girl Detective - Book 11 - Whispering Walls - © 2021 – The Phantom Friend Book 579 - © 2021 [Stave Two] – The Puzzle in the Pond Book 580 – [Stave Three] © 2021 Case 1-10130208421 ISBN 978-1-09837-635-2

Mary Eliska Girl Detective - Book 12 - Voice from the Cave – The Orinda Mystery Book 50 - © 2021 Case 1-10130208421 © 2021 TXu 2-264-787 Case 1-10557865731 ISBN 978-1-09837-636-9

Mary Eliska Girl Detective - Book 13 - The Clock Strikes Thirteen - © 2021 Case 1-10130208421 ISBN 978-1-09837-637-6

Mary Eliska Girl Detective - Book 14 - The Santa Claus Bank Robbery - © 2021 1-10156100271 [Staves 5 & 6 Republished Book 11]

Mary Eliska Girl Detective - Book 15 - The Deserted Yacht - [Republished as Book 1 Stave 3]

Mary Eliska Girl Detective - Book 16 - The Mystery of the Sundial - [Republished as Book 4 Stave Three]

Mary Eliska Girl Detective - The Mystery of a Hansom Cab– Book 20 © 2022 TXu 2-307-367 Case No. © 2022 1-11231552371 318pp

Mary Eliska Girl Detective – The Mystery of Madame Midas– Book 21 © 2022 TXu 2-314-023 Case No. 1-11299310531 327pp

Mary Eliska Girl Detective - Book 28 – Behind the Green Door - [Republished as Book 1 Stave Two]

Mary Eliska Girl Detective - Book 29 - The Missing Formula - [Republished as Book 2 Stave Two]

Mary Eliska Girl Detective - Book 30 – Danger at the Drawbridge - [Republished as Book 1 Stave Two]

Mary Eliska Girl Detective - Book 31 - The Mystery of 31 New Inn - © 2021 ISBN 978-1-09837-694-9

Mary Eliska Girl Detective - Book 32 – Mary Eliska Finds A Clue - [Republished as Book 6 Stave Three]

Mary Eliska Girl Detective - Book 36 - The Eye of Osiris - © 2021 ISBN 978-1-09837-705-2

Mary Eliska Girl Detective - Book 37 - The Mystery of the Lost Key - [Republished as Book 6 Stave Two]

Mary Eliska Girl Detective - Book 38 - The Mystery of the Red Thumb Mark -

Wives Who Kill

Mary Eliska Girl Detective - Book 39 - The Uttermost Farthing - © 2021 ISBN 978-1-09837- 695-6

Mary Eliska Girl Detective - Books 40-48 - Doctor Thorndyke's Cases - © 2021 ISBN 978-1-09837-706-9

Mary Eliska Girl Detective - The Mystery of the Rainbow Feather – Book 41 © 2022 TXu 2-307370 Case No. 1-11231594691 234pp

Mary Eliska Girl Detective - The Mystery of The Silent House– Book 45 © 2022

Mary Eliska Girl Detective - Book 50 – The Orinda Mystery - ©2021 TXu 2-264-787 - [Book 12 Stave 2] The Orinda Mystery Book 50 - © 2021 Case 1-10130208421 © 2021 TXu 2-264-787

Mary Eliska Girl Detective - The Millionaire Mystery – Book 54 © 2022

Mary Eliska Girl Detective - The Mystery Whom God Hath Joined– Book 58 © 2022

Mary Eliska Girl Detective - Book 59 – Mary Eliska Girl Detective and the Lorelei Rupert Mystery – © 2021 - Case 1-10582290111©2021 TXu 2-265-775 - [Republished as Book 8 Stave Two]

Mary Eliska Girl Detective - The Mystery of a Coin of Edward VII - Book 63 © 2022 TXu 2-309-496 Case No. 1-11243958179 269pp

Mary Eliska Girl Detective - The Mystery of the Yellow Holly – Book 64 © 2022 TXu 2-309-497 Case No. 1-11243958228 366pp

Mary Eliska Girl Detective - The Mystery of The Girl From Malta– Book 65 –© 2022

Mary Eliska Girl Detective - The Mystery of the Mandarin's Fan - Book 68 © 2022 TXu 2-309-498 Case No. 1-11243958130 282pp

Mary Eliska Girl Detective - The Mystery of the Red Window – Book 69 © 2022 TXu 2-309-502 Case No. 1-11243958070 399pp

Mary Eliska Girl Detective - The Mystery of Lady Jim of Curzon Street – Book 73 © 2022 TXu 2-315-157 No. 1-11337674021 526pp

Mary Eliska Girl Detective - The Mystery of the Opal Serpent - Book 74 © 2022 TXu 2-313-114 Case No. 1-11277466081 298pp

Mademoiselle Mary Eliska and The Phantom of the Opera - Book 76 © 2022 TXu 2-298-864 Case1-11110548251 326pp

Mary Eliska Girl Detective - The Mystery of The Red-Headed Man - Book 81 © 2022 TXu 2-301-967 No. 1-11152531130

Mary Eliska Girl Detective – The Mystery of the Sacred Herb – Book 84 © 2022 TXu 2-313-113 Case No. 1-11277515711 344pp

Mary Eliska Girl Detective – The Mystery of the Sealed Message –Book 85 © 2022 TXu 2-313-112 Case No. 1-11277515950 296pp

Mary Eliska Girl Detective – The Mystery of the Green Mummy – Book 88 © 2022 TXu 2-310-325 Case No. 1-11277549430 282pp

Mary Eliska Girl Detective – The Mystery of the Disappearing Eye – Book 91 (1909) © 2022 329pp

Mary Eliska Girl Detective – The Mystery of the Solitary Farm - Book 92 © 2022 112pp

Mary Eliska Girl Detective – The Mystery of the Crowned Skull – Book 99 ©2022 TXu 2-309-552 Case No. 1-11263042361

Mary Eliska Girl Detective - The Mystery of Monsieur Judas– Book 104 © 2022

Mariticide Club

Mary Eliska Girl Detective – The Mystery Queen – Book 106 (1912) © 2022 294pp

Mary Eliska Girl Detective – The Mystery of Red Money – Book 107 © 2022 268pp

Mary Eliska Girl Detective – The Mystery of the Lost Parchment - Book 115 © 2022

Mary Eliska Girl Detective – The Mystery of Streets of Fear © 2022

Mary Eliska Girl Detective - Fantômas Captured - Book 176 - © 2022

Mary Eliska Girl Detective and the Mystery of the Harlequin Opal – Books 91, 92 and 93 © 2022 Case 1-11299311170

Mary Eliska Girl Detective Professor Brankel's Secret Book 2 ©2023 TXu 2-358-212 ©2021 1-11299173361 98pp

Mary Eliska Girl Detective - The Mystery of The Yellow Room – Book 70 © 2021 TXu 2-274-3701-10740460241 266pp

Mary Eliska Girl Detective – The Mystery of the White Room – Book 71 © 2022 TXu 2-301-956 Case No. 1-11152531001

Mademoiselle Rouletabille Mary Eliska Girl Detective - The Secret of the Night – Book 72 © 2021 TXu 2-295-430 Case No. 1-11064158121 294pp

Mary Eliska Girl Detective – The Guarded Heights – Book 73 © 2022 TXu 2-201-503 Case No. 1-11144498241

Mary Eliska Girl Detective – The Mystery of The Spider – Book 74 © 2022 TXu 2-301-934 Case No. 1-11152531030

Mary Eliska Girl Detective - The Temple of Death – The Bride of the Sun King – Book 75 © 2021 TXu 2-296-617 Case No. 1-11077748851

Mademoiselle Mary Eliska Girl Detective - The Phantom of the Opera – Book 76 © 2022 TXu 2-298-864 Case1-11110548251 326pp

Mary Eliska Girl Detective - The Mystery of The Abandoned Room – Book 77 © 2022 TXu 2-299-769 ISBN: 978-1-64314-738-3 Case No. 1-1119216531 559pp

Mary Eliska Girl Detective - The Mystery of The Gray Mask – Book 78 © 2022 TXu 2-300-373 Case No. 1-11125258241 261pp

Mary Eliska Girl Detective – The Mystery of the Scarlet Bat – Book 79 © 2022 TXu 2-301-961 Case No. 1-11152531059

Mary Eliska Girl Detective – The Mystery of The Secret Passage – Book 80 © 2022 TXu 2-301-964 Case No. 1-11152498331 278pages

Mary Eliska Girl Detective – The Mystery of the Red-Headed Man – Book 81 © 2022 TXu 2-301-967 Case No. 1-11152531130

Mary Eliska Girl Detective - Book 82 – The Pagan's Cup and Silver Bullet - © 2021 TXu 2-307-868 Case No. 1-11237102261 - ISBN 978-1-09837-420-4 and 978-1-09837-717-5

Mary Eliska Girl Detective - The Mystery of the Pagan's Cup - Book 82 © 2022 TXu 2-307-868 Case No. 1-11237102261 218pp

Mary Eliska Girl Detective - Book 86 - The Mystery of the Disappearing Eye © 2021 -

Mary Eliska Girl Detective - Book 88 - The Mystery of the Opal Serpent - © 2021 -TXu 2-313-114 Case No. 1-11277466081

Mary Eliska Girl Detective - Book 90 - The Mystery of the Yellow Holly - © 2021 - ISBN 978-1-09837-713-7

Mary Eliska Girl Detective - Books 91, 92, 93 Mystery of the Harlequin Opal © 2021

Wives Who Kill

Mary Eliska Girl Detective - Book 97 - The Mystery of the Sealed Message - © 2021 TXu 2-313-112

Mary Eliska Girl Detective – The Mystery of the Society of Flies - Book 106 © 2022 TXu 2-314-501 Case No. 1- 11326931241 299pp

Mary Eliska Girl Detective - The Mystery of The Peacock of Jewels– Book 107 © 2022 Case No. 1-10336308231 452pp

Mary Eliska Girl Detective - Book 108 - The Mystery of a Hansom Cab - © 2021 TXu 2-307-367 Case No. 1-11231552371

Mary Eliska Girl Detective - Book 134 – The Mystery of the Whispering Lane - © 2022 TXu 2-317-000 Case No. 1- 11354442141

Mary Eliska Girl Detective - Book 135 – The Mystery of the Caravan Crime - © 2022 TXu 2-316-997 Case No 1-11354441431

Mary Eliska Girl Detective - Book 423 - Vanishing Man © 2021 -

Mary Eliska Girl Detective - Book 543 - The Gentleman Who Vanished © 2021

Mary Eliska Girl Detective - Book 546 - The Lady From Nowhere - © 2021 – 1-10759399892

Mary Eliska Girl Detective - The Mystery of the Purple Fern Book 553 ©2021 TXu 2-315-921 Case No. 1-11338176181

Mary Eliska Girl Detective - Book 564 – The Mystery of the Wooden Hand - © 2022 TXu 2-316-088 Case No. 1- 11344674401

Mary Eliska Girl Detective - Book 566 - The Mystery of the Sycamore - ©2021 - [Republished as Book 8 Stave 2]

Mary Eliska Girl Detective - Book 567 - The Mystery of the Red House 1-10547943101 ©2021 TXu 2-264-820 ISBN 968-1-09838-972-7

Mary Eliska Girl Detective - Book 568 - The Little French Girl – by Anne Douglas Sedgwick - Fiction - [Published Book 3 Stave 2]

Mary Eliska Girl Detective - Book 569 - The Clue of the Gold Coin - ©2021 TXu 2-265-659- [Republished Book 7 Stave 2]

Mary Eliska Girl Detective - Book 570 - The Silver Ring Mystery - © 2021 TXu 2-265-652 [Published Book 7 Stave 3]

Mary Eliska Girl Detective - Book 571 - The Stowmarket Mystery - © 2021 Case 1-10595752961 ©2021 TXu 2-2662-430 - [Republished as Book 9 Stave 2]

Mary Eliska Girl Detective –The Mystery at Dark Cedars Book 572 © 2021 TXu 2-308-721 Case 1-10602161171

Mary Eliska Girl Detective - Book 572 – The Mystery at Dark Cedars - © 2021 TXu 2-308-721 Case No. 1- 10602161171 and Case No. 1-10595752961 - © 2021 [Book 10 Stave 2]

Mary Eliska Girl Detective - The Mystery of the Secret Band Book 573 ©2021 TXu 2-270-007 Case 1-10676090161

Mary Eliska Girl Detective - Book 573 – The Mystery of the Secret Band - © Case 1-10595752961 – [Republished Book 10 Stave 4]

Mary Eliska Girl Detective and the Mystery of the Fires - Book 574 © 2021 TXu 2-269-991 Case 1-10676148519

Mary Eliska Girl Detective - Book 574 – The Mystery of the Fires - © 2021 - Case 1-10595752961 - [Published Book10 Stave 3]

Mariticide Club

Mary Eliska Girl Detective - Book 575 - The Uttermost Parts of the Sea –- © 2021 - Case 1-10692479811 - ISBN 978-1-09839-778-4

Mary Eliska Girl Detective - Book 576 - The Polly Page Yacht Club – Fiction by Izola Louise Forrester - [Published Book 1 Stave 2]

Mary Eliska Girl Detective - Book 577 - The Vanishing Comrade - © 2021 - [Republished as Book 2 Stave 3]

Mary Eliska Girl Detective - Book 578 - The Mystery Girl - Fiction - [Republished as Book 4 Stave Two]

Mary Eliska Girl Detective - Book 579 – The Phantom Friend - © 2021- [Published Book 11 Stave 2]

Mary Eliska Girl Detective - Book 580 - The Puzzle in the Pond - ©2021 [Published Book11 Stave3]

Mary Eliska Girl Detective - Book 584 - The Last Stroke - © 2021 – Case No. 1-10759399851

Bedtime Stories for Bad Children – An Anthology of Ghost Stories - Volume 1 © 2022 TXu 2-333 - 189 Case No. 1-11616027741

Bedtime Stories for Bad Children – An Anthology of Grimm Stories – Vol 2 © 2022 TXu 2-333-962 - Case No. 1-11626445221

Disconcerting Stories for Grownups - Not To Tell to Children in Darkness at Bedtime - © 2022 TXu 2-336-941 Case No. 1-11701275891

Mary Eliska Girl Detective Girl Aviatrix Series

Volume 1

Book 1 - Mary Eliska Girl Detective Wins Her Wings © 2022 Case No. 1-11371703511

Book 2 - Mary Eliska Girl Detective - The Mystery Plane © 2022 Case No. 1-11371703511

Book 3 - Mary Eliska Girl Detective Solves the Conway Case © 2022 Case No. 1-11371703511

Book 4 - Mary Eliska Girl Detective – The Double Cousins © 2022 Case No. 1-11371703511

Book 5 - Mary Eliska Girl Detective - The Air Pilot Mystery © 2022 Case No. 1-11371703511

Volume 2

Book 6 - Mary Eliska Girl Detective - The Ocean Flight Mystery © 2022 Case No. 1-11371703511

Book 7 - Mary Eliska Girl Detective – Flying Girl © 2022 TXu 2-326-043 Case No. 1-11376521721

Book 8 - Mary Eliska Girl Detective - Flying Girl and Her Chum © 2022 TXu 2-326-043 No. 1-11376521721

Book 9 - Mary Eliska Girl Detective - The Hollywood Flight © 2022 TXu 2-326-043 Case No. 1-11376521721

Volume 3

Wives Who Kill

Book 10 - Mary Eliska Girl Detective – Gypsies of the Air © 2022 TXu 2-326-043 Case No. 1-11376521721

Book 11 - Mary Eliska Girl Detective - The Island Adventure © 2022 TXu 2-326-043 Case No. 1-11376521721

Book 12 - Mary Eliska Girl Detective – The Mystery of Seal Islands © 2022 TXu 2-326-043 NO. 1-11376521721

Book 13 - Mary Eliska Girl Detective - The Phantom Airship © 2022 TXu 2-326-043 Case No. 1-11376521721

Book 14 - Mary Eliska Girl Detective - Girl Pilots on Golden Wings – © 2022 TXu 2-326-043 Case 1-11376521721

Volume 4

Book 15 - Mary Eliska Girl Detective – The Sky Cruise © 2022 TXu 2-326-043 Case No. 1-11376521721

Book 16 - Mary Eliska Girl Detective – The Motor Butterfly © 2022 TXu 2-326-043 Case No. 1-11376521721

Book 17 - Mary Eliska Girl Detective - The Air Perilous Summer © 2022 TXu 2-326-043 Case No. 1-11376521721

Book 18 - Mary Eliska Girl Detective - On Adventure Island ©2022 TXu 2-326-043 No. 1-11376521721

Appendix 1: Amelia Earhart

Appendix 2: Women Aviators

Appendix 3: Charles Lindbergh

Preview Hawai'ian Bedtime Stories - Legends & Myths of Hawai'i ©2022 TXu 2-330-801

Other Books Published and Copyrighted by William A Stricklin

Volumes 5 through 10

Book 1 Girl Aviatrix Series - Mary Eliska Girl Detective Wins Her Wings © 2022 Case No. 1-11371703511

Book 2 Girl Aviatrix Series - Mary Eliska Girl Detective - The Mystery Plane © 2022 Case No. 1-11371703511

Book 3 Girl Aviatrix Series - Mary Eliska Girl Detective Solves the Conway Case © 2022 No. 1-11371703511

Book 4 Girl Aviatrix Series- Mary Eliska Girl Detective – The Double Cousins © 2022 Case No. 1-11371703511

Book 5 Girl Aviatrix Series- Mary Eliska Girl Detective - The Air Pilot Mystery © 2022 Case No 1-11371703511

Book 6 Girl Aviatrix Series- Mary Eliska Girl Detective - The Ocean Flight Mystery © 2022 Case 1-1137170351

Mariticide Club

Book 7 Girl Aviatrix Series- Mary Eliska Girl Detective – Flying Girl © 2022 Case No. 1-11376521721

Book 8 Girl Aviatrix Series- Mary Eliska Girl Detective - Flying Girl and Her Chum © 2022 No. 1-11376521721

Book 9 Girl Aviatrix Series - Mary Eliska Girl Detective - The Hollywood Flight © 2022 No. 1-11376521721

Book 10 Girl Aviatrix Series - Mary Eliska Girl Detective – Gypsies of the Air © 2022 Case No. 1-11376521721

Book 11 Girl Aviatrix Series - Mary Eliska Girl Detective - The Island Adventure © 2022 No. 1-11376521721

Book 12 Girl Aviatrix Series - Mary Eliska Girl Detective - The Mystery of Seal Islands © 2022 1-11376521721

Book 13 Girl Aviatrix Series - Mary Eliska Girl Detective - The Phantom Airship © 2022 No. 1-11376521721

Book 14 Girl Aviatrix Series- Mary Eliska Girl Detective - Girl Pilots on Golden Wings © 2022 1-11376521721

Book 15 Girl Aviatrix Series- Mary Eliska Girl Detective – The Sky Cruise © 2022 Case No. 1-11376521721

Book 16 Girl Aviatrix Series - Mary Eliska Girl Detective – The Motor Butterfly © 2022 No. 1-11376521721

Book 17 Girl Aviatrix Series - Mary Eliska Girl Detective - The Air Perilous Summer © 2022 1-1137652172

Book 18 Girl Aviatrix Series - Mary Eliska Girl Detective - On Adventure Island © 2022 No. 1-11376521721

Volume 11 © 2023 Case No. 1-12136217511

Book 19 Mary Eliska Girl Detective Girl Aviatrix The Sky Detective - How She Got Her Man © 2023 No. 1-12136217511

Book 20 Mary Eliska Girl Detective Girl Aviatrix Eagle of the Sky - Along the Air Lanes © 2023 Case No. 1-12136217511

Book 21 Mary Eliska Girl Detective Girl Aviatrix Wings Over Rockies - Cloud Chaser © 2023 1-12136217511

Volume 12 © 2023 Case No 1-12179904021

Book 22 Mary Eliska Girl Detective Girl Aviatrix The Sky Pilot's Great Chase and Dead Stick Landing No. 1-12179904021

Book 23 Mary Eliska Girl Detective Girl Aviatrix Trackers of the Fog Pack Flying Blind No. 1-12179904021

Book 24 Mary Eliska Girl Detective Girl Aviatrix Flying the Coast Skyways Swift Patrol No. 1-12179904021

Wives Who Kill

Liam McAdams Boy Aviator Stories Series

In Passing ã paˑsã Four Score and Seven – © 2023 TXu 2-373-861 ISBN 979-8-35091-176-3
Mariticide Club - Wives Who Kill Husbands Nonfiction © 2023 TXu 2-378-397 Case No 1-12662549461
Uxoricide Club - Husbands Who Kill Wives Nonfiction © 2023 TXu 2-380-728 Case No 1-12719760611
American Madams Nonfiction © 2023 TXu 2-379-571 ISBN 979-8-35091-340-8
Vice Presidents of the United States of America © 2023 Case No 1- 12812460821
Earliest History of the United States of America © 2023 TXu 2-389-729 Case No 1-12939010871
Political Scandals of the United States of America © 2023 Case No 1- 12938975211
Sixty-five First Ladies of the United States of America Nonfiction © 2023 Case No. 1-13025699681

FINIS.